MUMBAI & GOA

JANHAVI ACHAREKAR

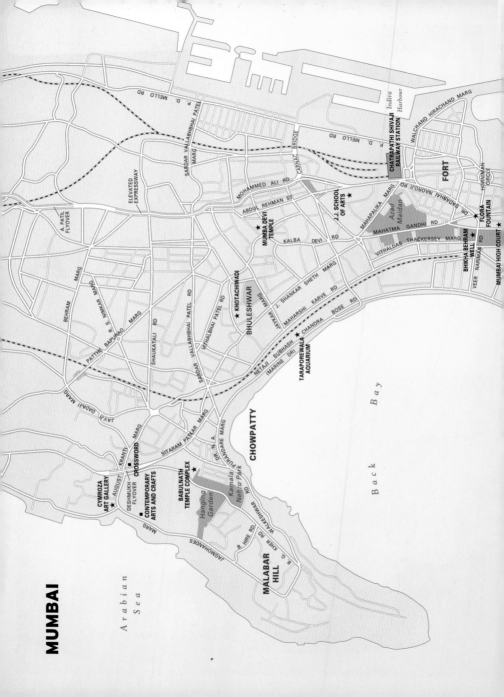

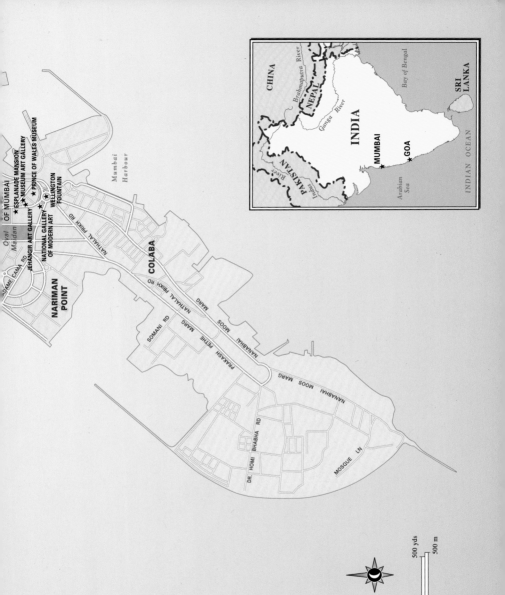

Dudhsagar Falls

Bhagwan Mahavir Wildlife Sanctuary

KARNATAKA

GOA

River

Uguem

Sanguem

Curdi

Curchorem-Cacora

Quepem

PALÁCIO DO DEAO

Colomba

Colomba

Pansimol (Piria)

Cotigao Wildlife Sanctuary

Astagal

Taljona

CASA BRAGANÇA

Chandor

Gaudongrem

Gaudongrem

Galgibaga River

Canacona

Chaudi

NH 17

Madgaon

River

Raja

NH 17

Sai River

Varca

Cavelossim

Mobor

Colva

Benaulim

Betalbatim

Paloem

Agonda

Cabo de Rama

Magdal

NH 17

5 mi

5 km

S e a

CHINA

NEPAL

Brahmaputra River

Ganga River

Bay of Bengal

INDIA

SRI LANKA

MUMBAI

GOA

PAKISTAN

River

Indus

Arabian Sea

INDIAN OCEAN

© AVALON TRAVEL

Contents

Discover Mumbai & Goa

It is nearly impossible to speak of Mumbai and Goa in the same breath. One is poised to become an international jet-setting megalopolis, while the other claims to provide respite from just that. One is concrete skyline and rush-hour traffic, while the other is synonymous with the restful, carefree attitude called *sossegarde*. Perhaps the one thing they have in common is the dramatic Arabian Sea. But even its chameleon waters adopt the character of each destination, turning crowded and carnival-like in Mumbai and then quiet and introspective, all aquamarine and gold, as they stretch sinuously along the Goan coastline.

People say that you have to be a little insane to live in Mumbai. Life here is really about living on the edge – commuters hang by their index fingers at the door of the local train, and speeding cars wend their way through traffic as if part of a video game. And crossing Mumbai's manic streets, you will come to realize, is a fine art learned only with time.

However, the people of Mumbai seem to have made peace with their city. Paeans have been sung about the city's famed spirit, seen in its throbbing nightlife, colorful festivals, and the shimmies of Bollywood cinema. Meanwhile, its magnificent colonial buildings stoically hold on to the city's historic past in the face of change, strangers to its dizzying new pace of life.

Mumbai's frenetic pace can only energize you or send you scuttling to the calmer vistas of Goa. Settle into the sandy soil of Goa and there's a sense of meditative calm that descends upon the visitor. Head to the nearest beach shack for a sip of the local brew – *feni*. And when it has shocked you out of your senses and sent you reeling into another time zone, brace yourself for the exhilarating unknown. Goa is not merely a geographical state in India, it is a state of mind. Goa is where you lose yourself among beer-guzzling neo-hippies, biker backpackers, melon-pink sunbathers, beach party revelers, and bazaar lurkers. It is a rollercoaster of sights and experiences ranging from beaches, coves, Indo-Portuguese casas, churches, carnivals, and flea markets, to luxury yachts and spas.

There's a proverb in Konkani, Goa's home language, that says "Open your true heart to a friend, show a smiling face to your enemy." Perhaps this is what Mumbai and Goa have in common; they are both large-hearted.

Planning Your Trip

▶ WHERE TO GO

Mumbai

Mumbai is a sprawling city that can be divided into several parts. Of primary interest to visitors, however, is the southern downtown region that includes the areas of Colaba, Kala Ghoda, Fort, and CST, stretching across to the sea-facing areas of Marine Drive and Chowpatty. While Central Mumbai has its fair share of sights, it has also developed as a burgeoning shopping district.

North Mumbai is where the city's ever-expanding suburbs lie and is now a throbbing, young, and vibrant center.

Panaji and Interior Goa

Goa's capital, Panaji, is representative of Portuguese Goa. The region's biggest draw is the heritage district of Old Goa (Velha Goa). Overshadowed by the sunny coastline is the

IF YOU HAVE...

- **FIVE DAYS:** Visit Colaba, the Fort and CST areas in Mumbai, and Candolim, Panaji, and Old Goa, or Madgaon and Velsao to Betalbatim in South Goa.

- **ONE WEEK:** Add Kala Ghoda and Marine Drive in Mumbai and Anjuna and Vagator in North Goa, or Colva and Benaulim in South Goa.

- **TWO WEEKS:** Add Central and North Mumbai and the Far North in Goa, or Varca, Cavelossim, and Palolem in South Goa.

- **THREE WEEKS:** Add Ajanta and Ellora Caves outside Mumbai, Ponda, and Far Eastern Goa.

seldom-visited deep interior, characterized by ancient Hindu temples and wildlife sanctuaries. Its largest town, Ponda, serves as a base for the neighboring temples and is the entry point to the Dudhsagar Falls and Bhagwan Mahavir Wildlife Sanctuary in Molem.

The Northern Coast

Goa's northern coast comprises a series of beaches that begin at Candolim and end at the northernmost tip of Terekhol (Tiracol) on the Maharashtra border. Anjuna and Vagator are frequented for their secluded golden beaches and full moon parties. The most pristine beaches are those of the Far North, where the golden sands attract even the rare olive ridley turtles that come to nest here in the winter months. In the northern interior are the ancient Arvalem Caves near Bicholim and a number of picturesque villages.

The Taj Mahal Palace and Tower overlooks Mumbai's Gateway of India.

A clay lamp lights up a Ganesha shrine in the courtyard of Gokarna's Shri Mahabaleshwar Temple outside Goa.

The Southern Coast

The southern coast is wonderfully secluded, and its many fishing villages and beaches remain untouched by tourist activity. Smaller beaches, framed by picturesque fields and villages, dot the coastline between Velsao and Betalbatim, even as Colva and Benaulim welcome visitors with a variety of water sports, boat rides, and dolphin trips. The most popular beach in the south is Palolem. Surrounded by islands and coves and lined with coco-huts, it is Goa's latest tourist hotspot.

Getaways Around Goa

To the south, in the neighboring state of Karnataka, are two of Goa's most popular getaways. Discovered in recent times by tourists seeking to maximize the Indian experience is the beach and pilgrim town of Gokarna. Reminiscent of the Goa beaches of old, its clean, white sands and negligible tourist activity are integral to its charm. The UNESCO World Heritage Site of Hampi lies farther southwest, its towering 15th-century stone temples attracting culture vultures and party animals alike.

Map labels:

- NH 8
- NH 222
- MUMBAI
- Ahmednagar
- Mumbai
- Pune
- 0 — 50 mi
- 0 — 50 km
- NH 211
- NH 4
- NH 9
- MAHARASHTRA
- Solapur
- NH 17
- *Arabian Sea*
- NH 218
- Bijaour
- KARNATAKA
- The Northern Coast
- NH 218
- NH 13
- Panaji and Interior Goa
- PANAJI
- NH 4
- GOA
- Hubli
- The Southern Coast
- NH 63
- NH 17
- Getaways Around Goa

a patch of green amid the sands of Goa's northern coast

▶ WHEN TO GO

Mumbai and Goa enjoy five months of pleasant weather. The best time to plan your holiday is the period from November through March. Although this is considered winter in these parts, this term is only relative to the other seasons, which include a wretched summer and a torrential monsoon. Moreover, with Mumbai's many cultural festivals and Goa's famous carnival being held during this time, it's no wonder this is peak season. Of course, prices are high during this period, especially in Goa, as hotel- and shack-owners are eager to make up for the lean season. Book your accommodations well in advance, especially around the time of the cultural festivals in Mumbai, Carnival in Goa, and on New Year's Eve at both places.

Even locals escape these parts in the searing summer temperatures, which peak in the month of May. Temperatures soar to 38°C, and humidity is almost always above 50 percent. The monsoon season, which lasts from June to September, is marked by unpredictable, heavy showers and empty beaches. If you're in Mumbai, try not to get caught in the floods that have been plaguing the city in recent years. The flip side, however, is that accommodations in Goa are much cheaper during the monsoon, often at half the high-season rate. If you're willing to trade the beach for a feel of local village life, you're likely to get an insider's view of Goa that you wouldn't get during peak season.

▶ BEFORE YOU GO

Passports and Visas

All foreign visitors must have a valid passport and visa to enter the country. Only citizens of India, Nepal, Bhutan, and the Maldives are exempt from carrying visas.

Vaccinations

Make sure you've taken the required shots, particularly your vaccination for tetanus, Hepatitis A and B, polio, typhoid, and chicken pox. Make sure you get anti-malarial tablets from your doctor, as both Mumbai and Goa are hotbeds for mosquitoes. Look out for World Health Organization (WHO) recommendations on their official website (www.who.int).

Travel Insurance

Travel insurance is a must as a safeguard against medical emergency or loss of luggage. It's best to arrange for travel and medical insurance before you set out, as there are no health policies to cover tourists in India. Contact your local insurance agent for an appropriate policy.

Transportation

Mumbai has an international and a domestic airport, Chhatrapati Shivaji Airport and Santacruz. For those traveling onward from Mumbai to other parts of the country, train and road travel are a scenic way to travel, but a number of budget airlines in the country reduce travel time by several hours or even days.

In Mumbai, walking and taking taxis and auto-rickshaws are better options than renting a vehicle, as driving in the city and finding parking can be a nightmare. For longer distances, consider hiring a car and driver. If you're here for the long haul, try braving the local trains and buses after you've settled down and figured out the routes.

In stark contrast, the open roads and winding village streets in Goa are best explored on your own, by car or on motorcycle, at a leisurely pace—no matter what the duration of your stay. Car and motorcycle rentals are widely available in Goa's tourist areas.

A car gets a ride on the ferry at Terekhol, Goa.

Mumbai's signature black-and-yellow taxi

Explore Mumbai & Goa

► THE BEST OF MUMBAI AND GOA

Day 1

Arrive in Mumbai. Overcome jet lag with an eye-opening taxi ride through Mumbai's crazy traffic. Head to the Gateway of India and take a ferry to the caves on Elephanta Island. Spend the afternoon in Colaba. Shop at Colaba Causeway, and have a meal at one of the many cafés and restaurants located here. If you have the energy for it, hit a popular nightspot.

Day 2

Begin the day at Chhatrapati Shivaji Terminus, then go to Mahatma Phule Market (Crawford Market) or Chor Bazaar. Take a heritage walk in the Fort area with Bombay Heritage Walks or with Mumbai Magic. If you prefer to do it on your own, head to the University of Mumbai and Rajabai Clock Tower, then walk towards Flora Fountain and end the walk at Horniman Circle and the Asiatic Society. Stop by the street booksellers.

Day 3

Dedicate the day to Mumbai's culture in the Kala Ghoda art district. Visit the Prince of Wales Museum and the many art galleries located around here. Take a break at the lovely Samovar café at the Jehangir Art Gallery and get your portrait sketched by one of the artists on the pavement gallery outside. Stop by at Max Mueller Bhavan or at the music store Rhythm House to ask for tickets to performances. If there's nothing of interest available, go to the National Centre for Performing Arts at Nariman Point and catch an evening show.

Roman goddess Flora turns her back to the Bombay Stock Exchange at Mumbai's Flora Fountain.

The Indian flag waves proudly amid 19th-century colonial architecture at the University of Mumbai.

BOLLYWOOD BLOCKBUSTER

Let's face it. In spite of its many interesting and varied facets, Mumbai is famous (or infamous) for the shimmer and shimmies of its film industry called Bollywood. Song and dance, melodrama and romance rule, as do the superstars who inspire countrywide mass hysteria. Mumbai is every Bollywood fan's dream destination – a fact that is fairly obvious from the number of onlookers gathered outside the homes of some of the popular stars.

Traditionally, Bollywood movies boasted Shakespearean plots and tragedy along the scales of Greek drama or of biblical proportions. Twins separated at birth were reunited by chance and blind people miraculously regained sight in moments of truth. Today, true to its name, Bollywood freely borrows from Hollywood. However, there is also a welcome experimentation in scripts and breaking of stereotypes, heralding (hopefully) a new phase in Indian cinema. The song and bling, meanwhile, are here to stay.

Begin your Bollywood blockbuster tour with a crash course.

STEP 1

Learn the names of **Bollywood's biggest stars** – Amitabh Bachchan, Shah Rukh Khan, Amir Khan, Salman Khan, Saif Ali Khan, Aishwarya Rai, Preity Zinta, Kareena Kapoor, and Priyanka Chopra. Lay your hands on the gossip magazines – *Filmfare, Stardust,* and *Cineblitz* are the big ones.

STEP 2

Try to catch a glimpse of the stars in person. Join the fans who gather outside the **star homes** of Shah Rukh Khan or Salman Khan in Bandstand (Bandra) or outside the bungalow of Amitabh Bachchan in Juhu. Visit **starry nightspots** like **Olive** (Pali Hill Tourist Hotel, Union Park) and **Aurus** (Nichani Kutir).

STEP 3

Go on a **Bollywood studios tour.** Visit **Film City** (off Western Express Hwy., Aarey Milk Colony Rd.) in the suburb of Goregaon. While we don't guarantee entry, **RK Studios** (Asha Compound, Sion-Trombay Rd., Chembur East) in the suburb of Chembur on the Central line is a historical Bollywood landmark. In Bandra, there's the equally iconic **Mehboob Studios** (Mount Mary Steps, near Bandstand, Bandra) near the Mount Mary steps and Bandstand. For fieldwork coupled with theory, enroll for the **Art in Bollywood** tour conducted by Mumbai Magic (cell tel. 91/98677-07414, www.mumbaimagic.com).

STEP 4

It's time to research your films. If you like old-fashioned action in the comfort of your fancy hotel, there's **Don** (the old 1970s version and the newer remake) or the iconic and evergreen **Sholay.** If you're one for tearjerkers, romance, and soppy family dramas, watch any of the films made by Karan Johar under the banner of BR Films. If you want to see the changing face of Bollywood or a telling commentary on contemporary Mumbai, watch **Chandni Bar** (a film on Mumbai's famous bar dancers) or **Page Three** by filmmaker Madhur Bhandarkar. For a look at Mumbai's famous "underworld" or mafia, watch **Company.** And if you prefer comedy, look out for any of the David Dhawan films starring actor **Govinda** or watch **Om Shanti Om,** a modern spoof on the good old '70s movies.

STEP 5

Depending on your preference, you may choose to view a Bollywood movie at one of Mumbai's old art deco cinema halls – **Regal, Eros, New Excelsior,** the newly restored **Metro cinema** – or at one of the new multiplexes, like **Imax, Inox,** or **Cinemax.** The latter has a premium cinema lounge called **Red Lounge** where you can recline in the cushioned comfort of private cubicles.

STEP 6

If you liked what you saw and are inspired to be a Bollywood actor, there's actor **Anupam Kher's acting academy** (Film Industry Welfare Trust House, near Ajivasan Hall, Juhu Rd., Santacruz, tel. 022/2660-5659, www.actorprepares.net) and filmmaker Subhash Ghai's **Whistling Woods International** (Goregaon East, tel. 022/ 3091-6000, www.whistlingwoods.net) located within Film City. Bollywood has plenty of bit parts for foreigners and it helps to be a good dancer.

Chhatrapati Shivaji Terminus in Mumbai, a UNESCO World Heritage Site

Day 4

Enter the ancient temple area of Banganga Tank at Malabar Hill, at the very end of the Marine Drive and Chowpatty area. Visit the nearby Mani Bhavan, Mahatma Gandhi's home, and the little hamlet called Khotachiwadi in the Girgaum area. In the evening, go for a stroll down Marine Drive, Mumbai's favorite seafront.

Day 5

Spend the day in Central Mumbai. Visit the Bhau Daji Lad Museum for some of Mumbai's finest historical artifacts. Have a meal at Gallops, the restaurant at the Mahalaxmi Race Course. Catch the sunset at the Haji Ali Mosque and Mausoleum.

Day 6

Discover the suburbs. Set off early in the morning for the Sanjay Gandhi National Park and join one of the many nature walks conducted by naturalists and wildlife enthusiasts. Visit the ancient Kanheri Caves within the park. On your way back, go to Juhu Beach and end your day on a high—at a Bandra resto-bar.

Day 7

Conclude your Mumbai sojourn with a day trip in the vicinity—to Vasai Fort if you're in the mood for heritage or to the islands of Manori or Madh if you want to see what Mumbai once looked like—a small fishing village and a beach. If you prefer to stay within city limits, catch a Bollywood film at one of Mumbai's old art deco cinema halls.

crowds and coconuts at Mumbai's Juhu Beach

GOAN FESTIVITY

Although Goa is in the festive mood all year long, two major festivals draw visitors by the droves. The state's most important event is the **Goa Carnival** – the state's last hurrah before the abstinence of the 40-day period of Lent. With three days of hedonistic revelry flagged off with colorful processions of parades, floats, and bands belting out Goan music to cheering crowds, it is reminiscent of a wild Brazilian extravaganza. The festival finds its origins in the feasting and merrymaking of ancient Rome and Greece, and was brought to the Portuguese colonies – where it was infused with flavor by African slaves. The carnival arrived in Goa in the 18th century, where it embraced the customs of the local village festivals. Today, it attracts thousands of tourists and locals. Highlights include the opening ceremony and the arrival of King Momo (derived from Momus, the Greek god of frolic), who orders his masked subjects in exotic costumes to indulge in wild feasting, drinking, and partying. The carnival opens in February on a *Sabado Gordo* or "Fat Saturday" and ends on Shrove Tuesday or "Fat Tuesday."

a Portuguese festival in Panaji's Latin Quarter

Meanwhile, the **International Film Festival of India** (IFFI, www.iffigoa.org), in November–December, is a world cinema festival à la Cannes. The organizers couldn't have chosen a better venue when they settled on Goa a few years ago. Films are screened across the city of Panaji at places such as the Kala Academy, INOX, and the nearby beaches. The film festival is one of the oldest and biggest in India, and boasts attendance by a variety of Indian and international celebrities. The "Cinema of the World" section features a selection of the year's best productions, screening close to 100 films from around 50 countries. Retrospectives, talent hunts, competitions, and awards light up this 11-day event, with the Golden Peacock award being given to the best film. The festival also works as a "film bazaar" where joint ventures between production houses are brokered and much money is involved.

Day 8

After a hectic Mumbai trip, dive headlong into the beaches of Goa. Head to the northern coast for a feel of the famous Goa vibe. Stay in Candolim if you want to be by the sea and yet be close enough to the historic sights of Panaji and Interior Goa. Go for a stroll down Candolim and Sinquerim Beaches and lunch at one of its famous beach shacks. Visit Fort Aguada and/or Calizz.

Day 9

Sign up for an activity with Goa's most reputed water-sports operator, Thunderwave, which operates from Sinquerim Beach. If you prefer a diving trip, head farther north to Baga and spend a good part of the day exploring the marine life of Goa with PADI-certified Barracuda Diving. After a day at sea, discover the nightlife in busy Baga.

Day 10

Alternate a day at the beach with the heritage trail of Panaji, Old Goa, and Ponda. Begin the day with an early-morning stroll around Panaji's charming Latin Quarter. Walk along the city's riverfront and visit its famous Church of Our Lady of the Immaculate Conception. Then go to Old Goa, where you can see the Basilica of Bom Jesus before you lunch at one of the spice plantations on your way to Ponda. Visit one or two temples to get a feel of pre-Portuguese Goa.

Day 11

Head to Anjuna and Vagator if you enjoy the hippie vibe, or farther north to the beaches of Morjim or Mandrem for a bit of peace and quiet. Visit the Chapora Fort in Vagator and spend the day on the beach or explore the Far North by taking a ferry to Fort Tiracol. If it's a Wednesday, visit Anjuna's Wednesday Flea Market instead. If it's a Friday, take a detour to Mapusa's Friday Bazaar. If it's

ramparts of the 17th-century Chapora Fort in Vagator, Goa

a Saturday, end the day at Ingo's Saturday Nite Bazaar.

Day 12

Head down to the southern coast via Madgaon. Drive past its beautiful Indo-Portuguese houses and visit a casa, such as Casa Araujo Alvares in nearby Loutolim, Casa Bragança in Chandor, or Palacio do Deao in Quepem. Catch the sunset at one of the nearby beaches, preferably at the iconic Zeebop on Utorda Beach.

Or head straight to the beach. Go beach-hopping from Velsao to Cavelossim, lunch at a riverside restaurant in Mobor, and watch fishermen bring in their fresh catch at Betul Jetty.

Day 13

Begin early and go farther south, stopping at Agonda Beach on the way to the magical destination of Palolem. Spend the day in Palolem, discovering its many coves and islands with a trusted boat operator.

Day 14

Relax on the beach. Treat yourself to a spa. Consider extending your holiday.

Latin Quarter in Panaji, Goa

▶ BEACHES, BARS, AND BAZAARS

Goa's bars and parties spill over onto the beach, as do its famous flea markets and night bazaars. Bazaars include live music, entertainment, and dancing, and the night markets are merely an excuse to prolong the party. Goa's beaches, bars, and bazaars are practically indistinguishable from one another, making each a little more colorful, a bit more vibrant, than it already is.

Day 1

Get into the thick of the crowds, stalls, and parties on the northern coast, in the stretch between Candolim and Baga. Start with a swim or water sports at Candolim and Sinquerim Beaches or at Baga Beach. Spend the afternoon browsing through the Tibetan Market in Baga before you settle into Shiro Poison for the night at Candolim, or get into the retro groove at Cavala. If you prefer the thrill of a casino, head down to Panaji for a night of beginner's luck at the cruise-ship casino MS *Caravela*. If you feel like you haven't had enough of the beach, simply relax at one of the many beachside shacks on this stretch that provide music and live entertainment.

Day 2

Go beach hopping on luxury yacht *Solita* in the day, and then bar-hopping on a fishing boat after dark, provided by Nerul restaurant Amigo's. The *Solita* takes you to the northern beaches and anchors at Coco Bay, where you can swim and sunbathe off the yacht. Or go diving with Barracuda Diving, which operates out of Baga. Set out on your bar-hopping boat ride later in the night with a local or travel on your own to Loungefly, Tito's, and Café Mambo's at Baga. If it's a Saturday, go to Mackie's Saturday Nite Bazaar for

Fishing boats take a break at Goa's Benaulim Beach.

some nocturnal entertainment, shopping, and partying.

Day 3

If it's a Wednesday, head straight to Anjuna's flea market. If it's a Friday, or any other day for that matter, take a detour to the Mapusa Friday Bazaar. The traditional market is partially open even on weekdays. Spend the rest of the day on Anjuna Beach or lounging around at Café Looda at the end of Anjuna market. In the evening, make your way to Shore Bar, Curlies, and on a Saturday, to Ingo's night bazaar.

Day 4

If you didn't get to go to a full moon or trance party in Anjuna, you may be in luck at Vagator. Locals will inform you about parties at Nine Bar, Primrose Bar, and Hill Top. Vagator's beaches are beautiful and there's a bit of street shopping, too. If you feel like heading farther north, Morjim is a lovely beach for a swim and dolphin sightings, while Mandrem is simply exquisite. In the evenings,

SHACKING UP IN GOA

Goa's most famous hippie legacy lies in its beach shacks. Hundreds of little makeshift huts supported by bamboo poles and covered by palm fronds come up in the tourist season, only to be dismantled in time for the monsoon. Their history goes back over four decades, when these cheap and temporary places were the only ones where traveling flower children could shack up for the night or enjoy a good Goan meal during the day. Soon, these shacks and "cocohuts" were where psychedelic drugs and rock and roll thrived — a legacy that was carried on by the trance and chemical generation of the 1990s.

Today, even the regular, permanent restaurants create a shack-like atmosphere to draw the crowds who like to lounge around with a beer, sunbathe on the deck chairs, and watch the world go by. After dark, the northern stretch of shacks, especially around **Calangute and Baga,** turns into a carnival as jugglers, acrobats, flame-throwers, and performers light up the night even as patrons tuck into the catch of the day. Shacks such as **Zanzibar** (Baga) and **Calamari** (Candolim) do brisk business for lunch and dinner; **Frank Zappa's Beach Shack** — one of the first hippie shacks in Candolim — and legendary Anjuna shacks like **Curlies** and **Shore Bar** are popular nightspots.

Most shacks rent rudimentary rooms in the form of beach huts with thatched roofs that are built on wooden stilts. Although basic (sometimes with a shared bathroom), they make for a pleasant stay, with the ocean at your doorstep. The southern coast, too, has a number of such accommodations, especially on the beaches of **Colva, Agonda,** and **Palolem.** Here, shack owners were originally permitted to build these temporary shelters as an alternate source of income by the government, but only on the condition that the structures would be brought down in the monsoon in adherence to coastal regulations and with regard to preservation of the environment. Shack owners also need to renew their license at the beginning of every new tourist season by paying the local governing body a nominal fee.

A shack undergoes construction after Goa's annual monsoon break.

Loekie Café at Arambol has live music and jam sessions in peak season.

without a second thought to Fisherman's Wharf in Mobor.

Day 5

The parties and bazaars thin out along the quiet southern coast but the beaches more than make up for it. The beach of Bogmalo is an ideal getaway from the crowds. And it's a tough choice between Utorda, Arossim, Varca, and Cavelossim if you want to spend the day by the sea. Zeebop by the Sea at Utorda is a great place to stay the morning and afternoon, right until sunset. After dark, hit Martin's Corner at Betalbatim for some cheery '80s music or to Shalom at Colva if you feel like some wine and a bit of atmosphere. For local style partying, go to Fiplee's at Benaulim, but for a romantic night with music and dancing by the riverside, head

Day 6

Begin the day with a refreshing early-morning swim (but don't venture too far out into the sea) at the small and quiet beach of Agonda. Spend the rest of the day in Palolem, discovering its many islands and coves. At night, experience a Silent Noise party or if you prefer to do it the good old-fashioned way, seek comfort in the loud beats of Cuba or Café Del Mar.

Day 7

Treat yourself to luxury yacht *Blue Diamond* and discover the unexplored southern islands around Rajbag. Give your holiday a happy end with a night out at The End in Rajbag.

► GOA'S INNER WORLD

For those who wish to be acquainted more intimately with this beautiful state, Goa is full of surprises. Not far from the beaches, it hides a treasure trove of islands, villages, forests, bird parks, heritage houses, and one of the largest waterfalls in India. Drive past the rustic setting, spend a day by the cascading waterfall, and explore the islands and sanctuaries at leisure. Goa's inner world cannot be hurried.

village of Salvador do Mundo, where you can visit the Houses of Goa Museum. Turn towards Calangute and you'll pass through the beautiful village of Saligao, known for its whitewashed neo-Gothic Church of Nossa Senhora Mae de Deus. Stop along Chogm Road at Nilaya's art and antiques store and café called Sangolda, named after the heritage village it is located in.

Day 1

From Ribandar and Old Goa, near Panaji, it's a short ferry ride to the Chorao and Divar Islands, the latter of which known for the Dr. Salim Ali Bird Sanctuary. From Panaji, you could also drive to the picturesque village of Britona, just across the Mandovi Bridge and take the luxury yacht *Solita* for a cruise down the river. Drive on to the lush

Day 2

From Mapusa it's a fairly straight and simple route to the wonderfully secluded village of Aldona, where locals, artists, and writers live amicably. Go westwards towards Anjuna and you will drive past the charming village of Assagao. Go eastwards and deeper into the interior, beyond Bicholim and you will reach the remote Arvalem Caves. There's a waterfall and a lake in the vicinity.

Day 3

Leave for a day of nature and adventure at the Bhagwan Mahavir Wildlife Sanctuary and Molem National Park, the Dudhsagar Waterfall, and the nearby temple of Tambdi Surla in Far Eastern Goa.

Day 4

Discover the interior urban landscape of the southern coast with the magnificent Indo-Portuguese casas of the villages of Loutolim and Chandor farther inland from Madgaon. Closer to the coast but

AYURVEDA SPAS

Where there are five-star resorts, there must be spas. Studded with luxury hotels, the southern coast is a delight for those seeking herbal indulgences and holistic experiences. With a range of aromatherapy, Ayurvedic, Thai, Balinese, Swedish, and other massages and treatments up on offer – along with whirlpool tub, steam, and sauna facilities – spa seekers are spoiled by all the choices.

Most visitors prefer to avail of treatments and therapies based on Ayurveda – the ancient Indian science of healing that uses natural and herbal remedies. A holistic method that believes in a healthy lifestyle achieved by balancing the spiritual with the emotional and physical forces, in harmony with nature, Ayurveda stresses the five great elements – earth, water, fire, air, and space. It believes that the life forces are guided by three natural elements or energies, known as *Vata* (air – movement, activity, inconsistency), *Pitta* (fire – heat, consistency, organization), and *Kapha* (water and earth – stability, lethargy, groundedness). Our bodies are believed to have each of these elements in varying degrees, the dominant element defining a person as a certain type, as either a *Vata, Pitta,* or *Kapha* personality and body type. Any imbalance in these forces is believed to bring about physical or mental ill health. Ayurveda treatments are specially designed for these various personality and body types and strive to harmonize their rhythms with those of the environment, with the help of herbal and natural oils, massages and foods.

Most spas offer a consultation with their Ayurvedic physician, who will help determine your "type" by understanding your personality traits and lifestyle choices. Once your

preparation for a traditional Ayurvedic massage

Ayurveda type has been determined, the physician will chart out a diet plan and recommend a spa treatment, and even advise the time of day when you should experience it.

Goa's southern coast boasts exceptional spas and resorts. Some of the best include **Sereno Spa** (Park Hyatt Goa, Arossim Beach), **Agua Spa** (Kenilworth Beach Resort and Spa, Utorda Beach), **Majorda Beach Resort** (Majorda Beach), **Jiva** (Taj Exotica, Benaulim), **Rejuvenation** (Soul Vacation, Colva Beach), **Spa Villa** (Holiday Inn Resort Goa, Mobor Beach, and **Ayurveda** (The Leela, Cavelossim).

seemingly far away from commercial beach activity are the unspoiled fishing villages of Velsao and Varca.

Day 5

Spend your last day spotting Goa's varied flora and fauna at the Cotigao Wildlife Sanctuary in the far south.

► MIX IT UP: MUMBAI MASALA

Mumbai is a masala, or a spicy mix of ingredients, both modern and traditional, the local and the global. If you have only five days in Mumbai, this itinerary will ensure that you experience its multiple worlds.

Colonial Architecture and the Skyline

Soak in the old Bombay charm at the Gateway of India and go on a heritage walking tour of the Fort and Kala Ghoda areas with a guide such as Bombay Heritage Walks. Spend the latter half of the day at Nariman Point and Marine Drive, taking in the sea and the city skyline, which includes skyscrapers and modern buildings looming large over the sea. View the sunset and the frenetic rush hour in this prime business district from the comfort of one of the many sea-facing five-star restaurants in the area.

Antiques and Boutiques

Mumbai's mix of tradition and modernity is best experienced with a tour of its markets. Bargain hard for antiques and artifacts at Chor Bazaar, buy flowers and spices at Crawford Market, and get clothes for cheap at the street-side market called Fashion Street. Later, for a look at Mumbai's designer clothes, visit the chic Courtyard, where the city's major designers have their boutiques. And don't forget the Bombay Stock Exchange at Dalal Street—it is Mumbai's most celebrated marketplace today.

The Rural and the Urban

Discover villages in the city. For all its modern facade, Mumbai's little *gaothans* (hamlets) and fishing villages continue to thrive. The hidden worlds of Khotachiwadi at Girgaum make for an interesting contrast with the upmarket urbane areas of Malabar Hill and Worli Seaface. Make sure you stop for a traditional Maharashtrian coastal lunch at Anantashram in Khotachiwadi.

Nature and the Concrete Jungle

Take the crowded local train from Churchgate on the Western line to the suburb of Borivli. Sanjay Gandhi National Park is a short ride from Borivli Station by auto-rickshaw. Breathe in the fresh air and

an antique gramophone for sale at Mumbai's Chor Bazaar

Sanjay Gandhi National Park

BAR-HOPPING IN MUMBAI

Mumbai's myriad bars cater to every audience, so you'll find everything from the cheapest country liquor to the most expensive single malts. The city has iconic budget bars and expensive destinations, and you'll even find some familiar ones (such as T.G.I. Friday's and the Hard Rock Cafe). Some nightspots enjoy short-lived popularity, while others are institutions – make sure you visit both kinds.

SOUTH MUMBAI
Begin your bar tour with live music at **Not Just Jazz by the Bay** (Soona Mahal, Marine Dr.) or with the view at **Dome** (Marine Dr.) – the stylish rooftop bar at the Hotel InterContinental. Pop in at **Indigo** (Mandalik Rd.) in Colaba and then at dive bar **Gokul** (opposite Badé Miyan, Tulloch Rd.), behind the Taj Hotel.

CENTRAL MUMBAI
Stop by for a game of snooker or to scrawl graffiti on the walls of **The Ghetto** (Bhulabhai Desai Rd.) in Mahalaxmi. Get to **Blue Frog** (Mathuradas Mills Compound, opposite Phoenix Mills) in the Lower Parel area, just in time for a live world-music performance accompanied by a visual display. Then visit Japanese fairytale palace **Shiro** (Bombay Dyeing Mill Compound) in Lower Parel.

NORTH MUMBAI
Head towards the suburbs and to celeb

hangout **Olive** (Pali Hill Tourist Hotel, Union Park) in Bandra. Shake a leg at the mega-discotheque **Poison** (Krystal, Waterfield Rd., Bandra) before you make your way to the car-turned-DJ-console suspended from the ceiling at "garage pub" **Toto's** (Pali Junction, Bandra). Pop in for a quick drink at the nearby budget bar **Janata** (Pali Naka, Bandra) before you head to Mumbai's hottest suburban nightspot: **China House** (off the Western Express Hwy., Santacruz East) at the Grand Hyatt. End the evening on the open wooden-deck beach bar of **Aurus** (Nichani Kutir, Juhu-Tara Rd.) in Juhu, watching the waves lap gently in the moonlight as the DJ plays your song.

Hop from the restaurant China House to its cool lounge, at the Grand Hyatt.

enjoy the open spaces and wildlife of the national park. Go on a nature walk or a lion safari. It is difficult to believe that tigers, leopards, lions, cobras, and porcupines inhabit this park, located within city limits. If you're in Mumbai during the winter months, go to the industrial area of Sewri in Central Mumbai for the bizarre sight of migratory flamingos in the bay.

The Local and the Global
End your trip with the ultimate Mumbai mix. Watch the city's famous *tiffin* transport system by seeing the *dabbawallas,* in action around lunchtime at Churchgate Station. Go to the area called Dhobi Ghat near Mahalaxmi and watch the city's washermen at work. Catch a popular Bollywood film (or a local festival if you're in luck), and try the street food at Chowpatty as you observe the city lights from the beach. Complete the day with a contrasting visit to Mumbai's hippest mall—High Street Phoenix.

MUMBAI

Nothing that anyone ever tells you will really prepare you for Mumbai. As soon as you step out of its newly renovated airport, the city will assault you with its sights, sounds, and smells. Mumbai's vast ocean is rivaled only by its sea of people, seen gushing out of railway stations and pouring out onto the streets during rush hour. As migrants settle into the city and adopt it as their new home (along with a tiny but growing resident foreign population), the 13-million-plus numbers, pretty much like the city's stock index, continue to rise. Celebrated commercial capital and the face of the new economically driven India, Mumbai straddles its contrasts and contradictions with astonishing ease. It surprises us with its vibrant nightlife and active cultural scene. It shocks us with its swelling slums and soaring realty rates. And it entertains us with its unique brand of commercial cinema, endearingly referred to as Bollywood. Visually, Mumbai provides a startling contrast of its concrete realities—British colonial buildings in the Indo-Saracenic style of architecture vie for attention with towering skyscrapers reminiscent of the Manhattan skyline. Heritage structures such as the 7th-century Elephanta Caves and the Haji Ali Mosque and Mausoleum emerge Poseidon-like from the Arabian Sea, lending the city its unique character.

The co-existence of contrasts—of the old and the new, the rich and the poor, the local and the global—is a recurring leitmotif in Mumbai. Shiny sedans overtake old black-and-yellow Fiat taxis, sprawling luxury apartments and penthouses overlook crowded slums,

© ASHIMA NARAIN

MUMBAI

HIGHLIGHTS

◖ **Gateway of India:** Mumbai's finest colonial remnant, the Gateway was built as the entry point into the city of Mumbai for King George V and Queen Mary (page 32).

◖ **Elephanta Island:** On an untouched island off the coast, the spectacular rock-sculpted caves of Elephanta are only an hour's boat ride from the Gateway (page 32).

◖ **Chhatrapati Shivaji Maharaj Vastu Sangrahalay (Prince of Wales Museum):** The city museum, a fine piece of colonial architecture, is known as much for its exterior as it is for the exhibits (page 35).

◖ **Chhatrapati Shivaji Terminus (Victoria Terminus):** Watch the Mumbai crowds in action or simply admire the colonial architecture of Mumbai's most significant train station, also a UNESCO World Heritage Site (page 40).

◖ **Mani Bhavan (Mahatma Gandhi Museum):** The former home of the man who got India its independence, Mani Bhavan is now a museum that displays Gandhi memorabilia, while its library is a great place for historical information (page 45).

◖ **Khotachiwadi:** Walk through narrow, winding lanes and past quaint wooden cottages at Khotachiwadi, a tiny 18th-century village in the heart of the city (page 46).

◖ **Banganga Tank:** A medieval stepped well surrounded by 18th-century temples, Banganga has both historical and religious significance, and is the setting for the spectacular Banganga music festival (page 47).

◖ **Haji Ali Mosque and Mausoleum:** An unusual mosque and mausoleum in the sea, Haji Ali is a 17th-century shrine dedicated to the saint of the same name (page 48).

◖ **Bhau Daji Lad Museum:** This wonderful museum documents the history of the city. Exhibits include the stone elephant that gave Elephanta Island its name and the statue of the black horse after which the Kala Ghoda art district is named (page 53).

◖ **Ajanta and Ellora:** These 3rd-century Buddhist rock-cut caves are one of India's most celebrated archaeological sites and a mere 40 minutes by air from Mumbai (page 112).

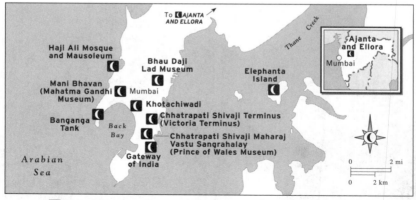

LOOK FOR ◖ TO FIND RECOMMENDED SIGHTS, ACTIVITIES, DINING, AND LODGING.

spanking new malls loom over lively traditional markets. And a national park teeters at the edge of the city, breathing oxygen into the carbon fumes of the concrete jungle. Of late, the city's migrant population has been tickled pink with its recent feathered addition; framed against the industrial landscape of the city in the winter months is the extraordinary sight of migratory flamingos that adds to the beauty and the madness of this schizophrenic city. And herein lies its charm.

In Mumbai, history and geography collude to bring you an extraordinary experience. Originally a group of seven islands passed on to the British as a dowry by the Portuguese, Mumbai has its fair share of architectural delights. However, its most dominant feature is the sea, framed by the Gateway of India at Colaba, adorned with the glittering Queen's Necklace by night and lined with beaches that resemble carnivals rather than seafronts. There's plenty to do here as well, ranging from heritage walks to nature trails and from art shows to discos. In Mumbai, shaking a leg at the latest nightspot is as important as shaking hands over an important business deal. The city youth take both jobs seriously, giving Mumbai its reputation as a city that never sleeps.

Of all the mixed feelings that you're likely to have about Mumbai, one feeling you will never experience is boredom. The city is always bustling with activity, eating and drinking, shopping, partying, and celebrating festivals both religious and cultural. Interestingly enough, the most enjoyable sights here are the ones conveying everyday life. Getting into the skin of the city is highly recommended, whether it means visiting Churchgate Station at lunch hour to observe the famous *dabbawallas* in action or going down to Dhobi Ghat to watch the city's dirty linen being washed in public. The true test of the city is met when visitors enter as foreigners and leave as locals. The day you jump into a suburban local train yelling *"Baaju Hato!"* ("Make way!"), sit through a three-hour Bollywood extravaganza, or stomach a spicy *paani puri* at Juhu Beach, rest assured that

you've passed the test. And that Mumbai welcomes you back with open arms.

HISTORY

Mumbai evolved from seven islands inhabited by Agris (salt-pan workers) and Kolis (a fishing community) as far back as the 2nd century B.C. It changed hands with shifting dynasties and empires until the Portuguese came along to discover the New World in the 16th century, fighting a battle with Arab traders and Sultan Bahadur Shah of Gujarat, to establish a small colony. The mosquito-infested islands were developed and flagged with churches and forts but were eventually passed on as dowry to the British, with the marriage of Catherine of Braganza to King Charles II. The British government, much like the Portuguese before them, failed to recognize the profitability of the islands and leased them out to the East India Company for a handsome rent of 10 pounds a year. The company realized the islands' potential and exploited the natural harbor to further its trade, developing the colony by building fortifications, churches, a mint, and a small hospital. The islands, now called Bombay, prospered and replaced Surat as the company headquarters in 1687. By this time, the city was awash with Arab traders eager to set up trade, Parsi migrants who had landed on the shores of Gujarat from Iran, as well as Jews who had arrived here from Armenia and Baghdad. The Queen took over the city in 1858, and it prospered with the cotton boom brought about by the American Civil War. Bombay grew to its present stature, complete with streets, buildings, commercial areas, and monuments from this point onward to the present day.

Today, Bombay is officially referred to by its Marathi appellation, Mumbai, and much of its colonial architecture has been renamed after Maratha king Shivaji—a manifestation of the megalomania of the right wing political party called the Shiv Sena that has been held responsible for communal tensions that scarred the city not so long ago. Having survived riots, floods, and terror attacks in recent times, the city that never sleeps continues to

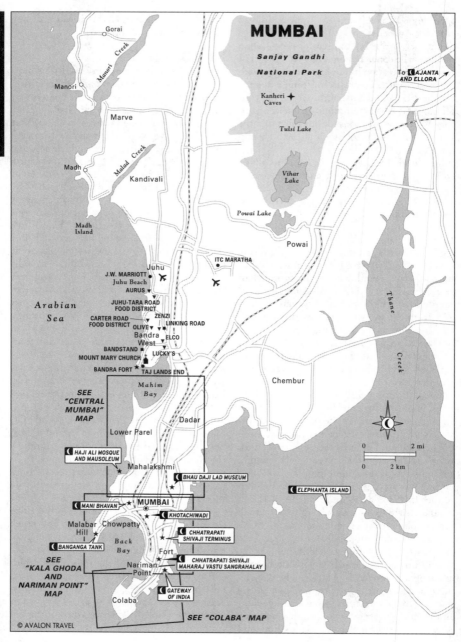

MUMBAI

Sanjay Gandhi

National Park

To **(AJANTA AND ELLORA**

Gorai

Manori Creek

Manori

Kanheri Caves

Tulsi Lake

Marve

Malad Creek

Madh

Vihar Lake

Kandivali

Madh Island

Powai Lake

Powai

ITC MARATHA

Juhu

Arabian Sea

J.W. MARRIOTT
Juhu Beach
AURUS

JUHU-TARA ROAD
FOOD DISTRICT

ZENZI

CARTER ROAD
FOOD DISTRICT

LINKING ROAD

OLIVE

Bandra West

ELCO

BANDSTAND

LUCKY'S

MOUNT MARY CHURCH

BANDRA FORT

TAJ LANDS END

Thane

Creek

Chembur

Mahim Bay

SEE "CENTRAL MUMBAI" MAP

Lower Parel

Dadar

0   2 mi

0   2 km

(HAJI ALI MOSQUE AND MAUSOLEUM

Mahalakshmi

(BHAU DAJI LAD MUSEUM

(ELEPHANTA ISLAND

(MANI BHAVAN

MUMBAI

Malabar Hill

Chowpatty

(KHOTACHIWADI

(BANGANGA TANK

Back Bay

(CHHATRAPATI SHIVAJI TERMINUS

Fort

SEE "KALA GHODA AND NARIMAN POINT" MAP

Nariman Point

(CHHATRAPATI SHIVAJI MAHARAJ VASTU SANGRAHALAY

Colaba

(GATEWAY OF INDIA

SEE "COLABA" MAP

© AVALON TRAVEL

make the maximum contribution to the national exchequer, even as it faces the threat of implosion, reeling as it does under the burden of an uncontrollable population and impossible infrastructural demands.

PLANNING YOUR TIME

A minimum of four days is required for a quick run-through of Mumbai's essential sights and sounds, if you're up to hectic sightseeing by day and frenzied partying at night. A week will allow you to comfortably experience most city highlights—architectural, artistic, culinary, and local. You could even include a day trip to the beaches of Manori and Madh or recreational activities at the national park. Two weeks will give you enough time for that and more, providing the opportunity to visit satellite towns and cities around Mumbai, the vineyards at Nasik, or the Ajanta and Ellora Caves near Aurangabad. If you are on an extended stay, make sure you explore the nooks and crannies of the city, discovering its many quirks and finer nuances, and living as locals do.

If you are pressed for time, it's best to look for accommodations in South Mumbai, as the major sights are located here. However, if time is not a constraint but budget is, it may be more economical to stay in the suburbs.

November to March is usually the best period to visit the city. This is when Mumbai's monsoon is left far behind and the oppressive October heat abates, giving way to a pleasant so-called winter. It is not surprising, therefore, that all of Mumbai's major events are held during this time, ranging from theater festivals in November to jazz concerts and arts festivals in February. Hotel bookings are usually available throughout the year, but you may want to book in advance to avoid disappointment during this peak tourist season.

Getting Around

Mumbai has a good public transport system and taxis are the best way to travel as long as you follow the local routine—of starting out early and returning late—to beat the traffic. Mumbai traffic is a nightmare and can eat into

© ASHIMA NARAIN

Ferries leave for Elephanta Island from the Gateway of India.

precious travel time. You can travel around the city by bus, taxi, and train—and also by auto-rickshaw in the suburbs starting from Bandra. Travel by train is the fastest but it is also the most crowded mode of transport. There are plenty of car rental agencies, but driving yourself is not recommended. Cars generally come with drivers and it is best to let them navigate the traffic and take care of parking for you. The city's BEST bus service also is efficient but you will need to research the routes and stops closest to your destination. Meanwhile, travel to the nearby islands is made easy with regular ferries, and if you want a prelude to Goa, you can extend your stay with a night or two at the cottages of Manori or the luxury hotels at Madh.

Safety

Once touted as the city of thieves and pick-pockets, Mumbai is now as safe as any big city in other parts of the world. Today, it is considered the safest city in India for single women, but it's best not to let down your guard. Instances of crime against tourists are few and far between, but the city has had its share of such incidents in the past.

Women are advised to stick to the women's compartment when traveling by train, and to ignore the stares, comments, and other harmless forms of unwanted attention that may come their way. However, "eve-teasing," as it is called here, is a criminal offence and any form of sexual harassment may be reported at the nearest police station. You should not accept drinks or rides offered by strangers at bars and should always keep your belongings close to your person, especially near tourist sights or in crowded places.

It's difficult for most tourists to get used to hawking and begging on the streets of Mumbai. Hawkers (vendors selling their wares on the street, such as peanut-sellers at Juhu Beach) and beggars—grim reminders of the city's economic inequalities—rarely pose a danger, but they are especially persistent with tourists. Maimed beggars and little children forced to beg on the streets can be a heartrending sight, but their earnings are often collected by a gang lord—or sometimes squandered by an alcoholic parent. If you find it difficult to turn a blind eye, you can carry a candy or two for the kids—but you may attract plenty more in the bargain.

ORIENTATION

Mumbai comprises seven islands fused together to bring you an elongated stretch of land that has eaten into its neighboring areas to keep up with its growing population. The original urban center is the part now known as downtown or South Mumbai; the rest of the city has expanded far into the north, well beyond the bustling suburb of Borivli, known for its national park that was once outside city limits. At the southernmost tip is the tourist area of Colaba, which leads to the Kala Ghoda, Fort, and CST areas, known for their historic sights and cultural events. Stretching from the business district of Nariman Point, the seaface at Marine Drive and Chowpatty connects downtown Mumbai to Central Mumbai where the Mahalaxmi Race Course and the shopping and commercial districts of Lower Parel are located. To the north, beyond Mahim, is the world of suburban Mumbai where auto-rickshaws ply residents from up-market Bandra, past the charming seaside suburb of Juhu and crowded Andheri, and into the green environs of Borivli to the far north. Both the domestic and international airports are located here, in Santacruz and Andheri, respectively, as are many five-star hotels, restaurants, bars, and malls.

Sights

Sightseeing in Mumbai is a combination of history, architecture, and daily activities. Mumbai's historical and architectural sights are marked by its striking Indo-Saracenic style of architecture that came into being primarily with the fusion of the Islamic and North Indian architecture in the 12th century. Its Islamic influences came from far-flung places like Syria, Persia, Egypt, and North Africa. On their arrival, the British fused features of these stylized buildings—arches, domes, minarets, pavilions, intricate grills—with Neo-Classical and Neo-Gothic architecture. In Mumbai, the largest example of this is the Chhatrapati Shivaji Terminus, which has marked additions to the Neo-Gothic style. Other great examples include the Chhatrapati Shivaji Museum, with its great onion-dome and numerous minarets, grills, and pavilions. The British Royal Engineers used local stone to experiment with color, good examples being the black and white General Post Office behind CST and the Elphinstone Building at Horniman Circle. In Mumbai especially, we find the additions of *jhilmils*—intricately designed eaves that hang over windows for protection from the sun and rain. The Horniman Circle, CST, and Fort areas are great for spotting variants of the Indo-Saracenic style.

Mumbai's historical and architectural sights are concentrated in and around South Mumbai starting from the iconic Gateway of India, a boat ride away from the UNESCO World Heritage Site of the Elephanta Caves. In the heart of the financial district are Flora Fountain and the old Town Hall, which houses the Asiatic Library. Not far away is the art district at Kala Ghoda, while Central Mumbai's chief attraction is the Haji Ali mosque. The suburbs too have a smattering of tourist attractions but what leaves visitors spellbound are Mumbai's everyday sights, such as the washermen at work in Dhobi Ghat and the *dabbawallas* (tiffin-carriers) in action at Churchgate Station.

COLABA

Mumbai is continually growing and spreading out with a population that continues to rise. However, its main sights are concentrated in the downtown areas of South Mumbai that once constituted the entire city and which remain today its epicenter. Here, the simultaneously posh and seedy area of Colaba is characterized by colonial architecture, sprawling mansions, and the first Indian-owned luxury hotel, The Taj. On the other hand, it is also filled with throngs of tourists, a busy streetside market, cheap lodges, and dark alleys that are best avoided.

It is difficult to believe that Colaba was once a sleepy fishing island populated by the Koli fisherfolk from whom it derives its name. Today, their numbers continue to dwindle, and they have been pushed to the fringes just as the seafront, where they continue to reside, has

A signboard welcomes visitors to Mumbai at the Gateway of India.

© ASHIMA NARAIN

been reclaimed to meet the demands of a metropolis bursting at its seams.

(Gateway of India

Among the many sights witnessed in the shadow of the massive arch of the Gateway of India are those of fluttering pigeons, flashing cameras, persistent peanut-sellers, beaming tourists, and unemployed hopefuls looking for a break in the city of their dreams. The arch and surrounding promenade (dominated by the Taj Mahal Hotel) are frequented by locals and tourists alike. As ferries toot before departing on the hour-long ride to the UNESCO World Heritage Site of the Elephanta Caves, the Gateway combines the perfect Mumbai experience of the sea, street food, colorful crowds, and rides in the garish Victoria—a silver horse carriage that was once colonial Mumbai's mode of transport. The point of entry to Mumbai harbor, it proves an excellent place for ship-spotting and provides a fine view of the annual sailing regatta in summer. In the monsoons, the esplanade is both favored and feared for its crashing waves.

Built in the Indo-Saracenic style of architecture, a combination of the Neo-Gothic and Mughal styles that characterizes much of Mumbai's colonial buildings, the grand Gateway marked the arrival of King George V and Queen Mary by ship in 1911 (and ironically, also witnessed the departure of British troops after India's Independence in 1948). Designed by architect George Wittet, the yellow basalt structure that was eventually completed only in 1927 is today the iconic monument of Mumbai.

(Elephanta Island

From the Gateway, it is a scenic ride by motorboat to the **Elephanta Caves** (9 A.M.–5:30 P.M. Tues.–Sun., Rs 250), located on Gharapuri Island, better known as Elephanta Island, 10 kilometers off the coast. As you lose sight of the grand arch and its ferries, you will chug past luxury yachts, naval and merchant ships, and an oil terminal before you see the island emerge from behind a curtain of sea mist. A temple complex of seven rock-cut Hindu caves, the island derives its name from a massive stone

The Taj Mahal Palace and Tower overlooks Mumbai's Gateway of India.

© ASHIMA NARAIN

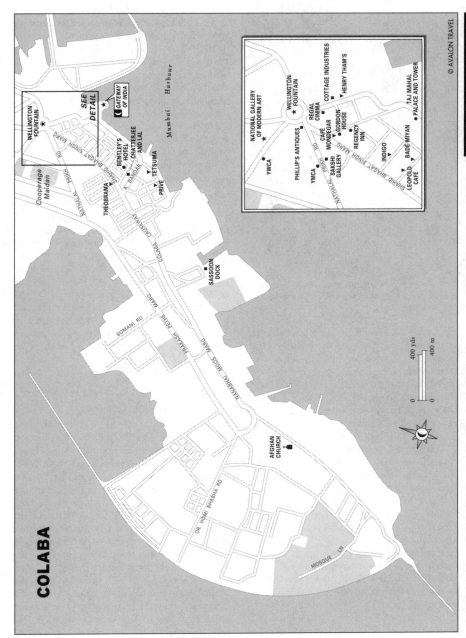

COLABA

Detail inset:
- NATIONAL GALLERY OF MODERN ART
- WELLINGTON FOUNTAIN
- COTTAGE INDUSTRIES
- HENRY THAM'S
- REGAL CINEMA
- TAJ MAHAL PALACE AND TOWER
- PHILLIP'S ANTIQUES
- CAFÉ MONDEGAR
- GORDON HOUSE
- YWCA
- YMCA
- REGENCY INN
- SAKSHI GALLERY
- INDIGO
- BADÉ MIYAN
- LEOPOLD CAFE
- SHAHID BHAGAT SINGH MARG
- NATHALAL PAREKH RD

Main map:
- WELLINGTON FOUNTAIN
- SEE DETAIL
- GATEWAY OF INDIA
- Mumbai Harbour
- Cooperage Maidan
- CHATTERJEE AND LAL
- BENTLEY'S HOTEL
- THEOBRAMA
- PRIVE
- TETSUMA
- SHAHID BHAGAT SINGH MARG
- NATHALAL PAREKH RD
- CAUSEWAY
- COLABA
- SASSOON DOCK
- SOMANI RD
- PRAKASH PETHE MARG
- NANABHAI MOOS MARG
- DR HOMI BHABHA RD
- AFGHAN CHURCH
- MOSQUE LN

0   400 yds
0   400 m

MUMBAI

© JANHAVI ACHAREKAR

The ancient temple complex of the Elephanta Caves surprises visitors with its location in the Arabian Sea.

elephant found on the shore (and which now rests at the Bhau Daji Lad Museum). Be it the *dvarapalas* (gigantic door-keepers), the colossal *trimurti* (three-headed image of the Hindu god Shiva as Creator, Protector and Destroyer), or the smaller shrines that dot the mountainside, these ancient caves showcase some magnificent examples of stone sculpture dating from the 7th to the 13th centuries A.D.

While the history of the caves is debated, it is believed that they were the handiwork of the artisans of a prosperous coastal kingdom whose capital was Gharapuri. The Portuguese called it the *ilha do elephanta* (Island of Elephant), but are believed to be responsible for more than its name change. Some say that they are to blame for the defacing of the sculptures, having used them for target practice. The damaged figures, however, are still as splendid as ever, especially those of Shiva as the trinity and as the *ardhanarinareshwar,* or the part male/part female form.

Boats depart from the Gateway of India every half-hour 9 A.M.–2:30 P.M. and return

at 5 P.M. Tuesday–Sunday (Rs 120). Luxury launches with tour guides are also available (tel. 022/2202-6364), and catamaran services run 10:30 A.M.–2 P.M. (tel. 022/2287-5473, Rs 150). Set aside three hours for the entire island, and choose a weekday to avoid crowds. It is a long walk and climb up a flight of steps (flanked by stalls selling souvenirs and eatables) before you get to the caves, so make sure you carry lots of water and wear a hat to avoid sunstroke. Keep food items and camera pouches close to your person, as the island is notorious for its aggressive monkeys.

Sassoon Docks

The only docks in Mumbai that allow complete access to the public, the Sassoon Docks are located off Colaba Causeway. Look out for the gate and clock tower at the entrance of the lane that leads to the docks. Built by Jewish businessman David Sassoon in the early 1800s, this was the port for his thriving cotton and opium trade. Today, a major part of Mumbai's Koli fishing community resides here; the best times to visit are around mid-morning and at sundown, when the fresh catch of fish is brought in to the docks from trawlers and launches for sale and also packed for frozen transport.

Afghan Church

Built to commemorate the martyrs of the first Afghan War (1835–1842), the Afghan Church (entry free, photography permitted) is a functional Presbyterian church built in the English Neo-Gothic style. Marked by a tall spire that was meant to be spotted from the harbor, the church is also known for some of the best stained glass of the period. The natural light streaming into the recently restored church reveals some well-cured woodwork, wrought iron, and encaustic floor tiles (geometric patterns embedded in the tiles) that were imported from England. Located in the naval area, the church is open from dawn to dusk, and you can even request the caretaker (who lives on the premises) to unlock the doors should you arrive late. If you're unclear about how to get there, take bus 123 from outside Churchgate Station, which will drop you near the church.

THE ART DISTRICT OF KALA GHODA

Kala Ghoda, literally translated, means "the black horse." The art district, easily accessible from the areas of Colaba, Fort, and Churchgate, derives its name from a stone statue that once stood here—of King Edward VII astride a horse. While the statue has long since been relocated to the Bhau Daji Lad Museum, the irreverent name lives on. In the seventies, Kala Ghoda was the domain of the city intelligentsia. Poets, writers, artists, and filmmakers met regularly at Samovar, the restaurant at Jehangir Art Gallery, and at Wayside Inn, a quaint café that has been replaced by the fancier Silk Route. Here, they discussed and debated ideas ranging from Marxism to the Cinema Nouvelle. The area was also immortalized by a Wayside Inn regular—the late Mumbai poet Arun Kolatkar—in his *Kala Ghoda Poems*.

The historic David Sassoon Library is a prominent landmark in the art district of Kala Ghoda.

© ASHIMA NARAIN

The precinct shelters some fine heritage structures from the turn of the century— examples like the **David Sassoon Library** and **Elphinstone College** are worth a look around. The city's oldest and most established art galleries are located here, as is the museum. The **Artists' Centre at Ador House,** closer to the naval area of Lion's Gate, was started by the city's earliest modern artists (called the Bombay Progressives) and was the first to host their debut group show. The **Max Mueller Bhavan,** where you can count on interesting Indo-German collaborations in the arts as well as screenings of German films, is just across the road from the crumbling Esplanade Mansion (previously Watson's Hotel) that was the first to screen Lumière brothers' films in India.

A new variation of the black horse is painted by a contemporary artist each year on the continuous facade of the building that houses the music store Rhythm House and the chic restaurants alongside.

The art district comes alive for nine days in February during the annual **Kala Ghoda festival.** A cultural medley that includes a range of events in art, theatre, music, dance, film, and literature, it transforms the area with its public art, installations, street shows, food court, handicraft stalls, and a carnival-like atmosphere.

🌙 Chhatrapati Shivaji Maharaj Vastu Sangrahalay (Prince of Wales Museum)

Previously known as the Prince of Wales Museum (tel. 022/2284-4484, www.bombaymuseum.org, 10:15 A.M.–6 P.M. Tues.– Sun., adult Indians Rs 15, foreigners Rs 300, students Rs 10, still/video photography Rs 200/2000), the city museum is located at the end of Kala Ghoda, toward the art deco–style Regal Cinema. The discreet blue **Wellington fountain,** just outside the museum, was built 200 years ago in commemoration of the duke's visit and marks the spot where the southern walls of the Bombay Fort once ended.

Inside the museum—another fine example of Indo-Saracenic architecture—are a

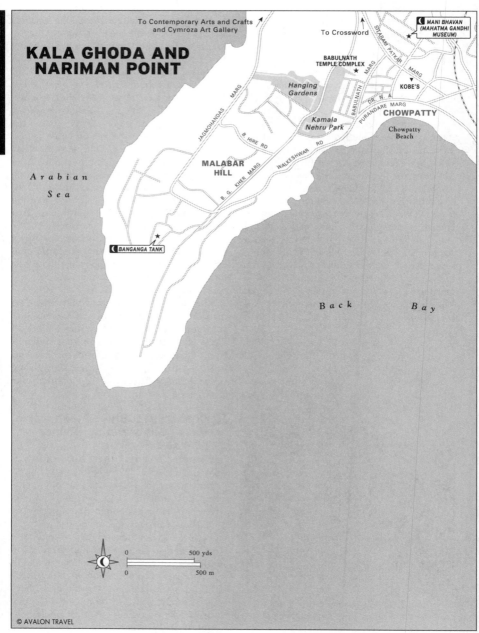

KALA GHODA AND NARIMAN POINT

To Contemporary Arts and Crafts and Cymroza Art Gallery

To Crossword

MANI BHAVAN (MAHATMA GANDHI MUSEUM)

BABULNATH TEMPLE COMPLEX

KOBE'S

JAGMOHANDAS MARG

Hanging Gardens

BABULNATH MARG

DR. N. A. PURANDARE MARG

SHABIN PATKAR MARG

CHOWPATTY

B. HIRE RD.

Kamala Nehru Park

Chowpatty Beach

Arabian

Sea

MALABAR HILL

B. G. KHER MARG

WALKESHWAR RD.

BANGANGA TANK

Back   Bay

0   500 yds

0   500 m

© AVALON TRAVEL

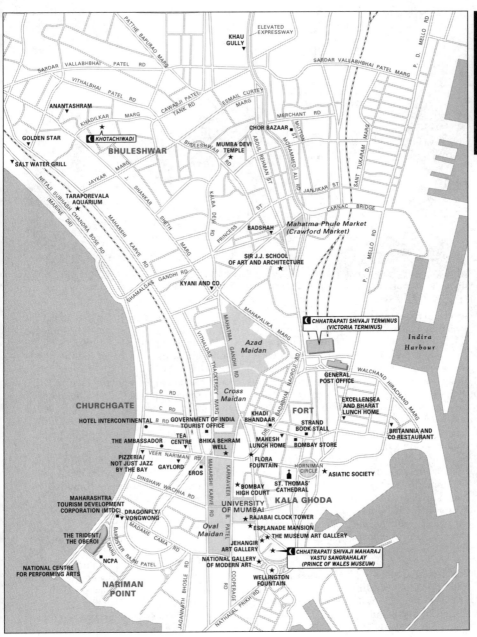

© ASHIMA NARAIN

Chhatrapati Shivaji Maharaj Vastu Sangrahalay (Prince of Wales Museum) houses art and historical artifacts.

spectacular internal dome, regal galleries, and sweeping staircases. The museum boasts a fine collection of various schools of miniature painting, as well as ancient bronze and stone sculptures. Some of the best statuettes from the Indus Valley Civilization through the various dynasties and religious schools may be found on the lower floor. There is an ornithological and marine collection in the natural history section, as well as crystal and miniature bottle collections in galleries on every floor. Apart from a small art collection comprising some Far Eastern art, a few Constables and paintings from the Flemish school, the museum also houses an Assyrian frieze in the Pre- and Proto History Gallery. Although the presentation of the objects could do with some improvement, the museum's cool interiors are ideal for loitering around on a muggy afternoon.

National Gallery of Modern Art

The National Gallery of Modern Art (NGMA) (tel. 022/2285-2457, www.ngmaindia.gov.in/ngma_mumbai.asp, 11 A.M.–6 P.M. Tues.–Sun., Indians Rs 10, foreigners Rs 150, photography prohibited), situated across the road from the museum, was commissioned as a public space in the early 1900s. Today, it exhibits the works of some of the finest contemporary artists and legendary greats. In the past, it has hosted the works of Picasso, Diego Rivera's photographs of Frida Kahlo, portraits by iconic Indian artist Ravi Varma from various royal collections, and, more recently, a retrospective of India's leading photographer, Raghu Rai. The gallery's stark white, modern interior is in contrast with its Neo-Classical facade. You can pick up some modestly priced prints of artists, or collect a commissioned portfolio of their works here.

Jehangir Art Gallery

Adjoining the museum, the Jehangir Art Gallery (tel. 022/2204-8212, 10 A.M.–7 P.M. daily, free, photography prohibited), houses two exhibition spaces, a charming restaurant, and a small art store (11 A.M.–6 P.M. daily). It's a great place to view contemporary art; you can simply stroll in to catch shows or buy works of both established and upcoming Indian artists,

THE MOST FAMILIAR NAME IN MUMBAI

Tourists will be struck by the number of roads, terminals, monuments, statues, and public buildings dedicated to Chhatrapati Shivaji – the 17th-century Maratha warrior king (and now the mascot of right-wing fundamentalist and popular revivalist party, the Shiv Sena).

Son of a Hindu general, Shahaji Bhonsale, who served the Bahmani and Deccan Sultanates, Shivaji rebelled against his father's rulers to found the Maratha empire. Known for his troops, who were trained in guerilla warfare, Shivaji was also the founder of India's first navy. The Maratha Navy was sizeable and controlled most of the sea along the coast of Maharashtra until the arrival of the Europeans. He also established seaside and hilltop forts at a number of locations across Maharashtra, and his exploits and conquests against the Mughal and Bijapur kings are legendary. Having captured his first fort (belonging to the Bijapur Sultanate) at the age of 17, he went on to win a number of battles in the region stretching from modern-day Maharashtra to Tamil Nadu, the southernmost state of India.

The subject of many a myth and folklore, Shivaji was pulled out of the dusty pages of history books in the 1960s by the Shiv Sena. The political party banks on Shivaji's martial and moral image to garner the support of the Maratha community and Marathi-speaking population of Mumbai and the rest of Maharashtra. The Sena has a stronghold in the local municipality, and while in power in the state government a few years ago, it busied itself by putting up Shivaji statues and changing nomenclatures across the city. Now both the international and domestic airports are named after Chhatrapati Shivaji, much to the distress of tourists who often mistake one for

© ASHIMA NARAIN

statue of Maratha warrior king Shivaji – the most familiar name in Mumbai

the other. The city's most important railway station, the Victoria Terminus, has been renamed the Chhatrapati Shivaji Terminus, while the Prince of Wales Museum is now officially known by its tongue-twisting appellation Chhatrapati Shivaji Vastu Sangrahalay (although locals generally refer to by its former name). The Sena also changed the name of the city from Bombay to Mumbai.

The latest in Shivaji news? The state government plans to erect a mammoth statue of the king – taller by a few feet than the Statue of Liberty – in the sea.

and then ponder over them at the gallery restaurant, Samovar.

For more, walk around the bend to **The Museum Art Gallery** (K Dubash Marg, Kala Ghoda, tel. 022/2284-4484, 11 A.M.–7 P.M. Mon.–Sat.) a space that often hosts shows of contemporary artists on the lower floor of the Max Mueller Bhavan. Max Mueller Bhavan is an Indo-German center that hosts cultural events and classes in German.

Esplanade Mansion (Watson's Hotel)

Located just off Kala Ghoda, across the road from Max Mueller Bhavan and Jehangir Art Gallery, is the dilapidated Watson's Hotel, now

A dilapidated building in present times, Esplanade Mansion, or Watson's Hotel, as it was once known, was the first to screen Lumière brothers' films in India.

known as Esplanade Mansion. Mumbai's first luxury hotel, and built only for Europeans, its erstwhile grandeur can only be imagined today. If you step into its dingy, dank interior, you will see the staircase that Mark Twain once climbed up. The first in India to screen the Lumière brothers' Cinematographe in 1896, the cast-iron structure, sadly, is on many endangered heritage lists today. You can go in for a look on weekdays when it is a bustling office complex.

FORT AND CHHATRAPATI SHIVAJI TERMINUS

To see the unbelievably vast Mumbai populace, all you need to do is visit the areas of Fort and Chhatrapati Shivaji Terminus (CST), which buzzes with activity at any time of day. Old-timers continue to refer to the Terminus and the area around it by its old name—VT, for Victoria Terminus. The Terminus spews millions of people during the peak hours of morning as they jostle to get to work, past roadside vendors and hawkers selling trivia. Passersby gawk as they rush past at the street

doctors—palmists, astrologers, and quacks offering their panaceas (including homegrown aphrodisiacs).

Nearby, the Mahatma Phule Market, previously known as Crawford Market, is ablaze with color as yellow marigolds and purple-pink asters vie for space with bright-yellow Alphonso mangoes within the heritage stone walls. A short walk from both Kala Ghoda and CST is the Fort area of Mumbai, dominated by the imposing Asiatic Society building with its white pillars and stone steps. The Bombay Stock Exchange and Reserve Bank of India's Mint and Monetary Museum are also located close by.

◖ Chhatrapati Shivaji Terminus (Victoria Terminus)

Even after the right-wing political party, the Shiv Sena, attempted to erase the colonial legacy of this magnificent building with a superficial name change, its architecture remains a fine combination of Victorian Gothic and Indian palace architecture that was recently awarded World Heritage status by UNESCO.

One cannot escape the statue of Queen Victoria either, as it continues to adorn the splendid dome constructed in 1888. The busiest monument in Mumbai, CST connects the city's eastern suburbs with downtown Mumbai, contributing to one-third of the six million who travel on the railway network every day. Lost amid the crowd are gargoyles and exotic animals carved in the interior and on the external facade. Don't miss the ceiling, especially the part in the portico that houses the ticket-office. Not all sections of the station are open to visitors, and videos are strictly prohibited on railway property. To see parts of the building where access is denied, visit whc.unesco.org/en/list/945. Make sure you buy a platform ticket (Rs 3) before you venture out of the ticketing area to get into the main station.

A stone's throw from here is the **General Post Office (GPO)** (St. George Rd., behind CST, Fort, tel. 022/2262-0956, 10 A.M.–5 P.M. Mon.–Sat.), a colonial building made of black basalt with marvelous hallways, spiraling stairways, and a stunning inner dome.

© ASHIMA NARAIN

Chhatrapati Shivaji Terminus, Mumbai's busiest landmark

Sir JJ School of Art and Architecture

Just across the north end of CST is the Sir JJ School of Art and Architecture (DN Rd., tel. 022/2262-1118, www.sirjjarchitecture.org, 8 A.M.–6 P.M. Mon.–Sat.). Built through the 1800s, this was among the first educational institutions in the city and has produced some of India's finest artists. Located within the green campus is the Dean's bungalow, a wooden cottage that was the birthplace of Rudyard Kipling (whose father, Lockwood Kipling, was one of the early principals and mentors of the institution). The bungalow has been vacant for a few years now; plans are in progress for its restoration and transformation into an art museum, cafeteria, and art store.

Mahatma Phule Market (Crawford Market)

Mumbai's largest municipal bazaar, Mahatma Phule Market (Mohammad Ali Rd., 8 A.M.–8 P.M. daily) still goes by its colonial name of Crawford Market. Built by the corrupt offices of Arthur Crawford, the controversial first municipal commissioner of Mumbai, it was later renamed after social reformer Mahatma Phule. Although a Grade I heritage structure that dates back to 1869, and the first building in the city to be lit with electricity, it was up for demolition by the municipality until prominent and ordinary citizens rose up in arms against the proposal to do so. A combination of fine Flemish and Norman architecture, this previously traditional market has adapted to modern times by stocking foreign cheeses, chocolates, and exotic fruits and vegetables from around the world—even as it continues to sell local spices and fresh flowers. Try and get to the market in the early hours of morning to see the fresh stock come in and visit the dingy by-lanes behind the market to see all kinds of meat on sale.

Bhika Behram Well and Flora Fountain

Across Azad Maidan and toward Churchgate Station is the Bhika Behram Well. A well enclosed within a non-descript compound, it

MUMBAI

© JANHAVI ACHAREKAR

The Mahatma Phule Market, or Crawford Market, is known for its fresh flowers, spices, fruits, and vegetables.

seems an aberration in an area bustling with activity and noisy with traffic.

Built in 1725—by Behram, a gentleman from the Zoroastrian émigré Parsi community, for thirsty fellow Parsis—the well has a perennial sweet-water source and is revered by the community. Its 300-year-old stained glass was recently vandalized and broken but has since been restored. Unfortunately, the site is open only to Parsis, but it is worth loitering around outside for a feel of the place.

Nearby, at what is now known as Hutatma Chowk, it is impossible to miss the ornate Flora Fountain. Though the fountain runs dry, it continues to be a central landmark, deriving its name from the Roman goddess Flora positioned at the base of the structure. Built in 1864, the fountain marks the approximate location of the western wall of the erstwhile fort.

The University of Mumbai and Vicinity

Down the road from Hutatma Chowk are some fascinating samples of Gothic architecture. At the intersecting University Road you will come across the **University of Mumbai building** (9 A.M.–5 P.M. Mon.–Sat.), built in the mid-1800s, but modeled on French castles of the 15th century, by Gilbert Scott, who also designed London's St. Pancras Station. Above the university library is India's own Big Ben, the **Rajabai Clock Tower,** a prominent city landmark (though entry is prohibited). Named after the mother of its principal donor, the tower makes for a splendid sight at night. Before you leave, visit the impressive University Convocation Hall for its fantastic ceiling and stained-glass windows.

Next to the university is the **Bombay High Court** (9 A.M.–5 P.M. Mon.–Sat.), a finely detailed Neo-Gothic building dating back to 1848. Look for carvings on the pillars and gargoyles on the terraces—you're likely to discover regional quirks in the Gothic form. Feel free to walk around the grounds and along the many corridors and balconies to catch sight of an interesting public hearing at one of the tribunals.

MUMBAI

© ASHIMA NARAIN

the Rajabai Clock Tower and Bombay Stock Exchange building

St. Thomas' Cathedral

Near the palatial Ready Money Mansion (named after its erstwhile occupant, whose philanthropy earned him this title) and toward Horniman Circle is St. Thomas' Cathedral (Veer Nariman Rd., 10 A.M.– 5:30 P.M. daily, free). Inside the cathedral rest finely carved marble memorials dedicated to British soldiers, civil servants, and noblemen and women who succumbed to the wars and malaria of the country. Built in 1718, the cathedral also has some fine stained-glass windows, a baptism well, and pews where royalty and Mother Teresa once rested their knees. Churchgate, now considered an altogether different area, derives its name from its proximity to the cathedral in the old days.

Asiatic Society

Near St. Thomas' Cathedral and in the heart of the Fort area is **Horniman Circle,** an open garden known to host cultural events that was once a parade ground and trading area

A SHARE IN THE ECONOMY

If you stand at Horniman Circle, you will see the **Bombay Stock Exchange** (BSE) building loom large over you. Then turn around to the circle and look at the banyan tree at the western end of the park, where it all began. A garden has replaced the vast ground where cotton, jute, tea, coal, and opium were once traded, and down the road, Dalal Street – where the BSE is now located – enjoys the significance of Wall Street in India.

The Exchange is the oldest in Asia, established as The Native Share and Stock Brokers' Association in 1875 (although in practice for nearly three decades before that) before it became the Bombay Stock Exchange. Today, it has the maximum number of listed companies in the world (6,000) and is the world's fifth in transaction numbers. The BSE SENSEX is India's first stock market index and is tracked widely around the world. India's booming economy has sent the SENSEX soaring to 21,000 points in the recent past. In 2007, the BSE became the largest stock exchange in Asia and the 10th largest in the world when the equity market capitalization of its listed companies reached a never-before high of US$1.79 trillion.

The city is always on the edge about the market's ups and downs, and the BSE has seen its share of scams and scandals. While barely 2 percent of the country invests in the Exchange, it is a city icon. The original traders included Armenians, Jews, Parsis, and various other Indian communities, but today the BSE is dominated by the Gujarati community. The trademark chaos of the BSE "ring" was replaced by online trading over a decade ago and it has rapidly reinvented itself with modern technology in the last few years. While recent recessionary trends have seen a few fortunes dip, the mood continues to be upbeat and investments in the market are as strong as ever.

for cotton and opium. At the gate that opens out to the cathedral is a banyan tree, believed to be the site of origin of the Bombay Stock Exchange. Looming large over Horniman Circle is a white Neo-Classical building with Doric columns that housed the old Town Hall and Asiatic Society (tel. 022/2266-0956, www.asiaticsociety.org, 10:30 A.M.–7 P.M. Mon.–Sat.). While the Asiatic Society is still in existence, the old Town Hall is now the city library. The society continues to fund scholarly research in Indology and boasts a collection of over 15,000 rare books, including a 400-year-old manuscript of Dante's *Divine Comedies* for which Mussolini famously bid £1 million. Its other collections include rare coins, archaeological discoveries, and around 3,000 manuscripts. Although entry is restricted only to members, a promise to maintain silence and abstain from photography will allow you a peek inside its rooms and staircases lined with busts of prominent Bombay rulers and noblemen.

© ASHIMA NARAIN

Mumbai's skyline as seen from Marine Drive

MARINE DRIVE, CHOWPATTY, AND VICINITY

Downtown Mumbai's seafront stretches out from Nariman Point at the far end and down Marine Drive, Chowpatty, and beyond. Lovers, unemployed youth, college students, joggers, and families out on a stroll occupy the promenade, faces turned to the Arabian Sea or the Manhattan-like skyline around it. At night, the row of glittering neon-orange streetlights along the promenade has earned them the collective sobriquet of the Queen's Necklace. The sea-facing Wilson College, a heritage educational institution, is illuminated with similar lights and makes for an exquisite nocturnal sight. Not far from Chowpatty Beach are a number of historical places of interest such as Mani Bhavan, Babulnath Temple, and Banganga Tank. The latter is located in Walkeshwar, in the posh neighborhood of Malabar Hill—the domain of South Mumbai's elite.

Nariman Point

The city's prime commercial area, Nariman Point, is fast losing out to the chic new business district of Lower Parel in Central Mumbai. Dominated by the towering Air India building and the Oberoi hotel, office space comes at a premium here, exceeding even Manhattan rates. The promenade by the sea gives a splendid view of the sunset, as hovering *chaiwallahs* (tea vendors), peanut-sellers, street-food stalls, and hawkers persuade you to try their treats and wares. There are a number of five-star hotels with sea-facing restaurants and bars, and in the distance, you can see the skyscrapers of Cuffe Parade. Small launches and stray fishing boats may be seen far out in the sea even as the Queen's Necklace lights up at dusk. At the farthest end of Nariman Point is the National Centre for Performing Arts, a complex of theaters, gardens, and art galleries where you can catch art exhibits, concerts, plays, and even the odd Broadway musical.

Taraporevala Aquarium

Located on Marine Drive and a mere five minute walk from Charni Road Station on the Western Railway, is the city's only aquarium (tel. 022/2282-1239, 10 A.M.–7 P.M. Tues.–Sun., adults Rs 15, children Rs 10, photography prohibited). While it has a sizeable collection of the region's sea life, the interior is dark and depressing and the conditions in which the marine creatures are kept are less than ideal. In the 1970s, it had a cheerful restaurant insensitively named Fish 'n' Chips, but the dull marine center gives little reason for a visit today—although plans for a makeover are on the anvil.

Chowpatty Beach

In Mumbai, don't let the word "beach" fool you. The city believes in using its beachfronts for family moments and social occasions. Instead of bikini-clad sunbathers, you are likely to see fully clothed lovers, heavily made-up new brides clinging to the arm of the other half, and overdressed families on an evening out. The beach is often merely an excuse to eat out or buy trivia but rarely, if ever, considered a place for a swim.

At the very end of the Queen's Necklace, Chowpatty carries the same festive air as the suburban Juhu Beach, albeit to a lesser extent. Eveningers snack at the food stalls, get a *champi maalish*—a vigorous, traditional head massage—from hopeful head masseurs, or simply gaze upon the ocean. The beach was once the venue for numerous political rallies, especially during the Independence movement. Today, it attracts large crowds during the various Hindu festivals that worship the full moon. It also proves to be an excellent vantage point for pictures of the Mumbai skyline—of the hill illuminated with neon signboards on one side and the sweeping art deco buildings of Marine Drive on the other.

◖ Mani Bhavan (Mahatma Gandhi Museum)

In the shade of the many trees that line Laburnum Road lies Mani Bhavan (19 Laburnum Rd., Gamdevi, tel. 022/2380-5864, www.gandhi-manibhavan.org, 9:30 A.M.–5:30 P.M. daily, free, donations accepted), former home of India's most revered figure, Mahatma Gandhi. Now preserved as a museum, this is where the leader of India's non-violent movement for Independence launched the civil disobedience movement. Visitors are presented with rare photographs, letters, personal belongings, and a diorama representation of his life. You may also spend time reading at the library or buy Gandhi stamps, books, and pamphlets at reasonable prices.

© JANHAVI ACHAREKAR

Chowpatty Beach, framed by the city skyline

Part of Gandhi's cremated remains were left to rest here from August 2006 to January 2008, after they were handed over to the museum by a businessman whose family had known the Mahatma and preserved his ashes. However, his proposal to exhibit the remains was quashed by Gandhi's descendants, and the ashes were immersed in the Arabian Sea on the 60th anniversary of the leader's assassination.

Babulnath Temple

At the northern end of Marine Drive stands the 200-year-old Babulnath Temple (5 A.M.–9 P.M. daily, open to all faiths). To enter, walk through the main archway and up a long stone stairway to the 305-meter-high hill. Devotees and visitors also have the option of taking an elevator (11 A.M.–6 P.M.). While the temple is dotted with smaller shrines along the steps, it is dedicated to Shiva—the Hindu god of destruction and regeneration—symbolized by the phallic *shivling* that may be found in the sanctum sanctorum. Monday is the holy day for worship in this temple, a day when devotees throng the *shivling*. From the top, the temple provides a bird's-eye view of the city.

◖ Khotachiwadi

A well-preserved *gaothan* (hamlet) of Hindu- and Portuguese-style cottages, Khotachiwadi is a heritage precinct that developed in the late 18th century. Located in the historic and crowded Girgaum area, just off Chowpatty, it housed members of the Pathare Prabhu (early Mumbai residents) and East Indian (Christian employees of the East India Company) communities. Its two-story wooden cottages, tucked among a maze of narrow lanes, are marked by precious antiques, trellises, and beautiful latticework. During the Khotachiwadi festival in May, the doors of these beautiful homes are left open for walk-in visitors by resident owners and the food and culture of these communities shared. Finding the entrance to this *gaothan* can be tricky—look for the lane cutting in from the bustling street opposite St. Teresa's Church.

Mumba Devi Temple

In the Bhuleshwar Market near Charni Road Station is the famous Mumba Devi Temple (5 A.M.–noon and 4–8 P.M. Tues.–Sun., free), whose deity Mumba—patron goddess of the Agri and Koli communities—is believed to have lent the city its name. The original temple and deity, believed to have been 600 years old at the time, were relocated in the mid-18th century from the previous site near present-day CST when the city began to expand rapidly. You can make an offering of fresh flowers to the goddess who, local legend says, seldom denies her devotees any favors.

Hanging Gardens and Kamala Nehru Park

The end of Marine Drive leads up to the affluent neighborhood of Malabar Hill, which derives its name from the famous pirates of Malabar on the southern coast, who hid in the jungles that once covered the hill. Today,

one of the many quaint heritage cottages found in the *gaothan* of Khotachiwadi

URBAN VILLAGES

Mumbai is a crucible of communities from across the country and the world, who arrived at this famous port-city and settled on its seven islands. Nowhere is this chapter of its history more alive than in the still-bustling *gaothans*, or villages in the city.

The most prominent among these is Khotachiwadi, a late-18th-century settlement dominated by the Christian East Indian community – a section of native Maharashtrians whose forefathers served the British East India Company as employees. Western in language, dress, religion, and habit, the East Indian community goes back 300 years. They rented or bought plots of land in Khotachiwadi – named after the owner or landlord, whose name was Khot – located in the heart of central Mumbai, in the area of Girgaum.

A heritage village in downtown Mumbai, Khotachiwadi continues to house the descendants of its original inhabitants and other trader communities that have settled since. The *gaothan* celebrates its own festival in the summer, when residents come together in an effort to showcase its culture in the form of performances, craft displays, food fiestas, and heritage walks, throwing open their doors to walk-in tourists.

Meanwhile, the suburbs have their own sleepy villages, such as Pali, Ranwar, Chimbai and Chuim villages in and around Bandra, and the Versova village in Andheri. Narrow lanes and winding paths are lined with the rare Mumbai cottage and fruit tree as cars maneuver their way through with great difficulty. Most former residents continue to live here, even as others sell out to builders dreaming of a fortune and designers hoping to turn a heritage house into a posh boutique. Most of the city *gaothans* are under threat from the construction boom, keeping heritage architects and activists busy.

© MANJIRI ACHREKAR-SMOTHERS

The medieval Banganga Tank resonates with the sounds of Indian classical music during the Banganga Festival.

the only green space in the area is provided by the Hanging Gardens (tel. 022/2363-3561, 5 A.M.–9 P.M. daily, free), known for their well-manicured lawns and hedges trimmed to resemble the shapes of various animals. The gardens offer stunning views of the city by day and of the Queen's Necklace at night. Across the garden is the Kamala Nehru Park, popular with children for the giant Old Woman's Shoe, which has a slide inside of it.

◖ Banganga Tank

A narrow lane near the Walkeshwar Bus Station on Malabar Hill leads down to the recently restored Banganga Tank (24 hr daily, free). One of the oldest parts of the city, Banganga is a large, stepped well or tank surrounded by 30 temples, two hermitages and several *gymkhanas*, or local gymnasiums. The steps were constructed during the Silhara Dynasty, between the 9th and 13th centuries A.D., but the water is believed to have been sourced with the help of an arrow shot by Lord Rama, deified monarch from the Hindu epic, *The Ramayana*. The largest temple here is that of Walkeshwara, or Lord of the Sand, dedicated to Lord Shiva. The tank, with its serene waters occupied by a large number of ducks, is the ideal location for the Banganga Festival that hosts Indian classical music performances by the country's maestros. An ancient medieval area in the heart of the city, surrounded by 18th-century temples, Banganga is a world away from the city's rush. It offers a slice of Hindu religious history to the surprised visitor.

CENTRAL MUMBAI

Central Mumbai is middle ground for both North and South Mumbai and best remembered for its phantasmagoric vision of the Haji Ali Mosque and Mausoleum jutting out into the sea. This part of the city also includes many contradictions. The washermen's area known as Dhobi Ghat and noisy bazaars are in stark contrast with Lower Parel's controversial mills-turned-malls, which have transformed a working-class locality into a chic commercial and residential address (often snobbishly referred to as "Upper Worli"). The dismal Byculla Zoo compares poorly with the equestrian activity at the Mahalaxmi Race Course, the venue

for Mumbai's fashionable derby. Science and religion coexist here—the Mahalaxmi and Siddhivinayak temples are a stone's throw away from the Nehru Science Centre. And, to level all differences, the ever-popular seaface at Worli provides respite to a mixed bag of people as it houses sprawling seaside mansions alongside a modest fishing colony.

❰ Haji Ali Mosque and Mausoleum

In 1631, the Muslim saint Pir Haji Ali Shah and a wealthy merchant built this grand mosque (Haji Ali, Mahalaxmi, pre-dawn–8 P.M. daily depending on the tide, free) out of marble on an island 500 meters off the shore. Legend has it that Haji Ali died on his way to Mecca and that his body floated back to the mosque, which thus came to house his mausoleum. The dome of the monument, built in the Indo-Islamic style of architecture, rises from the sea, and is particularly noteworthy when framed by a splendid sunset. A narrow strip of land connects the mosque to the mainland, and visitors can expect to encounter beggars, hawkers selling religious souvenirs, and stalls offering fried sweets that are a suspiciously bright shade of orange. The monument is a popular pilgrimage spot for all faiths; most visitors tie a thread at

© JANHAVI ACHAREKAR

Pilgrims make their way to the Haji Ali Mosque and Mausoleum on an offshore island.

An outdoor shrine leads to the entrance of the Mahalaxmi Temple.

the mausoleum for an answer to their prayers, or rest on the cool marble and enjoy a close view of the sea. It is important to keep track of the tides, however, as high tide submerges the access way from the mainland and is likely to leave you stranded on the island.

Dhobi Ghat

If you reach Mahalaxmi by train, climb the Bapurao Jagtap Bridge on Bapurao Jagtap Road at the station and walk eastward for a vantage view of Dhobi Ghat, where the city's dirty linen is washed in public. This is a housewife's fantasy, where a hundred men scrub and beat Mumbai's laundry clean in a long row of open cubicles, drying it later on seeming endless meters of clothesline. This sight can also been seen up close by wending your way through a maze of lanes. Be prepared, however, for a guided tour by a zealous *dhobi,* or washerman, who may demand a hefty fee at the end or charge you for use of camera.

Mahalaxmi Race Course

You can depend on this 130-hectare oval course (Dr. E. Moses Rd., tel. 022/2307-1401, www.rwitcraces.com) in the heart of the city for an impressive show of thundering hooves and shiny manes as novices learn to ride or professional jockeys spur their steeds onto winning the coveted cup at the Indian Derby, amid much betting, cheering and hat couture. The racecourse is also known for its restaurant, Gallops, and the newly opened Olive, where you can watch the horses being taken to their stables for a meal as you have yours. Entry is free for walking and exercises 6–9 A.M. and 5–8 P.M. daily. Tickets to watch the races are Rs 25, while derby tickets start at Rs 260.

Mahalaxmi Temple

Perched on a hilltop and facing the sea, this colorful, flower-bedecked temple (Bhulabhai Desai Rd., Breach Candy, 4 A.M.–11 P.M. daily) is dedicated to Laxmi, the Hindu goddess of wealth, and her consort Lord Vishnu. The story goes that an engineer employed by the East India Company on a land-reclamation project to connect the various islands of Bombay dreamed of an idol of the goddess in the sea—then recovered it in reality and built the temple for it.

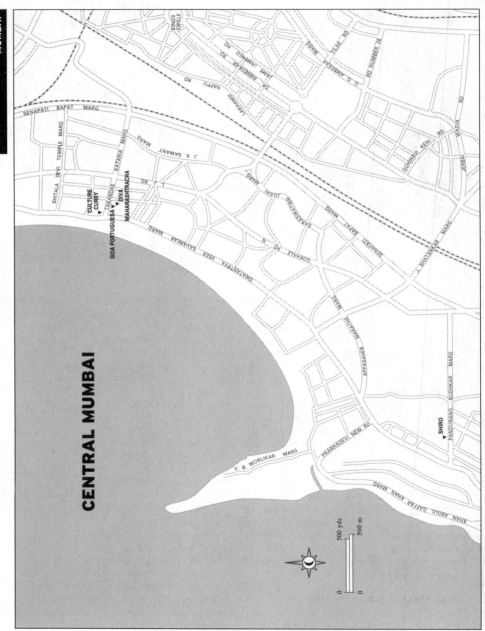

CENTRAL MUMBAI

KINGS CIRCLE

JAME JAMSHED RD

DR AMBEDKAR RD

NAPPU RD

LAKHAMSI

TILAK RD

RD NUMBER 28

D. D. AMBEKAR MARG

GOVINDJI KENI RD

WADIA RD

JERBA RD

SENAPATI BAPAT MARG

DEVI TEMPLE MARG

SHITALA

KATARIA MARG

J. K. SAWANT MARG

L. J. RD

JOSHI MARG

SARASWATIBAI

SENAPATI BAPAT MARG

J. BHATANKAR MARG

CULTURE CURRY

DIVA MAHARASHTRACHA

GOA PORTUGUESA

TAKANDAS

VEER SAVARKAR MARG

SWATANTRYA

GOKHALE RD (N)

MARG

APPASAHEB MARG

BUDHKAR MARG

SHIRO

PANDURANG

PRABHADEVI NEW RD

V. B. WORLIKAR MARG

KHAN ABDUL GAFFAR KHAN MARG

500 yds

500 m

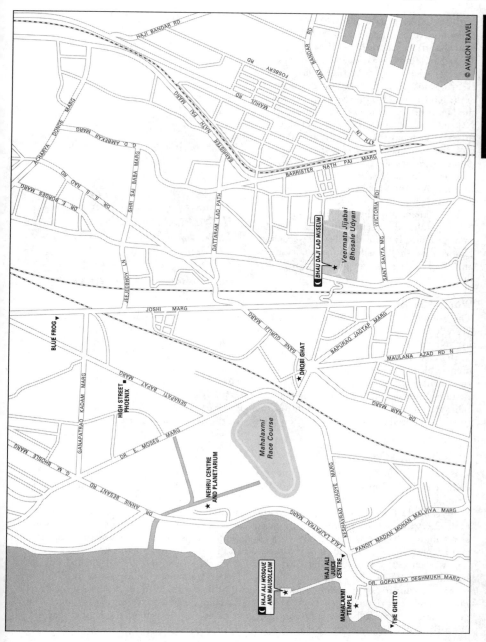

MUMBAI

© AVALON TRAVEL

Nehru Centre and Planetarium

This modern building (tel. 022/2496-4676, www.nehru-centre.org, 10:30 A.M.–5 P.M. Tues.–Sun., Rs 30) is a tribute to the first prime minister of Independent India, Jawaharlal Nehru, whose ideas and actions shaped much of the modern vision of the country. It includes the Discovery of India exhibit—named after Nehru's book by the same title—which comprises 14 galleries that cover the art, philosophy, and intellectual pursuits of the country. The cultural section has a separate wing for various performances, and an art gallery and information center are also located within the premises.

The Planetarium (English-language show 3 P.M., adults Rs 50, children Rs 25), on the same grounds, is a crowd-puller on weekends. Known for its high-quality projector, its shows and exhibitions make for an interesting family visit.

© ASHIMA NARAIN

A sculpture gazes upon the waters at Worli Seaface.

Worli Seaface

The saltwater-flecked promenade on Worli Seaface is ideal for an evening stroll or a jog. Not quite as manic as other seafronts in the city, it has its share of tranquil moments, blush sunsets, and monsoon spray. In the distance, you can see the ambitious Bandra-Worli sea-link route nearing completion while located all around are some of the finest residential and commercial properties in the city.

Siddhivinayak Temple

In the area of Prabhadevi, jutting out onto the main road, is the 200-year-old Siddhivinayak Temple (www.siddhivinayak.org, 4 A.M.– 9:30 P.M. daily, Pooja 4:30–5 A.M. and 8:30–9 P.M. daily), built two centuries ago as a tribute to Ganesh, the elephant-headed god believed to be the Remover of Obstacles. Easily reached by foot from Dadar Station or by cab from Worli, this temple has a high-security enclosure as protection from communal and terrorist attacks. Popular with politicians, Bollywood stars, and commoners alike, this high-profile shrine is most crowded at dawn on Tuesdays and Thursdays when devotees throng the shrine after having walked barefoot, often from tens of kilometers away.

Veermata Jijabai Bhosale Udyan (Byculla Zoo)

Located across the road from Byculla Station (in the east), and a short ride from CST on the Central line, the city zoo (tel. 022/2374-2162, 9 A.M.–5:30 P.M. daily, for walks only 6:30 A.M.–8 A.M. daily, adults Rs 5, children Rs 3, still photography Rs 10, video Rs 30) looks no different from when it was built in 1861. Animals are in a sorry state and confined in appalling conditions. The only saving grace, perhaps, is the wide green space within the premises that shelters some unique flora and fauna. Recently, naturalists and activists saved the space from demolition and talks of modernization are in progress, with the intent to build a café overlooking a vast enclosure housing big cats. At the moment, however, it remains a smelly, gloomy sight that may easily be skipped.

◖ Bhau Daji Lad Museum

The remarkable Bhau Daji Lad Museum (tel. 022/2375-7943, 10 A.M.–5 P.M. daily, adults Rs 100, children Rs 50, photography prohibited)

is the real attraction of Veermata Jijabai Bhosale Udyan (Byculla Zoo). Modeled upon the Victoria and Albert Museum in London, it was recently restored to its original glory

THE SLUMS OF MUMBAI

Scratch beneath the superficial glitz of the city and statistics will show that a shocking 55 percent of Mumbai's population lives in the slums. Of these, the majority can be found in the slum-complex of Dharavi, where nearly a million people live in an area of 200 hectares.

Leather shops, vegetable vendors, embroidery units, and recycling (of metal, plastic, and paper) all take place here – even as a million people bustle in and out of cramped pathways, jostling for space with stray animals, hutments, small factories, and low-income housing. The subject for many a popular documentary and movie, including Indian filmmaker Sudhir Mishra's *Dharavi* and the international sensation *Slumdog Millionaire*, the slum is the object of both fascination and revulsion. The place is a hotbed of crime by night, but attracts all kinds during the day, ranging from tourists who visit

the leather shops along its fringes to a never-ending inflow of new migrants who arrive here, hoping to make it big in the City of Dreams.

Situated between the Western Express highway and Western railway line on one side and the Central railway line and Eastern Express highway on the other, Dharavi is Asia's largest slum. It has an inadequate water supply and only one toilet per 1,400 residents; tanning units pollute the air and the polluted Mithi River passes through. Some houses are cramped and barely 14 square meters in size, while others are small cottages or low-income apartments.

The government has come up with several unsuccessful redevelopment and rehabilitation schemes in the past, and recently, an expat Indian has taken on the challenge of rehabilitating the residents of Dharavi.

© JANHAVI ACHAREKAR

a narrow lane lined with shops in Dharavi

with refurbished gilt work, grand staircases, wrought iron, and woodwork. The lighting is just right, as is the new arrangement of exhibits that cover a wide range of handicrafts and cultural artifacts of the subcontinent. On the first floor are beautiful paintings of the city, but the prized exhibits include maps of Bombay dating back as early as 1672. Peek into the garden outside to see the sculpted stone elephant that gave Elephanta Island its name, as well as the famous stone "Kala Ghoda" statue and a few headless statues of administrators.

NORTH MUMBAI

Once considered beyond city limits, the suburbs of North Mumbai are an indelible part of the city today. Indeed, this is where the young and the restless eat, drink, and party until the wee hours, zipping around in their fast cars while wearing designer sunglasses. The areas of Bandra and Juhu, previously quiet fishing villages dominated by fisherfolk and Goan Christian immigrants, are now upmarket residential areas inhabited by young singles, media professionals, celebrities, and foreign residents. They retain their character in pockets, in their hidden *gaothans,* villages where you can relive the old charm. Both areas host vibrant neighborhood festivals and you can even catch a free cultural performance at Bandra's Bandstand and Carter Road promenades on the odd Saturday evening. In the far suburb of Borivli is the last remnant of the city's fast-depleting reserve of greenery: Sanjay Gandhi National Park, which shelters a wealth of flora and fauna, maintaining the ecological balance of the city.

Mount Mary Church

Situated on a hillock overlooking the Arabian Sea, the Mount Mary Church in Bandra (Mount Mary, www.mountmarybandra.com, Sunday mass hourly from 6:30 A.M.) is frequented by people of all faiths and from around the country. This 17th-century church built by Jesuit priests is best known today for its annual fair—the Mount Mary Fair, or the Bandra Fair, held in September. During this time,

© ASHIMA NARAIN

a vegetable cart in the cosmopolitan suburb of Bandra

crowds throng the church to seek the blessings of Mother Mary and to light candles at the altar, causing Bandra's worst traffic jam annually. The fair is a treat for children who enjoy candy floss (cotton candy) and other goodies, along with a ride on the Ferris wheel.

Bandra Fort and Bandstand

Previously known as the Queen of the Suburbs, until the phrase took on a whole new meaning, Bandra—with its seaside promenade and street eats at Bandstand—is the suburban answer to Marine Drive. This area is often crowded with young couples and celebrity-gazers, so don't be surprised if you come upon a flock of people gawking at the opposite direction, their backs to the sea. In all likelihood, they are star-struck fans of Bollywood's leading actors, Shah Rukh Khan and Salman Khan, waiting for a glimpse of their favorite screen idols. The latter often indulges them by coming out onto his balcony, waving messiah-like and blowing kisses in the air.

At the very end of Bandstand, at Land's End, is the 17th-century Bandra Fort. Originally built as a watchtower by the Portuguese, it overlooks the sea on one side and an amphitheater (the venue for many open-air performances organized by zealous local residents) on the other. A charming ruin at one time, it now bears a hideous concrete look after a recent round of restoration went horribly wrong.

Juhu Beach

A carnival rather than a beach, Juhu (Juhu Tara Rd.) is a favorite weekend hangout for locals as well as visitors to Mumbai. Like the other city beaches, it is not recommended for swimming and flaunting your bikini here is a strict no-no. Marked by the absence of the usual seaside activity, the beach entertains instead with horse rides, fortune-telling robots, air rifle shooting, colorful pinwheels, and a food court serving various street eats. If you can stomach Mumbai's junk food, sample the *paani puri* (puffed canapés stuffed with sprouts and potatoes and doused in tangy water) or the *bhel puri* (a sweet-sour-spicy

© JANHAVI ACHAREKAR

A coconut seller looks on hopefully at the evening crowds at Mumbai's suburban Juhu Beach.

snack made of puffed rice and mixed with onion, potato, raw mango, and chili). The latter even finds itself in Mumbai vocabulary, its local meaning suggesting a hotchpotch or an unlikely mixture. The local ice-candy called *gola* is delicious, but not recommended unless made with mineral water. If you have "Bombay belly," stick to coconut water served in coconut shells (the flesh is scooped out later and good for eating).

Frequented for the local treats and bric-a-brac peddled on the shore, the beach is even more vibrant during the Ganesh festival in August and September, when a myriad of idols are immersed in the sea.

Gilbert Hill

A natural wonder that dates back around 65 million years, Gilbert Hill (Tipu Sultan Rd., 1.2 km from Andheri Station) in Andheri is a 60-meter-high column of basalt rock, created from molten lava. A protected national park under threat from property developers who carved out land from the hill, it has now been given the status of a heritage structure. A nondescript formation lost amid the fumes of passing traffic and neighboring rows of hutments, it has a small garden and two temples at the top that may be accessed by climbing a steep stairway. To reach the site, alight at Andheri Station on the Western Railway and take an auto-rickshaw to the hill. Although open to visitors throughout the day, the best hours to visit are before noon and after 4 P.M. to avoid the sun.

Film City

Located in the green suburb of Goregaon, off the Western Express Highway and on the Aarey Milk Colony Road, is Mumbai's Film City (11 A.M.–5 P.M.). Not quite Universal Studios, it is where most Bollywood films and Indian soaps are shot. Big productions are strictly off-limits but smaller studios may allow a peek if you prove to be an ardent fan. A garden here known as Chota Kashmir, meaning Little Kashmir, is where many of Bollywood's glitzy song sequences are shot.

The ancient Kanheri Caves in the Sanjay Gandhi National Park are the perfect getaway from the concrete jungle of Mumbai.

Sanjay Gandhi National Park and Kanheri Caves

Spread across the western suburbs of Goregaon and Borivli, and extending into the neighboring district of Thane, is the city's only green cover—the Sanjay Gandhi National Park, also referred to as Borivli National Park (Western Express Highway, Borivli, www.borivlinationalpark.com, 6 A.M.–6 P.M. Tues.–Sun., Rs 25, vehicle Rs 50). A thriving habitat for leopards, deer, birds, reptiles, insects, and other animals, the park makes for the perfect getaway from the chaos of the city. The park is 104 square kilometers in size, although illegal encroachments have reduced its total area. It also includes three lakes that contribute to the city's water supply, as well as the stunning Buddhist monastery in the Kanheri Caves (located on a small hillock about 7 km from the entrance, 9:30 A.M.–5:30 P.M. Tues.–Sun., entry Rs 120, still photography Rs 50, video Rs 200), which date as far back as the 2nd century B.C.

The main entrance to the park is about a kilometer from Borivli railway station and may be reached by auto-rickshaw from the station. It is advisable to take your own vehicle if you plan to go up to the Kanheri Caves, but the walk is wonderful if you set off early. You'll need to carry your own food and water, though, as there are few provisions within the park.

The **Nature Information Centre** (tel. 022/2884-1428, nicsgnp@vsnl.net, nicsgnp@yahoo.co.in), located near the main entrance, provides information on bird-watching excursions, walks to the butterfly garden, nature walks, and wildlife documentary screenings that are conducted for a modest fee. There's a lion and tiger safari (Rs 50) as well, conducted from the safety of a bus.

The best time to visit the park is from July through March, when the streams are full and the park is at its greenest. Avoid Sundays when the entire city seems to converge here. Inside the park, it is safer to stick to the main roads. Avoid straying alone and too far inside, as both animal and human attacks are not unknown. Steer clear of paths marked off by small barricades as they lead to prohibited areas like the core jungle or the lakes.

Gorai, Manori, and Madh

For a feel of old Bombay, visit the serene beaches of the far north where the landscape and culture have barely changed since the last century. To reach Gorai, which makes for an interesting getaway, take a ferry (7 A.M.–8 P.M. daily, round-trip Rs 30) from the Gorai jetty in Borivli. After alighting from the ferry, it is a short ride by auto-rickshaw or horse-cart to the fishing village and beach. There's an amusement park near here called Esselworld and an adjoining water park called Water Kingdom—the latter is generally filled with raucous, rowdy crowds and is best avoided. Ironically, in stark contrast, the Vipassana International Academy's **Global Pagoda** (tel. 022/2845-2111, www .dhamma.org, 8:30 A.M.–2:30 P.M. daily) is built alongside for anyone who may wish to practice the Vipassana technique of meditation.

Accessible by ferry from the same jetty, Manori is a tiny village dotted with cottages, chapels, and fishing boats. The beach may not be good enough for a swim but it is quiet and secluded. There's a charming resort called **Manoribel** (tel. 022/2845-2806, www.manoribel.com, Rs 832–2,420), and another called **Domonica** (tel. 022/2867-6591, Rs 600–900 d), should you wish to extend your stay.

Madh Island is a collection of fishing villages and expensive seaside bungalows. Other points of interest include an old fort and a 16th-century church in the village of Erangal. There are a couple of luxury resorts here. The island is easily reached by taking a train on the western line to Malad Station, then by auto-rickshaw after exiting on the western side of the station, or by ferry from Juhu-Versova. To get to the ferry, take an auto-rickshaw from Santacruz, Vile Parle, or Andheri stations.

GUIDED TOURS

Mumbai's enterprising individuals offer some excellent guided city tours. **Bombay Heritage Walks** (Navyug Niketan, ground floor, 185 Walkeshwar Rd., tel. 022/2369-0992, www .bombayheritagewalks.com, Rs 400 and up, free during the Kala Ghoda festival) was started by two young Mumbai architects—Abha Behl and Brinda Gaitonde. Regular walking tours around the downtown and other areas focus on the history and heritage of the city. Meanwhile, **Mumbai Magic** (cell tel. 91/98677-07414, www.mumbaimagic.com, costs vary) introduces visitors to various aspects of Mumbai with its Bazaar, Art, and Fort walks. It also organizes car tours and themed tours such as the Spirit of Dharavi and Mumbai Local tours.

Entertainment and Events

Mumbai is India's entertainment capital. It's where people work hard and party harder. It's where religious festivals cause traffic jams every other week. And where glitzy art openings and Bollywood events are splashed on the infamous Page 3. From bars and discos to colorful festivals, art shows, book readings, film premieres, and music performances, there's never a dull moment in the city. In keeping with the dichotomy of the city's social fabric, bars and discotheques are generally the domain of the affluent and the upwardly mobile. Mumbai's glitterati is famously fickle and its changing loyalties indicate the waxing and waning popularity of nightspots, often leading to the closure of many a successful bar. The masses, however, make merry on religious occasions with colorful processions and dancing on the streets. Owing to its cosmopolitan nature, Mumbai celebrates almost every religious festival in the country; considering the presence of Islam, Christianity, Hinduism, Zoroastrianism, Buddhism, and Judaism, among other religions, the city declares more public holidays than anywhere else in the country and most parts of the world.

The months between November and March are packed with neighborhood festivals and cultural events that range from theater and jazz festivals to all-night performances by the maestros of Indian classical music. Check local publications for event listings—Mumbai has a vibrant art scene with plenty of shows at its numerous galleries, while the Crossword chain of bookstores regularly hosts book readings at stores across the city. Activists and social organizations are also known to organize events. In 2008, Mumbai's sizable gay community held its first Pride March to protest the archaic section 377 of the Indian Penal Code, which declares homosexuality illegal (in July 2009, the Delhi High Court passed a path-breaking judgment that revoked section 377 and decriminalized consensual sex between same-sex adults).

NIGHTLIFE

A recent undercover survey conducted by a local daily showed that most upper-end bars in Mumbai have a bias toward foreigners. The bottom line is that with a bit of persuasion on your part, you can wheedle your way around the city's somewhat pretentious social scene. You may choose to be affronted by the attitude or simply revel in the attention. And once you've had enough of the air kissing and polite conversation, you can always head to the National Centre for Performing Arts or to Prithvi Theatre for some cerebral activity.

Live Music and Jazz

The city has some eclectic choices for live music and jazz. **Not Just Jazz by the Bay** (Soona Mahal, Marine Dr., tel. 022/2282-0957, www.mars-world.com/restaurants, noon–4 P.M. and 6 P.M.–1:30 A.M. daily, cover charge Rs 250) started out as Jazz by the Bay, until they decided to include music other than jazz. Indian jazz star Louis Banks has played here, as have a host of Indian and international bands. Its piano-like steps with keys lead to a guitar-shaped bar and a space scattered with musician coasters, posters, and crockery. Thursday, Friday, and Saturday nights are reserved for live music while Sundays through Wednesdays are karaoke nights. There's a

Mumbai's gay pride march

great buffet lunch here as well, but it's in the night that the place is packed.

Jazz, cigars, single malts, and spectacular ocean view are what you can expect at **Bayview Bar** (The Trident, Nariman Point, tel. 022/6632-6220, 8 P.M.–midnight daily), The Trident's signature bar. Corporate takeovers and business deals are conducted over live jazz performances and the finest cigars. The bar, not surprisingly, is a bit of an old boys' club. It serves martinis and other drinks in addition to a fine collection of single malts. (Under restoration after the November attacks.)

Blue Frog (Mathuradas Mills Compound, opposite Phoenix Mills, Lower Parel, tel. 022/4033-2300, www.bluefrog.co.in, 7 P.M.–1 A.M. Tues.–Sun., cover charge Rs 500 Fri.–Sat. or Rs 300 after 9 P.M. Sun., Tues.–Thurs.) is Mumbai's mecca for world music lovers and night creatures. This new club seems to have taken the party scene by storm, and for good reason. It hosts live international music, often coupling expert acoustics with a spectacular visual display. The amphitheater-style "pod" seating is bathed in violet hues, and an open area in the front makes way for ardent fans, giving it the feel of a rock concert. Food and drink are expensive but you'll find a host of people hurrying in before entry charges begin at 9 P.M., hovering around the bar and nursing their drink until the music begins. There's live music six days a week ranging from jazz gigs to rock, fusion, and experimental tunes, making this place a must-visit.

Resto-Bars and Lounges

Among Mumbai's first resto-bars, **Indigo** (Mandalik Rd., Colaba, tel. 022/6655-1010, 9 A.M.–midnight daily) sits in a delightful bungalow on a Colaba bylane. The food (mains Rs 1,200) is par excellence and the bar area is crowded. There's the Black Lounge as well and a soft candle-lit terrace for when things get too stuffy. Look out for the occasional live music performance—Indigo was the venue for the Daniel Pearl memorial night, when the slain reporter's friends from around the world performed at and attended this touching jazz

RESTO-BARS

If you're undecided between dinner and entertainment, or would like to begin with one and swing to the other, the uniquely Mumbai resto-bar is the place for you. As the name suggests, the resto-bar is usually a restaurant with an adjoining bar area where diners may enjoy their gourmet dinner, even as party-goers lounge in the bar area or dance the night away. Often, as the night progresses, the dining area is taken over by the bar crowd, and the result is often a night concluded with much revelry and loud music.

night. Pearl was an accomplished violinist who often performed here during his stay in the city.

Indigo's tiny neighbor **Busaba** (Mandalik Rd., Colaba, tel. 022/2204-3779, noon–3 P.M. and 6:30 P.M.–1 A.M. daily) is a chic resto-bar known for its Asian cuisine, fig mojitos, contemporary decor, and hip patrons.

Colaba's happening lounge and resto-bar **Oba** (behind Regal Cinema, Near Gordon House Hotel, Colaba, tel. 022/6524-7070, 7:30 P.M.–1:30 A.M.daily) is where celeb meets kitsch. Newly opened and still displaying teething trouble in the food and wine areas, its martinis (Rs 365) are recommended by the bartender. Animal prints, statues, and dimly lighted interiors make the décor as intriguing as the prices. A place that has piqued the curiosity of the crowds (at least in the initial stages) cannot be ignored in a hurry.

A giant Buddha, floating lotuses, Japanese-style wooden screens, a robata grill, and a fine selection of wines make **Tetsuma** (Dr. Minoo Desai Marg, Colaba, tel. 022/2287-6578, 12:30–3 P.M. and 7:30 P.M.–1:30 A.M. daily) a place for the swish set. This expensive Japanese lounge-restaurant and bar is known for its signature dishes—and as a place where wine, sake, and money flow freely. The sushi and Kobe beef served here are excellent, but some prefer the more economical Sunday brunch (Rs 1,600 with Indian liquor brands, or Rs 2,500 with foreign liquor brands) or the Chef's Banquet (Rs 1,700, unlimited food) on Mondays.

Next door to resto-bar Tetsuma and run by the same management is the equally exclusive **Privé** (Dr. Minoo Desai Marg, Colaba, tel. 022/2202-8700, 12:30 A.M.–3 P.M. and 7:30 P.M.–1:30 A.M. daily). A dim-lit lounge with boxed cubicles and partitions adorned with paisley and Gothic motifs, this is where noses and prices are up in the air. For Rs 95,000 a year, you can even get membership to their privileged Dom P lounge area—entitling members to the fine spirit that goes by the name of Dom Perignon. The place serves only starters, so if you want a spot of dinner before you embark on your expensive drinking spree, you'll need to go to Tetsuma.

If you can't find a seat at **Valhalla** (Eros Theater Building, 1st floor, east wing, Churchgate, tel. 022/6735-3535, www.valhalla .co.in, 8 A.M.–1:30 A.M. daily, Fri.–Sat. entry by invitation only after 10 P.M.), try the throne. Named after the paradisiacal place in Nordic mythology where warriors are welcomed after battle, this new hot spot is more like a resting place for those familiar with boardroom battles. Mumbai's first business lounge, it is quickly building a reputation for itself as a fine-dining and weekend hangout. A large throne dominates the décor, while the bar serves only the finest liquor. Known for its tapas and sangria, Valhalla is possibly the only lounge to open its elysian doors for breakfast, lunch, and high tea as well as dinner. The cuisine is traditional European (but is fast being "Indianized" to suit local tastes), and the menu boasts an authentic paella. Attached to the lounge are two snazzy conference rooms for corporate clients who choose to mix business with pleasure.

The Zen-like calm of the all-white rooftop bar at the InterContinental makes **Dome**

SLEEPLESS IN MUMBAI: CITY NIGHTLIFE

Mumbai is a city that never sleeps. Its nightlife includes everything from the shabby remnants of old-fashioned *mujra* places, which find their origins in the courtesan and nautch-girl days, to exclusive nightclubs and celebrity-filled lounges.

The city was once known for its controversial "dance bars" – bars with dancing girls (fully clothed in traditional attire) for a predominantly male audience – that were eventually declared illegal in the heat of protests by lawyers and activists. While the judgment has been stayed by the Supreme Court, the bars remain closed, depriving the dancers of their livelihood and often forcing them into prostitution.

Meanwhile, nightclubs and bars continue to bloom, albeit with a 1:30 A.M. curfew. Not long ago, you could dance the night away and nurse your drink until the early hours of morning. Today, bar owners grease the palms of corrupt cops to be able to stay open at all. The city also has its share of dry days, when bars and liquor shops remain closed in deference to a religious or political occasion, or a public holiday. However, the city has its secret suppli-

ers who deliver booze on the sly, ensuring that your party is not a damp squib. In recent times, the police have also adopted a zero-tolerance approach to drinking and driving after a series of alcohol-related accidents (involving celebrities and affluent kids) rocked the city.

But Mumbai's nightlife involves more than its bars. The city is beautiful after sundown when heritage monuments are illuminated with orange lights and ships twinkle in the distance. The glittering Queen's Necklace is a row of neon-orange streetlights along Marine Drive, best viewed from the gardens of Malabar Hill. The popular seafronts buzz with activity in the evening, well after the sun goes down and the billboards light up, as lovers canoodle amidst prying eyes and cops on the prowl. Sunset tours, such as Mumbai Magic's "An Evening in Mumbai" are conducted by knowledgeable tour guides. You can even hire a launch and spend a couple of hours watching the city lights from the sea. If you plan to explore the city by yourself, be prepared to encounter its seamier side.

(Hotel InterContinental, Marine Dr., tel. 022/6639-9999, www.intercontinental.com, 6 P.M.–1:30 A.M. daily) Mumbai's most ambient nightspot. Japanese cuisine is served under the stars and over the sea, while an enclosed dome houses the bar alongside the pool. Softly lit with flickering candles, this is also the most romantic place to watch the sun go down.

Japanese for "castle," **Shiro** (Bombay Dyeing Mill Compound, tel. 022/6615-6969, 7 P.M.–1:30 A.M. daily) is where Giant Robot meets Japanese fairy tale. This swish nightspot dominated by thirtysomethings is all stone, huge statues, and soaring ceiling. There are separate enclosures for dining where Japanese food and other Asian cuisines are served amid the red-flecked grey stone decor. The upstairs section with its four-poster seating is reminiscent of a Japanese boudoir, while the bar area downstairs is stocked with premium liquor from around the world—even boasting expensive Kauffmann vodka.

World fusion, salsa nights, and a international vibe are what set apart **Zenzi** (Waterfield Rd., Bandra, tel. 022/6643-0670, www.zenzi-india.com, 7.30 P.M.–1 A.M. daily) from the rest. This popular Bandra nightspot is always buzzing with regulars and new visitors who come here for the music belted out by its DJs and the special "learn-how" nights, and to socialize at the bar outside. It's also a place where young and struggling media professionals and models shamelessly network, hoping to bag their big assignment by simply hanging around and making new contacts.

A beautiful Mediterranean-style resto-bar, **Olive** (Pali Hill Tourist Hotel, Union Park, near Carter Rd., tel. 022/2605-8228, www.olivebarandkitchen.com, 7:30 P.M.–1:30 A.M. weekdays and also 12:30–4 P.M. Sun.) continues to be Bandra's trendiest nightspot, and is a favorite with celebrities, socialites, and Page 3 types. Its whitewashed walls, glowing candles, and Grecian urns in a lovely Bandra villa attract young men and women in designer outfits clearly out to be noticed. The sometimes-brusque staff has been known to ask patrons to clear the table for a celeb party or, quite simply, if they haven't ordered enough to set the cash registers ringing. The bar area is more friendly and provides a vantage point from where to observe the city's air-kissing flutterati. A sister establishment (also called Olive) at the Mahalaxmi Race Course in Central Mumbai is located just opposite the horse stables, and makes for a wonderful experience.

China House (Grand Hyatt, off the Western Express Hwy., Santacruz East, tel. 022/6676-1086, www.hyatt.com, 7:30 P.M.–1:30 A.M. daily) is Mumbai's most happening nightspot, at least in the suburbs. While China House offers dining, its chic new China Lounge is where the action is. Dancers, drinkers, PYTs, older businessmen, socialites, wannabes, and pretty much everyone who wants to be seen is here, packed like sardines on a Saturday night. Like the crowd and the cocktails, the music too is mixed, but tends toward the popular to please varied tastes.

Vie Lounge & Deck (102, Juhu-Tara Rd., tel. 022/2660-3003, www.vie.co.in, 4:30 P.M.–1:30 A.M. daily) is a resto-bar by the sea. Its wooden deck dotted with garden umbrellas projects out toward the beach, and the place opens early in the evening, allowing you to enjoy a beautiful sunset and the salty sea breeze along with your drink. There's an indoor restaurant and bar as well, but the lovely outdoor ambience is what brings in the crowd.

A short distance from Vie is another seaside resto-bar that attracts the crème de la crème of suburban Mumbai; **Aurus** (Nichani Kutir, Juhu-Tara Rd., tel. 022/6676-1086, 8 P.M.–1 A.M. daily) is where fine dining meets elegant wining. In the mellow, chandelier-lit ambience, the talented chef churns out dishes from the experimental molecular gastronomy menu, beginning with watermelon caviar and ending with the superb soufflé crepes. The outdoor bar area, flush with the vision of sand and sea, lies on the open deck; here you can book the "Aurus bed"—a four-poster seating area—if you assure a minimum tab of Rs 30,000 that night. The place comes alive with music on Friday nights. Try the kiwi-based Aurus Margarita.

Mangi Ferra (Gulmohur Cross Rd., JVPD Scheme, Vile Parle West, tel. 022/6675-1728, 1 P.M.–3 P.M. and 8 P.M.–1:30 A.M. daily) is named after the genus of the mango tree that grows in the area of this Juhu resto-bar. Known as much for its pizzas and pastas as it is for its cocktails and pleasing ambience, this is a great place to dine, unwind with a drink, or simply lounge around.

Theme Bars and Pubs

At old-world **Geoffrey's** (Marine Plaza, Marine Dr., tel. 022/2285-1212, 11:30 A.M.–1 A.M. daily), you can pretend to be in England, at least for a few hours. Wooden paneling, tan leather sofas, brass fittings, colonial prints, and memorabilia are matched with stiff-upper-lip service. Especially popular with the after-hours office crowds and during cricket matches, this is a good place to unwind.

Sports buffs will be overjoyed to know that the city has **Sports Bar** (High Street Phoenix, Lower Parel, tel. 022/2491-4000, noon–3:30 P.M. and 6:30 P.M.–12:30 A.M. daily). A casual atmosphere pervades the place with its pool table, basketball corner, dartboard, and sports memorabilia. Cricket matches and games are screened live on a large screen and you may even catch a glimpse of the odd sports celebrity. If you haven't had enough of sports already, you can head next door to the bowling alley of Bowling Co.

A quaint garage pub, **Toto's** (Pali Junction, Bandra, tel. 022/2600-5494, 6 P.M.–1 A.M. daily) was once Totlani's Garage. Spare auto parts from the erstwhile garage have accessorized the decor for nearly two decades now and the DJ console is a car that continues to stay suspended from the ceiling. The music and tariffs too remain unchanged—it's the same 1980s tape that plays Def Leppard and Air Supply in sequential order, and the booze is cheap. There's no dressing up required, as regulars turn up in hordes after work with sleeves rolled up and laptops in tow.

Nightclubs

Voodoo (Kamal Mansion, Behind Radio Club,

MUMBAI'S PAGE 3

In Mumbai, anything can be made available for a price. Even fame. Turn the pages of the colorful supplement of a leading daily and you will discover a phenomenon known as "Page 3."

In this capital of glitz and industry, commerce and glamour are united by mutual necessity. Aspiring models and starlets arrive in the hope of instant recognition, and publicity agents work overtime, even as event organizers look for pretty faces to fill boring parties. Mumbai's nightlife is forever buzzing with these famous, and infamous, Page 3 parties, which involve much air kissing, wine drinking, and flashing of designer wear and jewelry. Bollywood stars, artists, and unknown hopefuls all converge at these events, posing for the paparazzi, who will flash their pictures on Page 3 the next day.

The parties and ensuing publicity have invited criticism from the intelligentsia, but are the delight of corporations and small enterprises that find easy advertising in a paid-for celeb-filled party. It is rumored that many of the known faces are paid to party, while unknown aspirants often pay to be featured on the page. The workings of Page 3 have been well documented in a movie by the same name – part of a trilogy on Mumbai by filmmaker Madhur Bhandarkar. The Page 3 phenomenon has elicited both delight and ire among Mumbai residents and heralds the commodification of recognition in a city where money can buy you anything.

Colaba, tel. 022/2284-1959, 8 P.M.–1:30 A.M.) is Mumbai's landmark seedy bar, and the only nightclub in the city to host gay nights (Fridays and Saturdays). The notorious bar has leery men on the prowl and is teeming with male and female sex workers. Pushers and stags can get overwhelming, so this bar is certainly not for the faint-hearted.

The Ghetto (Bhulabhai Desai Rd., Mahalaxmi, tel. 022/2353-8418, 7 P.M.–1:30 A.M. daily) is a small bar that lives up to its name. The graffiti-scrawled walls of this dim-lit place draw a group of regulars who huddle together after work or class, hanging around the pool tables or in the shadow of Jim Morrison murals. Also frequented by young singles living around the area, it's hardly surprising that pitchers of beer (Rs 250) are downed by the gallon. Music is 1980s rock and the place often turns on its strobe and neon lights, exposing teeth and white underwear.

Poison (Krystal, Waterfield Rd., Bandra tel. 022/2642-3006, 7 P.M.–1:30 A.M. Tues.–Sat.) is a cavernous discotheque that brags of celebrity DJs, a hip clientele, and swish members. This is definitely a place that's high on cocktails and on energy. You can expect pounding music, bright lights, young men in tight T-shirts, and girls in short skirts. Music alternates between reggae, trance, hip-hop, house, and Bollywood tunes, according to the days of the week. It's not quite the place to sip elegantly over a conversation, unless of course you're in the exclusive members' lounge.

There's nothing terribly Hawaiian about **Hawaiian Shack** (16th Rd., Bandra, tel. 022/2605-8753, 6 P.M.–1:30 A.M. daily, weekend cover charge Rs 500) except for the floral attire of its overworked staff and bamboo decor. This three-level bar and discotheque is a favorite with local Bandra residents for its retro music. Madonna and George Michael play on the lower floor, while the upper levels cater to hip-hop and Indian tastes. Needless to say, the lower floor is the most crowded in this nostalgic suburb. The mobile DJ console moves up floors as well, adding to the excitement of the jostling crowds. Just when you think it's impossible to find a place to stand, you'll catch the odd couple breaking into a jive.

Like the money tossed around by its nouveau riche patrons, the new bar and discotheque **Bling** (Hotel Leela Kempinski, Sahar, tel. 022/6691-1234, 7 P.M.–1:30 A.M. Wed.–Sat., cover charge Rs 1,000 per couple) is all flash and dazzle. And not surprisingly. The bar has a starry connection—it is co-owned by Mumbai's celebrity DJ Aqeel, also part of a famous Bollywood family. That apart, its unabashed shine and shimmer include Swarovski-embedded spaces, mirror work, and glittering bathrooms. Cocktails are served in the bar area but the place also has a dance floor and private seating areas.

Karaoke Bars

Mumbai loves to be heard and there's proof of that in its karaoke bars. **Trafalgar Chowk** (Agnelo Building, off St. John the Baptist Rd., Bandra, tel. 022/2645-9151, 7:30 P.M.–1:30 A.M. daily) is a has-been resto-bar. Once popular for its food and drink, it now wears a deserted look after a change in management also resulted in a change of chef. The food is avoidable, so the only reason you should go here is for its karaoke room. A Sing Star karaoke system allows you to compete with friends over a couple of drinks. You can also rent out the place and have your own private karaoke party (Rs 10,000, includes all the people in the room).

Soul Fry (Pali Market, Bandra, tel. 022/2604-6892, 12:30–3 P.M. and 7:30 P.M.–12:30 A.M. daily) is more of a restaurant than a bar, but it's difficult to believe that on crowded Monday nights, when its fishing nets, menus suspended from the ceiling, and excellent Goan cuisine are lost amid the music. Spirits are high and flowing freely as the mike is passed from table to table, and old and new favorites sung, turning ordinary diners into stars for one night.

A merry bar in The Orchid, **Merlin's** (The Orchid, Nehru Rd., Vile Parle East, tel. 022/2616-4040, 4 P.M.–2:30 A.M., karaoke after 11 P.M. Tues.–Sun., happy hour 4–8 P.M., cover charge Rs 500 Fri. and Sat.) has a relaxed after-work air about it. Karaoke begins at 11 P.M., well after happy hour has ended and more than a couple of drinks downed. There's enthusiastic participation in the singing, but it's a pity that the grouchy old man who supervised the selection of songs is no longer around to add to the late-night madness.

Budget Bars

Mumbai's nightlife is incomplete without its budget bars—places dominated by bored-looking men (often prohibited from drinking by wives and mothers) who sit on mica-covered tables and benches, watching the odd cricket match or Bollywood movie on mute. If you're in pursuit of the original city nightlife, these are the places you should head.

Gokul (opposite Badé Miyan, Tulloch Rd., Apollo Bunder, Colaba, tel. 022/2284-8248, 11 A.M.–1 A.M. daily) is popular not only with the local men, but also with young men and women from advertising and journalism, up for a cheap drink, good food, and a bit of local adventure. If you're a rum drinker, don't shy away from ordering the excellent Indian-made brand of rum called Old Monk. Locals swear by it.

The one place you can depend on for your share of alcohol and food on a late night is **Janata** (Pali Naka, Bandra, tel. 022/2600-4049, noon–1:30 A.M. daily). A blink-and-miss kind of bar begun for the common man, it's where you'll occasionally chance upon a surprisingly sophisticated woman too. Not as dingy as it seems, Janata is a Bandra favorite—it's where old friends catch up, media professionals bitch about work, and women come in with or without male buddies to see what the hoo-ha is really about.

THE ARTS
Performing Arts

Mumbai has a tradition of theater, stemming from its roots in the vibrant Marathi drama culture. The city offers plenty of options to lovers of this medium, in English and local languages. For listings, pick up a copy of the latest *Time Out Mumbai* magazine or visit www.mumbaitheatreguide.com. Ticket prices vary but generally hover around the Rs 50–250 range, escalating to Rs 1,000 and up for international productions.

For experimental and international productions, you can rely on the **National Centre for Performing Arts (NCPA)** (Nariman Point, tel. 022/6622-3737, www.ncpamumbai.com, bookings 9 A.M.–7 P.M. daily). This large complex comprises five theaters, including the small Experimental and Little Theaters, and the grand Jamshed Bhabha Theater, known for its large, international productions. The

NCPA regularly hosts western classical music and dance performances by renowned Indian and international artistes.

Catch the local flavor at the quaint **Prithvi Theatre** (Janki Kutir, Juhu, tel. 022/2614-9546, www.prithvitheatre.org, bookings 10 A.M.–1 P.M. and 2–7 P.M. Tues.–Sun.), an informal and intimate space that hosts platform productions, children's theater workshops, English and local-language plays, poetry readings, documentary screenings, and literary talks. With its little bookshop, art exhibits, and café, the theater is also a hangout for struggling playwrights and aspiring filmmakers. It is known for its summer children's festival and the much-anticipated Prithvi Theatre Festival in November.

Other theaters include the massive **Bhabha Hall** (TIFR, Colaba, tel. 022/2282-4567) and **St. Andrew's Auditorium** (St. Andrew's College, Dominic Rd., Bandra, tel. 022/2651-3224, bookings 10 A.M.–6 P.M. daily), which often host traveling international productions and musicals. For a feel of local/regional theater, visit **Ravindra Natya Mandir** (PL Deshpande Maharashtra Kala Academy, Prabhadevi, tel. 022/2431-2956, 11 A.M.–10 P.M. Mon.–Sat.).

Shanmukhananda Hall (behind Gandhi Market, Sion-Matunga Scheme, tel. 022/2407-8888, www.shanmukhananda.org.in/Shanmukha/index.asp) is the best place to catch Indian classical music and dance performances. Keep a lookout for listings and make sure you buy tickets in advance.

Art Shows

In addition to the numerous galleries in the Kala Ghoda art district, Mumbai has a plethora of venues where you can view the latest public shows or gatecrash a fine wine-and-cheese opening. Listings are posted on the notice board outside the Jehangir Art Gallery and NGMA, and entry is generally free.

Previously located in the mill area of Lower Parel, **Sakshi Gallery** (Nathalal Parekh Marg, Colaba, tel. 022/6610-3424, www.sakshigallery.com, 11 A.M.–6 P.M. Mon.–Sat.) has moved closer to the art district. Its vast white

BEYOND BOLLYWOOD

There is more to Indian cinema than Bollywood. And there's more to Bollywood than its musicals, melodrama, gyrations, and glitter.

While star-studded big budget productions dominate the movie scene, Mumbai also puts out its share of alternative films. The Film and Television Institute of India in Pune has produced the country's finest actors and filmmakers, encouraging serious cinema and spawning India's Cinema Nouvelle in the 1970s and '80s. These were the best years of Indian filmmaking, and these decades were marked by art house films that ran parallel to popular cinema. Directors and filmmakers such as Sai Paranjpe, Saeed Mirza, Govind Nihalani, and Ketan Mehta told powerful stories of common people and local issues by creating compelling characters and plots. Paranjpe's movie *Disha* was a realistic look at the influx of migrants into Mumbai, with sensitively drawn characters and a touch of comedy. Mirza's *Salim Langde Pe Mat Ro* was a look at Mumbai's Muslim community, while Nihalani's *Ardh Satya* was a landmark film that explored the Mumbai underworld and told the story of a city cop. The era was also known for its brilliant comedies, the most memorable being Kundan Shah's social satire, *Jaane Bhi Do Yaaron*, where two photographers turn investigators and dis-

cover a scam between the city builders and corrupt authorities.

In recent years, the divide between popular Bollywood cinema and art house cinema has narrowed and directors such as Madhur Bhandarkar, Vishal Bhardwaj, and Sudhir Mishra have succeeded in creating films that are both serious and commercially viable. Bhandarkar's trilogy *Page 3, Corporate,* and *Fashion* are reflections of Mumbai's privileged sections of society, while his *Chandni Bar* takes a look at the city's dance bars and *Traffic Signal* focuses on street life. Bharadwaj's *Maqbool* adapts Shakespeare's *Macbeth* to the Mumbai underworld. He has also made another film, *Omkara*, a fine adaptation of *Othello*. Mishra's *Dharavi* is located in the famous city slum complex, while Ram Gopal Varma's *Company* tells the story of Dawood Ibrahim and Chota Rajan, India's notorious underworld dons. Other films include Anurag Kashyap's *Black Friday*, a controversial film about the 1993 blasts, and Anurag Basu's *Metro*, about life in the city.

Mumbai is also the base of a number of fine documentary filmmakers. Notable among these are Anand Patwardhan – whose film on the 1992–1993 Mumbai riots, *Ram ke Naam (In the name of God)*, was critically acclaimed – and feminist filmmakers Madhusree Dutta (known for *7 Islands and a Metro*) and Paromita Vora.

---

space includes a maze of smaller enclosures, giving it a galleries-within-a-gallery feel. It is known for some landmark art shows, having exhibited major retrospectives of established artists as well as coming-out shows of promising young debutants.

Not far from the art district, **Chatterjee and Lal** (Arthur Bunder Rd., Colaba, tel. 022/2283-0100, www.chatterjeeandlal.com, 11 A.M.–7 P.M. Mon.–Sat.) is named after the enterprising couple that runs the gallery. Dedicated to young artists, the space provides a platform for new forms of art, experimental media, and installations, without compromising on quality and high standards.

Instrumental in providing a space for

Mumbai's historic art movements, **Gallery Chemould** (behind VSNL Building, Fort, tel. 022/2200-0211, www.gallerychemould .com, 11 A.M.–7 P.M. Mon.–Sat.) was safely ensconced on the mezzanine of the Jehangir Art Gallery for many years. Today, it has located in the Fort area but continues to exhibit and encourage the finest Indian artistic talent.

Cymroza Art Gallery (Cumballa Hill, tel. 022/2367-1983, www.cymroza.com, 11 A.M.–7 P.M. Mon.–Sat.) is an established space for modern art. There's no shying away from popular culture either, and exhibitions of Bollywood film posters have been hosted in the past.

The glass facade of the **Tao Art Gallery** (Annie Besant Rd., Worli, tel. 022/2491-8585, www.taoartgallery.com, 10:30 A.M.–6:30 P.M. Mon.–Sat.) showcases its gigantic canvases to passersby who care to spare a glance. True to its name, this beautiful space by the sea exudes a Zen-like calm, and has an atrium that sheds light on exhibits.

Cinema

If you're in the mood for a movie, avoid going to the characterless multiplexes that are all the rage these days; instead, you can marry some sightseeing with entertainment at the art deco cinema halls of **Eros** (Cambata Building, opposite Churchgate Station, tel. 022/2282-2335, Rs 50–120), tel. 022/2282-2335, Rs 50–120) and **Regal** (Apollo Bunder, Colaba, tel. 022/2202-1017, Rs 60–140). Don't miss the velvet curtains, plush carpets, and gilt walls of the century-old **New Excelsior** (AK Nayak Marg, Fort, tel. 022/2207-3830, Rs 60–100) either. And if you must visit a multiplex, indulge yourself at the luxurious **Red Lounge** at Cinemax (Infiniti Mall, Andheri, tel. 022/2631-3355, www.cinemax.co.in, Rs 400), where you can relax in cushioned comfort while watching the latest flick.

The nonprofit **Vikalp** now screens films at Prithvi Theatre (20 Janki Kutir, Juhu Church Rd., Juhu, tel. 022/2614-9546, www.prithvitheatre.org) and hosts small gatherings and some of the best documentaries and social message films from around the world.

FESTIVALS AND EVENTS
January
MUMBAI FESTIVAL

Organized as a tribute to the zestful, never-say-die spirit of the city, the Mumbai festival (www.mumbaifestival.in) has a variety of events to choose from. Food, theatre, film, and art shows are hosted across the city in the month of January by a number of private and public groups, nonprofit bodies as well as international organizations. You can count on live jazz performances, seafood cookouts, handicraft exhibitions, and auto-rickshaw and fishing boat races to liven up your visit. While admission to some events is free, others require tickets. In the

past, the festival has hosted performances by jazz musicians Al Jarreau, guitarist Earl Klugh, pianist George Duke, and saxophonist Ravi Coltrane at the Gateway of India.

ELEPHANTA FESTIVAL

A celebration of Indian classical and folk dance and music, the Elephanta Festival (MTDC Reservation Division tel. 022/2202-6713, Rhythm House tel. 022/2284-2835, Gateway of India tel. 022/2284-1877, www.maharashtratourism.gov.in) is held with the spectacular cave complex as backdrop. Renowned artists from across the country perform at the Elephanta Caves on Gharapuri Island, showcasing the country's classical traditions of music and dance. Performances are held in the evening with mellow lighting in the scenic environs of the caves. The chief attraction is the illuminated idol of Shiva in the main cave of the island. Special launch services and meals are provided to visitors during the festival.

BANGANGA FESTIVAL

This two-day classical music extravaganza is held as a tribute to the heritage site of the Banganga Tank and Walkeshwar Temple. The Banganga Festival (MTDC Reservation Division tel. 022/2202-6713, Rhythm House tel. 022/2284-2835, Gateway of India tel. 022/2284-1877, www.maharashtratourism.gov.in) hosts concerts and live performances by the maestros of Indian classical music. Seating is arranged on the steps around the tank and the musicians perform on an elevated dais projected above the water. The tank and temple complex creates a sonorous effect and a surreal, magical atmosphere.

JANFEST

Another two-day Indian classical music recital, this one is held in the magnificent Neo-Gothic campus of St. Xavier's College. Janfest (www.indianmusicgroup.org) is organized by the campus' Indian Music Group. The festival is known to continue till the wee hours, welcoming the sunrise with strains of classical melody.

February
KALA GHODA ARTS FESTIVAL

A vibrant celebration of the art district in early to mid-February, the Kala Ghoda Arts Festival (www.kalaghodaassociation.com) is a culture vulture's delight. A wide range of events in art, literature, theatre, music, dance, and film is hosted simultaneously and the district turned into a pedestrian plaza lined with colorful installations, handicraft stalls, public art, a food court, and an amphitheater. Open-air dance performances, concerts, art shows in surrounding galleries, film screenings at Max Mueller Bhavan, and book readings at the David Sassoon Library make this nine-day festival a not-to-be-missed event. In the past, renowned figures such as tabla maestro Zakir Hussain and writers Indra Sinha and Paul Theroux have participated.

MUMBAI INTERNATIONAL FILM FESTIVAL

The Mumbai International Film Festival (www.miffindia.in) makes accessible feature films and documentaries from around the world. At the weeklong tribute to international cinema, the world's best films are screened back-to-back. To attend the festival, you'll need to buy a season pass for a nominal fee.

March
HOLI

The festival of color marks the end of winter and welcomes spring. According to Hindu mythology, it also represents the triumph of good over evil. Children and adults alike throw a psychedelic mix of colored powder known as *gulal*, dousing each other with water and hurling water balloons at unsuspecting passersby. A potent mixture of marijuana *(bhaang)* blended with dry fruit in milk is also drunk traditionally, making people silly and drowsy.

MAKAR SANKRANTI

Yet another spring festival, Makar Sankranti turns the Mumbai skyline into a sea of color as myriad kites of all shapes, sizes, and hues soar into the blue. This unique kite festival is best observed from the terrace of a high-rise so as to get a dramatic view of the fierce kite competitions that are a part of the celebration. On this day locals exchange *laddoos*, rounded sweets made of sesame and jaggery.

May
KHOTACHIWADI FESTIVAL

To experience the traditions and culture of Old Bombay, visit the Khotachiwadi Festival, celebrated in a quaint, 200-year-old hamlet well-hidden in the crowded Girgaum area. You can take a guided tour on the history of this *gaothan* as residents throw open their doors, turning their beautiful heritage homes into mini-museums. The festival showcases the hamlet's culture with performances and handicraft exhibitions. Traditional food items prepared by residents are sold and the festival is a good time to stock up on delicious pickles and chutney. If you have a taste for spice, pick up the tangy East Indian–style prawn pickle and pork items.

© ASHIMA NARAIN

A human pyramid goes wrong during celebrations of Gokulashtami.

MUMBAI

July
GOKULASHTAMI

A religious festival that provides a visual spectacle, Gokulashtami, or Janmashtami as it is also known, celebrates the birth of Lord Krishna. Hindu mythology is replete with stories of Baby Krishna's talent for stealing butter, as he did by breaking earthen pots hung high from the ceiling. Today, Mumbai's youth mimics Krishna's antics by participating in an activity called *Dahi Handi,* where human pyramids are formed to break earthen pots strung at a height of up to 30 meters. Occuring across the city in July–August, these feats are best viewed from the *chawls* (low-income community-housing societies) of Parel, Dadar, and Girgaum. The pyramids are surrounded by cheering spectators and revelers who sing, dance, and pour buckets of water on participants.

August
I-ROCK

Rock bands from around the country show their metal at I-Rock, or Independence Rock (www.independencerock.in)—held around Independence Day (August 15). With its tradition of head-banging among generations of Mumbai rockers, the festival dedicates its second day to the oldies—when you can catch some delightful classics from the 1970s.

GANESH CHATURTI

This 10-day festival, held around August–September to mark the birth of the elephant-headed god Ganesh, is unique to the city of Mumbai. The festival was started here in the 1900s as an occasion for public gatherings to promote religious and cultural harmony against the divisive policies of the British. Colorful idols of Ganesh are installed in homes and in community *pandals,* or tents. These tents generally house gigantic idols, often painstakingly decorated with a contemporary theme; rudimentary loudspeakers blare the Ganesh *arti,* or hymn, which is sometimes set to Bollywood film music. The largest and the most popular among them all is the giant idol known as Lalbaugcha Raja (www.lalbaugcharaja.com), or

worship of Ganesh, the god of Good Beginnings and Remover of Obstacles, during Ganesh Chaturti

© ASHIMA NARAIN

the King of Lalbaug. Idols are eventually immersed in the sea amid much pomp and fanfare, giving worshippers an excuse to get drunk and throw colored powder known as *gulal* at each other. The beaches of Chowpatty and Juhu are chockablock, as is traffic on the main and arterial roads of the city. The immersion makes for a fantastic sight if you steer clear of the crowds and observe it from a distance.

September
MOUNT MARY FESTIVAL

Celebrated at Mount Mary Church in Bandra on September 9–15, the Mount Mary Festival (also called the Bandra Fair) commemorates the birth of the Virgin Mary. Devotees flock from around the country to seek her blessings, asking for the fulfillment of desires or for relief from ailments. Wishes are conveyed by lighting symbolic candles (e.g., a heart-shaped candle for relief from heart disease, or a computer-shaped candle for a job with a multinational corporation). The festival is accompanied by a crowded fair popular with local residents for its joyrides and stalls selling treats and trinkets. If you must visit, beware of unruly crowds and keep your valuables close to your person. Women should be particularly cautious and wary of attending at all.

RAMZAN EID

Ramzan, the Islamic month of fasting, culminates with the festival of Eid—a time of celebration. The festival is best experienced in the Muslim-dominated areas of Mohammad Ali Road and nearby Bhendi Bazaar, where participants gather for delicious traditional Eid cuisine. Stalls sell embroidered caps, *kurtas* (traditional shirts), silver, and trinkets at the dazzling night market that takes over the street on the eve of the festival. Keep an eye on the lunar calendar to keep track of the festival, which generally falls around September–October.

NAVRATRI

A festival celebrated predominantly by the Gujarati community, Navratri is marked by nine nights of dancing that end with the burning of gigantic idols of Ravana, the demon king killed by Lord Rama in the epic *Ramayana*.

Shimmering mirror-work skirts swirl about as women and men in traditional attire dance all night to the rhythm of the *dandiya* dance—a blur of ornate wooden sticks struck against a similar pair held by dance partners to timed beats. The festival is celebrated around September–October and may be observed at the Mahalaxmi Temple or in the Gujarati-dominated suburbs of Vile Parle and Borivli.

October
DIWALI

India's famous festival of lights is a celebration of Lord Rama's return from exile after vanquishing the demon king Ravana. Celebrated with much enthusiasm in the city, houses are cleaned to welcome Laxmi, the goddess of wealth, and decorated with brightly colored paper lamps, fairy lights, and traditional earthen wick lamps called *diyas*. The three-day festival occurs around October–November and marks the beginning of the Hindu New Year. It is accompanied with rich sweets, the exchange of gifts, and noisy fireworks—which contribute immensely to the increasing levels of pollution in the city. Card parties and gambling precede the festival,

© ASHIMA NARAIN

Wax candles for sale during the Mount Mary Festival in Bandra.

MUMBAI

© ASHIMA NARAIN

Garlands, festoons, clay lamps, and ornaments are used to decorate homes during Diwali.

which ends with a *pooja,* or religious ceremony, in worship of the goddess Laxmi.

November
PRITHVI THEATRE FESTIVAL

Mumbai's most-awaited theater festival, Prithvi brings together the best of the country's talent in a whirlwind of plays, poetry readings, musicals, and workshops for both children and adults. From experimental adaptations of Beckett to original scripts in the Urdu language, the festival encompasses a wide range of events and audiences. While the focus is on the main venue, Prithvi itself, events are organized across public gardens and small theaters in the city.

CELEBRATE BANDRA FESTIVAL

Held every two years in November, the Celebrate Bandra Festival (www.celebrate-bandra.net) is a result of the concerted effort of enthusiastic residents of this chic suburb. A neighborhood festival, it is a kaleidoscope of events that include dance and music performances by the sea to poetry readings in parks, in addition to sporting events, workshops,

heritage walks, and a food festival. The history and culture of the suburb are woven into a different theme every year and finding local talent is rarely a problem among a resident population that comprises the country's leading artists, filmmakers, writers, and performers.

JAZZ UTSAV

Held around November–December, the Utsav is a medley of sorts as Indian jazz musicians play alongside international artists. Passes are precious and sold quickly; keep an eye on the NCPA (www.ncpamumbai.com) auditorium lists to catch the schedule.

December
CHRISTMAS

Christmas is widely celebrated in the city, across faiths and communities. Christian-dominated areas like Bandra are brightly lit, and Hill Road is lined with twinkling stalls and stores selling Christmas trees, ornaments, Santa hats, and festoons alongside traditional East Indian Christmas sweets, plum pudding, and marzipan. While old-timers complain about Midnight Mass ending long before midnight thanks to the recent noise curfew, the younger lot are only too happy to attend the various parties that rock the city on Christmas Eve. The festivity serves as a prelude to the grand, universal celebration on New Year's Eve—when traffic comes to a standstill from the sheer numbers of people and vehicles out on the streets.

Shopping

Like so much else in the city, shopping too has undergone a sea change in Mumbai. Gone are the days when Indian men in tailored trousers and demure women in saris shopped at the neighborhood shopping district. Today's urban Indian sports the same brands as her Western counterparts and you'll even find the odd Versace creation in the crowd. Malls arrived here only recently and have been embraced by upwardly mobile residents with open arms. High Street Phoenix in the emerging shopping district of Lower Parel and InOrbit and Hypercity in the suburbs have spawned ecosystems of their own. Hopefully, this development will not be at the cost of Mumbai's flea markets, bazaars, quirky local boutiques, and indigenous stores that contribute to the individuality of the city. A sad sign of changing times has been the dispersal of the street booksellers at Flora Fountain.

However, the flowers at Dadar Market continue to bloom and locally made handicrafts somehow find their way into snazzy lifestyle stores. Look out for exhibitions at the MMRDA ground in Bandra, when artisans from all over the country converge to sell their craft, and for the book sales at **Strand Book Stall** (Cowasji Patel St., Fort, tel. 022/2266-1994, www.strandbookstall.com, 10 A.M.–8 P.M. Mon.–Sat. and 10 A.M.–7 P.M. Sun.) and **Crossword** (main store at Kemp's Corner, tel. 022/2384-2001, www.crosswordbookstores.com, 11 A.M.–8:30 P.M. daily). Some of the best buys are still got off the streets and amid the organized chaos of the markets of Mumbai, you will discover experiences and freebies that locals take for granted—don't be surprised if the salesman at the sari store offers you tea or cola to sip on as you shop or, if at the end of your shopping trip you find your buys all neatly gift-wrapped or, better still, delivered home. In Mumbai, you get more bang for your buck.

STREET AND FLEA MARKETS

When you visit a market with a name as frank as this one, at **Chor Bazaar,** or Thieves' Market (Mutton St., near CST, 11 A.M.–7 P.M. Sat.–Thurs.), it's only natural to assume that what you see is what you get. The best place in Mumbai for antiques and quaint collectors items sold at throwaway prices, Chor Bazaar is where stolen goods were once sold. Today you

© JANHAVI ACHAREKAR

movie posters and bric-a-brac for sale at Chor Bazaar

can pick up anything (including period furniture, art, curios, LPs from the '60s, grandfather clocks, gramophones, old coins and posters, silver cutlery, swords and daggers, electronics, tools, and designer shoes) for a steal. However, make sure you bargain hard and beware of fake currency and false claims of antiquity—hawkers live up to the name of the market. Also located here is the **Mini Market** (tel. 022/2347-2427, 11 A.M.–8 P.M. daily, up to 7 P.M. in the month of Ramzan) where you can satisfy your interest in kitschy Bollywood posters.

Don't go expecting haute couture at the crowded stretch called **Fashion Street** (MG Rd., near Azad Maidan, Churchgate, 10 A.M.–7 P.M. Mon.–Sat.). A row of open stalls on the street opposite Bombay Gymkhana, this is where you're likely to find great street clothing at bargain prices, if you look (and push) hard enough. You can choose from a wide range of branded factory seconds as well as unbranded cottons, kids wear, and footwear. Ignore the signs saying "Fixed Price" and practice your haggling act instead by quoting an absurdly low price and then walking away—only to be called back to negotiate a good deal.

Once a famous landmark in itself, the large open-air street market comprising a cluster of **pavement booksellers,** in the area between Churchgate and Flora Fountain, is no more. A thriving center for students, academics, and bookworms, this was where secondhand books were bought, sold, and circulated for decades. Unfortunately, the municipality ordered the area to be cleared, displacing the booksellers. Today, they have dispersed and relocated to various streets around the same area. You'll find everything from old secondhand literary masterpieces to pirated bestsellers, academic books, and coffee-table writing on D.N. Road (Fort) as well as the northern and eastern corners of Flora Fountain. If you have a special request for a rare or banned book, you can be sure that it will be made available within 24 hours.

Mumbai's streets are famous for peddling pirated books and it's not unusual to have the latest Booker Prize winner thrust into your window at a traffic signal, for a ridiculously low rate. However, beware of such copies—not only will you deny the writer his or her due, you may find crucial pages blank or missing, often taking the thrill out of the latest thriller.

TRADITIONAL MARKETS

In Mumbai, all that glitters is, most likely, gold. In a country where jewelry implies much more than shiny metal and precious stone, even the poorest are likely to sport a 24-carat nose ring or *mangalsutra* (a black beaded necklace with gold pendant worn by married women). A symbol of social and marital standing, and a traditional tool for saving and investment, jewelry is one of the busiest industries in India. **Zaveri Bazaar** (behind Kalbadevi and west of Mohammad Ali Rd., Mon.–Sat.) is a bustling jewelers' market lined with traditional jewelry stores as well as gold-crafting and diamond-cutting workshops. The area is especially crowded during the Hindu festivals of Dussehra and Diwali, when it is considered auspicious to buy gold.

Next door to Zaveri Bazaar is the manic **Mangaldas Cloth Market** (11:30 A.M.–8 P.M. Mon.–Sat.). Mumbai's largest indoor cloth market, this where you can buy everything from linen to brocade for glitzy Indian weddings, at a wholesale rate. The market is a fascinating remnant of the city's prosperous cotton and fabric industry that grew in the 1800s and peaked in the early 20th century. Also located nearby is the Bhuleshwar Market, known for its flowers and pearl wholesalers.

However, the official wholesale flower market is the open **Dadar Flower and Vegetable Market** (Bapat Rd., Dadar, 6 A.M. until close daily), made up of numerous flower and vegetable sellers crammed around the bridge at Dadar Station on the western side. The heady scent of exotic and local flowers—including Chinese tea-roses, bright marigolds, pink lotuses, and frangipani—mingles with the smell of fresh greens, curry leaves, coriander, and mint being traded at wholesale rates. You may have to shout to be heard but the visit (and photo opportunity) is worth it.

SHOPPING DISTRICTS

For last-minute gift and souvenir shopping, there's simply no place like **Colaba Causeway.** On the stretch of street starting from Regal Cinema, this row of stores and streetside stalls sells everything from junk jewelry and silver trinkets to curios, handicrafts, sandalwood items, leather, antiques, shawls, shoes, sequined skirts, and embroidered bags. Bargaining is common practice here and you could easily walk away with an item for less than half the price of that available at a high-end store. However, don't forget to do a quick quality check before your purchase, especially inspecting fabric for tears or inconsistent weaves. Look for the Tantra brand of T-shirts, known for their cheeky India graffiti, and for cheap brocade and traditional Kolhapuri leather slippers. You'll find plenty of duplicated antiques as well, but if you're looking for something original and certainly more expensive, visit the reputed **Phillip's Antiques** (tel. 022/2202-0564, www.phillipsantiques.com, 10 A.M.–1:30

P.M. AND 2:30 P.M.–7 P.M. Mon.–Sat.) located diagonally opposite Regal Cinema.

If you're looking for Indian wear, specifically saris, visit the Dadar Market area for a wide variety of the six-yard (and ethnic Maharashtrian nine-yard) wear from across the country. The *zari*-bordered (gold brocade), handspun Kanjeevaram and Paithani saris may set you back by several thousand rupees or more, but the silks are worth their sheen.

For a wide choice between street shopping, malls, designer boutiques, and stores selling your favorite brands visit **Linking Road** in Bandra. Here, you can buy cheap shoes and clothes off the street or more expensive variants in the stores. Take your pick from leather bags, trendy clothes, and branded sneakers at many of the chic boutiques that line the street. At the end of your shopping escapade, try some of the street food available or visit the more expensive restaurants.

MALLS AND ARCADES

The very first mall equivalents in the city were the arcades that housed a number of emporia and boutiques in five-star hotels and at tourist-friendly locations. Although the crowd here has thinned somewhat thanks to competition from the newly sprouted malls, they remain the only places to house state emporia and sell original pashmina shawls or Kashmir carpets. The **World Trade Centre** (www.wtcmumbai.org) in Cuffe Parade has an arcade in addition to various offices. Here, you can buy handicrafts from Kashmir, semi-precious jewelry, as well as sandalwood and saris from the south. This is also the venue for a number of traveling exhibitions and for an annual food festival.

The **Taj Arcade** (Taj Mahal Hotel, Colaba) and **The Trident Shopping Arcade** (The Trident, Nariman Point) are great places for crystal, jewelry, brocades, bags, and shoes. Don't let the five-star ambience deter your bargaining urge. Most places mark up prices for foreigners and you could end up paying several times the actual price if you don't negotiate.

Part of the new breed of malls, **CR2**

© ASHIMA NARAIN

shop window of Phillip's Antiques at Colaba Causeway

MILLS TO MALLS: THE CONTROVERSY AROUND MUMBAI'S TEXTILE MILLS

Mumbai, the cotton mill capital in the 19th century, attracted a number of migrants from surrounding regions. The mills generated the maximum trade and employment in the city and the area of Girangaon in Parel was once bustling with the hum of hundreds of machines and the chatter of over 200,000 mill workers. The gradual decline of the mills began in the middle of the century and came to a close in the 1970s and '80s — when problems between the workers' union and mill owners came to a head, leading to an indefinite strike that eventually resulted in the closure of the mills. Initiated by union leader Datta Samant in 1982, the strike rendered the mills useless as workers demanded an increase in wages and better working conditions.

As the government and mill owners refused to negotiate, the mills eventually closed and thousands of workers were left unemployed. For two decades, the mills lay abandoned. Owners (many of the mills were government-owned) began to auction their sprawling properties to developers for unbelievable amounts as rates soared with the space crunch and property boom in the city. In the late 1990s, the first high-rises were constructed, as were commercial complexes and snazzy malls. Lower Parel, with its stretch of malls and enterprises, was transformed from a lower- and middle-class housing area to a posh new address, began to be called "Upper Worli."

Even as mill workers continued to fight for their dues and pending payments, heritage mill buildings were destroyed to make way for a brand new cityscape. There were protests against this widespread development from environmental and social activists. Social activists demanded fair settlement of the dues of the unemployed mill workers, while environmentalists protested the construction's lack of regulation and pointed to the dangers of the lack of city infrastructure. Activists filed petitions as the government made no effort to rehabilitate the workers or use these lands for middle-income housing projects and green spaces.

Writers such as Darryl D'Monte (*Ripping the Fabric: The Decline of Mumbai and Its Mills*) have chronicled the mill controversy. As workers' residences fell into economic gloom, the malls became the hippest part of town. Today, ad agencies, upmarket eateries, luxury stores, bars, and nightclubs light up mall-and-corporate complexes, such as High Street Phoenix (previously Phoenix Mills) and the Raghuvanshi and Sun Mill Complexes. The collective memory of a conflict that had once consumed the city, its population, and economy is slowly fading.

(Nariman Point, 10 A.M.–midnight daily) is downtown Mumbai's only mall—a place where you can shop for branded clothes, grab a bite, catch a movie, or simply use the restroom if you're passing by.

Atria Mall (Annie Besant Rd., Worli, www.atriamumbai.com, 9:30 A.M.–1 A.M. daily) is a place where mall molls buy trendy brands, eat sushi, and buy sexy lingerie. Nearby is **Heera Panna Shopping Centre** (Haji Ali Circle), Mumbai's original mall. It is known for good-quality electronics at bargain prices and for its brands as well as its fakes. You can even get your mobile phone or camera fixed here.

The most popular mall, however, is located in the emerging shopping district of Lower Parel. A sprawling shopping estate on old mill land, **High Street Phoenix** (www.highstreetphoenix.com, 11 A.M.–11 P.M. daily) is still referred to as Phoenix Mills. Where cotton was spun at the height of the textile era, you will now find brands like Puma, Nike, and Marks & Spencer's at lower rates than in the West; budget store Big Bazaar is known for its bargains, and there's plenty of home shopping and children's stores. A self-contained mall with a number of restaurants and bars, its central location is a draw for residents from across the city.

In the neighboring Raghuvanshi Mills are a number of lifestyle stores. Visit **Good**

Earth (Senapati Bapat Marg, Lower Parel, tel. 022/2495-1954, www.goodearthindia.com, 11 A.M.–8 P.M. daily) for its beautiful objets d'art and wonderful ambience.

DEPARTMENT AND DESIGNER STORES

Mumbai is India's fashion capital and there's proof of the city's obsession with clothes in its designer stores. If you haven't been invited to Mumbai Fashion Week, which showcases designers from all over the country, simply walk into places like **Courtyard** (near Radio Club, Colaba, tel. 022/6638-5479), **Kimaya** (Kemp's Corner, tel. 022/2386-2432, www.kimayastudio.com, 10:30 A.M.–8:30 P.M. daily), and **Ensemble** (130 Shahid Bhagat Singh Rd., Fort, tel. 022/2285-4603, 11 A.M.–7 P.M. Mon.–Sat.) for names such as Manish Malhotra, Narendra Kumar Ahmed, Manish Arora, Sabyasachi Mukherjee, Ritu Kumar, Anita Dongre and Sabina Singh, among others. Favorites are Sabyasachi for Indian wear, Narendra Kumar for dapper menswear, and Manish Arora for Bollywood and India kitsch.

A chain of stores that brings traditional handicrafts into the urban space, **FabIndia** (at Kala Ghoda, Bandra and InOrbit Mall, tel. 022/2262-6539, www.fabindia.com, 10 A.M.–7:45 P.M. daily) is a must-stop shop. By employing rural craftspeople and adapting their traditional techniques to produce contemporary designs and products, the store has gained popularity among locals and tourists alike. You'll find a variety of cotton *kurtas* (traditional long cotton shirts), *kurtis* (short *kurtas*), skirts, shirts, pants, and scarves made of natural fiber with colorful vegetable dyes and ethnic block prints. There's a separate home section, where you can buy everything from wooden furniture to curtains, lamps, linen, bath products, spices, and preserves.

Cottage Industries (Colaba, tel. 022/2281-8802, 10 A.M.–8 P.M. daily) is a reputed government-run enterprise that showcases the handicrafts and handlooms of the country. You can spend hours browsing

framed Hindu gods at FabIndia

© ASHIMA NARAIN

through the handcrafted products that make for great ethnic collectibles to gift or decorate the home with.

Bombay Store (PM Rd., Fort, tel. 022/2288-5048, www.bombaystore.com, 10:30 A.M.–7:30 and InOrbit Mall, tel. 022/2871-0013, 11 A.M.–9:30 P.M. daily) is a century-old historic outlet associated with freedom fighters and leaders of the pre-Independence era. Previously called Bombay Swadeshi, it specialized in indigenous items to aid the boycott of British and foreign goods. Today, it is frequented for its range of clothing, accessories, silver jewelry, leather, curios, home and healthcare products, and stationery, as well as exotic and herbal teas. Meanwhile, the posh **Ravissant** (Madame Cama Rd., Colaba, tel. 022/2287-3405, www.cest-ravissant.com, 10 A.M.–7:30 P.M. Mon.–Sat.) is a first-rate store for fine filigreed silver, handcrafted leather, and sparkling goblets, as well as fashion and interior accessories.

For Indian and Western wear as well as home accessories, walk into **Westside** (Kala Ghoda, tel. 022/6636-0500, www.mywestside.com, and off Kemp's Corner, tel. 022/2384-1729, 10:30 A.M.–8:30 P.M. daily). There's a perennial discount sale here where you're likely to chance upon a good bargain or two.

Indian brides will always shop at **Kala Niketan** (Marine Lines, tel. 022/2200-5001, and Juhu, tel. 022/2611-5689, 11 A.M.–7:30 P.M., Mon.–Sat.), where you can buy traditional Indian wear—lovely gauzy Indian fabric, brocade stoles and regional specialty saris. There's an in-house tailor here. You will also find the most exquisite saris at **Nalli's** (Mahalaxmi, tel. 022/2353-5577, 10 A.M.–8 P.M. daily), known for the finest silks in India. Specialties are naturally dyed raw silk and handspun saris.

SPECIALTY BOUTIQUES

You can pick up the finest stationary at **Chimanlal's** (Fort, tel. 022/2207-7717, www .chimanlals.com, 11 A.M.–7 P.M. Mon.–Sat.), known for its exquisite handmade paper, cards, and folders with pretty Indian motifs and ethnic block prints. this is where locals flock to get their wedding cards designed—definitely something to write home about.

Contemporary Arts and Crafts (Napean Sea Rd., tel. 022/2363-1979, www.cac.co.in, 10 A.M.–8 P.M. Mon.–Sat., 10 A.M.–7 P.M. Sun.) is the place for artsy accessories and home decor. You'll find an assortment of ceramics, handicrafts, furniture, knickknacks, wood carvings, and crystal collections—all at good quality and reasonably priced.

Anokhi (off Hughes Rd., tel. 022/2368-5308, www.anokhi.com, and Waterfield Rd., Bandra, tel. 022/2640-8263, 10 A.M.–7:30 P.M. Mon.–Sat.) brings you a piece of Rajasthan with its fine ethnic block-prints in womenswear and accessories. You'll find chic, contemporary designs in colorful, traditional motifs and patterns sourced from the villages of Rajasthan.

For trendy home furnishings, visit **Yamini** (Wodehouse Rd., Colaba, tel. 022/2218-4143, and 14th Rd., Khar, tel. 022/2646-3645, 10:30 A.M.–7:30 P.M.daily). You're sure to find unusual curtains, cushion covers, duvets, and

gift items. The store sources some of its materials from the southern state of Kerala to support the ailing cottage industry there.

Tresorie (Linking Rd., Santacruz, tel. 022/2660-8042, www.tresorie.com, 11 A.M.–8 P.M. daily) is an exclusive lifestyle store with everything from Belgian crystal and Italian crockery to candle stands and traditional Indian folk painting. There's a home accessories section as well as a floor for designer items.

The quaint **Dhoop** (off Carter Rd., Bandra, tel. 022/2649-8646, 11 A.M.–8:30 P.M. Mon.–Sat.) is known for its earthy handicrafts and accessories. You'll find natural fiber mats and lamps, jute, brassware, earthenware, lanterns, and more at this family-run store. Specialties include eco-friendly Ganesh idols for the Ganesh festival.

A tiny garage shop started by a couple of ad guys, **Loose Ends** (off Linking Rd., Bandra, tel. 022/2645-3777, www.looseendsindia.com, 11 A.M.–8:30 P.M. Tues.–Sun.) is a fun place with kitsch and popular culture driven over the edge. You'll find Che Guevara and Beatles lampshades, quirky Indian knickknacks, funky clocks, posters, bar accessories, bags, and clothes.

For cheap and unique clothes and accessories, visit **OMO** (Waterfield Rd., Bandra, tel. 022/6698-1804, 11 A.M.–8 P.M. Mon.–Sat.), short for On My Own. Here you'll find Indian fabric tailored to Western designs alongside handcrafted shoes, bags, and costume jewelry.

NONPROFIT VENTURES

Mumbai has a number of outlets run by nonprofit bodies whose proceeds go toward charity. Of these, **Khadi Bhandaar** (Dr DN Rd., Fort, tel. 022/2207-3280, 10:30 A.M.–6:30 P.M. Mon.–Sat.) is the oldest and most established. It supports the traditional *khadi* (handspun cotton) industry that was revived by Gandhi in the Independence era. The store is a great place for *khadi kurtas,* handspun raw silk, leather slippers, health foods, and handmade soap, among other handicrafts.

Akanksha (Voltas House 'C', TB Kadam Marg, Chinchpokli, tel. 022/2372-9880, www.akanksha.org), an organization that works toward the betterment of underprivileged children through formal and informal education, sells colorful greeting cards, gift bags, photo frames, and artworks produced by the kids. These products are also available at select stores in the city, including Bombay Store. **Life Trust** (Neelam Centre, SK Ahire Marg, Worli, tel. 022/2491-0287, www.lifetrustindia.org) is a similar body where income from student-made products contributes to the support of informal education for the underprivileged, and also toward developing improved teaching aids and skills.

Women's India Trust (23 Bombay Market, Tardeo, or Mogul Ln., Mahim, tel. 022/2446-2768, www.wit.org.in) is a good place to pick up handicrafts, ethnic toys, linen, and food preserves, and support the women's cause at the same time. Proceeds go toward the empowerment of unskilled and disadvantaged women through education and employment.

Sports and Recreation

At first glance, Mumbai is a concrete jungle with few open spaces. It's little wonder, therefore, that sports and recreation are relegated largely to schools and clubs. However, if there's one sport that sweeps the nation with its universal appeal, it has to be cricket. With the popularity of cricketers rivaling that of Bollywood stars, the game holds strange powers over the city (and the nation) and has the ability to clear traffic every time India plays a match. Crowds gather around shop fronts that display shiny new LCD TVs to catch the latest cricket score as they go about their daily business, and it's not unheard of for offices to schedule meetings around an important match.

The traditional game of *kushti* (wrestling) also has its followers, as do indoor activities like bowling. Despite its long coastline, the city only has one water sports operator—but you can go fishing on the lakes, if that's any

© JANHAVI ACHAREKAR

Jet Ski and speedboat rides at Mumbai's water sports complex, H2O, at Chowpatty Beach, are a great way to view the city skyline.

consolation. Mumbai's biggest surprise, however, is its national park in the far suburbs, where you can go on guided tours conducted by naturalists. And in the vast industrial wasteland of Sewri in the heart of the city is the shockingly pink sight of migratory flamingos feeding on toxic waste.

WATER SPORTS

Mumbai's only water sports complex, **H2O** (Chowpatty, tel. 022/2367-7546, info@h2osports.biz, 11 A.M.–10 P.M. daily Sept.–May), is located close to Chowpatty Beach. You can take a spin around the bay on a Jet Ski (Rs 250/10 min.) or go on a speedboat ride (Rs 175/hr) far out into the sea for a breathtaking view of the city skyline.

SPECTATOR SPORTS

If you want a glimpse of the next big cricket idol, go to **Shivaji Park** in Dadar and watch young players being groomed to become tomorrow's stars. This is where players like Sunil Gavaskar and Sachin Tendulkar were coached before they went on to become Indian cricket's biggest names. You can also visit the *maidans,* or open grounds (Oval, Cross, Azad), to watch numerous teams simultaneously at play, sharing the field in a city squeezed for space. Matches at the Wankhede (Navjivan Wadi, Marine Lines, tel. 022/2281-1795) and Brabourne (Dinshaw Vaccha Rd., Churchgate, tel. 022/6659-4198) stadiums in Churchgate require tickets, but the most popular matches are those played informally in the small by-lanes or *gullies* of the city, inspiring the term *"gully* cricket."

It's truly worthwhile to catch a game of *kushti*—traditional wrestling in mud courts with lithe, well-oiled young male participants coached at the *akhada,* or local gymnasium. The sport, unfortunately, is dying as most young people would rather participate in a WWF match. However, the sport may still be viewed at a few *kushti* schools in Girgaum and Dadar, and during competitions at some *akhadas.*

If you're in Mumbai in February, don your best hat and designer outfit and head

to the Indian Derby, held at the sprawling **Mahalaxmi Racecourse** (Keshavrao Khadye Marg, Mahalaxmi, tel. 022/2307-1401). There's a mad scramble for passes and coveted invitations to this glamorous event. The racing season lasts from November until April. You can also do a two-week riding course (Rs 30,000) at the Amateur Riders' Club (tel. 022/5600-5204, www.rwitc.com, office@arcmumbai.com) or go riding (Rs 800/hour) on your own. The restaurant Gallops, along the racecourse, is perfect for a meal in an equestrian ambience for those who wish to simply enjoy the spirit of the races from a distance.

While only members are allowed inside the colonial Bombay Gymkhana, South Mumbai's elitist club and sole venue for **rugby,** you can always cheat by watching from the adjoining Azad Maidan (between Mahatma Gandhi Rd., Mahapalika Marg, and Sterling Cinema Rd.). The sport is usually played between February and May.

INDOOR SPORTS

Bowling was all the rage when it first arrived here about a decade ago—hardly surprising for a city starved for recreation options. Although the craze has died down, it remains a popular social sport. **The Bowling Co** (High Street Phoenix, Lower Parel, tel. 022/2491-4000, 10:30 A.M.–12:30 A.M. daily, Rs 100–300), Mumbai's first bowling alley, remains the most popular.

At the **Hakone Bowling Café and Entertainment Centre** (Hiranandani Complex, Powai, tel. 022/4005-2121, www.hakonefun.com, 11 A.M.–9 P.M.daily, Rs 120 for four rounds), you can play mini-golf, do some indoor rock-climbing, try go-karting, and play a few arcade games in addition to bowling.

AMUSEMENT PARKS

Esselworld (near Gorai Beach, tel. 022/2845-2222 or 022/2884-7800, www.esselworld.com, 11 A.M.–7 P.M. daily, adults Rs 400, children Rs 300) and its adjoining water park, **Water Kingdom,** are generally crowded on weekends and filled with noisy, raucous crowds.

NATURE WALKS AND TREKS

The monsoon season and its successive months are the best times to go for a trek inside **Sanjay Gandhi National Park** (Borivli, tel. 022/2884-7800, nicsgnp@vsnl.net, nicsgnp@yahoo.co.in, 6 A.M.–7 P.M. daily, Rs 30). Nonprofit bodies within the park conduct butterfly walks, nature walks, and bird-watching tours. They also organize snake shows, documentary screenings, slide shows, and more, making your visit to the park a fun, educational experience. Tours usually fill, so it's best to book in advance to avoid disappointment. Walks may also be booked through the **World-Wide Fund for Nature** (National Insurance Building, DN Rd., tel. 022/2207-8105, 10 A.M.–5 P.M. Mon.–Fri.), **Bombay Natural History Society** (Hornbill House, Salim Ali Chowk, tel. 022/2282-1811, www.bnhs.org, 10 A.M.–5 P.M. Mon.–Sat.), or the Range Forest Officer at the **Forest Development Corporation and Management** (cell tel. 91/93240-60766).

A number of good Samaritans also conduct interesting walks through the park and surrounding jungles of Mumbai free of cost or for a negligible fee. Shardul Bajikar (cell tel. 91/98211-20494) and Hemant Tripathi (cell tel. 91/98701-63763) conduct nature walks, Adesh Shivkar (cell tel. 91/98204-55713, natureindiatours@gmail.com) leads bird-watching trips, and Saunak Pal (cell tel. 91/98505-14415, nisargtrust@gmail.com) specializes in snakes and amphibians.

If you're in the city in January, don't miss the annual **Bird Race** (www.indiabirdraces.com), where teams spread out across the city to track the maximum number of bird species. Accompanied by avid bird-watchers, this is an ideal way to discover the city.

For one-day, overnight, and long-stay field trips, call **Nature Knights** (www.natureknights.com) about their packages.

FLAMINGO-SPOTTING

Until recently, Sewri, a small industrial area along the Harbour line, looked just the way it sounded. Sewage waste from nearby industries was deposited on the shores of **Sewri**

The Sanjay Gandhi National Park makes for a great getaway within city limits.

© ASHIMA NARAIN

Bay, turning the mudflats into a dump for toxic waste. However, in an unforeseen turn of events, the site has turned into a birders' paradise. Thousands of flamingos descend upon the bay every year around November to feed on bacteria that thrive on the industrial waste. Dotting the shores with their pink plumage, these flamboyant birds provide the grey industrial landscape with much-needed visual relief. And they give the people of Mumbai another reason for an outing, binoculars and cameras in tow.

The birds may be viewed from Sewri or from **Chembur,** a suburb on the Central line. In Chembur, a group of enterprising Koli fishermen led by Waman Koli (Mahul Village, Chembur, cell tel. 91/98339-39051) have started ferry rides into the bay, offering a closer look at the beautiful birds. Be prepared, however, for an eardrum-shattering ride on a noisy, sputtering boat that traverses filthy, polluted waters. It's important to keep track of the tides as the birds are generally seen 2–3 hours before and after high tide.

PINK CITY

Tens of thousands of migratory flamingos flock to the unlikely location of Sewri Bay, an industrial area on the Harbour railway line. The muddy brown Sewri mudflats and the polluted, smoke-spewed grey horizon are dotted with the graceful pink of Lesser Flamingos between the months of November and May every year.

The birds feed on algae and bacteria that thrive on industrial waste, and have become a tourist attraction as well as a birder's delight. The feathered creatures arrived in the early 1990s, and the Mumbai Port authorities took them under wing, ensuring protection and maintenance of their habitat. Together with the authorities, environmentalists and bird lovers keep a watchful eye on the flamingos, protecting them from urban dangers and spreading awareness of their existence through events such as the Mumbai Bird Race.

The flamingos of Sewri make for a fine spectacle, their vibrant shades of pink reflected in the shimmering waters of the bay as they feed in the distant horizon. The birds are generally seen 2-3 hours before and after high tide, and fortunate onlookers have witnessed their rare courtship dance; in a city where the interaction between humans and nature is rare, this is a splendid example of the co-existence of the urbane and the natural.

The birds may be viewed from Sewri or from Chembur, a suburb on the Central line. In Chembur, a group of enterprising Koli fishermen led by Waman Koli (Mahul Village, Chembur, cell tel. 91/98339-39051) have started ferry rides into the polluted waters of the bay for curious bird-watchers.

The birds have been the subject of much interest ever since their arrival, and have been featured in an informative documentary titled *In the Pink* by city photographer and wildlife documentary filmmaker Ashima Narain.

ANGLING

In a city where honking at cars and talking loudly is the norm, you might think that finding a quiet spot for fishing could only be the pursuit of an unsound mind. However, the **Maharashtra State Angling Association** (tel. 022/2857-1780, powailake@hotmail.com) does just that; honorary members organize angling trips on the calm waters of the Powai Lake, providing momentary peace in the chaos of the city.

MUMBAI MARATHON

Held in January, the Mumbai Marathon (www.scmm.indiatimes.com) is the city's largest community sporting event. If you can't run the entire 42-kilometer stretch, try the 21-kilometer half-marathon or run for a cause on the seven-kilometer Dream Run. Participants include activists, celebrities, and common folk who come out on the streets of Mumbai, running past heritage monuments and the seaface in an electrifying atmosphere.

SPAS

Fraught with the pressures and rigors of the fast-paced city life, it's hardly surprising that local residents and visitors seek the relaxing comfort of a spa once in a while. Most five-star hotels in the city offer luxurious spa facilities and services, while traditional places like the **Kerala Ayurvedic Health Spa** (Neelkanth, Marine Dr., tel. 022/2288-3210, www.keralavaidyashala.com, 8 A.M.–8 P.M. daily) use ancient Ayurvedic treatments to heal both body and mind.

Rudra Spa (Kwality House, Kemp's Corner, tel. 022/2387-2363, 8 A.M.–9 P.M. daily) brings you special techniques ranging from foot-sole massages to aromatherapy in a wonderfully soothing ambience. This exclusive spa has lifelong members who swear by its rejuvenating powers.

If you're looking for something fun and exotic, try the **Franck Provost Salon and Spa** (Pali Danda Rd., Bandra, tel. 022/6703-6971, and Juhu Rd., Juhu, tel. 022/6702-1440, www.franckprovost-india.com, 11 A.M.–8 P.M.

Tues.–Sun.) for its Moroccan body wraps and hot stone therapy.

YOGA

Mumbai has a number of yoga institutes where its stressed-out denizens can seek respite from the urban rush. One of the oldest and most established is the **Ishwarlal Chunnilal Yogic Health Centre–Kaivalyadhama** (43 Marine Dr., tel. 022/2281-8417, 6:30–9:30 A.M. and 3:30–6:30 P.M. Mon.–Sat.). Known simply as Kaivalyadham, it imparts yoga lessons for a healthy mind and body, and conducts health checkups.

Teaching yoga in the famous B. K. S. Iyengar tradition, **Iyengar Yogashraya** (Elmac House, Senapati Bapat Marg, Lower Parel (W), tel. 022/2494-8416, 7 A.M.–8 P.M. Tues.–Fri. and 7 A.M.–4 P.M. Mon. and Sat.) is a branch of the famous Iyengar Yoga Institute started by the guru, one of a handful of yogis credited with introducing yoga to the West.

Purna Swasthya Yoga Therapy Center (Bhartiya Stree Seva Sangh, Behind Wilson College, Chowpatty, tel. 022/6505-7567, www.drpragna.com) specializes in medical yoga. They also run basic classes.

Yoga Training Centre (51, Jaihind Society, 11th N-S Rd., Juhu Scheme, tel. 022/2649-9020, www.traditional-yoga.com) runs basic sessions, weekend training sessions, specialized illness treatment, as well as three- to nine-month courses.

Shiv Holistic Yoga (tel. 022/3294-2844, www.yogathome.com) offers classes in the homes of clients and has a special class for foreigners. They run basic as well as advanced yoga classes.

Accommodations

In India, there's a catch phrase for the bare essentials of life—"*roti, kapda aur makaan*"—literally translated as "food, clothing, and lodging." While the first two are easily available, *makaan,* or lodging, comes at a heavy price. Mumbai is an expensive city, and with real estate prices beating even Manhattan rates, it is hardly surprising that hotel rates tend to be on the higher side as well. Five-star hotels abound and these, along with hotels that command a sea view, come at a premium. While budget options exist, these are often shabby, sleazy, or located in areas that are not recommended. A couple of youth hostels and some old establishments in downtown Mumbai are among the few reasonable budget options. Recently, the government proposed the idea of homestays, where willing residents open up their homes to tourists for a first-hand experience of the famed Indian hospitality. The idea has yet to take off but there's a website (www.allindiaguide.com/homestay/mumbai.html) where you can keep yourself updated on developments.

At one time, most visitors stayed in downtown Mumbai, over an hour's drive from the airport. Today, the expanding cluster of five-star hotels near the airport reflects the increasing number of business travelers to the city and of a shift in focus to other parts of the city. Downtown Mumbai, however, continues to be the location of choice for most visitors due to its concentration of tourist attractions.

Tariffs in most Mumbai hotels do not include taxes and are usually subject to change without notice, often varying according to season and reaching their peak in the winter months.

COLABA AND VICINITY
Under Rs 1,000

Colaba, being the tourist hub, has a wide range of hotels to suit both high and low budgets. Everyone from taxi drivers to touts lurking the streets will promise you the best hotel for cheap. To avoid being taken for a ride, book a room in advance. Located right behind the Taj, the **Salvation Army Hotel** (Red Shield House,

Colaba, tel. 022/2284-1824, red_shield@vsnl.net, Rs 150–897 includes breakfast or up to three meals) isn't exactly the lap of luxury, with its dank rooms and linen that looks like it could do with laundry. You can't miss the red signboard and Hindi music wafting from the sparse reception area. A lone waiter is usually found watching a Bollywood movie in the gloomy dining hall in the post-lunch afternoon hours, even as dreadlocked guests surf the Internet in the adjoining room.

YWCA International Center (Madame Cama Rd., Apollo Bunder, tel. 022/2282-6814, www.ywcaic.info, Rs 896–3,148) has basic but comfortable, clean rooms. There are one-, two-, three-, and four-bed rooms. The standard rooms look like they could do with a coat of paint, but the deluxe rooms on the upper floor have balconies overlooking the YMCA and YWCA grounds. Conveniently located in a quiet lane not far from the YMCA, the international guesthouse is well managed and admits men as well as entire families.

Rs 1,000-3,000

The **YMCA** (Nathalal Parekh Marg, tel. 022/2202-0079 or 022/2282-6384, www.ymcabombay.com, Rs 1,600 d and membership charges Rs 120) is the preferred choice of many young budget travelers, though damp walls and cramped spaces make it a less charming option than the YWCA. However, rooms are clean, the service is good, and the place fosters a stimulating atmosphere where you can meet fellow travelers and exchange local tips. A piano and table tennis in the community room at the entrance lend it a cheerful feel as children are tutored and visitors wait patiently to meet loved ones.

Nestled in a quiet shaded lane, **◖ Bentley's Hotel** (17 Oliver Rd., tel. 022/2288-2890, www.bentleyshotel.com, Rs 1,145–2,000) is a 1970s hotel located in a 1930s building. The spacious, tube-lit rooms with black-and-white checkered tile flooring have an art deco air about them and house some antique furniture. Located in a tranquil, residential area surprisingly close to the hustle and bustle of Colaba

Causeway, the hotel makes for an interesting stay at affordable rates.

Located in the grungy area of Crawford Market, **Hotel New Bengal** (DN Rd., near Crawford Market, tel. 022/2340-1951, www.hotelnewbengal.com, Rs 495–2,200) comes as a surprise. This well-managed business hotel makes for a great tourist stopover with clean, bright rooms at budget rates. There's a vast variety of rooms, ranging from single rooms with common baths to cheerful dorms and well-furnished deluxe rooms, including air-conditioning options. Close to the local community markets of Mohammad Ali Road, it is located in the center of action. There are several eateries around the hotel, in addition to Howrah, its famous Bengali restaurant.

If you have a taste for the artistic, coupled with a moderate budget, stay at the delightful **◖ Regency Inn** (18 Lansdowne House, MB Marg, Apollo Bunder, tel. 022/2202-0292, regency_inn@hotmail.com, Rs 1,500–4,000), situated in a 19th-century heritage building just behind the Taj and close to the Jamaat Art Gallery. Soft lighting, antiques, and Indian art disclose the touches of the owner, an art dealer who, in addition to aesthetic sensibilities, possesses a good measure of local knowledge. This pleasantly decorated, well-maintained old place has simple rooms but a lovely ambience, and an efficient staff. Book well in advance as the hotel's 20 rooms are always in demand.

A popular no-frills hotel, **The Strand** (Apollo Bunder, tel. 022/2288-2222, www.hotelstrand.com, Rs 2,000–3,500) boasts a beautiful location by the harbor. While living arrangements are purely functional, the sparse rooms are spacious, neat, and air-conditioned; the deluxe room on the upper floor has a long balcony and the sea-view rooms are great value for money. Guests have access to car rental, a doctor on call, and valet services.

Rs 3,000-10,000

Located amid a cluster of hotels in a quiet area off Colaba Causeway, **Hotel Godwin** (Garden Rd., tel. 022/2284-1226, hotelgodwin@mtnl.net.in, Rs 3,800–5,500) was once popular for its terrace resto-bar, Cloud 9, which offered a spectacular view of the surrounding cityscape. Sadly, Cloud 9 has closed and the terrace space, strewn with the erstwhile bar's beautiful white cast-iron chairs, is open only to private parties. The rooms in this three-star lodging, although cheery and recently renovated, wear a strangely vacant look these days. All rooms have wrought-iron and wood decor and are bright and airy. The smaller singles and doubles are good for the price, while the suites and deluxe rooms have a view. Use the elevator at your own risk!

Rs 10,000 and Up

Hotel Fariyas (off Arthur Rd., Colaba, tel. 022/2204-2911, www.fariyas.com, Rs 10,000–18,000) is a somewhat bland hotel, popular for its location and prices that are marginally lower than those of conventional star-rated hotels in the area. While a few rooms have balconies overlooking the sea, the ambience and furnishing leave a lot to be desired. For a few thousand rupees more, you can stay at the suites themed around Oxbridge, Agra, and oriental art. Helpful staff, a swimming pool, and classic rock at the on-site bar The Tavern do, however, make for a pleasant stay.

(Gordon House (Battery St., Apollo Bunder, tel. 022/2287-1122, www.ghhotel .com, Rs 8,500–17,000) is a boutique hotel located in a by-lane, away from the hustle and bustle of Colaba. A white stucco facade with shuttered windows leads into charming rooms themed in Scandinavian, Mediterranean, and country styles; original tiling and pleasant colors enhance the tasteful decor. The hotel has a good Asian restaurant, All Stir Fry, and a slightly jaded disco called Polly Esther—once Mumbai's hottest nightspot, and known for its retro music, menu cards designed like LPs, and waiters in Afro wigs. Run by star Mumbai restaurateur Sanjay Narang, this is a good alternative to the five-star hotels in the area—but you may want to avoid the rooms on the second floor, unless the thumping beats from the disco are likely to lull you to sleep. Room rates include breakfast.

The **Taj President** (Cuffe Parade, tel. 022/6665-0808, www.tajhotels.com, Rs 13,500–25,000) is a trim and efficient 280-room business hotel located in the posh Cuffe Parade area of Colaba. The hotel has elegantly designed rooms with wooden furniture, earthy colors, and spectacular views of the sea and surrounding cityscape. Part of the reputed Taj chain of hotels, it is known for its excellent Italian restaurant Trattoria and local coastal cuisine at Konkan Café. Rooms are of three types: Executive, Deluxe, and Deluxe Premium—ask for the recently renovated Deluxe rooms if you're one for luxuries like twin-headed massage showers and the latest in technology. The hotel also has Executive suites and new Deluxe suites.

Mumbai's landmark hotel, **(Taj Mahal Palace and Tower** (opposite Gateway of India, Apollo Bunder, tel. 6665-3366, www.tajhotels.com, Rs 16,500–300,000) reeked of Old World charm and luxury before its spectacular heritage wing and other parts were destroyed in Mumbai's horrific terrorist attack of November

the Taj Mahal Palace and Tower

© ASHIMA NARAIN

26, 2008. Built by Indian industrial giant Jamsetji Tata in 1903, it was British India's first Indian-owned luxury hotel. Known to host heads of state, royalty, rock stars, jet-setters, and awe-struck tourists with equal deference and hospitality, the hotel is an institution in itself. The latest ranking lists the Taj among the top 100 hotels in the world in *Institutional Investor Magazine*'s 2008/2009 survey. It also ranks among the top hotels in India, Asia, and the world, in several international rankings including the *Forbes* and *Conde Nast Traveller* lists. The Taj enjoys the most enviable location in the city with a vantage view of the Gateway and the harbor. The hotel offers a variety of rooms, ranging from Gateway-facing Tower rooms and Club Rooms with "invisible" butlers to the two Presidential suites. Service at is first-rate and the hotel lives up to the premium charged. It is also known to constantly reinvent itself and introduce pioneering restaurants like the Zodiac Grill, and the first dedicated Japanese cuisine restaurant in the city, Wasabi by Morimoto. The hotel has a number of bars, and you can also hire their luxury yacht (Rs 12,000/hour) for a romantic dinner on the bay.

The Taj Mahal's century-old palatial wing—once embellished with original art, period furniture, and Belgian crystal chandeliers—is no more, but the hotel management proved its mettle by reopening parts of the hotel within a month of the tragedy. Restoration is underway and the hotel intends to be fully functional within a year of the attack.

MARINE DRIVE AND CHOWPATTY
Rs 1,000-3,000

The Marine Drive/Chowpatty stretch is dotted with sea-facing five-star hotels, as well as cheap lodges and guesthouses. A popular low-range oceanview option is **Hotel Sea Green** (145, Marine Dr., tel. 022/2282-2294, www.seagreenhotel.com, Rs 2,250–3,350), a small but well-tended hotel known for its location, good service, and reasonably priced rooms. Rooms on the upper floor have a spectacular view of

the Arabian Sea but on the lower floors, you may have to trade the view for sounds of the traffic outside.

The **Sea Green South Hotel** next door (145 A, Marine Dr., tel. 022/6633-6535, www.seagreensouth.com, Rs 3,000 d), is a good inexpensive alternative.

Rs 3,000-10,000

The **Chateau Windsor Hotel** (86, V N Rd., Churchgate, tel. 022/6622-4455, www.chateauwindsor.com, Rs 3,100–4,500) is a stone's throw from Churchgate Station. While its plain, tube-lit rooms are spacious and have balconies, guests are hardly likely to stand and stare at the cityscape amid the sounds of traffic below. The hotel serves only breakfast, but there are plenty of eateries around, including popular Gaylord's across the road. The hotel also has Wi-Fi, an amenity that is rare in this price range.

The **West End Hotel** (opposite Bombay Hospital, New Marine Lines, tel. 022/2205-7484, www.westendhotelmumbai.com, Rs 3,600–5,400) provides four-star services for a mid-range price. Located away from the bustle of the main road, it is popular with tourists and foreigners who are temporarily stationed in the city for business. Rooms are neat and spacious with a 1970s-Mumbai-meets-contemporary-design look. The staff is helpful and you can even hire a mobile phone for the duration of your stay here. The hotel also has an in-house bar, multicuisine restaurant, and a coffee shop where you can unwind after a day out on the Mumbai streets.

It is difficult to miss the bright orange glow of the **Astoria Hotel** (J Tata Rd., Churchgate, tel. 022/6654-1234, www.astoriamumbai.com, Rs 5,000–8,500) through the peak-hour crowds of Churchgate. This recently renovated hotel has a history of jazz, but the nouveau look of its interior is deeply incongruous with its lovely brownstone facade. Like the exterior of the hotel, rooms are Old World—spacious and high-ceilinged—and so is the staff, which is old-fashioned and matter-of-fact.

Romanesque statues of Rubenesque women

CITY HELD HOSTAGE: MUMBAI'S TERRORIST ATTACKS

On November 26, 2008, 10 terrorists who had arrived by sea in the dead of the night, held Mumbai hostage for three days. They unleashed a wave of terror and violence that left around 170 dead and 300 injured.

The attacks targeted public places and prominent hotels, like the Chhatrapati Shivaji Terminus, Cama Hospital, The Taj Mahal Palace and Towers, The Oberoi and Trident Hotels, and Café Leopold in Colaba. The three hotels were held hostage, along with a Jewish cultural center, Nariman House, in Colaba; these sites were all the scenes of horrific civilian massacres. In the case of the hotels, they were also the scenes of miraculous escapes. At Nariman House, Mumbai-based Rabbi Gavriel and his wife Rivka – directors of an Orthodox Jewish center – were killed, while their toddler son, Moshe, was carried to safety by his Indian nanny. The attackers were well armed with weapons and communication systems, and the high drama lasted until November 29, ending after an intense operation by India's National Security Guards.

While nine terrorists were shot dead, one man, Ajmal Amir Kasab from Pakistan, was captured alive. He is currently under trial in India and has pleaded not guilty to the 86 charges leveled against him. He could face the death penalty if convicted. The attack left the city stunned, leaving an otherwise bustling center resembling a war zone. After the success of the anti-terror operation, the city and the nation reacted adversely – ministers resigned and recently improved relations with Pakistan were soured. The attacks showcased holes in intelligence, and while they were apparently targeted at tourists and were an attempt to cripple the country's tourist industry, more Indians than foreign nationals were killed. There emerged many uniformed and civilian heroes in the city, ranging from top cops killed in the line of duty to hotel staff, many of whom laid down their lives for guests by acting as human shields.

The restaurants of the Taj Mahal Palace and Tower and The Trident were reopened on December 21, 2008 (within a month of the tragedy) in a commendable restoration effort. Several guests who had narrowly escaped the scenes of violence returned in a show of solidarity against terrorism, together with the hotel management, politicians, top industrialists, Page 3 celebs, and hotel regulars. Guests at both hotels gave a standing ovation to the outstanding staffs at the emotional reopening.

strike a pose alongside dancing Natarajas (the Hindu god Shiva) in a lobby lit with suspended chandeliers and gold embellishments at **The Ambassador** (Churchgate extension, tel. 022/2204-1131, www.ambassadorindia.com, Rs 9,000–28,000). Once a prominent Mumbai landmark known for its revolving restaurant, called the Pearl of the Orient, the hotel is in need of an urgent makeover. While the restaurant is still popular for its fantastic view and palatable Asian cuisine, the rooms could do with some changes. It's strange that the lower-priced Executive rooms should be on the higher floor, commanding the best view with windows opening out to the sea. The Presidential Suite, in contrast, has an ungainly street view and a strange mélange of art and statuettes. The Duplex, Premier, and Superior rooms are more tastefully designed but the decor of the hotel, in general, is a clash of styles and art. If you leave your aesthetic sensibilities behind, the hotel provides some good mid-range options in a great location.

Rs 10,000 and Up

A small hotel with large rooms, **◖ Hotel InterContinental** (135 Marine Dr., tel. 022/3987-9999, www.mumbai.intercontinental.com, Rs 13,000–22,500)—like its star-rated neighbors—is known for its magnificent view of the ocean. Primarily a business hotel, it rates highest on comfort, and was the first in the Indian hospitality business to introduce a pillow and quilt menu. Rooms scan the surrounding seascape, and are tastefully designed and accessorized with the latest gizmos. From Korean, bamboo, and zero-headache pillows to Bose speakers, plasma TVs, DVD players, and music in the sea-view bathrooms, the hotel anticipates all your needs. The crescent-shaped suite has a large bathroom with a TV. Rooms even come equipped with a safe large enough to accommodate your laptop (complete with an electrical point for charging), making this boutique hotel one of Mumbai's finest. The hotel has a Sicilian restaurant, Corleone, and an Indian restaurant called Kebab Korner, in addition to Czar, a vodka bar, and the spectacular rooftop resto-bar Dome.

Hotel Marine Plaza (29 Marine Dr., tel. 022/2285-1212, www.hotelmarineplaza .com, Rs 14,000–25,000) is a relatively new entrant to the stretch of Mumbai's high-end seaside hotels. The rooms at this four-star property rooms command a fine view of the sea and the Queen's Necklace. The ceiling of the lobby presents a view of the glass bottom of the swimming pool above. The hotel's art deco–inspired look is accompanied by no-frill rooms and a suite with a romantic sunset view. Popular for its English-style pub, Geoffrey's, Hotel Marine Plaza also has two restaurants—Oriental Blossom and Bayview—that provide a beautiful sea view.

The Trident, Nariman Point (Nariman Point, tel. 022/6632-4343, www.tridenthotels.com, Rs 16,000–80,000) and its sister hotel **The Oberoi** (tel. 022/6632-5757, www .oberoimumbai.com, Rs 21,000–150,000), like their rival the Taj, were the sites of high drama and tragedy during the terrorist attacks of November 26, 2008. The Trident reopened within weeks of the terrible event, but the Oberoi—the most affected of the two—is still under restoration. Previously one property under the name the Oberoi, the two hotels have undergone three management changes in recent times. Today the twin hotels are run by the same management and share a common passageway. They have distinct identities, however, with The Oberoi positioned as a five-star hotel and The Trident as a luxury five-star. The hotels have been known to host celebrity guests, including the likes of Bill Clinton and Michael Jackson. Both hotels are placed for the perfect panorama of the city skyline—rooms enjoy breathtaking ocean views and a lovely open rooftop pool presents the perfect vision of azure sky and blue sea. On the downside, The Oberoi's proximity to the adjoining high-rises in the business district of Nariman Point gives their higher floors a view of the pool and the poolside rooms. All rooms in The Trident come with a personal butler and both the hotels are known for their restaurants, bars, and spa, Shanti, all of which were the scenes of violence in November 2008. While the spa and some restaurants—like Frangipani, serving Mediterranean cuisine, and the pan-Asian India Jones—have reopened and continue to serve their signature dishes, others won't be fully functional until the end of 2009. The Oberoi is also popular with tourists, local residents, and employees of the swank offices in neighboring buildings for its café and shopping arcade.

NORTH MUMBAI

North Mumbai is increasingly the choice for business travelers and long-term foreign residents in the city. The trend is reflected in the numerous star-rated hotels located around the airports and in upmarket suburban areas such as Bandra and Juhu. If you're in Mumbai on a tight schedule, we recommend the more convenient options downtown, as the traffic-ridden commute to and from North Mumbai will eat into precious sightseeing time. If you have a tight budget, however, the suburbs have some convenient options.

Rs 1,000–3,000

Hotel Jewel Palace (Fifth Rd., near Khar Railway Station, tel. 022/2604-5488, Rs 2,000–3,000) is a small, pleasant place in a not-so-pleasant location. Situated on the corner of Khar market, the hotel is a short walk from

Khar Station on the Western line. While rooms are clean and comfortable, the surroundings leave much to be desired. Be prepared to have your senses assaulted by the sights and smells of the vegetable market and by the din of vendors and passing trains. However, there's consolation in the fact that the hotel is well located if you intend to travel downtown by train. It also provides free airport transfer and has an in-house restaurant that may easily be given a miss for the numerous Bandra eateries and nightspots close by.

Rs 3,000-10,000

Royal Inn (opposite Khar Tel Exchange, tel. 022/2649-5151, Rs 4,000–7,000) is a small, uninspiring hotel near the shopping district of Linking Road. Located in the heart of Bandra, it provides easy access to the surrounding sights and eats. Rooms are simple but good for the price.

Don't let the posh Pali Hill address of **Executive Enclave** (Dr. Ambedkar Rd., Pali Hill, Bandra, tel. 022/6696-9000, www.executiveenclave.com, Rs 5,500–8,500) fool you. Located on an arterial road, it overlooks a vast hutment area and has been the victim of road repairs lately. However, this predominantly business hotel is a great option for those with a moderate budget. Professionally managed with compact but clean rooms, the hotel also provides free airport transfer, Wi-Fi, as well as complementary bedtime tea and a buffet breakfast. The efficient staff make sure that you're well looked after.

You'll find a variety of good mid-range accommodations near the domestic airport. **Hotel Airlink** (off Nehru Rd., near domestic terminal, tel. 022/6726-7000, www.hotelairlink.com, Rs 4,000–6,000) is a nice enough place for the price, with small, well-maintained rooms and pleasant staff. You may need to book in advance, however, as rooms are limited. A restaurant on the hotel premises whips up some decent fare.

For Rs 1,000 more, it's worth going to **Avion** (opposite the domestic terminal, tel. 022/2611-6958, www.avionhotel.com, Rs 6,300–7,400) for its simple but spacious rooms and sheer proximity to the airport. The hotel also provides emergency laundry services at reasonable rates and has a 24-hour check-in and check-out facility. Room rates include buffet breakfast and dinner, as well as airport transfer.

At **C Hotel Kings International** (Juhu Tara Rd., tel. 022/2618-4381/4382/4383, www.kingsinternational.com, Rs 5,500–12,000), you can expect the service, meals, and luxury of a high-end hotel without the price to match. Rooms are large and well designed, with twin, double, and suite options (rates differ for single and double occupancy), and there's easy access to currency exchange and car rentals. The hotel has some popular restaurants, including Alfredo's for Italian and Temple Flower for Asian cuisine.

Hotel Citizen (Juhu Tara Rd., tel. 022/6693-2525 or 022/2660-7273, www.citizenhotel-mumbai.com, Rs 6,000–12,000) prides itself for being right next to the beach. All rooms are bright and airy and come with a sea view. Avoid the ostentatious suite; the deluxe and executive rooms are pleasantly cheerful. This is a good seafront option if you don't want to pay five-star prices.

Hotel Metro International (Andheri Kurla Rd., tel. 022/6694-1010, www.uniquehotelsindia.com, Rs 3,500–6,000) is a pleasant-enough mid-range option near the international airport. You can choose between its small, basic rooms and a relatively inexpensive presidential suite with contemporary decor. They also have a sister hotel in Bandra called Metro Palace.

Tunga Paradise (MIDC Central Rd., Andheri, tel. 022/6789-8900, www.tunga-hotels.com, Rs 6,500–7,750) may be a better alternative. At the heart of the northern commercial district and a short distance from the international airport, this business hotel comes with spacious rooms, good service, and the necessary amenities. It also has a two restaurants and a bar. A traveler's pit stop rather than delight, it is not ideally located if you intend to travel around the city.

Rs 10,000 and Up

Located, as the name suggests, at Land's End on the rocky Bandra shore close to the Bandra Fort, **Taj Lands End** (Bandstand, Bandra, tel. 022/6668-1234, www.tajhotels.com, Rs 19,000–24,500) is yet another beautiful property owned by the Taj. Its large, elegant rooms have the next best view after Marine Drive. The hotel has a range of rooms, including expensive club rooms with butler service (women get female butlers) and a presidential suite. There's a non-smoking floor, as well as a "ladies only" floor. A popular venue for business and lunch meetings, its lobby bar is packed even on weekday afternoons. Meanwhile, signature East Asian restaurant Ming Yang, Indian cuisine Masala Bay, and newly opened health restaurant/bar Pure are frequented by locals and Bollywood stars. The poolside is a great place to relax and watch the sun go down.

Rising high above the Juhu traffic is the nouveau palatial facade of the most high-profile luxury hotel in the suburbs. The ◖ **J. W. Marriott** (Juhu Tara Rd., tel. 022/6693-3000, www.marriott.com, Rs 16,500) is the playground of the suburban rich and famous—with Bollywood stars, industrialists, politicians, and others converging here for business and pleasure. The hotel offers spacious and well-designed rooms with numerous amenities. It has a café with a spectacular view of the sea; dining options ranging from Thai and teppanyaki to the hugely popular Italian restaurant, Mezzo Mezzo; the fancy Quan Spa; and the Enigma nightclub.

If you prefer to stay close to the international airport, the **ITC Maratha** (Sahar, tel. 022/2830-3030, www.itcwelcomgroup.in, Rs 28,000–100,000) is a stunning red stone building modeled on Indian palaces (with latticed windows, brocade, etc.). Like the rest of the sprawling super-premium property, the rooms sport Indian exotica and are tastefully accessorized with ethnic handicrafts. The exclusive new wing, called ITC One, features butler service, as do rooms in The Towers. There's a presidential suite as well, the price of which

is disclosed on request. Guests enjoy perks in the form of complimentary breakfast and free cocktail hours. Dakshin and Dum Pukht—restaurants par excellence—attract businesspeople, jet-setters, and the who's who.

Once Mumbai's most talked about hotel and the first real five-star property in the suburbs, **Hotel Leela Kempinski's** (Sahar, tel. 022/6691-1234, www.theleela.com, Rs 16,000–100,000) days of glory have long faded. However, it continues to deliver good service thanks to a staff that takes hospitality seriously. Large, neat rooms as well as a spa and naturopathy center help you relax on arrival while a bar and a nice Indian garden meal or Chinese cuisine in the cellar serve to refresh you after a long day.

Le Royal Meridien (Sahar, tel. 022/2838-0000, www.starwoodhotels.com, Rs 16,000–35,000) is a classy colonial-style hotel near the airport. Its European elegance, the stunning Crystal Lounge, and rooms with charming four-poster beds are sure to make your stay memorable. The Royal Club rooms have a pillow and herbal soap menu, while the premium rooms come with a Mercedes or BMW airport pickup. There's a Cigar Divan as well, where you can listen to live jazz amid single malts and Habanos. The LM100 team—culinary experts, artists, and culturati—constantly innovate and reinvent the space.

New to the area, the **Hyatt Regency** (Sahar, tel. 022/6696-1234 or toll-free U.S. tel. 800/633-7313, www.mumbai.regency .hyatt.com, Rs 12,500–22,000) is known for excellent service and its contemporary design. The Italian marble and glass facade houses spacious rooms and a restaurant/bar, while a large pool, tennis courts, and spa make for a pleasant stay. Its sister hotel, the Grand Hyatt, is located about 20 minutes from the airport and close to the upcoming business district of Bandra-Kurla.

InterContinental The Grand (Sahar, tel. 022/6699-2222, www.thegrandhotels.net, Rs 18,000–100,000) is a vast hotel with a beautiful eight-story atrium lobby dominated by a giant trident in tribute to Lord Shiva. In addition to well-designed deluxe rooms, it also has designer suites and club-class accommodations. The hotel has 21 service apartments for long-stay patrons and a number of restaurants, a lounge, and a spa. The hotel is popular among business travelers thanks to its proximity to the airport.

Food

Mumbai's gastronomical fare is aptly represented by *bhel puri*—a street eat that has a load of ingredients thrown in for good measure. Mumbai truly is a melting pot—and this is reflected in the city's vast array of regional and international restaurants. There's traditional local coastal food, or Gomantak cuisine, as well as cheap South Indian food at budget Udipi restaurants. North Indian food and Mughlai cuisine, which finds its origins in the Mughal era, is available at nearly every Indian and multicuisine restaurant, and the city also has its share of Bengali and Parsi joints.

There are eateries to suit all budgets. Some of the cheapest and best foods are available off the streets of Mumbai, ranging from the ubiquitous *chaat* (a broad term that includes tangy streetside snacks like the *bhel puri* and *paani puri*) to the "Indian burger" called *vada pav*—as well as the sweets and meats found on Mohammad Ali Road during the month of Ramzaan.

Some of the city's local restaurants are institutions in themselves. The Irani cafes and Maharashtrian lunch homes, or *khanavals,* have a history of serving the common man and are known for their matter-of-fact service and economic fare. On the other hand, swish mall eateries serve everything from Italian and Lebanese to Japanese and pan-Asian cuisines.

A vendor sells roasted peanuts and gram on city streets.

Mumbai also has its own hybrid variety of Chinese cuisine that involves fiery red sauces and dishes, such as Paneer Manchurian, that would intrigue the Chinese. The result isn't bad, and it's worth trying just to be able to say that you've sampled some "Indian Chinese" on your visit to the city.

Coffee culture has taken the city by storm in recent years, with chains such as Mocha, Café Coffee Day, and Barista drawing youth to their selection of international coffees. Mumbai is also proud of the old faithfuls, known simply as *coffeewallas,* who carry their brew around in metal containers and can be heard ringing their bicycles until the wee hours.

The city has a few juice bars that offer wheatgrass and other shots, but the streetside juice-and-fruit stalls also bring fresh fruit, sliced and aesthetically presented. Ice cream is big in Mumbai and gelato is all the rage right now (try Amoré, Amici's, or the rich, creamy, fruity flavors of Natural's).

And, lastly, if you're homesick (or just sick), there's always McDonald's, Subway, Domino's, and KFC. With local variants, of course.

COLABA

Colaba has almost as many restaurants as its vast number of tourists, and the choice can be daunting. The seedy-looking joints often offer excellent food, while fine dining is best enjoyed in the glamorous five-star restaurants and resto-bars that are better known as nightspots.

Five-Star Dining

Colaba is known for its gourmet five-star restaurants, located within the two Taj hotels. The venues of Mumbai's November 2008 terrorist attacks, the five restaurants of the Taj Mahal Palace and Towers were reopened in a commendable restoration effort, and with an emotional reopening ceremony, within just three weeks of the tragedy. Of these, the **Zodiac Grill** (Taj Mahal Palace and Towers, tel. 022/6665-3366 ext. 311, 12:30–2:45 P.M. and 7–11:45 P.M. Mon.–Sat., 7–11:45 P.M. Sun., Rs 4,000 and up) continues its tradition

of fine dining, complete with caviar and crystal. Known for its excellent and expensive gourmet delights, ranging from French goose liver to vegetarian delicacies, the restaurant is a celeb favorite.

Konkan Café (Taj President, tel. 022/6665-0808, 12:30–2:45 P.M. and 7–11:45 P.M., Rs 1,000), at the Taj President, is the place for gourmet Indian cuisine. Its *thalis* (all-you-can-eat platters) and spicy coastal delicacies from the Konkan region are served in an authentic courtyard ambience reminiscent of a grand Konkani home.

Cafés and Patisseries

Colaba has a number of well-established eateries that draw a steady stream of regular patrons. Among these are its famous cafés that often double up as bars or as full-fledged restaurants. Noise levels can be high and you may need to shout above the hum of music and conversation to be heard, but no trip to Mumbai is complete without a visit to these cafés.

Leopold Café (Colaba Causeway, opposite Colaba Police Station, tel. 022/2282-8185, www.leopoldcafe.com, 8 A.M.–1 A.M. daily, mains Rs 200–300, cocktails Rs 250) is *the* tourist place in Colaba. At this 140-year-old institution, you can have breakfast, meals, and snacks, or simply relax with a chilled beer. While the meals here—Indian, East Asian, and Continental (a sweeping term used generously by Indians for any kind of bland, Western cuisine)—are nothing out of the ordinary, the world gathers here to exchange travel tips and rest their tired feet. Dominated by tourists, often here on a long stay, "Leo's" as the place is lovingly known, is also popular for its five-foot-tall chilled beer tower and for upper floor bar. The legendary café was acknowledged by author Gregory David Roberts in his book *Shantaram.* Leo's is now famous as the first scene of Mumbai's heinous November 2008 attacks, and the unfilled bullet holes in the café walls continue to be both a tourist attraction and a grim reminder of the event.

A short walk down the Causeway from

DELIVERY FROM HOME: THE *DABBAWALLAS* (TIFFIN CARRIERS)

Mumbai's biggest management gurus do not believe in power dressing or in carrying laptops. Instead, they wear the traditional white *kurta* and Gandhi cap as they transport aluminum *dabbas* (tiffins). Around 200,000 tiffins, containing freshly cooked lunches, are picked up every day from homes in the North Mumbai suburbs and transported by 5,000 *dabbawallas* to the offices of South Mumbai. These meals are transported by bicycle, handcarts, and wooden crates precariously balanced on the head – and by the local train. The train ride is punctuated by hundreds of men sorting thousands of *dabbas* with the help of a highly sophisticated, century-old manual coding system (using colors and numbers) devised by the *dabbawallas* themselves. Due to the *dabbawallas'* efficient service and high degree of professionalism, it's said that no matter what the circumstances, the local trains and the *dabbawallas* will continue to be on time.

The *dabbawallas'* management skills have been studied and lauded by the most reputed business schools the world over; even Stanford University has sent students to Mumbai to observe and learn from the *dabbawallas*. These extraordinary men have also been paid visits by the likes of Prince Charles (whose wedding they were invited to!) and Richard Branson. They are regularly called upon to lead seminars and conduct lectures at Indian and international business schools and corporate offices – all after work hours, of course.

The biggest surprise? Most of these enterprising men are illiterate, while the rest have barely completed eighth grade. Their website, www.mydabbawala.com, allows you to book their exceptional services online. You can catch them live and in action around 11:30 A.M. on weekdays at Churchgate Station or even enroll in their "A Day with a *Dabbawalla*" tour for a unique experience of the city.

© JANHAVI ACHAREKAR

The complex manual coding system devised by the *dabbawallas* brings corporate Mumbai its weekday lunches.

Leopold Café, and on the corner of the lane before Regal Cinema, is another Colaba landmark—**Café Mondegar** (Metro House, Causeway, tel. 022/2202-0591, 8 A.M.–1 A.M. daily, mains Rs 275). Famous for its mural of the Mumbai life painted by Goan cartoonist Mario Miranda, "Mondy's" is small and cheery. An old jukebox, red-and-white checkered tablecloths, and a display of souvenirs add to the charm of this quaint café. Locals

and tourists congregate here for steak and fries downed with a chilled beer.

Sandwiches and pasta may not be within the scope of gastronomic interest during your visit to Mumbai, but you may want to give your taste buds some respite from spice at **Café Churchill** (Colaba Causeway, opposite Cusrow Baug, tel. 022/2284-4689, noon–midnight, mains Rs 275). This tiny hole-in-the-wall keeps you waiting for a table, but the delicious

Italian and Continental fare are well worth it. Try the mixed seafood pasta or cheddar-baked chicken and wash it down with a chilled iced tea. Don't leave without sampling the divine cheesecake, among other desserts.

Café Basilico (Sentinel House, next to Radio Club, Apollo Bunder, tel. 022/6634-5670, www.cafebasilico.com, 7:30 A.M.–1 A.M. daily, and at Pali Naka, Bandra, tel. 022/6703-9999, noon–1 A.M. daily, mains Rs 250–300, Sunday brunch adults Rs 500, children Rs 400) is a bistro and deli with mellow ambience. The international cuisine includes Moroccan wraps, Mediterranean salads, and seafood in various culinary styles. Popular for its Sunday brunch, Basilico is also known for delicious cold cuts, cheeses, and freshly baked bread.

If you want the view but not the price of some of the expensive restaurants and bars in the area, head straight to **Starlit Café** (Hotel Harbour View, opposite Radio Club, Apollo Bunder, Colaba, tel. 022/2282-1089, 6 A.M.–midnight daily). This modest terrace café is where you can drink in the view along with some beer and kebabs. Mumbai's smog may not always allow you a view of the stars, but you can be assured of seeing the twinkling lights of ships along the stunning harbor.

In one of the fast-disappearing heritage bungalows of Colaba, **Moshé's** (7, Minoo Manor, Cuffe Parade, tel. 022/2216-1226, 7:30 A.M.–midnight daily, mains Rs 350) is the original café of the chain of the same name. Celebrity chef Moshé Shek's first signature eatery serves a combination of Mediterranean and Jewish home-style cooking. Fresh fondues, creamy risottos, Turkish turlu turlu (roasted vegetables), and hameem (Jewish pot roast) are topped off with some excellent and innovative desserts. In the patisserie section, you can buy focaccia and olive bread; or try gooey brownies and a delicious chocolate-something called "Delilah" with coffee or wine within the restaurant or in the leafy courtyard outside.

Indigo Deli (opposite Dhanraj Mahal, Apollo Bunder, 9 A.M.–noon daily, mains Rs 250–400) is an extension of famous restaurateurs Rahul and Malini Akerkar's chic resto-bar Indigo.

With a wooden floor, high ceiling, and walls stacked with rows of wine bottles reached by climbing up a tall ladder, the deli is the more casual of the two spots. Try the lamb risotto, soufflés, and homemade ice cream, and take their cold cuts, cheeses, and preserves to go.

Arguably the finest patisserie in Mumbai, (**Theobroma** (Shop 24, Cusrow Baug, tel. 022/6529-2929, 11 A.M.–11 P.M. daily, sandwiches Rs 120, desserts Rs 50–90) is the scientific name of the genus of the cacao tree—and translates as "food of the gods." Divine is indeed the right word to describe the melt-in-your-mouth brownies, cheesecakes, and pastries. This small but busy patisserie/chocolaterie is run by a friendly mother-daughter pair known to serve a mean chili-vodka cheesecake, as well as a host of freshly baked goodies that include quiches, breads and cookies. Some of the treats—like the chocolate-and-orange "Tiered Temptation" pastry, with beautiful orange floral motifs painted onto the chocolate—are as appealing to artistic sensibilities as they are to the taste buds. Don't miss the delicious macaroons that ooze strawberry jam.

Grills and Street Eats

The best part of **Koyla** (Gulf Hotel, Arthur Bunder Rd., tel. 022/6636-4727, 7 P.M.–1 A.M. daily, mains Rs 400–600) is its view. Located on the rooftop of a nondescript hotel, the restaurant overlooks the harbor, and serves delicious charcoal-grilled Indian items under the stars. The only downside here is the absence of alcohol but the lantern-lit ambience is intoxicating enough.

A street eatery that became so popular it turned into a small restaurant, (**Badé Miyan** (behind the Taj, near Gordon House, tel. 022/2284-8038, 7 P.M. until close daily, Rs 40–80) is one of those places you should be thankful for after a long night of drinking. It has the street swarming until the wee hours with pub-crawlers, executives and the odd celebrity waiting patiently to grab a bite of succulent grilled meat. Known for its tandoori char-grilled items, Badé Miyan rustles up some excellent kebabs, rolls, and tandoori chicken,

022/2284-1972, 11 A.M.–11 P.M. daily, mains Rs 30–50) serves everything but pasta. A chain of restaurants that rustles up great Mumbai street food in a hygienic manner, Kailash Parbat is a great place to dig into your street eats, uninhibited. In addition to *chaat*, you can try the *ragda pattice* (potato patties dunked in chickpea curry) and *pav bhaji* (a gravy made up of finely blended vegetables served with chopped onion and bread) or sample regional specialties like *bhee masala*, a preparation made with lotus stem. The Indian desserts are not to be missed either, and you can decide between the sweet-syrupy *gulab jamun* or the more subtle *malai kulfi* (a creamy Indian variant of ice cream).

KALA GHODA
Indian

Kala Ghoda's iconic restaurant **《 Samovar** (Jehangir Art Gallery, tel. 022/2284-8000, 11 A.M.–7:30 P.M. Mon.–Sat., Rs 50–150) is nothing short of a legend. This lovely café overlooking the museum grounds is located within the Jehangir Art Gallery and has been a long-standing hangout for artists, poets, writers, and actors. The place is famous for its *kheema parathas* (rotis stuffed with mincemeat) and piping hot *pakodas* (vegetable fritters). It was recently saved from closure thanks to vehement protests from the city's artistic community.

Across the road from Max Mueller Bhavan, **《 Chetna** (tel. 022/2284-4968, www.chetana.com/r.htm, 11 A.M.–7:30 P.M. daily, Rs 250) is famous for its Rajasthani and Gujarati *thalis* (unlimited platters). A jumble of vegetables, curries, dal (lentils), rotis laced with ghee (clarified butter), rice, and sweets is all served one one plate—only to be replenished by persuasive waiters whose job is to ensure that you leave only after you've eaten enough to last you for a week. To digest the deliciously rich food, try the spiced buttermilk called *chaas* or the spicy digestive drink *jaljeera* that comes with the *thali*. Or if you feel like a little adventure, end your meal with chilled beer from the bar. If you'd rather have something light, early evenings are reserved for snacks and savories.

© ASHIMA NARAIN

a tropical fruit mix made to look visually appealing at a street fruit-and-juice stall

as well as the odd *keeri-kaleji* (udder and liver) and *bheja* (goat brain) coupled with the deliciously soft, white *roomali roti*. The aroma is tantalizing and lasts until dawn, when the final tikka has been tucked into and the last *baida roti* (a meat-and-egg wrap) wolfed down.

Next door, mammoth cauldrons keep curries bubbling at **Baghdadi** (Tulloch Rd., tel. 022/2202-8027, 7 A.M.–midnight daily, mains Rs 40–60), famed for its cheap and spicy meat delicacies. This hard-nosed, no-frills eatery provides seating on classroom-style benches that may require you to share space with strangers. The cuisine is low on hygiene and high on oil, meant only for those with robust stomachs. The *kheema pav* (spicy mincemeat with bread) is a breakfast favorite, while the *paya* (trotters) and beef biryani (spiced rice with meat) are crowd-pullers at lunchtime. It's no wonder that Baghdadi discourages patrons from over-staying—the place is especially crowded for lunch, making it difficult to find seating.

Safely ensconced in Pasta Lane, **Kailash Parbat** (Sheela Mahal, 1st Pasta Lane, tel.

You can't miss the massive, inscribed wooden door of **Khyber** (145 MG Rd., tel. 022/2267-3227, www.khyberrestaurant.com, 12:30–3:30 P.M. and 7:30–11:30 P.M. daily, mains Rs 250 and up)—a Kala Ghoda landmark that pooh-poohs the need for a signboard. With an ambience as rich as its delicious northwest frontier cuisine, Khyber continues to serve old favorites like its succulent chicken and fish kebabs, biryani, and the famous Khyber *raan* (lamb), along with vegetarian dishes like *paneer makhanwala* (cottage cheese in a spicy, buttery gravy) and black dal. The luxurious private dining areas are adorned with fine art by the likes of Indian stalwarts such as M. F. Husain and Anjolie Ela Menon. Avoid the Bandra branch and go for the authentic dining experience instead.

Seafood

Another old favorite, **(Trishna** (Sai Baba Marg, tel. 022/2270-3213, noon–3:30 P.M. and 6 P.M.–12:15 A.M., mains Rs 200) is a seafood lover's paradise. The spicy South Indian coastal cuisine is par excellence, with everything from squid and pomfret to tiger prawns, shark, lobster, and a few cursory vegetarian dishes thrown in. The butter-pepper-garlic king crab, local ladyfish, and fish koliwada are to die for. It's not surprising that Trishna has an impressive list of patrons that includes corporate honchos, sports celebrities, and heads of state.

East Asian

Opposite Max Mueller Bhavan, **Joss** (30 K Dubhash Marg, tel. 022/6635-6908, 12:30–3 P.M. and 7:30 P.M.–midnight daily, mains Rs 400, drinks Rs 300) whips up excellent East Asian fare (from sushi to Thai, Indonesian, and Korean dishes). Vegetarians are delighted by the variety, with the Balinese coconut and basil curry a hot favorite. For fish- and meat-eaters, the sea bass reigns supreme from amid the wide choice of Japanese dishes available. There's some interesting dessert sushi as well, not to mention the Kahlua chocolate soufflé.

FORT AND CST

The Fort area is full of commercial establishments that have ensured the presence of a wide variety of restaurants. Office-workers and visitors have a choice of cheap, fast lunches as well as extended, siesta-inducing *thali* meals.

Multicuisine

Mocambo (Phirozeshah Mehta Rd, tel. 022/2287-0458, 9 A.M.–11:30 P.M. daily, mains Rs 250), once a common man's café, is now an upmarket restaurant boasting a celebrity clientele. Its menu is set by the same chef as Café Churchill's, though the trademark grilled items and creamy pastas are supplemented with traditional Parsi and Goan dishes here. Try the pork chops or a dish called Chicken Flamingo, along with beer and other guzzlers. The desserts, in keeping with Churchill standards, are excellent, and you would do well to end a good meal with some Irish Bailey Walnut.

If you thought a "sizzler" referred to that attractive young man or woman seated at the table next to yours, you're mistaken. The sizzler is a uniquely Mumbai phenomenon—a sizzling dish of chicken, fish, steak, or cottage cheese, served with vegetables and fries, that smokes and sputters its way to your table. **Fountain Sizzlers** (Flora Fountain, opposite HSBC, tel. 022/2267-5315, 11:30 A.M.–11:45 P.M. daily, mains Rs 150) is where lawyers from the adjoining firms tuck into a jolly beef pepper steak or a cottage cheese shashlik sizzler. This delightful little eatery believes in quick lunches to make way for the waiting populace outside, and even serves dessert sizzlers.

Seafood

A legendary Fort area establishment, **(Mahesh Lunch Home** (Cowasji Patel St., tel. 022/2287-0938, 11:30 A.M.–3:30 P.M. and 6 P.M.–midnight daily, mains Rs 200) is famous for its local and South Indian coastal cuisine. It's known for its clams, squid, and thick coconut *gassis*— curries served with rice or a *neer dosa* (a thin, soft crepe-like item made of rice flour). If you have a taste for spice, try the fried *surmai* (seer fish); if not, the butter garlic crab is equally good. The busy restaurant gets its fresh catch from the nearby docks early in the morning. There's also a vegetarian menu that includes standard Indian fare.

At **Excellensea and Bharat Lunch Home** (Bharat House, Mint Rd., tel. 022/2261-8991, 11:30 A.M.–midnight daily, mains Rs 150–200), a fish tank allows you to make a live catch that is then cooked South Indian style. Should you find it difficult to make up your mind, you can order the wholesome seafood *thali* to sample a bit of everything available.

East Asian

Located in a nook, **5 Spice** (Perin Nariman St., tel. 022/2266-6435, 11:30 A.M.–3 P.M. and 7 P.M.–12:30 A.M., mains Rs 150) cheerfully serves "Indian Chinese" food alongside wok dishes and other Asian cuisines. In addition to the mandatory red sauces are stewed noodles and rice combinations, as well as plenty of veggies flavored with bamboo shoots and lemongrass. Starters are scrumptious, as are desserts. (They even challenge you to lick clean the dessert aptly named "Mission Impossible.") Popular with students and young executives from neighboring offices, the restaurant is crowded for lunch and a 15-minute wait is typical.

Indian

The city's first Parsi restaurant, **Jimmy Boy** (11 Bank St., Fort, tel. 022/2266-2503 or 022/2270-0880, noon–3 P.M. daily, mains Rs 200) is a quaint old place dedicated to the delicious food of this minority community. Try the *patra-ni-macchi* (pomfret stuffed with chutney, wrapped in banana leaves, and slow cooked), the *jardaloo* (apricot) chicken, or the famous *dhansak* (lentils served with vegetables, mutton, or chicken). Few pass up the opportunity to attend a Parsi wedding, since these occasions are notorious for their delectable fare (which involves a set menu served on banana leaves at an official sit-down dinner). Now, you too can partake of the experience with the *lagan-nu-bhonu* (literally translated as "wedding feast") served at Jimmy Boy.

Britannia and Co Restaurant (Wakefield House, Ballard Estate, tel. 022/2261-5264, 11:30 A.M.–3:30 P.M. Mon.–Sat., Rs 70–250) runs on its Berry Pulao (Rs 120), an aromatic preparation of rice with vegetables, chicken, or mutton, and garnished with berries imported especially from Iran. This eatery specializes in Parsi and Iranian food, and its ambience is as unique as its menu. A crumbling old place with surly waiters and a garlanded photo of the owner's deceased pet rooster, this is a must-visit. To complete the experience, order a raspberry soda.

If you're vegetarian and wondering whatever happened to good old greens in a vastly vegetarian country, head to **Rajdhani** (opposite Mangaldas Market, near Crawford Market, tel. 022/2342-6919, 7–10:30 P.M. daily, Rs 200) for its superbly rich traditional Rajasthani *thali* or the sweetened Gujarati *thali*. Piping hot ghee-laden rotis are served with purely vegetarian cuisine, and you can even sample Rajasthani specialties such as *dal-batti* (flour dumplings soaked in ghee and served with dal). The food is as authentic as it can get and also as greasy.

A deceptively small-looking eatery lost amid the crowd and bustle of Crawford Market, **Badshah** (opposite Crawford Market, tel. 022/2342-1943, 7 A.M.–12:30 A.M. daily) is a century-old establishment that draws crowds from far and wide. Like its name, which means king, Badshah reigns over the recipe for the indescribable *falooda*—a rose-flavored milk-based drink that is a shock of pink with floating chunks of rose jelly, sweet yellow vermicelli, takmaria seeds, and topped with a dollop of vanilla ice cream. Mastery over the recipe has encouraged experimentation, which has led to variants of this unusual drink, but it's best to start off with the traditional Royal *falooda*. The eatery also serves juices, milkshakes, and local snacks, but it's the *falooda* that's the crowd-puller.

Grills and Street Eats

For a truly authentic culinary experience, make sure you're on **Khau Gully**—literally translated as Food Street, but known more commonly as Mohammad Ali Road—to celebrate Eid. Here you can feast on traditional Muslim dishes such as biryani, *bheja masala*, roasted liver, and various beef and mutton curries (meals around Rs 200). You can participate in the *iftaar* feast or the breaking of the daily Ramzan fast with the Islamic community at this predominantly Muslim area. Lined with open street stalls and restaurants, this lane comes alive after sunset to mark the end of the fast, before it is resumed after sunrise the next day. Khau Gully has a terrific sweet tooth as well with desserts such as *phirni* (a traditional milk-based dessert), *kheer* (traditional rice or vermicelli pudding), and *malpuas* (sweet fritters) to dream about the next fasting day. As for the intestinally challenged, merely watching this grand nocturnal feast itself can be quite a treat.

The rest of the year, the street turns into a non-descript local eating area missing the variety of food and visitors, as well as the festive atmosphere, with most food stalls closing a little past midnight.

CHURCHGATE AND NARIMAN POINT

Once Mumbai's most important business district, this area is dotted with food options ranging from street food to the sea-view restaurants.

East Asian

❰ VongWong (Express Towers, Nariman Point, tel. 022/2287-5633, 12:30–3 P.M. and 7:30–11:45 P.M., full meal Rs 1,500) is a bold and exclusive restaurant in the most prominent building of this commercial area. Its strategic location ensures a steady flow of corporate heads and investment bankers, who often work out of the same building. Meals feature Thai and Chinese delicacies prepared to perfection. There's a lovely view of the city and a private dining area as well. The adjoining bar, Dragonfly, is run by the same management.

Cafés and Patisseries
Gaylord (Mayfair, Vir Nariman Rd., Church-

gate, tel. 022/2282-1259, 12:30 P.M.–3:30 P.M. and 7 P.M.–12:30 A.M. daily, mains Rs 300, pastry Rs 30–80) is an old favorite that houses two establishments. Dinner at the inner restaurant is an elegant affair, with a choice of Indian and Continental dishes. In the courtyard is the patisserie, where you can enjoy freshly baked breads, cookies, pies, and pastries.

A minute away from Churchgate Station is the recently renovated **Tea Centre** (Resham Bhavan, Churchgate, tel. 022/2281-9142, 8:30 A.M.–10:30 P.M. daily, tea Rs 40–120, snacks Rs 80–120, meals Rs 115 and up). Great for breakfast, lunch, or dinner, this is a tea drinker's paradise, with vast varieties of tea from all over. Try the ginger-, mint-, and lemongrass-infused masala chai or the delicious Kashmiri kahwa. The food is also excellent, with a range of soups, pastas, and risottos in addition to an Indian menu.

Soak in the old Bombay charm of **Kyani and Co.** (Jer Mahal estate, opposite Metro Cinema, tel. 022/2201-1492, 6:30 A.M.–9 P.M. daily, cakes Rs 6–20), one of the last surviving Irani cafés. Known to serve tepid tea, cakes, cookies, and oven-warm *bun-maska* (buns slathered with butter), it's visited for its century-old furniture and charm. The waiters, however, are less than charming, but don't let their no-nonsense attitude daunt you. The almond *mawa* cupcakes, caramel custard, and bread pudding are must-tries.

Italian
With a location that's as remarkable as its pizzas is **Pizzeria** (Soona Mahal, Marine Dr., tel. 022/2284-3646, 11:30 A.M.–1 A.M. daily, pizzas Rs 200 and up). This lovely sea-facing eatery is attached to popular resto-bar/nightspot Not Just Jazz by the Bay, and is next door to Gaylord's. Try the Indian-style masala, chicken tikka or Bombay masala pizza if you feel like something different. The place also serves pastas, salads, and coolers.

Indian
Jafferbhai's (near Gol Masjid, Dhobi Talao, Marine Lines, tel. 022/2208-4613, www

.jafferbhaisdelhidarbar.com, 11:30 A.M.–midnight daily, mains Rs 175) is Mumbai's oldest chain of Mughlai food. The original restaurant at Nagpada Junction near Grant Road is the central kitchen, from where its legendary biryani is sent to sister outlets all over the city. Try the various gravies, *paya, murg kali mirch* (roasted pepper chicken), *seekh kebab,* a rice-and-meat dish called *khichda,* and the famous mutton biryani. Delhi Darbar, another Mughlai chain, is run by the same family.

MARINE DRIVE AND CHOWPATTY

Like the adjoining areas of Churchgate and Nariman Point, Marine Drive also has a fine stretch of street food as well as five-star restaurants.

Five-Star Dining

The InterContinental dishes out excellent Sicilian fare at **Corleone** (Hotel InterContinental, Marine Dr., tel. 022/23987-9999, 12:30–3 P.M. and 7:30 P.M.–3 A.M. daily, mains Rs 425 and up) and gourmet kebabs at **Kebab Korner** (Hotel InterContinental, Marine Dr., tel. 022/6639-9999, 12:30–2:45 P.M. and 7:30–11:45 P.M., mains Rs 500–1,000).

Multicuisine

The chic **Salt Water Grill** (H2O water sports complex, Chowpatty, tel. 022/2368-5485, 4–11:30 P.M. daily, mains Rs 400 and up) is a lovely seafront restaurant that specializes in gourmet European dishes. Its delightful ambience is coupled with dishes such as chicken liver pate with apple marmalade and delicious calamari. Closed for renovation, the restaurant will be opened in a new avatar by mid-2009.

Kobe's (Hughes Rd., Chowpatty, tel. 022/2363-2174, 9:30 A.M.–11:30 P.M., mains Rs 200) is Mumbai's original sizzler chain. You'll come out smelling of smoke but the Prawn Shashlik, Satellite Steak and Chicken Pepper are worth their sizzle in gold. Vegetarians can try the Veg Cheese Sizzler, among a variety of options.

Indian

To experience the Mumbai of the 1960s, visit the two-level **☾ Crystal Lunch Home** (near Wilson College, Chowpatty, tel. 022/2369-1482, noon–3 P.M. and 7–11 P.M. daily, Rs 50–75) facing Chowpatty Beach. With flaking paint and a tiny boom box that continues to play the same Bollywood songs as it did back in the golden era, this is a place where time stands still. The cramped budget eatery is known for its home-style North Indian cooking. The stuffed *parathas* (thick rotis) are delicious, as is the *rajma chawal* (a gravy of kidney beans served with rice) and deliciously sweet *kheer.* This is the regular haunt of office workers, students living in nearby hostels, and visitors who like their Indian meal amid crumbling walls and whirring table fans.

Golden Star (Sakina Manzil, opposite Charni Road Station, tel. 022/2363-1983, 11 A.M.–3 P.M. and 7–10:30 P.M. daily, www.goldenstarthali.com, Rs 195–225), a popular *thali* joint, is located in the crowded jewelers' district. The restaurant serves Gujarati and Rajasthani cuisine, and celebrates the two in the form of an annual food festival held in January.

Seafood

☾ Anantashram (Khotachiwadi, Girgaum, noon–2 P.M. and 7–9 P.M. Mon.–Sat., Rs 80) is a historic eatery located in Girgaum's heritage area of Khotachiwadi. Owned by the Khadpe family, this restaurant has served generations of immigrants craving delicious, home-style Maharashtrian and Saraswat cooking. It is known as much for its budget seafood as it is for its spartan interior, pajama-clad waiters, and loads of attitude. Plates may be banged down upon your table by easily miffed waiters, but it's all a part of the experience—and the fried pomfret and *teesrya* (clams) are worth it. The restaurant was recently saved from closure by ardent protests and pleas from locals, celebrities among them.

MUMBAI

CENTRAL MUMBAI

Central Mumbai brings together food from all over the country, from local Maharashtrian to South Indian and Bengali. The burgeoning commercial district of Lower Parel and new five-star properties like the ITC Grand Central have brought about a number of up-market eateries. However, the heart of the city is also throbbing with the small, modest variety. While there's a concentration of Maharashtrian *khanavals* in the Dadar area, you'll get the fluffiest *idlis* (steamed rice cakes) and crispiest *dosas* (crepe-like rice preparations) at the South Indian cafés and "tiffin rooms" of Matunga and Mahim on the Western line. Primarily middle-class community huddles, these areas are also known for small community centers like **Kutumb Sakhi** (Dada Gokhale Rd., Mahim, tel. 022/2446-2804, 8 A.M.–8 P.M. daily, Rs 20) that provide traditional Maharashtrian takeaway at budget rates—and supply a source of income to the underprivileged women who help run it.

South Indian cuisine is popular in multicultural Mumbai where the *idli*, or steamed rice cake, is a staple at southern cuisine restaurants.

Seafood

If you want to sample the seafood-rich Bengali cuisine, go to **Oh, Calcutta!** (Hotel Rosewood, Tulsiwadi Ln., Tardeo, tel. 022/2496-3115, noon–3 P.M. and 7 P.M.–midnight, meals Rs 500) for the real thing. Named after the famous musical, the restaurant does indeed give you something to sing about. Calcutta nostalgia prevails and you won't miss the replica of the controversial hand-rickshaw outside this eatery. Once inside, you'll find it difficult to think beyond the *doi maach* (fish in yogurt and mustard sauce), an all-time Bengali favorite, or the *ileesh* (Hilsa fish) preparations. The river fish is brought down from Kolkata (Calcutta) and mouthwatering Bengali sweets like *mishti doi* (yogurt sweetened with jaggery) are sourced from their own sweet shop, called Sweet Bengal.

For coastal cuisine from the Malvan region of Maharashtra, visit **Gajalee** (Phoenix Mill Compound, tel. 022/2495-0667, 11:30 A.M.–3:30 P.M. and 7:30–11:45 P.M. daily, mains Rs 250) is a branch of the famous restaurant located in the suburb of Vile Parle. Try the crisp-fried fish called the Bombay duck, oyster masala, or the shark and clam dishes. There are plenty of options for vegetarians as well—all served in a wonderfully smoke-free environment.

Fresh Catch (next to Mahim Fire Brigade, Mahim, tel. 022/2444-8942, noon–3:30 P.M. and 7 P.M.–11:30 P.M. daily, Rs 300) is a small eatery that specializes in the coastal cuisine of the Karwar region of Karnataka. Its menu includes traditionally prepared crab *xec xec* (crab cooked in a thick gravy) and Bombay duck fried to a crisp.

Indian

Swati Snacks (opposite Bhatia Hospital, Tardeo, tel. 022/2492-0994, 11 A.M.–11 P.M. daily, Rs 60–100) is a popular vegetarian eatery that serves great Mumbai snacks as well as unusual Gujarati cuisine items like *panki* (rice pancakes steamed in banana leaf and

© ASHIMA NARAIN

served with spicy chutney) and *dal dhokli* (lentils with soft wheat-flour chunks). There's also freshly made ice cream and fruit juices (try some sugarcane juice here—the ones on the streets could give you jaundice) as well as sinful Indian sweets like the *malpua.*

A restaurateur couple, the Awchats, run a trio of kitschy eateries where each showcases a regional cuisine. **Goa Portuguesa** (opposite Mahim Head Post Office, tel. 022/2444-0202, noon–3 P.M. and 7 P.M.–midnight daily, www.goaportuguesa.com, mains Rs 200) was the first A-list Goan restaurant complete with *vindaloo,* sausage *pulao,* and Goan guitarists singing Elvis Presley numbers. The neighboring **Culture Curry** (tel. 022/2446-8260, noon–3:30 P.M. and 7 P.M.–12:30 A.M. daily, www.culturecurry.com, mains Rs 200) specializes in South Indian dishes—and the ambience is unabashedly South Indian pop. It is possibly the only restaurant in Mumbai to serve cuisine from the Coorg region of Karnataka. **Diva Maharashtracha** (tel. 022/2292-9092, 7 P.M.–12:30 A.M. daily, Rs 200 mains), the newest entrant, has a Maharashtra-highway-restaurant-meets-Peshwa-palace kind of look, with red lights and ornate metal carvings. While local Maharashtrian specialties flow freely, the food is overpriced and no match for the good old *khanaval.* You're likely to meet the chatty owner, Suhas Awchat, who's sure to hand you one of his unusual business cards.

Café Noorani (Haji Ali Circle, tel. 022/2494-4753, 10 A.M.–1 A.M. daily, mains Rs 150) is a small no-frills place known for its North Indian Muslim style of cooking. The *kheema* (mincemeat) and biryani reign supreme, as do their mutton curries. If you're looking for ambience, you may not approve of the Formica-covered tables and benches for seating, but you can take some kebab rolls to go instead.

Grills and Street Eats

The vegetarian equivalent of popular streetside restaurant Badé Miyan, **Sardar Pav Bhaji** (opposite Tardeo Bus Depot, tel. 022/2494-0208, noon–2 A.M. daily, Rs 60) is so tiny that it can barely accommodate even a few patrons. However, the crowd milling about outside is unmindful of the unappetizing environment (located next to a public toilet) and only too happy to eat the buttery, piping hot *pav bhaji* on bikes, in parked cars, or wherever they can park themselves. The "Sardar Special," the best of the greasy mish-mash of vegetables served with bread, is a favorite with late-night bar-hoppers and families alike.

If you're looking for a quick bite (milkshakes, fruit platters, and snacks) and a great view, stop by **Haji Ali Juice Centre** (Haji Ali Circle, tel. 022/2351-7632, 5 A.M.–1:30 A.M., www.hajialijuice.com, Rs 40 and up). Located on the main road, just before the neck of land leading up to the Haji Ali Mosque, the juice center is a tiny place that allows only a handful of patrons into its cramped seating. Try their seasonal milkshakes, especially the mango variants in summer or the most expensive item on their menu card—the dry fruit milkshake (Rs 150). In the past, most visitors preferred to park their cars facing the mosque and the sea, taking in the colors of the sunset as they sipped on their fresh fruit juices. However, the Mumbai traffic police have put an end to all that and you can only get takeaway or grab a hurried bite before you leave.

Multicuisine

A place that's sure to set your appetite racing, **◖ Gallops** (Mahalaxmi Race Course, tel. 022/2307-1448, noon–midnight daily, meals Rs 500) is the ideal combination of good food, a great view, and a memorable experience. Located right along the racecourse, its colonial ambience and view of the horses amid the greens make it a charming dining option. The racing season is the best time for a visit if you are looking for excitement, though Gallops is also popular for breakfast, when horses are led back to their stables. But the horses are not the only focus here—the roast lamb in wine sauce and green *pahadi kebab* are winners, too.

East Asian

Although located in one of Mumbai's busiest malls, **Lemon Grass** (Phoenix Mill Compound, tel. 022/2495-9999, noon–3:30 P.M. and 7 P.M.–12:30 A.M. daily, meals Rs 400) is a delightful Southeast Asian cuisine restaurant with a distinctly un-mallish ambience. An open staircase leads up to warm wooden decor and the friendly staff serve everything from Burmese *khauswey* to Mongolian stir-fry. The vegetarian dishes are good as well, and there's a host of desserts to choose from.

NORTH MUMBAI

North Mumbai is where the action is. Families, young couples, and singles seem to be eating out more than ever, and the areas of Bandra, Juhu and Andheri buzz with activity well past the witching hour. The suburbs are known for numerous eateries, big and small, as well as areas that have turned into food districts for the variety of culinary options that they have to offer. However, eateries tend to disappear as quickly as they had mushroomed

and it is best to verify the existence of popular restaurants before you land up there. Prices are equally mercurial, and dependent on the increasing costs of vegetables and victuals in times of inflation.

Food Districts

The sea-facing cluster of open cafés at Bandra's **Carter Road** exudes a young and joyous vibe. This recently established food district has the perfect seaside ambience coupled with a selection of cuisines. Sipping coffee at the breezy Café Coffee Day is merely an excuse to gaze upon the sea—as is a languorous meal at kebab and tandoori joints like Kareem's. This stretch is also known for sandwiches, crepes, desserts, ice cream, pastas, and Asian cuisine. For excellent pan-Asian food, visit tiny Kwikwok, run by the same management as Kareem's. Ask for their watered-down but excellent version of Tibetan *thupka,* a broth with vegetables and meat. Albeit away from the sea, at the end (or beginning) of this stretch, Out of the Blue—the restaurant at Hotel Pali Hills—is a great

© JANHAVI ACHAREKAR

A *chaat,* or street food stall, displays its goodies at Juhu Beach.

place for a romantic dinner and wine amid art and live music.

Juhu Beach is filled with eating options at its food court and makeshift stalls, and **Juhu-Tara Road,** which leads to the beach, is lined with a number of restaurants. There's Indian *thali* at The Class; vegetarians will be delighted with the all-veg Italian menu of Little Italy; and for a close view of the sea and piping hot *pakodas* with beer, there's no place like the old Sea View restaurant at Hotel Citizen. There are a number of star-rated hotels here as well, with 24-hour coffee shops and poolside Sunday brunches.

The suburb of Andheri has a number of food districts, especially in its shopping and entertainment areas. **Link Road** has emerged as a gastronome's hangout with the arrival of restaurant chains such as Trishna for seafood, Red Box Café for international fare, and China Gate for excellent East Asian cuisine. Moviegoers and shoppers from the nearby Fame Adlabs and Infinity Mall unwind with wine and romance at Myst, at the many Indian restaurants around, and at the ever-popular Mainland China. Several restaurants on these stretches also offer hookahs, and guests can choose from a wide range of flavored tobacco.

Seafood

Of the numerous restaurants in the suburbs, a few are must-visits. **Highway Gomantak** (Gandhi Nagar, Western Express Highway, Bandra, tel. 022/2640-9692, 11:30 A.M.–3:30 P.M. and 7–11 P.M. Fri.–Wed., meals Rs 200) is a simple, family-run eatery that serves the coastal cuisine of the Konkan and Goan regions. You can sample seafood *thalis,* and a variety of clam, fish, and prawn dishes cooked as per secret family recipes. Try the stuffed pomfret and the fried *mandeli* fish or mussels for a taste of the authentic.

Indian

There was a time when every party in Bandra was graced by biryani from **Lucky's** (junction of Bandra Station and SV Rd., tel. 022/2644-

2973, 9 A.M.–12:30 A.M. daily, Rs 200), the most celebrated biryani joint in the suburbs. Lucky's delivers giant aluminum vessels filled with its deliciously aromatic mutton or chicken biryani, and serves Mughlai dishes in the noisy Old World atmosphere of its restaurant, giving you a glimpse of the hustle and bustle of the adjoining road and station.

A profusion of colorful pinwheels, large bunches of flutes and mirrorwork walls make the decor of ◖ **Urban Tadka** (Juhu-Versova Link Rd., Seven Bungalows, Andheri, tel. 022/2632-8172, noon–3:30 P.M. and 7 P.M.–12:45 A.M. daily, Rs 300) as loud as its acoustics. Though it's not quite the place for a romantic dinner (especially on weekends), the vigorous Punjabi music and ambience lend to the flavor of the cuisine. Try the *nimbu* (lime) chicken and the sugarcane-vodka cocktail. The vegetarian menu is refreshingly different with its *tandoori arbi* (coal-fired cocoyam) and *paneer-aur-mirchi-ka-saalan* (a gravy of cottage cheese and green peppers). End the meal by sharing a tall glass of the incredibly heavy lassi (a traditional Punjabi yogurt drink) and keep the afternoon free for siesta!

Grills and Street Eats

One of the many Mumbai success stories, multi-level ◖ **Elco** (Elco Market, Hill Rd., Bandra, tel. 022/2643-7206, 9 A.M.–12:30 A.M. daily, Rs 150–200) was once a street stall. Rumor has it that the stall's loyal clientele saw the owner rise from rags to riches, move from hovel to multiple apartments, and rest his once-tired feet in luxury cars. If the story is indeed true, then the man deserves every penny he has earned for his consistent *chaat* recipes and entrepreneurial skills. Elco was among the first in Mumbai to emphasize hygiene by using mineral water in its *paani puri,* so you can be assured of cleanliness—even if you eat at the restaurant's street-side seating (never mind the fumes from the traffic). However, if you prefer the din of the crowded restaurant upstairs to the sounds of the street, you could always queue up for a table.

At **Barbecue Nation** (Dr. Ambedkar Rd.

and Pali Hill Junction, Bandra, tel. 022/6682-4434, noon–3:30 P.M. and 7:30 P.M.–11:30 P.M. daily, fixed menu Rs 500), a set menu of barbecued starters is followed by a dinner buffet and presented in a lounge-like ambience. Vegetarians will be happy with the attention paid to their menu, which includes some excellent barbecued mushrooms, potatoes, and beetroot, in addition to other interesting items. Meat-eaters can gorge on delicious lamb and fish on skewers. Most diners find it difficult to move on to the buffet after the lavish beginning to the meal, but you may want to save your appetite for the variety of Indian dishes, if not for the desserts.

Italian

If discerning Italian friends say that this restaurant reminds them of their mother's cooking, then there must be something special about **Mia Cucina** (Gasper Enclave, Pali Naka, Bandra, tel. 022/6671-0158, 12:30 P.M.–midnight daily, Rs 300). This small eatery—with its arches, spice jars, Italian-style posters and accessories—lends the flavor of a mama-and-papa village restaurant, and has even passed the true test of one by perfecting the art of its panna cotta. Superlative pizzas, pastas, and stand-alone dishes like the stuffed zucchini and the Chicken scallopini make this a must-visit for fans of Italian cuisine.

Multicuisine

Yoko's (309, SV Rd., Santacruz, tel. 022/2649-1528, 11:30 A.M.–11:30 P.M. daily, Rs 300), the restaurant that introduced the sizzler to the suburbs, hasn't lost its sizzle—and continues to expand across the city. From sizzling chicken to Italian-style vegetarian sizzlers, famous iced tea and sizzling brownies, Yoko's has it all. Patrons end their meals with a grand finale of sweet *paan* (betel nut bits, coconut, sugar, honey, and a variety of other things wrapped in betel leaf) at the open stall located just outside the restaurant. To find the restaurant, look for a row of florists lined up alongside the entrance.

Information and Services

INFORMATION
Tourist Information

The **Government of India** tourist office is located just across from Churchgate Station in downtown Mumbai (tel. 022/2207-4333, www.incredibleindia.com, 8:30 A.M.–6 P.M. Mon.–Fri., until 2 P.M. Sat.) and offers maps, travel brochures, upcoming festival announcements, as well as a list of recommended hotels and bookings.

The **Maharashtra Tourism Development Corporation (MTDC)** office (Express Towers, Nariman Point, tel. 022/2202-4482, www.maharashtratourism.gov.in, 9:45 A.M.–5:30 P.M. Mon.–Fri., until 3 P.M. Sat.) is helpful with bookings and information for travel, accommodation, and tours. Try to get a booking on the Deccan Odyssey, a luxurious train ride touring the best attractions of the state.

Information is also available at **tourist booths,** manned by MTDC at the Gateway of India (Colaba, tel. 022/2284-1877, 10 A.M.–5 P.M.) and by the Government of India at the domestic airport (Santacruz, tel. 022/2615-6920, 7 A.M.–11 P.M.) as well as the international airport (Sahar, tel. 022/2682-9248, 24 hours).

Newspapers

Mumbai has a number of local English dailies, of which the *Times of India* is the most widely read. The *Times* is also the most controversial, for its share of celebrity gossip and "Page 3" culture, and it comes with its local gossip supplement called the *Bombay Times* and daily tabloid, *Mumbai Mirror.* For more stimulating reading, pick up the *Hindustan Times.* Most newspapers, *Bombay Times* included, carry daily event listings, but the local edition of the weekly *Time Out* magazine is the most comprehensive in its coverage and listing of local events.

Hospitals, Emergency Services, and Pharmacies

An increasingly popular destination for medical tourists, Mumbai has no dearth of efficient hospitals or qualified doctors. Though the larger hospitals are known for their reliable and advanced medical facilities, beware of the city's smaller (and shadier) clinics and hospitals, which may be involved in medical scams and money rackets.

There are 24-hour emergency rooms in the major city hospitals, including **Bombay Hospital** (Marine Lines, tel. 022/2206-7676), **Breach Candy Hospital** (Bhulabhai Desai Rd., tel. 022/2363-3651), **Jaslok Hospital** (Peddar Rd., tel. 022/2493-3333), Hinduja Hospital (Mahim, tel. 022/2445-2222), and **Lilavati Hospital** (Bandra Reclamation, tel. 022/2645-5920). For **ambulance services,** dial 1298 from a landline or call 022/2385-3130. For privately operated ambulances, call cell tel. 91/98331-69329 or 022/2385-3130.

All hospitals have 24-hour pharmacies, and there are a number of day and night pharmacies all over the city. Don't be alarmed if you see a sign saying "chemist" or "druggist"—the local term for pharmacy. **Wordell Chemist** (Churchgate, tel. 022/2242-0768, 24 hours), **Noble Chemist** (Charni Rd., tel. 022/2385-3130, 24 hours), and **Bandra Medical Store** (Hill Rd., Bandra, tel. 022/2642-3757, 24 hours) are among the city's most established pharmacies, stocking everything from personal items and toiletries to medical supplies.

Police

Dial 100 for the 24-hour police helpline but don't be surprised if your call is unattended. Some important police stations to know are the ones in **Colaba** (Near Electric House, Shahid Bagat Singh Rd., tel. 022/2285-6817), **Cuffe Parade** (Near World Trade Centre, tel. 022/2218-8009), **Worli** (Dr Annie Besant Rd., tel. 022/2494-0303), **Bandra** (Hill Rd., tel. 022/2642-3021), and at the **domestic airport** (Santacruz, tel. 022/2611-7309).

SERVICES
Money

The Indian rupee is the standard currency used throughout the country, except for high-end hotels and restaurants or stores located in tourist dominated areas, which accept dollars and euros. The value of the rupee keeps fluctuating in the international market but is generally pegged at anywhere between 40 to 50 rupees to a dollar.

There are 24-hour ATMs scattered throughout the city, and with the number of banks operating here, there's one at every corner—especially around malls or commercial areas. Some ATMs are linked with international networks and will dispense cash at an added charge. Most banks have their main office in the downtown areas but have branches and ATMs all over the city. Some of the major banks include **Citibank** (DN Rd., Fort, tel. 022/2269-5757, www.citibank.co.in, 10:30 A.M.–2 P.M. Mon.–Fri.), **HSBC** (MG Rd., Flora Fountain, tel. 022/4042-2424, www.hsbc.co.in, 9:30 A.M.–5 P.M. Mon.–Sat.), and **American Express** (DN Rd., Fort, tel. 022/2280-2001, 10:30 A.M.–2:30 P.M. Mon.–Fri. and until 12:30 P.M. Sat.).

In major tourist areas like Colaba and Fort, there are innumerable moneychangers—but beware of street touts promising good rates, as you're most likely to get swindled. You can exchange foreign currency at the 24-hour counter in the airport and at reliable foreign exchange dealers such as **Thomas Cook** (Dr. DN Rd., Fort, tel. 022/2207-8556, 9:30 A.M.–6 P.M. Mon.–Sat.), **Forties Financial Services** (Dr. DN Rd., Fort, tel. 022/2207-3191, 9 A.M.–6 P.M. Mon.–Fri.), and **Standard Chartered** (MG Rd., Hutatma Chowk, tel. 022/2204-7198, 9 A.M.–6 P.M. Mon.–Sat.).

Western Union also provides money transfer services at most post offices and licensed shops.

Internet and Telephone

Almost all mid- to high-range hotels provide Internet access, and there are Internet cafés scattered all over the city. Hourly rates are about Rs 20–40.

At phone booths marked "STD-ISD-PCO," you can make local, national, and international calls, and can fax documents. Calls to Europe cost around Rs 7 per minute; to the United States, it's about Rs 5 per minute. If you're in India for a long duration, it's worth getting a pre-paid mobile connection offered by local service providers such as Airtel and Vodafone. However, if your phone was purchased in the United States, you may have to unlock it at a local electronics store for a small fee to be able to make local calls.

To make local calls from your mobile phone, dial the area code for Mumbai (022) before you dial the local number. If you have a Vodafone connection, you can even buy their international calling card, which allows you to make international calls at cheaper rates.

There are a number of information services that work as a 24-hour telephonic phone directory. Of these, **Just Dial** (tel. 022/2888-8888 or 022/2222-2222) is known for its efficient services and will even text message the required numbers to your mobile phone for free.

Post Offices

The **General Post Office** (tel. 022/2262-1671, 9 A.M.–8 P.M. Mon.–Sat. and 10 A.M.–5 P.M. Sun.) near CST Station provides a number of services, including Poste Restante and speedpost. Visit the philately section to get the latest issues of stamps.

Private operators like **DHL** (tel. 022/2283-7187, www.dhl.co.in, 9:30 A.M.–6 P.M. Mon.–Fri.), **Fly King Courier Services** (tel. 022/2283-3996, www.flykingonline .com, 9 A.M.–6 P.M. Mon.–Fri.), **Blue Dart** (tel. 022/2282-29495, www.bluedart.com, 9 A.M.–7 P.M. Mon.–Sat.), and **FedEx** (cell tel. 91/18002-096161, 9 A.M.–9 P.M. Mon.–Sat.) have offices all over the city to provide national and international courier services.

For one-day courier services within the

© ASHIMA NARAIN

Letter boxes can be found throughout the city.

city, try local agency **Vichare** (tel. 022/2283-3996).

Immigration

The **Foreigners' Registration Office** (tel. 022/2262-0111, ext. 266, 9 A.M.–7 P.M. Mon.–Sat.) is located behind the Times of India Building opposite CST Station and attends to queries on various visa and immigration requirements. If you intend to extend your stay over six months, make sure that you register here within two weeks of arrival. Visa extension is generally not possible unless in the case of extreme emergency.

Travel Agencies

A number of travel agents are conveniently located near most hotels and around the CST area. **Akbar Travels** (www.akbartravelsofindia.com, 10 A.M.–7 P.M. Mon.–Sat.) has offices opposite CST (tel. 022/2263-3434) and Crawford Market (tel. 022/2340-3434), where everything from tour packages to car rentals and flight requirements are efficiently handled. Larger travel companies like **Thomas Cook** (Thomas Cook Building, Fort, tel. 022/2204-8556, 10 A.M.–6 P.M. Mon.–Sat.) and **Cox and Kings** (Turner Morrison Building, Bank St., Fort, tel. 022/2207-3065, 10 A.M.–6 P.M. Mon.–Sat.) also have offices in the Fort area.

Launderettes

Most hotels provide laundry services and there are launderettes all over the city. A wash and iron press at these local outlets costs around Rs 30 per item of clothing, while dry cleaning costs Rs 50–150. In Colaba, there's **Akash Dry Cleaners** (Wodehouse Rd., tel. 022/6516-1616, 10 A.M.–6 P.M. Mon.–Sat.), and in Churchgate, the reputed **Beauty Art** (Veer Nariman Rd., tel. 022/2282-1039, 9 A.M.–2 P.M. and 4–7 P.M. Mon.–Sat.). In Bandra and around, you can call **IFB**

Launderette (tel. 022/5584-1282 or cell tel. 91/92244-24420) for pick up and delivery.

The *dhobis* (local washermen) will do your laundry for even less money, but don't expect sophisticated cleaning processes and gadgets such as washing machines or dry cleaning. Clothes are simply hand-washed, then beaten and left to dry in the open before they are ironed to a crisp and delivered to your doorstep.

Storage

Left luggage offices (tel. 022/2615-6500) at the international and domestic terminals of the airport charge Rs 50–250 per day depending on the size of the bag. There is a cloak room for left luggage at CST Station, behind platform 13, where you can leave your luggage for around Rs 40 a day. Make sure that your bags are locked and sealed.

Getting There and Around

GETTING THERE
Air

Unless you're arriving from other parts of India, you will land at Mumbai's **Chhatrapati Shivaji International Airport**, jet-lagged and befuddled with the crowds, touts, and taxi drivers swarming around you. The domestic (tel. 2626400) and international (tel. 022/2681-3000) terminals are four kilometers apart, but connected by a free shuttle service every half-hour.

From the Airport

Transportation is easily available from the airport and includes taxi, auto-rickshaw, bus service, and car rental. Taxis cost around Rs 16 per kilometer; it takes about two hours to reach downtown Mumbai from the international airport. If you are taking a black-and-yellow taxi, make sure you pick up a prepaid coupon from the official counter. From the airport to downtown Mumbai costs approximately Rs 375 by prepaid taxi and Rs 650 by air-conditioned

cabs. The efficient **Meru** (tel. 022/4422-4422, www.merucabs.com, 24 hours) private cab service also operates within the city. It is not necessary to tip the driver and there are no extra charges for luggage.

Auto-rickshaws are noisy, three-tired vehicles that ply the suburbs beyond Bandra and are not permitted to go into town. Demand to see the tariff conversion card in order to be able to interpret the archaic meters. The cost is around Rs 9 per kilometer.

The local **BEST** (Brihanmumbai Electric Supply & Transport, www.bestundertaking.com) bus service runs between the airport terminals and downtown Mumbai every half-hour, but is not recommended if you are carrying heavy luggage. Private coach services are also available and may be booked at the tourism counter in the international terminal.

Car-rental services such as **Avis** (tel. 022/6556-4697, 24 hours) are lcoated inside the domestic and international terminals.

MUMBAI

MUMBAI'S SUBURBAN TRAIN NETWORK

Mumbai's local train network is a metaphor for life in the city. The "Mumbai local," as it is known, is where friendships are struck, gossip shared, spats initiated and resolved, matches for arranged marriages made, religious hymns and Bollywood songs sung, business deals closed, news on the stock market shared, card games won, and, on the odd occasion, premature babies delivered. The trains have seen the darker side as well, with robbery, rape, acid attacks, death, and terrorist attacks in recent times. In short, the local train is where the drama of life is played out every day.

The city has three train routes – the Western, Central, and Harbour routes – that connect the suburbs to the downtown areas. Aptly called the lifeline of the city, these trains are a welcome relief from the unpredictable nature of Mumbai traffic with their precise timings and punctuality. The swiftest and most reliable mode of transport in Mumbai, the trains ferry the city's millions from 4 A.M.–1:30 A.M. every day, groaning under the load of the rush hours that last 8–10:30 A.M. toward downtown and 5–8 P.M. toward the suburbs.

The crowds, especially to an outsider, are unimaginable. Men and women resort to bestial pushing, jumping into the moving train to secure themselves a seat, even before it comes to a halt. Commuters often leap in and block a seat for friends by placing handkerchiefs, newspapers, handbags, or anything that comes to hand. The last ones to get in are the most unfortunate, often hanging precariously, grasping doors and windows with only a finger and a foothold. Others clamber up to sit on the roof, oblivious to the danger of electrocution that lies overhead. It is hardly surprising that rail accidents occur daily as people fall to their death or get run over while crossing the tracks in their hurry to get to work on time – and these tragedies seldom deter regulars from traveling as they do, on the fastest and cheapest mode of transport across the city.

Mumbai's class system is starkly visible on the train. Local trains have separate first- and second-class compartments, divided by ticket price and the quality of seats. As trains are a mass mode of transport, the second-class sections tend to be more crowded. Amid this chaos, vendors jostle their way through the crowds, selling everything from snacks to hairclips, their wares held safely above the crowds.

Separate "ladies' compartments" are meant to protect women from sexual harassment in these mobile cans of sardines, where close physical proximity is unavoidable. A few years ago, separate "ladies' locals" were introduced – a sign of increasing numbers of urban working women.

Mumbai's local trains are rarely delayed and come to a standstill only on days of heavy downpour during the monsoon. On July 11, 2006, when terrorists planted bombs in seven local trains on the Western line during rush hour, hundreds of lives were lost and train services suspended. But in keeping with their reputation, and the celebrated spirit of the city, the trains were back on track the same day.

© JANHAVI ACHAREKAR

Local trains ferry seven million passengers every day.

From the Train Terminals

Most trains arriving from the southern part of the country come to **Lokmanya Tilak Terminus** in the eastern suburb of Kurla, at **Dadar Terminus,** or downtown at the **Chhatrapati Shivaji Terminus.** Trains from the north arrive at the **Mumbai Central Terminus** and at the **Bandra Terminus.** If your train arrives at the Lokmanya Tilak Terminus or at Bandra Terminus, you can opt for a taxi to go downtown or take a short auto-ride to the local suburban stations of **Kurla** or **Bandra,** from where trains can be taken to South Mumbai or the northern suburbs.

By Bus

Buses from most parts of the country terminate their journey close to major railway stations within the city. Before booking your journey ask the operator if the bus terminates at **Borivli, Bandra, Dadar, Mumbai Central,** or **Marine Lines.** If you plan to stay downtown, take a bus that drops you off at one of the latter three stations or at Churchgate, all on the Western line. There are plenty of taxis, rickshaws, trains, and BEST buses from these stations.

By Car

If coming from the north of the country you will enter the city by the **Western Express Highway.** If coming from the south, you'll take the **Eastern Express Highway.** Both highways terminate centrally in the city, merging into major roads that take you downtown.

GETTING AROUND
Taxi and Auto-Rickshaw

The city is filled with the quaint old black-and-yellow Fiat taxis and three-tired auto-rickshaws (restricted to the northern suburbs). These taxis charge a minimum fare of Rs 16 per kilometer, while the auto-rickshaws charge Rs 9 per kilometer. When traveling by the black-and-yellow taxi or auto-rickshaw, demand to see the tariff card, as drivers often take advantage of outdated meters by quoting a higher rate.

Blue-and-silver air-conditioned cabs and the

Mumbai's quaint black-and-yellow taxis

© ASHIMA NARAIN

private **Meru** cabs (tel. 022/4422-4422, www .merucabs.com, 24 hours) are available at a higher rate. The **Priyadarshini Taxi Service** (tel. 022/4033-1444, cell tel. 91/93208-45064) has female drivers for women traveling alone in the city and late at night.

Car Rental

Car-rental services such as **Avis** (domestic and international airports, tel. 022/6556-4697, 24 hours), **Car Care** (Dongersi Rd., Malabar Hill, tel. 022/2367-7724, 24 hours), and **Hertz** (Mahakali Caves Rd., Andheri East, tel. 022/6570-1692, 24 hours) are available at a rate of approximately Rs 1,500 per 100 kilometers, inclusive of driver, fuel, and insurance. However, given the dismal traffic and parking situations in the city, it is easier to take a taxi for point-to-point travel.

Train

Called the "lifeline" of Mumbai, the city rail network transports a whopping seven million passengers every day. The network includes three lines: the **Western** route, which runs

Mumbai's BEST buses are the cheapest way to travel across the city.

from Churchgate to Virar (and farther), and the **Central** and **Harbour** routes, which ply from CST to the satellite township of Navi Mumbai (New Bombay), Karjat, and beyond. These local trains, or "Mumbai locals" as they are known, are the quickest—and most uncomfortable—means of transport in Mumbai. Efficient and punctual, they tend to be unimaginably crowded, especially during peak hours (8–10:30 A.M. toward downtown and 5–8 P.M. toward the suburbs). Railway timetables and prepaid coupons are available at all major stations. The minimum fare is Rs 4 and return tickets are available for a round-trip.

Trains stop for barely 10 seconds and it might take a little local help to learn the station codes on the platform indicators. There are first-class compartments that cost 12 times the general fare, but they are equally crowded during peak hours. There are separate second-class and first-class compartments for women, as well as a compartment for commuters with disabilities.

Bus

Mumbai's cheap and efficient **BEST** bus service (www.bestundertaking.com) connects all parts of the city at a minimum fare of Rs 4. Its numerous, complicated routes are not easily figured out. Booklet guides available at railway stations come in handy, and it pays to ask for help from the generally genial crowd around the bus stops. Once you're aboard, bus conductors are helpful and will indicate your stop as long as you have the requisite change for your ticket. You can also get prepaid GO cards at railway stations and bus depots.

Around Mumbai

"If you've come all the way, you may as well stay" is the mantra of many travelers who turn a brief sojourn in Mumbai into an extended sabbatical. If you're one of those blessed with the luxury of time, don't pass up the opportunity to pack in the surrounding sights and getaways from the city. These escapades range from day trips to weekend excursions and short holidays to vineyards, beaches, hill stations, archaeological wonders, and satellite townships around the city.

VASAI FORT

A day trip from Mumbai, the historic Vasai Fort is a two-hour drive or train ride away. It's difficult to believe that the moss-covered ruins of the fort were once the pride of Portuguese rulers. Deserted and ill-maintained, the fort's high arches lead to the old Portuguese town, now inhabited by wild foliage, various species of insects, and the odd monkey. In the old days, however, this was the capital of the Portuguese colony—attracting a Maratha siege and, eventually, a successful attack by the British. Gifted as a mark of gratitude by the Sultan of Gujarat in 1534 for the Portuguese help in fending off the Mughals, Bassein, as it was then known, was the center of Portuguese trade.

In the fishing village of Vasai, the many churches and large Christian population are the only indication of the region's history, apart from the ruined fort. A great place to commune with history, the fort makes for a worthwhile solo trip. Make sure you pack your own sandwiches, though, as there's precious little in terms of food options here. You could, however, get a local fishing family to cook you some spicy fried fish or, if you're driving down, stop at Dara's Dhaba for a highway-style *dhaba* lunch.

Getting There

Vasai is a train ride from Mumbai on the Western line. The trip takes about an hour and a half, with a round-trip fare of Rs 26 for second class and Rs 300 for first class. After alighting at Vasai Road Station, the onward journey is by auto-rickshaw, costing about Rs 40 and lasting about half an hour.

By road, Vasai is roughly two hours and less than 80 kilometers away, on the Mumbai–Ahmedabad highway.

VINEYARDS AT NASIK

A four-hour drive from Mumbai takes you to India's wine country. Wait a minute, Indian wine did we say? Most visitors are surprised (and skeptical) to know that Maharashtra has more than 30 wineries, and the major players export their products—even to France. Visit the temple town of Nasik and you'll see acres of green vineyards on the outskirts tended by a bunch of passionate farmers-turned-oenophiles dedicated to injecting the wine culture into a country that can hardly tell its wine from its whisky.

While most of the wineries are in the nascent stages of development and ill-equipped to conduct wine tours, pioneers such as Chateau Indage and Sula have country-style wine bars, and the latter runs regular guided tours and tasting in addition to renting out Beyond, their spectacular vineyard villa. Up-and-coming wineries such as **Renaissance** (Mumbai-Agra Highway, near Ojhar village, tel. 02550/329-303) and **Vinsura** (Mumbai-Aurangabad Rd. at MIDC Vinchur, near Lasalgaon, tel. 02550/261-751) conduct informal wine-tasting sessions on request and have plans for wine bars. While there's not much to be said about the factory-like appearance of the Vinsura winery, it is worth a visit for a meeting with the winemaker M. P. Sharma—an elderly gentleman in a tweed cap and twirling moustache who is ever-willing to share his knowledge on wine.

The city of Nasik itself is at once a fast-growing business center and a pilgrimage spot known for its ancient temples. The heady mix of wine and religion has resulted in a conservative Maharashtrian population that can tell its

MUMBAI

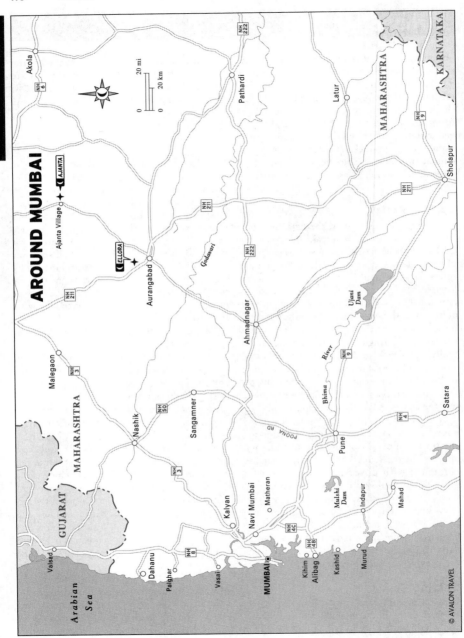

AROUND MUMBAI

© AVALON TRAVEL

Sula Chenin Blanc from its Ivy Zinfandel—a fact reflected in the town's emerging wine lounges and bars. International winemakers, many of whom are consultants to the Nasik wineries, have given a thumbs-up sign to Indian wines. Some of the wines are recipients of international awards and from the warm welcome that they have received across the country and internationally, it looks like the wine culture is here to stay.

Wineries

Nasik is full of eateries that serve everything from the local *misal pav* (a mix of sprouts, onion, and fried semolina strips in a spicy gravy served with locally baked bread) to fine wine and expensive cheeses. However, for an authentic vineyard experience, head to **Sula Vineyards** (off the Gangapur–Savargaon Rd., tel. 91/99700-90010, www.sulawines.com, 11 A.M.–10 P.M. Mon.–Thurs. and 11 A.M.–11 P.M. Fri.–Sat., harvest and crush season Jan.–Mar.). You won't get dinner here, but the fine selection of wines, cheeses, and cold cuts is enough to regale your taste buds as you take in the breathtaking view. Hotel management graduates take you on a guided tour (hourly from 11 A.M., Rs. 150) of the yellow-and-blue winery, concluding with a tasting session at The Bar. You can buy the various Sula brands, a few foreign wines, and souvenirs before you order a bite to eat (cheese and meat platter with wine Rs 200–400). Try their fruity Chenin Blanc or the Dindori Reserve, matured in oak barrels.

Cellar Door (Patil Plaza, Canara Corner, Nasik, tel. 0253/231-8226, meal with wine Rs 500–1,000) is Nasik's first wine lounge. The only place in town where you can choose from a host of Indian and foreign wines, this pleasant rooftop bar and eatery is also known for its great entrées and an Indian menu carefully tailored to complement its wines.

Not quite on the Mumbai–Nasik Highway, the Chateau Indage vineyards and "rural" wine bar **Ivy** (Narayangaon, tel. 021/2295-2838 or 020/2295-2839, 11 A.M.–11 P.M. daily, meal with wine Rs 250–500) involve a picturesque

three-hour drive from Mumbai or Nasik. The ivy on the small, open, country-style bar provides the desired effect. You can gaze upon the surrounding vineyards and a faux chateau as you have the Indian lunch buffet accompanied by a selection of wines. Try the Tiger Hill and Chantilli brands, or call for a bottle of Marquise de Pompadour champagne (they refuse to call it sparkling wine) if you feel like celebrating. Since there are no accommodations in the vicinity, Ivy is best as a day trip.

Accommodations

Nasik city has a wide range of luxury and budget accommodations, including the high-end Taj Group and the no-frills Ginger chain of hotels. For a memorable stay, move to the outskirts and book Sula's **Beyond** (3 km from the Sula winery, off Gangapur–Savargaon Rd., tel. 91/99700-90010, www.sulawines.com, weekdays Rs 16,000, weekends Rs 20,000 for up nine people with breakfast, lunch, and dinner), a sprawling Mediterranean-style bungalow overlooking its own vineyards and the Gangapur Dam in the distance. The place comes with a pool, an in-house cook, complimentary wine tasting sessions, and access to kayaking.

Chateau Indage's **Tiger Hill Resort** (Mumbai–Agra Highway, tel. 022/2404-2501 or 0253/233-6274, www.tigerhillvineyards .com, Rs 2,800–4,800 including breakfast) is located nowhere close to its vineyards, which lie three hours away at Narayangaon. However, its cluster of cottages, garden restaurant, and well-stocked wine bar make for a pleasant getaway if you ignore the truck traffic outside.

Getting There

Nasik is a major station on the Central Railway circuit. The station, 44 kilometers from the town center, is well connected by a number of trains; the Panchavati Express is the fastest train that runs daily between Mumbai and Nasik. By road, Nasik is a three- to five-hour journey, depending on traffic, on National Highway 3 (also known as the Mumbai–Agra Highway). Buses run by the state government and private operators connect the two cities, with Trimbakeshwar (28 km from Nasik) being the major stop on this route.

◖ AJANTA AND ELLORA

Some 400 kilometers from Mumbai and 107 kilometers from the city of Aurangabad, the rock-cut honeycomb-like caves of Ajanta (Sahyadri Hills, Ajanta Village, 9 A.M.–5:30 P.M. Tues.–Sun., Indian Rs 10, foreigner US$5, photography and entry to certain caves prohibited) are safely hidden in the forested Sahyadri Hills of Maharashtra. A few kilometers away, the mammoth Kailasa temple of the Ellora caves (Charanadri Hills, Verul Village, 9 A.M.–5:30 P.M. Wed.–Mon.) rises above the arid countryside. Entry to the caves is free, but there's a fee to explore the temple (Indian Rs 10, foreigner US$10, video camera Rs 25). Flash photography is strictly forbidden, but the guide will turn on the lights if you purchase a "light pass" (Rs 5).

This UNESCO World Heritage Site is one of India's prized archaeological discoveries. It is difficult to believe that its forgotten landscape was once a busy trade route and an important seat of Buddhism. While both the Ajanta and Ellora cave temples began to take shape in the 3rd century B.C., the focus shifted to Ellora toward the 8th century A.D. Carved out of the mountainside and beautifully preserved from wind and rain, Ajanta was rediscovered in 1819 when a group of British soldiers chanced upon the caves. The 30 caves provided a rocky canvas for ancient artisans, who painted intricate, colorful scenes from the Jataka Tales (fables narrated by the Buddha) and from the life of the Buddha. In contrast, the 34 caves at Ellora are beautifully sculpted and can be seen to herald the return of Hinduism after its long hiatus, signaling the twilight years of the Buddhist era.

A steep climb up the rocky mountainside leads up to the dark cells of Ajanta. Inside, a profusion of color startles the unsuspecting visitor with its freshness. Intricate illustrations adorn the cave temples and their *viharas* (monasteries).

In contrast, the Ellora caves display cleaner strokes in sculpture, with bold flourishes that are indicative of changing times. They serve as a dramatic backdrop to the Ellora Festival of Dance and Music during the last week of Novemeber, when the country's foremost Indian classical musicians and dancers perform within the Kailasa Temple, reviving briefly, the former glory of this spectacular site.

Contact the Maharashtra Tourism Development Corporation for more information about the caves (tel. 022/2202-4482, www.maharashtratourism.gov.in).

Accommodations and Food

There are few options for lodging and eating near the caves, so some visitors prefer to stay at one the many hotels in nearby Aurangabad.

Hotel Kailas (tel. 091/02437-244543, www .hotelkailas.com, Rs 900–2,000) features a cluster of stone cottages just opposite the Ellora caves. This lovely boutique hotel is beautifully furnished and landscaped, and receives a steady stream of guests from around the world. It also has a restaurant and a bar.

Getting There

By air, Aurangabad is a mere 40 minutes from Mumbai and easily reached by domestic carriers like Indian Airlines, Jet Airways, and Deccan. From here, taxis are available to go to the caves.

By train, the Tapovan Express and Devgiri Express ply daily from Mumbai to Aurangabad. There are a number of bus services to Ellora from Aurangabad Central Bus Station, including the MTDC service.

By road, Aurangabad is 400 kilometers from Mumbai; state and private buses run regularly between the two cities. If you plan to drive yourself, you can take the route via Nasik or through Pune—the cities are well connected by the Mumbai–Agra highway and the Mumbai–Pune expressway.

MATHERAN

Red earth, horses, a "toy train," deep ravines, and bungalows with endless verandahs make

Matheran (entry fee Rs 25) Maharashtra's most charming hill station. The perfect getaway from Mumbai's pollution and traffic, this quaint colonial town provides respite with its fresh mountain air, forested walks, and a ban on vehicles. With horses being the favorite mode of transport, Matheran seems caught in a time warp—and its equine population is outnumbered only by its bold simian population. The monkeys of Matheran are the stuff of lore, known to mimic human actions, snatch foodstuffs, and even provide comic relief by sporting the odd undergarment stolen from the rooms of unfortunate travelers.

The most interesting feature of the hill station, however, is its miniature train, known affectionately as the "toy train." Vehicles are allotted parking just before the ascent into town, so Matheran is best reached by its Raj-era narrow-gauge train (currently up for contention for UNESCO World Heritage status) that chugs along the misty mountainside.

The hill town is known for its numerous "points"—Panorama Point, Porcupine Point, Echo Point, and Louisa Point, among others. These places provide stunning views of the surrounding vistas, including perpendicular cliffs and deep ravines, monsoon waterfalls and rose sunsets.

Matheran is best avoided in the summer months, when noisy holiday crowds from Mumbai and Pune descend upon the hill town. The place is best enjoyed in the quiet season, when you can visit the Charlotte Lake undisturbed or trek up its rugged hillside, gazing upon the dramatic mountainscape and the city lights below.

Accommodations and Food

Matheran has some beautiful heritage bungalows-turned-hotels, the most remarkable of which is **The Verandah in the Forest** (Barr House, tel. 02148/230296, www.neemrana-hotels.com, weekdays Rs 2,000–4,500, weekends Rs 2,500–5,000). This lovely colonial property—with its high ceiling, stained glass, old-world dining area lit with silver candelabras, and rooms furnished with antiques—is

the ultimate heritage experience in Matheran. There are a wide variety of rooms, ranging from the smaller single rooms to the grand rooms and luxury suites, all of which are named after prominent citizens of colonial India.

Another heritage favorite is the 80-year-old **Lord's Central Hotel** (tel. 02148/30228, www.lordsmatheran.com, Rs 1,600–2,300), run by the Lords, a Parsi family. The hotel is known for its sweeping view of the valley and has a number of cottages and rooms with vast verandahs and mountain views. The hotel has a pool and a dining room that serves all meals.

Getting There

Take a Karjat-bound local train to Neral Station on the Central line from Chhatrapati Shivaji Terminus in Mumbai. From Neral, the toy train runs to and from Matheran about four times a day. Alternately, there are tourist taxis that take you up to Dasturi Naka—the last point to allow vehicular access before entry into the hill town. If you have your own car, you can park (Rs 30/day) at Dasturi Naka, from where it is a half-hour walk or ride into Matheran.

PUNE

Once a sleepy town for students and pensioners, and an important military base, Pune has emerged as India's newest IT and business hub—and Maharashtra's cultural capital. Pune's rich past is evident as educational institutions, military academies, and software companies go about their daily business amid the backdrop of its historic stone buildings and bustling *peths* (marketplaces). Women race their scooters and bikes alongside their male counterparts, and the city is abuzz with an active international populace and an academic community.

The capital of the Maratha empire, Pune was taken over by the Peshwa rulers before the British finally turned the city into the alternate administrative headquarters for the Bombay Presidency. The city is therefore a potpourri of tradition and modernity, and of the artistic and the commercial.

The palace of the Peshwas, **Shaniwar Wada** (Shivaji Rd., 8 A.M.–6:30 P.M. daily, Rs 2 Sat.–Thurs., free on Fri) dominates the cityscape as much as the **Osho Meditation Resort** (17 Koregaon Park, tel. 020/612-8562, www.osho.com, 9 A.M.–3:30 P.M. daily, photography prohibited)—famous for Bhagwan Rajneesh's spiritual philosophy borrowed from various world religions and infused with a generous dose of hedonism.

Pune is characterized by its famous Shrewsbury biscuits and its *khanavals,* by the chic global food village ABC Farms and its vibrant nightlife, by the Ganesh festival and a rich legacy of the arts. It is also known for its beautiful landscape and historical sights that include the Khadakvasla Dam, Mulshi Lake, Shivaji's Sinhagad Fort, and the neighboring hill stations of Lonavla and Khandala. With its great standard of living, cosmopolitan culture, and casual outlook toward life, Pune is fast turning into an alternate choice of residence for the people of Mumbai.

Accommodations
Hotel Sunderban (19 Koregaon Park, tel. 020/2612-4949, www.tghotels.com, Rs 700–7,500) is a heritage hotel located next to the Osho ashram and built in the art deco style of architecture. There is a wide choice of living arrangements, ranging from economy rooms to the spacious Osho suite and grand studio rooms with kitchenettes.

Taj Blue Diamond (11 Koregaon Rd., tel. 020/6602-5555, www.tajhotels.com, Rs 14,000–23,000) is a landmark property that is part of the famous Taj Group. A top-notch business hotel, it offers 110 rooms and suites that offer the best in comfort and design. The hotel and its fine dining restaurants are efficiently managed, in keeping with the Taj reputation.

Food
Pune has plenty of eating options, ranging from traditional *khanavals* to German bakeries and sophisticated gourmet options at fine dining restaurants. **ABC Farms** (35/36 Koregaon Park, Ghorpadi, Pune, www.abcfarmsindia.com), a cluster of individual restaurants located on a farming estate, is unique to the city. Within the leafy environs of the park is a wide selection of cuisines ranging from the traditional Parsi *dhansak* at Parwara to the spicy Hyderabad cuisine of Golconda. There's also the Swiss Cheese Farm, the Shisha Café, and a restaurant called Soul that belts out music from the 1950s, '60s, and '70s.

In the old days, when residents of Mumbai heard of friends or family traveling to Pune, there was only one favor to ask for: *bakarvadi* (a fried mini-roll with a crust of chickpea flour and a sweet-spicy filling) from **Chitale Bandhu** (777, Sadashiv Peth, Bajirao Rd., tel. 020/2447-3208, www.chitalebandhu.in, 8 A.M.–1 P.M. and 3:30–8:30 P.M. daily). At this famous local establishment, locals and visitors stock up on traditional Maharashtrian snacks and other delights, including *bakarvadi, samosa, chivda* (crisp, beaten rice flavored with peanuts and spices), *kachori* (a rounded version of the *bakarvadi*), and a variety of Indian *mithai* (sweets), including the typically Maharashtrian *ale paak* (crystallized ginger cubes).

Getting There
Pune is 160 kilometers from Mumbai. The easiest way to get there is by the famous Mumbai–Pune expressway, which turned a previously long and bumpy ride into a smooth two-hour cruise. Many private and state-owned luxury buses also ply this route, departing from Dadar Station in Mumbai.

By rail, Mumbai and Pune are connected by fast commuter trains like the Deccan Queen and Shatabdi Express, which leave from Mumbai's Chhatrapati Shivaji Terminus as well as Dadar Station. Travel time is 3.5 hours from one city to the other.

You can also fly to Pune's airport at Lohegaon, located around 12 kilometers from the main city center and connected to Mumbai by most domestic carriers. A handful of international flights also arrive and depart from here.

ALIBAG, KIHIM, AND KASHID

Only three hours by road from Mumbai, and less than that by ferry, is the beginning of the Konkan coast, Maharashtra's long stretch of whispering palms and white sands. Known for its fishing villages, seaside forts and coconut-topped seafood curries, the coast comprises a string of small beaches.

Alibag is a popular getaway from Mumbai, and crowds arrive here by the hordes on weekends. While the beach itself is nothing to write home about—full of black sand, un-derwear-clad male swimmers, and crowded food stalls—a horse cart ride to the ruins of the Kolaba Fort built by Shivaji makes for a memorable experience. Alibag also has a 150-year-old geomagnetic observatory. Near the bus station lies Angrewada, the home of Kanhoji Angre, the man who founded Alibag. You may need to ask its present-day owners for a look around the ornate 17th-century house. Nearby, at Akshi, are ancient stone tablets, temples, and the twin sea forts of Undheri and Khanderi.

If you're looking for a place in the sun where you can set your deck chair and relax, Kihim is just 11 kilometers from Alibag. The beach here is better, the sand whiter, and old beach bunga-lows line the seafront. MTDC rents tents and local villagers will be happy to provide a cook-out under the stars for a small fee.

The most picturesque of the nearby beaches, however, is the deserted Kashid Beach. Known for its glistening sand and exotic birds, Kashid is the perfect combination of ocean, forest, and history. The ruins of an old Portuguese fort lie close to a solitary lighthouse and near its emerald waters is the verdant green of the Phansad Bird Sanctuary, which shelters rare birds and butterflies.

Accommodation and Food

Kashid Beach Resort (P.O. Kashid, tel. 02144/278501, Rs 5,000) is a hillside resort that overlooks the sea. All the rooms have sea views and offer easy access to the beach and surrounding nature trails. The resort organizes barbeques and parties, and has a restaurant that serves everything from Chinese food to regional Konkani-style specialties.

Getting There

Alibag can be reached by the Central Railway. The nearest Central Railway stations are at Panvel, 85 kilometers away, and at Roha, 50 kilometers away. Alibag is well connected to all the major cities in western Maharashtra by road. Regular buses are available from Mumbai, and if you're driving, you can take the Mumbai–Goa–Ernakulam National Highway (NH17). Continue straight at Wadkhal Naka, a little ahead of Pen. From Pune, you can take the Mumbai–Pune Expressway and take the Khopoli exit. From there, drive toward Pen and then cross the Mumbai–Goa Highway to proceed toward Alibag.

However, the best way to reach Alibag is by sea. Ferries and catamarans are available from the Gateway of India in Mumbai to Rewas, where you can proceed by bus to Alibag. Note that service is suspended during the rains (June–Sept.).

MURUD-JANJIRA

Not far from Kashid, the coastal region of Murud-Janjira is known better for its fantas-tic fortress than for its beach. The sea fort of Janjira stands apart from other coastal forts in that it is relatively well preserved, and because it was built not by the warrior king Shivaji but, rather, by his enemy. The 350-year-old fort was the domain of the Siddis—Abyssinian warriors who landed on Indian shores from Africa. The fort was built Siddi Johar, and was rumored to be impregnable, surviving failed attacks by the Marathas, the British, and the Portuguese.

Today, the victorious fort is attacked by throngs of people who come here for a glimpse of history amid white sands and endless ocean. Descendants of the Siddi community continue to exist in small numbers in the coastal town. While they have adopted the local language, dress, and customs, they continue to pass down some of their own unique traditions to new generations.

Murud-Janjira also has a second claim to fame: the inaccessible Padmadurg Fort. Now known as Kasa Fort, this fortress was built in a fit of egotistical fervor by Shivaji's son, Sambhaji, but proved to be a less-than-fitting answer to the magnificent Janjira Fort.

A perfect beach, fascinating forts, a private palace belonging to the descendants of the erstwhile Siddi Nawab, a waterfall, and chilled *sol kadi* (a spicy-sour drink of coconut and a local fruit called *kokum*) on the beach make Murud-Janjira an interesting destination full of history and culture.

Accommodation and Food

Golden Swan Resort (Darbar Rd., tel. 02144/274078, www.goldenswan.com, Rs 1,700–15,600) is a lovely seaside resort comprising a number of rooms, cottages, and beach houses with views of Kasa Fort and the Nawab's palace. An on-site multicuisine restaurant dishes out local food and other specialties, but the place to go to for a typical coastal meal is the rudimentary **Patil Khanaval** (Maruti Naka, Murud). Run by five brothers, this simple *khanaval* has a few tables set up beneath coconut palms on the beach. It is known for its delicious Konkani-style seafood preparations and fresh catch of fish. Try the fried pomfret, prawn curry, and numerous types of local fish (served pickled, salted, and dried).

Getting There

Murud is 165 kilometers and five hours from Mumbai by road. State Transport buses travel to Murud from Mumbai via Revdanda, Alibag (52 km), Panvel and Rewas (75 km), and from Pune (230 km) via Mahad. From Mumbai, these buses depart from Mumbai Central for Murud's Durbar Road. By rail, the nearest station is Roha, 122 kilometers away, and the Konkan Kanya on the Central route departs from Mumbai. The onward journey from Roha and Panvel is by bus.

The most convenient way to get to Murud, however, is by ferry from the Mazgaon Ferry Wharf in Mumbai to Rewas, 23 kilometers from Murud, or by catamaran from the Gateway of India to Mandwa. Ferry services are available from 6 A.M.–6 P.M. daily, but are suspended during the monsoon (June–Sept.).

PANAJI AND INTERIOR GOA

If it were left to the Goans, *bebinca* would be the national dessert—if there could be such a thing. There's *bebinca* in every nook and corner of Goa and if you apply a little last course philosophy, you'll agree that this 16-layer dessert is representative of Goan society itself.

There's no better starting point than the very heart of the state—Goa's capital, Panaji, and the central interior—with their nuances and myriad influences. If you picture Goa to be all golden sand and aquamarine beaches, Panaji and the interior landscape will defy all logic. They present to you, instead, Mediterranean yellow and terra-cotta-hued houses versus emerald forests; churches and temples alongside carnivals and chariot festivals; and riverside serenity together with cruise-ship casinos. There's urbanity, heritage,

and wildlife. All at once. And thrown in for good measure are the fine beaches and islands in the vicinity, ranging from the beautiful Miramar and Dona Paula beaches to the Divar and Chorao Islands.

Most tourists only ever explore the topmost layer of Goa: the coastline. Those who care to sink their teeth deeper inside chance upon a veritable treasure trove of history and culture. Their findings lead them, at first, along Panaji's Church Square, then into the cheery Latin Quarter with its Portuguese-sounding street names and bright little houses, and to the riverfront with its many ferries and cruise ships. They lose themselves in the quaint bar-cafés, giddy with *feni* and the joy of culinary discovery. Nights sparkle with possibilities. Panaji's floating casinos and cruises provide

© ASHIMA NARAIN

HIGHLIGHTS

◖ Church of Our Lady of the Immaculate Conception: Also known as Panjim Church, this whitewashed structure with zigzag diagonal steps is a prominent Panaji landmark (page 124).

◖ St. Sebastian Chapel: Located in the charming Latin Quarter of Fontainhas, this chapel and its surrounding alleys lined with brightly colored heritage houses make for a delightful discovery (page 125).

◖ Basilica of Bom Jesus: Goa's most important monument, the Basilica of Bom Jesus in Old Goa houses the miraculously intact remains of the state's most venerated saint, St. Francis Xavier (page 150).

◖ Sé Cathedral: Although overshadowed by the Basilica of Bom Jesus, the Sé Cathedral in Old Goa is believed to be the largest in Asia and is larger than any church in Portugal (page 152).

◖ Spice Plantations: Ponda may be known for its temples, but it is worthwhile stopping over at one of its many spice plantations for a traditional Hindu Goan meal. The **Savoi Plantation** at Savoi Verem is particularly picturesque and serves a wonderful set meal in its rustic environs (page 156).

◖ Tambdi Surla: Goa's oldest and most beautiful temple, Tambdi Surla is a Shiva shrine located in a village by the same name, close to the Karnataka border. The temple dates back to Goa's 11th-century Kadamba dynasty (page 163).

◖ Bhagwan Mahavir Wildlife Sanctuary and Molem National Park: Wildlife walks, bird-watching tours, and nature treks are all possible in this vast sanctuary (page 164).

◖ Dudhsagar Falls: One of the highest waterfalls in India gushes in the forested precincts of Bhagwan Mahavir Wildlife Sanctuary and Molem National Park gushes (page 165).

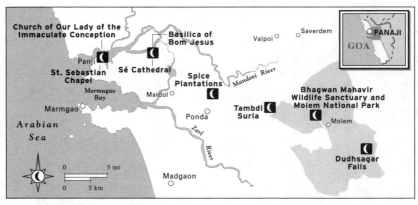

LOOK FOR ◖ TO FIND RECOMMENDED SIGHTS, ACTIVITIES, DINING, AND LODGING.

both entertainment and sightseeing, but the most important sights lie a few layers deeper.

A visit to Old Goa will give you the state's colonial history in a nutshell—from the spot where Portuguese governor Afonso de Albuquerque first set sight on Adil Shah's capital (and Portugal's jewel in the crown) to the ferries at Viceroy's Arch, where future viceroys would be handed the ceremonial key to Goa. Among the many churches and monuments, is Goa's most-visited building—the Basilica of Bom Jesus, which is the resting place of St. Francis Xavier's miraculously preserved remains. The route from Panaji into the hinterland takes you deeper into the region's history as you go through Old Goa, past Adil Shah's mosque—Safa Masjid—and toward the temples of Ponda or Hindu Goa. Both culture and landscape change color as soaring lamp-towers rise above temple courtyards and lush spice plantations merge with green forests. As if to present an appropriate soundtrack for a more pristine Goa, the countryside is filled with the chirping of birds and resounds with the roar of the mighty Dudhsagar Falls. Nature and heritage enthusiasts have it good, as wild animals roam the state's national park and sanctuaries, and an ancient temple survives to tell the tale of pre-Portuguese Goa.

Peel the layers and Panaji and interior Goa make for an exciting, uncharted holiday. This region will be overwhelm you with its multiple flavors and cater to varied tastes. Either way, be sure to enjoy it—the aftertaste will most certainly be sweet.

HISTORY

Goan history goes back to pre-historic times—to the Neolithic and Mesolithic eras, according to rock carvings and stone tools found in the region. Later, after centuries of Sumerian, Phoenician, and Buddhist influences, it entered its most glorious phase under the Hindu Kadamba dynasty around the 11th century A.D. Goa flourished under Kadamba rule and became an important port for trade with merchants arriving all the way from Sumatra and Arabia. However, the Kadamba empire declined and a brief stint by the Yadava dynasty was cut short by the Delhi Sultanate and the Muslim Bahmani rulers of the Deccan region of western India. The 14th century was a turbulent period in the history of the region as Hindu temples were destroyed by these Islamic invasions. The Hindu Vijayanagar empire briefly gained control over Goa and restored peace in 1378, only to lose it once again to the Bahmani kings in 1472. As the Bahmani Sultanate fragmented, Goa came under the rule of the Sultan Yusuf Adil Shah of Bijapur (in modern-day Karnataka). Under his rule, Old Goa developed into a major port known for its shipbuilding and great international trade—so much so that it attracted the attention of Afonso de Albuquerque of Portugal, successor of Vasco da Gama, who had only a decade before reached the shores of Southern India. In March 1510, Albuquerque launched his attack on Old Goa, but Adil Shah responded with a surprise counter-attack, leaving Albuquerque and his troops stranded on the river in Goa's treacherous monsoon season. A few months later, in November, the Portuguese divested control over Goa and Albuquerque led a horrific massacre before establishing his rule over the territory. Christian missionaries belonging to different orders—the Dominicans, Franciscans, Jesuits, and others—soon arrived by the shipload to win over new souls for Christendom. Old Goa became one of the richest cities in the world as trade flourished and churches, educational institutions, and hospitals emerged in an effort to make it a grander destination than even Lisbon.

However, Goa Dourada, or "Golden Goa" as it came to be known, was marred by the plague, which was brought here by a ship from Europe in 1635. This was followed by a cholera epidemic. The surviving populace moved to Panjim, which went on to become the new capital, called Nova (New) Goa, in 1843. Only the missionaries remained to look after the churches and institutions of Old Goa; when they too were ordered to leave Goa, apparently owing to their interference in the administration, the erstwhile capital went to seed and the monuments and buildings were left in a state of disrepair.

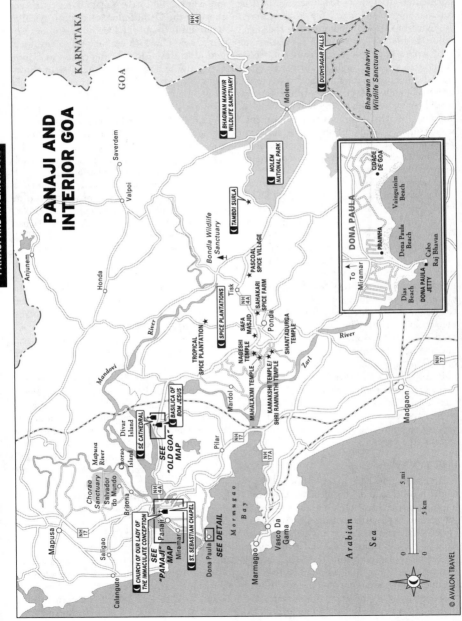

PANAJI AND INTERIOR GOA

PANAJI AND INTERIOR GOA

KARNATAKA

GOA

NH 4A

Anjunem

Saverdem

Valpoi

Honda

River

Mandovi

Bondla Wildlife Sanctuary

BHAGWAN MAHAVIR WILDLIFE SANCTUARY

Molem

DUDHSAGAR FALLS

Bhagwan Mahavir Wildlife Sanctuary

MOLEM NATIONAL PARK

TAMBDI SURLA

PASCOAL SPICE VILLAGE

SPICE PLANTATIONS

Tisk

TROPICAL SPICE PLANTATION

SAFA MASJID

NH 4A

SAHAKARI SPICE FARM

Ponda

NAGESHI TEMPLE

MAHALAXMI TEMPLE

KAMAKSHI TEMPLE

SHRI RAMNATH TEMPLE

SHANTADURGA TEMPLE

Zuari

River

NH 17

Mapusa River

Chorao Island

Divar Island

Chorao Sanctuary

Salvador do Mundo

Britona

SÉ CATHEDRAL

BASILICA OF BOM JESUS

"OLD GOA" MAP

SEE

Mardol

Pilar

NH 17

NH 17A

Madgaon

Mapusa

NH 17

Saligao

Calangute

Panaji

Miramar

Dona Paula

CHURCH OF OUR LADY OF THE IMMACULATE CONCEPTION

SEE "PANAJI" MAP

ST. SEBASTIAN CHAPEL

SEE DETAIL

Mormugao Bay

Vasco Da Gama

Marmagao

Arabian Sea

DONA PAULA

CIDADE DE GOA

PRAINHA

Vainguinim Beach

Dona Paula Beach

To Miramar

Cabo Raj Bhavan

Dias Beach

DONA PAULA JETTY

5 mi

5 km

0

0

© AVALON TRAVEL

© MANJIRI ACHREKAR-SMOTHER

view of the monuments of Old Goa and the surrounding countryside

Meanwhile, the Goan Inquisition forced a mass exodus of the Hindu population to other regions and pushed them into the interior, inaccessible parts. The area of Ponda continued to be ruled by the Marathas who sheltered the Hindus and carried on the reconstruction of temples destroyed by the Portuguese. However, this region and other remaining areas were soon captured by the Portuguese; it was only in the Liberation of 1961, when the Indian army took over Goa in a bloodless coup, that it became a part of India. The capital, Panjim, became Panaji, and other places too went back to their pre-Portuguese appellations. Initial moves to assimilate the region into neighboring states were resisted by the Goans and it was declared a Union Territory. Finally, in May 1987, Goa became India's 25th state and Konkani was recognized as one of the country's official languages. Goa emerged as a tourist hub soon after its independence and was a mecca in the hippie era. Today, it remains a predominantly tourism-run economy.

PLANNING YOUR TIME

If you intend to do a thorough exploration, set aside about a week for Panaji and interior Goa. While the city itself may be covered in a day or two, the surrounding beaches of Miramar and Dona Paula, and islands like Divar and Chorao, merit a longer visit. It is possible to see

Old Goa and visit a spice plantation and the temples around Ponda in a single day, using Panaji as base. However, for a leisurely and in-depth experience in these parts, visitors often base themselves in the wildlife sanctuaries for a few days of birdlife and nature. If you're a beach enthusiast who's merely curious about the sights here, three or four days should be enough time for you to soak in the landscape before you move on to the sunny coast.

Interior Goa is both beautiful and inaccessible during the monsoon months (June–Sept.). River cruises from the Mandovi jetty in Panaji are suspended and irregular ferries ply to the islands of Chorao and Divar, depending on the weather. The sanctuaries may be open (entry is usually at your own risk) but the Dudhsagar Falls within the Bhagwan Mahavir Sanctuary and Molem National Park are closed. While the greenery is worth braving the rain for, it may not be all that practical to make a trip into the hinterland, as you could find yourself stranded in a heavy downpour with little or no mobile network coverage for long stretches. However, if you want to avail of the cheap monsoon rates at hotels and don't mind being indoors for long periods of time, this is a great time for bargains. In peak season, visitors often plan their visit around the Goa Carnival, which takes place in Panaji in February.

PANAJI AND INTERIOR GOA

Panaji (Panjim)

A visit to Goa's capital city of Panaji will prove that there's more to this destination than sand and sea. Those who venture beyond the beaches discover a tiny city whose riverine landscape and charming neighborhoods are its main attractions. The Latin quarter of Fontainhas and its neighboring Sao Tome are the finest representatives of Portuguese Goa—with crooked lanes and narrow alleys lined with cheerfully painted houses that show off traditional oyster-shell windows and hand-painted *azulejo* tiles. Nearby, the posh residential area of Altinho Hill gives visitors a wonderful view of the city. Meanwhile, the city's most significant structure—the Church of Our Lady of the Immaculate Conception—looms large over Church Square, casting its shadow over busy city streets. And nearby, as the sea gives way to the sinuous Mandovi River, the historic Old Secretariat undergoes its transformation into a museum that will, hopefully, represent Goan history better than the rather lackluster Goa State Museum.

On the outskirts of Panaji is the area of Campal, just before the areas of Miramar and Dona Paula. Here, the city's cultural hub, the Kala Academy, continues to preserve and showcase the artistic traditions of the state in a vibrant and stimulating atmosphere. And just as Panaji turns all notions of Goa around in your head, you visit the adjoining beaches of Miramar and Dona Paula, which make you realize that, in Goa, the sea is never really far behind.

SIGHTS
Church Square and Around

Panaji's historic Church Square is the very heart of the city. Here, the Church of Our Lady of the Immaculate Conception looks upon the bustle of everyday life in all its whitewashed glory. People from nearby offices rush past the Municipal Garden, browse through the old Singbal's Bookstore, and meander into the famous George restaurant. A short walk behind the church leads to the riverfront, the

© ASHIMA NARAIN

The Church of Our Lady of the Immaculate Conception is Panaji's most important landmark.

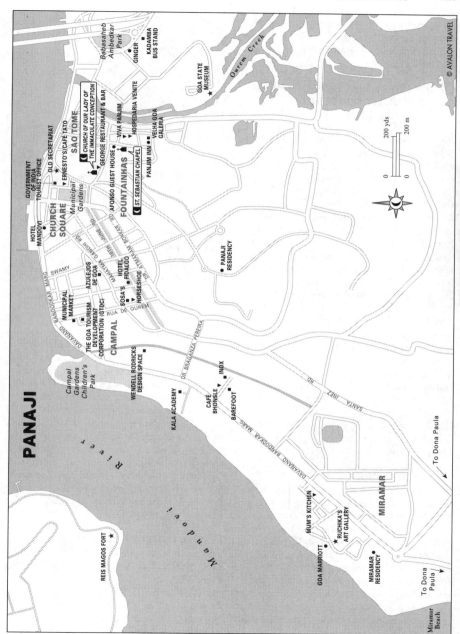

© AVALON TRAVEL

PANAJI

Mandovi River

REIS MAGOS FORT

Campal Gardens Children's Park

PANAJI

Ourem Creek

Babasaheb Ambedkar Park

GINGER

KADAMBA BUS STAND

GOA STATE MUSEUM

VIVA PANJIM

HOSPEDARIA VENITE

VELHA GOA GALERIA

GEORGE RESTAURANT & BAR

CHURCH OF OUR LADY OF THE IMMACULATE CONCEPTION

ERNESTO'S/CAFÉ TATO

SAO TOME

OLD SECRETARIAT

GOVERNMENT OF INDIA TOURIST OFFICE

AFONSO GUEST HOUSE

PANJIM INN

ST. SEBASTIAN CHAPEL

FOUNTAINHAS

PANAJI RESIDENCY

HOTEL MANDOVI

CHURCH SQUARE

Municipal Gardens

SWAMY

AZULEJOS DE GOA

HOTEL FIDALGO

SOSA'S

HORSESHOE

MAHATMA GANDHI RD

DR. DADA VAIDYA RD

18TH JUNE RD

RUA DE OUREM

MUNICIPAL MARKET

THE GOA TOURISM DEVELOPMENT CORPORATION (GTDC)

CAMPAL

BANDODKAR MARG

DAYANAND

WENDELL RODRICKS DESIGN SPACE

DR. BRAGANZA PEREIRA

KALA ACADEMY

CAFÉ BHONSLE

INOX

BAREFOOT

DAYANAND BANDODKAR MARG

SANTA INEZ RD

To Dona Paula

MIRAMAR

MUM'S KITCHEN

RUCHIKA'S ART GALLERY

GOA MARRIOTT

MIRAMAR RESIDENCY

To Dona Paula

Miramar Beach

200 yds

200 m

busy area by the Mandovi River that's home to the Old Secretariat, other historic buildings, and numerous hotels—and where cruise boats and ferries depart.

☾ CHURCH OF OUR LADY OF THE IMMACULATE CONCEPTION

Goa's defining landmark, the Church of Our Lady of the Immaculate Conception, or **Panjim Church** (9 a.m.–12:30 p.m. and 3:30–5:30 p.m. weekdays and 11 a.m.–12:30 p.m. and 3:30–5 p.m. Sun. and holidays), as it is commonly known, is an imposing structure that presides over the honking cars and bikes in the bustling Church Square area. Overlooking the tourist office, Singbal's bookstore, and the everyday sights of Panaji, the church was where Portuguese sailors said a prayer of thanks after a safe journey across the seas. Built in 1541 and renovated in 1619, the structure was bestowed its unique identity with the addition of a striking staircase in 1870. Red laterite steps lead in an attractive zigzag pattern to the white facade that houses the giant church bell, once hung in St. Augustine's Church in Old Goa. The stark simplicity of the whitewashed exterior is in contrast with interior of the church, where gilded Baroque decorations vie with marble statues, ornate chandeliers, and plastic flowers. The church has three altars—dedicated to the Virgin Mary, Jesus, and Our Lady of the Rosary—as well as a chapel of St. Francis Xavier. Mass is held daily in English, Konkani, and Portuguese.

OLD SECRETARIAT

The yellow-and-white building along the riverfront known as the Old Secretariat was once the luxurious summer palace of the ruler Adil Shah. The building dates to the 16th century and is the oldest standing building in Panaji. The Portuguese used the building as a Viceregal Lodge, and referred to it as "Idalcao's Palace"—a Portuguese corruption of the erstwhile ruler's name. Until recently, the Old Secretariat housed the Goan Assembly and government offices; it is currently being renovated and there are plans to transform it into a museum.

© ASHIMA NARAIN

A sculpture commemmorates Goa's famous hypnotist-priest, Abbé Faria, near the Old Secretariat.

Alongside the Old Secretariat is the intriguing sculpture of what appears to be a man attempting to strangle a woman. This statue actually depicts one of Goa's most famous priests hypnotizing a subject. The priest, Abbé Faria, was among the first to exercise the power of suggestion known as hypnosis. A resident of Candolim who found himself in prestigious institutions in Europe and later in the thick of the French Revolution, the Abbé cut a sensational figure in 18th-century Europe. A contemporary of Anton Mesmer, whose name is now synonymous with hypnosis, Faria was even fictionalized by Alexandre Dumas in *The Count of Monte Cristo.*

INSTITUTE MENEZES BRAGANZA

The Institute Menezes Braganza (tel. 0832/242-5730, 9:30 A.M.–1:15 P.M. and 2 P.M.–5:45 P.M. daily, closed on second Sat. of the month, membership fee Rs 200) is located above the unassuming Central Library, east of the Old Secretariat. Its main attraction is a blue-and-white *azulejo* mural depicting the Portuguese colonization of the East. Founded in 1832, the library is the oldest in India and has an interesting collection of rare books from the 18th century. The Institute was previously called Institute Vasco da Gama, but was renamed after Goan freedom fighter Menezes Braganza.

Fontainhas and Sao Tome

A heritage area located behind Patto Bridge and overlooking Ourem Creek, the old Latin quarter of Fontainhas is a maze of narrow alleys with names such as Rua de Ourem and Rua de Natal. Lined with quaint houses painted in bright terra-cotta, amber, and blue, this heritage district is named after the natural fountains, or springs, in the area. Ideal for an amble, the cobblestone streets are marked by tiny houses-turned-restaurants with cheery balconies that overlook the narrow streets. Important Fontainhas landmarks include the

post-siesta in Fontainhas

St. Sebastian Chapel; a wishing well and the egg-yolk yellow Afonso guesthouse alongside the chapel add to the charm. The Panjim Inn and Panjim Pousada, once grand Fontainhas homes, have been restored to their former glory as heritage hotels—and are worth a look from the inside.

The 300-year-old Panjim Inn makes for a good starting point for a leisurely walk along the winding lanes. Back alleys house the Velha Goa Galeria (with its collection of hand-painted *azulejo* tiles), an arts center called Gallery Gitanjali (part of Panjim Inn), and a Portuguese-funded foundation called the Fundaçao Oriente that originally supported itself with the gambling incomes of Macau. A short walk away is Altinho Hill, home to the chief minister and the archbishop (who resides in the grand archbishop's palace). The Maruti Temple located at the top of the hillock commands a fine view of the city.

Alongside Fontainhas is Sao Tome, another heritage quarter. Located alongside Rua de Ourem creek, Sao Tome is a picturesque extension of Fontainhas with its brightly colored Mediterranean-style houses, offices, and news presses that seem incongruous with the rest of Panaji city. Its church pre-dates the St. Sebastian Chapel and lies near the Head Post Office, formerly a tobacco trade house, and the building alongside that was once the mint. The open area in front of the post office and mint was the site of public executions during Portuguese times. It was here that the masterminds of the unsuccessful Pinto Revolt—where members of the Goan clergy from the Pinto family protested against racial prejudice—were executed in 1843.

◀ ST. SEBASTIAN CHAPEL

A Fontainhas landmark, the St. Sebastian Chapel (St. Sebastian Rd., tel. 0832/242-0448) is more than 125 years old. Its unusual wooden crucifix, which depicts Christ with his eyes open, was witness to the horrific inquisitions at the Palace of Inquisitions in Old Goa. The chapel is filled with collectibles and relics from the churches of Old Goa—including the images of

The St. Sebastian Chapel in Fontainhas is filled with relics from the churches of Old Goa.

St. Joseph and Our Lady of Livramento that were part of St. Joseph's Church, which that once stood in the old capital. A statue of Mary and three intricately designed screens from a church in the erstwhile Portuguese territory of Diu, in the Gujarat region, are other items of interest here. The chapel is open only for mass in the mornings (7–7:45 A.M. daily in Konkani, 8:30–9:15 A.M. Sun. in English) and for sightseeing once a week (7:45–8:30 A.M. Sun).

BISHOP'S PALACE

Bishop's Palace is a sprawling property located atop the quiet Altinho Hill, and is the archbishop's residence. Built in 1894, it has 12 crosses to depict the Stations of the Cross, in memory of Christ's walk to his crucifixion. The grandeur of the whitewashed palace with its silver-shining statue of Christ was originally meant to symbolize the rise of the archbishop to a patriarch. The entrance also bears the coat of arms of Goa's first patriarch, Dom Antonio Sebastio Valente. The palace may be admired from the outside (entry is prohibited), and a

Christmas mass held in the open courtyard every year allows visitors.

MARUTI TEMPLE

High up on Altinho Hill, the Maruti Temple (dawn–dusk daily, photography prohibited inside the temple, open to all faiths) is a Hindu shrine dedicated to the simian bachelor god known as Lord Hanuman or Maruti. An unspectacular building but for its location, the white marble steps lead up to the central shrine and offer a bird's-eye view of the city. The temple makes for a beautiful sight at night, with its twinkling lights and waving orange flag. Thousands throng this place of worship during the Maruti Fair in February.

MAHALAXMI TEMPLE

At the base of Altinho Hill, on Dada Vaidya Road, is the historic Mahalaxmi Temple (6:30 A.M.–9:30 P.M., photography prohibited inside the temple, open to all faiths). People selling religious souvenirs and flowers line the entrance, beseeching you to make offerings to the deity. The inside of the temple resembles an ordinary community hall and provides escape from the afternoon sun to students and young people from the neighborhood. Surrounding the temple are smaller shrines dedicated to other deities from the Hindu pantheon.

The liberal Portuguese governor Conde De Rio Pardo permitted the construction of the Mahalaxmi temple—making this the first Hindu temple to be allowed by the Portuguese after 300 years of religious persecution. Built in 1818, it was renovated to its current marble-and-concrete state in 1983. The deity had been previously housed in Taleigaon village and then moved to Bicholim in the 16th century to protect it from the Portuguese. It lay hidden there for centuries until a resident of Panaji, Narayan Kamat Mhamai, discovered it and brought it home. Today, the original shrine is stored in a box in the sanctum sanctorum, alongside the newer idol.

GOA STATE MUSEUM

Located in the Patto area, the State Museum

© JANHAVI ACHAREKAR

Bishop's Palace, the archbishop's residence, crowns Panaji's Altinho Hill.

(EDC Complex, southwest of Kadamba bus stand, tel. 0832/243-8006, www.goamuseum.nic.in, 9:30 A.M.–5:30 P.M. Mon.–Fri., free, photography permitted) is an uninviting building that wears a vacant look. Its 14 galleries housing artifacts and paintings are disappointingly bare; the only saving grace, perhaps, is the massive spot-lit wooden chariot from Chandreshwar at Quepem, which occupies pride of place at the center of the lower floor. The sculpture gallery showcases a collection of Hindu archeological findings from Goa, as well as Jain bronzes and stone sculptures dating to the 11th century A.D. There is also a Christian art gallery, a modest numismatics gallery, and an interesting lottery draw machine imported from Portugal in 1947. In the furniture gallery lies the infamous table of the Goa Inquisition that was initiated, ironically, by the state's most venerated figure—St. Francis Xavier. It was on this table that terrible punishments were meted out against Hindus for practicing religious rituals.

The museum also has two art galleries that display paintings by renowned Goans and other Indian artists. The corridors are lined with a display of photographs that include an image captioned "Symbolic Way of Carrying Arrested Thief."

Campal

From the riverfront, it's an easy drive through widening roads to the elite neighborhood of Campal—the last Panaji locality before you hit the beaches of Miramar and Dona Paula. Grand old colonial homes and designer boutiques line up opposite the picturesque Campal Children's Park. Nearby is Panaji's cultural hub—the Kala Academy—where you can catch local *tiatr* (theater), music and dance performances, and art shows by prominent Goan artists and others. There is also a small garden on the premises where you can gaze upon the river.

CAMPAL CHILDREN'S PARK

A lovely piece of landscape in an urban setting, the Campal Children's Park is a long stretch of sand and casuarina trees swaying on the banks of the river. The park makes for a pleasant stroll in the evenings and is a popular hangout with families and young people. The swings and slides are a hit with children from Panaji and the nearby areas of Miramar and Dona Paula.

ENTERTAINMENT AND EVENTS

Panaji lacks the vibrant and varied nightlife of the Goan beaches, but it makes up for it with its floating casinos and active cultural scene. The cruise-ship casino *Caravela* provides nightly entertainment with blackjack and live music. The Goa Tourism Development Corporation (GTDC) runs themed cruises, which are often full in the peak season—but if you're not one for loud music and raucous crowds, it's best to stick to some of the city's pleasant restaurants and bars. Culture vultures will be delighted with events at the Kala Academy, and even if you're not quite familiar with the local language, it's worth going to a short performance of the traditional vaudeville-style theater called *tiatr,* or to one of the many local music festivals.

The capital also celebrates major festivals, both religious and cultural. The popular **Goa Carnival,** undoubtedly Goa's biggest tourist draw, is the time to see the capital at its festive (and crowded) best. For the last few years, Panaji has been the venue of choice for the International Film Festival of India (IFFI)—when the best of world cinema is screened at the city's snazziest cinema hall, INOX, as well as at the Kala Academy and the nearby beach of Miramar.

Nightlife

After dark, Panaji's riverfront lights up as its many cruise boats and floating casinos twinkle in the dark waters. On the river, food, entertainment, and sightseeing are rolled into one as visitors enjoy good food, music, and the city's many sights by night.

The Goa Tourism Development Corporation (GTDC) conducts **"Festive Nights on Board"** cruises (8:45–10:45 P.M., Rs 450, includes dinner buffet) on its two boats—the *Santa Monica* and the *Shantadurga.* There's live music and traditional Goan dances onboard as the boats circle the river. GTDC also organizes hour-long **sunset and sundown cruises** (departures at 6, 6:30, 7:15, and 7:45 P.M. daily, Rs 150) and a **dinner cruise** (8:30–10:30 P.M. Wed. and Sat., Rs 400, includes snacks and dinner buffet).

Hour-long evening river cruises are also conducted by **Emerald Waters Cruises** (near

© ASHIMA NARAIN

Dancers add to the festivity at the three-day Goa Carnival.

GOA'S BIG THREE

Goa has produced an illustrious lot of artists and achievers who have been received by the country and the world with much critical acclaim. Among the first to be noticed outside of the state, cartoonist **Mario Miranda** is a Goan legend. His goggle-eyed characters may be seen across the state, framed as paintings, found as murals, or reproduced as ceramic tiles. Educated in Mumbai and England, Miranda began work with an advertising agency before he shot to fame as a cartoonist with the *Illustrated Weekly of India* and then with the *Times of India*. His characters – such as Miss Nimbupani (Miss Lemonade) – were dearly loved by Indian readers and he brought alive through his art the people of Goa and Mumbai. A large Mario mural may be seen in popular Café Mondegar in downtown Mumbai, and his cartoons have also featured in international publications such as *MAD* and *Punch*. With several books and awards to his credit, the artist now leads a reclusive life with his family in his beautiful ancestral casa in the Goan village of Loutolim.

If there's any contemporary Goan to have made a name for himself in Goa, India, and abroad, it has to be fashion designer **Wendell Rodericks.** In keeping with his belief that one must bring something of one's own culture and identity into fashion, his clothes capture the essence of Goa, reflecting its breezy feel, seaside nature, and mood of *sossegarde* with flowing whites and minimalist linens. Inspired by "yoga, Ayurveda, and Gandhi," Wendell's creations are non-elitist and ecofriendly. His affordable prices and vegetable and natural dyes (created with old and forgotten recipes) contribute toward the development and environmental protection of the state, as part of a larger ecological program. As chairman of Green Goa Works – a nonprofit environmental organization – the designer is involved with major Goan issues, ranging from garbage management to fighting internal inimical forces to preserve the Goan way of life. Tourism and natural beauty go hand in hand, believes the designer. "If we don't preserve the environment then tourism is lost, and at the same time, tourism must respect the environment," he says, pointing out that children residing along the northern beach of Anjuna cannot study at night because of the noisy raves on that stretch – and that residents in the tourist-populated parts of Goa are facing a scarcity of fish, which is first supplied to the many hotels and restaurants there.

Meanwhile, the popularity of singer **Remo Fernandes** may have waned but this rock musician was among the first Goan songwriters and composers to cut an album, as well as to have public performances of Western-style rock and pop music, and Indian fusion. Fernandes was an 1980s icon with his albums *Pack that Smack* and *Bombay City,* and was known for his socio-political lyrics and influences of world music. He created original soundtracks for Bollywood films and has performed with Led Zeppelin and Jethro Tull in concert. Based in Siolim, Goa, the singer continues to write and compose songs, although to a vastly diminished audience.

National Theatre, tel. 0832/243-1192, departure 6:15, 7:30 and 8:45 P.M. daily mid-Oct.–Apr., Rs 150) and **Royal Cruises** (below Mandovi Bridge, tel. 0832/243-7887, departure 6, 7:15 and 8:30 P.M. daily mid-Oct.–Apr., Rs 150). The boats depart from the Santa Monica jetty and include entertainment in the form of cultural programs, live music, or DJs.

Panaji's hot nightspots, however, are its cruise-ship casinos, which are dominated by domestic tourists armed with wads of notes. These are Goa's only live gaming casinos (the state prohibits on-shore live gaming). The ships cruise up and down the Mandovi River, leaving behind a trail of music and fairy lights reflected in the water. The pioneer among these is the **MS *Caravela*** (Fisheries Jetty, Dayanand Bandodkar Marg, tel. 0832/223-4044, sales@casinogoa.biz), which operates all-night dinner cruises (embarkation 7:30–8:30 P.M., returns to the jetty every hour throughout the night, final return at 6 A.M., entry fee Rs 1,500 Mon.–Thurs. and Rs 1,800 Fri.–Sat., includes dinner buffet and drinks, children not allowed). You can try your hand at roulette, blackjack, baccarat, poker, and slot machines (gaming limits range Rs 100–50,000). There's live music, a restaurant, a sun deck, and a suite for celebrity guests. The 66-meter ship accommodates up to 300 guests, but a strict dress code denies entry to those in shorts, cropped pants, or sandals. There's also a two-hour sunset cruise (embarkation time 5–5:15 P.M., entry fee Rs 600 adults and RS 300 children Mon.–Thurs., adults Rs 750 and children Rs 350, Fri.–Sat., Rs 200 extra to entry casino, includes snack buffet and drinks) for those who want to make a quick buck or simply enjoy the view.

All cruise services are suspended in the monsoon season, and the floating casinos, although operational, are safely docked at the jetty.

The Arts

Goa's tradition of the arts is well represented at Panaji's **Kala Academy** (Dayanand Bandodkar Marg, Campal, tel. 0832/242-0451, 9 A.M.–9 P.M. daily). The state's leading cultural institution hosts a variety of events, ranging from classical music (both Indian and Western) and dance concerts to art exhibits and theater. There's no better place than Kala Academy to experience Goa's famous *tiatr* (traditional theater). Faux balconies with caricature cutouts of *tiatr*'s diverse audience lend to the ambience of the auditorium within this sprawling cultural complex. The art gallery hosts exhibits and also conducts workshop, while an open arena by the river is used as a venue for cultural activities and the sale of handicrafts. There's an amphitheater and a number of auditoria for cultural events. The Academy also conducts courses in Indian classical dance and music, and in Western classical music. It hosts several arts festivals, including the Kesarbai Kerkar Music Festival; Monte Music Festival; *tiatr* festivals and competitions; and the Pop, Beat & Jazz Music Festival.

The heritage quarter of Fontainhas is the ideal location for an art gallery. **Gallery Gitanjali** (E-212, 31st January Rd., Fontainhas, tel. 0832/222-6523, www.gallerygitanjali.com, 9:30 A.M.–7 P.M. daily) is a lovely space housed in the heritage building of "Panjim People's," whose doors are always open to passersby. A part of the Panjim Inn complex, this art gallery exhibits the works of both Indian and foreign artists. Its objets d'art often spill over into the hotel premises of Panjim Inn and Panjim Pousada and the trail continues well into the dining areas and even the rooms. The gallery is also a popular venue for book launches and other cultural events.

In the beautiful riverfront location of Campal, Panaji's four-screen, stadium-style cinema hall, **INOX** (Old GMC Heritage precinct, Dayanand Bandodkar Rd., Campal, tel. 0832/242-0999, goa@inox.co.in) is located in the heritage neighborhood of the 150 year old Goa Medical College. It screens the latest movies, and is the venue for Goa's famous film festival, IFFI.

Festivals and Events
FONTAINHAS FESTIVAL

The Fontainhas Festival is an eight-day arts festival that celebrates the heritage and culture of the Latin quarter. Held in January or February, the festival is a medley of art and music and is unique in that private homes are turned to art galleries, showcasing the works of local and other renowned artists. The festival attracts hordes of tourists every year, who also come for its vibrant live performances by artistes such as Goa's premier musician, Remo Fernandes. The festival is at once large and intimate, giving tourists a first-hand experience of the famous Fontainhas charm and a peep inside both its history and its daily life.

MARUTI FAIR

Every temple in Goa celebrates an annual *zatra* (fair)—a time when the idol of the temple deity is brought out in a wooden chariot or procession. Stalls selling trinkets, religious souvenirs, and food are set up in the temple premises and it is a time for merrymaking and religiosity all at once. The Maruti Temple on Altinho Hill, dedicated to the bachelor monkey-god Lord Hanuman, celebrates the temple festival, the Maruti Fair, in February. People from around the state throng the brightly colored temple with its triumphant flags that overlook the city.

SHIGMO

Shigmo heralds spring, celebrating the arrival of the season with colorful processions on the streets of Panaji around the month of March. Shigmo is similar to Holi, the festival of color, which is celebrated in other parts of the country. Shigmo is observed over a period of five days, and colored powder—known as *gulal*—is playfully smeared on the faces of revelers on the fifth day of the celebration. Processions are led by competing bands playing traditional musical instruments and are enlivened with floats and folk dances from across the state.

SAO JOAO

Sao Joao, the feast of St. John the Baptist, is a fun festival celebrated across Goa on June 24. Young boys wearing laurels on their heads leap into village wells while clutching bottles of *feni,* the local brew, in their hands. The festival commemorates the story of St. John jumping with excitement when still in his mother's womb, in anticipation of the birth of Jesus (the news of which the Virgin Mary had come to share with her cousin, his mother). On this day, girls are given fruit baskets by their mothers and this merry procession is also accompanied by wooden boats that set sail in nearby waters.

GANESH CHATURTI

Mumbai's biggest festival is also one of Goa's most-awaited celebrations. Ganesh festivities here tend to be more private, however, with fewer public or community *pandals* (tents) than in Mumbai. The festival falls around the time of the harvesting season in Goa, in August–September, making it a dual celebration of sorts. Religious songs, cymbals, and drums accompany the immersion of the idol at the end of the 10-day period. After the festival, beaches

are often awash with marigold flowers from the immersion celebrations and handcrafted Ganesh idols made of cane that have drifted back to shore.

FEAST OF OUR LADY OF THE IMMACULATE CONCEPTION

This three-day feast is held on December 8 every year. Goa's most important church is brightly lit with beautiful lights at night, accentuating the zigzag pattern of its magnificent steps. By day, Church Square is transformed with a profusion of stalls selling religious trinkets, sweets, and handicrafts. Devotees flock from all over to celebrate the miraculous conception of Jesus by the Virgin Mary. In addition to the fair, the church also conducts a special service.

MUSIC FESTIVALS

The Kala Academy (Dayanand Bandodkar Marg, Campal, tel. 0832/242-0451) hosts a number of music festivals, ranging from Indian classical music to jazz. The **Kesarbai Kerkar Music Festival,** held in November, brings together some of the most renowned classical Indian musicians and vocalists. Recitals are accompanied with dance performances by acclaimed artists.

The two-day **Pop, Beat and Jazz Music Festival,** held in February, also draws big crowds. Local bands play and compete with each other at the Kala Academy, showcasing Goa's musical talent. The Academy also helps organize the spectacular Monte Music Festival held at the Chapel of Our Lady of the Mount in Old Goa.

GOA HERITAGE FESTIVAL

This event is held over two days in the heritage precinct of Campal. Organized by the Department of Tourism together with the Goa Heritage Action Group, this cultural festival exhibits the artworks of local artists in its colorful, historical backdrop. Goan music and folk dances form an important aspect of the celebrations, as do the various traditional delicacies that are served here. Proceeds from the festival are then plowed back into the maintenance of heritage structures.

SHOPPING

While Panaji lacks the shopping options that Mumbai has to offer, its stores and markets offer the ambience of a quaint town. Colorful old residences-turned-stores decorated with hand-painted ceramic *azulejo* tiles and winding wooden staircases lead up to local artifacts and designer clothes. A throbbing municipal market displays its sense of humor with Mario Miranda cartoons on its walls. A vibrant street brings you the vast Goan produce of cashew nuts and sweetens your palate with *bebinca*.

Panaji's claim to fame on the handicrafts front lies not in its government-run emporia but in its *azulejo* boutiques. The blue-and-white flourishes on ceramic nameplates and colorful floral motifs seen across Goa are the happier products of Portuguese colonization. A Persian creation adopted by the Spanish and the Portuguese, the traditional *azulejo* tile has come to represent Goan art. The hand-painted, glazed ceramic tiles are available at select places in the form of framed art, murals, coasters, and other innovative items that make for great souvenirs.

© JANHAVI ACHAREKAR

Goan cartoonist Mario Miranda's mural at Panaji's Municipal Market

Shopping Districts and Markets

In spite of the designer boutiques and sophisticated shopping options that Panaji has to offer, its most vibrant markets are the traditional ones. The **Municipal Market** (Dayanand Bandodkar Marg, 6 A.M.–7 P.M. daily) is where you will find everything from local produce to electronic gadgets. However, its most interesting features are the large and colorful Mario Miranda murals that mirror the activity and buzz of the market, caricaturing its noisy fish and vegetable vendors, tourists, and buyers. The two-level market is occupied by vendors selling fresh fruit and greens, local flowers, fish, pickles, spices, and preserves on the lower level; the upper level has stalls selling toys, clothes, shoes, and mobile phones. The market is especially popular for its mangoes and fresh catch of tiger prawns, crab, squid, lobster, mackerel, shark, and local varieties of fish.

A long street lined with shops and stalls, **18th June Road** offers a variety of treats ranging from cashew nuts to Goan sweets, masalas, books, and handicrafts. Named after a protest launched against the Portuguese government in 1946, the street is located in the city center, parallel to MG Road and extending right up to the Municipal Garden. Always bustling with activity, it is a good place to visit if you're looking to stock up on your curries and spices or carry home some *bebinca*.

Art, Books, and Handicrafts

Panjim Art Gallery (Church Square, opposite Municipal Garden, cell tel. 91/98221-68703, panjimartgallery@gmail.com, 10 A.M.–1 P.M. and 3–7:30 P.M. Mon.–Sat., 10 A.M.–1 P.M. Sun.) is a modest, inconspicuous place near the church that exhibits and sells works of well-known and emerging Goan artists.

Velha Goa Galeria (next to Panjim Inn, Rua de Ourem, tel. 0832/242-6628,

9:30 A.M.–1 P.M. and 3–7:30 P.M. Mon.–Sat.) is the place for traditional handpainted *azulejo* tiles and nameplates, glassware, and ceramic souvenirs. The gallery doesn't ship outside of Goa, so if you like the lovely latticed ceramic tiles fitted snugly on wood (which make unusual table tops), you'll have to lug them home yourself.

A delightful residential gallery, **Azulejos de Goa** (MG Rd., opposite Club National, next to sales tax office, tel. 0832/243-1900, cell tel. 91/98509-30253, www.azulejosdegoa.com, 9:30 A.M.–6:30 P.M. Mon.–Sat.) is the home and exhibition space of *azulejo* artist Orlando de Noronha. Colorful *azulejo* murals cheer up the exterior of the house and street, while the interior exhibits the artist's own work as well as that of other local artists. You can browse through the catalog, buy smaller *azulejos* at reasonable rates, or commission the artist to create some especially for you. Noronha learned his art in Lisbon—the homeland of the *azulejo* tile—and much of the *azulejo* art that you see in and around Goa is his handiwork. Noronha

has also taken to customizing crockery, reproduced in the style of old Macau, and emblazoned with the buyer's family name.

The government-run handicrafts emporium **Aparant** (Crafts Complex, Neugi Nagar, Rua de Ourem, tel. 0832/222-8157, goahandicrafts@sify.com, 9:30 A.M.–1 P.M. and 2–6 P.M. Mon.–Sat.) has several branches across the city that house a disappointing collection of seashell, lacquer, and coir souvenirs in the form of key-chains, clocks, lamps, and curios. It has the odd piece of furniture, *azulejo* tiles, and some junk jewelry as well.

A quaint old store that sells all kinds of musical instruments, **Pedro Fernandes & Co.** (near Head Post Office, tel. 0832/222-6642, musicdoctor@rediffmail.com, 9 A.M.–7:30 P.M. Mon.–Sat.) is a tiny place. Here you can find guitars and drums, as well as Indian instruments like the cymbals, sitar, and rare *santoor* and *sarod*. You can exchange old for new at a nominal rate or buy second-hand. The clientele comes from all over the world.

Singbal's Book House (Church Square,

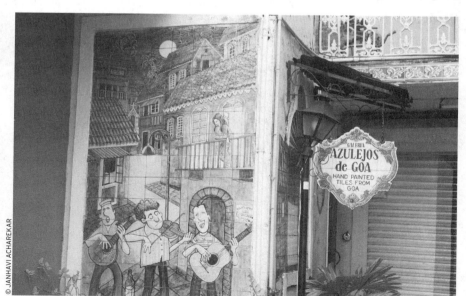

Azulejo artist Orlando de Noronha displays his talent at his home studio.

tel. 0832/242-5747, singbalbookouse36@
rediffmail.com, 9:30 A.M.–1 P.M. and 3:30–
7:30 P.M. Mon.–Sat.) is another old Panaji favorite. Established in the 1940s, this bookstore,
located opposite the church, retains its old-
world charm—complete with original name
board and whirring fans. In keeping with the
archaic decor, customers are not allowed entry
into the books section but are attended instead
by the staff, who present options on a counter. Works of fiction and non-fiction, as well
as books of academic interest and textbooks
are available, and there is a small circulatory
library section too.

If you're looking for specific books on
Goa, **Bookfair** (Hotel Mandovi, Dayanand
Bandodkar Marg, tel. 0832/222-4405,
9:30 A.M.–1 P.M. and 2:30–9 P.M., daily) is a
tiny but popular bookstore in town. You'll find
plenty of literature on the history, culture and
fiction of Goa and a small collection of children's books as well. The helpful staff will aid
you in your search for anything ranging from
academic to travel writing.

Boutiques and Designer Stores

An old Goan home converted into a specialty
boutique, **Barefoot** (1/26, 31st January Rd.,
tel. 0832/243-6815, barefootgoa@sancharnet.
in, 10 A.M.–8 P.M. Mon.–Sat.) presents a small
but charming collection of home decor items
and Indian apparel. The home stuff is typically Goan, with ceramic tiles, Jesus figurines,
wooden furniture items, and curios such as
lamps and candlestands in glass and mosaic.

If you missed out on it during your
visit to Mumbai, **Bombay Store** (5/214,
Rua de Natal, Mala, Fontainhas, tel.
0832/223-0223, www.thebombaystore.com,
10:30 A.M.–8 P.M. daily) has a new outlet
in Panaji's pretty Fontainhas area. You'll
find a wide range of artifacts, herbal teas,
home decor, and jewelry, as well as Indian
and Western wear. The original outlet in
Mumbai is of historical significance and
associated with freedom fighters and leaders of the pre-Independence era. Previously
called Bombay Swadeshi, it specialized

© ASHIMA NARAIN

**Goan designers display their creations at
Sosa's.**

in indigenous items to aid the boycott of
British and foreign goods.

Sosa's (E 245, Rua de Ourem, tel.
0832/222-8063, 10 A.M.–7 P.M. Mon.–Sat.)
is a chic designer boutique that showcases
the creations of Goan designers and others. A
glass-and-silk entrance leads to designer wear
juxtaposed with black-and-white photos. There
are plenty of cottons, linen, and beads—perfect for the Goan climate. Look out for the
seasonal collection of Goan designer Savio Jon,
among others. Although pricey, there's an exclusive range of outré creations for both men
and women here.

The showcase of Goa's premier designer,
Wendell Rodricks Design Space (158, near
Luis Gomes Garden, Campal, tel. 0832/223-
8177, www.wendellrodricks.com, 10 A.M.–6:30
P.M. Mon.–Sat.) is a lovely old Goan home-
turned-boutique where the vast white space
offsets the trademark white creations. Rodricks
is known for his bold whites and pastels, cool
linens and cottons. He has also created a special line of designer bed linen for well-known

Indian brand Bombay Dyeing. His bedroom creations are available at all Bombay Dyeing outlets and major department stores. The designer is also known for his active role in the preservation of Goan heritage, culture, and the environment. His latest collection is made of eco-friendly materials using vegetable and other natural dyes, including skirts dyed with guava leaves.

SPORTS AND RECREATION

The city's old quarters make for wonderful self-guided walking and cycling tours, taking the unsuspecting visitor through narrow alleys and heritage homes with bright colors and tiled roofs. On the riverfront, a number of operators conduct river cruises. The government-run Goa Tourism Development Corporation (GTDC) also conducts themed and guided river tours for tourists, ranging from dolphin cruises to Goa-by-night tours. However, all riverside activity comes to a stop during the monsoon months between June and October when the waters are rough and the downpour is torrential.

Cruise ships and ferries traverse the Mandovi River.

River Cruises

The Mandovi River is a hub of activity with its ferries, cruises, and floating casinos. **GTDC** (Santa Monica jetty, tel. 0832/243-7496, www .goa-tourism.com, 9:30 A.M.–1:15 P.M. and 2–5:45 P.M. Mon.–Fri.) organizes a number of river cruises that depart from the Panaji jetty, going down the Mandovi and into the Zuari Bay or up to Aldona and to a mineral water spring. The **Dolphin Cruise** (8:30–10:30 A.M. Wed., Sat., and Sun., Rs 250, includes refreshments) takes visitors to areas where they can view sea dolphins and muddy-brown river dolphins at close quarters. Similarly, the **"Backwater Thrills"** cruise (9:30 A.M.–4 P.M. Tue. and Fri., Rs 700, includes refreshments and lunch) leads tourists through thick mangroves into the river's deep end—to Chorao and Divar Islands as well as to Old Goa. The cruise includes a visit to the Savoi Spice Plantation, where a traditional meal is served on banana leaves.

Bird-Watching Tours

GTDC (Santa Monica jetty, tel. 0832/243-7496, www.goa-tourism.com, 9:30 A.M.–1:15 P.M. and 2–5:45 P.M. Mon.–Fri.) used to regularly conduct two special river tours for bird-watchers and nature enthusiasts: **"Wings & Fins"** took visitors to Dr. Salim Ali Bird Sanctuary at Chorao Island, while the **"Birds & Breakfast"** tour took guests down the Cumbarjua Canal, a short drive from Panaji, for sightings of Goa's rich bird life over breakfast. These tours were discontinued in 2008, but they are sometimes conducted by special request—depending on the number of passengers available.

Backwoods Camp (Matkan, Tambdi Surla, cell tel. 91/98221-39859, www.backwoodsgoa.com, Rs 1,200–1,800), based in the Bhagwan Mahavir Sanctuary, conducts a three-hour cruise up the Zuari River and into the Cumbarjua Canal, for sightings of the elusive collared kingfisher and other birds, the Indian crocodile, and the Indo-Pacific hump-backed dolphin. Prices include pick-up and drop-off between Panjim, Calangute, Baga, and Arpora.

Guided Tours

GTDC (tel. 0832/243-7496, www.goa-tourism.com) also conducts a number of guided tours departing from Panaji. These include numerous day trips to North Goa, South Goa, and Dudhsagar Falls, as well as themed church and temple tours. There's also the special **"Goa by Night"** tour (6:30–9:30 P.M., Rs 200) that begins with a sunset cruise on the Mandovi and takes you through the city's nocturnal sights and its beautifully lit monuments—the Old Secretariat, the Church of Our Lady of Immaculate Conception, the Maruti Temple, and the twinkling lights of the city seen from the top of Altinho Hill.

ACCOMMODATIONS

Panaji has a good mix of budget hotels, high-end stays,, and charming heritage options. All hotels in Goa adjust their rates according to the season; the year is divided into low season (Jun–Sept.), high season (Oct.–Dec. 23 and Jan. 3–May), and the Christmas/New Year period (Dec. 24–Jan. 2), where tariffs are even higher. Taxes are charged separately, and rates, in general, are subject to change without notice.

Church Square and Around
UNDER RS 1,000

Hotel Republica (opposite Old Secretariat, tel. 0832/222-4630, Rs 400–1,000) is easily recognized from the riverfront by the long, brightly colored staircase that leads up to this Goan home-turned-budget-hotel. An old house that looks like it has seen better days, Republica is popular with backpackers. It has damp walls and flaking paint, but the building has lovely old windows with a river view, and rooms are adequately large—although not exactly what you'd call luxurious. If you're on a budget trip, this place is a good value, especially during peak season.

RS 1,000–3,000

Located near the Old Secretariat and over-looking the Panaji jetty is the somber-looking GTDC-run **Panaji Residency** (MG Rd., tel. 0832/222-7103, www.goa-tourism.com, Rs 915–2,535). There are three types of rooms: those without air-conditioning, those with air-conditioning, and deluxe rooms (with a/c). While all rooms have pleasant balconies, living arrangements are simple and basic—the lower-priced double room without air-conditioning has damp walls and is less than aesthetic. The higher-priced rooms are a shade better and offer a partial river view. Ruchira, a popular terrace restaurant, is located on the premises, as are the Aparant handicrafts store and an Internet café. You can make bookings here for any of the GTDC guided tours and river cruises.

A pleasant mid-range alternative in the heart of the city, **Hotel Nova Goa** (Dr. Atmaram Borkar Rd., tel. 0832/222-6231, www.hotel-novagoa.com, Rs 2,300–4,200) has a swimming pool and in-house restaurant, and rooms are comfortable and equipped with modern amenities. The hotel has no great views, although the deluxe suites and some superior-category rooms do overlook the pool.

Ginger (Pato Complex, near Kadamba bus stand, tel. 0832/664-3333, www.gingerhotels.com, Rs 1,999–2,499) in the city center is part of India's new chain of no-frills hotels. The chain is unique for providing modern facilities with minimum fuss. Guests check themselves in at the self-check-in kiosk. Rooms are of three types—single, twin-bedded and double. All are contemporary in design and equipped with air-conditioning, mini-refrigerator, LCD TV, and coffeemaker. The hotel also has vending machines, currency-exchange facilities, an Internet zone, a gym, and a restaurant.

RS 3,000–10,000

Located in the busy shopping area of 18th June Road, the four-star **Ⓒ Hotel Fidalgo** (18th June Rd., tel. 0832/222-6291, www .hotelfidalgo-goa.com, Rs 2,300–15,500) is known better for its amenities than for an ambient location—but is a stone's throw, nevertheless, from the waterfront and other Panaji sights. The hotel is luxurious, especially for the price, and has a swimming pool, traditional health spa, and a cluster of six different restaurants under the umbrella of the "Fidalgo Food Enclave." Its 103 rooms are contemporary in design and come in club, premium, and executive classes—and all include complimentary breakfast.

Fontainhas and Sao Tome
UNDER RS 1,000

A charming Fontainhas home converted into a lodge, **Afonso Guest House** (near St. Sebastian Chapel, Fontainhas-Mala, tel. 0832/222-2359, Rs 800) is painted a bright yellow, with oyster-shell windows, *azulejo* tiles, and a lovely terrace. This pretty, well-maintained guesthouse continues to be part of a residential house and is run by the family that lives there. The rooms, unfortunately, are small

and do not carry the same look as the exterior, but are clean, comfortable, and well-kept, making this one of Panaji's best budget options.

RS 1,000-3,000

Panjim Inn and Panjim Pousada (E-212, 31st January Rd., tel. 0832/222-8136, www .panjiminn.com, Rs 990–3,600) are two lovely heritage hotels run by the Silveira-Sukhija family. Panjim Inn was the first Fontainhas home to be turned into a hotel (25 years ago), and its success inspired the establishment of the Panjim Pousada. The two are an interesting study in contrasts. Panjim Inn was built in the late 19th century by Francis Assis D'Silveira, a landed gentleman, and is a Portuguese-style house that belongs to the family. The Pousada, a 1930s home that belonged to the Hindu Ghanekar family, is a courtyard-style home purchased in later years. The houses are located next to each other and are filled with antique furniture and artifacts collected by the present owner over the years. Rosewood

© ASHIMA NARAIN

Panjim Inn in the Fontainhas area was the first heritage home to be turned into a hotel.

almirahs, four-poster beds, carved chairs, and marble-top tables retain the old character of the rooms. Old-world verandahs and balconies overlook the busy Fontainhas streets or the Ourem creek, while old family photographs and art works from Gallery Gitanjali—part of the Panjim Inn complex—adorn the walls. Across the street is the third and latest hotel in the complex, the Panjim Pousada. The three hotels share a restaurant and terrace café where the owner, Mr. Ajit Sukhija, and his son Jack often interact with guests. There's a wonderfully warm feeling to this well-managed heritage hotel complex, which often encourages visitors to extend their stay.

The Casa chain of boutique hotels also has a small heritage house-turned-hotel near the St. Sebastian's Chapel in Fontainhas. **Casa Fontainas** (tel. 0832/225-3205, cell tel. 91/99606-05416, www.casaboutiquehotels .com, Rs 3,000) only has two bedrooms, furnished with wooden antiques and restored to original glory. Ideal for a family or two couples looking for privacy, the place also has an in-house cook who rustles up authentic Goan dishes.

RS 3,000–10,000

◀ Panjim People's (E-212, 31st January Rd., tel. 0832/222-8136, www.panjiminn .com, Rs 4,500–7,200) lies just across the road from Panjim Inn and Panjim Pousada. Built in the 1880s, this exclusive heritage hotel was a prominent Fontainhas school until recently. There are only four rooms here, all of which are luxurious, complete with original artworks and lovely mosaic-tiled bathrooms. Large windows framed by gilded pelmets and lace curtains let in the morning sunlight, giving you a truly authentic Goan heritage experience. Gallery Gitanjali is housed on the ground floor.

Campal
RS 3,000–10,000

Once Panaji's leading hotel, **Hotel Mandovi** (Dayanand Bandodkar Marg, Campal, tel. 0832/222-4405, www.hotelmandovigoa .com, Rs 1,900–7,500) is not as high-end as

© ASHIMA NARAIN

Casa Fontainhas is another heritage hotel.

it used to be. Charming nonetheless, it gives the feel of an old Goan home in the comfort and convenience of a hotel. The Mandovi may have slipped down the price ladder and in star perception, but not in the quality of rooms and service, making it great value for money. Rooms are large, furnished with antiques and ornate mirrors, and painted in traditional Goan colors; the spacious deluxe suites offer a view of the river. The hotel has a bar called High Tide, a seafood restaurant by the name of Riorico, the A Pastelaria bakery, and a tiny but well-stocked bookshop called Bookfair.

FOOD

Panaji's setting—with its flowing river and ferries, winding lanes and colorful heritage districts—makes even the most run-down café appear romantic. The city eateries are proud of their heritage and are situated in old homes and charming districts with tiny, wooden balconies overlooking the riverside or busy streets. Coupled with the tantalizing curries and spices of Goan cuisine, this proves to be a heady combination. It's no wonder customers tend to extend their visit—often hanging around for a game of cards or for one more of the local King's beer—long after they've wolfed down a sumptuous meal.

Church Square

Some of the oldest and most established eateries in Goa are located in the bustling Church Square area. **George Restaurant & Bar** (near Mary Immaculate Conception Church, tel. 0832/242-6820, cell tel. 91/98224-87722, 11 A.M.–5 P.M. and 6–10:30 P.M. Mon.–Sat., mains Rs 50 and up) was established in 1957, when Goa was still under Portuguese rule, and it continues to provide excellent local cuisine at cheap prices. In the old days, customers (including the Portuguese) were known to keep monthly accounts at the restaurant, paying up only at the end of the month. Today, regulars frequent this place for breakfast or soup on their way to work, while tourists drop in to refresh themselves with a beer and sausage *pulao* (spiced rice with sausage bits) after a visit to the church that overlooks the tiny restaurant. George now offers Chinese cuisine, too, but it would be a shame to trade the home-style Goan cooking for it. Try any of the seafood preparations, as well as the beef and pork items on the menu, especially the beef soup, steaks, and pork *sorpotel.* They also serve roasted suckling pig for Christmas. The friendly second-generation owner, Eddie Jorge, is always ready to share the history of the place with interested customers. A simple eatery with an air-conditioned section upstairs, this is a great place to watch the world go by.

Established in 1922, **Mr. Baker** (Jesuit House, opposite Municipal Garden, tel. 0832/222-4622, 8:30 A.M.–1 P.M. and 3–7:45 P.M. Mon.–Sat.) is a small bakery with a longstanding reputation. While it has reinvented its look to keep with changing times, its baked goodies remain traditional and low-priced. Try the delicious rum balls, coconut cookies, *bebinca,* fruit cakes, and other treats available at unbelievably low prices. They also serve sandwiches, puffs, and egg chops, and bake wedding cakes.

Next door to Mr. Baker is vibrant **Ernesto's** (1st floor, Souza Towers, near Municipal Garden, tel. 0832/325-6213, ernestosgoa@gmail.com, 11 A.M.–3 P.M. and 6:30–11 P.M. daily, mains Rs 70–250), a restaurant and pub located on the premises of the historical Club Vasco da Gama. Once a lively social club for Portuguese naval officers and upper-class Goans, it was at the height of its glory from the time it was established in 1909 until the Goan Liberation in 1961. Members would come to relax with a drink, play cards, socialize, or simply hang around all day. Today, the restaurant is the entrepreneurial venture of its young owner, Ernesto Alvares, who is attempting to revive the old club culture. The food is as inviting as its cheery ambience and retro charm. Seafood and steaks are specialties, and there are regular food festivals to add to the varied menu. In the bar area, good music adds to the ambience. Ernesto's success has inspired plans for another branch in an old Portuguese-style house on Altinho Hill.

In the same building, **Café Tato** (Souza Towers, Rua Travessa de Revolucao, near Municipal Garden, tel. 0832/242-6690, 7 A.M.–8:30 P.M. Mon.–Sat.) is a small local eatery with subsidized food—famous for its cheap *bhaji puri* (Rs 25), spiced potato served with small fluffy *puris* or deep-fried wheat bread. Here you can observe daily Goan life at close quarters.

Café Bhonsle (near Cine National, tel. 0832/242-6000, 6 A.M.–8 P.M. Mon.–Sat. and 6 A.M.–noon Sun.) is also popular with the working class for its cheap local snacks, vegetarian cuisine, and *bhaji puri* (Rs 23). It;s also where young Goans head for an early-morning breakfast after a night of partying. Its bench-style seating and no-frills ambience may surprise the unsuspecting tourist, but you can rest assured that the kitchen is clean and food hygienically prepared.

An old favorite for its Goan seafood preparations, **Ritz Classic** (18th June Rd., tel. 0832/664-4796, noon–3 P.M. and 7–11 P.M. daily, mains Rs 150) is a busy place that's always exuding the coconut-rich aromas of fish curry. Not known for its ambience, the place more than makes up for the simplicity of its environment with authentic Goan cooking. Try the seafood platter here or other fish preparations, either fried or dried.

Located alongside the Old Secretariat, **Ruchira** (1st floor, Panaji Residency, tel. 0832/223-1059, 11 A.M.–3:30 P.M. and 7–11 P.M. daily, mains Rs 30–100) is a terrace restaurant overlooking the Mandovi River and jetty. It serves eclectic fare ranging from North Indian to Chinese and Continental, but the specialty here, like most Panaji restaurants, is Goan-style seafood.

Fontainhas and Sao Tome

The quaint Latin quarter is home to a host of delightful little eateries that spice up the street life of this heritage district. Worthy of a special mention, ◖ **Hospedaria Venite** (31st January Rd., tel. 0832/242-5537, 9 A.M.–3 P.M. and 7–10:30 P.M. Mon.–Sat., mains Rs 100 and up) is a charming place with wooden floorboards, colorful wall art, and cramped balconies for two where you'll trade comfort for a novel dining experience. The menu is varied and dominated by seafood—you may choose from Mediterranean or Goan dishes. There are limited but great vegetarian options and deliciously juicy steaks. The bar serves some excellent *feni* cocktails (Rs 70) amid graffiti-streaked walls. Try the Coco Fling (palm *feni,* mint, and lime juice) or the Goa Libre (*feni,* cola, lemon, and ice).

On the same street, ◖ **Viva Panjim** (31st January Rd., tel. 0832/242-2405, 8 A.M.–3:30 P.M. and 7–10:30 P.M. Mon.–Sat., mains Rs 120 and up) offers Goan fare with a wonderful courtyard dining experience. The seafood platter is a specialty, as are the prawn curry-rice and various *vindaloos.* An old Goan home-turned-restaurant, the eatery is a favorite for its old-world ambience, with whirring table fans providing a respite from the spicy curries.

A popular eatery with a loyal clientele, ◖ **Avanti** (Rua de Ourem, tel. 0832/242-7179, 11 A.M.–3 P.M. and 7–11 P.M. Mon.–Sat., mains Rs 100 and up) is where you can sample a good home-cooked Goan meal. Located along the Ourem creek, this is another Fontainhas favorite.

At **Horseshoe** (Rua de Ourem, tel. 0832/243-1788, 12–2:30 P.M. and 7–10:30 P.M. Mon.–Sat., mains Rs 150 and up), you can expect authentic Goan-Portuguese cuisine. The chef whips up various original dishes (like the *galinha piri piri*) with the help of recipes learned from his days in Portugal and Angola.

Don't let the run-down exterior of **Corina Restaurant & Bar** (at the foot of New Patto Bridge, near the GPO, tel. 0832/2425-740, 12–2:30 P.M. and 7–10:30 P.M. Mon.–Sat., mains Rs 100) deter you from entering this haven for lovers of Goan cuisine. The restaurant offers no-frills dining in a less-than-charming ambience to ardent foodies.

Campal

At **Riorico** (Hotel Mandovi, Dayanand Bandodkar Rd., tel. 0832/222-4405, www .hotelmandovigoa.com, 12:30–3 P.M. and 7–11 P.M. daily, mains Rs 175–1,000), the charming, old-world atmosphere complements the Goan-Portuguese cuisine. The high ceiling with chandeliers, carved wooden furniture, and river view make this a popular place with tourists and locals alike. Located in the once-famous Hotel Mandovi, the restaurant has been serving authentic Goan and Portuguese dishes for decades. If you've had enough of fish-curry-rice already, try the Portuguese seafood *caldeirada* or the fish Mornay. The restaurant gets its fresh catch every day from the river, and also serves North Indian and Chinese dishes.

INFORMATION AND SERVICES
Tourist Information

The **Government of India tourist office** (Communidade Building, Church Square, tel. 0832/222-3412, indiatourismgoa@ sancharnet.in, 9:30 A.M.–6 P.M. Mon.–Fri. and 10 A.M.–1 P.M. Sat.) is located diagonally opposite the Church of Our Lady of the Immaculate Conception. You can get maps, brochures, and any other tourist information you require.

The services of trained, government-approved guides are also available on request.

The **Goa Tourism Development Corporation (GTDC)** (Trionora Apartments, Dr. Alvares Costa Rd., tel. 0832/222-6515, www.goa-tourism.com, 9:30 A.M.–1:15 P.M. and 2–5:45 P.M. Mon.–Fri.) provides maps and brochures and organizes a number of tours and river cruises led by government-approved guides.

Hospitals, Emergency Services, and Pharmacies

Goa has a number of reputed medical colleges, ambulance services, and hospitals, some of which are located in Panaji. These include the **KLES Hospital Liaison Office** (St. Inez, tel. 0832/222-5601), **Goa Medical College** (Bambolim, tel. 0832/245-8725 or emergency helpline 102), **Indian Red Cross** (18th June Rd., tel. 0832/222-4601), **Laxmibai Talaulikar Memorial Hospital** (Dada Vaidya Rd., tel. 0832/242-5625), and **Panjim Ambulance and Welfare Trust** (Hotel Manoshanti, behind EDC House, tel. 0832/222-7997).

There are a number of pharmacies across Panaji, in addition to those attached to hospitals. These include **Farmacia Universal** (Fontainhas-Mala, tel. 0832/222-3740), **Neha Chemists and Druggists** (Fontainhas-Mala, tel. 0832/242-1313), and **Jeevan Rekha Medical Stores** (Padmavati Towers, 18th June Rd., tel. 0832/243-5946)—all of which are open 24 hours a day.

The headquarters of the Goa Police are located near Azad Maidan in Panaji. However, in case of emergency, **dial 100** for the 24-hour police helpline or try the **Police Control Room** (tel. 0832/242-8400).

Money

High-end hotels, restaurants, and stores may accept U.S. dollars or euros, and most places accept Visa and MasterCard. There are also plenty of 24-hour ATMs all over Panaji, including those at **Centurion Bank** (MG Rd., tel. 0832/222-9112, www.centurionbank.com), **HDFC** (18th June Rd., tel. 0832/242-1922, www.hdfc.com), and **ING**

Vysya (MG Rd., tel. 0832/222-9705, www.ingvysyabank.com).

There are plenty of money-changers in the city center; it's best to go with the reputed ones at state banks, leading hotels and shops, and travel agents. Visitors can go to **Thomas Cook** (8, Alcon Chambers, Dayanand Bandodkar Marg, tel. 0832/222-1312, 9:30 A.M.–6:30 P.M. Mon.–Sat.), **Amex** (14, Alcon Chambers, Dayanand Bandodkar Marg, tel. 0832/243-2645, 9:30 A.M.–6:30 P.M. Mon.–Sat.), or **Pheroze Framroze & Co.** (Mahalaxmi Chambers, tel. 0832/242-1398, 9:30 A.M.–6 P.M. Mon.–Sat.).

Postal Services

The **Head Post Office** (MG Rd., tel. 0832/222-3704, 9:30 A.M.–1 P.M. and 2–5:30 P.M. Mon.–Sat.) is a lovely old building that offers speedpost, registered letter booking (9:30 A.M.–4:30 P.M.), and money orders (9:30 A.M.–3:30 P.M.). Late-evening speedpost booking facilities are also available 6–8 P.M.

Internet and Telephone

Most high-end hotels provide Internet access, and there are a number of Internet cafés all over the city center, especially on 18th June Road. Rates are about Rs 30 per hour. Similarly, there are a number of phone booths marked "STD-ISD-PCO" from where you can make local, national, and international calls and fax documents. Calls to Europe cost around Rs 7 per minute; to the United States, the rate is about Rs 5 per minute. If you're going to be in India for awhile, it's worth getting a pre-paid mobile connection, offered by local service providers such as Airtel and Vodafone. However, if your phone was purchased in the United States, you might have to unlock it at a local electronics store for a small fee to be able to make local calls (perhaps easier to do in Mumbai). For local calls made by mobile phones, dial the area code for Goa (0832) before you dial the local number. If you have a Vodafone connection, you can buy their international calling card, which allows you to make international calls at cheaper rates.

Goa also has a 24-hour helpline that works as a telephonic phone directory. You may dial 0832/2412121 to get any number in the state.

GETTING THERE
Air
While Goa does not have a dedicated international airport, a host of domestic flights and a few charter airlines arrive at Dabolim Airport (tel. 0832/540-806), 29 kilometers south of Panaji, near Vasco. An increasing number of budget flights have begun to arrive here from Mumbai and other destinations in India, leading to plans for another airport farther north at Mopa. If you're booking your flight from Mumbai or any other destination in India, you will get the best deals on www.cleartrip.com or www.makemytrip.com.

On arrival, it is useful to keep in mind that Goa is a relatively small state; even if you plan to stay in the remote interior, it's best to take a cab from the airport. You can book a prepaid taxi to Panaji for Rs 500 at the airport counter. There is no bus service to or from the airport.

Rail
India's west coast is connected by a number of trains, which you can book online (at www.irctc.co.in or www.cleartrip.com). The Konkan Railway (www.konkanrailway.com, ticket from Mumbai Rs 1,500) assures a scenic ride to Goa from Mumbai. To get to Panaji, you will need to alight at **Karmali,** about 12 kilometers east of the town center.

Once you've arrived at Karmali, the onward journey to Panaji costs around Rs 250 by taxi, or Rs 200 by auto-rickshaw. The local Kadamba bus service offers stage carriages from Karmali to Panaji for Rs 20.

Panaji is well connected by train to other parts of Goa. The main stations are at Madgaon and Vasco da Gama in the south and Tivim in the north.

Bus
Both private and state buses connect Panaji with other parts of Goa, Mumbai and other destinations in Maharashtra, and to Karnataka and Andhra Pradesh. **Paulo Travels** (Monalisa, Hill Rd., Bandra, Mumbai, tel. 022/2645-2624 and G1, Cardozo Building, near Kadamba bus stand, Panaji, tel. 0832/243-8531, www.paulotravels.com, fares Rs 350–750) is most popular and recommended bus service. Its Volvo sleeper and seater luxury coaches make the 12-hour journey more comfortable than trips with other providers. State-run buses have counters at the Panaji bus terminus. Luxury and air-conditioned buses are available to Mumbai, Bangalore, Hampi, and other destinations. Most private interstate buses arrive and depart from a separate bus stand next to the Mandovi Bridge.

GETTING AROUND
Car and Taxi
Car rentals and taxi are the best way to get around Goa—but the worst in terms of quality of service and attitude. Owners and middlemen lure customers with bargain prices, but drivers—who are often kept in the dark about these rates—can be unrelenting at the end of a long day. Panaji has a number of such services that take you around the city and outside. While black-and-yellow taxis are available for short distances, it's the tourist taxis that are prevalent. Rates vary depending on the type of vehicle you hire and the whims of the driver/owner. And if you happen to stay in a posh hotel, be prepared to be overcharged. Remember to bargain hard, especially during low season.

Car rentals generally come with a driver, although self-drive cars are also available. Drivers are usually as clueless about directions as you are, unless you intend to visit only the popular tourist hotspots. Rates vary from Rs 800–1,400 for eight hours and then Rs 10–14 per kilometer after that. Smaller hatchbacks like the Hyundai Santro are cheaper than larger cars like the Toyota Innova or luxury cars like the Honda City. There's a Rs 100–150 charge for keeping the driver late and Rs 250–300 for keeping him overnight (and it's rare to find a driver who will stay the night willingly). If you think you're being clever by relieving the driver on reaching your destination, think again—taxis charge for the return journey irrespective of whether you're in the car or not, so if your end destination is a considerable distance from your starting point then you end up paying for two long taxi rides instead of one.

Self-drive cars are not much cheaper (Rs 100–200 less per day), but may be marginally easier on your blood pressure. An international driving license is required, in addition to good road sense (Goa is not known for its road signs) and parking skills. Make sure you check the car well before you set out on your journey, as damages have to be compensated on return of the vehicle and you don't want to pay for something you didn't do.

Though it can be difficult to find a good taxi/car rental operator in Goa, **Joey's** (near Hotel Mandovi, Campal, tel. 0832/222-8989, open 24 hrs) is a pricey but professionally run option. Independent driver Paul (cell tel. 91/98221-42692) operates in and out of the city too. You can also rent a vehicle from the **Goa Tourism Development Corporation (GTDC)** (Trionora Apartments, Dr. Alvares Costa Rd., tel. 0832/222-6515, www.goa-tourism.com, 9:30 A.M.–1:15 P.M. and 2–5:45 P.M. Mon.–Fri.).

Motorcycle and Bicycle

Motorcycle taxis, known as "pilots," are also available throughout Panaji. Their origins go back to the hippie era, when motorcycles became a favored form of transport. Licensed motorcycles have a yellow front mudguard and can be found at motorcycle taxi stands in main city areas. They charge Rs 10–15 per kilometer.

Motorcycle rentals do an even brisker business. Even families and mama-and-papa outfits rent out motorbikes and scooters, which are easily available at every nook and corner. Rentals cost Rs 250–500 per day, depending on the type and model of the two-wheeler hired, and the season. In Panaji, **Paulo Travels** (G1, Cardozo Building, near Kadamba bus stand, Panaji, tel. 0832/243-8531, www.paulotravels .com) rents out two-wheelers. An international license is required and some places may ask

for your passport details and a small security deposit. Do not leave your passport with them at any cost.

Bicycles are also easily hired in Goa, and make for a pleasant ride along beaches and fields. Look out for signs that say Bicycle Rental in the city center, and sometimes in the backyards of residential houses. Bicycle rental costs Rs 30–50 per day. Both motorcycle and bicycle rentals cost less during low season.

Bus

Goa's state-run bus service **Kadamba (KTC)** (tel. 0832/243-8031, min. fare Rs 5) provides local bus services and also connects Panaji to Old Goa, Ponda, Mapusa, Madgaon, Vasco, and the various Goan beaches through nonstop shuttle services. The shuttles require tickets to be bought at the KTC counter before boarding, but the regular buses provide tickets on board. A shuttle from Panaji to Ponda costs around Rs 20.

Ferry

River cruises are popular for sightseeing on the Mandovi River, and local ferries are a regular means of transport at inland river crossings in

an evening cruise on the Mandovi River

and around Panaji. Passengers get a free ride, but vehicles are generally charged Rs 3–20, depending on the type of vehicle. From near Panaji, the main ferries are from Dona Paula to Mormugao, Old Goa to Divar Island, and from Ribandar to Chorao Island, departing every half-hour or so. Some ferry services are suspended from June to September, during the monsoon season.

BRITONA AND SALVADOR DO MUNDO

Within easy distance of the capital are two of Goa's most picturesque villages. The urbanity of Panaji melts into a rustic landscape at the villages of Britona and Salvador do Mundo.

Only two kilometers from Panaji, Britona is a traditional village hidden amid greenery along the banks of the Mandovi River. The village is known for its quiet charm and its beautiful houses—as well as for the 17th-century **Nossa Senhora de Penha de Franca Church** (Our Lady of the Rock of France, believed to protect seafarers on their voyage), which can be visited only for mass (7–10 A.M. Sun.). Britona has some wonderful cottages and heritage accommodations, and is the departure and arrival point for the luxury yacht *Solita*.

Meanwhile, in Salvador do Mundo, a leafy village only six kilometers from Panaji, is architect Gerard Da Cunha's **Houses of Goa Museum** (674, near Nisha's playschool, Torda, Salvador do Mundo, tel. 0832/241-0711, www.archgoa.org, 10 A.M.–7:30 P.M. Tues.–Sun., adults Rs 100, Rs 25 on Sun.; children Rs 25), which showcases Goan architecture in its unusual triangular, ship-like structure. The museum presents illustrations of Goan history by cartoonist Mario Miranda and a chronology of world architecture in addition to photographs, architectural designs, and plans of prominent old Goan houses. It explains the various elements of the Goan house and also displays remnants of heritage houses (columns,

doors, and wooden carvings, for example). The building has a theater on its third and uppermost level. The museum offers a guided tour (9:30 A.M.–1:30 P.M., Rs 1,000 per person, advance notification required), conducted by Da Cunha himself, of historical houses and temples in beautiful Salvador do Mundo. Should the museum be of little interest to you, the village itself is lovely, with lush greenery, a shaded hillock, pretty houses, and a lake.

Sports and Recreation

The luxury yacht *Solita* (departure/arrival from Britona jetty, opposite Village Panchayat, Britona, tel. 91/98221-80826, www.solita.co.in, Rs 1,000 per pp or Rs 10,000/hour plus tax for private charter, Oct.–Apr.), a sleek white beauty, cruises around the northern coastline. The ride offers a beautiful view of Panaji town and of river dolphins as the yacht goes past the Nossa Senhora de Penha de Franca Church, the Salim Ali bird sanctuary, and the fort of Reis Magos from the River Mandovi; the yacht then heads into the Arabian Sea, where it anchors and allows guests to swim in the waters, before proceeding to Fort Aguada for a beautiful sunset. The *Solita* also goes on sunset cruises—drinks served on board, and meals may be arranged. The yacht comes with a crew of four, including the captain, an engineer, and two deck hands or stewards, and has two small cabins for rest and relaxation. It accommodates a maximum of 26 guests and is popular during the Christmas/New Year period, although prices are doubled during this time.

Getting There and Around

Britona and Salvador do Mundo lie northeast of the Mandovi Bridge and are easily accessible by road from Panaji. A bus from the city center costs Rs 10 to Britona, and about Rs 15 to Salvador do Mundo. By taxi, it is Rs 80–100 to Britona, and Rs 200 to Salvador do Mundo.

Miramar and Dona Paula

On the outskirts of Panaji are the beaches of Miramar and Dona Paula. Not quite part of the city and yet not really separate from it, these two adjoining seaside areas are both prestigious residential addresses, as well as popular tourist destinations. They offer the best of both worlds—the city and its seafront. While both beaches are considered unsafe for swimming, they are popular venues for recreation. The sandy stretch of Miramar sees plenty of beach volleyball and some water sports while the Dona Paula jetty serves as a popular promenade for evening strolls and the occasional dolphin sighting. Water scooters and boating are popular here and a flight of steps leads up to a spot that provides a bird's-eye view of the surrounding seascape. Dominated by a number of resorts, including the five-star Goa Marriott and Cidade de Goa, Miramar and Dona Paula also offer a number of dining and entertainment options.

SIGHTS
Cabo Raj Bhavan
At Dona Paula, the Cabo Raj Bhavan (westernmost end of Dona Paula, www.rajbhavangoa.org) was previously a fortress, then the summer residence of the Goan archbishop, and then the official residence of the Portuguese governor-general in 1866—before it turned into the present-day residence of Goa's governor. On Sunday mornings, the 500-year-old chapel next to the main residence is opened to public for Mass. Inside the chapel are a gilded altar and a beautiful pulpit, as well as old gravestones. Among these is the grave of a lady called Dona Paula—rumored to have been the paramour of one of the governor-generals of Goa—after whom the beach is named.

Art Galleries
Miramar has its own gallery, **Ruchika's Art Gallery** (4th floor, Casa del Sol, opposite Goa Marriott, Miramar, tel. 0832/246-5875, www.ruchikasart.com, 11 A.M.–6 P.M. Mon.–Sat.). A vast white space on the upper floor of a residential building, it exhibits the works of local artists and others. It also curates themed exhibits—such as one with a Ganesh theme during

marigold offerings from a Ganesh festival, washed ashore at Miramar Beach

the Ganesh festival, when small clay models of the elephant-headed god created by local schoolchildren were displayed.

Close by is **Harshada Art Gallery** (opposite Goa Marriott, Miramar, cell tel. 91/98812-55587, www.harshadakerkar.com)—the private studio of Harshada Kerkar, who belongs to Goa's premier artist family. It's not quite a public gallery for viewing, but the friendly artist welcomes the occasional, curious visitor into the studio to take a look at her recent works.

ENTERTAINMENT AND EVENTS
Casinos and Nightclubs

Miramar and Dona Paula are self-sufficient in their nightlife options, comprising five-star nightclubs and casinos that draw even the Panaji crowds. At the casino at the Goa Marriott, **Winners** (Goa Marriott, Miramar Beach, tel. 0832/246-3333, www.goamarriottresort.com, 24 hours, entry fee Rs 200), you can try your hand at poker, roulette, blackjack, or slot machines. The "semi-live" casino (only offshore casinos in Goa hold a license for live gaming) has digitally operated games and is dominated by domestic tourists, mostly men, out for a gamble.

At Cidade de Goa, the small, semi-live casino **Goldfinger** (Cidade de Goa, Vainguinim Beach, Dona Paula, tel. 0832/245-4545, ajayathapa@hotmail.com, 24 hours) is where the action is. Whirring roulette tables, games of baccarat, and clinking slot machines are operated under the eagle eyes of the affable owner, who also runs the Goldfinger chain in Kathmandu, Nepal. Drinks flow freely and so does the currency, as guests hope to make a quick buck.

In the nearby Vainguinim Valley Resort, **Chances** (Vainguinim Valley Resort, Machado's Cove, Dona Paula, tel. 0832/245-2201, chances@vainguinimvalleyresort.com, 24 hours), one of the largest casinos around, scores on size. Here you can play the exciting horse derby, in addition to the usual games. The casino has 35 slot machines and its spacious interior is usually filled with locals.

Most visitors prefer to party at the nearby beaches of North Goa, a short drive from Panaji. However, if you're looking for some indoor fun, there's **Ozone** (Goa Marriott, Miramar Beach, tel. 0832/246-3333, www.goamarriottresort.com). A small bar known for its retro music and karaoke, it is currently under renovation and will soon be re-opened as a pub. Meanwhile, Cidade de Goa has an alfresco bar called **Bar Latino** (Cidade de Goa, Vainguinim Beach, tel. 0832/245-4545, www.cidadedegoa.com, 10:30–2 A.M. daily) where you can enjoy live music and performances every evening by the pool.

SPORTS AND RECREATION

Aquatic Watersports (tel. 0832/325-2854, www.drishtiadventures.com) operates from five-star resort Cidade de Goa. Run by the same management as H2O in Mumbai, they offer dolphin cruises, banana rides, Jet Skiing, snorkeling, parasailing, windsurfing, kayaking, and a host of other activities and boat tours. They are known for their "underwater sea walk"—a walk along the sea bed at Baina Beach, farther south—and conduct PADI-certified dive training.

ACCOMMODATIONS

Rates in these five-star-dominated areas tend to swing wildly between seasons. Guests are lured with attractive rates and packages during the monsoon months, but the peak season makes up for the lull with higher rates.

Rs 3,000-10,000

The GTDC-run **Miramar Residency** (Miramar Beach, tel. 0832/246-3811, www.goa-tourism.com, Rs 970–6,100) is preferred over its sister hotel at Panaji. A cluster of cottages and apartments by the beach, the hotel has clean, comfortable rooms and green lawns. It is also one of the few hotels that is sensitive to the needs of the physically challenged. There are four types of rooms, ranging from doubles without air-conditioning to larger air-conditioned rooms and a suite. There's an in-house restaurant that serves local cuisine.

A resort located in a secluded palm grove, **Prainha** (Dona Paula Beach, tel. 0832/245-3881, www.prainha.com, Rs 3,000–6,500) has its own private beach. Its delightful multi-level terraced cottages overlook Dona Paula Beach, with rooms that have high wooden ceilings and antique furniture. The cottages have French windows leading to the sea, while apartments come with balconies that offer lush green treetop views. For those who prefer the safety of a swimming pool to Dona Paula's rough sea, there's an outdoor pool. The hotel has a bar called Harbour Lights and an alfresco restaurant called Palm Grove that serves both local and international cuisine.

Rs 10,000 and Up

Goa's original five-star—and one of the state's first luxury hotels—(**Cidade de Goa** (Vainguinim Beach, Dona Paula, tel. 0832/245-4545, www.cidadedegoa.com, Rs 12,500–14,750) greets you with colorful murals of Vasco da Gama's journey. Well furnished and aesthetically appealing, the rooms have wall art and themes varying from Rajasthani to Portuguese. Some of the deluxe rooms offer direct access to the beach, while the lobby (dominated by statues of the explorer) and the lobby bar, Taverna, offer a view of the sea. A kiddie pool and park make this a great place for families, and the hotel also offers complimentary babysitting services. There's an on-site water-sports operator, a library, health center, tennis, spa, and even an in-house tarot card reader and numerologist. For entertainment, there's a casino and the alfresco Bar Latino. The Portuguese restaurant Alfama hosts traditional fado dance performances and there are a wide choice of eateries to choose from.

A vast ocean-view lobby lined with waiters offering pomegranate-flavored lime juice greets visitors at the (**Goa Marriott** (Miramar Beach, tel. 0832/246-3333, www.goamarriottresort.com, prices upon request). An excellent hotel that combines five-star comfort with the feel of home, the Goa Marriott attracts both business travelers and families. The place, in general, is well-managed by its genial and efficient staff. The old Goan-Portuguese architecture on the outside melds into a pleasant and contemporary look in the rooms. Bayview rooms have a magnificent perspective on the harbor, while garden-view rooms overlook pretty, well-manicured lawns. Executive rooms, meanwhile, provide access to the executive lounge, where guests can avail themselves of free Internet, use the library and bar, or help themselves to breakfast and dinner buffets. The hotel also has cheerful one- and two-bedroom suites with kitchenettes for long-stay visitors. The Goa Marriott is known for its spa, an outdoor pool (with poolside bar) by the beach, and an open seafood restaurant called Simply Fish that does barbeques during tourist season. There's also a 24-hour deli, a patisserie, and the Chinese restaurant, Wan Hao, which is managed by an all-female staff. For entertainment, the hotel offers a casino and a pub, and there's a kid zone with childcare services. Look out for special packages as well as daily activities organized for guests.

FOOD
Miramar

With a name that articulate, you simply can't go wrong at (**Simply Fish** (Goa Marriott, Miramar Beach, tel. 0832/246-3333, www.goamarriottresort.com, 7–11 P.M. daily, mains Rs 300 and up). This popular seafood grill at the Goa Marriott has a delightful ambience and great food. Diners sit under the starry night sky or in the shadow of a cheerful ceramic Mario Miranda mural—from where the chef hands out his signature barbecue specialties. Diners gorge on the lobster cappuccino, seafood in lemon sauce, or the spicy fried masala fish dishes, seeking occasional relief in a chilled beer or the calming sound of the sea.

For home-style Goan cooking coupled with a pleasing ambience, there's no better place than (**Mum's Kitchen** (Martins Building, Panaji-Miramar Rd., cell tel. 91/98221-75559, 11 A.M.–11 P.M. daily, mains Rs 100 and up). A restaurant that claims to preserve the state's culinary heritage, Mum's Kitchen serves a variety of traditional Goan dishes. In addition to the spicy vindaloos, *cafreals,* and *xacutis* served with rice cakes called *sannas,* try the *chourico* sausages and a deliciously spiced chicken dish called *guisado de galinha.*

Dona Paula

An old Miramar-Dona Paula favorite, **Martin's Beach Corner** (Caranzalem, Dona Paula-Miramar, tel. 0832/246-4877, 11 A.M.–3 P.M. and 7–11 P.M. daily, mains Rs 70 and up) has a deceptively simple appearance, but the shack-like entrance opens out to the sea. Here you can try local seafood specialties along with a chilled beer or *feni.* Try the pork items as well, especially the *sorpotel,* as well as the deliciously spicy fried mussels.

Locals swear by **Goan Delicacy** (Hawaii Beach, Dona Paula, tel. 0832/224-356, 8 A.M.–11:30 P.M. daily, mains Rs 30 and up), a small restaurant that overlooks Dona Paula's Hawaii Beach. Although this place is frequented primarily for the view, the food isn't bad. The place serves everything from spaghetti Bolognese to Goan and tandoori cuisine at inexpensive, local prices. The restaurant also organizes special barbeque nights in peak season.

At yet another seaside location, **Sea Pebble** (Dona Paula jetty, tel. 0832/245-6554, 11 A.M.–11 P.M. daily, mains Rs 70 and up), in the Dona Paula cove, brings you seascape along with local and international cuisine. A place that invites a leisurely meal and a drink, it specializes in fried tiger prawns and crumb-fried mullet.

If you're looking for a fine dining experience or a romantic candlelight dinner coupled with a bit of entertainment, try **(Alfama** (Cidade de Goa, Vainguinim Beach, tel. 0832/245-4545, www.cidadedegoa.com, 7:30–11 P.M. daily, Rs 1,000–1,500 for a three-course meal). Named after a town square in Lisbon, the restaurant serves Portuguese cuisine from the colonies, including dishes from Brazil and Mozambique, in addition to Goan-Portuguese dishes. Designed like a Portuguese casa, its dim-lit interior is a profusion of arches, steps, and balconies. There's a traditional fado music and dance performance every second Tuesday evening and local musicians regularly serenade diners.

GETTING THERE AND AROUND

Miramar and Dona Paula are on the fringes of Panaji and easily accessible by all modes of city transport. Taxis are generally available outside city hotels, restaurants, and the bus station. A taxi ride from the bus station near Mandovi Bridge in Panaji should cost about Rs 100–120. Buses are also available from this bus station and a ride to the beaches costs around Rs 8.

Old Goa (Velha Goa)

About 10 kilometers from Panaji, the deserted city called Old Goa, or Velha Goa, is a picturesque drive along the glistening waters of the Mandovi and past the area of Ribandar. Here itself, halfway to Old Goa, visitors are given a taste of history with Portuguese-style homes.

On reaching the ghost town of Old Goa, you'll see the skeletal remains of a once-vibrant metropolis. Its history goes back to the 11th century, when the Hindu Kadamba dynasty established a small settlement here, later to be taken over by the Vijayanagar empire and then the Bahmani Muslims. In the 15th century, it was the alternate capital of the ruler of Bijapur in present-day Karnataka—the Bahmani king Adil Shah. A wealthy, thriving port, it was attacked in March 1510 by the Portuguese, led by Afonso de Albuquerque. The story goes that Adil Shah launched a surprise counterattack, forcing Afonso and his troops into the river, leaving them stranded there during the terrible monsoon months until their supplies ran out. Taking pity on them, the people of the nearby village of Taleigaon offered them their rice crop; thus began the custom of offering the first crop to the governor, a practice that continues in Goa to this day. In November 1510, the Portuguese troops attacked the Bahmani capital with renewed vigor and succeeded in capturing the city. It became the capital of Portuguese Goa, and the construction of its magnificent churches and buildings was carried out under the Franciscan, Dominican, and Jesuit orders that followed suit in their missionary zeal.

Old Goa was built in the image of Lisbon and was at the height of its glory when it was destroyed by the plague, brought here in 1635 by a ship that had arrived from Europe. Survivors fled the city and settled in Panjim—present-day Panaji—which became the new capital of the Portuguese empire, leaving the old city in a state of neglect. In 1835, when the religious orders were asked to leave by the Portuguese government, the churches and monuments fell into ruins and were left exposed to the elements; they were eventually restored in the 20th century and given World Heritage status by UNESCO.

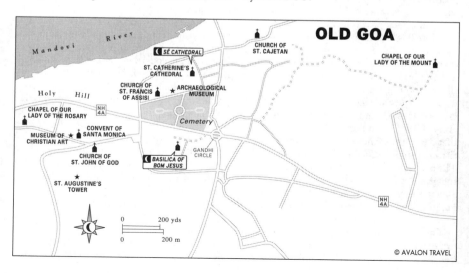

© ASHIMA NARAIN

The Basilica of Bom Jesus in Old Goa is the state's biggest pilgrim and tourist attraction.

SIGHTS
◖ Basilica of Bom Jesus

Old Goa's most celebrated church, the Basilica (near Gandhi Circle, 9 A.M.–6:30 P.M. Mon.–Sat. and 11:30 A.M.–6:30 P.M. Sun., photography of persons prohibited, videography prohibited) is known more for the miraculously intact body of St. Francis Xavier that rests here than for its magnificent gold altar dedicated to Baby Jesus. The body of the saint lies in a silver casket at an elevation so that only the wrist, part of the face, and robe are visible to visitors. It is opened to the public only once every 10 years at an event called the Exposition that draws thousands of pilgrims and tourists; the next one is scheduled for the year 2014. The marble-and-jasper tomb, commissioned by the grand duke of Tuscany and sculpted over 10 years by Florentine artist Giovanni Batista Foggini, was offered in exchange for a pillow that the saint had rested his head on.

The basilica itself is a marvelous piece of architecture with a red laterite exterior, embellished in Baroque style. Inside, under the soaring ceiling, is the grand gold-painted (previously gold leaf) altar of Bom Jesus. Below the statue of Baby Jesus is the founder of the Jesuit order—St. Ignatius de Loyola—installed by the powerful Jesuit priests of the time. The intricately carved pulpit is one of the finest pieces of craftsmanship in Old Goa and was in use at a time when church services were delivered facing the altar instead of the people gathered there. A rotating bible stand, beautifully carved wooden doors, and a small altar dedicated to St. Anthony are other attractions. There's an art gallery (9 A.M.–5 P.M. daily, entry Rs 2, photography prohibited) upstairs that exhibits the religious paintings of Goan artist Dom Martin, as well as a photo gallery and wooden sculptures of the saints. Downstairs, on your way out, is the statue of Francis Xavier and an arch with newly discovered frescoes.

Church of St. Francis of Assisi and Archeological Museum

This magnificent church (8:45 A.M.–5:30 P.M. daily, free, photography of persons prohibited) was built by the Franciscan priests in 1521 and rebuilt in 1661 after the original building was pulled down. It is known for its beautiful murals, which depict the life of the saint, and for its exquisitely carved and ornate interior. The carved gravestones on the church floor date back to the 16th century, while the adjoining convent of St. Francis of Assisi has been turned into an archeological museum and portrait gallery (tel. 0832/228-5299, 10 A.M.–5 P.M. Sat.–Thurs., adults Rs 5, children free, photography prohibited). The museum exhibits antiquarian objects and portraits of Portuguese governors and viceroys. These include the 3.6-meter-high bronze statue of Afonso de Albuquerque that was cast while he was still alive, and that of Portugal's national poet, Luis Vaz de Camoens, holding in his hand his poem *Os Lusiades,* which describes the journey of Vasco da Gama. Also on display are statues, Hindu sculptures, pillars, weapons, stamps, and other objects of historical interest.

As you make your way from the church to the Sé Cathedral, you will come across the

THE LIFE OF ST. FRANCIS XAVIER

A distant glimpse of the jostling crowds at the annual Feast of St. Francis Xavier celebrated at the Basilica of Bom Jesus in Old Goa is enough to arouse the visitor's curiosity in Goa's most venerated figure. Born in Navarre, Spain, in 1506, the saint was a young nobleman pursuing his letters in Philosophy when he met St. Ignatius of Loyola. Ignatious changed his life forever, and the young Francis went on to study for priesthood until 1535. Soon after, he was ordained into Loyola's newly formed Jesuit society, and in 1542, sent on his first mission to Goa. Here, he is said to have founded schools and churches, and ironically, also initiated the terrible Goan Inquisition – eventually carried out in 1560 – where thousands of Hindus were brutally tortured and burned at the stake for practicing their religious rites and rituals.

Francis Xavier himself only spent six months in Goa, traveling to Malacca, Japan, Africa, and China on his mission to convert people to Christianity. It was on Sancian Island in China that he faced resistance from the local people and eventually caught a fever and died in 1552. It's said that his body was coated with quicklime (to aid decomposition) and buried on the island.

However, when he was exhumed after four months, his body was intact. The miraculously preserved remains were then interred in Malacca and lay there for a year and eight months, only to be dug up again. The body was in the same state of preservation as before and was brought to Goa in 1554 for its first Exposition.

News of the miracle reached far and wide, leaving everyone with the desire for a relic of the saint. A Portuguese noblewoman is said to have bitten off a toe during an Exposition, while the Pope himself acquired the right forearm in 1615. The rest of the arm was sent to the Japanese Jesuits in 1913. Various parts of the saint's body rest in places across the world; one of his fingernails may be found in the private chapel of Casa Perreira-Bragança in Chandor. He was finally canonized in 1622 and his remains, laid to rest in a silver casket (crafted, by a quirk of fate, at the hands of a Hindu silversmith) at the Basilica of Bom Jesus. The body continues to be an object of curiosity and interest, drawing hundreds of thousands of pilgrims every year and at the Exposition that continues to be held every 10 years.

PANAJI AND INTERIOR GOA

© ASHIMA NARAIN

The Basilica of Bom Jesus in Old Goa carries the miraculously preserved remains of St. Francis Xavier.

former **Archbishop's Residence** (9:30 A.M.–5:30 P.M. Tues.–Sun., Rs 20, photography prohibited), which displays some paintings, antique furniture, and statues of saints.

Nearby is the first chapel built in Old Goa—**St Catherine's Chapel** (8:45 A.M.–5:30 P.M. daily, free, photography of persons prohibited). This plain construction was built by Afonso de Albuquerque in 1510 and was rebuilt twice, most recently in 1952. There's not much to see inside except for a small, simple altar and some graves.

☾ Sé Cathedral

The largest church in Asia and larger than any in Portugal, the Sé, or St. Catherine's Cathedral (7 A.M.–6 P.M. daily, free, photography of persons prohibited), lies across the road from the Basilica of Bom Jesus and is easily recognized by its asymmetrical exterior. One of its two towers was struck by lightning and collapsed in 1776, while the other holds the "Golden Bell" that tolled before the gruesome acts of the Inquisition were committed, and was heard all the way up to Panjim. The cathedral derives its name from the fact that it was the seat of the Bishop (the word *sé*, in Portuguese, means "seat"). Built in 1562 but consecrated in 1640, it has an intricately detailed Corinthian interior with a beautiful, gilded altar later dedicated to St. Catherine of Alexandria and which narrates her story in the form of painted panels. There are eight chapels and 15 altars in all, with the relics of the Blessed Martyrs of Cuncolim (whose failed attempt at the conversion of Mughal emperor Akbar resulted in their murder) resting in the altar of St. Anne.

Also found within the Cathedral, behind an ornate, lattice door, is the **Miraculous Cross,** believed to have cured leprosy and skin diseases. It is also known as the Growing Cross, because it was fitted into the custom-made door with difficulty as it expanded in size (now believed to have been due to the moisture of the monsoon) when brought down from its hilltop location after news of its healing powers spread far and wide. Today, the cross is kept in a box

© JANHAVI ACHAREKAR

the Chapel of the Blessed Sacrament, seen through an ornate filigree door, in the Sé Cathedral, Old Goa

and has a small opening on the side where devotees may touch it. The beautiful Chapel of the Blessed Sacrament, located within the cathedral, is also known for its intricate Persian-style filigree door.

Just outside Sé Cathedral is the Senate Square. Old Goa was once known for its Senate House and also had a royal hospital, a mint, and a gun foundry.

Church of St. Cajetan

This hauntingly quiet church (near the jetty and Viceroy's Arch, 8:30 A.M.–5:30 P.M. daily, free, photography of persons prohibited) was built by Italian friars of the Theatine order and was modeled in the image of St. Peter's Basilica in Rome. Ornately carved and gilded in Baroque style, its pulpit is unusual for its carvings, which display cashew motifs and Hindu influences—a unique local touch. Located behind the church are old catacombs where entry is prohibited.

In the open, on the road leading to the church, is the **Gate of Adil Shah's Palace.**

The only pre-Portuguese remnant of the old Bahmani capital, this was once the entrance to a magnificent palace that also served as a residence to various Portuguese governors until 1695. The palace eventually fell to ruin and came down in 1820. The gate itself resembles Hindu temple architecture—raising questions of its origins, which may lie in the pillaging of Hindu temples during the monarch's reign.

Viceroy's Arch

Near the riverfront, watching over the jetty that takes ferries to Divar Island, is Viceroy's Arch. This grand gateway was once the entry point to Old Goa for its Portuguese governors and others who arrived by ship. It was built in 1597 to commemorate Vasco da Gama's arrival in India, by his grandson Francisco da Gama, who went on to become the viceroy of Goa. The red laterite structure depicts a "native" figure kneeling at the feet of a missionary and its facade has a stone statue of da Gama. All viceroys were made to enter through the arch where they were handed the symbolic key to the capital.

Chapel of Our Lady of the Mount

On the other side of the Church of St. Cajetan, a steep climb takes you to Chapel of Our Lady of the Mount, which offers the most spectacular view of the old capital. From here, the single tower of the Sé Cathedral is easily visible, as is the river surrounded by thick vegetation. The church's whitewashed facade and open courtyard with its breathtaking backdrop are the venue for the Monte Music Festival, where the musical performances combined with the awe-inspiring setting make for a unique experience. The festival is held over four evenings in November. The interior of the chapel is usually closed but is open during festivals.

Holy Hill

If you come down the slope from Our Lady of the Mount, past Gandhi Circle and up toward Holy Hill, you will come across another cluster of old churches and monuments. Near the base of the hill is the **Church of St. John of God,**

The Chapel of Our Lady of the Mount serves as a dramatic backdrop to the Monte Music Festival.

built in 1685 as a sanitarium by the Order of Hospitallers of St. John of God. Today it is a home for the elderly, managed by the Franciscan sisters. A short distance from here is the ruined **St. Augustine's Tower,** the sole reminder to the Church of St. Augustine, built in 1602 by the Augustinian friars. The church complex is said to have included eight chapels, a monastery, and library, making it larger than the basilica. Today, the obelisk-like red laterite projectile looms large over the winding road that leads up the hill, a lonely remnant of its glorious past. Opposite the tower is the largest convent in Asia, the **Convent of Santa Monica,** which houses the **Museum of Christian Art** (tel. 0832/228-5299, 9:30 A.M.–5 P.M. daily, adults Rs 20, students Rs 5, children under 12 free, photography prohibited). While the convent is out of bounds for visitors, entry is permitted to its small but beautiful chapel. The museum showcases religious art, sculptures, ornaments, robes, and artifacts from Portugal and Portuguese Goa. On display are also beautiful figurines, crosses, and traditional objets d'art gifted in marriage, crafted from ivory or studded with precious stones.

Perched atop Holy Hill is the tranquil **Chapel of Our Lady of the Rosary** (9:30 A.M.–5:30 P.M. daily, free, photography of persons prohibited)—a simple church with a view of the river. It was here that Afonso de Albuquerque looked upon the capital of Adil Shah and decided to make it his own. One of the first buildings in Old Goa, it was built in the mid-16th century in the Manueline style with fortress-like turrets and a tower with the same view that charmed the Portuguese governor.

Pilar Monastery and Seminary

From Velha Goa, it's only a short distance to Goa Velha. Visitors often confuse the two, but Goa Velha is a small place distinct from Velha Goa (Old Goa). The village was the capital of the Kadamba dynasty between the 11th and 14th centuries. Today, it's a quiet town visited by Catholic pilgrims, who come to visit Pilar Monastery and Seminary. This nondescript attraction is reached by a winding road up a hillock that offers a beautiful view of the old town, the Zuari River, surrounding villages, and paddy fields. Built in 1613, the building itself is unremarkable but it includes the **Church of Our Lady of Pilar** (tel. 0832/221-8549, 8:30 A.M.–5:30 P.M. daily, photography permitted) that houses the original statue of Our Lady, brought by the Capuchins of Spain. There's a statue of St. Francis Xavier; an exquisitely carved Baroque church door ;and an ornate, gilded pulpit. There are traces of fading frescoes on the inside walls and in the cloisters around the garden. Farther up, in the new seminary is a museum (tel. 0832/221-8521, 8:30 A.M.–1 P.M. and 2:30–5:30 P.M. daily, free, photography prohibited) that showcases relics from the Kadamba era, as well as paintings, sculptures, and manuscripts.

Goa Velha is also known for its annual Procession of All Saints, held just before Easter. It is a 15-minute drive from Old Goa via the village of Neura, and 10 kilometers from Panaji on the road to Madgaon via Bambolim.

Chorao and Divar Islands

The islands of Chorao and Divar on the River Mandovi, present the lush rural Goan landscape at its best. Life on these islands has remained unchanged for many years and locals have resisted bridges in an attempt to conserve their natural and cultural heritage.

A ferry ride (every half-hour, free for passengers, fee for vehicles) from the Ribandar wharf on the Panaji-Old Goa Road takes you to Chorao Island. The Chorao village is marked by mud huts, Portuguese-style houses, and a church; the western half of the island is a protected area called the **Dr. Salim Ali Bird Sanctuary** (7 A.M.–5:30 P.M. daily, Rs 50, still/video photography Rs 30/150), named after the famous Indian ornithologist. At 1.8 square kilometers, it is the smallest wildlife sanctuary in Goa, but it is densely populated with mangroves, a variety of resident and migratory birds, as well as the Indian crocodile, python, flying fox, otter, and mudskipper. The birdlife on this island includes the kingfisher, pheasant-tailed jacana, green bee-eater, red-wattled lapwing, sandpiper, tailor-bird, purple moorhen, stork, cormorant, and pin-tail duck, among others. To enter, permission is required from the chief wildlife warden (Forest Department, Junta House, Panaji, tel. 0832/222-5926). The Forest Department also has an office on the island that grants entry and provides boats (Rs 900) to help maneuver through the creeks and waterways of the island. October–June is the ideal time to visit.

Similarly, ferries (every half-hour, free for passengers, fee for vehicles) depart regularly through the day from the Viceroy's Arch in Old Goa to Divar Island across the Mandovi. A pleasant day trip, the island is ideal for picnickers and visitors looking for leisurely walks amid paddy fields, or to simply commune with nature. The landscape is dotted with old Portuguese villas and the Divar hill here presents some scenic views of the river. On the hilltop is the Church of Our Lady of Compassion. The island celebrates a colorful festival called Bonderam in the month of August, but ferries may not be available for the journey during the monsoon months.

ENTERTAINMENT AND EVENTS

A short distance from Old Goa, the village of Goa Velha is the only place (apart from Rome) to celebrate the **Procession of All Saints.** Held on the first Monday before Easter, the procession begins at St. Andrew's Church, from where life-size statues of the saints are carried through the village streets in floats and amid throngs of devotees. The procession ends with a lively fair in the evening, with stalls and eateries selling their treats and wares on the road just outside the church.

A cultural event held in the picturesque venue of the Chapel of Our Lady of the Mount, the **Monte Music Festival** is organized by Dona Paula hotel Cidade de Goa (tel. 0832/245-4545, www.cidadedegoa.com) and the Fundaçao Oriente in association with the Kala Academy (tel. 0832/242-0451) of Panaji. Held over four evenings in November, the festival showcases the duality of Goan culture by presenting a medley of the Indian and Western classical traditions—alternating Indian instruments such as the sitar and sarod with western Baroque music. The festival is spread across the chapel and courtyard performances see the performers framed by the setting sun, amid the mesmerizing background landscape of the Mandovi and the islands of Divar and Chorao.

Most churches of Old Goa celebrate the feasts of their saints, but the most important event here is the **Feast of St. Francis Xavier,** held on the third of December every year to commemorate the anniversary of the saint's death. Marked by processions and folk dances and attended by thousands, the feast is celebrated at the Basilica of Bom Jesus, which shelters the mortal remains of the saint. The basilica also allows the public viewing of the body in an event called the Exposition, which occurs every 10 years. Millions of people from all over the country and the world gather here on this occasion. The last Exposition was held in 2004, and the next is scheduled for 2014.

ACCOMMODATIONS AND FOOD

There are few options for lodging and food in the deserted erstwhile capital, with only some sub-standard hotels, small wayside cafés, and the run-down GTDC-operated **Old Goa Residency** (behind Basilica of Bom Jesus, tel. 0832/228-5327, www.goa-tourism.com, Rs 600–1,800). Most visitors prefer to stay in Panaji and make a day trip of Old Goa, but if you must stay longer, the apartment-style lodging offers budget rates and basic rooms, some with air-conditioning and balconies. There's a garden on the premises and Sukhsagar restaurant serves local and North Indian cuisine. Around the parking area near the churches are a few food stalls and an open café that offer refreshments.

GETTING THERE AND AROUND

It's a short ride to Old Goa from Panaji (via Ribandar) by either bus or taxi. Buses ply frequently from the Kadamba bus stand to the Basilica of Bom Jesus—the journey takes around 20 minutes and costs Rs 6 (Rs 20 if you take the shuttle). Buses to Ponda and Marcel also stop at Old Goa. Taxis, shared taxis, and auto-rickshaws are also available, but charge Rs 200–300 one-way. The GTDC has guided bus tours from Panaji that include Old Goa. Once there, it is easy to walk around the old capital or take a taxi or auto-rickshaw to get around.

Ponda

The colorful temples and lush greens of the countryside around Ponda are in stark contrast with the deserted churches of Old Goa. Outside the temples, rows of women in traditional saris sell floral offerings (garlands and baskets of lilies and lotuses). Some, like the Mangeshi Temple, are lined with stalls selling clothes and shells along with religious souvenirs (and even the odd tattoo artist). Most shrines have residences for pilgrims, who flock here during festivals to participate in the vibrant fairs and processions.

The town of Ponda itself is a characterless place, filled with concrete buildings, traffic, and crowds. Visitors generally prefer to stay in Panaji and make a day trip of the temples scattered around Ponda, often stopping in Old Goa and the spice plantations on the way. The cultural distinctions are sharp; Ponda allows a peek into Hindu Goa and to a turbulent chapter in the region's history. The last province to be captured by the Portuguese, it was ruled by Shahu Maharaj, the grandson of Maratha warrior Shivaji, until it was acquired by the conquistadors in 1764. Deities from temples destroyed by the Portuguese were patiently kept in secrecy, for centuries in some cases, and brought here to be installed in the newer shrines. Today, the modern-looking concrete temples have been renovated so often that very little remains of their history—apart from the original deities.

◖ SPICE PLANTATIONS

Once you've sampled Goan cuisine, it's only natural to be curious about the ingredients that go into its making. Cinnamon, clove, cumin, turmeric, cardamom, Portuguese chili (2,800 times spicier than the regular chili!), and a variety of other spices grow among the lush spice plantations of inner Goa. Camouflaged among the tropical forests of the region, these plantations, or spice farms, are concentrated around Ponda and are open to tourists. Visitors are given a traditional welcome and a guided tour around the property, followed by a sumptuous lunch. The spice plantations of restaurant-starved Ponda are a popular stop for tourists on their way to the temples from Panaji and Old Goa, helping them combine a local meal with a traditional experience.

Some of the plantations, like the **Sahakari Spice Farm** (Curti, 2 km from Ponda, tel. 0832/2312394, cell tel. 91/94220-57312, www.sahakarifarms.com, 9:30 A.M.–4 P.M. daily, Rs 300) have a history that goes back 350 years. The owner, Madhav Sahakari, belongs to the seventh generation of the family that owns this 52-hectare plot of land—one hectare of which is used to show visitors around. After a traditional welcome with a garland and *kumkum* (a spot of red powder on the forehead), visitors are given a shot of *feni*. A trained guide then takes guests through the spice tour, where you can see and taste fresh cinnamon, pepper, nutmeg, vanilla, coffee, herbs, betel leaf, areca nut,

© JANHAVI ACHAREKAR

A spice tour is the highlight of a visit to a Goan spice plantation.

pimento, and a variety of other spices. Visitors may also opt for an elephant ride (Rs 500) or spend a day with an elephant—and can even help bathe of the pachyderm. At the end of the tour, the guide pours a little spring water down your back to soothe your tired spine. A traditional Hindu lunch on a banana leaf then awaits you—a variety of vegetables, spiced rice, rotis, and some fish or chicken. The sweet saffron rice is a must-try.

The most charming of all plantations, the **Savoi Plantation** (Savoi Verem, tel. 0832/234-0272, cell tel. 91/98221-33309, 10:30 A.M.–3:30 P.M. daily, Rs 150 with snacks, Rs 300 with lunch) is a serene, shaded place with fewer crowds than the more touristy Sahakari Spice Farm. Turmeric, ginger, basil, cinnamon, and a host of spices are grown organically and demonstrated to visitors in this beautiful rural setting. The farm restaurant serves a buffet lunch with traditional Hindu preparations and there are two village-style mud huts where guests can stay overnight (Rs 3,000 each, accommodates two people).

A riverside property, **Pascoal Spice Village** (Ponda-Belgaum Rd., Khandepar, near Usgao, tel. 0832/234-4268, 9 A.M.–5 P.M. daily, Rs 100, meals à la carte) is conveniently located en route to Far Eastern Goa. While the plantation has a lovely lawn, a nursery, and a river flowing through it, the vegetation is not quite as lush as that of the others. Turmeric, ginger, cardamom, pepper, and other spices are grown here, along with fruits like pineapple. In addition to the plantation tour, visitors may also feed fish and go on a boat ride along the river. The farm restaurant serves a village-style lunch along with *feni*. The plantation also has cottages (Rs 500 without a/c, Rs 900 with a/c) should you wish to extend your stay.

The **Tropical Spice Plantation** (Keri, 6 km from Ponda, tel. 0832/234-0329, 8:30 A.M.–5 P.M. daily, Rs 300) is equidistant from Ponda and the Mahalsa Narayani Temple. Along with the usual spice tour, its added attractions include a lovely lake as well as elephant rides (Rs 500) and baths (Rs 600). The plantation itself comes across as a little

sparse compared to the others, but offers a hearty Goan meal with a drink at the end of the tour.

SIGHTS
Shri Mangeshi Temple
Dedicated to Mangesh, an incarnation of Lord Shiva, the Mangeshi Temple (Panaji-Ponda Rd., Priol, 6 A.M.–10 P.M. daily, photography prohibited inside the temple, open to all faiths) originally stood in Cortalim. It was moved to its present location in the 16th century to escape the pillaging of the Portuguese; the temple, in its present form, was built in the 18th century. A beautiful water tank located near the entrance is one of the oldest parts of the structure. The temple is easily distinguished by its towering white *deepastambha* (lamp-tower) in the open courtyard.

The structure is a fascinating fusion of various styles of architecture. The dome above the sanctum sanctorum resembles that of a church, specifically St. Cajetan's in Old Goa. The bell on the tower, an alien concept within Hindu

© JANHAVI ACHAREKAR

The *deepastambha* bears a church-style bell that rings hourly.

PANAJI AND INTERIOR GOA

temples, mimics the Portuguese churches of Goa and rings hourly, like a church bell. Meanwhile, the domed roofs outside are distinctly Islamic in style.

Inside the temple is a disappointing combination of marble and concrete. The only historical reminder is its *shivling,* the phallic temple deity (covered after the *arti,* or prayer service, at noon) that was rescued from the original temple in 1561 and preserved in a secret place until the temple was rebuilt in its current location.

Shri Mahalsa Narayani Temple

A temple built in worship of the goddess Mahalsa, the female incarnation of Lord Vishnu, the Mahalsa Narayani Temple (1 km from the Shri Mangeshi Temple, off the Panaji-Ponda Rd., Mardol, 6:30 A.M.– 8:30 P.M. daily, photography prohibited inside the temple, open to all faiths) is the most pristine of the Ponda temples. The 18th-century temple has preserved its marble-floored *mandapa* (hall), which leads to beautiful carved wooden pillars and the detailed panels inside. The deity that rests in the sanctum sanctorum originally stood in Salcete, farther south, but was smuggled here from Verna to protect it from destruction by the Portuguese colonizers. The temple has an unusual *deepastambha,* made of the *panchadhaatu* or an alloy of five metals (gold, silver, copper, iron, zinc) considered sacred in Hinduism. The soaring lamp-tower, at 21 meters, is believed to be the highest found in any temple, and comprises 21 tiers, with the tortoise Kurma—another avatar of Vishnu—as its base. The lamp-tower is lit with wick-and-oil lamps during festivals and makes for a spellbinding sight.

Nageshi Temple

The Nageshi Temple (Farmagudi-Kavlem-Ponda Rd., Bandora, 8:30 A.M.–8:30 P.M. daily, photography prohibited inside the temple, open to all faiths) exudes a calm that is lacking in other temples. Walk past

its colorful *deepastambha* decorated with protruding *nagas* (serpents), and toward the entrance of the temple—you will come upon the green waters of its hundred-year-old tank, surrounded by swaying palm trees. The courtyard has an old stone inscription and sculpture, while inside, the *shivling* is glimpsed past the *sabhamandapa* (central hall). The hall is richly decorated with wooden carvings that depict scenes from the Hindu epic of the *Ramayana.* Built in 1413, the temple is dedicated to the deity of Nageshi, the serpent-incarnation of Lord Shiva, and is one of the few to remain at its original site.

Shri Mahalaxmi Temple

Located close to the Nageshi Temple, the Shri Mahalaxmi Temple (300 m from the Nageshi Temple, Farmagudi-Kavlem-Ponda Rd., 7 A.M.–8:30 P.M. daily, photography prohibited inside the temple, open to all faiths) pays tribute to its chief deities—Lord Vishnu and his consort Laxmi—with an ornate and detailed *mandapa.* A gallery filled with 24 painted and wooden images, mostly of Vishnu, greets pilgrims upon entry into the temple. The original temple was located in Colva, on the southern coast, but was moved here to protect it from the Goan Inquisition. The goddess was worshipped by the Silahara kings (750–1,030 A.D.) and the early Kadamba rulers of Goa.

Safa Masjid

Built in 1560, the Safa Masjid (Farmagudi-Bondla Rd., restricted entry) is Goa's most important mosque. This beautiful vision in white and laterite red emerges from its green surroundings along the road to the Shantadurga temple. Built by Ibrahim Adil Shah of Bijapur, the mosque was originally surrounded by beautiful gardens but was abandoned during Portuguese rule and fell into neglect until its recent restoration by the Archaeological Survey of India. Today, men and young boys from the neighborhood may be seen sporting white skullcaps and emerging from the building after the morning prayers.

© JANHAVI ACHAREKAR

The 16th-century Safa Masjid, Goa's most important mosque, stands tall amid Hindu temples in Ponda.

Shantadurga Temple

The sprawling Shantadurga Temple (off the Panaji-Ponda Rd., 3.5 km from Ponda, in Kavlem, 7 A.M.–9 P.M. daily, photography prohibited inside the temple, open to all faiths) dates back to 1738, when it was built by the reigning Shahu Maharaj. A modern-looking structure, it has a tall *deepastambha* and a water tank. Dedicated to the goddess Parvati, Shiva's consort, and a striking balance of two avatars—the peaceful Shanta and the violent or martial goddess Durga—the temple is also known locally as Santeri. The incarnation of Shantadurga is believed to have played mediator between the gods Shiva and Vishnu during a battle between the two.

The original temple of Shantadurga once stood on the southern coast of Cavelossim. The current building displays the influence of Portuguese architecture with its pyramid-style tiled roof and dome over the sanctum sanctorum. Like the lamp-tower of the Mahalsa Narayani Temple, the idol of the deity too is made of the *panchadhaatu,* with a *shivling* and the images of Vishnu and Shiva on either side of it.

Shri Ramnathi Temple

Another Shiva shrine, the Shri Ramnathi temple (near Shantadurga Temple in Kavlem, Bandora, 6 A.M.–9:30 P.M. daily, photography prohibited inside the temple, open to all faiths) is dedicated to Lord Ramnath—an incarnation of the Hindu god who plays an important role in the epic *Ramayana*. Within the temple is a cluster of four more shrines—together, the five are known as Shri Ramnath Panchyatan. The *shivling* and deity in the sanctum sanctorum lay in Loutolim in South Goa before they were brought here to safety in 1566. The shrine is located near the Shantadurga Temple and is distinguished by a silver screen decorated with images of animals and flowers.

Kamakshi Temple

The Kamakshi Temple (12 km south of Ponda, Shiroda, 7 A.M.–9 P.M. daily, photography prohibited inside the temple, open to all faiths) is dedicated to another incarnation of the goddess Parvati, known as Kamakshi. Originally located in Salcete, the shrine was moved to its present location around the year 1564. The temple also houses smaller shrines dedicated to deities Shantadurga, Laxmi Narayan, and Rayeshwar.

Bondla Wildlife Sanctuary

You know you've reached the Bondla Wildlife Sanctuary (via Usgaon, tel. 0832/293-5800, 9:30 A.M.–5 P.M. Fri.–Wed., adults Rs 5, children Rs 2, vehicles Rs 50, photography Rs 20) when you read a sign that says "Drive slow, wild animals have right of way." Greenery, streams, and monsoon waterfalls greet visitors on arrival. Not far from the temples of Ponda, this is the smallest of all the sanctuaries in Goa. Spread over eight kilometers, it is home to a deer park and shelters leopards, gaurs (Indian bison), wild boars, sloth bears, panthers, jackals, cobras, and many species of birds and butterflies. The sanctuary has a garden and mini-zoo as well as a nature education center. It offers living arrangements—cottages, rooms, and dormitories—for visitors who wish to stay the night, while an in-house restaurant serves local home-style cooking.

ENTERTAINMENT AND EVENTS
Temple Festivals

Every temple in Goa celebrates its *zatra* (temple fair), no different from the "feasts" celebrated by the various churches here. The atmosphere is festive and the temple deity is brought out in a palanquin or a chariot as part of a colorful procession. Thousands flock to offer their prayers and to worship the honored god or goddess. Each of the temples in Ponda celebrates its own *zatra* and throngs of pilgrims arrive here during this time. The pilgrims' lodging within the temples is generally teeming with occupants, even as they bathe in the water tanks and participate in religious ceremonies. Celebrations involve much pomp and gaiety, with makeshift stalls selling toys, treats, and religious souvenirs on the temple premises.

floral offerings for sale outside the temples of Ponda

The **Mangeshi Temple Festival** (Mangeshi Temple, Priol), also called the *Manguirish zatra* is one of the most vibrant celebrations in Ponda. It takes place around February, on a date selected on the basis of the lunar calendar. The temple deities are brought out on a chariot that is then parked on the right side of the temple for public viewing.

The **Mahalsa Narayani Temple Festival** (Mahalsa Narayani Temple, Mardol) is held February with a *vijayarathotsav* (chariot festival) and a special *puja* (religious ceremony) in the months of August and September.

The **Shantadurga Temple Festival** (Shantadurga Temple, Kavlem) is an eight-day affair, also celebrated in February.

Other temples such as the Nageshi and Ramnathi in Bandora organize *zatras* around Hindu festivals such as *Mahashivratri* (celebratory worship of Hindu god Shiva) and *Dassera* (a celebration of the triumph of good over evil, of the victory of Lord Rama over Ravana in the epic *Ramayana*).

SPORTS AND RECREATION

Goa's interior offers plenty of opportunity for adventure and recreation. While there are no organized tours, Ponda's surrounding countryside is ideal for independent trekking and hiking. Wildlife-viewing and bird-watching are possible at the **Bondla Wildlife Sanctuary** (via Usgaon, tel. 0832/293-5800, 9:30 A.M.–5 P.M. Fri.–Wed., adults Rs 5, children Rs 2, vehicles Rs 50, photography Rs 20), where you can spot animals such as leopards, panthers, deer, wild boar ,and birds such as peacocks, drongos, Paradise flycatchers, hornbills, sunbirds, and green bee-eaters. There's a treetop watchtower and the sanctuary sometimes conducts special safaris for visitors. It also offers **elephant rides** (11 A.M.–noon and 4–5 P.M.) and plenty of wildlife trails for visitors to follow. Those interested in trekking on their own in the interior will be disappointed with the absence of maps and trails, but the staff at the sanctuary office should be able to guide you.

The Bondla Wildlife Sanctuary is home to several species of mammals, birds, reptiles, and insects.

ACCOMMODATIONS AND FOOD

There are only two reasonably good lodging options in and around Ponda—the Bondla Wildlife Sanctuary and the GTDC cottages in Farmagudi. There are surprisingly few eateries, considering the number of pilgrims who descend upon the place during festivals. While both accommodations have restaurants that whip up palatable fare, the spice plantations in the area are the best places to go for an authentic local meal.

Bondla Wildlife Sanctuary

If you're looking for a nature retreat, the Bondla Wildlife Sanctuary (via Usgaon, tel. 0832/293-5800, Rs 350–700) offers cottage-style accommodations within the park. It also has dormitories (Rs 75 per bed) for groups of at least 20 people. Rooms are simple and basic, but offer proximity to wildlife. Visitors come here for the nocturnal sounds of the jungle rather than the comforts of home. The sanctuary has an in-house restaurant called **The Den** (tel. 0832/293-5800, Rs 50–150).

Farmagudi Residency

GTDC's Farmagudi Residency (tel. 0832/233-5122, www.goa-tourism.com, Rs 600–1,660) in the village of Farmagudi near Ponda is the preferred alternative to the chaos of Ponda town. This well-maintained hillside resort is made up of multi-level cottages that overlook manicured lawns. Rooms are bright and airy and the resort also offers dormitory facilities (Rs 120–200 per bed) to groups. The Residency has a cottage-restaurant, **Hilltop Restaurant and Bar** (tel. 0832/233-5122, 7 A.M.–11 P.M. daily, mains Rs 30–120) that serves local and North Indian cuisine.

INFORMATION AND SERVICES
Tourist Information

GTDC's **Farmagudi Residency** (tel. 0832/233-5122, www.goa-tourism.com) is the best place near Ponda for tourist information.

PANAJI AND INTERIOR GOA

© JANHAVI ACHAREKAR

BEYOND TOURISM: COMMUNITY WORK AND CULTURAL INTEGRATION

The discovery of Goa by the Western world led to an unprecedented growth in tourism, dividing the beaches from the interior. As a result, while tourists enjoyed the sand and the surf, a sense of alienation descended upon local residents and villagers, who could no longer identify with the new culture of their home state.

Local concerns have grown as the Goan countryside, and therefore its geographical identity, is systematically eroded to give way to modern concrete structures. However, a number of artist and activist groups have come together to preserve, in the face of tourism, the old Goa that they once knew. One such body is the Goa Writers' Group – a set of Goan and other writers who have made the state their home. Started by Goan expat writer Victor Rangel-Ribeiro and Margaret Mascarenhas, the group meets in and around Panaji or at members' residences, once a month on Fridays. They critique works, discuss ideas, and act on issues that need to be tackled to preserve the Goan heritage. Well-known author Amitav Ghosh resides in Goa for six months of the year and participates in the activities of the group, as does Goa's premier writer, Maria Aurora Couto.

Meanwhile, using theater as an instrument of change is Isabel St. Rita Vaz's Mustard Seed Art Company. Mustard Seed strives to portray the real Goa – the one that goes beyond the beaches and the tourist attractions. The theater company writes scripts inspired by social concerns and politics in the state. Vaz is also involved in community work, actively raising funds for AIDS and other causes.

Finnish writer Iikka Veklahathi first visited Goa as a tourist and then lived in the village of Carmona, just off the southern coast near Varca, for a year. The Goan environment, having contributed greatly to his writing, compelled him to give back in some way. When Saxtti Kids – a pre-primary village school – was set up in the village, Iikka and his visiting family and friends contributed toward building a toy library for the school. These toys are now part of a circulating library that the village kids use on a day-to-day basis. Saxtti Kids also allows tourists to interact with the children, by telling stories of their countries at sessions on the school premises. Goan writer Savia Viegas, who runs the organization, feels that many tourists consume the Goan landscape without really knowing it. Giving back is a great way to show your appreciation – and to end your holiday. For a storytelling appointment, or to make a donation, email saxtti@gmail.com.

Tourists can also contribute to Arz (Plot. No-71, next to ESI Dispensary, Sancoale Industrial Estate, Zuari Nagar, Vasco, tel. 0832/255-5446, cell tel. 91/94224-38109, www.arzindia .org), an organization working to combating human trafficking for commercial sexual exploitation in Goa. Arz has been appointed by the Goa Police as a nodal organization to fight human trafficking in Goa.

You can make inquiries and obtain maps/brochures at the office.

Hospitals

Ponda is well equipped with medical facilities. It has a number of nursing homes and hospitals, including **Sushrusha Nursing Home** (Radhakrishna Apartments, near Maruti Temple, Ponda, tel. 0832/231-5610) and **Central Hospital** (Usgaon, tel. 0832/234-4221).

Police

In case of emergency, **dial 100** for the 24-hour police helpline or try the **Ponda Police Station** (Ponda, tel. 0832/231-3101). There's also a police outpost near the temples—**Farmagudi Outpost** (Farmagudi, tel. 0832/233-5339).

Money

For currency exchange, you're better off going to Ponda town, although there are a few banks and travel agents located en route to some of the temples. **Centurion Bank** (Commerce Centre, Tisca-Ponda, tel. 0832/231-9112, 9:30 A.M.–1 P.M. Mon.–Sat.) and **Vishwakamal Travels** (4, Kazi Building, tel. 0832/231-2724, 10 A.M.–5:30 P.M. daily) are both options. **Corporation Bank** (Ramnathi, Ponda, tel. 0832/233-5266) also has an ATM.

Postal Services

Ponda Post Office (near old bus stand, Dada Vaidya Chowk, tel. 0832/231-2892, 9:30 A.M.–4 P.M. Mon.–Sat.) is where to go for speedpost services and registered letter booking.

GETTING THERE AND AROUND

It's a short distance along the National Highway 17 to Ponda from Old Goa, and the same bus that takes you to Old Goa from Panaji generally carries on ahead to Ponda. There's also a shuttle service (Rs 20 per person) to Ponda that leaves from the Kadamba Bus Stand (Patto area, Panaji). A taxi to Bondla sanctuary from Ponda costs Rs 350.

If you intend to travel to the spice plantations or to the Bondla Wildlife Sanctuary, it is wiser to rent a car or taxi, although you can get to the sanctuary by taking a bus to Usgaon village from Ponda bus station and then a taxi to the park entrance.

Far Eastern Goa

As you venture deeper into the interior, the kaleidoscopic Goan landscape morphs magically from sand and sea to fields, forests, and waterfalls. While Goa's lush hinterland is sadly overshadowed by its coastal cousins, there's no doubt that there's a whole world to be discovered in its villages and national parks. Farther inside from the temples of Ponda and the Bondla Wildlife Sanctuary is a countryside crisscrossed by streams, betel plantations, inhabited only by tribals, villagers, and wildlife. At the very eastern end of the state is the remote medieval temple of Tambdi Surla—Goa's most interesting shrine—lost amid thick foliage and hidden from the prying eyes of regular tourist traffic. Not far away, the Bhagwan Mahavir Wildlife Sanctuary and Molem National Park present a wealth of wildlife and offer accommodations to jungle enthusiasts. Meanwhile, it's a small climb to the magnificent Dudhsagar Falls—the second largest in India—and it's a shame that the cascading waterfall is closed to visitors in the monsoon (for reasons of safety) when it is at its most glorious.

SIGHTS
◖ Tambdi Surla

Easily the best of Goa's temples, this black basalt shrine (Tambdi Surla village, at the edge of Bhagwan Mahavir Wildlife Sanctuary and

A stone tablet bears a sculpture of intertwined cobras at the temple of Tambdi Surla.

Molem National Park, 8:30 A.M.–5:30 P.M. daily, free, photography permitted, open to all faiths) is dedicated to the god Mahadev, or Lord Shiva. It dates back to the 11th–12th century A.D., when the Kadamba dynasty was at the peak of its glory. The oldest and most pristine of all Goan temples, it escaped the destruction of the Portuguese Inquisition only because of the inaccessibility of its location, which remains remote even to this day. Situated on the banks of the Surla River in the village of Tambdi Surla (from which it derives its name), the temple has a beautifully carved facade and a geometric structure with snugly fitted stone blocks that stand free of mortar or any binding substance. Within the temple is a statue of Nandi, the mount of Lord Shiva, and on the tower above the sanctum sanctorum are carvings of the Hindu Trinity—Brahma, Vishnu, and Shiva. A stone tablet with a sculpture of intertwined cobras adds to the mystical charm. The temple faces eastward, allowing the first rays of the morning sun to fall on the deity. At dusk, it exudes a magical calm when the wick-and-oil lamps are lit, transporting the shrine and its visitors back to medieval times.

◖ Bhagwan Mahavir Wildlife Sanctuary and Molem National Park

Goa's largest wildlife sanctuary at 240 square kilometers, the Bhagwan Mahavir Wildlife Sanctuary and Molem National Park (Molem village, 9 A.M.–5:30 P.M. daily, photography Rs 30, videography Rs 150) are densely vegetated with thick, evergreen forests and inhabited by a variety of wild animals—including panthers, bison, wild boar, deer, sloth bears, and more. The Molem National Park, a part of the larger sanctuary, is a haven for various species of resident and migratory birds, including the exotic fairy bluebird, Paradise flycatcher, Malabar pied hornbill, green bee-eater, shrike, rare species of kingfishers, and the singing Malabar whistling thrush, among others. Visitors can observe wildlife at close quarters from a number of watchtowers around watering holes. The park also has several "points" (places that serve as vantage points). Among them is Sunset Point, where visitors can soak in the beautiful landscape and the twilight hues of the setting sun.

© JANHAVI ACHAREKAR

Goa's oldest and most beautiful temple, the Mahadev temple of Tambdi Surla, dates back to the 11th-century Kadamba dynasty.

◖ Dudhsagar Falls

A 90-minute drive through Molem, on the Goa-Karnataka border, are the gushing Dudhsagar Falls. Literally translated as "Milky Sea," Dudhsagar Falls are 300 meters high (600 meters from source) and emerge from the Mandovi River, spraying mist as they cascade over a mighty cliff. One of the highest falls in India, their deafening roar may be heard over the gorge known as the Devil's Canyon, even as they pool at the bottom. Unfortunately, the din of tourists and revelers may be heard even above the sound of the waterfall. This area is quiet and at its most beautiful in the monsoon, but is cordoned off because of the danger of strong currents and uncontrollable flow of water. The forested landscape surrounding the falls is equally spectacular and ideal for a walk, though there are no marked or organized trails.

SPORTS AND RECREATION

A remote temple, lush national park, and one of the highest waterfalls in India make for a heady combination as far as adventure and recreation go. Far Eastern Goa provides myriad opportunities to wildlife-enthusiasts and birders, who can go on wildlife and bird trails at the **Bhagwan Mahavir Wildlife Sanctuary and Molem National Park** (Molem village, 9 A.M.–5:30 P.M. daily, photography Rs 30, videography Rs 150). The sanctuary has a birding lodge called **Backwoods Camp** (Matkan, Tambdi Surla, cell tel. 91/98221-39859, www. backwoodsgoa.com), run by a bunch of passionate birders. They organize professional birdwatching tours in the area (even into the nearby Bondla Sanctuary) with camping and meals.

The dense forest around the Tambdi Surla Temple and the path from Molem to Dudhsagar also make for excellent self-guided bird trails, where sightings of the vivid Malabar trogon and flame-throated bulbul are common. Non-birders will find it just as pleasant to go trekking and hiking along the same trails. There's also a GTDC-conducted guided tour called the **Dudhsagar Special** (GTDC, Trionora Apartments, Dr. Alvares Costa Rd., tel. 0832/222-6515, www.goa-tourism.com,

9:30 A.M.–1:15 P.M. and 2–5:45 P.M. Mon.–Fri.) that leaves from a number of departure points in Goa, including Panaji. The coach tour goes deep into interior Goa via Old Goa and past Ponda, Tambdi Surla, and Molem to the Dudhsagar Falls.

ACCOMMODATIONS AND FOOD

Your accommodations become more limited the deeper you travel into Far Eastern Goa. Rooms and tents are provided by the tourism department inside the Bhagwan Mahavir Sanctuary and Molem National Park (Molem village, Oct.–May, Rs 200–500). Living arrangements are basic and the place is closed for the monsoon. The sanctuary also has a restaurant that cooks meals as per your requirements.

Located in the heart of the Bhagwan Mahavir Sanctuary and Molem National Park, ◖ **Backwoods Camp** (Matkan, Tambdi Surla, cell tel. 91/98221-39859, www.backwoodsgoa.com) is a haven for birders. The camp offers special tours and the rates are inclusive of professional guides, transport, accommodations, and meals. Guests arriving from Panaji, Calangute, Baga, or Arpora even get picked up and dropped off. The tour packages start with a minimum of three days/two nights in order to be able to do some meaningful bird-watching; accommodations includes safari-style tents and cottages (Rs 5,500), as well as farmhouse rooms (Rs 6,500). Prices are slightly higher for the four-day/three-night package (Rs 8,000–9000), with every additional night another Rs 2,500–2750. Children below eight years of age are free, and the camp admits groups of up to 12 people. The rooms have attached bathrooms and verandahs overlooking the forest. The site, in general, has electricity, generators, and running water, as well as a small library and bar. This delightful eco-friendly, back-to-nature camp is an ideal getaway for nature enthusiasts—and a surprising find in these remote parts.

Located at Chorla Ghat, near the Karnataka border, **Wildernest** (Swapnagandha, off Sankhali, Chorla Ghats, tel. 91/98814-02665, www.wildernest-goa.com, Rs 3,800–10,000) is one of the country's finest nature resorts. Located in the beautiful Swapnagandha Valley and overlooking the Vazra Falls, this little piece of paradise seems almost miraculous in both location and offerings. Strictly for nature-lovers, the rustic resort has breathtaking infinity pool and vast tracts of surrounding forest populated by rare birds. It's managed by staff who, according to a guest, are "very clued in." Rural and back-to-nature accommodations in the form of private eco-huts are complemented by traditional cuisine at the in-house restaurant and cocktails at a garden bar called Cloud 9. Resident wildlife experts conduct reptile, butterfly, and bird walks for guests, in addition to giving talks on these subjects. A great place for treks, hikes, or quite simply to get away from urban life, Wildernest is exactly what its name conveys—a cozy nest in the wilderness.

GETTING THERE AND AROUND

From the Bondla sanctuary, you will need to carry on by car or taxi to Tambdi Surla via Valpoi, and then take the road to Molem. From Ponda, Tambdi Surla is a half-hour drive on the NH4. The bus ride from Ponda costs Rs 25, while a taxi costs around Rs 350.

To get to Molem directly from Panaji (65 km), drive along the NH4A, also known as the Panaji-Belgaum Highway; the drive takes about 1.5 hours. You can also take a bus to Ponda and then change to a bus that goes to Belgaum in Karnataka or to Londa, both of which stop at Molem on the way.

Dudhsagar Falls are located within the sanctuary and may be reached by Jeep through the park. If you want to get there by train, you will need to alight at Collem Railway Station (6 km from Dudhsagar Falls) and take a taxi for the onward journey. For the sake of convenience, however, it is advisable to hire a taxi for the day, starting from Panaji.

The Goa Tourism Development Corporation (GTDC) also conducts guided tours (Trionora Apartments, Dr. Alvares Costa Rd., Panaji, tel. 0832/222-6515, www.goa-tourism.com, 9:30 A.M.–1:15 P.M. and 2–5:45 P.M. Mon.–Fri.) to these places, starting from Panaji.

THE NORTHERN COAST

Transformed from a cluster of secluded fishing villages into a hippie paradise in the psychedelic 1960s, the northern coast of Goa is now a shadow of its former self. Lined with rows of identical shacks known for their excellent seafood, English breakfast, and Goan curries, the northern beaches are dotted with sunbathing tourists. The recent increase in the number of budget flights available within India has created an influx of domestic tourists, causing popular beaches, such as Baga and Calangute, to become even more crowded in peak season. During the day, tattoo artists, trinket sellers, ice-cream vendors, and water sports add to the melee, while sundown brings with it fire shows and acrobatics on the beach, night markets, and the occasional "full moon party." The nude beaches have long disappeared, but the drugs and parties have not; at the beaches of Anjuna and Vagator, in spite of the official clamp-down, those with an ear to the ground are in the loop as far as Goa's raves are concerned.

However, those looking for solitude are pleasantly surprised by the smaller and more secluded beaches of northern Goa. In the far north, the little-known beach of Mandrem is a picture of tranquility, while Morjim is nesting ground for olive ridley turtles. And at the lush Maharashtra border is Goa's northernmost point, the blissfully calm Keri Beach, watched over by the impressive Fort Tiracol. The northern coast is also where heritage and nature commune to present a dramatic landscape—the spectacular Chapora Fort in Vagator is proof enough. Closer to where the action is,

© JANHAVI ACHAREKAR

HIGHLIGHTS

◖ **Fort Aguada:** Once a stopover for Portuguese ships, this 17th-century fort presents a fantastic view of the sea and houses an old lighthouse (page 170).

◖ **Calizz:** You can witness the old Goan way of life at this museum, which offers a guided tour of its colorful heritage homes filled with antiques and artifacts (page 172).

◖ **Nightlife in Baga:** If you want to experience Goa's party-hearty scene, head to Baga, where you can choose between raucous nightclubs, live music, and retro nights (page 184).

◖ **Anjuna's Wednesday Flea Market:** The biggest draw in the north, Anjuna's Wednesday flea market is a crowded affair with a plethora of stalls that sell everything from clothes and trinkets to handicrafts and hammocks (page 199).

◖ **Chapora Fort:** It's a short and worthwhile climb up to the ruins of Goa's most scenic sea fort – sure to take your breath away with its spectacular view of the Vagator coastline (page 205).

◖ **Mandrem:** Goa's little secret with golden sunsets, fishing boats, and a handful of resorts, Mandrem is a lovely beach unspoiled by the commercialization of the north (page 212).

◖ **Yoga in Arambol:** If you're looking for some peace and calm, Arambol has several yoga retreats, including the famous Himalayan Iyengar Yoga Centre (page 214).

◖ **Fort Tiracol:** A 17th century Maratha fort on the Goa-Maharashtra border, the fort is now a heritage hotel whose interior and 100-year-old chapel are open to the public. It is reached by ferry and offers a spectacular view of Keri Beach (page 218).

LOOK FOR ◖ TO FIND RECOMMENDED SIGHTS, ACTIVITIES, DINING, AND LODGING.

near Candolim, is Goa's famous Fort Aguada with its vast view of the ocean.

Not far inland and within easy distance of the beaches are some of Goa's prettiest villages. The drive to Calangute from Panaji is made lovelier by the picturesque landscape of heritage village Sangolda and the 19th-century neo-Gothic church at Saligao. Today, villages such as Aldona near Mapusa are also home to a growing community of artists and writers who come here seeking respite from urban life and inspiration from the Goan countryside and culture. The northern coast is incredibly diverse, appealing to both the party-goer and nature-lover, and to those who wish to simply be amidst sand and sea and watch the world go by.

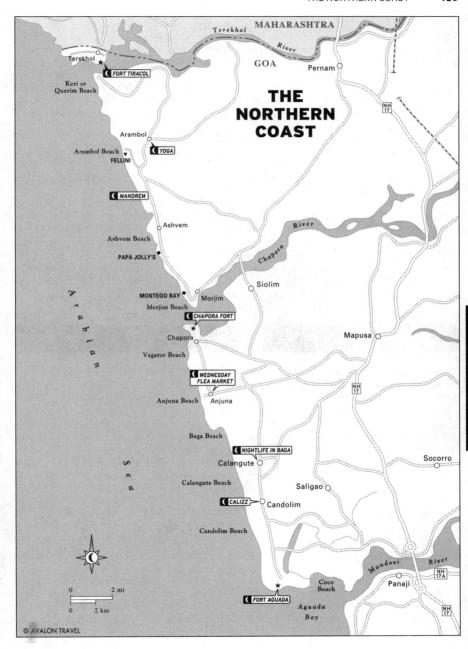

© AVALON TRAVEL

PLANNING YOUR TIME

The northern coast is the most popular destination in Goa, and any stay here requires planning and booking in advance. Unless you're a compulsive beach-hopper, it's usually best to use one or two beaches as base and then travel around to the various sights, nightspots, and markets. Five days is plenty of time in the north—enough to soak up the sun and explore the surroundings. You may want to plan your stay around a Wednesday or a Saturday, to make sure that you don't miss out on the biggest flea markets in the region. Most flea markets are only open during the high season, between November and May. This is also the time for good weather, just after the monsoon.

The beaches are vacant in the monsoon, between June and September, and most restaurants and bars are shut. Some semblance of activity exists along the Candolim–Calangute–Baga stretch, but the coast farther north is strangely quiet. Most hotels too are closed, suffering the ravages of weather before they are spruced up again, magically transformed for the next tourist season. However, if you want to soak in the atmosphere more than the sun, this is a good time to book a boutique hotel and watch the rain beat down on the palm trees from the luxury of your designer suite.

SAFETY

While the northern coast is relatively safe, there have been instances of drug-related crime in recent years, the most famous being the Scarlet Keeling rape and murder case in Anjuna, which occurred in March 2008. Illegal drugs continue to be sold discreetly in the face of police vigilance, and there are a number of tourists languishing in the Aguada jail for drug use and trafficking. Steer clear of the beaches at night and keep out of trouble in general—corrupt cops seeking bribes are known to target foreigners.

Candolim

It is difficult to sum up Candolim in a nutshell. Images of this stretch of beach and entertainment are fragmented, divided as they are between three beaches, more sights than most of coastal Goa, and the best activities, dining, and entertainment. The first in line of a series of beaches leading up to the far northern coast, the Candolim area is also the most conveniently located. Equidistant from both the heritage sights of Panaji and Old Goa as well as the sun, sand, and parties of Anjuna and Vagator, it appeals to a wide range of tourists. Charter tourists, backpackers, and domestic visitors comb the beaches, swarm the Aguada fort and lighthouse, and shop and eat around the market area.

No longer a sleepy fishing village, Candolim does, however, still have its moments. These include calm sunsets at Coco Beach, where the Mandovi River meets the sea, and quiet lunches by the Nerul River. The first to herald luxury tourism, this is also where the Taj Group of Hotels developed their flagship Goan property, the Fort Aguada Beach Resort. Today, Candolim is lined with innumerable lodges and small hotels, churches and pretty houses, restaurants and shops, all gaily lit with festive lights during the peak season. Adding to its appeal is the recently opened museum, Calizz, turning this stretch into what its baseline aptly captures—"the heart of Goa."

SIGHTS
◖ Fort Aguada

A quiet, winding road leads up to the ruins of the impregnable Fort Aguada (Fort Aguada Rd., 9:30 A.M.–5:30 P.M. daily, free, photography allowed) that loom over the surrounding seascape. Built on the mouth of the Mandovi River, overlooking Sinquerim Beach, the fort dates back to 1612, when it was meant to guard against attacks from the Dutch and the

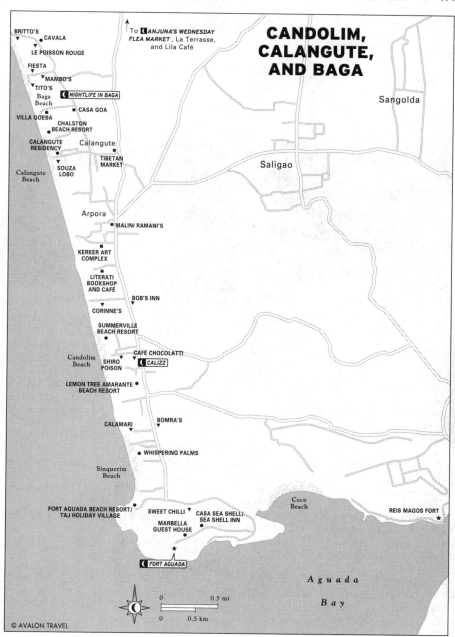

CANDOLIM, CALANGUTE, AND BAGA

To **ANJUNA'S WEDNESDAY FLEA MARKET**, La Terrasse, and Lila Café

BRITTO'S
CAVALA
LE POISSON ROUGE
FIESTA
MAMBO'S
TITO'S
NIGHTLIFE IN BAGA
Baga Beach
CASA GOA
VILLA GOESA
CHALSTON BEACH RESORT
CALANGUTE RESIDENCY
Calangute
SOUZA LOBO
TIBETAN MARKET
Calangute Beach

Sangolda

Saligao

Arpora
MALINI RAMANI'S
KERKER ART COMPLEX
LITERATI BOOKSHOP AND CAFÉ
BOB'S INN
CORINNE'S
SUMMERVILLE BEACH RESORT
CAFÉ CHOCOLATTI
Candolim Beach
SHIRO
POISON
CALIZZ
LEMON TREE AMARANTE BEACH RESORT
BOMRA'S
CALAMARI
WHISPERING PALMS
Sinquerim Beach
Coco Beach
REIS MAGOS FORT
FORT AGUADA BEACH RESORT/ TAJ HOLIDAY VILLAGE
SWEET CHILLI
CASA SEA SHELL/ SEA SHELL INN
MARBELLA GUEST HOUSE
FORT AGUADA

Aguada Bay

0   0.5 mi
0   0.5 km

© AVALON TRAVEL

© ASHIMA NARAIN

The ruins of Fort Aguada, with its old lighthouse, offer a view of the surrounding ocean.

Marathas. It was named after the Portuguese word for water—*agua*—not for the surrounding ocean, but for its three freshwater springs, which turned this destination into a pit stop for ships arriving from Portugal. Protected by a deep moat, the ramparts house an old lighthouse (4–5 P.M. daily) that predates the fort by nearly four decades and which once displayed the bell of the Church of St. Augustine in Old Goa before it was taken to the Church of Our Lady of Immaculate Conception in Panaji. From the fort, you can also see the 17th-century Church of St. Lawrence (open only for Mass at 8 A.M. sun.), dedicated to the saint of sailors.

Meanwhile, beneath the fort and alongside the sprawling estate of a Mumbai millionaire lies the Aguada Jail—once the main citadel of the fort, but now home to a number of inmates doing time for drug charges.

Sinquerim Beach

North of Fort Aguada, Sinquerim Beach is a golden stretch of sand dominated by luxury Taj Aguada hotel and the marooned *River Princess*. Calm and picturesque, it is the beginning of a continuous strip of land that extends to the Baga River in the north. It begins at Fort Aguada, turns into Candolim, and then extends into the Calangute and Baga beaches, all of which are named after fishing villages that lie alongside. Sinquerim is also known for water sports, and the sky above the beach is often dotted with parasailors.

Candolim Beach

A quiet fishing-village-turned-hippie-discovery-turned-popular-tourist- resort, Candolim has been reincarnated several times over the last few decades. This strip of beach, which connects the neighboring beaches of Sinquerim and Calangute, has a 17th-century church and is home to a tiny fishing village.

◖ Calizz

Calizz (Bammon Vaddo, tel. 0832/325-5555, www.calizz.com, 11 A.M.–8:30 P.M. daily Oct.–Apr. and 11 A.M.–8:30 P.M. Mon.–Sat. May–Sept., Rs 300 including guided tour and tea/coffee) is the labor of love of Goan resident Laxmikant Kudchadkar, who has made it his passion to showcase old Goan life for visitors. A cluster of heritage homes spanning various architectural styles and eras, this wonderful museum is a veritable treasure trove of antiques and artifacts. The guided tour begins with the Portuguese-style house of Dona Bertha, built in 1804. Having dedicated, according to custom, her three sons to God, the people, and the devil—that is, to priesthood, medicine, and law, respectively—she proceeded to accommodate their offices and themed rooms within the sprawling family home. Every room has been meticulously designed and decorated, showcasing original frescoes and period furniture, as well as relevant artifacts and objets d'art collected by Kudchadkar over the years. The house also has a beautiful private chapel and a trading house, Casa de Tobago, where the family traded in tobacco.

Next door is the pre-Portuguese Hindu home of a Goan Brahmin woman called Laxmibai. The traditional Hindu style of architecture and its earthy hues are in stark contrast with the house of Dona Bertha. Whereas Dona Bertha's residence has an impressive display of glassware, four-poster beds, and objects from around the world, Laxmibai's house is an example of Spartan living and showcases traditional items such as brass bells and lamps collected by the entrepreneur-collector (don't miss the traditional sex-education toys). Adjoining Laxmibai's house is that of the landlord, Gopala Pilgaonkar (perhaps the only dissonant chord in the museum, with its kitschy new plaster-of-Paris models of Hindu deities), and at the farthest end are the huts of a carpenter and a fisherman. Even the restaurant is true to its ambience, with a 150-year-old mirror suspended from the ceiling and a 70-year-old two-propeller fan. With all this painstaking effort and eye for detail, it's no wonder that Calizz, open only since 2007, has already won a tourism award.

Reis Magos Fort and Church

Three kilometers from Fort Aguada, in the

© ASHIMA NARAIN

THE NORTHERN COAST

grinding stones and pestles, remnants of old Goa, on display at Calizz

village of Verem, is a fort called the Reis Magos. It's located on a path going uphill from the church of the same name and dedicated to the three Magi kings. Originally built in 1551, the fort was rebuilt in 1709 and then turned into a jail soon after Liberation. It was also briefly occupied by the British army (1798–1813). At one time, it was where high officials stopped on their way to and from Lisbon. The most spectacular feature of this nondescript structure is its sweeping view of the Mandovi River meeting the sea at Coco Beach.

The church was built in 1555 and is known for the Festa dos Reis Magos, a feast celebrating the journey of the three kings with a joyous and colorful procession. A freshwater spring flows alongside, and within the church premises rest the remains of Dom Luis de Ataide, who was twice appointed viceroy of Goa and Portuguese India.

Covered with dense foliage, the once-forgotten fort is now undergoing fervent restoration and will soon be transformed into a cultural center.

Coco Beach

Located at the estuary of the Mandovi River, Coco Beach offers a close view of Panaji and the Cabo Raj Bhavan. The beach was once a scenic stretch hidden from the tourist eye and away from the crowded northern stretch. Changes in tide and weather patterns have caused the beach to shrink to a narrow strip, but it does have a few loyal European visitors in peak season, when it is lined with shacks and makeshift restaurants. In the low season, the beach is deserted and is the domain of the local fisherfolk, who may be seen taking their boats out to sea to bring back their fresh catch. Fishing is popular on the rocky seafront and the water is generally safe for swimming.

ENTERTAINMENT AND EVENTS

The northern coast is Goa's most vibrant stretch, lined with shacks that double up as restaurants and bars. After dark, the long strip of beach from Candolim to Anjuna turns into an open stage as local performers—hired by select shacks—display traditional acrobatics and rope-walking, often accompanied by drummers and flame-throwers. The mood is festive and the party, very clearly, is on the beach. However, for those who wish to shake a leg, there are also a few nightspots that host Goa's busy DJs and some great live bands.

Bars and Discotheques

A short distance from Fort Aguada, **Sweet Chilli** (house no. 54, Sinquerim, tel. 0832/247-9446, sweetchillilounge@rediffmail.com, 11 A.M.–12:30 A.M. daily) is a vast open area twinkling with fairy lights. Its bamboo-covered bar is known for its cocktails (Rs 180–280) and there's a live band playing every day during peak season (Fri.–Sun. in low season). Wednesday is Carnival night and there's jazz on Friday nights, in addition to Western, Indian, and Goan Portuguese music through the week. The place also hosts special Goan nights and performers like the African Cats—jugglers from Africa.

On the same road, leading to Candolim, is **Butter** (tel. 91/98221-26262, 7 P.M.–3 A.M. daily), which raises some eyebrows for its

Fishermen bring in their fresh catch at Coco Beach.

© JANHAVI ACHAREKAR

baseline, which says "Spread your night." Sprawling over an open space with several bar and dancing areas, it has an enclosed discotheque that is usually filled with domestic tourists—teenagers, twenty-somethings, and hangers-on—grooving to the latest (and loudest) beats. The bar area outside provides a breather and there's a separate lounge area as well. There's a proposed Sky Bar on the terrace, and the DJ list includes the illustrious Carl Cox of Sunburn fame. While many dismiss the place for being "wannabe," others come here for special deals on cheap booze.

Two of Mumbai's hippest nightclubs have joined hands in Goa, with upmarket Japanese-inspired Shiro's and discotheque Poison coming together as **Shiro Poison** (Candolim Beach, tel. 0832/645-1718, 5 P.M.–2 A.M. daily). The place buzzes with activity every night during tourist season. Everyone from Mumbai's famous DJ Aqeel to Goa's hottest DJs play at the nightclub's full moon parties and Sundown Sundays. The latest beachside party hotspot, it has an outdoor lounge with a stunning sea view as well as an indoor dance floor. Large statues carry forward the Japanese castle/fairy-tale themes of the chain, while the sushi, sashimi, and yakitori are sheer haiku.

Located right on the beach, **Frank Zappa's Beach Shack** (Candolim Beach, www.frank-zappas.com, 11 A.M.–11 P.M. daily) is known more for its relaxed seaside ambience, well-stocked bar, and music than for its cuisine. One of the first hippie shacks on this stretch, the previously German-owned place was known to be fiercely loyal to Frank Zappa's music. Today, its Goan owners organize fire shows and performances, barbecue-and-disco nights on Tuesdays, and parties through the Christmas and New Year's week. Zappa's offers both Goan cuisine and Western fare, including a good suckling pig roast for Christmas.

SHOPPING

Like the rest of the northern coast, Candolim is filled with small, transient boutiques and rows of nameless street stalls selling everything from handicrafts to beachwear. A few stores merit a

THE HIPPIE LEGACY

The hippie movement was born in the 1960s, the same decade that Goa gained Liberation. It was a long journey from San Francisco to Goa's beaches, and it often involved a train ride on the Direct-Orient Express, which passed through Turkey and into Asia. Once discovered, Goa became the mecca of the nomadic flower children who lived on peace, drugs, rock, and sex. Their adoption of Eastern philosophy ensured that it was always a hippie hotspot, and long-haired, bare-chested men and women were often found smoking a chillum (pipe) with many a holy man.

Goa's secluded shores made for ideal nudist beaches and getaways from society. The Anjuna flea market was born out of hippie necessity and started out as a barter bazaar. The "Goa Freaks" paved the way for the destination's famous party culture by introducing their brand of drug- and alcohol-filled full moon parties. The most famous of the neo-hippies was Goa Gil, or Gilbert Levey, responsible for turning Anjuna into a party destination. Dressed like the holy men he hung around with, his matted hair and saffron robes added to his mystical aura – even as he continued to DJ, playing techno, house, and trance music at Goa's famous rave parties well into the 1990s.

Today, Goa's unique character is derived from its hippie legacy – its flea markets, parties, fashion, and even the beach shacks that line the shores are all a result of the hippie lifestyle and their adoption of Goa as a second home. Today, the last of the hippies still remain while the neo-hippies carry on the tradition, although not quite in the same league.

THE NORTHERN COAST

special mention, however, for their home decor and other items. **Soto Haus** (1266/F, Anna Vaddo, tel. 0832/248-9983, www.sotodecor .com, 10 A.M.–7 P.M. Mon.–Sat.) is the brainchild of Swiss artists Thomas and Sonja. Wares include original artworks, as well as artsy lamps and original furniture made with ecofriendly

WATER SPORTS SAFETY

Reverberating with the squeal and roar of boats and revelers, Goan beaches are a haven for thrill-seekers and operators alike. The northern beaches, being more commercial in nature, tend to see more activity than the southern ones, although water sports across the coastline include parasailing, Jet Skiing, banana boat rides, ringo rides, kayaking, snorkeling, and, in some places, windsurfing and diving. Operators for dolphin-sighting trips and island trips are a dime a dozen, even at the most remote beaches.

While sailing was popularized by the Goa Yachting Association, water sports first arrived here with windsurfing, brought to India by John Lucas in 1979. Among the first trained operators in the state, Derrick Menezes recalls the time when Lucas, assisted by Martin Poetz (who continues to live in Goa) initiated the state into aquatic adventure. Having trained in and taught at windsurfing schools in England and Greece, Menezes is considered one of the pioneering operators here. The first to introduce paragliding at the five-star hotels and to start an international windsurfing school, he has trained most of the recommended water-sports operators. However, Menezes expresses concern over safety norms, warning against fly-by-

night operators. He ought to know. Affiliated to the erstwhile National Institute of Watersports and having aided the government and tourism department with regard to safety measures, he makes a clear distinction between non-skilled and skilled sports. While the former includes boat rides, Jet Skiing, and ski rings, the latter includes diving, windsurfing, and parasailing. While most operators in the "no skill, high thrill" category pose little danger, it is operators who offer skilled sports that one needs to be wary of. There have been serious accidents in the past; operators at Colva on the southern coast, particularly, are best avoided.

Among the few operators recommended for skilled water sports are **Thunderwave** (Taj Fort Aguada, Sinquerim, tel. 0832/247-9779, cell tel. 91/98221-76985) and the PADI 5-star certified **Barracuda Diving** (Sun Village Resort, Baga-Arpora, tel. 0832/227-9409, cell tel. 91/98221-82402, www.barracudadiving.com). A shipbuilding consultant to the United Nations, Menezes also organizes the occasional thrill for celebrity clients and large groups under the aegis of his company **Ocean Blue Services** (2/133, Pequeno Morod, Saligao, cell tel. 91/98221-24457, derrick_menezes@ oceanblue.in).

materials such as banana and papaya leaves and tree bark.

Yamini (Acron Arcade, Fort Aguada Rd., tel. 0832/564-367, 10 A.M.–10 P.M. daily) is part of a chain of trendy home stores found in Mumbai and elsewhere in the country. This is the place for interesting curtains, cushion covers, duvets, and gift items to take home. The store also sources some its materials from the southern state of Kerala to support the ailing cottage industry there.

SPORTS AND RECREATION

There's plenty to do in the Candolim area, including a wide variety of water sports and marine activity. Most hotels will lead you in the right direction as far as these activities are

concerned, and there are plenty of tour operators by the beach should you wish to go for a dolphin sighting. Swimming is generally safe if you keep track of the tides, and at the end of the day, there are a number of spas where you can relax with aromatherapy and traditional Ayurvedic massages and treatments.

Water Sports and Boat Tours

Considered Goa's safest and best water-sports operator, **Thunderwave** (tel. 0832/247-9779, cell tel. 91/98221-76985) operates from the Taj Fort Aguada and offers parasailing, banana rides, ringo rides, Jet Skiing, sea walks, dolphin rides, and water-skiing.

John's Boat Cruises (near Marquis Beach Resort, Dando Vaddo, tel. 0832/247-9780, cell

ASHIMA NARAIN

Parasailing is one of many popular water sports in Goa.

The **InterContinental** (Rajbag, tel. 0832/264-3288, www.intercontinental.com), on the southern coast, has its own water sports managed by Captain Paul Moore. The highlight is their luxury boat – the **Blue Diamond.**

Closer to Panaji, in Britona, is the departure point of another luxury yacht, the **Solita** (286, Boa Viagem Rd., Naikavaddo, Calangute, tel. 91/98221-80826, www.solita.co.in), ideal for pleasure trips.

tel. 91/98221-82814) provides a houseboat on the backwaters in addition to fishing trips and dolphin cruises.

Spas

A Goan-Portuguese-style spa with an uninhibited sea view, **Jiva** (Fort Aguada Beach Resort, Sinquerim, tel. 0832/664-5858, www.tajhotels .com, 8 A.M.–8 P.M. daily) offers a variety of spa treatments along with yoga and meditation. Balinese and Thai massages are included on the spa menu, as are Ayurvedic treatments, which performed by trained masseurs and masseuses after consultation with an Ayurvedic physician. The spa boasts both invigorating and relaxing signature treatments, including the Jivaniya—an energizing treatment—and the

Pehlwan Malish, or wrestler's massage. Every treatment room has a personal soak pool, making the experience a luxurious one.

Snip Salon and Spa (Candolim, tel. 0832/242-0898, www.snip.co.in, 9 A.M.–9 P.M. daily) takes care of both health and beauty needs. Offerings include massages (Swedish, aromatherapy, and Ayurvedic), floral footbaths, beauty treatments, and hair styling. The spa also has a reflexology area and aims to provide five-star ambience and service at affordable rates.

ACCOMMODATIONS

Candolim has a variety of accommodations, ranging from beach shacks and small guest houses to lovely boutique hotels and luxury five-star properties. The Taj Fort Aguada was the first five-star property in Goa, and continues to be one of the most reputed. Like all accommodations in Goa, these hotels change their tariffs according to the season—the year is divided into low season (June–Sept.), high season (Oct.–Dec. 23 and Jan. 3–May), and the Christmas/New Year period (Dec. 24–Jan. 2), which sees rates increase even further. Taxes are charged separately. and rates, in general, are subject to change without notice.

A number of beachside shacks line the secluded Coco Beach in peak season, but have not been included here owing to their transitory nature. A walk down the northern beaches and arterial roads will also reveal apartments and villas for rent, which usually come and go with every season. If you're in a group, you may want to explore this option.

Under Rs 1,000

Candolim has few good budget options but the all-time favorites with backpackers and budget tourists are the twin hotels **Casa Sea Shell** (Fort Aguada Rd., Candolim, tel. 0832/247-9879, seashellgoa@hotmail.com, Rs 750–1,850) and **Sea Shell Inn** (Fort Aguada Rd., Candolim, tel. 0832/227-6131, seashellgoa@hotmail.com, Rs 1,000, closed June–Sept.). Run by the same family, the former is an old Goan home-turned-hotel while the latter is a newer building. Although rooms are basic, the hotels are a mere five- to ten-minute walk from the beach and are good value for money. They may lack the facilities of the more posh hotels that may be found down the road, but they have a delightful restaurant (decorated with fairy lights in peak season) and facilities to hire a refrigerator!

Rs 1,000–3,000

A charming little place, **Corinne's** (Escrivao Vaddo, Candolim, tel. 0832/645-2249, www.corinnesgoa.com, Rs 1,500) is the newest entrant on the block. Primarily a restaurant and bar, its three rooms are simple and well maintained. Just off the main road, it lies in a quiet lane opposite Bob's Inn. The comfortable rooms are nicely decorated and have little balconies and attached bathrooms. Music from the restaurant might be disturbing if you want to turn in early for the night, but this inn-like accommodation is a great value. However, as with all hotels in Goa, rates soar during the Christmas and New Year week, going up to as much as Rs 4,500 per night.

Summerville Beach Resort (Taj Holiday Village Rd., Dando, Candolim, tel. 0832/247-9075, Rs 1,600–2,200) is located close to the beach and is a great bargain. The comfortable rooms (studios and suites with television) come with sea- or pool-facing balconies. The resort organizes poolside barbecues and has a restaurant and pub.

Rs 3,000–10,000

A beautiful Portuguese-style villa, **◖ Marbella Guest House** (Fort Aguada Beach Road, tel. 0832/247-9551, www.marbellagoa.com, Rs 1,350–6,300) lies in Sinquerim Village—a stone's throw away from Fort Aguada and the adjoining beaches of Candolim and Sinquerim. Tucked away in a quiet, shaded lane, this lovely boutique hotel lies within easy access of the attractions of North Goa but well away from their commercial activity. It has three rooms and luxurious suites (each with a historical or floral theme) that are generally booked well in advance. They include well-designed bathrooms, air-conditioning, and cable television. There's also a restaurant (8 A.M.–10 P.M. daily, snacks and drinks available 24 hrs) on the premises. The Marbella is worth visiting even in the monsoon or low season, when its shaded terraces are ideal for sipping *feni* on rainy afternoons—and this makes a great romantic getaway for couples who want to stay in. In addition to the exotic decor (rooms with a historical theme have period-style furniture and fine architectural details), the suites offer picturesque views of the surrounding hills and countryside. The Rajasthani and Moghul Suites, in particular, are worth a look, even if a stay at Marbella eludes you.

Casablanca Beach Resort (Wadi,

Candolim, tel. 0832/247-9224, www
.casablanca.com, Rs 2,500–4,500) has a great
seaside location. Its air-conditioned suites and
terrace rooms are clean and comfortable and
there's a pool, Ayurvedic massage parlor, and
a poolside restaurant and bar.

Not far from the beach, **Aldeia Santa Rita
Resort** (Candolim Beach, near Kingfisher
Villa, tel. 0832/247-9868, Rs 4,000–8,000) is a
Portuguese villa-style resort with Mediterranean
colors and balconies and terraces that overlook
green lawns. Rooms are of two types—standard
and superior—and come with a small sit-out
each. A pool, indoor recreation, and a restaurant and bar add to the appeal. Aesthetically
designed and efficiently managed, the resort
makes for a great Goan experience.

Whispering Palms (Sinquerim Beach, tel.
0832/665-1515, www.whisperingpalms.com,
Rs 6,100–10,000) is another beautiful resort in
the area. Its 106 spacious, well-designed rooms
come with private balconies or terraces that
overlook the pool or surrounding foliage. The
resort has alfresco dining with live music and
offers direct access to the beach. It also has a
whirlpool tub, gym, library, and babysitting facilities. There are barbecues in the evenings, as
well as indoor recreation and entertainment.

Rs 10,000 and Up

Goa's first luxury hotel, **◖ Fort Aguada
Beach Resort** (Sinquerim, tel. 0832/664-
5858, www.tajhotels.com, rates upon request)
is built amid the remains of the original 16th-
century fortress. A sprawling property with
its own stretch of golden beach, it comprises
a spread of cottages, restaurants, and bars.
Over the years, this landmark five-star hotel
has turned into a destination in its own right,
attracting both international and domestic
tourists. Rooms are both sea-facing and garden-facing, with a private sit-out. In addition,
the hotel has lovely hilltop cottages, terrace
suites, and private villas that come with a lawn
and a verandah. Restaurants Fish Tail and
Morisco are known for their seafood, while Il
Camino serves great Italian fare. The hotel is

also popular for its spa and activities such as
tennis, squash, rappelling, and rock climbing.
Guests may also use the facilities at their sister
hotel, Taj Holiday Village.

The **Taj Holiday Village** (Sinquerim, tel.
0832/664-5858, www.tajhotels.com, rates
upon request) keeps up the Taj reputation with
its villas and cottages located around scenic
gardens and facing the sea. Most cottages come
with a balcony or a lawn, while villas have a private lawn. Meanwhile, the Luxury Villa Sunset
View has a bedroom, living room, kitchen, and
private lawn, in addition to a breathtaking view
of the sea and the Goan sunset. The hotel has
a number of dining options; it's particularly
popular for its Thai restaurant, Banyan Tree,
which derives its name from the 300-year-old
tree beneath which it is located. Beach House
serves authentic Goan fare, while Jungle Jam
is a special restaurant for kids. There's a pool
bar as well as a 24-hour café, and there's a five-
hole golf course among other recreational facilities. Popular with families, tourists, and
corporate clients, both Taj properties are old
five-star favorites.

◖ Lemon Tree Amarante Beach Resort
(Vadi, Candolim, tel. 0832/398-8188, www
.lemontreehotels.com, Rs 10,500–33,000) is
a lovely new boutique hotel with the facilities of a five-star property. Close to the beach,
its Portuguese-style rooms offer the best of
the Goan experience. The resort offers a variety of living arrangements, from standard
and garden-facing rooms to terrace studios.
Artworks and artifacts, a lovely pool (reminiscent of a slice of lime), and tasteful furnishings make for a pleasant stay. In spite of their
nostalgic charm, rooms are equipped with the
latest gizmos, like flat-screen TVs and DVD
players. The hotel has some excellent restaurants, including Candolim's best East Asian
restaurant, Republic of Noodles. There's also
a multi-cuisine café called Citrus. Meanwhile,
opposite the main hotel is a separate heritage
block where high-end villa-style rooms and
suites with exclusive pools offer both luxury
and privacy.

THE NORTHERN COAST

FOOD

You're likely to find Candolim quiet in the low season, with most of its popular shacks and restaurants closed for the monsoon. In peak season, however, the area buzzes with activity and is bathed in bright lights after dark from the myriad restaurants that line the entire stretch. There's no dearth of dining options and you'll find all kinds of world cuisine here. From seafood on the shacks that fringe the beach to fine dining at specialty eateries and five-star restaurants, Candolim has it all. A word of caution, however: Before you order that alluringly large fresh catch of the day, make sure you inquire about the price first, or you're likely to be in for an unpleasant surprise. Most restaurant menus do not list seafood rates and charge according to the size of the catch.

Signature dishes are served at **Banyan Tree** (Taj Holiday Village, Sinquerim, tel. 0832/664-5858, www.tajhotels.com, noon–2:30 P.M. and 7:30–10:30 P.M. daily), the Thai restaurant at the Taj Holiday Village. The restaurant is known as much for its green curry and crispy fried fish dished out by chef Danny as it is for its superlative ambience. The dining area is spread beneath a 300-year-old banyan tree, which inspired the restaurant's name.

The terrace restaurant **Santa Lucia** (Fort Aguada Rd., tel. 0832/561-5213, 6:30–11 P.M. daily, mains Rs 200 and up) rustles up excellent Italian fare. Known for home-style pasta and a few Swiss specialties, this is a great place to relax and soak in the atmosphere after a day on the beach.

While its name may do nothing to whet your appetite, the pan-Asian cuisine at **C Republic of Noodles** (Lemon Tree Amarante Beach Resort, Candolim, tel. 0832/320-2000, joeces@rediffmail.com, 11 A.M.–3 P.M. and 7–11 P.M. daily Oct.–May and 7–11 P.M. daily June–Sept., mains Rs 180 and up) is nothing short of delicious. New to Candolim but already declared the number-one fine dining restaurant in Goa and one of the top 20 in Asia, it boasts a chef trained at the Royal Palace in Thailand. Here you can sample the best of Burmese, Vietnamese, Indonesian, Singaporean, and Hunan cuisine, in addition to Thai specialties. If you have a taste for spice, try the jungle chicken curry, a spicy Thai signature dish. The spare ribs served here are also a delicacy. The place is also popular for its Sunday brunches (Rs 1,200) and cocktails (Rs 250 and up), which have entertaining names like the Pissed-Off Japanese Farmer and the Neutered Purple Squirrel. Republic of Noodles is a must-visit if you're in this part of the state.

Giving tough competition to Republic of Noodles is the quiet Burmese restaurant called **C Bomra's** (opposite Kamal Retreat, Souza Vaddo, Candolim, cell tel. 91/98221-06236, bawmra@yahoo.com, 7–11 P.M. daily Oct.–Apr., lunch available upon request with 24 hours prior notification, mains Rs 250 and up). Named after its affable Burmese chef-owner, who divides his time between Goa and London, the restaurant specializes in modern Burmese cooking and Kachin cuisine. The menu changes seasonally—with innovations like black pomfret miso and warm chicken liver with chili garlic and ginger. There are also a few dishes that remain on the menu year-round due to their popularity: the tea leaf salad (which is supreme), the beef salad, and spicy mussel curry are runaway hits. Seared tuna with wasabi; steamed snapper with lemongrass, chili, fish sauce, and jaggery; and slow-cooked pork belly with lentils, apple chutney, and cashew nut crust are also popular delicacies. The dessert list is equally intriguing, with the tamarind chili ice cream begging to be sampled. Not only does the creative chef reinterpret traditional Burmese cooking, he also shakes a mean cocktail. Try the lime- and ginger-infused vodka to end the evening on a high note.

The whitewashed **Café Chocolatti** (Fort Aguada Rd., tel. 0832/247-9340, mains Rs 200 and up), run by the Rebelos, built its reputation on chocolate and cold salads. This is the place you ought to head if you're in the mood for light eats or comfort food. Choose from a variety of sandwiches or try out some home-baked goodies in the patisserie area. The brownies here are legendary.

FENI: WHERE GOA BECOMES A STATE OF MIND

Feni is to Goa what tequila is to Mexico. Brewed either from cashew apple or from coconut, this wonderfully potent drink lends to the good times and flavor of Goa. Drunk on the beaches, in the villages, on farms, in five-star hotels, and pretty much everywhere in the state, the harmless-looking clear drink is consumed as a shot, with lemonade, with salt and lime, or as a cocktail. *Feni* is not as benign as it looks, however, and its high level of alcohol – about 40 percent – can have you laughing silly. If you're a first-timer, remember that *feni*, especially the cashew variety, is an acquired taste and can be overwhelmingly strong. It's best to stick to palm or coconut *feni*, mixed with lemonade.

Introduced to Goa by the Portuguese, who also brought the cashew apple to the state, the drink only gained in popularity after Liberation when the departure of the colonizers left a vast vacuum of products. Today, *feni* bottles come in all shapes and sizes and are known especially for their quaint packaging; they're even available in bottles shaped like guitars and sailors.

Big Boss was the brand to bottle and package the drink, which was previously considered the poor man's poison; Big Boss is now synonymous with *feni*, just as *feni* is synonymous with Goa. The owner of Big Boss, Mac Vaz, is also the president of the Feni Association, which comprises the 2,000-odd distillers that exist in the region. The Association is attempting to patent the drink, which would then come under the WTO umbrella, thus preventing anyone from outside the state to stake their claim on the name – pretty much like Champagne. This move, they hope, will change perceptions of the drink from that of country liquor to "heritage liquor."

The *feni*-making process involves the fermentation and double-distillation of crushed cashew apples in copper pots. Another drink, known as *urak*, is the product of the first distillation. Not as strong as the final brew, *urak* is a popular summer drink. Coconut or palm *feni* is similarly fermented and distilled from coconut toddy.

Meanwhile, it is only natural that the land of *feni* be famous for its blissful approach to life called *sossegarde*. Goans believe in taking it easy, and the word, borrowed from the Portuguese dictionary, couldn't capture more appropriately the essence of their philosophy. Now corrupted to the more Konkani-sounding *susegaad*, it translates, quite simply, to "minimum effort, maximum relaxation." The monsoon months especially, when there is a lull in both tourism and agriculture, see an extended period of *sossegarde* before they gear up once again for the busy season. Come to Goa and you'll soon realize that *feni* and *sossegarde* go hand-in-hand. The two lend to the wonderfully laid-back, carefree attitude of this destination and make for a potent combination – turning Goa into a state of mind, rather than a destination.

THE NORTHERN COAST

© JANHAVI ACHAREKAR

Feni bottles come in various shapes and sizes, including guitars, violins, and sailors.

A celebrated hippie hangout from the old days, **Bob's Inn** (Ann Vaddo, Candolim, tel. 0832/227-6402, 11 A.M.–3 P.M. and 7–11 P.M. daily, mains Rs 90 and up) is a lovely, old house-turned-restaurant run by the Lawande family. The now sober-looking present owner, Bob's brother (Bob is no more), was once a long-haired hippie, and he will willingly share stories of the old days, even citing book references when it comes to the story of Lord Lucan—an Englishman who was charged with murder and on the run from Scotland Yard during the 1970s. Known to locals as "Jungle Harry," Lord Lucan had made Bob's Inn his haunt. The alias came from his enthusiasm for leading tourists into the nearby jungles of Goa—territory with which he was obviously familiar—for wildlife treks. The restaurant is a great place to exchange stories—of Lord Lucan or otherwise—as you tuck into some great Goan-style seafood. The seafood platter and crumb-fried mussels are an absolute must, as are the Goan curries, washed down with some good palm *feni* and Bob Marley music.

Candolim seems to be the place in Goa for East Asian cuisine, and on the long, illustrious list is **Cuckoo Zen Garden** (house no. 1127, near Bob's Inn, Candolim, tel. 91/98221-26031, www.cuckoozen.com, 7–11 P.M. Mon.–Sat. Oct.–Apr., mains Rs 150 and up), the only place in town for authentic Japanese and Chinese fare. You can be assured of good homemade noodles, excellent sushi and sashimi platters, and miso soup. A little sake will go down well in this Korean-run place with great food and an ambience to match.

At the end of the lane opposite Bob's Inn is **Corinne's** (Escrivao Vaddo, Candolim, tel. 0832/645-2249, www.corinnesgoa.com, 5 P.M.–midnight Mon.–Sat. Oct.–Apr., mains Rs 150 and up)—the new favorite for authentic Goan cuisine. Named after its ex-stewardess chef-owner, who was egged on to open this delightful little space by family, Corinne's is known for its local fare. Specialties include prawn curry rice with *kismar* (dry prawns with coconut), *sorpotel* served with *sannas* (rice cakes), and prawn *risois* (savory prawn puffs).

The restaurant also has a bar and an open courtyard that is ideal for parties.

A small hole-in-the-wall known to few until recently, **Lloyd's** (near Snip Salon and Spa, Candolim, tel. 91/94224-38230, 7 P.M.–6 A.M. Mon.–Sat., mains Rs 100 and up) is where Goans end up after a long night of partying. The only place to serve basic home-cooked Goan-style food until the wee hours of morning, this place was once a well-kept secret among the party-hearty set. You will find all the spicy Goan sauces *xacutis* and *cafreals* here, along with alcohol—if you haven't had enough already. You may even find the odd Candolim restaurateur here; most owners of fine dining restaurants in this area swear by the food at Lloyd's, although some claim that the quality has been inconsistent lately.

La Fenice (near Tarcar Ice Factory, Candolim, tel. 0832/228-1182, 11 A.M.–10 P.M. daily, mains Rs 150 and up) is a pretty terrace restaurant that specializes in Italian cuisine. A lovely setting and home-style pastas with wine make this a favorite with tourists. Try the creamy seafood pasta with salmon as well as the steaks.

One of Candolim's most popular beach shacks, **Calamari** (Sinquerim-Candolim beach stretch, tel. 0832/309-0506, cell tel. 91/93261-02242, 8:30 A.M.–9:30 P.M. daily Oct.–Apr., mains Rs 150 and up), as suggested by its name, is excellent for seafood. The seafood salads and butter garlic prawns are favorites, and guests on deck chairs enjoy drinks on the beach. At night, it's an ideal dinner place, with a wooden deck that juts out onto the beach, softly framed by lamps and curtains and a view of the marooned ship *River Princess*.

No well-informed visitor to Candolim leaves without a meal at ◖ **Amigo's** (under Nerul Bridge, tel. 0832/240-1123, 11 A.M.–10:30 P.M. daily, mains Rs 150 and up). Equally appealing for its location as for its home-style Goan cuisine, this quaint eatery is situated on the banks of the Nerul River. The menu is best left to the owners, who organize a fresh catch with help from the local fisherfolk. Try their tiger prawns and king crab, as well as various fish preparations, as you sit in the leafy environs and gaze upon the shimmering waters of the river. They also organize local bar-hopping boat tours upon request.

INFORMATION AND SERVICES
Hospitals and Pharmacies

Candolim has adequate health and medical facilities that include **Bosio Hospital** (Pinto's Vaddo, Candolim, tel. 0832/248-9034). There are plenty of pharmacies and provision stores as well. Perhaps the most conveniently located is **Ayush Medical Stores** (Shop no. 6, Pinto's Vaddo, Candolim, tel. 0832/691-0173, 8:30 A.M.–10 P.M. daily).

Money

Since Candolim is a prime tourist area, there is no dearth of ATMs or money changers in town. **Gauri Tours and Forex** (289, Bammon Vaddo, Candolim, tel. 0832/247-9492, 9 A.M.–9 P.M. Mon.–Sat.) handles both travel and currency needs. Meanwhile, you can accept money transfer and use the ATM services at **Canara Bank** (Santa Durga, Pinto's Vaddo, Candolim, tel. 0832/248-9187, 9:30 A.M.–1:30 P.M. and 2–3 P.M. Mon.–Fri. and 9:30 A.M.–noon Sat.)

and **Corporation Bank** (opposite Kamat Holiday Homes, Candolim, tel. 0832/227-7062, 9:30 A.M.–1:30 P.M. and 2–3 P.M. Mon.–Fri. and 9:30 A.M.–noon Sat.).

Internet

Most hotels in Candolim have Internet facilities, or should be able to point you in the right direction. At Candolim Market, there's **Sify I-Way** (Laxmi Apartments, 9 A.M.–10 P.M. daily).

GETTING THERE AND AROUND

From the Dabolim Airport, Candolim is an hour's drive and costs about Rs 600 for a taxi. By train, you will need to alight at Thivim, from where it is a half-hour ride by taxi, costing approximately Rs 350. Meanwhile, the nearest interstate bus station is at Mapusa, from where you can take a local bus or taxi onward to Candolim. The distance from Mapusa is 14 kilometers.

A number of buses ply the way between Candolim and the neighboring beaches. For motorcycle rental, it is best to inquire with your hotel's reception desk, as operators change with every season.

THE NORTHERN COAST

Calangute and Baga

If you're looking for a quiet romantic holiday or a family vacation, it's best to turn the page. Possibly the most commercial beaches in Goa, Calangute and Baga are crowded with sunbathers, hangers-on, and raucous tourists. Busy with a multitude of water-sports activities that range from parasailing and water-skiing to banana boat rides and dolphin trips, the beach has little space to spare in the peak season. While domestic tourists have made Calangute their domain in recent years, introducing even the Delhi variety of street food, or *chaat,* on the beach, Baga remains Goa's undisputed party destination. In the narrow lanes leading to the beach, alternately sharing elbowroom

are clothes-and-trinket stalls and discos blaring loud music. A youth haven and party hotspot, this stretch is a melee in peak season with its many clubs, night bazaars, and beach activities. Meanwhile, neo-hippies have taken on from where the original hippies left off, selling their goods and grooving to the music at the area's vibrant night markets.

A hippie discovery in the 1960s, Calangute has seen a sea change in the last few decades. Wedged between Candolim in the south and Baga farther north, this was where open-air rock, pop, and beat shows took place. Today, it has a varied profile of tourists, ranging from backpackers, charter tourists, and domestic

fishing boats by the Baga River

visitors to Israelis on their year off after compulsory military training and duty. Meanwhile, Baga also boasts a river and a "hilltop," both of which are overshadowed by its crowded beach. The once-virgin sands are now filled with sunbathing tourists on deck chairs, tattoo artists, and often, gawking voyeurs. Lined by rows of identical shacks, the beach is now a mere excuse for revelry, attracting a motley crowd of first-time Goa-goers and die-hard fans who return year after year.

SIGHTS

These areas also offer a slice of history. As you travel inland from the coast and toward the beautiful village of Saligao (3 km), you will discover the 18th-century **Church of St Alex.**

Then, on the Chogum Road in Saligao, on the road from Calangute to Panaji, is the spectacular **Church of Nossa Senhora Mae de Deus** (Our Lady, Mother of God). Built in 1873, this is one of the few neo-Gothic churches in Goa. A sight to behold at night, the church may be seen amid the fields, lit in all its glory. The statue of the Virgin Mary—believed

to be miraculous and brought from the ruins of the Convent of Mother of God in Old Goa—rests here, as does an old stone bearing an inscription and brought from the same ruins.

ENTERTAINMENT AND EVENTS

Calangute and Baga are possibly the only parts of Goa where entertainment and beach activity are on par with each other. A wide range of bars, beach shacks, and discotheques are sure to dazzle the first-timer, with a couple of shows and flame-throwing performances thrown in for good measure. Combining shopping with entertainment, to provide "shoppertainment," are night markets with music and live performances. Zestful and youthful, the nightlife in these parts is characterized by its sheer energy and variety. Meanwhile, for the artistically inclined, there's also a bit of fine art at the Kerkar Art Complex.

(Nightlife

Baga's most famous nightclub **Tito's** (Tito's Lane, Baga, tel. 0832/227-9895, www.titosgoa

© JANHAVI ACHAREKAR

.com, 10 P.M.–4 A.M. daily, Rs 500 per couple) even has a lane named after it. This multi-level discotheque flashes with strobe lights and is infused with Bollywood music, hip-hop beats, and raw, unabashed energy. It attracts young men and women from all walks of life, who jostle for space amid jugglers and performers. Local and visiting DJs, as well as special events like salsa and karaoke nights, keep this club at the top of the party list.

By the beach, and run by the same management as the famous Tito's, **Café Mambo's** (Tito's Lane, Baga, tel. 0832/227-9895, 7 P.M.–3:30 A.M. daily, Rs 500 per couple) sports a casual air, and its DJs belt out hip-hop, house, and trance music. During Christmas and New Year's, however, the crowds outside both Tito's and Mambo's can get unruly.

While teenagers and twenty-somethings make a beeline for Tito's and Mambo's, the thirty-and-above crowd turns to lovely **Cavala** (Saunta Vaddo, Baga, tel. 0832/227-6090, www.cavala.com, 9 A.M.–midnight daily) for its retro nights and fantastic ambience. Loyal fans brave even the worst rainy weather to hear live music on Wednesday and Saturday nights. Dimly lit and with a crowd of eclectic locals and tourists milling around the bar, this is a great place to enjoy the real Goan vibe.

Nearby, the erstwhile Kamasutra Lounge is undergoing a makeover as Take Five, a new restaurant/nightspot that will soon join the ranks of its illustrious neighbors.

A lovely, open, whitewashed space—resembling the dining room of a medieval English castle with its long bar table and candelabras—**Loungefly** (Baga Beach Road, Saunta Waddo, cell tel. 91/99234-47137, 8 P.M.–4 A.M. daily, Rs 500 per couple, Rs 700 for singles) attracts a sophisticated crowd. One of Goa's largest lounge bars, with the longest bar table to boot, Loungefly also has a eight-meter-high sundeck. You can listen to some great lounge music here or shake a leg on the dance floor as you down a few cocktails.

Pubs

If you're in the mood for an Irish pub, head to

Molly Malone's (Maddo Vaddo, Calangute, tel. 0832/561-5325, www.goatravel.co.uk, 9 A.M.–midnight daily) for a Guinness and some live music—and if you feel like some traditional Irish stew, try it along with their specialty steaks and pies (mains Rs 190 and up). The pub hosts some form of entertainment every day with the help of local and French musicians, and it even organizes quiz shows. Space is rarely a problem here.

Fine Arts

In the midst of all the hip-hop and trance, **Kerkar Art Complex** (Gaurawaddo, Calangute, tel. 0832/227-6017, www.subodh-kerkar.com, 9 A.M.–10 P.M. daily) is a surprising discovery. The erstwhile family home of prominent Goan painter and sculptor Subodh Kerkar has been turned into a haven for art lovers with an open-air auditorium that hosts Indian classical music and dance performances every Tuesday (6:45–8:30 P.M.) in tourist season. The art gallery exhibits Kerkar's paintings and installations as well as a few works of contemporary Indian artists. The complex also has an artists' retreat, as well as a restaurant.

SHOPPING

Calangute and Baga offer some of the best and most entertaining shopping experiences in Goa. From silver jewelry at the Tibetan Market to bright lights, live performances, and foot-tapping music at Mackie's Nite Bazaar, this stretch is vibrant and fun. Handicrafts, souvenirs, clothes, bags, and beachwear are displayed at rows of merry stalls that line the roads leading to the beaches. In addition to the stalls and the Saturday flea markets, Calangute and Baga also have their very own designer clothing store and a quaint bookshop.

Night Markets

Live bands, acrobats, Goan food, and *feni*-laced cocktails are as much the highlight of the carnival-like **Mackie's Saturday Nite Bazaar** (Arpora-Baga, cell tel. 91/98221-43661, www.mackiesnitebazaar.com, from 6 P.M. Sat. Nov.–Apr.) as are its many handicrafts, hippie clothing, and trinkets. Situated by the Baga River and shaded by coconut groves, the bazaar makes for atmospheric shopping. Brightly colored lamps and fairy lights add to the festive feel, as do tattoo artists, hairstylists, and fortune-tellers. Also popular for its dance floor and bar, Mackie's draws crowds from across the northern coast.

Bazaars, Street Stalls, and Flea Markets

T-shirts and bags saying "Free Tibet," strung alongside silver trinkets, will greet you at the **Tibetan Market** (near the post office, Calangute) on Saturdays—a much-awaited bazaar where Tibetan textiles, crafts, and silver jewelry are available for bargain prices. Beautifully crafted rings, bracelets, pendants, and souvenirs are displayed in this brightly lit space on the road to the beach.

For some local flavor, visit the **Calangute Bazaar,** near the Calangute post office, where goods and wares are up for display on the open

The Tibetan Market is among the more peaceful sections of the manic Calangute Bazaar.

street. Clothes, eats, and CDs are sold here every Saturday.

A colorful profusion of stalls flash mirror-work and brocade bags as well as linen clothing, all the way to the beach. These temporary makeshift shops are propped up with the help of bamboo and cloth after the monsoon season. Artisans from Kashmir are also seen on this stretch, selling traditional Kashmiri handicrafts and carpets.

Clothing

Flowing fabric, bold prints, kitsch, and bling greet you at designer **Malini Ramani's** boutique (house no. 156, opposite St. Anthony's Chapel, Calangute, tel. 0832/227-5305, www .maliniramani.com, 11 A.M.–8 P.M. daily). The Delhi designer has turned this beach destination into her base and has a lovely old home-turned-store that displays her glitzy creations and accessories. Animal prints, striking Indian *kurtas,* and beachwear are found at this designer store patronized by those clearly out to be noticed.

Arts and Handicrafts

As you find your way around the area, it's impossible not to notice **Casa Goa** (Cobravado, Calangute, tel. 0832/228-1048, cezarpinto@ hotmail.com, 10 A.M.–8 P.M. daily). A beautiful blue-and-white Portuguese-style house restored to exhibit Goan art and artifacts, it sells everything from antique furniture to unusual objets d'art. You can pick up metal-sculpted bowls, candlesticks, and bric-a-brac, in addition to paintings by local artists.

Go inland from Calangute, past Saligao and toward the village of Sangolda for one of Goa's finest specialty boutiques: Nilaya's **Sangolda** (E2-6, Chogm Rd., tel. 0832/240-9310, sangolda@sancharnet.in, 10 A.M.–7 P.M. Mon.–Sat.) is a treasure house of antiques, reproductions, and objets d'art. Beautifully carved chests, unusual almirahs, sculptures, and metal art are presented in an aesthetic display around the 130-year-old heritage-house-turned store, which is owned by glamorous couple Hari and Claudia Ajwani of Nilaya

Hermitage fame. There's also a lovely café (10 A.M.–6 P.M. daily, Rs 130–150) that serves tea and sandwiches.

Bookstores

Book-lovers will be delighted with **Literati Bookshop and Café** (E/I-282, Gaura Vaddo, Calangute, tel. 0832/227-7740, books@literati-goa.com, 10 A.M.–6:30 P.M. Mon.–Sat.). A bookstore that wends its way through a charming old house, this is where you can buy new bestsellers as well as secondhand books. Book releases and book clubs are hosted here regularly with an impressive turnout of both authors and readers. The store has an entire section dedicated to Goa and Goan literature, while refreshments, snacks, and pasta (Rs 80) are served in the open verandahs or inside the nooks and crannies of the store. Ask for some refreshing *kokum* juice as you browse through the titles.

SPORTS AND RECREATION

Owing to the commercial nature of both the beaches, Calangute and Baga are a haven for water-sports operators. It is best to go by recommendation rather than risk an unknown operator. While boat trips are fairly safe, parasailing, Jet Skiing, and other activities need a reliable operator. It is worth driving down to Candolim to book these services through Thunderwave (tel. 0832/247-9779, cell tel. 91/98221-76985).

Meanwhile, diving enthusiasts will be pleased to know that **Barracuda Diving** (Sun Village Resort, Baga-Arpora, tel. 0832/227-9409, cell tel. 91/98221-82402, www.barracudadiving.com) is a PADI 5-star certified center. Though diving isn't very popular in Goa (owing to its murky waters), Barracuda's Venkat Charloo and Karen Gregory conduct courses and organize dive trips (Rs 3,000). Both are qualified PADI instructors with a passion for the sport and international experience. The Barracuda team organizes scuba diving and snorkeling (Rs 1,000) trips to Grande Island—known for its coral, shipwrecks, and amazing aquatic life. The sea

© JANHAVI ACHAREKAR

The hum of Jet Skis and motorboats mingles with the sounds of the ocean at Baga Beach.

life here includes barracudas, angelfish, parrotfish, snappers, sergeant majors, sting rays, reef tip sharks, and mullets. Favorite dive sites include Suzy's Wreck—a cargo ship called the SS *Rita* that breeds a variety of fish life. Umma Gumma Reef and Shelter Cove—known for its coral—are among other sites. Barracuda also conducts beginner and instructor courses that range from the Discover Scuba Diving course (Rs 3,500, inclusive of equipment rental) to the PADI Divemaster and Rescue courses (Rs 25,000, inclusive of equipment rental).

ACCOMMODATIONS

Calangute and Baga have some superb accommodations choices. There are innumerable options to suit all budgets, as both luxury boutique hotels and cheap budget places line the beaches and the roads leading to them. Also available are apartment rentals and villas that come and go with every season, but are advertised with the help of signboards and local people.

THE NORTHERN COAST

Under Rs 1,000

A simple resort attached to an old family home, **Shelsta** (Cobra Vaddo, Baga Rd., tel. 0832/227-6069, Rs 500–1,500) seems to expand with every tourist season. Located in the midst of the Baga chaos, with a Subway in its courtyard, it is not exactly a solitude-seeker's dream—but it's close enough to Baga Beach and its bars to attract the party set. The whitewashed resort has terra-cotta tiles and arches, and is well managed and maintained. Rooms are small but clean and comfortable and have little balconies that overlook a bit of greenery. Overall, it's a good value.

Rs 1,000-3,000

Located just above Log Cabin Pub, **The Cross Road Inn** (Porba Vaddo, Calangute, tel. 0832/227-9662, www.travelinggoa.com/thecrossroadinn, Rs 800–1,800) is a simple place with comfortable and reasonably aesthetic rooms. Conveniently located, this is a nice-enough place to use as a budget base.

Located right on the beach is one of GTDC's best properties—the **Calangute Residency** (Calangute Beach, tel. 0832/227-6024, www .goa-tourism.com, Rs 970–3,500). Rooms are clean, spacious, and tastefully furnished, with balconies that open out to the sea. The Residency also has some pretty cottages with antique furniture, while the suites have separate balconies for the bedroom and the living room. The hotel also has a restaurant and a garden, and it contributes to environmental protection with its waste-water management.

The artistically inclined will be delighted by Kerkar Art Complex's **Kerkar Retreat** (Gaurawaddo, Calangute, tel. 0832/227-6017, www.subodhkerkar.com, Rs 1,500–2,500). Comprising five rooms within the art complex, this lodging offers something of an artist's retreat coupled with a homestay. Rooms are simple but tastefully furnished, and, needless to say, strewn with paintings, sculptures, and objets d'art. Guests have access to a ceramic studio, where they may paint and sculpt. The Retreat also has a kitchen where guests can exercise their culinary skills (when they're

not dining at Waves, the restaurant within the complex) and an open terrace for relaxing in the evenings.

A family-run hotel attached to a well-known beach shack by the same name, **Chalston Beach Resort** (Cobra Vaddo, Calangute, tel. 0832/227-6174, cell tel. 91/98221-02149, www.chalstoningoa.com, Rs 1,400–2,500) is a lovely getaway with direct access to the beach. Beautiful rooms with balconies overlook the sea, pool, and gardens, and provide a relaxing ambience. Efficient service and good food and drink add to the experience, making this a great bargain.

Rs 3,000-10,000

Red laterite walls covered with ivy and white arches with wrought-iron Veronese balconies can only mean one place: ◼ **Cavala** (Baga-Sauntavaddo, tel. 0832/227-6090, www .cavala.com, Rs 750–6,500). A charming boutique hotel with a Mediterranean feel to it, Cavala is a Baga institution. Established during the hippie years, it has acquired a set of loyal guests who come here year after year for its quaint rooms, countryside views, warm service, good food, live music, and fantastic bar nights. Rooms are simple yet lovely, with mosaic-tiled bathrooms and seahorse motifs. While most of the single and double rooms overlook the vast green paddy fields behind the resort, the suites are located across the road, amid tropical foliage and overlooking the pool. All rooms come with balconies or sit-outs, while the suites (named after exotic beach destinations) have small terraces. Open year-round, Cavala makes for an especially beautiful stay in the monsoon if you happen to be here in the low season (bird-watchers, especially, will be delighted with the profusion of kingfishers and bright green bee-eaters, among other feathered varieties). The owner, Marius Monteiro, personally oversees the daily administration and maintenance of the place and is often found mingling with guests-turned-friends at the bar. Room rates include a hearty breakfast with the option of traditionally baked bread called *poi*. Close to the beach, and yet a world away from it, Cavala makes for a delightful stay.

Another beautiful boutique hotel, **(Presa di Goa** (Arais Wado, Nagoa, tel. 0832/240-9067, www.presadigoa.com, Rs 1,450–9,000) is a quiet, seven-room Portuguese-style house in the village of Nagoa, three kilometers from Calangute beach. Surrounded by palm trees and lush greenery, it gives you the best of both worlds—the country and the beach. Its bright blue exterior with exquisite tilework is offset by the azure outdoor pool. The detailed decor displays the painstaking effort taken by its soft-spoken director, a Luxembourg resident who now calls Goa home. The rooms are painted in colorful hues and tastefully furnished with colonial antiques that have been collected over the years. Four-poster beds, planter's chairs, and elegant *almirahs* make for an almost luxurious stay at mid-range prices. The hotel has two deluxe rooms and five junior suites; each room is named after a different bloom and has been given a unique look and design. Particularly innovative is the three-bed suite with a little room for a child or an extra person. The hotel has an open restaurant and bar on the premises, located around the pool, and plenty of old-world charm that brings people back year after year.

A pretty Calangute resort, **Villa Goesa** (Cobra Vaddo, tel. 0832/228-1120, Rs 1,200–8,000) stands apart for its old Goan charm and proximity to the beach. Set amid palm trees and pleasant lawns, rooms have terraces and balconies as well as access to a pool. Apart from serving local and other cuisines at the restaurant and bar, the resort also organizes barbecues and live music.

Rs 10,000 and Up

For a piece of Bali in Baga, there's **Casa Baga** (40/7, Saunta Vaddo, Baga, tel. 0832/228-2931, www.casaboutiquehotels.com, Rs 3,500–14,000), part of the Casa chain of hotels found across Goa. Its Balinese-style rooms are furnished with bamboo and carved wood, with lovely wooden decks and sit-outs. The pagoda-style Lotus Pond Restaurant, a rooftop

bar with an ocean view, a 24-hour coffee shop, and a pool add to its charm.

A high-end boutique hotel, the **(Pousada Tauma** (Porba Vaddo, Calangute, tel. 0832/227-9061, www.pousada-tauma.com, Rs 9,200–34,800) is worth the money. Its open, surreal architecture uses red laterite stone, sea-shells, and metal-crafted banisters, giving it the appearance of a rustic castle. The interior, similarly, is superlative—the multi-level cottage-rooms, centered around the pool, are all decorated with nature themes (sea, field, garden, and mountain). Soothing colors, beautiful wooden colonial furniture, and large windows make it a pleasure to be indoors in Goa. The hotel also has an Ayurvedic spa and a restaurant and bar. Spa treatments follow a consultation with the in-house Ayurvedic doctor and use traditional therapeutic methods such as copper baths for spinal treatment as well as herbal applications and massages for other ailments.

FOOD
Calangute

One of the first restaurants to appear on Calangute Beach, **Souza Lobo** (Calangute Beach, Umta Vaddo, tel. 0832/228-1234, www.souzalobo.com, 9 A.M.–10 P.M. daily, mains Rs 100 and up) was once a tradition. Its Goan-style seafood continues to be legendary, but the aroma of its kingfish and lobster thermidor has been overwhelmed by the smells of fried savories from the North Indian street-food stall outside. Known for its red snapper, live music, and open view of the beach, it draws a regular stream of loyal old-timers.

There's no dearth of small cafés on this popular stretch, and yet old-timers and first-timers alike make it a point to visit **(Infantaria Pastalaria Restaurant, Bakery & Bar** (Calangute-Baga junction, tel. 0832/227-7421, 7 A.M.–midnight daily, mains Rs 100–650). A modest-looking place with a small bakery and no great view but for the road and passing beach traffic, its bakes and meals are the toast of the northern coast. The soups, pastas, *sorpotels,* and brownies are excellent while the baked goodies and pastries sell like, well, hot cakes.

Stop by for a quick meal, halt for takeaway, or simply pop in for coffee (or beer). Infantaria is not to be missed.

Art and cuisine come together to form a unique fusion at **Waves** (Gaura Vaddo, Calangute, tel. 0832/227-6017, www.subodh-kerkar.com, 8 A.M.–2 P.M. and 6–11 P.M. daily Oct.–Apr., mains Rs 200), the restaurant at Kerkar Art Complex. You can try authentic Hindu Goan fare, as well as fine European cuisine, much of the menu being the creation of artist Kerkar himself. The mussel preparations and the spiced beef are specialties, while there's plenty of traditional fare for vegetarians. Surrounded by art and bathed in soft light, this makes for an exquisite dining experience.

An outdoor restaurant housed in the courtyard of an artist's residential home, ◖ **I-95** (Castello Vermelho, 1/115 Gaura Vaddo, Calangute, tel. 0832/227-5213, www.i95goa.com, 7–11 P.M. daily Oct.–Apr., mains Rs 350 and up) is all the rage. An art gallery on the lower floor of the house is usually open until late, and sees restaurant patrons flit in and out of its vast white space (which exhibits works by the resident and other artists). The restaurant is run by two enterprising young couples previously employed by a cruise liner, thus providing a clue to the origin of the intriguing name (I-95 is the form required to be filled by new employees—a sort of license to sail). The cuisine is an assorted pick of dishes from around the world—ranging from Indian *chettinad* (spicy south Indian cuisine from Tamil Nadu) to tapas, pasta, pizza, and East Asian fare. Try the beef Wellington, blue cheese–stuffed beef tornadoes, smoked salmon, and freshly baked breads as you soak in the lovely ambience and good music. The food is consistent, the wine list is exhaustive, and the owners are always around, mingling with guests who almost always return.

It's a short drive from Calangute to Porvorim, if you want to dine at the restaurant where bikini serial killer Charles Sobhraj was caught over two decades ago. Once known for its local cuisine, **O'Coqueiro** (Alto-Porvorim, tel. 0832/241-7806, ocoqueirogoa@dataone.

in, 11 A.M.–3 P.M. and 6:30–midnight daily, mains Rs 150 and up) became famous for its role in the capture of the notorious criminal now doing time in Nepal. In a bizarre turn, the restaurant recently sealed this association by installing a statue of Sobhraj in its patio. Thankfully, it continues to serve a good pork *sorpotel,* steak, lobster thermidor, and prawn curry rice.

Baga

An old favorite, ◖ **Britto's** (Baga Beach, tel. 0832/227-7331, 8:30 A.M.–11:30 P.M. daily, mains Rs 100 and up) is great for breakfast, lunch, and dinner. You can lounge with a book here and gaze upon the sea, watching time go by as you sip on your King's beer. A tad crowded in the peak season, it remains, nevertheless, a recommended venue for both Goan and Western-style cuisines. Try the calamari, meat platter, and various Goan seafood curries, and end a spectacular meal with the equally commendable desserts.

Zanzibar (Baga Beach, 9 A.M.–11 P.M. daily Oct.–Apr., mains Rs 150 and up) is another popular Baga shack known for its fresh catch and great Goan-style seafood. Like the others, it offers a close sea view and some fantastic prawn dishes.

An old Portuguese beach villa is now ◖ **Fiesta** (Saunta Vaddo, opposite Tito's, Baga, tel. 0832/227-9894, www.fiestagoa.com, 7–11 P.M. Wed.–Mon. Oct.–Apr., mains Rs 300), a restaurant with a reputation for outstanding contemporary European cuisine and posh patrons. Its French-style steaks, lobster dishes, and wood-fired pizzas are must-tries, as are its desserts and cocktails—all served in an equally dazzling ambience. This is a great place for a romantic night, but you'll need to book your table in advance.

Fado music and food prepared by an attorney-chef greet you at **Casa Portuguesa** (Beach Rd., Baga, tel. 0832/227-7331, www.casa-portuguesa-goa.com, 7–11 P.M. daily Oct.–Apr., mains Rs 200 and up), a heritage house transformed into a Portuguese restaurant with open-air dining. The menu includes authentic

© ASHIMA NARAIN

Goa's popular Baga Beach is lined with shacks and crowded with deck chairs occupied by sunbathers.

recipes prepared using traditional methods. The Portuguese soups, seafood, and Goan-style *chouricos* are especially popular and this is one of the few places where you will get to sample *cabidela de pato,* a traditional Portuguese duck preparation. There are also a variety of vegetarian dishes and great desserts—making this an excellent choice for dinner.

Something of an institution **Lila Café** (Baga Creek, tel. 0832/227-9843, 9 A.M.–6 P.M. Wed.–Mon. Oct.–Apr., mains Rs 150) is a German-owned bakery and restaurant, legendary for its fresh bread and croissants. A great breakfast and daytime place, this is where you can count on a hearty farmer's breakfast and sample some excellent European specialties and salads. If you feel like some traditional goulash or smoked fish (kingfish is a specialty), this is where you ought to wend your way.

If you're craving Italian, think first of atmospheric ◖ **J&A's Little Italy** (Baga Creek, cell tel. 91/98231-39488, 6 P.M.–midnight daily Oct.–Apr., mains Rs 300 and up). This Italian restaurant is known for the best salads, pastas, and antipasti in these parts. Try

the seafood pastas, pizzas, carpaccio, the fillet steak, or the excellent vegetarian dishes. Desserts are fantastic, with the baked lemon cheesecake topping the list.

Chic black and white decor, good music, and soft candlelight can only mean one thing: the classic French touch. One of the many French restaurants in Goa, **La Terrasse** (Baga Creek, tel. 0832/395-0832, www.laterrasse.in, 6:30–10:30 P.M. daily Oct.–Apr., mains Rs 200 and up) serves authentic dishes from the South of France. Perched on the hilltop, with both outdoor and indoor seating, La Terrasse offers a sweeping view of the creek along with a choice of some excellent French wines and plenty of romance.

For more French cuisine, try **Le Restaurant Francais** (Milky Way Restaurant, Baga Rd., cell tel. 91/98221-21712, 7:30–10:30 P.M. Wed.–Mon. Oct.–Apr., mains Rs 200 and up)—a garden restaurant with a new theme for its decor every season. The French trio that runs the place believes in experimental cooking and the result is a wonderful crucible of contemporary French cuisine. The *croustillant* *de sardines* is a delicacy, and a *mise en bouche* (starter) comes on the house once you've placed your order.

At **Le Poisson Rouge** (opposite Baga bridge, tel. 0832/324-5800, cell tel. 91/98238-50276, www.lepoissonrouge-goa.com, 7–11 P.M. daily Nov.–May, mains Rs 200 and up), it's got to be fish. The name of the restaurant suggests that the red snapper (steamed and stuffed with *re-ichad masala* and prawns) is worth trying, but the black pomfret and kingfish preparations are equally good. The asparagus and tomato risotto and the *filet de boeuf* aren't bad either at this mixed-cuisine restaurant, where Goan food is given a French accent by the chef from Normandy. Dining under the stars and in the night-shadow of swaying palm trees ensures that your experience is better than *comme ci comme ca.*

C **Cavala** (Baga-Sauntavaddo, tel. 0832/227-6090, www.cavala.com, 7:30 A.M.–11 P.M. daily, mains Rs 250 and up) is as admired for its food as it is for its drink and hospitality. Its cheerful outdoor ambience, good music, and beautiful decor make the perfect accompaniments for its multi-cuisine fare. Known for its spicy, Goan-style curries and seafood, it can also rustle up good pasta, moussaka, and other European-style dishes.

It is worth traveling to Saligaon for the legendary chicken *cafreal* at **Florentine** (Pequeno Morod, Saligao, tel. 0832/227-8122, 11 A.M.–3 P.M. and 6–10:30 P.M. daily, mains Rs 100 and up). Though old-timers cluck that they don't make it like they used to, this non-descript restaurant continues to dish out the local Goan delicacy (and other chicken and fish preparations) to its varied clientele. The service is quick and efficient, in keeping with its large turnover of patrons.

INFORMATION AND SERVICES
Tourist Information
The **Goa Tourism Development Corporation (GTDC)** (Calangute Residency, Calangute Beach, tel. 0832/227-6024, www.goa-tourism.com, 9:30 A.M.–1:15 P.M. and 2–5:45 P.M.

Mon.–Fri.) provides maps and information on guided tours.

Hospitals and Pharmacies
Calangute and Baga have a number of medical clinics and pharmacies, such as **Dharwadkar Clinic** (near St. Alex Church, Calangute, tel. 0832/227-6588), **Large Scale Medical Centre** (Calangute Market, tel. 0832/227-6666, 24 hr), and **Ayush Chemist & Druggist** (Cobra Vaddo, Baga, cell tel. 91/99232-12624, 8:30 A.M.–10 P.M. daily).

Police
In case of emergency, **dial 100** for the 24-hour police helpline or try the **Calangute Police Station** (tel. 0832/227-8284) or the **Tourist Police Booths** (tel. 0832/228-1238).

Money
Paul Merchants Ltd (Shop G3, G4, Colonia, De Braganza Phase III, Candolim Rd., Calangute, tel. 0832/227-5054, www.paul-merchants.net, 9 A.M.–8 P.M. Mon.–Sat. and 10 A.M.–5 P.M. Sun.) are Western Union money transfer agents and will also meet all your foreign exchange needs. **Wall Street Finance Ltd** (D-6 Tourist Complex, Naik Vaddo, Calangute, tel. 0832/227-6607, 9:30 A.M.–6 P.M. Mon.–Sat.) and **Gouri Tours & Forex** (Baga Rd., tel. 0832/227-9938, 9 A.M.–9 P.M. Mon.–Sat.) also exchange currency.

There are plenty of ATMs in the area, including **HDFC** (near The Grand, Calangute-Candolim Rd.) and **ICICI** (Baga Rd.).

Postal Services
The **Calangute Post Office** (near St. Alex Church, tel. 0832/227-6030, 9 A.M.–5 P.M. Mon.–Fri.) does speedpost as well as registered letter booking.

Internet
Being a tourist area, this stretch has plenty of Internet cafés, including **Sify I-Way** (Shop no. 1, Sunshine Complex, Baga Rd., 9 A.M.–9 P.M. daily) and **Indo Cyber Café** (Saunta Vaddo, Baga, tel. 0832/227-7582,

9 A.M.–8:30 P.M. daily). The rate is Rs 40–60 per hour.

GETTING THERE AND AROUND

From Dabolim Airport, Calangute and Baga take a little over an hour by taxi, which costs around Rs 650. By train, you will need to alight at Thivim, from where it is a half-hour ride by taxi, costing approximately Rs 350.

The nearest interstate bus station is at Mapusa, from where you can take a local bus or taxi onward to Calangute. The ride takes about 15 minutes and costs Rs 130 by taxi. It takes half an hour by bus and costs Rs 15. There are buses every 15 minutes. A number of buses also ply between these and neighboring beaches.

For motorcycle rental, it is best to inquire at your hotel reception as operators change with every season.

Mapusa

The hub for the northern beaches, Mapusa is a crowded, charmless town but for its vibrant, traditional market. Packed with glum, low-rise buildings located along its undulating slopes and around the market area, it sees fewer tourists than its coastal neighbors. On Fridays, however, locals and visitors alike throng the massive municipal market at the entry point of town. Flowers, fish, spices, pottery, and everything that you can possibly find under the Goan sun vie for attention here, in a chaotic and colorful display. Meanwhile, small and local eateries and bars are scattered in and around the market, turning it into a food and entertainment zone in addition to a shopping and sightseeing attraction. Mapusa, pronounced "Mhapsa," derives its name from the market where the Konkani word *map* translates to "measure."

There's not much to see around the town besides the market. Visitors generally prefer to

THE NORTHERN COAST

© JANHAVI ACHAREKAR

the 16th-century Church of Our Lady of Miracles in Mapusa

stay at the nearby beaches or in Panaji, and drive down on market day.

SIGHTS

The **Bodgeshwar Temple** (opposite Hanuman Theatre) is dedicated to the town's chief deity. It was built around the "bodgo" tree under which Lord Bodgeshwar is believed to have sat. It is also known for the traditional *tiatr* performances that take place at the Hanuman Theatre just opposite the temple.

Meanwhile, the well-kept **Church of Our Lady of Miracles** (St Jerome Rd.) is a white-washed structure reached through the narrow lanes and honking traffic of the dusty town. Previously dedicated to St. Jerome, the 16th-century church is also known as the Milagres Church and celebrates an annual feast during Easter.

Just two kilometers south of Mapusa, a little off the Mapusa-Panaji highway (NH17) is the **Monte de Guirim Monastery** (off the Panaji-Mapusa Hwy.). Ask for "Monte Giri" to reach this quiet hillside school and monastery, which houses an old chapel known for its five beautiful altars. Entry to the chapel is permitted, but access to other parts of the monastery are prohibited; the only other attraction is the bird's-eye view of the surrounding countryside.

FRIDAY BAZAAR

People jostle for space just as sights and smells compete for attention at Mapusa's biggest attraction: its lively bazaar (8 A.M.–7 P.M. Fri.). The otherwise unexceptional town comes alive just before the weekend as vendors hawk their wares in the enormous municipal market. Dried fish, fresh flowers and vegetables, traditional baked goods and sweets, jewelry, pottery, spices and local curries, fireworks, music and DVDs are all up for sale at the enclosed stalls and open spaces of this vast ground. This is a great place to stock up on your Goan masalas, cashew nuts, *bebinca* (a multi-layered traditional sweet made from egg, jaggery, and coconut milk), and other local treats and knickknacks. The market is great for a bit of local flavor and photo opportunities. If you

slippers on display at Mapusa's famous Friday bazaar

© ASHIMA NARAIN

can't make it on a Friday, the permanent stalls are open through the week.

ACCOMMODATIONS

Mapusa is not known for its accommodations. If you bypass Mapusa and head to Corjuem Island in Aldona instead, the surreal boutique villa Panchavatti will take you to another world.

Under Rs 1,000

Despite its run-down exterior, the **Mapusa Youth Hostel** (Goa-Mumbai Rd., Peddem, tel. 0832/225-7534, yhmapusa@sancharnet.in, Rs 40 for members, Rs 60 for non-members, Rs 10 for linen) is a breath of fresh air. It is equally attractive for unbelievable rates and its location in the Peddem area—providing respite from the crowds of the market town, yet adequately near to it. The hostel has an open courtyard and compound, while the interior is simple but clean. Dorms are of two types—three-bedded and eight-bedded—and are popular with students and backpackers.

Rs 1,000-3,000

Mapusa's only recommendable hotel, **Hotel Satyaheera** (opposite Kadamba bus stand, tel. 0832/226-2849, satya_goa@sancharnet.in, Rs 590–1,300) is located in the heart of town, just outside the municipal market. Neat and clean rooms provide refuge from the din outside. Functional and as well maintained as possible, the hotel may not be a preferred alternative but is a good option if you're looking at a stopover or last-minute stay. The place is efficiently and professionally managed, and has a popular terrace restaurant and bar called Ruchira.

Not far from Satyaheera is the less-than-aesthetic GTDC-run **Mapusa Residency** (opposite Kadamba Bus Stand, Gandhi Chowk, tel. 0832/226-2794, www.goa-tourism.com, Rs 650–2,945). Rooms are basic. Some are air-conditioned and some are not. There's a so-so bar and restaurant frequented by locals, as well as a small shopping arcade. You can make bookings for the GTDC's sightseeing tours and

river cruises from here. For the price, however, Satyaheera is the better option.

Rs 3,000-10,000

A veritable paradise in the middle of nowhere, **◖ Panchavatti** (Corjuem Island, Aldona, tel. 91/98225-80632, www.islaingoa.com, Rs 8,000–9,000 Oct.–May) is a luxury boutique hotel in Corjuem, farther inland from Mapusa. An exquisitely designed four-bedroom villa, it boasts the unique touch of its owner, Loulou Van Damme. Gauzy curtains, deep pinks and blues, romantic arches, and antique furniture make this a work of art. The property overlooks the Mapusa River, has a pond, and is surrounded by splendid gardens, hills, and orchards. Room rates include all meals and an excellent in-house chef prepares international cuisine for guests in a pleasant outdoor ambience. Panchavatti is ideal for those seeking a private retreat or soul-searching vacation.

FOOD

Mapusa's restaurants, bars, and bakeries are clustered around the market area and are particularly crowded on Fridays. Seafood and local cuisine, as always, are popular with visitors. Mapusa is also known for its quaint soda parlor, **Hanuman Soda,** located next to Hotel Satyaheera.

◖ Ruchira Bar and Restaurant (Hotel Satyaheera, near Hanuman Temple, opposite Kadamba bus stand, tel. 0832/226-3869, cell tel. 91/98221-03529, satya_goa@sancharnet.in, 11 A.M.–3:30 P.M. and 7–11 P.M. daily, mains Rs 30 and up), a branch of its namesake in Panaji, is a terrace eatery that offers a view of the busy Mapusa market. Frequented by locals and tourists alike, it is known for its seafood, particularly kingfish. There's regular North Indian fare as well and an air-conditioned section for those seeking respite from the local spice and heat. Some say that the place is overrated, but it remains Mapusa's most popular restaurant.

Café Xavier (141 Municipal Market, tel. 0832/226-2229, 8 A.M.–8:30 P.M. Mon.–Sat., mains Rs 40 and up) is a great place for local cuisine in the traditional ambience of the bazaar. An old favorite, this is where you can sample some authentic *sorpotel* (a traditional pork dish), mutton *xacuti,* beef chili fry, and kingfish.

Owned by the same family as Café Xavier, **Golden Oven** (9, Ramchandra Building, opposite Municipal Market, tel. 0832/226-4210, 8 A.M.–8:30 P.M. Mon.–Sat.) is the only local café with a contemporary look and feel—in stark contrast with its surroundings. Try the many traditional snacks and baked goods, sweets and savories, including the delicious egg chops, pastries, and the pork and sausage items that are available at throwaway rates. There's also a **Golden Oven 2** (Fred Villa, Morad, tel. 0832/225-3010) in town.

A quaint old place, (**Bertsy Bar and Restaurant** (opposite Municipal Market, tel. 0832/226-2841, 9 A.M.–11 P.M. daily, mains Rs 150 and up) resembles an English pub in incongruous surroundings. This small family-run eatery has a well-stocked bar area replete with wine racks and a wide variety of liquor; it seems a world away from the market and everything outside. A dimly lit interior, multi-cuisine options, and plenty of beer make it popular with tourists.

Away from the market buzz and located along a quiet slope, **Stomach Bar and Restaurant** (near Cinema Alankar, tel. 0832/226-3190, 11 A.M.–3:15 P.M. and 7–10:15 P.M. Mon.–Sat., Rs 50) is a great place for Goan-style seafood. The fish *thali* (all-you-can-eat platter) is a gastronome's delight with its authentic flavors and low price.

INFORMATION AND SERVICES
Tourist Information
The **Goa Tourism Development Corporation (GTDC)** (Mapusa Residency, tel. 0832/226-2794, www.goa-tourism.com, 9:30 A.M.–1:15 P.M. and 2–5:45 P.M. Mon.–Fri.) provides maps and information on guided tours and river cruises.

Hospitals and Pharmacies
Mapusa has a number of hospitals and health clinics, including the **Mapusa Clinic & Research Centre** (near St. Britto High School, tel. 0832/226-3343), **Asilo Hospital** (near Milagres Church, tel. 0832/226-2372), and **Holy Cross General Remanso Hospital** (near Milagres Church, Rajvado, tel. 0832/226-2466). You can also get medical supplies and toiletries from **Bardez Bazar** (Morod-Mapusa, tel. 0832/225-0618, 24 hr).

Police
In case of emergency, **dial 100** for the 24-hour police helpline or try the **Mapusa Police Station** (near the Mahalaxmi Temple/ St. Britto's School, tel. 0832/226-2231).

Money
Go to **Pink Panther** (1, Coscar Building, tel. 0832/226-3180, http://pinkpanthergoa.com, 10 A.M.–5 P.M. daily) for currency exchange, travelers checks, and travel assistance.

Bank of India (near Municipal Garden, tel. 0832/226-2371) has an ATM, while **Allahabad Bank** (Hotel Satyaheera, tel. 0832/226-2801, 10 A.M.–2 P.M.) accepts money transfers.

Postal Services
The **Mapusa Post Office** (near the Mahlaxmi Temple/St. Britto's School, tel. 0832/226-2235, 9 A.M.–5:30 P.M. Mon.–Fri.) does speedpost, as well as registered letter booking.

Internet
Mapusa has a number of Internet cafes, including **Cyber Space** (3rd floor, Communidade Ghor, Angod-Mapusa, tel. 0832/226-3911, 9 A.M.–9 P.M. Mon.–Sat., Rs 32/hr) and **Tape Rollers Iway Cybercafe** (Jelanza Apts., opposite mosque, Angod-Mapusa, tel. 0832/226-3911, 9 A.M.–9 P.M. Mon.–Sat., Rs 32/hr).

GETTING THERE AND AROUND
From Dabolim Airport, the drive by pre-paid taxi to Mapusa takes slightly over an hour and costs around Rs 700.

On the Konkan Railway, Mapusa Road is the nearest station—just six kilometers northeast of Mapusa's town center. Trains also stop at Thivim, 12 kilometers away. From here, it's a short journey into Mapusa by bus (around Rs 5), auto-rickshaw (Rs 80), or taxi (Rs 125). If you're traveling by bus from Mumbai to Goa, you can disembark at Mapusa.

Within Goa, there are frequent bus departures between Mapusa and Panaji, Madgaon, Chapora, and Candolim, and hourly buses to and from Calangute and Anjuna. Hiring a motorcycle taxi to the nearby beaches of Anjuna or Calangute costs around Rs 30–35 and is a 15-minute ride. By auto-rickshaw, it costs around Rs 75.

ARVALEM CAVES AND WATERFALL

About two hours from Mapusa, and approximately 10 kilometers south of Bicholim, the Arvalem Caves (Arvalem, 8:30 A.M.–5:30 P.M. daily, free, photography allowed) date back to the 5th or 6th century A.D. These red laterite rock-cut caves are believed to have been carved by traveling Buddhist monks. They house an ancient *shivling* that bears an inscription in the Sanskrit and Brahmi scripts. The caves also have a mythological connection and are believed to have played a role in the Hindu epic *Mahabharata,* giving shelter to the five brothers called the Pandavas. Down the road is the gushing Arvalem Waterfall, spewing mist and water at pilgrim-revelers who come to visit the **Rudreshwar Temple** (6 A.M.–7:30 P.M. daily), which shares its courtyard with the falls.

Getting There

The Arvalem Caves and Waterfall are located on a lonely stretch with few road signs. It is best to hire a taxi (around Rs 450) from Mapusa toward Bicholim. The caves and waterfall are within 10 kilometers of Bicholim (turn right at the bus stand) and near the village of Sanquelim.

ALDONA

Only eight kilometers from Mapusa and reached by the Mapusa bypass, the beautiful village of Aldona is home to a small community

© JANHAVI ACHAREKAR

The Arvalem Waterfall is a short walk from the ancient rock-cut Arvalem Caves near Bicholim.

THE NORTHERN COAST

of writers and artists, including renowned Goan author Maria Aurora Couto.

The picturesque, winding lanes of this sleepy village lead to the **Church of St. Thomas,** built high above the Mapusa River in 1596. The whitewashed church, also known as the St. Tome Church, is reached by a flight of steps carved into a cliff. Its history and legends are as colorful as the frescoes and sculptures that adorn the interior. It celebrates Dia dos Ladroes (Day of Thieves) in June, in memory of a robbery thwarted by local women—though some believe that the attack was averted by divine intervention.

Just two kilometers from Aldona, if you follow the bridge to Corjuem Island, you will reach an 18th-century Portuguese fort. **Corjuem Fort** is an old laterite structure that is believed to have protected the Portuguese from the Marathas.

To get to Aldona from Mapusa, cross the NH17. Take the first left after crossing the highway, and follow the road straight for eight kilometers to Aldona.

Anjuna

A hippie destination turned rave haven, Anjuna is one of the most vibrant beaches in Goa. Brought alive by its full moon parties, famous Wednesday flea market, and assorted bars, it draws an interesting mix of visitors from all over the world. The first sanctuary for the hippies who landed on Indian shores in the 1960s, it became famous in the '90s for its *chatai* parties, held at a secret location called Disco Valley where trance and drugs were the norm. The term came from the *chatais,* or the Indian straw mats used as seating in the open landscape by vendors selling tea and eatables to quell the hunger of marijuana-happy trippers. The full moon parties involved much wild revelry, but Anjuna's psychedelic nightlife was nipped in the bud by the government's clamp-down on raves. While the raves are no more, you will find reminders in the form of images of the Hindu god Shiva—icon of the revelers—everywhere. The nightlife, however, continues in its many bars.

Anjuna also brings in the crowd for its famous flea market. A place filled with hawkers selling everything from silver trinkets and clothes to musical instruments, textiles and handicrafts, it is a vast and colorful profusion of makeshift stalls on an open ground. The atmosphere is festive, while juice-and-beer stalls as well as shacks like Café Looda provide shoppers with a place to rest their weary feet. Anjuna offers a bit of history too, for those who are able to tear themselves away from its beautiful beach. The Church of St. Michael the Archangel goes back to times of Portuguese missionary zeal, while a few historical homes have been turned into heritage hotels. The hedonistic beach destination, filled with young visitors seeking answers to existential conundrums, also offers a bit of yoga along with the meditative calm of its ocean.

NIGHTLIFE

Anjuna's legendary nightlife has toned down since the 1990s, but the tradition is carried on with trance nights at some of the beachside shacks. Once famous hilltop nightclubs Club Cabana and Paradiso, with their high stone walls and multiple terraces overlooking the sea, were where the swish set once partied the night away. Today, Club Cabana is closed due to legal complications, while Paradiso has reopened to a modest crowd. **Club Paradiso** (North Anjuna Beach, cell tel. 91/93261-00013, 10 P.M.–5 A.M. daily) is a vast, white cave-like space overlooking a ground-level open area. Compensating for the slowdown in activity at these two legendary clubs are shacks that turn into party zones at night, playing trance music and serving excellent cocktails. **Curlies** (South Anjuna Beach, tel. 91/98221-68628, 6 A.M.–4 A.M. daily) is where all the action is. Located right on the beach, this is where revelers go quiet only when they watch the sunset or sunrise, whichever they can get first. Trance

The countryside is dotted with little churches and shrines on the way to Anjuna.

© JANHAVI ACHAREKAR

Bags, trinkets, clothes, and handicrafts are among the many things for sale at Anjuna's Wednesday Flea Market.

takes over the night and the party ends only when the sun comes up.

Hanging by the edge of Anjuna market, with a spectacular view of the sea, **Café Looda** (tel. 0832/562-9323, 8:30 A.M.–11:30 P.M. daily Oct.–Apr., mains Rs 100 and up) hosts live music every Wednesday, ranging from reggae to rock. A sort of open mike session, there is no quality control and it can get quite noisy.

The almost podium-style seating of **Shore Bar** (Anjuna Beach, 8 A.M.–11 P.M. daily, mains Rs 150 and up), its large images of Shiva in the background, and surreal choice of music—Tchaikovsky by day and trance by night—will make you feel like you're at a rave even if you're not. Apart from its unique ambience, which also includes a close view of the sea, the place is known for its singular cocktails like the Bob Marley—an excellent mix of Malibu rum, pineapple, lime, and mint—and good food.

SHOPPING
◖ Wednesday Flea Market

Painted elephants, Rajasthani women in traditional outfits, musicians, and rows of colorful stalls can only mean one thing: Anjuna's biggest attraction, the Wednesday flea market (8 A.M.–6 P.M. Wed. Nov.–Apr.). The origins of the market lie in the 1960s, when hippies bartered or sold their personal belongings every time they ran out of money.

Today, the market offers plenty of interesting shopping and photo opportunities, and both come at a price. Don't think that you can get away with taking a photo of the elephants or the traditionally dressed musicians holding up a "Welcome to Anjuna Market" sign. Chances are, you'll be chased and hounded until you tip your models, who make a living from posing for the tourist cameras. The stalls are no less aggressive, and bargaining is common practice as you sift through jewelry, beachwear, handbags, Ganesh idols, bedspreads, cushion covers, traditional musical instruments, souvenirs, and handicrafts. Check items thoroughly before you buy and quote less than half the price demanded. Beware of scamsters and hold your belongings close to your person.

The enclosed Tibetan market—where silver jewelry, traditional handicrafts, and "Free Tibet" bags and T-shirts are sold—is a bit more genuine. The flea market, in general, can seem repetitive, as most stalls sell the same stuff. However, it's worth walking to the end to rest at Café Looda with some live music and beer.

Shops and Markets

Near the Wednesday flea market and known for its popular restaurant, Sublime, is **Artjuna**

(Montero Vado, Flea Market Rd., tel. 91/98224-84051, 10 A.M.–9 P.M. daily Oct.–Apr.). Here you'll find artsy objects, leather items like trendy belts, handicrafts, and souvenirs of a more superior quality than the ones found at the flea market.

On the road to Anjuna is another Saturday night market. A bazaar that resembles a fair, **Ingo's Saturday Nite Bazaar** (Arpora-Anjuna Rd., cell tel. 91/93261-26200, www.ingosbazaar.com, Nov.–Apr.) is a hippie market and beer garden. Artisans from all over the country display their wares alongside dreadlocked foreign tourists on extended stays. A world market in a sense, items sold here range from local souvenirs, tie-dye scarves, mirrorwork clothes, and Rajasthani artifacts to handmade shoes and French-made curtains. You can buy trinkets, clothes, and artifacts found at the Colaba Causeway market in Mumbai for a steal, and bargaining is common. The atmosphere is celebratory, with food and drinks flowing freely as live performances and fire shows light up the night. You can even get a massage or your hair braided, amid acts by belly dancers and jugglers. A flea market with a party at the heart of its maze of flimsy, curtained stalls, Ingo's is one of Goa's most vibrant markets.

SPORTS AND RECREATION

Anjuna has its share of water sports operators, but it's best to go with the reliable ones in Candolim or Baga. Meanwhile, there's a **go kart racing track** (55, Anjuna-Calangute Rd., Arpora, tel. 91/98224-80823, 4–10 P.M. Tues.–Sun. Oct.–Apr. and 3–7 P.M. Tues.–Sun. May–Sept., Rs 150 for 10 laps) close by if you feel like a thrill.

For those who've had enough of adventure or debauchery, help is at hand. Beer is replaced with herbal tea and fish with vegetarian meals for students of the **Purple Valley Yoga Centre** (Hotel Bougainvillea/Granpa's Inn, tel. 91/93705-68639, www.brahmani-yoga.com, Nov.–Apr.), which conducts yoga classes in the shade of a tree in the garden of a charming heritage hotel. The Ashtanga and Hatha branches of yoga are taught here by qualified international instructors. You can book classes in advance or walk in. For a more intense course, sign up for the two-week retreats in the nearby village of Assagao.

ACCOMMODATIONS

Anjuna caters to a varied cartel of tourists, ranging from the neo-hippie budget traveler to the rich and famous. Among these are heritage homes and the luxury boutique hotel Nilaya Hermitage, owned by tycoon Hari Ajwani and his Parisian wife, Claudia.

Under Rs 1,000

Palacete Rodrigues (Mazal Vaddo, tel. 0832/227-3358, palacetterodrigues@rediffmail.com, Rs 650–1,050, Sept.–Apr.) is a 400-year-old Portuguese villa that offers rooms at budget rates. Impressive from the outside, with a large Portuguese-style verandah and patio, the place is owned by the family that continues to live in the old section of the house. Rooms, however, have been ill-restored with modern-day window grills and decor, taking away from the heritage charm. Some have air-conditioning. Single rooms and the newly constructed rooms outside the house may not rate highly on aesthetics but are a great value. The saving grace is the family home with its antiques and artifacts, carved chairs and chandeliers. The grand dining room in this part of the house is open to guests and is especially festive during Christmas and New Year's.

Rs 1,000–3,000

One of the best mid-range options in Anjuna, **Hotel Bougainvillea** (Gaun Vaddo, tel. 0832/227-3270, www.granpasinn.com, Rs 850–4,350, breakfast included), also known as Granpa's Inn, is a well-maintained 200-year-old Portuguese-style house with rooms in the heritage part as well as the newer sections of the property. Old family photos adorn the walls of the historical house and the friendly daughter-in-law who now manages the place will show you a sepia picture of the matriarch as a young girl. (Be sure to ask her the story behind the upper floor of the house.) Carved furniture and antiques are spread around the reception area while the garden turns into an open café. There's a lovely pool with aesthetically designed suites clustered around it, and rooms with simple but tasteful furnishing. Suites have lovely outdoor showers and a poolside terrace. For yogis, there's a yoga center that conducts courses in the shade of a large tree in the tropical garden. There's snooker and a pool bar, and modern amenities offered in a heritage ambience.

An azure pool and a grand restaurant-and-recreation area surrounded by mango, banyan, and palm trees greet you at the serene **Lotus Inn** (Zor Vaddo, tel. 0832/227-4015, Rs 800–5500). Charming cottage-style rooms are marked by bright colors and wooden furniture, with individual balconies; suites are spacious, and have private verandahs. The resort has a multi-cuisine restaurant and hosts parties on Sundays. It also has recreational facilities including a spa, health club, and indoor games.

Rs 3,000-10,000
An eco-resort with designer architecture, **(Laguna Anjuna** (Soranto Vaddo, tel. 0832/227-4305, www.lagunaanjuna.com, Rs 3,200–14,000) was built in the traditional Portuguese-style using local materials. This laterite and terra-cotta resort has its own "lagoon"—a lovely turquoise pool shaded by tropical plants with outdoor showers among the trees. Its cottage-style suites are individualistic in both architecture and interior design, with a unique classical-meets-contemporary look. While the one-bedroom suite accommodates two people, the two-bedroom unit is great for families. A verandah-bar and ambient restaurant add to the romance in the air, making this the top pick for people who want a pleasant retreat rather than a hotel.

One more in this excellent chain of boutique hotels, **(Casa Anjuna** (D'Mello Vaddo 66, tel. 0832/227-4123, www.casaboutique-hotels.com, Rs 3,500–18,000) is a beautiful old Portuguese mansion-turned-hotel located close to the beach. The sprawling property has beautiful rooms furnished with colonial-style furniture, antiques, and collector's items. Four-poster beds, wood, and wrought iron lend to its old-world feel, as do the charming balconies. The hotel also has a rooftop restaurant that presents Goan-style seafood along with a view. The Casa is located in the midst of a lush garden, providing the perfect getaway within easy proximity of the sea.

Yoga, Ayurveda, and natural living converge at **Yoga Magic** (Grand Chinvar Vaddo, tel. 0832/652-3796, www.yogamagic.net) to bring you a holistic holiday. A camp with a yoga temple carved out of mud and clay, its resident teachers conduct courses on various styles of yoga, including Ashtanga, Iyengar, Kundalini, and Scaravelli. Meditation, chanting, and breathing techniques are also taught here, along with healing and Ayurvedic massage training. Tents and suites are both made of ecofriendly materials. Thatched roofs, arched windows, and gauzy drapes make for a luxurious back-to-nature stay in the tents, while the wood-and-stone suites are quaint and rustic, with a wrought-iron staircase leading up to a meditation mezzanine. Food is organic, home-grown, vegetarian, and usually served on a banana leaf. Rates include breakfast, evening refreshments, and dinner, but yoga lessons (Rs 300 per class), therapies (Rs 750), and massage training (Rs 10,000) are charged separately. The camp offers two packages—the one- to six-night package (Rs 2,750–4,250 daily) and the seven-night package (Rs 17,500–27,500 for the week).

Rs 10,000 and Up
A quiet, forested path leads up to the fairy-tale palace called **(Nilaya Hermitage** (Arpora-Bhati, tel. 0832/227-6794, www.nilayahermitage.com, Rs 21,000–27,600, Aug.–May). One of Goa's prized jewels and premier boutique hotels, it is owned by millionaire Hari Ajwani and his Parisian fashion stylist wife Claudia. A popular celeb hangout, it has hosted the likes of Giorgio Armani and Kate Moss. A romantic citadel perched atop a hill, its classical-contemporary, Indian-Mediterranean look is woven into an unusual theme—that of elements of

nature. Cheery reds, yellows, and blues light up the 12 large and elegant rooms (earth, sun, water and fire show up as visual motifs in the decor). Antiques and designer furniture are strewn around the hotel, as are the latest gadgets and gizmos. Perhaps the most striking feature of the hotel is its music room, a soothing blue-and-white space with floor seating and excellent acoustics. The chic interior of this luxurious modern-day palace is coupled with a lovely outdoor pool and views of the surrounding greenery. Room rates include breakfast, a set-menu dinner, airport transfer, wellness and sports facilities, and taxes for two people (a minimum stay of three nights is a prerequisite). In the off-season months of May, August, and September, discounts may be negotiated.

FOOD

Anjuna's nightspots double up as great daytime hangouts. **Curlies** (South Anjuna Beach, tel. 91/98221-68628, 6 A.M.–4 A.M. daily) is on the beach, and is known better for its trance music than for its food. You will, however, find a range of multi-cuisine options here.

Hanging by the edge of Anjuna market, with a spectacular view of the sea, **Café Looda** (tel. 0832/562-9323, 8:30 A.M.–11:30 P.M. daily Oct.–Apr., mains Rs 100 and up) hosts live music every Wednesday. It serves seafood, along with multi-cuisine options ranging from pasta to traditional Goan curries. This is a popular flea market hangout.

The beachside **Shore Bar** (Anjuna Beach, 8 A.M.–11 P.M. daily, mains Rs 150 and up) has a unique ambience and sea view. The food isn't bad, and ranges from Goan fish curry rice to baba ghanoush and European fare.

At (**Sublime** (Montero Vado, Flea Market Rd., cell tel. 91/98224-84051, 6:30–11 P.M. daily Oct.–Apr., mains Rs 260), the accomplished chef rustles up some great deep-fried oysters, tuna, cucumber and mint salad, and beef with blue cheese and potatoes. The open-air fine-dining restaurant is atmospheric, with colorful overhanging lamps and tables neatly laid out under the trees.

Pick your own seafood at **Xavier's** (Praia de San Miguel, tel. 0832/227-3402, 9 A.M.–11 P.M. daily, Rs 150 and up), an old beachside multi-cuisine favorite. Known for its fresh catch and local-style fish preparations, it also serves European and Chinese fare. It's best to stick to the prawn curry rice or the lobster if you're seeking some truly local flavor.

If you feel like some good home-cooked Italian food, head to **Basilico** (D'mello Vaddo, tel. 0832/227-3721, 11 A.M.–midnight daily, mains Rs 150 and up). A beautiful garden restaurant known for its wood-fired pizzas and pastas, it has a surprisingly wide choice of salads and mains for vegetarians.

Vegetarians will be delighted to know that soy rules in a corner of Anjuna. (**Bean Me Up Soya Station** (Soranto Vaddo, tel. 0832/227-3977, 9:30 A.M.–10:30 P.M. daily Oct.–Apr., mains Rs 120) is a small place with a big veggie menu. You can expect some excellent meat substitutes, tofu preparations, and salads here. The tofu Thai curry and tofu "soyabean" are both excellent dishes, while salads are served with homemade dressing. There's also organic tea and coffee.

It's difficult to miss the signs that point to **Blue Tao Organic Restaurant and Café** (875/2, Anjuna Main Rd., tel. 0832/309-0829, 9:30 A.M.–10:30 P.M. daily, mains Rs 100). Known for its all-natural menu, this garden restaurant serves organic juices, fresh salads, and herbal tea. A great place for breakfast and snacks, it also has an impressive tofu menu. The organic farm salads, tempeh curry rice, and vegan cocktails are also particularly good. The ambience complements the cuisine, with soothing classical music and cultural performances.

Another place that will appeal to vegetarians and those looking for a cleansing experience is **Yoga Magic** (Grand Chinvar Vaddo, tel. 0832/652-3796, www.yogamagic.net, 9 A.M.–10 P.M. Sun.–Fri., *thali* Rs 400). This organic, vegetarian restaurant attached to the yoga camp of the same name is known for its experimental natural and Indian fare.

Patrons can eat their greens and lentils in a special *thali* (unlimited platter) served on a banana leaf.

A cliffhanger with a spectacular view of the sea, **Zooris** (North Anjuna Beach, 11 A.M.– 11 P.M. daily, mains Rs 120 and up) is situated next to Club Paradiso. Visited as much for its location and sea breeze as for its menu, it serves a variety of cuisines, including Italian, Mexican, and Israeli specialties.

INFORMATION AND SERVICES
Hospitals and Pharmacies
Medical help and supplies are available at **St. Anthony Hospital & Research Centre** (near petrol pump, cell tel. 91/98224-86688) and **St. Michael's Pharmacy** (Soranto Vaddo, tel. 0832/227-4439, 8:30 A.M.–9:30 P.M. daily).

Police
In case of emergency, **dial 100** for the 24-hour police helpline or try the **Anjuna Police Station** (Anjuna Rd., tel. 0832/227-3233).

Money
Anjuna has a number of foreign exchange dealers such as **Nehal Travels** (St. Anthony Prai, Anjuna Beach, tel. 0832/227-3288, 9 A.M.– 10 P.M. daily), **Oxford Arcade** (D'Mello Vaddo, tel. 0832/227-3436, 8:30 A.M.–9 P.M. Mon.–Sat.), and **Connexions** (St. Michael's Pharmacy, Soranto Vaddo, tel. 0832/227-4347, 9:30 A.M.–10 P.M. daily), as well as ATMs such as **HDFC** (Mazal Vaddo) and **Bank of Goa** (Soranto Vaddo).

Postal Services
For postal services, the **Anjuna Post Office** (near the football grounds, tel. 0832/227-3221, 9 A.M.–5 P.M. Mon.–Fri.) is easily accessible.

Internet
Anjuna has a number of Internet cafés, such as **Sify I-Way** (Mazal Vaddo, 9 A.M.–9 P.M. daily), **Nehal Travels** (St. Anthony Prai, Anjuna Beach, tel. 0832/227-3288, 9 A.M.– 10 P.M. daily), **Connexions** (St. Michael's Pharmacy, Soranto Vaddo, tel. 0832/227-4347, 9:30 A.M.–10 P.M. daily), and **Manali Computers** (near Star Co., tel. 0832/227-3980, 9:30 A.M.–9:30 P.M. daily). Rates hover around Rs 40 per hour.

GETTING THERE AND AROUND
From Dabolim Airport, Anjuna is 50 kilometers and an hour and fifteen minutes away by taxi, which costs Rs 750.

From the Thivim train station, Anjuna is less than half an hour away; the cab ride costs around Rs 350.

Anjuna is easily accessible from other parts of Goa and is only 10 kilometers from Mapusa, from where you can take a pre-paid taxi (Rs 130) or a Siolim bus (Rs 15, every half-hour) that stops at Vagator junction.

If driving from Panaji (32 km away), take the NH17 to Mapusa and turn left to Anjuna via Assagao. Once you're in Anjuna, you may rent a motorcycle or scooter (ask at your hotel reception), or take buses or local taxis to travel around.

Vagator

Swaying palm trees, a crescent beach, and a magnificent fort with an unparalleled view of the sea are what make Vagator different from the other beaches. Its two beaches—Big Vagator and Ozran (or Little Vagator)—draw an interesting mix of tourists. Big Vagator is a haven for domestic tourists, while Ozran is a secluded cove ideal for trance-and-pot-happy neo-hippies. And high above the two, a steep climb leads unsuspecting visitors up to the romantic arches of the Chapora Fort, startling them with the sudden and spectacular view of the vast ocean on one side and the Chapora River on the other. The charming Chapora village is only a stone's throw away from the beaches, with its quiet, shaded by-lanes and rustic atmosphere.

Vagator has a distinctly young tourist population and is famous for places like Nine Bar, where revelers drink and dance the night away, leaving the nearby beaches only after having witnessed a breathtaking sunrise. A plethora of budget accommodations line this stretch to cater to backpackers, while a number of quaint eateries and street-side stalls selling clothes and trinkets pop up during the peak season. Although the raves have officially ended, underground parties continue—guests are informed by word of mouth. This tantalizing mix of solitude and psychedelics, river and ocean, village and beach make Vagator a unique and irresistible destination.

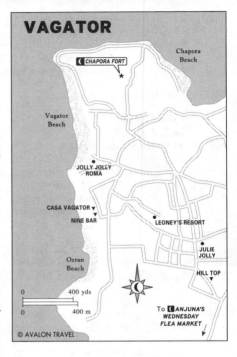

SIGHTS
Big Vagator Beach

A spectacular stretch of sand and sea, Big Vagator Beach can be viewed from the dramatic ramparts of the Chapora Fort and from the concrete benches on the road above. Tourists, here to enjoy the view, are surrounded by persuasive trinket sellers, who, in turn, come here for the tourists. The beach is crowded with domestic visitors and swimmers in peak season, but can be hauntingly quiet in the off-season, its sounds of the sea broken only by the sighing of palm fronds swaying in the monsoon breeze.

Ozran (Little Vagator)

A sandy cove shaded by palm trees at the southern end of Vagator, Ozran, also called Little Vagator, is a picturesque small beach offering seclusion and a bit of quiet, far from the frenzy of Anjuna and the crowds of Big Vagator. Another spectator to the wild and wonderful hippie era, Ozran has a famous rock carving of Shiva from its hippie days and was known for its raves and full moon parties until recently. Even today, its bars are patronized by a large number of international partiers who celebrate until sunrise.

© JANHAVI ACHAREKAR

view of Big Vagator Beach from the ruins of the Chapora Fort

(Chapora Fort

Only the ramparts of the fort remain, but it still has an air of grandeur and a dramatic view. Built by Sultan Adil Shah of Bijapur, after whom the Chapora fort was named—"Shah-pura"—it was captured and rebuilt by the Portuguese in 1617. In 1684, it was lost to the Marathas and eventually recaptured in 1741. The fort was abandoned in 1892 but continues to draw tourists to its haunting beauty and sweeping views of the Arabian Sea and the Chapora River.

NIGHTLIFE

Vagator's wild raves and full-moon parties may have ended, but ravers continue to find an outlet in the area's iconic bars. The famous **Nine Bar** (above Ozran, near Casa Vagator, 6 P.M.–midnight daily Oct.–Apr.) has a tunnel-like entrance that leads into an open space crowded with revelers and with a fantastic view of Little Vagator Beach. There's a bar on the side that serves all kinds of liquor, and trance plays in the background, working up the mood for an all-night high.

An unspectacular café with a seedy-looking indoor nightclub, **Primrose Bar** (Coutinho Vaddo, tel. 0832/227-3210, 5 P.M.–3 A.M. daily Oct.–Apr.) has a government-office canteen look on the outside with its display of sandwiches, pastries, and baked items. There's an extensive food menu as well that includes everything from Goan seafood and North Indian–style cuisine to Italian pasta. Inside is another story. The discotheque is cramped with ravers tripping on trance music and other stuff. The place is open until the early hours, attracting crowds from other bars that close earlier.

High up and away from the beach is the newly renovated **Hill Top** (cell tel. 91/98221-51690, 9 A.M.–11 P.M. daily Nov.–Apr.), an open bar shaded by trees and surrounded by gardens. Seemingly in the middle of nowhere, this is the ideal location for an impromptu techno and trance party.

ACCOMMODATIONS

Vagator is a backpacker's paradise and its many budget and mid-range hotels are usually filled with dreadlocked tourists and techno-trippers. That said, this trance destination has a number of good, comfortable and value-for-money accommodations such as Bethany Inn and the more upmarket Casa Vagator.

THE NORTHERN COAST

© JANHAVI ACHAREKAR

The Chapora Fort offers one of the best views in Goa.

Under Rs 1,000

A quiet house shielded by a garden from the frenzied partying at the bar area, **Hill Top** (Vagator, cell tel. 91/98221-51690, Rs 600) is a small place with a few basic rooms. The location is pretty enough and the rates equally attractive (though they rise to about Rs 2,000 during Christmas and New Year's). The beach is a short ride away.

A name that's sure to bring some jollity, **Jolly Jolly Roma** (Vagator Beach Rd., tel. 0832/227-3001, www.hoteljollygoa.com, Rs 990–1,560 Oct.–Apr.) is part of a family of three hotels owned by the same management. The property comprises a simple set of cottages close to the beach. Each has a sit-out and is shaded from the activity outside by trees and foliage, offering seclusion and tranquility. Rooms are basic—twin-bedded, double-bedded, and air-conditioned. The resort, like most other hotels in the Vagator area, offers facilities for Western Union money transfer, taxi and bike hire, travel bookings, and a doctor on

call. Needless to say, for the price, the place is jolly good.

Rs 1,000–3,000

[Bethany Inn (Vagator Rd., tel. 0832/227-3731, www.bethanyinn.com, Rs 450–2,500) is a clean, well-maintained place with a bit of greenery and rooms with large windows and balconies. Popular with tourists, the double rooms are small but pleasant and comfortable, while the larger suites are spacious and come with large balconies. Rooms are air-conditioned, and the inn's facilities include a money changer, travel agency, Internet, taxi service, and a doctor on call.

It is difficult to miss the bright red facade of the cottages at **Julie Jolly** (Ozran, tel. 0832/227-3620, www.hoteljollygoa.com, Rs 990–3,660, rates increase during Christmas and New Year's and dip in the low season)—a popular budget option for the party-hearty lot that has been upgraded in price and facilities. Part of the same Jolly family, it is close to the nightly action of the area. Rooms are basic and simple, but sought after for their proximity to nightspots and the beach. Equipped with a kitchen and bar counter, the cottages also have access to a pool. Like its sister hotel, it offers facilities for money transfer, taxi and bike hire, travel bookings, and a doctor on call.

Rs 3,000–10,000

A tranquil getaway with a sea view, **Alcove Resort** (Ozran Beach, tel. 0832/227-4491, www.alcovegoa.com, Rs 1,000–5,500) is a lovely self-contained property with beautiful tiled-roof cottages and gardens in addition to standard rooms and suites. Aesthetically appealing sea-view suites and rooms facing the pool make for a comfortable and luxurious stay, and are well worth the price. The resort also has a bar, a multi-cuisine restaurant, Internet facilities, and money exchange, and organizes boat and sightseeing tours.

A lovely cluster of villas by a pool and amidst beautiful gardens, **Leoney's Resort** (Ozran Beach Rd., tel. 0832/227-3634, www

.leoneyresort.com, Rs 1,300–4,700) is only a short walk from the beach. Accommodation options include deluxe rooms, suites, and whitewashed Goan-Portuguese-style cottages. Cottages are well designed and spacious, and are kept bright and cheerful with a skylight; rooms are pleasant and comfortable. All categories of rooms are furnished with cane and wooden furniture and come with four-poster beds. The resort also has a restaurant, Ayurvedic massage facilities, a money changer, Internet and phone facilities, as well as bikes and taxis for hire.

A heritage hotel in the beautiful interior but easily accessible from Vagator, the award-winning **⟨C Siolim House** (Wadi, Siolim, tel. 0832/227-2138, www.siolimhouse.com, Rs 6,300–7,900) is a 300-year-old residence with a history. The family home of the erstwhile governor of Macau, its restored Goan-Portuguese architecture is marked by a beautiful yellow facade and a wooden-beamed interior filled with antiques. Its seven bedrooms and sprawling suites (named after ancient ports along the coast) are furnished with four-poster beds, rocking chairs, chandeliers, and traditional oyster-shell windows. Painted in bright colors with sunlight filtering through sheer drapes, the rooms have equally grand bathrooms. The house has a landscaped garden, a pool, and top-notch service, but maintains the appearance and feel of a private home, making for an atmospheric stay. It is equipped with all the modern amenities, including wireless Internet. The staff prepares home-style Goan meals and can arrange for car hire, massages, yoga, barbecues, and excursions around the area.

Rs 10,000 and Up

Another superb product of this impressive chain, **⟨C Casa Vagator** (tel. 0832/225-3205, Rs 5,000–24,000) is a veritable paradise. It's located next to the famous Nine Bar and offers private access to the beach. The beautiful white-and-yellow structure is accentuated by individually designed rooms furnished with antiques and original artworks. While some rooms have private verandahs or sit-outs, the crowning glory is the fantastic ocean-view penthouse. An amazement of terraces and an outdoor "sunset lounge," it's equipped with a home theater and an equally luxurious bathroom with a whirlpool tub. A multi-cuisine restaurant on the premises affords a beautiful view and serves global fare in addition to Goan-style cuisine. There's a terrace bar, a pool, and a wonderful ambience that is disturbed every evening, unfortunately, by the thumping sound of disco beats from the neighboring bar.

FOOD

Most Vagator restaurants rarely see the next season, but **Baba Yaga** (House 408, Main Rd., Chapora, tel. 0832/227-3339, 11 A.M.–midnight daily Nov.–Apr., mains Rs 200 and up) and a few others are permanent hangouts for the area's Russian tourist population. Located in the Chapora market area, its small, hole-in-the-wall entrance leads up to a rooftop bar and restaurant serving Russian specialties and Ukrainian delicacies. The place is a haven for vodka drinkers and after a couple of shots, you're likely to believe that you've been transported to Russia—thanks in no small measure to the Russian folk art and decor.

A place that will have you saying "Blistering Barnacles!," **TinTin Bar & Restaurant** (Big Vagator Beach Rd., cell tel. 91/98813-47762, 8 A.M.–midnight daily, mains Rs 100 and up) was inspired by Belgian creator Hergé's famous comic book character—a theme seen in the decor as well as the menu. Known for its seafood, European dishes, and Goan cuisine, the restaurant is also frequented for its pub-like atmosphere and cocktails (Rs 150 and up). On Christmas and New Year's Eve, they organize live entertainment in the form of Captain Haddock bartenders and Bianca Castafiore singers.

Most visitors are surprised to know that authentic ratatouille and bouillabaisse are available in the area. **⟨C Le Bluebird** (Ozran, tel. 0832/227-3695, 9 A.M.–2 P.M. and 7–11 P.M. daily Nov.–Apr., mains Rs 200 and up) has made a name for itself, though, and offers a wide selection of wines along with its traditional French menu. The steaks, in particular, are supremely good.

Perched on a cliff above Ozran is the beautifully located **[Alcove Restaurant** (Ozran, 8 A.M.–11 P.M. daily, mains Rs 100 and up), known for its amazing sunsets and Goan-style cuisine. Try the seafood preparations, especially the tiger prawns and the curries, as you enjoy the ocean view.

Overlooking Ozran is the newly opened Greek Taverna and Vagator's most atmospheric restaurant **Thalassa** (Little Vagator, cell tel. 91/985003-3537, marikettyindia@hotmail. com, 7–11 P.M. daily, mains Rs 150 and up). Run by Mariketty, a vivacious Greek who arrived in Goa during the hippie era, this is where you can sample some authentic and traditional Greek food off a menu that promises to reinvent itself with every season. Try the souvlaki wraps, kebabs, salads, and the excellent desserts amid a white outdoor ambience with a view of the sea from atop a cliff.

INFORMATION AND SERVICES
Money
While the larger beach town of Anjuna with its many hospitals, pharmacies, banks, and post office lies close by, most resorts in Vagator—both budget and mid-range—will provide money services. **Alcove Resort** (Ozran Beach, tel. 0832/227-4491) has a foreign exchange counter, as do **Soniya Travels** (Chapora, tel.

0832/227-3344, 9:30 A.M.–10 P.M. daily) and **Travel Cash Online** (Bethany Inn, Vagator Rd., tel. 0832/227-3731, 10 A.M.–10 P.M. daily)—which even gives cash advances on credit cards and conducts money transfers through Western Union.

Internet
Almost all of Vagator's popular resorts and money changers offer Internet access (at about Rs 50/hr).

GETTING THERE AND AROUND
Only a short distance from Anjuna, Vagator takes about an hour and a half and Rs 750 by taxi from Dabolim Airport. The closest train station is Thivim, about half an hour away and Rs 350 by cab. It is well connected to other Goan destinations by both pre-paid taxi and bus. Vagator is only 10 kilometers away from Mapusa and most buses from Mapusa to Anjuna carry on to Vagator and Chapora. You can take a Siolim bus and get down at Vagator junction, and then take a motorcycle taxi to the beach.

Driving from Panaji (32 km away), take the NH17 to Mapusa and turn left to Anjuna via Assagao and then left again from outside Anjuna village to Vagator.

Siolim Village lies on the southern bank of the Chapora River and is best reached by taxi from Vagator. From Vagator, it is a six kilometer drive via Chapora Village.

The Far North Coast

The far northern coast of Goa holds the dubious distinction of sheltering a surprising mix of visitors—olive ridley turtles and the Russian land mafia—both of which have dwindled in number in recent years. This continuous strip of beach just across the Chapora River from Morjim to Keri—covering Ashvem, Mandrem, Arambol, and right up to Terekhol—makes for an interesting journey with dolphin encounters and sandy coves, riverine nooks and techno bars, virgin sands and old forts on the way. Both geographical and cultural landscape are distinct in character from the rest of the region as tourist population and commercial activity become scant, thinning out to reveal a dramatic marine and inland topography comprising rock formations and dense foliage.

Local residents, too, are rural in character, but the area has seen a surprising new phenomenon in recent times: the mass influx of Russian tourists. A hip destination for affluent Russians and a lucrative one for its mafia, the far north now welcomes its new clientele with Russian cuisine, plush accommodations, and Russian-language food menus. You won't be left wanting for good vodka in these parts.

While Morjim, the tiny Ashvem, and the tranquil Mandrem are quiet and soulful, Arambol is where the action is. Discos, trance bars, pool, and pot make for a heady combination as Shiva images and filthy sands offset the dramatic natural rock formations at the far end of the beach. The landscape is then redeemed by Keri, the northernmost beach, with its calm casuarinas and ferry to the hauntingly quiet Fort Terekhol.

Meanwhile, farther inland in the Pernem district is the 17th-century **Deshprabhu House**—a large complex of houses with 13 courtyards and the estate of the Hindu family that ruled the entire region until it was awarded the title of viscount (viscondes de Pernem) in exchange for a merger of its territory with the rest of Portuguese Goa. The property is generally off-limits to tourists, although that depends entirely on the whims of its present-day owner and descendant of the family who continues to live here. It is located near Pernem town, just off the Morjim-Pernem road.

MORJIM AND ASHVEM

It's easy to tell why Morjim is a nesting site of the olive ridley turtle. Its peace and calm have been maintained in no small measure by the efforts of local residents who are passionate about ecological conservation in this protected area. Although they say that the nesting pattern has changed since the tsunami and that fewer hatchings take place now than they did before, the place remains a veritable treasure trove for lovers of nature. While water sports are slowly making their way into these parts, a dolphin ride into the sea means an assured sighting of at least three dolphins (or else you get your money back) and even the odd swordfish or two. In the monsoon months, the sandy

Rest, relaxation, and recreation are the essentials of a Goan holiday.

stretch is overrun with creepers and wildflowers, wearing a vacant look. Away from the shacks and hammocks of Morjim Beach are the quiet, winding lanes of the village. Only slightly farther (another kilometer) is the sleepy fishing village of Ashvem, recognized by its green ponds, rows of fishing boats, and bamboo huts or "coco-huts."

Sports and Recreation

Beach activity in these parts is generally quiet and restricted to swimming and dolphin trips. Dolphin sightings are best done with Francis (cell tel. 91/96041-07620), who takes a personal interest in informing you about the marine and other life of the region as you head toward the surrounding beaches. For Rs 350 per person, the trip is well worth it. And if you don't spot a dolphin on an early morning ride, you get your money back.

Accommodations

Morjim is a small beach, but it has a surprisingly good range of accommodations, including beach shacks, tents, and luxury boutique stays that remain open only in the tourist season.

RS 3,000–10,000

Among Morjim's favorite budget shacks is **Mojito** (Vithaldas Vaddo, Morjim, cell tel. 91/98232-76520, Rs 950–2,950, Oct.–Apr.)—a group of beachside huts on wooden stilts that come with attached bathrooms. Strewn with colorful hammocks, the thatched-roof, ecofriendly accommodation has an English pub-style bar and a restaurant (8 A.M.–midnight daily Oct.–Apr., mains Rs 150) that serves both Indian and European cuisine.

Topping the list of accommodations— as far as both quality and location—is Alvin Fernandes' [**Montego Bay** (Vithaldas Vaddo, Morjim, tel. 0832/651-1254, cell tel. 91/98221-50847, www.montegobaygoa.com, Rs 2,000–9,500, Oct.–Apr.). A motley cluster of striped tents, log cabins, a beach house, and a casa make up this cheerful beach resort. Tents are well kept and come with attached

Tents and outdoor seating make for a relaxing time at Morjim Beach.

© ASHIMA NARAIN

bathrooms (with cold showers). Beds are draped with mosquito nets; to avoid being bitten, ask for the tents closer to the sea and away from the foliage. The resort has quaint log cabins with sit-outs and well-equipped bathrooms, but the star rooms lie in the beach house and the casa. The upper room of the casa affords a fantastic view of the sea, while the beach house is the original Fernandes home now spruced up for visitors, complete with living room, verandah, bedroom, and a kitchen equipped with a refrigerator. Montego Bay is also known for its restaurant, which is particularly good for seafood and pasta. Breakfast is included in room rates, service is excellent, and the owner looks into the daily management himself, ensuring that a high standard of quality is always maintained.

Close by is the Zen-like exclusive boutique hotel [**Ku** (Gaudo Vaddo, Morjim, cell tel. 91/93261-23570, Oct.–Apr., Rs 5,000) run by European couple Marie and Chris. With its Japanese-style garden, a delightful restaurant, and two Japanese-inspired rooms, it makes for a wonderful living and dining experience.

The rooms are natural, with Japanese-style screen doors and low beds, and are shaded by trees. The appealing treehouse-style structure has an open-plan living area at the top for the owners, while the restaurant and lounge are spread over top and bottom, with a view of the surrounding fields. At the restaurant (12:30–5:30 P.M. daily, dinner by reservation), a French chef who whips up excellent Spanish and East Asian delicacies. A surprising getaway in the middle of nowhere, Ku spells sophistication and originality.

Closer to Ashvem, **Papa Jolly's** (House no. 749/A, Morjim-Ashvem Rd., tel. 0832/224-4113, www.papajollysgoa.com, Rs 4,500–14,200, Oct.–Apr.) has surprisingly pleasant rooms and a sea view. The themed rooms are large and have balconies that open out to a beautiful view of Morjim beach. Inside, four-poster beds and soft lighting are teamed with modern-day gadgets, including an LCD TV and a whirlpool tub in the bathroom. All rooms are air-conditioned and the resort has a pool where guests can cool off. It also has facilities for Ayurvedic massage, yoga, and meditation; a restaurant and bar; and Internet access. Tariffs are inclusive of breakfast.

RS 10,000 AND UP

A short distance from Montego Bay, a narrow path leads to the newly developed ◖ **Sur La Mer** (Morjim-Ashvem Rd., tel. 0832/645-3102, cell tel. 91/98500-56742, www.surlamergoa .com, Rs 10,000–40,000, Oct.–Apr.). A luxurious resort built around a central courtyard with a pool, it has an elegant Rajasthani-style interior. Rooms are of two types—royal and deluxe—and are well furnished with canopied beds and carved wood antiques. Every room has a balcony (with the option of a mountain or an ocean view), LCD television, and DVD player. There's a Maharaja suite, too, but the highlight of the resort is the spectacular penthouse, which offers a stunning and intimate view of the sea. It also comes with a steam room and butler service. The resort has a restaurant and bar area, as well as a spa. It also boasts a wide selection of books, in both English and Russian, for patrons to borrow.

Food

Morjim has a varied mix of restaurants that draw a motley crowd from the nearby resorts, in search of a different ambience or cuisine. **Mojito** (Vithaldas Vaddo, Morjim, cell tel. 91/98232-76520, 8 A.M.–midnight daily Oct.–Apr., mains Rs 150) is an English pub-style bar and restaurant that serves both Indian and European cuisine. The colorful hammocks add to its charming beachside ambience, encouraging guests to relax even as the food arrives.

Known better for its beachside tents, **Montego Bay** (Vithaldas Vaddo, Morjim, tel. 0832/651-1254, cell tel. 91/98221-50847, www.montegobaygoa.com, 8 A.M.–midnight daily Oct.–Apr., mains Rs 100 and up) serves local seafood preparations and first-rate pasta—in the open and in the covered reception area, which is usually gaily lit with twinkling fairy lights.

Frequented by the region's Russian tourist and long-stay population, **Glavfish** (Vithaldas Vaddo, cell tel. 91/98812-87433, 8 A.M.–midnight daily Oct.–Apr., mains Rs 300) is where you can enjoy a beautiful sunset and a traditional creamy *syrniki* (cottage cheese pancake) on a wooden bench. One of the first restaurants here, Glavfish pushed up the property prices in the region. It screens the odd Russian movie in the evening.

Che Guevera is alive and well at the beachside shack of **Café del Mar** (Turtle Beach, Temb Vaddo, Morjim, cell tel. 91/98225-81928, sach6437@rediffmail.com, mains Rs 150 and up), which is decorated with posters and wall hangings of the revolutionary. This hippie den serves excellent Mediterranean salads, seafood, and pasta. Lounge music and floor seating add to the ambience, making this a vibrant lunch and dinner hangout.

Boutique hotel ◖ **Ku** (Gaudo Vaddo, Morjim, cell tel. 91/93261-23570, 12:30–5:30 P.M. daily, dinner by reservation

Oct.–Apr., mains Rs 250 and up) has a delightful restaurant reached through a Japanese-inspired garden. The restaurant and lounge are spread over two levels, with a view of the surrounding fields. Prices are steep—a pot of tea costs Rs 100—and there's no fixed menu, but it boasts a French chef whose repertoire includes sashimi, Vietnamese soup, Spanish *jamon,* and Thai specialties.

On the way to Ashvem, the restaurant at **Papa Jolly's** (House no. 749/A, Morjim-Ashvem Road, tel. 0832/224-4113, www .papajollysgoa.com, 7 A.M.–11 P.M. daily Oct.–Apr., mains Rs 120 and up) serves everything from Goan-style seafood to Mediterranean and Chinese cuisine.

At luxury resort **◖ Sur La Mer** (Morjim-Ashvem Rd., tel. 0832/645-3102, cell tel. 91/98500-56742, www.surlamergoa.com, noon–11 P.M. daily Oct.–Apr., mains Rs 100 and up), the restaurant serves French, Italian, and Indian cuisine, with Goan-style seafood preparations. Lobster and pasta are specialties here and are accompanied with a fine selection of wine.

◖ La Plage (Ashvem, cell tel. 91/98221-21712, 8:30 A.M.–10:30 P.M. daily Nov.–Apr., mains Rs 250 and up) is a French restaurant par excellence, and one of the finest in Goa. Must-haves include the caramelized tuna, ceviche, and chocolate pudding. The beachside ambience is a plus, although the famous French attitude, some complain, is not.

Getting There and Around

Morjim is easily reached via the Siolim Bridge—a taxi ride from Dabolim Airport costs Rs 850 and takes about an hour and a half.

From the Thivim rail station, it is a 40-minute taxi ride that costs Rs 500.

From Panaji by car, take the NH17 and go past Mapusa and onto the Siolim Bridge.

A number of buses (Rs 20, every 20 minutes) also ply to Morjim from Mapusa and Pernem bus stations.

A ferry service (free, Rs 10 for vehicles) runs every half-hour between Chapora and Morjim, across the Chapora River.

◖ MANDREM

Mandrem (pronounced Maand-ray) offers the solitude of the Goan beaches of yore, complete with blush sunsets and golden sands. One of the most enchanting beaches that Goa has to offer, it has only a smattering of resorts and restaurants, without the noisy water sports or the frenzied parties of its neighbor, Arambol. The narrow strip of beach is ideal for a swim or a stroll and is lined only with the occasional coco-hut. Charming bamboo bridges are slung across sandy moats created by the high tide. The air is exhilarating and rural, with only fishing boats for company in the quiet waters. The nearby Mandrem village makes for an interesting cycling excursion with its picturesque river and rural scenes together with the old Ravalnatha temple. Meanwhile, a handful of resorts in the vicinity, especially the luxury boutique hotel Elsewhere, contribute toward making this the ideal getaway.

Sports and Recreation

Mandrem's charm lies in the absence of sport, though dolphin rides are conducted by local

© ASHIMA NARAIN

A bamboo bridge leads to the quiet, picturesque Mandrem Beach.

fishermen (ask for information at your resort). Traditional massage therapy is available at **Riva Ayurvedic Health Spa** (Mandrem Beach, tel. 0832/224-7088, www.rivaresorts.com), a part of the tranquil Riva Beach Resort. Both relaxing and curative treatments are available here and are carried out only after a thorough consultation with the practitioner.

Dunes Holiday Village (Mandrem Beach, tel. 0832/229-7219, www.dunesgoa.com) offers yoga. Lessons are conducted on specially created yoga platforms in the yoga center. Walk-ins are permitted.

Accommodations

Mandrem has a select but excellent choice beachfront huts and resorts with attached restaurants.

Swaying palm trees, endless rows of bamboo cottages connected to the almost private beach by a wooden bridge, and sun beds in the blue horizon make **(Riva Beach Resort** (Mandrem Beach, tel. 0832/224-7088, www .rivaresorts.com, Rs 600–2,500, Oct.–Apr.) one of the most romantic settings on the northern coast. Although basic in amenities, the resort has a wide variety of accommodations to suit various budgets, ranging from the cheaper tree houses and huts with shared bathrooms to bamboo cottages, cheerful tents, beachfront and air-conditioned huts, among others. There's an Ayurveda health center, and the resort has a sea-facing bar and restaurant called Waves. The hotel arranges for bike and taxi hire, and has money changing, travel services, and phone and Internet facilities.

Another group of beachfront shacks, **Dunes Holiday Village** (Mandrem Beach, tel. 0832/224-7071, www.dunesgoa.com, Rs 600–1,500 hut, Oct.–Apr.) offers value-for-money accommodations by the sea. Huts come with shared or attached bathrooms, and there's a larger family room that is available on request. An open-air restaurant serves multi-cuisine buffets in a vibrant atmosphere, and there's a yoga center as well as facilities for Ayurvedic massage. The resort has indoor recreation and also organizes Indian classical music concerts.

It arranges for bike and taxi hire, dolphin trips, and has money changing, travel, and phone and Internet facilities.

An unusual Portuguese-style house with a soft corner for its feline occupants, **(Villa River Cat** (Junaswada, Mandrem River, tel. 0832/224-7928, www.villarivercat.com, Rs 1,600–3,300) is a riverine getaway with a view of the sea. Designed using local materials by animal-lover and owner Rinoo Sehgal, this lovely resort has a lush garden and a verandah strewn with hammocks. Rooms are spacious with large windows and balconies, and are crammed with objets d'art. Especially receptive to artists and writers, the house functions as a creative commune and rooms are equipped with painting materials. In addition, a library, telescope, massage therapy, and yoga lessons ensure that boredom never sets in. The Miau restaurant serves great home-style cooking. The atmosphere is homey and guests invariably leave as friends.

The name is telling and the location does it justice at **(Elsewhere** (Mandrem, cell tel. 91/98200-37387, www.aseascape.com, Rs 13,000–33,600 daily, 40,000–116,000/week, Oct.–Apr.), a resort that is altogether something else. Dating back to 1886, this is the ancestral home of photographer Denzil Sequeira. Wedged between river and ocean, and cooled by palm trees, this unique beach house is now a boutique hotel that offers modern comforts in a heritage ambience. Luxurious tents and brightly painted beach houses supplement the sprawling rooms of the main house, some of which are furnished with four-poster beds and equipped with World Space Radio, as well as Internet. The tents are lovely and face the creek, their curtains billowing in the private sit-out and wooden deck. Meals are served at the restaurant shack, while a car and driver are available at an extra charge.

Food

Mandrem's handful of beach resorts have attached restaurants for guests. Riva Beach Resort has a sea-facing bar and restaurant called **Waves** (Mandrem Beach, tel. 0832/224-7088, www.rivaresorts.com, 8 A.M.–midnight daily Oct.–Apr., mains Rs 120 and up) that serves Goan, Mexican, Chinese, and European specialties, and hosts the occasional DJ night.

Dunes Holiday Village (Mandrem Beach, tel. 0832/224-7071, www.dunesgoa.com, 8 A.M.–5 P.M. and 6–11 P.M. daily, mains Rs 150 and up) has a multi-cuisine restaurant that serves open-air buffet-style meals; guests also have the option of ordering à la carte.

Miau (Villa River Cat, Junaswada, Mandrem River, tel. 0832/224-7928, www.villarivercat .com, 8 A.M.–10 P.M. daily, mains Rs 350, prior notification required for dinner) is the restaurant of the lovely riverside Villa River Cat resort. It serves great home-style cooking and European cuisine, and guests are encouraged to participate in the culinary process.

Getting There and Around

From Dabolim Airport, Mandrem is less than two hours and a taxi ride (costing Rs 850) away. From Thivim, the journey by road takes less than an hour and costs Rs 500. By road, you may take the scenic coastal route from Morjim (go south toward Agarvado and turn right at the first junction) or take the ferry (every 30 minutes, 6 A.M.–9:30 P.M., passengers free, vehicle Rs 10) across the Chapora River, or the Colvale bridge.

ARAMBOL (HARMAL)

With its rows of beach shacks, polluted sands, and noisy water sports, it is difficult to imagine Arambol (also known locally as Harmal) as an idyllic golden getaway of the hippie era. Today, the beach is fast turning into a melee akin to the chaos of Baga or Calangute. Pleasure boat trips and water sports such as Jet Skiing and parasailing have transformed this former hippie paradise into a thrill-seeker's haven. Street stalls selling clothes, crafts, and musical instruments lead up to bars and cafés that often host live music and the occasional trance party.

In the crevices of Arambol village, some semblance of peace is maintained in the form of yoga and meditation. However, Arambol

© ASHIMA NARAIN

A former hippie paradise, Arambol Beach is a yoga and trance party destination today.

retains its unique identity with its unusual rock formation that easily distinguishes it from the other beaches. Jutting out of the sea with a sense of renewed purpose, the rocky projectiles are visible from anywhere on the beach. A lake and forest are hemmed in by the shoreline and many a beautiful sunset catches the silhouette of the occasional surfer.

Sports and Recreation

Although Arambol has water-sports operators galore, none are recommended due to their fly-by-night tendencies. Windsurfing and kitesurfing are also popular activities here, but surfers are advised against coming close to the rocky northern end of the beach.

◖ Yoga

Arambol is famous for yoga. The **Himalayan Iyengar Yoga Centre** (Madhlo Vaddo, near Pia Guesthouse, www.hiyogacentre.com, 1–3 P.M. daily) conducts five-day initiation courses, as well as advanced and intensive courses in the Iyengar tradition of Hatha yoga. Different meditation techniques as well *pranayama* (breathing techniques) are taught by a disciple of B. K. S. Iyengar. Teacher's training courses are also offered. Classes are conducted in the spacious and brightly lit center, which is surrounded by palm and mango trees.

The Italian-run **Samsara Beach Resort** (near temple, tel. 91/98226-88471, www.samsara.20m.com) promotes healthy living and conducts twice-daily yoga classes. Monthly courses are held in the peak season and both Iyengar as well as Ashtanga yoga are taught to beginners and veterans alike by qualified teachers.

Accommodations

A hippie paradise, Arambol is made up of budget beach shacks and guesthouses. Living arrangements are wonderfully cheap and tend to be basic but comfortable.

Run by a local Goan family, the respected budget accommodation **Relax Inn** (Arambol Beach, tel. 0832/651-0856, Rs 450–500, Oct.–Apr.) is a spread of beach huts sprinkled around the rocky end of the beach. Rooms are

functional and come with an attached bathroom that has a hot and cold shower. If you intend to be on the beach all day, the shack is a good enough place to rest for the night.

Another good option in Arambol, **Lamuella Guesthouse** (Arambol Beach Rd., tel. 0832/561-4563, Rs 500–700, Oct.–Apr.) is an Israeli-run place that welcomes all nationalities. Rooms are bright, spacious, and almost luxurious in comparison to the shacks on the beach.

Located atop a dune, **Samsara Beach Resort** (near the temple, Arambol Beach, tel. 91/98226-88471, www.samsara.20m.com, Rs 700–1,000, Oct.–Apr.) is positioned as a health resort. Beach huts and rooms are accompanied by a yoga center, and there's a restaurant serving healthy Italian-style food, herbal tea, and fresh juices. Living arrangements are clean and well maintained by the Italian management. While the beach huts have common bathrooms, rooms come with an attached bath. Both categories of lodging enjoy a stunning sea view. Guests can relax

© ASHIMA NARAIN

A beachside juice bar and bakery displays its variety of healthy beverages.

PROPERTY AND THE RUSSIAN LAND MAFIA

Much has been debated about the real estate scenario in Goa. Entrepreneurs, hoteliers, and tourists (both domestic and foreign) have each demanded their slice of Goa in recent years, sending land prices skyrocketing and making good property scarce for local Goans. While beachfront areas were traditionally handed over in dowry (for their lack of profitability in an agricultural society), they are now a much sought-after luxury. Today, the tourist-dominated northern coast, especially, is saturated, overcrowded, and overpriced. Although foreign nationals are not legally permitted to own property in Goa, they can form a company with an Indian director and share a 70-30 ownership equation.

It is only natural that the property boom has been accompanied by fraud and intrigue. Pushing up the prices further is Goa's notorious Russian land mafia. While the boom in the Russian economy continues to bring affluent and peaceful Russian nationals to Goan shores – making it fashionable in Russia to take beach holidays in Goa – its prostitution and drug mafia (that some say operates from Turkey) has been known to turn Goa, as a property consultant calls it, into "a place of transaction." Only three to four years old, the mafia is believed to have made an entry into the beach state with the help of businessmen in the Delhi black market. A proposed new airport at Mopa in the far north led them to acquire large tracts of land in Morjim and around. In their eagerness to launder illegal money, property was bought at generous and inflated rates, far higher than the actual going rates. Hotel tariffs too were controlled by booking and blocking rooms – often for periods of 6-10 years. However, the activity slowed down somewhat when plans for the airport were stalled owing to protests by prominent five-star hotels in South Goa. Today, with the same plans being renewed, one can only wait and watch to see what happens.

In the meantime, builders and developers from Mumbai and Delhi had begun to show an interest in replicating high-rises across Goa. The apathy of the government alarmed and prompted prominent local residents and activists into taking action. The Urban Task plan has put certain property rules and regulations in place to preserve the Goan land and heritage, and to make Goans feel less – to quote an activist-resident – like "lesser halves."

with yoga, meditation, and Thai massages, or simply lounge around on the hammocks slung around the property.

Food

Most of Arambol's beach shack restaurants double up as eateries during the day and party places at night. The **C Samsara Beach Resort** (near the temple, Arambol Beach, tel. 91/98226-88471, www.samsara.20m.com, 8 A.M.–midnight daily Oct.–Apr., mains Rs 200) has a terrace restaurant and bar with a sweeping bay view. Brightly lit with colorful lanterns and fairy lights, it serves great Italian cuisine accompanied by both cocktails as well as health and energy drinks. Try their herbal tea and pastas.

For true-blue home-cooked Italian cuisine, go to **Fellini** (Arambol Beach, cell tel. 91/98814-61224, 11 A.M.–11 P.M. daily Oct.–Apr., mains Rs 200 and up). Seafood, gnocchi, and wood-fired pizzas have made this spot a favorite hangout.

The popular **German Bakery** (Arambol Beach, cell tel. 91/98221-59699, 7:30 A.M.–11 P.M. daily Oct.–Apr.) is decorated with Shiva images in a seaside, beach shack atmosphere. Try the *kombucha* (health tea) here, along with various baked goodies. Sweet and savory items are served, along with light mains and a range of iced teas and juices.

Authentic Israeli food is available in a colorful tie-dye ambience at **Little Mango Tree** (Arambol Beach, cell tel. 91/93720-49176, kps_ajay2002@yahoo.com, 7 A.M.–midnight daily Oct.–Apr., mains Rs 90 and up). You can sample dishes such as *sabich* and *shakshuka* with hummus salad as you gaze upon the sea from this shack.

Tucked away in a lane just before the beach is the ordinary-looking **Rice Bowl** (Socoilo Vaddo, cell tel. 91/98507-27329, 8 A.M.–11 P.M. daily, mains Rs 150 and up). It specializes in Tibetan and Far Eastern fare, and serves some extraordinary East Asian–style noodles and dumplings.

For live music and jam sessions, ◖ **Loekie Café** (Arambol Beach Rd., tel. 0832/652-9632, www.loekiecafe.com, 7 A.M.–11:30 P.M. daily, mains Rs 50 and up) is a vibrant place with a great mix of patrons. The lamp-lit café serves multi-cuisine fare, including European, Chinese, Goan, and tandoori items, and specializes in seafood. Sundays and Thursdays are reserved for music performances, turning the place into one big party.

Nearby, **Blue Sea Horse** (Socoilo Vaddo, tel. 0832/651-5232, 7 A.M.–midnight daily, mains Rs 65 and up) serves a variety of cuisine to cater to its mixed bag of clientele. Italian, Chinese, tandoori, Portuguese, and various seafood preparations are coupled with a wide selection of liquor at the bar. For entertainment, they provide pool tables, screen movies, and organize live music at night.

Getting There and Around

Arambol takes nearly two hours to reach from Dabolim Airport and costs Rs 850. From Thivim Station, taxis cost Rs 600 and take around an hour to get there. You can also take a bus from Mapusa and alight on the main road near the Our Lady of Mount Carmel Church.

TEREKHOL (TIRACOL)

From Arambol, a beautiful, scenic route leads to the northernmost tip of Goa: Keri Beach and Terekhol. As you go up north, past Siolim and the rush of Goan-Portuguese houses, the landscape transforms into lush greenery and dense vegetation, quaint villages, and Hindu architecture. This area presents, almost, a prelude to the neighboring state of Maharashtra. As you wait for a ferry across the calm Terekhol River to take you to Terekhol village, you can stroll on the deserted **Keri Beach,** which is dotted with casuarinas and untouched by tourism. At the village, a winding path leads up to its beautiful fort, now a heritage hotel.

© JANHAVI ACHAREKAR

THE NORTHERN COAST

The nothernmost beach in Goa, Keri is a beautiful combination of casuarina trees, river, and ocean.

⟨ Fort Tiracol

The 17th-century Fort Tiracol (8 A.M.–6 P.M. daily, free) was built by the Marathas and then conquered for its strategic location by the Portuguese in 1764. Having successfully withstood a failed rebellion by the Goans in 1825, the fort stood guard until it fell to seed, only to be revived as a boutique hotel by Nilaya Hermitage. The beautiful yellow-and-white structure stands tall over Terekhol, a village populated by some 200 people, and its turrets present an uninhibited view of the curvature of Keri Beach, the lull of the estuary, and the contrasting whooshes of the vast, open sea. Inside, in the courtyard, is the century-old **St. Anthony's Chapel** (open for mass 8–11 A.M. Sun.)—a mute witness to history, brought alive on Sundays and festive occasions when the all-Christian population of the village throngs here to offer its prayers.

Accommodations and Food

Nilaya Hermitage's ⟨ **Fort Tiracol** (Terekhol, Pernem, tel. 0832/652-9653, www.forttiracol.com, Rs 7,600–13,500) is Terekhol's only hotel. The crumbling fort was given a facelift by its glitzy management (millionaire Hari Ajwani and his Parisian wife Claudia, who also own the glamorous boutique hotel Nilaya Hermitage in Arpora). Now the property boasts beautiful white-and-amber décor, with seven themed rooms named after every day of the week. At once public and private property, the fort is filled with interesting crevices, hidden windows, steep staircases, and gleaming turrets. Ideal for those seeking solitude, a romantic getaway, or to commune with the sand and the sea, this beautiful heritage hotel offers the most spectacular ocean view in Goa. The two suites are appropriately named Friday and Sunday, and rooms come with private balconies or open out into the rampart-terraces of the fort. Tastefully furnished and filled with antiques, they make for a wonderfully private holiday. The hotel also has private boats for pleasure trips and dolphin sightings. An Ayurvedic massage parlor and yoga lessons complete the perfect holiday.

The hotel offers alfresco dining, with candlelit tables neatly laid out under the stars on one of the rampart-promenades. Room rates include breakfast and Goan-style dinner at the **Fort Tiracol restaurant** (8 A.M.–9 P.M. daily, mains Rs 180 and up, dinner reservations required), which serves fresh catch from the sea. Also open to non-guests, the restaurant offers an unparalleled view of the ocean and, sometimes, of dolphins. The enclosed bar area adjoining the restaurant has an impressive selection of wines and liquor from around the world.

Getting There and Around

Although buses from Mapusa go to Keri, from where you can take the onward ferry (6:15 A.M.–10 P.M. every half-hour, passengers free, vehicles Rs 10 one-way), it is best to arrange for your own transport (the hotel provides a speedboat if you're a guest). Terekhol has no transport and you will require a vehicle to take you up to the fort. From Dabolim Airport, Terekhol is roughly a two-hour journey by taxi and costs around Rs 1,000. If the new airport transpires at Mopa as planned, this journey will be considerably reduced.

THE SOUTHERN COAST

It is difficult to believe that the discovery of golden Southern Goa was the result of mass impatience. In 1986, when the collapse of the Mandovi Bridge led to interminable waits for the ferry to the northern beaches, it drove desperate tourists to explore other options. The southern beaches came as a pleasant surprise, and as word of their pristine beauty spread amid backpacking circles, a steady trickle of loyal fans returned every year.

Inspired by the response, a number of luxury hotels followed suit, occupying prime beachside property and creating five-star bubbles for the rich and famous alongside makeshift beach shacks.

Until recently, however, the southern coast was relatively isolated, enjoyed only by a select few. Although more and more tourists are let in on this secret every year, the beaches here continue to be cleaner and quieter than those up north. Even as commercial activity and frenzied partying catches up in popular destinations like Palolem, others offer delightful insights into the Goan fishing and village culture. The beach of Bogmalo, just south of the airport, is a wonderfully secluded spot, as are the beaches of Velsao and Arossim. The action heats up toward Betalbatim, and continues up to Benaulim as a number of resorts and local nightspots light up the stretch. At Varca and Cavelossim, the southern coast is at its most beautiful, meeting the River Sal at the Mobor Peninsula and offering a glimpse of the traditional fishing culture at the Betul Jetty. In the far south, the beaches are shaded by forested hills, and it is not unusual to

© ASHIMA NARAIN

HIGHLIGHTS

◖ Casa Araujo Alvares: Beautiful Indo-Portuguese Casa Araujo Alvares comes complete with original furniture and antiques, and a guided tour (page 227).

◖ Casa Bragança: One of Goa's most prominent stately mansions comprises the Casa Bragança Pereira and the adjoining Casa Menezes Bragança, both of which offer a glimpse into their days of forgotten glory (page 229).

◖ Palacio do Deao: The 18th-century house of the founder of Quepem town has been restored to perfection by its present-day owner-residents, who give guided tours of this wonderful remnant of Indo-Portuguese architecture (page 230).

◖ Utorda Beach: Utorda boasts blue waters, golden sands, and a restaurant-shack called Zeebop by the Sea. It is one of Goa's most magical beaches and a great destination even for a day trip (page 236).

◖ Varca: This fishing village and beach lie forgotten in the sands of time, if such a thing were possible in Goa. Varca is easily one of Goa's most beautiful, and wonderfully secluded, beaches (page 248).

◖ Cavelossim: With a beach, a river, and a view of a jetty where you can watch the fishermen bring in their fresh catch, Cavelossim presents an interesting geographical and cultural landscape (page 249).

◖ Palolem: If you think that pristine waters overlooked by green hills and butterflies sounds like paradise, it probably is. It's not without reason that Palolem is also called Paradise Beach (page 256).

LOOK FOR ◖ TO FIND RECOMMENDED SIGHTS, ACTIVITIES, DINING, AND LODGING.

find a forgotten cove or a lonely island in the ocean. Beaches like Agonda and Patnem take the visitor on a nostalgic trip, back to an unspoiled Goa.

What comes as a surprise to many, however, is the historical legacy of these parts. Southern Goa is known for its large colonial-style houses, called casas, seen in and around the city of Madgaon. In the old village of Chandor is Goa's largest

residence—the impressive Casa Bragança, an Indo-Portuguese mansion that stretches across an entire street. Farther into the southern interior are the prehistoric rock carvings at Pansimol and the splendid Palacio do Deao at Quepem. Churches and temples lie scattered around, and a wildlife sanctuary—Cotigao—completes the tourist trail. Needless to say, those who come to the southern coast are rarely disappointed.

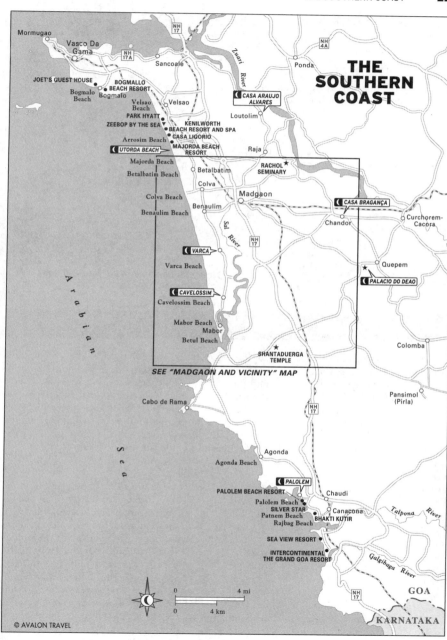

THE SOUTHERN COAST

Mormugao

Vasco Da Gama

NH 17

NH 17A

Sancoale

NH 4A

Ponda

THE SOUTHERN COAST

Zuari River

JOET'S GUEST HOUSE

BOGMALLO BEACH RESORT

Bogmalo Beach

Bogmalo

Velsao Beach

Velsao

CASA ARAUJO ALVARES

Loutolim

PARK HYATT

ZEEBOP BY THE SEA

Arrosim Beach

KENILWORTH BEACH RESORT AND SPA

CASA LIGORIO

UTORDA BEACH

MAJORDA BEACH RESORT

Raja

Majorda Beach

Betalbatim Beach

Betalbatim

RACHOL SEMINARY ★

Colva

Colva Beach

Benaulim

Madgaon

CASA BRAGANÇA

Benaulim Beach

Chandor

Curchorem-Cacora

Sal River

NH 17

VARCA

Varca Beach

Quepem

★

PALACIO DO DEAO

CAVELOSSIM

Cavelossim Beach

Colomba

Mabor Beach

Mabor

Betul Beach

SHANTADUERGA TEMPLE ★

Pansimol (Pirla)

SEE "MADGAON AND VICINITY" MAP

A r a b i a n   S e a

Cabo de Rama

NH 17

Agonda

Agonda Beach

PALOLEM

PALOLEM BEACH RESORT

Chaudi

Palolem Beach

SILVER STAR

Patnem Beach

Canacona

Rajbag Beach

BHAKTI KUTIR

Talpona River

SEA VIEW RESORT

INTERCONTINENTAL THE GRAND GOA RESORT

Galgibaga River

0   4 mi

0   4 km

GOA

NH 17

KARNATAKA

© AVALON TRAVEL

PLANNING YOUR TIME

Southern Goa is meant to be enjoyed at leisure and it would be a shame to rush a holiday here. Most visitors prefer to park themselves at one or two quiet beaches rather than indulge in frenzied beach hopping. A minimum of four or five days is recommended to capture the feel of the coast and tour any heritage sights in the vicinity. The southern stretch is vast, however, and if you intend to cover more than one beach, or complete the heritage trail thoroughly, make sure you stay longer—about a week—to balance out leisure and sightseeing activities.

The southern coast is dead in the monsoon (unlike the north, which shows some signs of life). Shacks and cabanas are dismantled and the beaches unrecognizable in the torrential downpours. However, for those booked in the five-star properties, luxury compensates for the lack of beach activity.

© ASHIMA NARAIN

Time stands still at 450-year-old Casa Bragança in Chandor.

Madgaon (Margao)

In the south of Goa, all roads lead to Madgaon. Also known as Margao, the buzzing commercial town is the largest in these parts and the second largest in Goa. The hub for the southern coast and interior south alike, it has a number of sights and heritage attractions. Somewhat underrated, Madgaon is not as mundane as it is often made out to be. Previously the cultural center of the state, its former glory has dimmed somewhat since the Goan Liberation of 1961, although one can get an occasional glimpse of its bygone splendor in the form of the grand Indo-Portuguese mansions that line its Holy Spirit Church Square (Largo de Igreja). Once a prominent town populated by affluent Goan and Portuguese families, it is now a crowded, dusty place where nostalgia and modernity vie with each other in the form of its old mansions and newer, unappealing concrete buildings. It is, nevertheless, dotted with charming heritage attractions in and around town, and is also within easy distance of the villages of Loutolim and Chandor—known for their magnificent casas. Meanwhile only an hour away, in Quepem, is the lovely restored mansion called Palacio do Deao and the scenic environs of the Chandreshwar temple. And further in the interior, in Prila (Sanguem) is the pre-historic rock art of Pansimol, along the banks of the Kushavati River.

SIGHTS

Taken over by the Portuguese in the mid-16th century, Madgaon was once an important marketplace and Hindu town, filled with temples and ashrams that were destroyed by the conquistadors. Within the city, the famous landmark is the **Church of the Holy Spirit** (6–9 A.M. Mon.–Sat. and 5:30–11 A.M. Sun., free, photography permitted), a lovely whitewashed structure that dates back to 1564. Rebuilt four times after being gutted by a fire (most recently in 1675), its simple exterior leads into vast, baroque grandeur. Gold leaf, stucco, and mellow candle-lamps light up the statues of Jesus and the Virgin Mary, while a splendid altar, high dome, and five bays lend to its character.

From the Church of the Holy Spirit, you can take the road that goes left toward Borda. Just where the road forks, is the grand, terracotta-and-white Da Silva House, also known as the **House of Seven Gables.** The gables from which the 17th-century mansion derives its name have long since reduced in number, and entry is prohibited, but it remains one of the prominent homes in Madgaon.

On Monte Hill is the **Chapel of Our Lady of Mercy,** from where you can get a bird's-eye view of the beautiful countryside and distant coastline.

SHOPPING

Madgaon has plenty of modern stores and amenities. Although long-stay tourists from the nearby beaches come here only to stock up on supplies, the local **Madgaon Market** (near the Kadamba bus stand) makes for an interesting experience. A melee of fish, vegetables, and noise, the market is brought alive by flower sellers and stalls filled with cashew nuts and other produce. This is a great place to stock up on your *masalas* or simply observe the local flavor.

ACCOMMODATIONS

Madgaon is not quite the destination of choice in terms of accommodation. It does, however, have two basic hotels with uninspiring city views.

Among the better accommodations that Madgaon has to offer, **Hotel Nanutel** (Padre Miranda Rd., tel. 0832/272-6700, www.nanuindia.com, Rs 1,300–3,000) is a functional place located in the city center and close enough to Madgaon Station. Rooms come in three categories—deluxe, executive, and suite—and are clean and simple, though not great on aesthetics. While the deluxe rooms overlook the crowded street, executive rooms and suites have a redeeming view of a neighboring park. The staff is friendly and makes

© JANHAVI ACHAREKAR

THE SOUTHERN COAST

Madgaon's Church of the Holy Spirit has a beautiful baroque interior and carved altar.

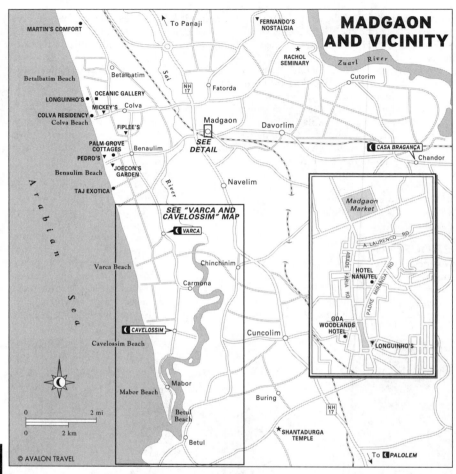

for a pleasant enough stay. The hotel also has a multi-cuisine restaurant, Utsav, and a bar called Zodiac.

The other alternative is the **Goa Woodlands Hotel** (Miguel Loyola Furtado Rd., opposite city bus stand, tel. 0832/273-8732, www .goawoodlandshotel.com, Rs 1,300–2,000), a bright new building with neon signs leading up to its restaurants, bar, and shopping area. Rooms are equipped with modern amenities, and the suites, particularly, are spacious and airy. Painted in bright colors, rooms are

cheerful or jarring, depending on your point of view. The suites are spacious and the hotel also has "king" and "queen" suites, each with a separate living area and bedroom. There are two in-house restaurants (one is vegetarian), as well as a bar, lounge, and conference area.

FOOD

Surprisingly, for a city this prominent, there are few good restaurants. The recommended ones, however, more than make up for the scarcity. A popular stopover for tourists on the way to Big

Foot at Loutolim is **Peppers** (15/604, Gold Rd., Pajifond, tel. 0832/271-1125, cell tel. 91/98221-33506, 11 A.M.–3 P.M. and 6:30–11 P.M. daily, mains Rs 80 and up), a charming old Goan house restored and transformed into a vibrant restaurant. Known for its Goan and Portuguese cuisine and its experimental menu, Peppers draws a number of Portuguese guests and other clients. Its chef-owner believes in changing the menu often to keep the element of surprise, and organizes food festivals on a regular basis. On Fridays and weekends, the place comes alive with jazz music and performances by local one-man bands. Diners delight in the Goan platters, steaks, and sizzlers, as they sit along lovely balconies overlooking a sloping road.

In the heart of the city, 【 **Longuinho's** (Dr. Antonio Dias Building, Luis Miranda Rd., opposite Madgaon Municipality, tel. 0832/273-9908, 8 A.M.–11 P.M. daily, mains Rs 80 and up) is a Madgaon institution. Established in 1950, it maintains its old-world look and charm in addition to a traditional Goan menu. Known particularly for its local seafood preparations, it draws a loyal set of clients who return for the fantastic prawn patties, mussels, and stuffed crabs, as well as various curries and sausage dishes.

Panaji's favorite haunt for *bhaji puri* has a branch in Madgaon. **Café Tato** (Apna Bazar Complex, Varde Valaulikar Rd., Madgaon, tel. 0832/273-6014, 7 A.M.–8:30 P.M. Mon.–Sat., *bhaji puri* Rs 25) is a simple eatery located just behind the Collectorate. Apart from its famous spiced potato served with small fluffy *puris* (deep-fried wheat bread), the café also serves great vegetarian food in an all-you-can-eat platters called *thalis.*

In Raia, there's a quaint place strewn with bric-a-brac and known for its fantastic seafood. 【 **Fernando's Nostalgia** (608, Margarida's Haunt, No Bairro Ozro, Raia, tel. 0832/277-7054, cell tel. 91/98221-51296, nostalgiagoa@ yahoo.co.in, 11 A.M.–3 P.M. and 7–11 P.M. daily, mains Rs 70 and up) is named after late chef Fernando da Costa, who combined an old-world atmosphere with traditional Goan cuisine. Tucked away in a little lane that could easily be missed, and in the leafy courtyard of the family home, this is where antiques meet the traditional beef *rollado,* and old posters look over patrons relishing pork *sorpotel* with *sannas.* The ambience is lovely and the food is exceptional.

INFORMATION AND SERVICES
Tourist Information
The **Goa Tourism Development Corporation (GTDC)** (Margao Residency, Luis Miranda Rd., tel. 0832/271-5528, www.goa-tourism.com, 9:30 A.M.–1 P.M. and 2–5:30 P.M. Mon.–Fri.) provides maps and brochures and also organizes a number of guided tours.

Hospitals and Pharmacies
Madgaon is known for its medical facilities at **Apollo Victor Hospital** (near Carmelite Monastery, Aquem, tel. 0832/272-8888) and **Hospicio** (Rua do Miranda Rd., tel. 0832/270-5664). It also has a number of pharmacies, such as **Apollo Pharmacy** (near old railway station, Malbhat, tel. 0832/272-0090, 24 hr) and **GAPL Medi Centre** (near Hospicio Hospital, tel. 0832/271-0965, 24 hr).

Police
In case of emergency, **dial 100** for the 24-hour police helpline or try the **Madgaon Police Station** (tel. 0832/270-5095).

Money
Madgaon has plenty of money changers, banks, and ATMs. You can change money at **Travco Holidays** (6 Ranghavi, opposite Madgaon Municipal Building, tel. 0832/271-3207, 9 A.M.–6 P.M. Mon.–Sat.), **Thomas Cook** (5 Mabai Hotel, opposite Municipal Garden, tel. 0832/271-4768, 9:30 A.M.–6 P.M. Mon.–Sat.), and **Weizmann Forex** (Shop no. 1, Minguel Miranda, near Mohidin petrol pump, tel. 0832/273-3280, 9:30 A.M.–6:30 P.M. Mon.–Sat.). ATMs are available at **HDFC Bank** (Plot no. 27, Madgaon), **Centurion Bank** (off Luis Miranda Rd.), and **UTI** (at the roundabout south of the bus station).

Postal Services

Madgaon Post Office (near Municipal Gardens, tel. 0832/271-5791, 9:30 A.M.–1 P.M. and 2–5:30 P.M. Mon.–Fri.) is easily accessible. Speedpost and registered letter booking may also be done here.

Internet

Internet cafés are easily found in and around Madgaon. These include **Cyber Inn** (ground floor, Kalika Chambers, behind Grace Church, tel. 0832/273-3232, 9 A.M.–9 P.M. Mon.–Sat.), **Phoenix** (Apna Bazaar, Varde Valaulikar Rd., tel. 0832/271-2430, 9 A.M.–9 P.M. Mon.–Sat.), and **Cyberocks** (Shop 5, Reliance Residency, Colmarod, Navelim, tel. 0832/270-2407, 9 A.M.–9 P.M. daily). Rates usually hover at Rs 15–25 per hour.

GETTING THERE AND AROUND

Madgaon Station (Station Rd., 2 km east of the city center, tel. 0832/270-3950) is the main southern stop on the Konkan Railway, with direct trains to and from Mumbai. The city bus stand, located in the center of town, is where buses depart regularly to go to the southern beaches, as well as to Panaji, Mapusa, and the northern beaches. A number of interstate buses also ply from here to destinations such as Mumbai, Karwar, Gokarna, and Mangalore. From Dabolim Airport, it is a 40-minute taxi ride that costs Rs 450.

Vicinity of Madgaon

RACHOL SEMINARY

Seven kilometers away from the city is the serene Rachol Seminary (Raia, Rachol, 9–11 A.M. and 3–5 P.M. Mon.–Sat. and 9 A.M.–5 P.M. Sun. and holidays, free, photography permitted). This large church and Jesuit seminary, established in 1576 and 1610, respectively, were once located within the Rachol Fort. The magnificent church is dedicated to St. Ignatius Loyola, founder of the Jesuit order, and to St. Francis Xavier. Beautiful murals and a carved altar—as well as the figure of the Menino Jesus, famed for its miraculous powers—face the pews, which are lighted by shafts of sunlight filtering in through its open windows. Distinguished by its carved wooden panel along the chancel, this is one of the most ornate church interiors in Goa. In the corridors are murals from the 17th and 18th centuries, which, sadly, have been defaced by bats and need urgent protection. A number of religious relics and artifacts lie strewn around the seminary, which once included a hospital, a school, and a printing press.

Outside the seminary are the remains of the stone gateway to the Rachol Fort, built by the Bahmani kings, captured by the Vijaynagar rulers, and then given to the Portuguese in 1520 for their support against the Bahmani sultans.

© JANHAVI ACHAREKAR

The Rachol Seminary is known for its beautiful murals and ornate church interiors.

© JANHAVI ACHAREKAR

Casa Araujo Alvares in Loutolim is reminiscent of a bygone era.

LOUTOLIM

Loutolim (sometimes pronounced "lot-lay") lies 10 kilometers northeast of Madgaon and, like Chandor, houses some of Goa's most spectacular colonial mansions. Most tourists do the Big Foot (Ancestral Goa) and Casa Araujo Alvares route.

Big Foot (Ancestral Goa)

Big Foot, or Ancestral Goa, (Loutolim, tel. 0832/277-7034, www.ancestralgoa.com, 10 A.M.–6 P.M. daily, adults Rs 50 for museum or Rs 100 for casa, children Rs 25 for museum or Rs 50 for casa—rates include a guided tour, still/video photography Rs 10/20) is a disappointing display of the life and culture of Goa, portrayed mostly through sculptures and plaster-of-Paris models. The museum was established by the Alvares family, which also owns 252-year-old Casa Alvares. The place exhibits India's longest laterite sculpture, created by a member of the Alvares family, and demonstrates the *feni* distillation process.

◖ Casa Araujo Alvares

Across the road from Big Foot and part of the same complex, Casa Araujo Alvares (Loutolim,

tel. 0832/277-7034, www.ancestralgoa.com, 10 A.M.–6 P.M. daily, adults Rs 50 for museum or Rs 100 for casa, children Rs 25 for museum or Rs 50 for casa—rates include a guided tour, still/video photography Rs 10/20) is of greater interest. Impeccably maintained, this beautiful mansion with its grand stairway and imposing *balcao* (portico) displays the family crest before you embark on your guided tour around the house. Built on a higher plinth to indicate the wealthy status of its owner, it also has the trademark rooster—the national bird of Portugal—which was seen perched atop most colonial houses of the era. The casa displays all the original furniture and artifacts of the period, ranging from hat stands and four-poster beds to mirrors, glazed jars, and objects acquired during the family's travels to Macau and Seychelles. The house has a private altar and a Judgement House, while valuable objects were hidden in a safe area to protect them from burglaries carried out by the Rane group of robbers who, oddly enough, informed the household they planned to rob. The house is a cultural revelation with its well-equipped kitchen and ancient heating system in the bathrooms. The most spectacular part, however, is

THE SOUTHERN COAST

THE INDO-PORTUGUESE HOUSES OF THE SOUTH

The beaches may be exquisite, but competing with Goa's natural splendor are the magnificent "casas" – old heritage houses – built in the Indo-Portuguese style of architecture. Large oyster-shell windows, a grand *entrada* (entrance), beautiful *balcaos* (porches) and wide verandahs distinguish these lavish works of art from houses anywhere else in the country, or the world.

A product of the Portuguese influence melded with the pre-Portuguese Hindu style and yet distinctly Goan Catholic in character, the houses – says prominent Goan architect Gerald da Cunha – were an assertion of the newly created Goan Christian identity. A symbol of affluence – for it was only the rich who could afford to build these luxurious, opulent villas – they are found across the state. Prominent in the southern parts, brightly colored casas may be seen in the interior, near a beach, or they may startle you by emerging out of nowhere, as you suddenly turn around a bend. Scattered mostly in and around Madgaon, where the casas of distinguished residents continue to stand as stoic witnesses to over a century of the town's history, these beautiful houses are a reflection of dramatic social and cultural changes within the state. Various architectural features and the interiors indicated the status of the owners (mostly aristocrats and land owners – beneficiaries of the Portuguese), the status of the women of the house, and international travels of the residents. A high plinth, such as the one in Loutolim's **Casa Alvares** was a symbol of wealth and power – and the women now enjoyed a status at par with the men of the house as the traditional Hindu courtyard house with small windows that cloistered them gave way to a dramatic new mansion with open verandahs facing the street, large windows with wrought-iron balconies, and *balcaos* with seats made of concrete meant for socializing and interactions. Crowning these splendid architectural gems was a sculpted rooster – the national bird of Portugal.

The grand *entradas* of these houses led into splendid ballrooms and parlors, long dining tables with silver candelabras, Belgian chandeliers, *azulejo* tiles, antique furniture, and expensive artifacts. Many houses, like the **Casa Bragança** in Chandor, had private chapels and were painted in bright colors – blues, yellows, and terra-cottas. Made of laterite and plastered with mortar, the walls were often adorned with Rococo-style embellishments on the outside and floral frescoes on the inside. The houses had beautiful eaves and decorative cornices but were also built keeping in mind Goa's erratic weather. The openness in the architecture, with the house centered around a large courtyard (a legacy of the Hindu courtyard house) together with ventilated roof tiles were meant to facilitate the summer breeze; while in two-story houses, the lower floor housed the horse stables so as to heat the upper floor with their warmth. The casas were also built in a way that they were monsoon friendly.

While most of Goa's beautiful casas are concentrated around the city of Madgaon, Quepem, and in the villages of Loutolim and Chandor, the bright blue *Rebello House*, a private residence, in northern Anjuna is also a lovely example of the Indo-Portuguese architecture.

the parlor area near the entrance, with its open French windows, gilded mirror, and beautiful chandeliers.

Loutolim Mansions

There are 35 palatial houses in Loutolim alone, most of which are private residences even today. One such place is the **Miranda House** (near the square, Loutolim), an 18th-century mansion with a rich history. It's now the home of famous Goan artist Mario Miranda (and is not open to the public unless you happen to know the family). Similarly, the **Roque Caetan Miranda House** (south of the square) and the imposing **Salvador Costa House** (western side of Loutolim) are worth seeing from the outside. The current owner of the Salvador Costa House, Dr. Adelia Costa, sometimes accepts visitors on request and by prior appointment (tel. 0832/242-5142).

The **Figueiredo Mansion** (no. 376, Loutolim, tel. 0832/277-7028, donations accepted) is open to visitors—and even doubles up as a bed-and-breakfast, where the owner organizes traditional Goan-Portuguese meals (Rs 800) by prior notification. The elderly owner, Maria de Lourdes de Albuquerque, is a Figueiredo descendant and divides her time between Goa and Lisbon.

The houses are located within easy distance of each other—mostly walking distance around the square—and are distinguished by their names or numbers.

Accommodations

The beautiful Indo-Portuguese casa by the name of **Figueiredo Mansion** (Loutolim, tel. 0832/277-7028, Rs 3,800–4,800) offers five rooms for bed-and-breakfast-style homestays. The elderly owner, Maria de Lourdes de Albuquerque, is a keen cook who organizes traditional Goan-Portuguese meals (Rs 800/person) by prior notification.

Getting There

From Madgaon, it is best to hire a private vehicle or taxi to go to Loutolim. Take the road to Ponda and then take the second left turn. The drive is about 20–30 minutes.

CHANDOR

In the village of Chandor, 15 kilometers east of Madgaon, are some of the state's grandest casas. The famous Casa Bragança, now split into two wings, and the equally significant Fernandes House were once the homes of rich landowners. Today, their landed property has all but disappeared, taken over by the government after Liberation. The grandeur remains, however, surviving on donations made by visitors.

◖ Casa Bragança

Chandor is home to two of Goa's most splendid casas: the 450-year-old Casa Bragança Pereira (diagonally opposite Chandor Church, tel. 0832/278-4227, 10 A.M.–6 P.M. daily, donations accepted, photography allowed) and the adjoining Casa Menezes Bragança (tel. 0832/278-4201, 10 A.M.–6 P.M. daily, donations accepted, photography allowed in moderation). The east and west wings of one casa divided between two brothers, both sections continue to be inhabited by descendants of the once-prominent family; donations contribute to the maintenance of the vast mansion, whose occupants have seen better days. The stately home with 28 balconies stretches across the street and belonged to the illustrious Bragança family, inextricably linked with the history of Goa.

© ASHIMA NARAIN

Chairs gifted by the King of Portugal occupy pride of place in the grand ballroom of Casa Bragança.

The Bragança Pereira part of the casa has a vast ballroom that displays gilded mirrors and antique furniture, including ornate, carved chairs with the family coat of arms, gifted by the King of Portugal. The grand salon is a treasure trove of antiquities with Belgian chandeliers and interesting objets d'art. The house also has a private chapel with a relic—the fingernail of St. Francis Xavier.

Next door, visitors are shown around the Menezes Bragança house by the sprightly 90-year-old lady of the house, who lives in this sprawling property by herself. Chinese porcelain, crystal from Brazil, old family portraits, and a library that boasts the largest private collection in Goa occupy this section—the lovelier of the two wings.

Meanwhile old photographs and an eerie stillness may be found in both sections, freezing them, almost, in a time warp.

Fernandes House

A five-minute walk from Chandor Church, farther into the village, is Chandor's other grand casa: the Fernandes House (tel. 0832/278-4245, 10 A.M.–5 P.M. Mon.–Sat. by appointment). The previous generations of this 500-year-old house were related to the Braganças by marriage and were a hybrid lot as far as religion goes—the original Hindu inhabitants turned Muslim and successively converted to Christianity. These changes in faith are reflected in archaeological findings around the property. The house is believed to have been built in place of the original Hindu home, remnants of which have been found in the form of a temple entrance, ancient Hindu sculptures, and documents written in the old Modi script. The architecture, however, is Indo-Portuguese and alongside Hindu carvings on its doors and a 7th century stone pillar are Chinese porcelain and European furniture (including an 18th-century love seat). The house is also known for its secret tunnel, built for escape in case of attack.

Getting There

From Madgaon, it is about a half hour by road to Chandor. It is best to hire a private vehicle or taxi. For Chandor, go via Curtorlim and ask for Chandor Church.

QUEPEM

The small, dusty town of Quepem (pronounced "ke-pay") is 14 kilometers south of Madgaon. Though the town itself is quite unremarkable, it houses the beautiful Palacio do Deao, the 18th-century home of the town's founder. Nearby is the ancient Chandreshwar-Bhutnath Temple, where a major religious festival is celebrated.

◖ Palacio do Deao

The Palacio do Deao (opposite Holy Cross Church, cell tel. 91/98231-75639, www.palaciododeao.com, 10 A.M.–5 P.M. Sat.–Thurs., by appointment on Fri. and after 5 P.M., donations accepted, photography allowed) is a beautifully restored 18th-century house. This bright yellow and white structure, presiding over its lush gardens and the Kushavati River, is as much the labor of love of its erstwhile priest-owner as it is of the young couple

the beautifully restored Palacio do Deao

that has painstakingly restored it. Built in 1787 by Jose Paulo, a Portuguese priest who went on to become dean of the church and the founder of Quepem town, the house was his alternate residence and getaway. The Palacio is a fine combination of traditional Indian and Portuguese architecture—with a wide staircase leading directly into an altar reminiscent of the *garbhagriha* (assembly hall) found in Hindu temples. The house has a parlor with finely carved antique rosewood and teak furniture, as well as canopied beds and an unusual toilet. Traditional oyster-shell doors and windows are accentuated by flowing drapes, while chandeliers and plaques adorn the ceiling and walls. The Palacio also has a library and the owners encourage visitors to spend the day browsing through the impressive collection or relaxing in the garden. Games of carom and chess are kept here for visitors to while their time as they wait for an Indo-Portuguese lunch (Rs 400 pp) served in the open belvedere that overlooks the river. Meals are served on request and with prior notification. The place also hosts cultural events and weddings. Perhaps the most striking feature of the Palacio is its well-maintained garden, in which stands a gazebo where Jose Paulo once addressed gatherings.

The Palacio lay in neglect for years, until owners Celia and Ruben Vasco da Gama restored it to its original glory, referring to illustrations and books with information on the house and its style of architecture. Ruben, an engineer by profession, is passionate about restoring heritage houses and will willingly show you photos of the transformation of the Palacio. The friendly couple take visitors on a guided tour around the house themselves, letting their dogs and children run freely around the place. And in case you wonder what the flat-screen TV is doing, discreetly positioned next to a four-poster bed in one of the bedrooms, Celia and Ruben will apologetically explain that they reside in the Palacio.

Chandreshwar-Bhutnath Temple

Perched atop the Chandranath Hill near the village of Paroda—once part of the capital of the Bhoja empire, Chandrapur—is the Chandreshwar-Bhutnath Temple. The drive to the temple is more spectacular than the temple itself, and it is not unusual to encounter a monkey or a mongoose on the way. Dedicated to Lord Shiva's incarnation as the Moon God or Chandreshwar, the ancient temple is known for its *shivling,* which is bathed in moonlight on nights when there's a full moon. Approached from the side is the little shrine dedicated to Bhutnath or the Lord of Ghosts.

Believed to date back to the 8th century, and reached after a short uphill climb on foot, the temple is now a modern-looking concrete structure. An ancient wooden-carved chariot that once stood here now lies at the Goa State Museum in Panaji. A palanquin is displayed in the temple and the courtyard is a venue for festivity during the Mahashivratri festival. The temple is opened on the whims of the caretaker or resident priest; afternoons, especially during lunch, are a particularly bad time to visit. However, should entry into the temple elude you, the surrounding view is wonderful and makes up for the disappointment.

Getting There

To get to the Chandreshwar Temple, a hired vehicle is a must for the uphill drive. Located on the Chandranath Hill, it is about 14 kilometers from Madgaon, on the road to Quepem. Turn right just before the village of Paroda to go up the hill.

PANSIMOL ROCK ART

If prehistoric rock art sounds exciting to you, think again. Be prepared for poor road signs, bad roads, and a supposedly protected heritage site that allows you to step all over its ancient rock carvings. In the southern interior, at Pansai in the Sanguem district, are Goa's gems from the Stone Age—found in an idyllic location by the Kushavati River. The carvings date back 20,000–30,000 years and depict ancient fertility symbols, hunts, dancing women, animals, and birds; unfortunately, the carvings are open to the elements and tourists are allowed to walk freely over them. The government's

THE SOUTHERN COAST

plan to present an aerial view of the site by constructing an overhead viewing gallery and cafeteria seems to have come to naught, so one can only hope the best for the future of Pansimol.

Getting There

The carvings may be found in the Pansai area of Prila village in the Sanguem district and are best reached by taxi—an hour's drive—from Madgaon. Make sure you have a driver who knows the way, as the place is difficult to find. Take the NH17 toward Rivona, via Tilamol, and then to the village of Colomb—from where you will have to keep your eyes peeled for signs saying Protected Site. Then take the dirt road toward the river. Avoid coming here from the far south as milestones are missing and road signs scarce—if you must, however, turn into Pansai from Dandolem (pronounced "Dando-lay").

© ASHIMA NARAIN

This prehistoric rock-cut labyrinth at Pansimol dates back 20,000–30,000 years.

Vasco da Gama and Bogmalo

Although named after the great explorer, there's not much to discover in Vasco. Now a city known only for its proximity to Dabolim Airport, it was once one of the most important ports in India. Located on the western Mormugao Peninsula and overlooking the Zuari River, it was taken over by the Portuguese in 1543. More than a century later, when plans were afoot to move the capital from Old Goa, Vasco was developed by its then-viceroy in the hope that it would be Portuguese Goa's next capital. While Panaji pipped Vasco to the post, the city continued to be a prominent one. Today, Vasco is an important shipping center and commercial town, but nothing more than that.

Visitors looking for solitude are often surprised to find the near-private **Bogmalo Beach** on the outskirts of Vasco. The seclusion and golden sands of this softly curving beach are in stark contrast with Vasco and the more commercial coastlines farther north and south. Stray swimmers dot the waters even as beach shacks and restaurants reduce in number. While Bogmalo is fairly safe, avoid straying too far late at night. Its ambience is that of a tiny fishing village, and it also has some of the most charming resorts, with direct access to the beach. The ideal getaway for those fatigued with the crowds at the more popular beaches, and for those seeking to snatch some quiet, private moments.

SIGHTS

Bogmalo has a **Naval Aviation Museum** (Bogmalo Rd., Dabolim, tel. 0832/510-183, 10:30 A.M.–5:30 P.M. Tues.–Sun., adults Rs 20, children Rs 5, physically challenged free, still photography Rs 20, video Rs 50). While its location, overlooking the ocean, is spectacular, the museum itself is sparse and unremarkable. A collection of aircraft—including a Super Constellation, Sea Hawk, and the World War II Fairy Firefly fighters—is supplemented by indoor galleries that display everything from torpedoes and bombs to pilot safety equipment. The musuem does, however, have an interesting collection of photographs of the Goa Liberation.

A beautiful 10-kilometer drive from Bogmalo leads to the tiny crescent-shaped **Hollant Beach.** With just one rundown bar and restaurant, the beach sees more fisherfolk and local residents than it does tourists. However, its fishing boats, palm trees, and the picturesque drive there make for an interesting excursion from Bogmalo.

Twelve kilometers from Hollant and through Vasco city is the characterless **Baina Beach.** Known only for its water sports, including an underwater sea walk, the beach sees a few adventure enthusiasts.

SPORTS AND RECREATION

Baina is one of the few southern beaches to offer good water sports, organized by **Drishti Adventures** (H2O Complex, Baina Beach, tel. 0832/324-6052, h2o.goa@drishtiadventures.com), who also run the H2O Complex in Mumbai. Drishti offers dolphin and crocodile cruises, island trips, kayaking, Jet Skiing, parasailing, windsurfing, snorkeling, and scuba diving. Their glass-bottomed boat rides (Rs 180 pp, Nov.–May) and underwater walk (Rs 1,800 pp, 8 A.M.–4 P.M. daily every 30 min., Nov.–May) are extremely popular. The walk involves going 12 feet down to the sea bed with a dive helmet to see marinelife from close quarters. Drishti also has scuba diving courses (Rs 2,500–15,000) for various levels, ranging from pleasure dives to advanced rescue courses.

The **Coconut Creek Resort** (Bimut Vaddo, Bogmalo, tel. 0832/253-8100, coconutcreek@dataone.in) also organizes water sports in collaboration with **Betty's Place** in Cavelossim (Mobor, tel. 0832/287-1456, www.bettysgoa .com). The resort arranges day trips called "The Day Out on Betty's Boat" (details available at hotel reception) from Mobor Beach that include dolphin sightings and bird-watching.

© JANHAVI ACHAREKAR

The tiny Hollant Beach is a fisherman's haunt.

ACCOMMODATIONS

Bogmalo's three evergreen favorites, for both accommodations and dining, are famous beach-shack-turned-guesthouse Joet's, its more posh sister resort Coconut Creek, and the five-star Bogmallo Beach Resort.

The mid-range seaside sibling of the higher-end Coconut Creek Resort, **(Joet's Guest House** (Bogmalo Beach, tel. 0832/253-8036, joets@sancharnet.in, Rs 2,900–6,000, Oct.–Apr.) is right on the beach. Rooms are simple but airy and well kept, attracting a loyal clientele that also delights in the food, drink, and retro music at its popular bar and restaurant. Access to the pool, games, and fitness facilities at Coconut Creek are a plus. The staff is friendly, the bar is well stocked, and the ocean is close at hand, making for a heady mix and adding to the appeal of this Bogmalo favorite.

A short distance from Joet's, **(Coconut Creek Resort** (Bimut Vaddo, Bogmalo, tel. 0832/253-8100, coconutcreek@dataone.in, Rs 4,500–10,000, Oct.–Apr.) is a secluded paradise in a palm grove. Large colonnades and lovely cottage-style rooms surround a turquoise pool shaded by coconut trees. Rooms are tastefully decorated with wooden furniture and bamboo blinds, and equipped with modern amenities and gadgets. Private sit-outs and bay windows offer a lovely view of the pool and surrounding gardens, while Balinese beds and contemporary bathrooms make the stay comfortable. This private getaway has an atmospheric poolside restaurant and also offers massage therapy, water sports, health facilities, Internet, and currency exchange, and has a gift shop on the premises. The staff is lovely and the place makes for an idyllic vacation, far from the madding crowd of the northern beaches.

The largest resort in the area, **Bogmallo Beach Resort** (Bogmalo Beach, tel. 0832/253-8222, www.bogmallobeachresort .com, Rs 4,000–10,500) is a sprawling star-rated property with 126 rooms and a spectacular view of the beach. The hotel has well-furnished sea-facing deluxe rooms and spacious executive suites with a sitting area, bedroom, and balcony with a breathtaking ocean view. Equipped with air-conditioning, television, and electronic safes, the stay is made comfortable by a pleasant staff. Farther down the road, the resort also has more basic but charming palm-fringed beach huts available at a lower tariff. Hammocks and Ayurvedic treatment are the highlight of these cottages, where experienced practitioners offer a variety of treatments and therapies. The resort also has a squash court and gymnasium, and organizes water sports on request. It has a number of dining options, as well as live music in the evenings at its lobby bar, called the Sunset Bar, where guests can unwind with cocktails (Rs 190 and up) and snacks. Guests can also lounge around by Gazebo, the poolside bar (cocktails Rs 190 and up).

FOOD

Bogmalo's best eateries the ones attached to its popular hotels. **(Joet's Bar and Restaurant** (Bogmalo Beach, tel. 0832/253-8036, joets@ sancharnet.in, 7 A.M.–closing daily Oct.–Apr., mains Rs 150 and up) offers a combination of seafood and retro music at the part-open-air restaurant downstairs. Try the kingfish, red snapper, and mussel dishes here, along with a varied choice of liquors.

The lovely **Coconut Creek Resort** has a beautifully colonnaded and ambient poolside restaurant (Bimut Vaddo, Bogmalo, tel. 0832/253-8100, coconutcreek@dataone.in, 7 A.M.–11 P.M. daily Oct.–Apr., mains Rs 200 and up) in a palm grove. It is known for its steaks, pastas, and Goan preparations—together with alfresco dining and barbecues.

The Bogmallo Beach Resort has a number of restaurants. **Nautilus** (tel. 0832/253-8222, www.bogmallobeachresort.com, 12:30–2:45 P.M. and 7:30–10:45 P.M. daily, mains Rs 200 and up) is a multi-cuisine restaurant, while the lovely seaside coffee shop, **The Verandah** (7 A.M.–11 P.M. daily, mains Rs 200 and up), offers bites and nibbles, coffees and milkshakes—as well as steaks, tandoori dishes, and Goan fare. Meanwhile, the seafront restaurant, **Coconut Grove** (12:30–2:45 P.M. and 7:30–10:45 P.M. daily, Rs 190 and up) serves everything from Hungarian beef goulash to pasta, beer-battered calamari, and Goan dishes like prawn *balchao*.

INFORMATION AND SERVICES
Hospitals and Pharmacies

Being a major city, Vasco has good medical centers, such as **Vasco Hospital** (Cottage Hospital, Chicalim, Vasco, tel. 0832/254-0864), **Dr. Kamat's Nursing Home** (behind La Paz Hotel, Vasco, tel. 0832/254-1353), **Sanjeevani Hospital** (near Old MPT Hospital, Vasco, tel. 0832/251-0024), **Apollo Pharmacy** (Chase Chambers, opposite La Paz, Vasco, tel. 0832/251-3681, 24 hr).

Police

In case of emergency, **dial 100** for the 24-hour police helpline or try the **Vasco Police Station** (tel. 0832/251-2304).

Money

Most Bogmalo resorts offer currency exchange facilities. Both ATMs and currency exchange are available in Vasco at **State Bank of India** (Satyawan Building, FL Gomes Rd., tel. 0832/250-0102, 10 A.M.–5 P.M. Mon.–Fri. and 10 A.M.–12:30 P.M. Fri.) while **ICICI Bank** (Raj Tara Building, Tilak Maidan, Vasco) and **HDFC Bank** (Damodar Building, Swatantra Path, Vasco) also have ATM facilities.

Postal Services

The **Vasco Post Office** (NH17A, tel. 0832/251-2264, 9:30 A.M.–1 P.M. and 2–5:30 P.M. Mon.–Fri.) is easily accessible. Speedpost and registered letter booking may also be done here.

GETTING THERE AND AROUND

Vasco and Bogmalo are a mere 15-minute drive from Dabolim Airport; a taxi costs around Rs 200. From Madgaon Station, it takes a little over half an hour and costs Rs 400. Vasco is also a major station and trains starting from here go to various destinations in the country. Interstate buses arrive at the Kadamba Bus Terminal, 3 kilometers east of town, while auto-rickshaws and motorcycle taxis—found at the corner of Swatantra Path and Dr. Rajendra Prasad Avenue—may be used to travel around the area.

Velsao to Betalbatim

If Bogmalo was a quiet interlude between the noisy north and the vibrant south, then the long stretch of beach between Velsao and Majorda is just the beginning of the party. The secluded **Velsao Beach** is a small, sandy belt marked by a fishing village and little tourist activity. Great for sunsets and a bit of local flavor, it makes for a short day trip from the neighboring Arossim. The beachfront of the village of Cansaulim, **Arossim Beach** itself is a beautiful stretch lined with beached boats and old Portuguese casas; it's dominated by the sprawling five-star Park Hyatt, whose candlelit wooden deck may be seen from the waters at night. Sandpipers mark its quiet, sandy shores that carry on ahead to **Utorda Beach.**

A place for rose sunsets and quiet family moments by the sea, Utorda is famous for its beach shack, Zeebop by the Sea. Palm trees, rickety bridges, and untouched sands make this one of the prettiest beaches on the stretch. At night, it is lit with the earthen lamps of Zeebop and is alive with music as guests delight in the fresh catch of the day. Farther south is the famous **Majorda Beach,** known for its star-rated beach resorts. Believed to be the birthplace of toddy-infused bread, first baked by the Jesuits, it is known for its small local bakeries as well as its shacks. Close to **Betalbatim Beach,** the two make for an intoxicating vacation with the perfect combination of sun, sand, and festivity. The winding lanes of Betalbatim village lead

THE SOUTHERN COAST

© JANHAVI ACHAREKAR

White sands and palm trees mark the beachfront along the Park Hyatt at Arossim.

to paddy fields, palm trees, and quaint Goan houses. Here, the popular restaurant Martin's Corner is an institution in itself and its live music plays into the night, drawing customers from across Goa.

◖ UTORDA BEACH

The near-absence of seaside accommodations at Utorda are the source of both joy and sorrow. It is precisely this lack of beachside activity that maintains the magically pristine nature of the golden stretch. And yet, the sheer beauty of the beach, with its inviting blue waves, makes day-trippers want to stay the night. Luckily, even those who cannot afford to stay at the star-rated Kenilworth Hotel can partake of its seaside splendor. The atmospheric and homey Zeebop by the Sea has changing rooms and an outdoor shower for those who wish to spend a lazy day on the beach, bathing in the superlative waters and gorging on the choicest seafood. A great place to unwind, Utorda is where you can simply relax by the sea and enjoy a moving sunset.

ENTERTAINMENT AND EVENTS

Restaurant **Martin's Corner** (Binvaddo, Betalbatim, 11 A.M.–3 P.M. and 6 P.M.–midnight daily) doubles up as a nightspot with its live music, as local bands belt out popular retro favorites and other numbers.

The lounge bar at the Park Hyatt, **Praia de Luz** (Arossim Beach, tel. 0832/272-1234, www.goa.park.hyatt.com, 11 A.M.–1 A.M. daily) offers a beautiful view of the sunset, along with a fine selection of wines, cocktails, and appetizers. A great place to relax over fine liquor, it also hosts live performances.

The **R.E.D. Entertainment Centre** (Utorda Beach, tel. 0832/669-8888, www.kenilworth-hotels.com) at the Kenilworth Beach Resort and Spa has a bar, discotheque, and casino.

The Majorda Beach Resort is known for its casino, **Treasures** (Majorda Beach, tel. 0832/668-1111, www.majordabeachresort.com), where you can try your luck at roulette or on the slot machines.

SPORTS AND RECREATION
Water Sports

The beaches on this stretch are generally quiet, but most resorts will organize water sports for guests. The Park Hyatt Goa (tel. 0832/272-1234, www.goa.park.hyatt.com) and Kenilworth (tel. 0832/669-8888, www.kenilworthhotels.com) arrange for Jet Skiing, fun rides, island trips, and dolphin cruises.

Go Kart Racing

The track at **Goa Kart Racing** (near Tata Indica showroom, Belloy-Nuvem, tel. 0832/279-1300, 4–10 P.M. Tues.–Sun. Oct.–Apr. and 3:30–7 P.M. Tues.–Sun. May.–Sept., Rs 150 for 10 laps Oct.–Apr. and Rs 130 May–Sept.) is situated on a hill, with a steep and narrow road leading to the top. The drive uphill is worth it—the track offers a spectacular view of the coastline and the unforgettable experience of racing against the backdrop of the ocean.

Spas

Apart from swimming and tanning on these beautiful beaches, visitors can treat themselves to the excellent spas at the host of five-star properties. The best, undoubtedly, is the **Sereno Spa** (Park Hyatt Goa, Arossim Beach, tel. 0832/272-1234, www.goa.park.hyatt.com) at the Park Hyatt Goa Resort and Spa. Awarded the top spa in Asia and the world, it offers holistic healing in the form of Ayurveda, yoga, and meditation. Its outdoor sunlit ambience, relaxation areas, and soothing massage

© ASHIMA NARAIN

One of Goa's prettiest beaches, Utorda Beach, also boasts the most beautiful sunsets.

rooms—named after the floral and spicy fragrances that envelop them—lend it a Zen-like serenity. Friendly Ayurvedic doctors attired in calming whites offer a detailed consultation to guests, helping them understand their Ayurvedic body type and then recommending treatments (Rs 3,500 and up), to be carried out by expert massage therapists. The spa has luxurious treatment suites—some with an open plunge pool—with an outdoor view as well as open-air therapy pavilions. Centered around the Courtyard of Tranquility and surrounded by gardens, this is the ideal place for a healing experience. In addition to the regular massages and treatments, the spa also offers a range of therapy packages such as a rejuvenation program, a beauty and indulgence program, and a stress-management program. If you want to feel one with nature, try the Marine Ritual (Rs 9,000), which uses seaweed and minerals.

The **Agua Spa** (Kenilworth Beach Resort and Spa, Utorda Beach, tel. 0832/669-8888, www.kenilworthhotels.com) is a small peaceful spa exuding the light and fragrance of flickering, scented candles. Their menu includes a number of treatments and massage therapies including Balinese, Swedish, Shiatsu, and Ayurvedic methods. The spa also specializes in a number of bath and beauty rituals, such as the milk and rose bath ritual (Rs 1,500) and a number of lengthy rejuvenation rituals (Rs 7,500–25,000) that require up to 10 days of treatment. The Agua Signature ritual (Rs 7,000) is one of the most elaborate, with sand peeling, hot-stone therapy, and chakra healing. It also offers a number of Ayurvedic herbal treatments (Rs 1,500–3,600) and beauty treatments.

The **Majorda Beach Resort** (Majorda Beach, tel. 0832/668-1111, www.majordabeachresort.com) has a spa that offers the Kalari form of Ayurvedic massage (Rs 1,500–2,500). In this massage, the masseur uses his feet as well as his hands for an effective massage, using medicated herbal oils. The spa also has a hydrotherapeutic whirlpool tub, as well as steam and sauna facilities.

ACCOMMODATIONS

Like most of the southern coast, this stretch is dominated by high-end resorts and five-star properties. The Park Hyatt is one of the best in Goa, and the area also has two lovely Indo-Portuguese mansions that offer homestays.

Rs 1,000-3,000

A short walk from the beach, ◖ **Casa Andrade** (House no. 194, Arossim, tel. 0832/275-4147, www.casaandrade.com, Rs 1,500–5,000) is a magnificent 150-year-old Indo-Portuguese mansion with rooms spread across two wings. Its green facade leads into a black and white mosaic-tiled interior filled with antique furniture. While one wing has four rooms (complete with four-poster beds, carved almirahs, and a common kitchen), the other has two bedrooms on the upper floor and a large one on the lower floor. Some rooms are air-conditioned, while those in the two-story old section of the house have a shared bathroom. The house also has a private chapel and a garden. While complimentary breakfast and evening meals are served with prior notice, guests are also free to cook in the common kitchen. The elderly couple that owns the house will be happy to share the history of the place and treat you as houseguests, rather than customers.

Don't go expecting similar colonial architecture at **Casa Ligorio** (near Kenilworth Beach Resort, Utorda, tel. 0832/275-5405, www.casaligorio.com, Rs 1,200–3,000). This unattractive but good-value resort is a recent construction with basic accommodations. Rooms are air-conditioned and have private balconies with a view of the surrounding gardens, while the beach is a five-minute-walk away. Although a bit run-down, the place is quiet enough and offers budget rates in a stretch dominated by five-stars.

Popular Betalbatim restaurant Martin's Corner runs its own lodging. **Martin's Comfort** (Ranvaddo, Betalbatim, tel. 0832/288-0765, www.martinscomfort.com, Rs 3,000–4,500) offers comfortable and contemporary rooms within a few meters of the beach. It has 18 air-conditioned deluxe rooms with a balcony, and, true to its name, modern comforts—including television and intercom. The hotel also has a restaurant, Carafina, although it may be worthwhile going to Martin's Corner for the ambience. There's a pool as well as Internet and currency exchange.

Rs 3,000-10,000

Another beautifully restored old house, ◖ **Vivenda dos Palhacos** (Costa Vaddo, Majorda, tel. 0832/322-1119, www.vivenda-goa.com, Rs 3,500–10,850) combines the colonial architecture of an old Portuguese-style house with the traditional style of an older adjoining Hindu house. The two, together, have five bedrooms, as well as a cottage in the pool and garden area at the back. The rooms are themed, with names of old colonial towns and Calcutta suburbs. While Ooty is airy and bright with a soothing white look, Konnager has a four-poster bed and a spacious verandah. Ballygunge and Alipore are bathed in colorful hues, while Madras has a skylight and an outdoor shower. A charming bar, dining room, and a pool make this an almost exclusive getaway. The entire house is also rented out to groups by the owners, a British but resident Indian brother-sister duo.

Rs 10,000 and Up

Right on Utorda Beach, **Kenilworth Beach Resort and Spa** (Utorda Beach, tel. 0832/669-8888, www.kenilworthhotels.com, rates upon request) is a low-profile but pleasant hotel. Though it hosts mostly corporate customers, it's a family-friendly place with a pool, restaurants, bars, and landscaped gardens that open out onto the beach. Its garden-view and deluxe rooms offer a private access to the garden with an exclusive sit-out, while the superior deluxe rooms on the upper floor have a balcony with a pool view. The sprawling property also has executive suites that are both spacious and luxurious, with similar views. Elegantly and tastefully furnished, all rooms have five-star amenities and creature comforts. Service is efficient and the hotel offers plenty of dining and drinking options, ranging from its Italian trattoria,

Portofino; Mallika, with Indian Northern Frontier cuisine; poolside café Aquarius; and beachfront Sea Hawk, with Goan cuisine. A lobby bar, pool bar, and entertainment center add to the excitement. Meanwhile, the Agua Spa offers a range of beauty and massage treatments in a pleasing ambience. The hotel also organizes dolphin and sunset cruises, fishing trips, and a variety of water sports for guests.

One of Goa's oldest and favorite five-star deluxe family resorts, **Majorda Beach Resort** (Majorda Beach, tel. 0832/668-1111, www .majordabeachresort.com, Rs 5,300–19,000) is a vast property with over 120 rooms and 10 cottages and suites. Rooms are spacious and have balconies with a view of the ocean or the gardens. In addition, the resort has a casino, discotheque, and several lively restaurants: a seafood grill called Sea Shells, a garden café, a tea lounge and bar, a coffee shop, and a multicuisine restaurant called Laguna. There are plenty of activities for guests—who have the option of swimming in the only indoor pool in Goa, in addition to the outdoor one. The resort has tennis and squash courts, a fitness center, and Ayurvedic massage therapy, and also organizes water sports.

However, the cream of the crop is most definitely the ◖ **Park Hyatt Goa Resort and Spa** (Arossim Beach, tel. 0832/272-1234, www.goa.park.hyatt.com, 7,000–125,000). A five-star that beats most luxury hotels in location, quality of accommodation, dining, and service, this is where landscaped gardens meet the beach and courtyard cafés lead to wooden decked restaurants by the sea. Its international vibe, busy cafés, and chic decor make for a refreshing luxury experience. The staff—even the senior management—is hands-on, personalizing holidays for repeat customers. Rooms and suites are contemporary, à la mode, and inviting. Designed like a contemporary Indo-Portuguese village with its open courtyards, canals, and bridges, rooms resemble Portuguese-style villas or *pousadas*. Rooms are bright and airy, with views of a lagoon and lawn, and access to a hidden private garden and verandah. The bathrooms are the

most defining features of the rooms, with their striking neon lights, flower arrangements, and sunken tubs. The deluxe category of rooms also has a lovely outdoor rain shower area tiled in cheerful colors. The resort has a number of seafacing rooms with balconies and verandahs for ocean-gazing, while its sun-kissed suites are beautifully furnished with large living areas, a king-sized bedroom, luxurious bathrooms, and a sea view. However, the grand Imperador Suite is the show stealer, with its intimate ocean view and sprawling living and dining areas, in addition to a spacious bedroom and kitchen. Rounded windows and bamboo blinds, an open sunken bath and an additional jetted spa tub, private garden, and verandah make for a premier luxury experience.

Meanwhile, the Sereno Spa at the Park Hyatt Goa is synonymous with the hotel. It has an impressive reputation, and has been named the top spa in the world. The hotel also has a lounge bar and a number of outstanding restaurants.

FOOD

Known for the legendary beach shack Zeebop, for popular restaurant Martin's Corner, and for its excellent fine dining, this stretch between Arossim and Betalbatim is popular for dining. At the top of this illustrious list is the varied slew of restaurants at the Park Hyatt. Deserving special mention is the atmospheric fine dining Goan cuisine **Casa Sarita** (Park Hyatt Goa Resort and Spa, Arossim Beach, tel. 0832/272-1234, www.goa.park.hyatt.com, noon–3 P.M. and 6:30–11 P.M. daily, mains Rs 425 and up)—named after its Goan chef Sarita, who works magic in the open kitchen as you take in the casa-like ambience with its oyster-shell French windows and placemats. The restaurant serves your regular vindaloos and *cafreals,* in addition to traditional Hindu vegetarian cuisine. Try the wonderfully innovative *kokum* dip that's served before your meal and round off a fantastic meal with the dessert called *pudim de papaya* (papaya pudding). Chef Sarita also conducts culinary lessons in Goan cooking; inquiries may be made at the hotel.

If you're one for the outdoors, the open wooden-decked restaurant **The Palms** (Park Hyatt Goa Resort and Spa, Arossim Beach, tel. 0832/272-1234, www.goa.park .hyatt.com, 10 A.M.–11 P.M. daily Oct.–Apr., seafood priced by weight) may be more appealing. New in 2008, this beachside restaurant is already one of the most popular eateries in the area. Ambience and cuisine play an equal role here as the deliberate absence of music welcomes the sound of the ocean waves. Candles light up the tables as the expert chef, Asif, prepares experimental cuisine that includes fantastic grilled seafood, salads, and dessert under the stars.

Meanwhile, a small beach shack with a big reputation, **(Zeebop by the Sea** (opposite Kenilworth Beach Resort, Utorda Beach, tel. 0832/275-5333, zeebop@sify.com, 10 A.M.–11 P.M. daily Oct.–Apr., mains Rs 200 and up), is a Goan legend. Customers come from far and wide to this beachfront Goan seafood restaurant for its fried prawns and fish curries. Try the lobster preparations as well as the fresh pomfret and crab *xec xec*. The shack is a landmark and has foot-tapping live music five days a week. It is also rented out for weddings and parties. The intriguing name, in case you were wondering, has no history behind it. It was simply the first one to come to mind when the owner, Sergio Dias, was contemplating names.

In the same league—not quite as consistent these days, but still as enjoyable for the ambience—is **(Martin's Corner** (Binvaddo, Betalbatim, 11 A.M.–3 P.M. and 6 P.M.–midnight daily, mains Rs 150 and up). What started as a corner store is today a thriving restaurant and nightspot where excellent local bands play even as you tuck into some fantastic king crab and lobster preparations. Known for its Goan specialties such as pork

© ASHIMA NARAIN

Great for a swim and seafood, restaurant-shack Zeebop by the Sea enjoys Goa's most picturesque location.

sorpotel and mutton *xacuti*, as well as its seafood, Martin's has slowed down somewhat in service and quality. However, the atmosphere is electric, cocktails unique (try the Betalbatim Delight), and the colorful caricatures of Goan life only add to the cheery ambience as you wait in line for a table at this popular restaurant.

GETTING THERE AND AROUND
Both Dabolim Airport and Madgaon Station are equidistant from this stretch of beaches. A taxi from either takes 15–30 minutes and costs around Rs 300 to get to these beaches. Once here, you can hire a private taxi or a motorcycle if needed.

Colva and Benaulim

Once a 25-kilometer stretch of pristine white sand, Colva is now a beach reveler's paradise. Water sports, hawkers, young honeymooners, and others have turned this once-elite colonial getaway into something akin to Mumbai's Juhu Beach.

Colva Beach is somewhat similar to the more commercial northern beaches, its beach shacks and nightspots overshadowing a 17th-century church famous for its statue of the Menino Jesus (which now lies in the Rachol Seminary). Fishing boats line the stretch as fishermen continue to bring in their catch of the day, unmindful of the crowds. Even as bright parasails shoot over the palm trees of Colva, the party continues down the stretch at **Benaulim Beach,** two kilometers farther south. Although commercial, the beach has a relaxed air and offers a degree of seclusion. Here, popular beachside shacks vie with popular garden restaurants and the beautiful five-star property of the Taj Exotica. Live music and a festive air envelop the beach at night while antique and handicraft stores add to the melee. Believed by Hindus to be the spot where Lord Parashurama—an incarnation of Vishnu—shot his arrow into the sea, causing the waters to recede and create Goa, Benaulim is an unlikely combination of mythology, religion and beach culture. It is also known for its village and the 16th-century **Church of St. John the Baptist,** located at Monte Hill. Mass is held at 8 A.M. daily. Built in 1581, the church is known for its classic architecture and Italian marble spires.

ENTERTAINMENT AND EVENTS

Colva and Benaulim are full of nightspots and popular hangouts that draw tourists and locals alike. One such place, **Boomerang** (Colva Beach, tel. 0832/278-8249,

© ASHIMA NARAIN

fishing boats, Colva Beach

THE SOUTHERN COAST

www.boomerangcolva.com, no fixed hours but open morning to night, Oct.–Apr.) is a beach bar that serves cocktails and wine. It has a dance floor, hosts beach parties in the peak season, and serves grilled seafood as you watch sports on its gigantic screens.

At boutique hotel Soul Vacation, **Shalom** (Colva Beach, tel. 0832/278-8144, www.soul-vacation.in, 8 A.M.–midnight daily) is popular for its margaritas and Moroccan delights. Ambient and dimly lit, with gauzy curtains flowing in the breeze, this is a great place to sample classic Mediterranean cuisine or to simply lounge in a calm atmosphere.

Just off the road to Benaulim Beach, in a narrow lane to the right, **Fiplee's** (near Maria Hall, Benaulim, tel. 0832/277-0123, www .fiplees.com, 7:30 P.M.–2 A.M. daily) is a self-confessed "restaurant, pub and leisure zone." Locals hang out here for the snooker table and games, as well as live music and karaoke nights. The red-and-black interior is dingy but for good reason—its discotheque belts out favorites played by local and visiting DJs. The choice of music is varied to include pop, reggae, country, and jazz.

Just before the Taj Exotica, on the right hand side is **Joecon's Garden** (near Taj Exotica, Benaulim, tel. 0832/277-0077, www.joecon-sgarden.com, 11:30 A.M.–midnight daily), a lovely open-air garden restaurant and bar. Although open through the day, fairy lights and live music light up the atmosphere after dark. The bar is well stocked (cocktails Rs 120 and up), the staff is friendly, and the seafood is excellent.

Both Goan beats and sitar sounds waft out of **Pedro's** (Benaulim Beach, tel. 0832/277-0563, 10 A.M.–10 P.M. daily). As popular for its music as it is for its fiery curries, this beach shack organizes live performances on weekend that include local Goan bands and classical Indian music. In accompaniment are a variety of cocktails at the bar.

Nearby, the owner of the previously popular Coco's Beach Shack has opened **Roger's Beach Shack** (Benaulim Beach, cell tel. 91/98224-88079, 7 A.M.–midnight daily),

which, in the Coco's tradition, hosts live music every day of the week except for Mondays and Wednesdays. The food is authentic Goan, just like the music.

SHOPPING

While Colva and Benaulim have the usual street stalls selling clothes and such, Benaulim also has a few specialty stores. Kashmir handicrafts store **Oceanic Gallery** (1346, Mazil Vaddo, near Holy Trinity Church, Benaulim, tel. 0832/277-1659, oceanic.gallery@edutca-reers.com, 9:30 A.M.–8:30 P.M. daily) is located in an old colonial house that used to be home to artsy Manthan. Papier maché, carved wood, and textiles are strewn around the place, and flirtatious sales boys try to charm you into buying their wares.

Just around the corner from here is **The Museum Company** (1239, Mazil Vaddo, near Holy Trinity Church, Benaulim, tel. 0832/277-0843, fortroyale-chennai@hotmail. com, 9 A.M.–10 P.M. daily), where antique furniture and handicrafts vie for attention with the lovely white-and-yellow Indo-Portuguese structure that they are housed in. Carved wood antiques and replicas are shipped here from various parts of the country, as are Kashmir handicrafts, carpets, and jewelry.

SPORTS AND RECREATION
Water Sports

Apart from lending their waters for a good swim, the beaches of Colva and Benaulim are both famous and infamous for their water sports. It is possible to go parasailing, Jet Skiing, and on banana boat rides, but tourists are warned against sports involving "skill." Colva's water-sports operators are notoriously commercial, paying little heed to safety measures. This stretch is known for serious accidents in the past and visitors are advised to stick to dolphin and fishing trips. A number of operators may be found on the beach and some even take you on an island trip (Rs 7,000) that includes lunch. You can also check at your hotel reception or at the more popular beach shacks that also organize boat trips.

© ASHIMA NARAIN

parasailing over Colva Beach

Spas

This stretch is known for its holistic and beauty indulgences. Taj's **Jiva** (Taj Exotica, Cal Vaddo, Benaulim, tel. 0832/277-1234, www.tajhotels.com, 7 A.M.–8 P.M. daily) offers a varied experience with an in-hotel spa, a secluded Ayurvedic center, and an outdoor massage pavilion. The in-hotel spa—bathed in incense and oils—welcomes guests with herbal tea, and specializes in aromatherapy, Swedish, Balinese, and Thai massages. Try their signature Jivaniya energizing treatment or the Pehlwan Malish—the wrestler's massage. The spa has relaxation rooms, as well as a whirlpool tub, often made special for couples with champagne and music. The Ayurvedic Spa, meanwhile, is located in the tranquil environs outside the main hotel area and offers the traditional Kerala spa experience. Treatments are carried out by trained masseurs and therapists after a consultation with the Ayurvedic doctor. Soothing music, oil lamps, and tranquil surroundings make this a private and healing experience. The beachside outdoor pavilion, on the other hand, is the perfect way to commune with the sea. Guests can have massages outdoors while luxuriating in warm rays and the sound of the ocean.

Rejuvenation (Soul Vacation, Colva Beach, tel. 0832/278-8144, www.soulvacation.in, 9 A.M.–7 P.M. daily), at the boutique hotel, Soul Vacation, also offers outdoor massage experiences. This open-air spa, in a soothing white ambience with flowing curtains, provides relaxing aromatherapy treatments. It then goes a step further by providing an outdoor whirlpool tub and sets the mood for a romantic twosome with wine and scented candles.

ACCOMMODATIONS

Colva and Benaulim have a strange mix of budget and luxury accommodation. The luxury properties afford guests surprising privacy and seclusion in the face of commercial beach activity.

Under Rs 1,000

Away from the hustle and bustle of the main center, **Succorina Cottages** (1711/A, Vas Vaddo, Benaulim, tel. 0832/277-0365, Rs 250) is located in a quiet area about one kilometer south of the fishing village of Benaulim. A set of clean rooms have views of field and ocean. Since this property is somewhat distant from the beach, you may need to arrange for your own vehicle or cycle. However, it is unbelievably low-priced and the staff make your stay as pleasant as possible.

Rs 1,000–3,000

La Ben (Colva Beach Rd., tel. 0832/278-8040, www.laben.net, Rs 400–1,400) is another good-value budget hotel near Colva Beach. It has a lovely rooftop restaurant and clean, modest rooms with balconies that overlook a lawn and palm trees. The staff are helpful.

Colva Residency (Colva Beach, tel. 0832/278-8047, www.goa-tourism.com, Rs 915–2,100) is a sprawling Goa Tourism Development Corporation (GTDC) property located amidst gardens and facing the sea. One of the better GTDC properties, rooms are airy and well kept, with balconies overlooking the scenic surroundings. There are 47 rooms (some with a/c) as well as a garden restaurant serving Goan cuisine that blares local and reggae music all day long.

Within walking distance of Colva Beach, **Star Beach Resort** (near football ground, Colva, tel. 0832/278-8166, www.starbeach-resortgoa.com, Rs 600–2,500) is a great value. Rooms are simply furnished but spacious and have balconies with a view. They come with a television, refrigerator, and air-conditioning. There are two types—standard and deluxe—but you can also inquire about the availability of cottages. The resort has a pool, a restaurant, travel and money-exchange counters, and an Ayurvedic massage facilities.

Surrounded by palm trees, **Camilson's Beach Resort** (Ambeaxir, Sernabatim, Colva, tel. 0832/277-1582, www.camilsons.in, Rs 600–2,500) is a quiet resort in the Sernabatim Beach area toward Benaulim. Rooms are comfortable and tastefully furnished with carved wood beds and other furniture. They also come with great private terrace areas and a view of the surrounding landscape. The resort has a beachfront restaurant good for spotting dolphins as you sample Goan seafood and other specialties.

The name is indicative of the ambience at ◖ **Palm Grove Cottages** (Tamdi Mati, 149 Vas Vaddo, Benaulim, tel. 0832/277-0059, www.palmgrovegoa.com, Rs 960–1,680), a peaceful mid-range retreat surrounded by beautiful gardens and palm trees. The place is generally well managed and the beach is a short distance away. Rooms are minimalist, bright, and airy, with cheerful balconies that have a view of the lush greenery. Those in the new block are luxurious. The beautiful gazebo-style restaurant dishes out local seafood preparations, as well as North Indian, Chinese, and European dishes. The resort offers traditional Ayurvedic massage therapy and treatment in consultation with the in-house Ayurvedic doctor. It also has a pub, a well-stocked library, and travel and money-changing facilities.

Rs 3,000-10,000

Longuinho's Beach Resort (Colva Beach, tel. 0832/278-8068, www.longuinhos.net, Rs 1,500–6,500) is a modern building surrounded by greenery and gardens, just along Colva Beach. It has the same ownership as Longuinho's, the famous Madgaon restaurant. Rooms are clean and pleasant, and offer a magnificent sea view from their private balconies. The resort also has a pool for guests. At A Tartaruga (Portuguese for sea turtle), guests can choose from among traditional Goa, North Indian, and European delicacies, along with cocktails. Meanwhile, Coco del Mar is an open-air restaurant where buffets are served amid live music.

A small boutique hotel not far from the beach, ◖ **Soul Vacation** (Colva Beach, tel. 0832/278-8144, www.soulvacation.in, Rs 3,500–7,000 includes breakfast) is part of the Shalom chain of hotels. This is a chic resort with designer rooms, Mediterranean lounge, restaurant, spa, and plenty of other frills to make for a great vacation—at incredibly

© ASHIMA NARAIN

Star-rated and boutique hotels abound in southern Goa.

Beach chairs and thatched umbrellas line Benaulim Beach outside the Taj Exotica.

reasonable rates for all it offers. Soothing white decor lends to the spirit of the place. Stylish rooms are tastefully furnished in calm, pastel hues and come with modern gadgets and amenities. All rooms have lounge seating, while the luxury rooms are more spacious and come with a writing desk. The hotel boasts of one of the finest Mediterranean restaurants in these parts, Shalom, known for its Lebanese and Spanish specialties as well as its white plaster-and-wood decor. There's a lovely poolside lounge area as well—which doubles up as a nightspot—distinguished by its outdoor boudoir-esque appearance, complete with flowing white drapes and mellow lighting. To go with the soul-nourishing theme, there's a spa and whirlpool tub, as well as activities such as yoga, painting, and pottery.

Rs 10,000 and Up

The queen bee of luxury resorts, the 🌑 **Taj Exotica** (Cal Vaddo, Benaulim, tel. 0832/277-1234, www.tajhotels.com, Rs 17,500–143,000) has 23 hectares of greenery and private villas that offer a sanctuary from the clamor of the main beach areas. A variety of restaurants, including the wonderfully ambient Lobster Shack by the sea, a lounge bar, nine-hole golf course, and the Jiva Spa—with its separate Ayurveda Center—make for a complete vacation. Accommodations are elegant and classical, with deluxe rooms and suites, as well as two- and four-bedroom villas. Deluxe rooms and sea-view villas have an ocean view, while the garden-view villas open out into the lush lawns. In addition, the hotel offers sunset pool villa rooms where beautiful Goan-Portuguese architecture is coupled with a wide verandah and sit-out overlooking a private pool. Suites come with private whirlpool tubs and the two-bedroom Presidential villas are positively luxurious—with 24-hour butler service, among other perks. The villas are painted in beautiful earthy colors and combine luxury with a feeling of home. The outside pool area is beautiful, providing the feel of a private garden. The hotel has an excellent travel desk that can take care of your sightseeing needs, while the beach area maintained by the hotel is lined with deck chairs for its guests and looked over by a watchful lifeguard. The hotel offers facilities for a number sports, including archery and cricket. And apart from business facilities, there are babysitting and library services. In keeping with the famed Taj hospitality, the staff are both efficient and friendly, doing all they can to ensure that your stay is a comfortable one.

FOOD

Colva and Benaulim are known for bars that double up as restaurants. There's a fine line dividing places such as Fiplee's or Pedro's in Benaulim from **Mickey's** (near football ground, Colva Beach, tel. 0832/278-9125, mickeyscolvagoa@yahoo.co.in, 11:30 A.M.–3 P.M. and 6:30 P.M.–midnight daily, mains Rs 100 and up)—an open air restaurant and bar popular with both locals and tourists. Local cuisine is served here, with seafood (as always) being the hot favorite. Mickey's is also known for its weekend entertainment, when live music infuses the air with a festive spirit. Saturdays see a one-man band, while Sundays are popular for karaoke night.

Right alongside Colva Beach is its most famous restaurant-shack: **Kentuckee** (tel. 0832/278-8107, 8 A.M.–2 P.M. and 6 P.M.–midnight daily, mains Rs 100 and up). One of the best places in the area for a good Goan meal, it serves everything from spicy vindaloos to authentic pastas. Be sure to ask for the catch of the day—and confirm the price before you place your order! They serve an excellent catfish preparation, which can cost Rs 1,000 or more, depending on its size. The shack comes alive with live jazz performances on Fridays, Saturdays, and Sundays, making it a great local hangout.

Fiplee's (near Maria Hall, Benaulim, tel. 0832/277-0123, www.fiplees.com, 7:30 P.M.–2 A.M. daily, mains Rs 150 and up)—"restaurant, pub and leisure zone"—serves some decent Goan food as well as Chinese, European, and North Indian dishes. Locals and tourists also come here for the live music and karaoke nights, as well as the snooker table and games.

Similarly, the open-air **Joecon's Garden** (near Taj Exotica, Benaulim, tel. 0832/277-0077, www.joeconsgarden.com, 11:30 A.M.–midnight daily, mains Rs 85 and up) is known for its great ambience, live music, cocktails, and excellent seafood. While the lobster is supreme,

the fish curry rice, king prawn *balchao,* steaks, and sizzlers are also popular.

At **Pedro's** (Benaulim Beach, tel. 0832/277-0563, 10 A.M.–10 P.M. daily, mains Rs 80 and up), Goan-style seafood accompanies local Goan bands and classical Indian music on weekends. Try the spicy shark *amotic* (shark curry rice), pork *sorpotel,* and steaks, along with a variety of cocktails at the bar.

For live music every day of the week (except for Mondays and Wednesdays) along with authentic Goan cuisine, head to **Roger's Beach Shack** (Benaulim Beach, cell tel. 91/98224-88079, 7 A.M.–midnight daily), run by the previous owner of the popular Coco's Beach Shack. It specializes in seafood preparations, with North Indian and Chinese fare for variety.

A great place to watch the sunset, **Johncy's Beach Shack** (Benaulim Beach, tel. 0832/277-1390, 7–1 A.M. daily, mains Rs 150 and up) is known for its wide choice of menu. It serves Goan, European, and Chinese fare, but is most popular for its traditional seafood preparations. Any Monday blues are chased away with a seafood festival and cocktail party, while beach volleyball is an added attraction.

Among the various restaurants at the Taj Exotica, the one that deserves special mention is the beachfront **Lobster Shack** (Taj Exotica, Cal Vaddo, Benaulim, tel. 0832/277-1234, www.tajhotels.com, noon–10:30 P.M. daily Oct.–Apr., sandwiches Rs 375 and up, seafood Rs 275–350 per 100 gm). Overlooking Benaulim Beach, the Lobster Shack is a great place to unwind with a book, sandwich, and a beer. Perfect for a lazy day by the beach, lunch is served until 6 P.M. At night, it turns festive with live music and candlelight, as patrons select their meal from among the live seafood display, or down a cocktail by the bar. Needless to say, lobster is a specialty here and served with a choice of sauces. There is a selection of meat as well, and intriguing appetizers such as the chilled watermelon soup spiked with lemongrass.

Another Taj favorite is **Miguel Arcanjo** (Taj Exotica, Cal Vaddo, Benaulim, tel. 0832/277-1234, www.tajhotels.com,

12:30–2:45 P.M. and 7:30–10:45 P.M. daily, mains Rs 625 and up), named after the late Goan chef Miguel A Mascarenhas, a Taj employee, and the first to popularize Western cuisine in the country. The restaurant lives up to his name as a variety of Mediterranean cuisines carry on the tradition with dishes such as Lebanese mezze, Spanish paella, and a variety of risottos. Seafood junkies will appreciate the oven-baked red snapper and the shrimp glazed with honey and garlic. Lamb chops, too, are a specialty. Desserts, such as chocolate mousse or poached pear with vanilla bean custard, are divine. Coupled with an excellent meal is a fantastic sea view and mariachi-style singers singing old favorites and local Goan songs.

INFORMATION AND SERVICES
Tourist Information

The **Goa Tourism Development Corporation (GTDC)** (Colva Residency, Colva Beach, tel. 0832/278-8047, www.goa-tourism.com, 9:30 A.M.–1 P.M. and 2–5:30 P.M. Mon.–Fri.) provides maps and brochures and also organizes a number of guided tours.

Pharmacies

Medical supplies and toiletries are available at **Colva Medical Stores** (Colva Crossroad, below Concha Resort, tel. 0832/278-8591) and **Menino Jesus Medical Stores** (Shop no. 5, Sanzgiri Arcade, Colva, tel. 0832/278-9555, 8 A.M.–9:30 P.M. Mon.–Sat. and 8 A.M.–1:30 P.M. Sun.).

Police

In case of emergency, **dial 100** for the 24-hour police helpline or try the **Colva Police Station** (along Varca Rd., tel. 0832/278-8396).

Money

GK Tourist Center (Vasvaddo Beach Rd., near Maria Hall, Benaulim, tel. 0832/277-0471, 9 A.M.–10 P.M. daily) and **Meeting Point Travel** (Colva Beach Rd., tel. 0832/278-8003, 9 A.M.–6 P.M. daily) change money and cash traveler's checks. ATMs are few and far between, but you can go to **Bank of Baroda** (Maria House, Benaulim, tel. 0832/277-0116, and near Colva Church, Colva, tel. 0832/278-0528).

Postal Services

Postal needs are met at the **Colva Post Office** (tel. 0832/278-8505, 9:30 A.M.–1 P.M. and 2–5:30 P.M. Mon.–Fri.). Speedpost and registered letter booking facilities are available here.

Internet

There are a number of places where you can surf the Internet for about Rs 40 per hour. Try **GK Tourist Center** (Vasvaddo Beach Rd., near Maria Hall, Benaulim, tel. 0832/277-0471, 9 A.M.–10 P.M. daily), **Hello Mae** (Colva Beach Rd., tel. 0832/278-0108, 7:30 A.M.–11 P.M. daily), **New Horizon** (1595 Benaulim Beach Rd., tel. 0832/277-1218, 9 A.M.–10 P.M. daily), or **Sify I-way** (road to Taj Exotica, Benaulim, 9 A.M.–1:45 P.M. and 3–8:30 P.M.).

GETTING THERE AND AROUND

From Dabolim Airport, Colva and Benaulim take less than an hour by taxi and cost Rs 450–500. By train, Madgaon—about 15–20 minutes away—is the closest station, and costs Rs 150–200 by taxi. There are regular bus services as well from both Madgaon and Vasco. Buses leave from the Kadamba Bus Stand and stop at a crossing called Maria Hall in Benaulim.

THE SOUTHERN COAST

Varca and Cavelossim

Varca and Cavelossim surprise you with their idyllic beauty. This is where soft white sand meets the sea undisturbed, and where the ocean meets the River Sal. It's no wonder, then, that these pristine beaches, watched over by swaying palm trees and dolphins, have been claimed by a dazzle of exclusive five-stars that play host to a number of charter tourists every year.

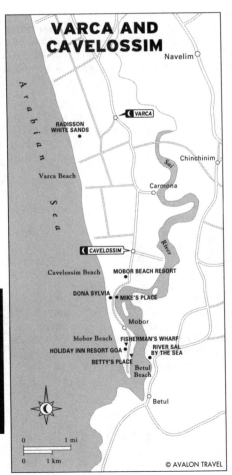

Pretty fishing villages, lined with thatched houses, starkly contrast with their five-star neighbors. And across the river from Mobor Beach at the end of Cavelossim, birds of prey keep a watchful eye, swooping down behind the turned backs of unsuspecting fishermen busy sorting piles of giant catfish from among pomfrets and other fish. To experience the spirit of a traditional fishing village, head to Betul, just across the River Sal. At the **Betul Jetty,** fishing boats and trawlers bring in their fresh treasures from in and around the Mobor Peninsula, where the river meets the Arabian Sea. The fishermen are busy but also curious and friendly, and often show off their biggest catch to those who are willing. From the jetty, you can also see the twinkling lights of riverside restaurant Fisherman's Wharf at Mobor.

Meanwhile, not far into the interior, in the village of Fatorpa, is the **Shantadurga Temple,** famous for its fair held around December. The image of the deity of Shantadurga—an incarnation of Shiva's consort—is from the original shrine that stood in Cuncolim prior to being destroyed by the Portuguese in the 16th century.

Between the two, Varca and Cavelossim present to the crowd-weary traveler a fresh geographical and cultural landscape as well as a unique rustic getaway.

◖ VARCA

Distinguished by black lava rocks that dot its white sands, Varca is the more secluded of the beaches on this stretch. Its solitude is broken only by a couple of five-star properties. Varca's glistening sands are offset by the characteristic thatched roofs of its quaint fishing village, where fisherfolk continue to bring in their fresh catch, oblivious to the changes elsewhere in the Goan landscape. This very unselfconsciousness—of the place, of this virgin beach that is also a study in rural life—lends to its irresistible charm.

© ASHIMA NARAIN

Fishermen call it a day at Betul Jetty.

C CAVELOSSIM

Cavelossim is busier than Varca but no less beautiful. Its main street is lined with shops and it even has a shopping arcade (called Luisa by the Sea). At the farthest end of Cavelossim is the seahorse snout of **Mobor Beach.** Here, river and sea meet to present a beautifully rustic landscape marked by a view of the jetty across the river. A luxury hotel, The Leela, dominates the beach in the face of environmental concern. From riverside restaurant, Fisherman's Wharf, there's a clear view of fishermen bringing in their fresh catch at the jetty by day, and of the red and green lights of fishing boats coming in after dark.

ENTERTAINMENT AND EVENTS
Casinos

Where there are five-stars, there's bound to be a casino. At **Hacienda de Oro** (Holiday Inn Resort Goa, Mobor Beach, Cavelossim, tel. 0832/287-1303, www.holidayinngoa.com, 11 A.M.–3 A.M. daily, entry Rs 200), you can play baccarat, blackjack, slots, and roulette.

Las Vegas (The Leela, Mobor Beach,

Cavelossim, tel. 0832/287-1234, www.theleela .com, 24 hr daily, entry Rs 200) offers mechanical casino games, roulette, six-lane Derby, slot machines, blackjack, and baccarat.

Live Music, Bars, and Discotheques

For those who want to shake a leg, **Aqua** (The Leela, Mobor Beach, Cavelossim, tel. 0832/287-1234, www.theleela.com, 7 P.M.–1 A.M. Tues.–Sun., open only to guests in Jan.–Feb.) is an entertainment lounge with separate semi-private lounges as well as a cigar divan. It turns into a full-fledged discotheque at night with laser lights and all.

If you want to have fun at more affordable rates, some beach shacks and restaurants organize live music. The popular riverside restaurant **Fisherman's Wharf** (next to Holiday Inn, Mobor, Cavelossim, tel. 0832/287-1317, fishermanswharfgoa@gmail.com, 11 A.M.–midnight daily) has live retro music every night. Their well-stocked bar has a wide selection of wines and is known for its excellent margaritas, drawing both locals as well as guests from the neighboring five-stars. As the night progresses and

THE SOUTHERN COAST

spirits soar, an open area in front of the bar turns into a dance floor.

Betty's Place (near The Leela, Mobor, tel. 0832/287-1456, www.bettysgoa.com, 7–11 P.M. daily Oct.–Apr., mains Rs 150 and up) organizes fire shows and karaoke nights. It also runs two beachside shacks: **Betty's Shade** (outside Holiday Inn Resort, Mobor Beach, Cavelossim, tel. 91/98504-80390, 9:30 A.M.–10:30 P.M. daily Oct.–Apr.) and **Betty's Shack** (near The Leela, Mobor Beach, Cavelossim, tel. 91/98504-80390, 9:30 A.M.–10:30 P.M. daily Oct.–Apr.). These spots provide live music on Sundays and Tuesdays, and a beach party with dance performances, limbo dancing and fireworks on Fridays.

SPORTS AND RECREATION

There's plenty to do in Varca and Cavelossim, with their plethora of water-sports operators and five-star spas. As with other beaches in Goa, beware of operators without the required safety measures, and stick to the "non-skilled" variety of water sports—namely, dolphin trips and boat rides. This stretch also has guided cycle tours and a number of golf courses.

Water Sports

Most hotels organize water sports for guests, or dolphin trips at the very least. The Leela offers parasailing, ringo rides, banana rides, fishing trips, backwater cruises, and water-skiing, among other activities.

Betty's Place (near The Leela, Mobor, tel. 0832/287-1456, www.bettysgoa.com) is a well-known operator in these parts. They organize day cruises (Rs 750) starting from the River Sal pier that include drinks and lunch. Fishing rods and bait are provided for anglers. They also offer deep-sea fishing trips. The Great Escape (Rs 600) is a day-long boat trip to the beaches off Mobor that are not accessible by land, and includes dolphin sighting and a barbecue. There's a two-hour sunset cruise (Rs 300) down the River Sal that includes bird-watching, and they also customize trips for large groups.

fresh catch, Betul Jetty

© ASHIMA NARAIN

Fisherman's Wharf (next to Holiday Inn, Mobor, Cavelossim, tel. 0832/287-1317, fishermanswharfgoa@gmail.com, 11 A.M.–midnight daily) offers several water sports, including ringo rides and Jet Skiing. Fishing trips have a happy ending as guests are given the option of barbecuing their catch.

Jack's Watersports (behind Hathi Mahal, Mobor, Cavelossim, tel. 0832/287-1132) offers boat rides, river cruises, and bird-watching trips, in addition to other water sports, while **Gavy Cruises** (Mobor, Cavelossim, tel. 0832/287-1146) offers crab-fishing trips.

Cycle Tours

For those who wish to explore the picturesque villages and countryside around the beaches, **Cycle Goa** (Shop 7, Mobor Beach Resort, Cavelossim, cell tel. 91/98223-80054, www.cyclegoa.com) is run by two British tourists who decided to stay in Goa. They conduct tours with specific itineraries for cycling enthusiasts, including half-day village tours, a ride to the Cabo de Rama Fort, day trips, and two-week trips. Tours are usually charged in British currency.

Spas

The Varca-Cavelossim stretch offers some of the choicest spas on the southern coast. Nearly all the star-rated resorts have their own staff of trained masseurs and spa practitioners. Among these, **Spa Villa** (Holiday Inn Resort Goa, Mobor Beach, Cavelossim, tel. 0832/287-1303, www.holidayinngoa.com) offers Thai therapies, Swedish massages, aroma massages, and Ayurvedic treatments. **Ayurveda** (The Leela, Mobor, Cavelossim, tel. 0832/287-1234, www.theleela.com) offers authentic Ayurvedic treatment from Kerala that includes a consultation with an Ayurvedic doctor at their Ayurvedic Rejuvenation Centre.

ACCOMMODATIONS

Studded with five-stars and mostly upmarket timeshare resorts, the beaches of Varca and Cavelossim have little to offer the budget tourist—mainly basic (and sometimes, unsafe) hotels near the beach or homestays in the fishing villages. For the luxury tourist however, this is a five-star paradise, with the spectacular Radisson and The Leela emerging as the clear winners.

Under Rs 1,000

The only budget hotel in the region lies across the river at Betul. **River Sal by the Sea** (Zuem, Betul, tel. 0832/277-3276, Rs 800–1,200, Oct.–Apr.) is known for its superb riverside location. Although waning in popularity in recent times, the place is nevertheless the best option for the price. There's a little swimming pool on the premises and all rooms have a pool and river view. The rooms aren't fancy, but the no-frills resort gives little reason to complain. The open-air restaurant here is legendary—for both riverside location and cuisine—and specializes in Goan-style seafood. The fish, not surprisingly, is fresh from the river and both hotel and restaurant

guests are provided with a free ferry service across the river.

Rs 1,000–3,000

Among the few low- to mid-range options in these parts, the one that stands out is the **Mobor Beach Resort** (Mobor, Cavelossim, tel. 0832/287-1170, www.moborbeachresort.net, Rs 2,000–2,500). With a pool, restaurant, pub, Internet access, shopping mall, live music, yoga, Ayurveda, and even a "naturist's roof terrace," it's an excellent value. The resort offers studio rooms and suites, all tastefully furnished and with beautiful views from their open balconies. Suites are air-conditioned and have a separate bedroom and a sitting area with a sofa bed. Equipped with a refrigerator and microwave, they make for a great family stay. While studios are smaller, they have the same amenities as the suites. The resort has plenty to offer in terms of dining and entertainment, and also has private access to the beach. Tour operator Cycle Goa works out of the resort.

Another superb low-range option is **(Mike's Place** (opposite Dona Sylvia, Mobor, Cavelossim, tel. 0832/287-1248, Rs 2,000–2,500). A simple but pleasant resort with a Goan feel thanks to its balconies and *balcaos,* it's within walking distance of the beach and the river. Rooms are clean, comfortable, and airy, often bringing back old customers. The place is well maintained by its friendly and efficient staff. Although no match in facilities with the neighboring luxury resorts, Mike's Place makes for a great stay. It also offers free transportation to Mike's Beach Oasis Shack.

Rs 3,000–10,000

A sprawling five-star, **Dona Sylvia** (Mobor Village, Cavelossim, tel. 0832/287-1888, www.donasylvia.com, Rs 7,000 and up) is something of a Mediterranean village on the shores of Goa. Its colorful villas, cottages, and profusion of terraces and verandahs are surrounded by lawns and flowers. Rooms and suites are pleasant enough and, more importantly, bright and airy. The resort has multi-cuisine, open air, and "fusion grill" restaurants, in addition to a pub and bar. An Ayurvedic spa managed by trained doctors and masseurs is located on the premises, as are a health club and aromatherapy center. Meanwhile, live entertainment, water sports, tennis, a swimming pool, a kids club, and a shopping center make this a popular place with tourists. The hotel also offers all-inclusive three-night/four-day packages.

Rs 10,000 and Up

Varca and Cavelossim together have the maximum number of five-star and luxury resorts in Goa. The **Ramada Caravela Goa Resort** (Varca Beach Rd., Varca, tel. 0832/274-5200, www.caravelabeachresort.com, Rs 8,000–77,000) is a massive beachfront property, designed by the architects of Sun City in Africa and owned by the same group that manages the cruise-ship casino MS *Caravela* in Panaji. Surrounded by beautiful gardens, its sunlit atrium and a Mario Miranda mural lead to over 200 rooms, suites, and villas. Well-furnished rooms with balconies have a view of the ocean, surrounding gardens, and pool. The resort also offers yoga, golf, water sports, an Ayurvedic clinic, and a spa. Attentive staff, solitude, and one of the most beautiful beaches in Goa make this an ideal getaway.

A vast and luxurious property near Varca Beach, **Country Inns and Suites by Carlson** (Pedda, Uttar Doxi, Varca, tel. 0832/669-7272, www.countryinns.com/goain, Rs 9,500–31,500) brings in Goan flavor with Portuguese country-style rooms and suites built around courtyards and gardens. Rooms are cheerful and contemporary in design and the ambience of the hotel, overall, is charming. In addition to a restaurant and a bar, guests have access to the pool, spa, and whirlpool tub, among other facilities. The place is well managed by a professional staff and has a special appeal for families due to its kid zone.

Close by, the ◖ **Radisson White Sands** (Pedda, Varca, tel. 0832/272-7272 and U.S. toll-free 800-1800-333, www.radisson.com/goain, Rs 11,000–55,000) is a spectacular luxury hotel that has recently been refurbished.

Its rooms offer some of the best views of Varca Beach, while the suites are a statement in elegance and sophistication. Rooms have whirlpool baths and private sit-outs among a whole host of luxuries, while suites have separate dining, sitting, and bedroom areas (and in some cases, a whirlpool tub). The pick of the lot, however, are the magnificent Radisson Suites, which come with a four-poster bed and a sprawling living area. The hotel also offers air-conditioned tents by the beach and rooms designed for guests with special needs. It has six restaurants and bars that serve everything from teppenyaki to grilled seafood, and from sake to *feni*.

Although it's a has-been five-star that has enjoyed better seasons, **Holiday Inn Resort Goa** (Mobor Beach, Cavelossim, tel. 0832/287-1303, www.holidayinngoa.com, Rs 5,300–24,000) is still worth considering. It has a pool, spa, casino, disco, tennis, and a host of other activities and facilities that make for a pleasant stay. Rooms are large and well appointed, and have a view of the pool or garden; one room is dedicated to customers with special needs. The resort also has Goan-Portuguese garden suites that have a private balcony and whirlpool tub. The family-friendly "kids' room" is a sprawling suite with a bunk bed for children—with a Treasure Island mural, games, and soft toys. Meanwhile, the most exclusive room in the resort—the Sunset Suite—offers an intimate and spectacular view of the sunset from its private balcony. The resort has a number of dining options, including a 24-hour café that serves traditional Goan cuisine, a pan-Asian restaurant, an Indian village-style diner, a fish grill, and a bar.

Next door is the ◖ **The Leela** (Mobor, Cavelossim, tel. 0832/287-1234, www.theleela .com, rates upon request), also referred to as The Leela Palace, alluding to its architectural resemblance to an Indian summer palace. A vast, open lobby with traditional Indian lamps and marigold flowers leads into the sprawling beachside property surrounded by lush greenery. The hotel comprises Portuguese-style villas, lagoon suites, and a new complex of one-bedroom suites and a pool called The Club. All rooms have lovely terraces, while deluxe suites come with private plunge pools. The Leela makes for a secluded getaway for those seeking solitude and, at the same time, offers activity and entertainment to those who desire it. The luxury hotel complex includes seven restaurants, a discotheque, casino, spa, sports (including a 12-hole golf course), games, and a children's activity center.

FOOD

Varca and Cavelossim have a variety of fine-dining restaurants, as well as a number of beach shacks and restaurants serving great local cuisine. At the top of this list is **Fisherman's Wharf** (next to Holiday Inn, Mobor, Cavelossim, tel. 0832/287-1317, fishermanswharfgoa@gmail.com, 11 A.M.–midnight daily, mains Rs 150 and up), a lovely open-air restaurant by the River Sal and just across the Betul jetty. Its relaxed air translates into relaxed rules—like lunch service until early evening. Known for its local-style seafood, it draws patrons from the surrounding five stars (and even from North Goa) for its grilled items, calamari, and crab dishes. A great place to bird-watch or simply watch the ferries glide past, it also doubles up as a nightspot and entertainment zone with its excellent bar, live music, and water sports. If you'd like to go fishing, you'll be provided with tackle—and can have your proud catch cooked by the chef. Alternately,

you can be provided with a barbecue set and marinade for an outdoor grill under a canopy. The restaurant is also planning a "fish bazaar" that will allow you to pick your fish and then include it in a set meal with salad and dessert.

A local favorite, **Betty's Place** (near The Leela, Mobor, tel. 0832/287-1456, www.bettysgoa.com, 7–11 P.M. daily Oct.–Apr., mains Rs 150 and up) is a garden restaurant known for its local cuisine. While seafood preparations such as crab masala and prawn curry are popular, there are also a variety of steaks and tandoori items on the menu. The restaurant has a bar and organizes evening entertainment, such as fire shows and karaoke nights.

GETTING THERE AND AROUND

Varca and Cavelossim take a little over an hour to reach from Dabolim Airport by cab. The journey costs around Rs 650. A taxi ride from Madgaon Station should take half an hour and cost Rs 400.

To get to Betul, it's best to take a ferry across the river from Cavelossim. The ferry will drop you off at Assolna, from where it is a short distance to Betul. However, you can also come directly from Madgaon by bus—buses to Chinchinim will stop at Betul village.

Meanwhile, cycles and scooters may be hired from the villages for exploration—your hotel reception ought to be able to help you arrange local transport.

Palolem and Vicinity

After the rural charm of the fishing village of Betul, the southern seascape takes on a different hue in the district of Canacona. As if miraculously, sands turn whiter and the sea becomes more blue. Meanwhile, above palm trees and a soaring cliff is the solitary Cabo de Rama Fort, keeping watch over the ebb and flow of the tide below. Farther south, at Agonda, it seems as if time has stood still. A few modest village resorts, beach huts, and friendly rural folk add cheer to the vacation of tourists seeking a more pristine Goa—away from the hustle bustle of the crowds and the disco beats of parties only a few kilometers away in Palolem.

In Palolem, the psychedelic colors of the sky at sunset reflect the mindset of its party-happy backpacking visitors. By day, the beach is a beautiful crescent curve surrounded by green hillocks and leafy islands inhabited by butterflies. At dusk, graceful palms take a bow as bathers leave the beach, trading the sound of the ocean for the soundless pounds of party tracks at Palolem's Silent Noise parties. The beach then stretches over to Patnem—where peace reigns once again—and ends at Rajbag in a grand and fitting finale with the coming together of river and sea, witnessed by the only sign of tourist life: the InterContinental.

AGONDA

As you make your way from Betul to the far south, chancing upon the tranquil Agonda Beach is nothing short of sweet serendipity. The beautiful coastal drive leads you through hills and plains, with the ocean in plain view all along, guiding you toward your destination. Agonda Beach has almost negligible tourist activity. It works to Agonda's advantage, presenting an equivalent, almost, of northern counterpart Mandrem. A secluded beach lined with palm groves, beach huts, and a scatter of small, village accommodations, it has succeeded in preserving its precious solitude by fighting off big hotel development. A church and a small canal along the village road add

to the rustic charm. A safe, rural place where you're likely to be well cared for by friendly village folk, this is where village Goa meets the beach.

Cabo de Rama Fort

On the way—just 12 kilometers short of Agonda—a small detour leads to the ruined Cabo de Rama Fort, standing sentinel over the Arabian Sea—much like the Chapora Fort of Vagator. Unlike Chapora, however, the ill-maintained fort cuts a sorry figure from up close, although the view it affords is just as stunning. The present fort dates to 1763, when it was rebuilt by the Portuguese, from the original structure built by the former Hindu rulers. Local legend also says that this was a rest stop for Lord Rama, protagonist of the Hindu epic **Ramayana.** Today, the undergrowth of tangled shrubs makes way, briefly, for an old stone

In the face of tourism, pristine Agonda Beach retains its strong rural flavor.

© ASHIMA NARAIN

The ruins of the Cabo de Rama Fort afford a sweeping view of the Arabian Sea.

stairway leading up to a platform rimmed with ramparts and cannons, once part of a magnificent fort (that was later used as a prison until 1955). In contrast, within the fort compound, is the whitewashed and impeccably kept St. Anthony's Church.

Accommodations and Food

Agonda is one of the least commercially active beaches in Goa; it saw little tourist activity before its first resort, Dunhill, arrived in 1982. Today, it remains wonderfully unspoiled, thanks to the efforts of the villagers, and offers only a handful of shacks, beach huts, and basic budget hotels that offer home-cooked meals and cocktails. That said, the beach is currently witness to building activity at Praia de Agonda (praiadeagonda@gmail.com)—a new eco-resort that will offer tennis courts and a swimming pool on the premises. Agonda being a tiny village, most accommodation and restaurants tend to be on the beach itself or on the village road parallel to the beach.

Responsible for placing Agonda on the tourist map, **Dunhill Resort** (Agonda Beach, tel.

0832/264-7328, dunhill_resort@rediffmail. com, Rs 300–600) is a simple property owned and managed by the Fernandes family since 1982. A shaded village-style construction, it has a few small and basic but comfortable rooms with clean bathrooms. It also has an open restaurant area with an awning where home-style local food, as well as Italian and European dishes, are served. Taxi services are arranged for guests.

Another old favorite, **Dersy Cottages** (Tambdem, Agonda Beach, tel. 0832/264-7503, Rs 300–400) is an unattractive construction without much of a view. It offers both beach huts and cramped, functional rooms with clean bathrooms. Outside, in the bar and restaurant area, everything from home-cooked pork chops to steak, grilled fish and local dishes are served along with beer and cocktails. Here, too, taxi services are arranged for guests.

Farther down the road, **River-Side** (Agonda Beach, tel. 0832/264-7021, Rs 300–500) is located off the beach and along a small canal. Rooms open out to the canal and have clean bathrooms, as well as a kitchen area. If you want to stay closer to the beach, they also have a few beach huts. They have a restaurant and bar by the same name along the beach that serves local cuisine, as well as Chinese and Italian dishes.

Meanwhile, at the far end, is the quiet cluster of cottages called **Forget Me Not** (Agonda Beach, tel. 0832/264-7611, Rs 300–600). These rustic cottages are simple but come with attached bathrooms and have a vegetarian restaurant that serves home-cooked meals.

Don't let the name deceive you, because surprisingly good accommodations are available at **Common Home** (House no. 398/I, Wahl, Agonda Beach, tel. 0832/264-7890, www.commonhomeindia.com, Rs 500–1,500). Beautifully furnished rooms with carved wood and air-conditioning are available on this lovely property with some sea view. The place also offers beach huts and has a lawn in front. There's a vegetarian restaurant that serves *puri bhaji* and an all-you-can-eat vegetarian platter *(thaali)* for Rs 75.

THE SOUTHERN COAST

Common Home is a beautiful property, right on the beach.

The newly built **Cuba** (Agonda Beach, cell tel. 91/98221-83775, www.cubagoa.com, Rs 1,000–3,500) is part of the larger chain of beach shacks found along the Goan coast. Large, well-furnished, and air-conditioned beach bungalows are equipped with modern amenities, including safes. The resort also has five un-air-conditioned rooms at a lower rate. The beach restaurant and bar are known for good local cuisine and a vibrant nightlife. The hotel arranges airport transfer for guests.

Getting There and Around

Agonda is about two hours from Dabolim Airport; taxi fare costs about Rs 1,100. From Madgaon Station, it is around 40 kilometers and costs Rs 620 by pre-paid taxi. A number of buses from Madgaon and Canacona also stop at Agonda. Once there, most of the shacks and resorts provide taxis and rent bikes for visits to neighboring beaches and sights.

◖ PALOLEM

A crescent beach covered with soft, white sand and shaded by swaying palm trees, Palolem is South Goa's most popular destination. From its view of the tiny Green Island, which emerges from the sea like a psychedelic fantasy, to its endless row of bamboo shacks and flame-throwers at night, Palolem is like an exotic extravaganza from the Moulin Rouge. Also known as Paradise Beach, it was until recently as isolated as Varca, but has become the place of choice for young budget travelers and backpackers.

Palolem is also a major party destination, known particularly for its Silent Noise parties—an innovative solution to the 10 P.M. noise curfew. Young revelers groove to the beats belted out by a host of international DJs...on their headphones. Like Palolem's silent party animals, the beach has a number of quirks, including the colorful butterflies that flit above your boat even when you're far out at sea. It is no wonder, therefore, that one of its major attractions is **Butterfly Beach,** accessed by boat. A number of tour operators organize trips to this little piece of paradise, with barbecues on the beach.

Palolem's soft white sands and clear waters are looked over by its surrounding thickly forested hills and islands. From the sea, it is a

Palolem's beautiful beach is framed by green hillocks, secret coves, and palm trees.

© ASHIMA NARAIN

THE SOUTHERN COAST

spectacular sight of undulating beach hemmed in by tall palms and alternating coves and hillocks. Lined by makeshift beach shacks and cheap, rudimentary accommodations, it also offers a "back to nature" experience at places such as Bhakti Kutir. On the beach, meanwhile, sunbathers lie sprawled on the sand and water-sports operators lure tourists with promises of dolphin sightings and money-back guarantees. At the northern end of the beach is **Palolem Island,** connected to the headland by a strip of land that allows you to walk there during low tide. At the southern end is the unimpressive little cove, **Colomb Bay**—a tiny stretch of rocks and sand lined with fishing boats and residual oil from the sea.

Nightlife

Palolem has the most vibrant nightlife in the south, and is often compared to Anjuna on the northern coast. Once popular for all-night raves, it is now known for its unique **Silent Noise parties** (tel. 91/97309-35334, www .silentnoise.in), held at a beachside location called Neptune's Point that comprises a grassy field, sand, rocks, and a breathtaking view of the Palolem coastline. Low on noise but big on visuals, the parties are a visual spectacle with their large image-flashing AV screens, disco lights, fire dancers, circus acts, tarot card readers and bonfires. House, electro, retro and other beats bombard headphones while onlookers can only see dancers grooving to the sounds of silence.

For traditional party animals, a number of noisy parties still take place at Palolem's beach shacks. Parties can sometimes get rowdy here, but **Café Del Mar** (Palolem Beach, cell tel. 91/98232-76520, 24 hr, Oct.–Apr.) is where young party-goers head for a night out. A popular watering hole that serves both alcohol and food (good kebabs and grilled items) until the wee hours, it is not unusual to see a scuffle at this wood-and-bamboo shack where revelers dance to the thumping beats of pop and house music played by DJs, or of international musicians performing live.

Part of a chain of beach shacks across Goa,

Cuba (Palolem Beach, cell tel. 91/98221-83775, www.cubagoa.com, 8 A.M.–midnight daily, Oct.–Apr.) is a beach bar with a relaxed vibe. Littered with beanbags, it is known for its Mexican food and live performances. Especially crowded during football matches, it also has a pool table and is the ideal place to chill out or shake a leg.

Packed even in the low season, **Silver Star** (Palolem Beach, tel. 0832/264-3113, 24 hr daily) is open 24/7. A beachside hotel with basic rooms and a restaurant-shack, it turns into a party zone after dark. The revelry continues until well after the stipulated 10 P.M. deadline, thanks largely to the local clout of the two brothers who own the place. A local DJ plays popular tracks in the makeshift discotheque area even as a wooden cross, outside, keeps guard.

Shopping

Palolem has plenty of streetside shopping, and stalls are assembled as soon as the monsoon ends. Hippie clothing, beach wear, bags, trinkets, handicrafts, and all other items and souvenirs that are available in the bustling markets of North Goa may be found here.

Sports and Recreation

Palolem offers varied activities for recreation, ranging from water sports on the beach to wildlife-viewing at the nearby Cotigao Wildlife Sanctuary. Some shacks and hotels provide kayaks and cycles and most will be able to guide you to a boat operator.

BOAT TRIPS

There are plenty of operators who will solicit their boat services—everything from early-morning dolphin cruises to fishing and overnight island trips—at the beach. Be sure to bargain hard—and inquire at your hotel about the ever-changing standard rate—before you finally agree upon a price. Taxi operators such as **Mr. Dolphin** (Palolem Beach, tel. 0832/264-4614) also arrange for dolphin cruises. However, be sure to confirm the rate once again before you get on to the boat or you may be in for a rude surprise once you're at sea.

YOGA

Holistic resort **Bhakti Kutir** (296, Colomb, Palolem, tel. 0832/264-3469, www.bhakti-kutir.com) offers yoga lessons (8–9:30 A.M. daily, Rs 200; 10–11 A.M. daily, Rs150; and 4–5 P.M. daily, Rs 150) in the tradition of T. Krishnamacharya, in January and February. Also open to non-guests, the course is for both beginners and practicing students.

Accommodations

When tourists first began to arrive on the Palolem shores, a few rudimentary coco-huts and thatched shacks went up to accommodate them. Living arrangements were basic and bathrooms were mostly shared. Today, a total of 62 shacks line the beach and a number of resorts, big and small, lie scattered around the beach and its environs. Visitors, meanwhile, come to Palolem in droves, fueling the constant demand for lodging—and often settle for a small windowless room with a pig toilet as long as there's the beach at the doorstep.

UNDER RS 1,000

A good beachside budget option, **Silver Star** (Palolem Beach, tel. 0832/264-3113, Rs 300–1,000) is a concrete structure with cramped, basic rooms and shared verandahs. Bathrooms are attached and living arrangements are clean and comfortable. Avoid the rooms near the restaurant area, however, or you'll be left wide-eyed at night by the pounding beats of the disco. The resort has a lovely ocean-facing restaurant-shack where friendly and efficient waiters serve Goan and European fare, as well as cocktails from a well-stocked bar. Open 24/7, it is also known for its all-night parties.

At the far northern end of the beach, accessed by a footbridge by the riverside, are the beach huts of **Ordosounsar** (Palolem Beach Riverside, cell tel. 91/98224-88769, www.ordosounsar.com, Rs 500–1,000). Made of bamboo, on stilts, and with thatched roofs, the huts are secluded and have shared bathrooms.

The resort also has basic rooms at ground level with attached baths. A restaurant serves local cuisine. Strewn with hammocks and with a recreation area and bar, this is one of the better shack accommodations in the area.

RS 1,000-3,000

Occupying the vantage point on Palolem Beach is the **⟨ Palolem Beach Resort** (tel. 0832/264-3054, www.goainns.com/palolembeachresort, Rs 1,000–2,000). One of the nicer places to stay, the resort comprises both cottages and tents with the option of attached bathrooms. Located amid lawns and gardens, and shaded by palm trees, cottages have little verandahs and balconies. All rooms are equipped with wardrobes and TVs, and some have air-conditioning. The resort has an Ayurvedic massage parlor and a lovely café with an intimate view of the sea and its various islands. Goan, North Indian, and European dishes are served here, along with beer and cocktails.

John Douglas Coutinho's **⟨ Ciaran's** (Palolem Beach, tel. 0832/264-3477, www.ciarans.com, Rs 2,500–3,900) is a fabulous option with its wood-and-coir cottages or cabanas. Dismantled and lovingly re-constructed each season, all accommodations are made from local materials such as bamboo, mud, straw, and coir. The result is a cluster of extremely attractive rooms with attached baths and sit-outs, and two cottages even have air-conditioning. The resort has garden cottages, ocean-view cottages, and sundeck cottages—which have lovely roof seating and rooftop day beds with a clear view of the sea. The resort is strewn with hammocks and has plenty of nooks where guests can lounge around, reading a book from the in-house library. The restaurant is laid out in the open and serves both Goan as well as European cuisine. It is especially known for its seafood and for its excellent Christmas dinner.

If you're one for natural living, healthy eating, yoga, Ayurveda, and the like, **⟨ Bhakti Kutir** (296, Colomb, Palolem, tel. 0832/264-3469, www.bhaktikutir.com, Rs 800–3,000) is the place for you. A small, forested haven that creates its own ecofriendly world, away from the mad rush of the beach parties, Bhakti Kutir ("House of Devotion") is run by a Goan-German couple. Situated on a small hillock 200 meters above the beach, this unusual back-to-nature place overlooks Colomb Bay. Wooden Kerala-style cottages and cabanas are shaded by dense foliage, while a community-and-restaurant area with an open kitchen turns strangers into family within no time at this warm and friendly eco-resort. The German owner, Ute, is seen chatting with her guests, who are free to use the kitchen for an interactive cooking experience. Cabanas are made from natural local materials such as bamboo, mud, and straw, and come with attached ecofriendly compost toilets. If you're not one for roughing it out, however, be warned that the foliage attracts mosquitoes, hot water (in a bucket) takes a while, and water runs out quickly in the morning. The resort also offers Ayurvedic massage treatments and courses as well as yoga and meditation. Close enough to the beach and yet a serene, secluded getaway that brings together like-minded people, Bhakti Kutir makes for a calming, meditative living experience.

Opposite Bhakti Kutir, is the new me-too resort, **Sevas** (Palolem-Colomb, tel. 0832/264-3977, www.sevaspalolem.com, Rs 400–1,500, Oct.–Apr.). Unlike its pioneering neighbor, however, it offers basic huts and cabanas with thatched roofs and bamboo walls. En-suite bathroom facilities are available, as are larger family cottages with laterite walls and tiled roofing. The resort also has a restaurant that serves local Goan meals, and offers Ayurvedic massages, currency exchange, and Internet facilities.

A little way from the beach but charming nevertheless, **Oceanic Hotel** (Timbavaddu, Palolem, tel. 0832/264-3059, www.hotel-oceanic.com, Rs 750–3,500) is an ambient resort owned by an English couple and located on a terraced hillock between the beaches of Palolem and Patnem. It makes up for its lack of proximity to the sea with a swimming pool and is a great place for families, with its baby monitors and kids pool. Living arrangements are tasteful and comfortable—standard rooms are simple, while double rooms have a balcony, and deluxe rooms come with the option of air-conditioning. There's a poolside restaurant that serves everything from Goan, Chinese, and European dishes to baby food, and the hotel also organizes live classical Indian music. There are a number of amenities, including massage therapy and free wireless Internet. Friendly staff, good management, and peaceful surroundings make this a pleasant option.

Food

Palolem's restaurants and shacks are located in and around the beach, or on its main street parallel to the beach. Beach shacks and nightspots such as **Cuba** (Palolem Beach, cell tel. 91/98221-83775, www.cubagoa.com, 8 A.M.–midnight daily, Oct.–Apr., mains Rs 70 and up) and **Silver Star** (Palolem Beach, tel. 0832/264-3113, 24 hr daily, mains Rs 70 and up) also serve excellent food and double up as popular eating joints during the day.

◖ **Smuggler's Inn** (Palolem, tel. 0832/264-3354, smugglers_goa@yahoo.co.in, 9 A.M.–11 P.M. daily, mains Rs 150 and up) on the main street greets you with the line, "Old smugglers never die, they only smell that way." Its fun, cheerful decor with pirate murals was painted by the British expat owner's husband, a ship's captain. Known for its delicious steaks and pastas, burgers and healthy salads, the quaint restaurant also has plenty of options for vegetarians. Frequented as much for its ambience as it is for its cuisine, it has two DVD lounges for people who get "beached out" and organizes theme nights. Weekends are reserved for football, while weeknights year-round include special dance nights, ladies' nights, and corporate nights. The cocktail lounge serves a variety of liquors to go with the meals.

Down the road is another delightful British-owned restaurant with an amusing name: **Cheeky Chapatti** (Palolem, ljlowy@hotmail.com, 9 A.M.–11 P.M. daily, mains Rs 100 and up) serves everything from South Indian cuisine to Italian fare and Sunday roasts with fish.

Also known for excellent salads and wraps, the menu changes with every season. Christmas meals tend to be special, usually with a bit of lobster thrown in.

An old beachside favorite, **Dropadi Bar & Restaurant** (Palolem Beach, cell tel. 91/93261-27437, www.goyam.net, 9 A.M.–midnight daily Aug.–Apr., mains Rs 100 and up) is a simple shack known for its local and other cuisines. A great place for breakfast, lunch, and dinner, this is where all the Palolem beach bums gorge on spicy curries, tandoori, and pasta.

Information and Services

Palolem has a number of places where you can change money and use the Internet. Located on the main street near the beach are **Bliss Travels** (263/3, near Main gate, Palolem Beach, tel. 0832/264-3456, blisstravels@rediffmail.com, 8:30 A.M.–10 P.M.daily May–Sept. and 8:30 A.M.–midnight daily Oct.–Apr., Rs 50 per hour) and **Dolphin Travels** (Palolem Beach, tel. 0832/264-5236, 8 A.M.–11 P.M. daily, Rs 40 per hour). **Rainbow Travels** (Palolem Beach, tel. 0832/264-3912, sitaben@hotmail.com, 9 A.M.–6 P.M. daily) does currency exchange and gives advances on credit and debit cards. There are no ATMs in Palolem, although the nearest town, Chaudi, farther south, has ATMs at HDFC, Canara Bank, and State Bank of India.

Getting There and Around

From Dabolim Aiport, Palolem is nearly a two-hour journey that costs about Rs 1,200 by cab. Not all trains halt at the nearest railway station at Canacona, so you will most likely need to alight at Madgaon. From here, it is an hour's journey by cab, costing Rs 800. Alternately, you may also take a direct bus from Madgaon to Palolem or one that stops at Chaudi, taking an auto-rickshaw for the onward journey.

To get around Palolem, it is best to hire a cycle or a motorcycle if you find the walk tiresome. Most hotels, travel agents, and money-changers will be able to help you. Bikes generally cost Rs 150–300 per day.

MALLIKARJUN TEMPLE

Just five kilometers from Chaudi, the nearest town to Palolem, this historical temple dates back to the 16th century. Rebuilt in 1778, and dedicated to Mallikarjun—an incarnation of Lord Shiva—it is also houses a number of other deities. It is known for its wooden pillars with intricate carvings as well as scenes from the epic *Mahabharata*. According to local myth, the temple lies on the spot where Shiva and his consort, Parvati, came together after a period of separation from each other. An annual temple festival is celebrated here every year when the deity is carried out in a public procession on a chariot.

You can hire a taxi or an auto-rickshaw to go to the temple from either Palolem or Chaudi.

© ASHIMA NARAIN

The Cotigao Wildlife Sanctuary shelters a wealth of wildlife, including deer, black panthers, and king cobras.

COTIGAO WILDLIFE SANCTUARY

Located in southeastern Goa, the Cotigao Wildlife Sanctuary (Hathipal, Poinginim, Canacona, tel. 0832/296-5601, adults Rs 5, children Rs 2, car Rs 50, bike Rs 20, photography Rs 25, videography Rs 100) stretches over an area of about 85 square kilometers and borders the neighboring state of Karnataka. Home to a wealth of flora and fauna, the sanctuary shelters rare animals such as the black panther and the king cobra, as well as the sloth bear, leopard, flying squirrel, barking deer, pangolin, Russel's viper, crested serpent eagle and black-headed oriole, among others. The sanctuary has several treetop watchtowers built around watering holes, but unless you stay in the sanctuary itself, there's little likelihood of spotting anything other than monkeys. In case of disappointment, there's a deer park and a rescue shelter where snakes and animals found outside of their natural habitat are displayed to visitors before they are released back into the wild.

Accommodations and Food

The Cotigao Wildlife Sanctuary offers **tents and simple cottages** (tel. 0832/296-5601, Rs 250–500) within park limits. Tents and cottages are large enough to accommodate four people, while the Peacock Cottage is a spacious suite with a verandah and red-tile roof. The sanctuary also has a 24-hour garden restaurant.

Just outside of the sanctuary is a more pleasant alternative: spice plantation **Pepper Valley** (Dabemola, Partagal, tel. 0832/264-2370, Oct.–Apr.) offers accommodations and a restaurant. Its huts are basic but beautifully shaded by cashew and spice trees on the banks of the river Talpona. It has a restaurant and small bar overlooking the plantation where you can try the seafood platter, Goan-style chicken, and vegetarian dishes seasoned with spices from the surroundings.

Getting There

From Palolem, the Cotigao sanctuary is best reached by private vehicle, motorcycle, or taxi, and is a 20-minute drive, just off the NH 17 to Karwar.

PATNEM AND RAJBAG

Just 1.5 kilometers south of Palolem and Colomb Bay, away from the beach parties and water sports, is quiet Patnem Beach. An unspoiled version of Palolem, this vast stretch of sand sees a few beached boats, the stray sun bed, and mostly, clear blue waters. The marked absence of tourist activity lends to the wonderful seclusion and relaxed air of this piece of the golden southern coast. Few people come to Patnem by choice, however, and usually find themselves here when accommodations in Palolem are scarce—only to be pleasantly surprised.

Two kilometers farther south from Patnem, Rajbag Beach is the southernmost tourist-accessible point in Goa. Stretching to the mouth of the Talpona River, Rajbag is one of the most isolated and romantic of beaches in Goa. Practically the private beach of luxury hotel the InterContinental, access to Rajbag is only through the hotel premises. Some of the most beautiful sunsets may be viewed from here and the hotel even offers tent accommodations on the seashore. In contrast with the sprawling five-star, at the farthest end of the property is the rural scene of fisherfolk seeking their catch, and of women washing clothes along the river.

Nightlife

Serene Rajbag is slowly developing a nightlife of its own. The InterContinental serves cocktails, wine, and cigars at its Mario Miranda–inspired **Very Feni** (noon–midnight daily, cocktails Rs 250 and up). Visitors can groove on the dance floor here to music belted out by the DJ.

Guests at the InterContinental can also enjoy the sunken, poolside bar **Gazebo** (11 A.M.–7 P.M. daily, cocktails Rs 250 and up).

However, the newest entrant on this stretch is **The End** (Rajbag Beach, cell tel. 98221-83775, www.cubagoa.com), yet another addition to the Cuba family. Sun beds, music, and river and ocean views give way to parties and entertainment after dark. Known for good cocktails and tapas, The End heralds the end of Rajbag's peace and quiet.

Sports and Recreation
WATER SPORTS

The **InterContinental** is the only luxury hotel in Goa to organize its own water sports managed by British expat Captain Paul Moore. A jocular ship's captain who is full of adventure stories (and artistic talents—he also owns the popular Smuggler's Inn in Palolem, where he painted the pirate murals himself), he organizes snorkeling, Jet Skiing, ringo rides, and scuba diving with the help of hotel staff specially trained by him. Safety norms are strictly adhered to. However, the apple of his eye is the beautiful luxury yacht, the MV *Blue Diamond* (Rs 18,000/hour, accommodates up to 12 people). A lovely boat that has everything from a bar to a sun deck and a smaller inflatable boat attached to it for ferrying people, it is hired out to guests as well as the rich and the famous. It is also used for trips to surrounding islands that others cannot access. The *Blue Diamond* as well as the water sports are open to non-guests and Captain Paul is happy to customize trips. From group trips and parties to romantic twosomes with champagne and caviar, the boat has seen some good times and is the pride of the InterContinental.

GOLF

The lush greens of the golf course at the **InterContinental** are offset by the rose sunset on the beach in the background. Nine-hole (Rs 1,455 for non-guests, includes tax, green fees, golf set, and caddy) and 18-hole (Rs 2,265 for non-guests, includes tax, green fees, golf set and caddy) golfing are available and free to guests. The hotel also hosts tournaments and has a golf professional on staff for lessons.

SPA

If you're looking for a bit of pampering, the **Rejuve Spa** at the InterContinental is one

The golf course at the InterContinental is open to guests and non-guests.

of the most luxurious in Goa, made up of 10 rooms, including a spa suite. Thai specialists, Swedish massage experts, and Kerala Ayurvedic therapists and masseurs impart various treatments (Rs 1,000–5,000) to both guests and non-guests. The spa menu is varied and there's a whirlpool bath, a hydrotherapy tub, an outdoor plunge pool, and an ambient chilled pool. Each treatment room has a private relaxation area and you can treat your tired feet to a foot massage or reflexology (Rs 1,000–2,000). You can also get an Ayurvedic consultation (Rs 1,500) with the resident doctor, who will then recommend the therapy most suited to your body type.

Accommodations and Food

Apart from the Oceanic Hotel located midway between Palolem and Patnem, there's not very much in terms of accommodations as you go down to the far south. Patnem has a smattering of beach shacks and small guesthouses, with new ones coming up as Palolem

© ASHIMA NARAIN

THE SOUTHERN COAST

begins to get crowded. Rajbag has only one hotel—the five-star InterContinental Grand Goa Resort—but even this beach has seen some construction activity of late with the Cuba Royal Resort (www.cubagoa.com) to be opened shortly.

Just around the corner from the beach but not on the beach itself, **Sea View Resort** (Patnem Beach, tel. 0832/264-3110, www. seaviewpatnem.com, Rs 350–3,500) is a cluster of family-run cottages and rooms. The Goan-style cottages are a good value, and have a skylight as well as a verandah and a little lawn in front. The resort also has a few air-conditioned rooms, with the deluxe rooms being a bit more spacious than the rest. The un-air-conditioned deluxe rooms have a little kitchen area, and all rooms are clean and well kept. The resort has numerous facilities, including an Internet café and an Ayurvedic massage center. Attached to the resort is the **Sea View Restaurant and Bar** (7:30 A.M.–10:30 P.M. daily, mains Rs 80 and up), which serves a variety of cuisines including Goan, North Indian, Italian, and Mexican.

Part of the popular chain, **Cuba** (Patnem Beach, cell tel. 91/98221-83775, Rs 2,000–4,500) has shack and cottage accommodations on the beach. Shaded by palm trees and facing the ocean, rooms are beautifully designed and have thatched roofs and little sit-outs. While the exteriors are painted in cheerful hues, the interiors are comfortable and all rooms have attached baths. The resort has a restaurant-shack and bar in the tradition of the Cuba chain, which serves a variety of cuisines and cocktails.

You know you're home and dry when you arrive at **Home** (Patnem Beach, tel. 0832/264-3916, www.homeispatnem.com, Rs 1,500–2,200 high season, negotiable in the low season). A small guesthouse that resembles a village home with its Spartan rooms and tiled roof, this is the best option for accommodation in Patnem. Located on the beach, rooms are simple but have verandahs that overlook the surrounding garden and ocean. The resort

also has a restaurant (9 A.M.–sunset daily) that serves great juices, vegetarian dishes, spicy curries, and coffee.

The sprawling 34-hectare **InterContinental Grand Goa Resort** (Rajbag Beach, tel. 0832/266-7777, www. intercontinental.com, Rs 8,500–25,000) calls itself an "all suites hotel." With the largest rooms in Goa and more suites than any other five-star property, this magnificent resort is the only one on this beautiful stretch with the sea, quite literally, at its doorstep. The beach is almost private, as the only access is through the InterContinental property—although there are plans for a separate access as other resorts and restaurants slowly make inroads here. A vast golf course is framed by the ocean, while a spa, luxury yacht, swimming pool, tennis, and squash courts provide plenty of opportunities for recreation and relaxation.

As you enter the lobby, a combination of Goan architecture and five-star opulence

© ASHIMA NARAIN

The InterContinental Grand Goa Resort

greets you. And don't be surprised if, along with your traditional welcome of a shell garland, you hear the guest relations officer speak Russian. This is the favored accommodation for Russian charter tourists, as well as a popular venue for weddings, corporate seminars, and other events. The beautiful sunlit property comprises elegant pool- and sea-facing rooms with classical decor and the latest in gadgets and technology. The hotel also has bright, airy, and comfortable Executive Club rooms. Occupying pride of place, however, are the magnificent Luxury and Presidential suites. All suites have a spectacular sea view and include butler service and limo transfer. While luxury suites have one bedroom and doors that open out to a verandah or a balcony, the two grand Presidential suites have a sprawling living area and two large bedrooms. In addition, the hotel also houses a cluster of magnificent villas with private pools. If you're looking for a closer sea view, the InterContinental also has luxury tent accommodation on the beach.

Dining options in the hotel include the seafood grill **Sea BQ** (12:30–3 P.M. and 7–11 P.M. daily), which has a set menu (Rs 1,200) where fish, crab, lobster, and tiger prawns are all prepared before you teppenyaki-style. **Canacona** (7:30–10:30 A.M., 12:30–3 P.M., and 7:30–11 P.M. daily, mains Rs 300 and up) serves good dinner buffets—Indian, East Asian, and Continental—as well as à la carte meals that include pastas and wood-fired pizzas. **Sirocco** (5:30–11 P.M. daily, mains Rs 400 and up) serves Mediterranean fare, and the beachfront restaurant **Corta's** (5:30–11 P.M. daily Oct.–Apr., mains Rs 400 and up) specializes in Goan cuisine. And if you want to simply relax with a drink, head to the hotel's two bars.

Getting There and Around

Patnem is 65 kilometers from Dabolim Aiport; it's nearly two hours by taxi, and costs about Rs 1,000. Not all trains halt at the nearest railway station at Canacona, so you will most likely need to alight at Madgaon. From here, it is an hour's journey by cab, costing around Rs 800. Alternately, you may also take a direct bus from Madgaon to Palolem via Canacona Station (the Patnem stop is just outside Sea View Resort) or one thats at Chaudi, taking an auto-rickshaw for the onward journey.

For Rajbag, the InterContinental has an airport shuttle for guests that charges $20 one-way. By train, Madgaon Station is 35 kilometers away and taxis charge a little over Rs 1,000. Buses are also available from Madgaon to Chaudi, from where it is one kilometer to Rajbag by auto-rickshaw.

To get around the far south, check with your hotel or shack for cycle or motorcycle hire. Bikes generally cost Rs 150–300 per day.

GETAWAYS AROUND GOA

Within easy reach of Goa, in the neighboring states of Karnataka and Maharashtra, are some of the most spectacular sights and destinations in the country. Over the years, the typical Goan holiday has come to include many of these for a richer, fuller experience. The best of these satellite destinations lie in the relatively undiscovered state of Karnataka. Under-rated and under-sold, Karnataka makes for a breezy drive down from Goa. Its shady, winding roads open out along the breathtaking golden coast of Karwar, tracing its sinuous curves, overlooking stray fishing boats on deserted beaches, dishing out a montage of seaside village scenes and readying the traveler for the quiet beaches of Gokarna. Just over two hours by road from the Goa border, Gokarna resembles the Goan shores of yore, with its near-untouched sands

and absence of commercial activity. Perhaps what distinguishes this destination from Goa is its cliffhanging palms and forests looking down upon clear beaches that are both visual spectacles and soulful getaways.

While Gokarna is close enough to Goa, Hampi is infinitely more magical. Its gigantic boulders and pink-grey monuments reminisce over a glorious past even as pilgrims and tourists lose themselves amid this surreal setting. The River Tungabhadra brings relief to a rocky landscape, as does the occasional paddy field. The small temple town and UNESCO World Heritage Site also receive a regular stream of tourists from Goa, by train and on bike (often heading straight to a rave before they get to the monuments). At Hampi Bazaar, hippie bikers and travel agents have replaced the spice

© JANHAVI ACHAREKAR

HIGHLIGHTS

🌙 **Om Beach:** Swimming, trekking, and ocean-gazing are all possible at Gokarna's famous Om Beach, which gets it name from its unique shape – that of the Hindu symbol Om. A beautiful beach coupled with a green mountainside, it presents a quieter alternative to Goa (page 269).

🌙 **Virupaksha Temple:** The soaring tower of Hampi's central and most significant monument rises from among boulders and ruins to present an elaborate interior and a lovable temple elephant (page 277).

🌙 **Vitthala Temple:** A splendid complex marked by a beautiful stone chariot and 56 musical pillars, this is the venue for the spectacular Hampi Festival (page 278).

🌙 **The Royal Group of Monuments:** A combination of intricate Vijayanagar carving and Islamic architecture, this royal complex is made up of the lovely Lotus Mahal, the Queen's Bath, the Hazara Rama Temple, and the grand Elephant Stables, among other monuments (page 279).

🌙 **Daroji Bear Sanctuary:** A road lined with sunflowers and boulders takes you to the Daroji Bear Sanctuary at Kamalapuram near Hampi, where you can view the sloth bear amid picturesque environs (page 281).

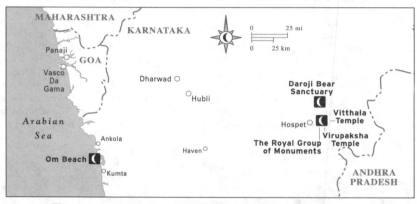

LOOK FOR 🌙 TO FIND RECOMMENDED SIGHTS, ACTIVITIES, DINING, AND LODGING.

merchants and gemstone traders of its medieval past, while small terrace cafés gaze alternately at the ruins and the goings on at the Bazaar.

Much has been said about the wonders of Hampi, and ballads have been sung about its glory. But no matter how much you've heard or read about it, you will find that it is as magnificent and awe-inspiring as you had wished it to be. The ancient city does not disappoint—and it makes a fitting end to a fantastic Goan holiday.

PLANNING YOUR TIME

If you're planning to head to Gokarna and Hampi after a Goan holiday, chances are that you are pressed for time. If you must choose between the two, Hampi is the obvious choice. Gokarna is closer to Goa—a mere three hours from Palolem in the south—but is not half as magical as Hampi; two or three days is ample time for its beaches and temples. A day's trip from Goa and about 10 hours from Gokarna, Hampi deserves a minimum

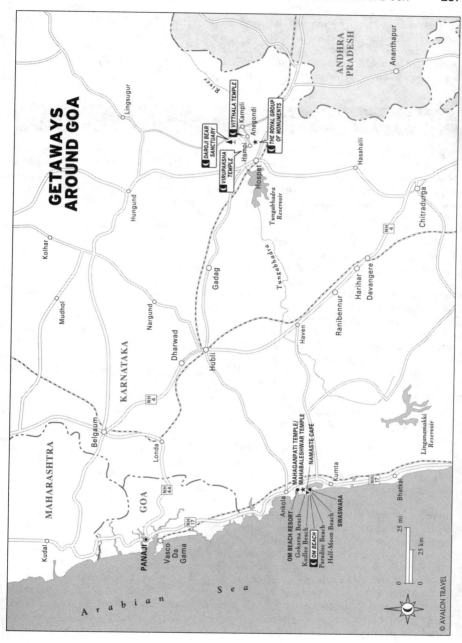

GETAWAYS AROUND GOA

ANDHRA PRADESH

Ananthapur

Lingsugur

River

VITTHALA TEMPLE

Kampli
Anegondi

DAROJI BEAR SANCTUARY

THE ROYAL GROUP OF MONUMENTS

VIRUPAKSHA TEMPLE

Hampi

Hungund

Hospet

Hasahalli

Kolhar

Tungabhadra Reservoir

Chitradurga

NH 4

Mudhol

Gadag

Tungabhadra

Nargund

Harihar
Davangere

Ranibennur

Haven

KARNATAKA

Dharwad

Hubli

NH 4

Belgaum

Lingamamakki Reservoir

Londa

NH 4A

MAHAGANPATI TEMPLE/
MAHABALESHWAR TEMPLE

NAMASTE CAFE

MAHARASHTRA

GOA

NH 17

Kumta

NH 17

Bhatkal

Kudal

PANAJI

Vasco Da Gama

NH 17

Ankola

OM BEACH RESORT
Gokarna Beach
Kudlee Beach
OM BEACH
Paradise Beach
Half-Moon Beach

SWASWARA

Arabian Sea

25 mi

25 km

0

0

© AVALON TRAVEL

of three or four days to be able to take in its surreal beauty and cover its vast expanse of ancient temples and monuments. There are a number of other historical sights and other attractions within easy distance of Hampi, such as the ancient temples of Badami, Aihole, and Pattadakkal. The Tungabhadra Dam and the Daroji Bear Sanctuary also lie close by. A week will allow you to cover these, together with Hampi.

Gokarna

A paradoxical pilgrim and hippie paradise, Gokarna is a 1970s Goa doppelganger. A lazy traditional town with a plethora of soaring cliffs that overlook virgin beaches, it's no wonder this destination is drawing dreadlocked tourists from Goa by the busloads and on bikes. With its medieval temples steeped in mythology, Gokarna is the perfect combination of mysticism and natural landscape, attracting foreign visitors for the exotica and oceana that make up the Great Indian Experience. Visitors range from neo-hippies to pilgrims and even those seeking Ayurveda, yoga, and a bit of solitude—for some, a fitting end to the excesses of a Goan holiday. Its resorts are therefore geared to cater to those seeking holistic living while on the beach, the party continues as shacks and stalls blare music, serving chilled beer and local food.

Gokarna means "cow's ear"; it's named after the ear-shaped confluence of the Rivers Gangavali and Agnashini. To tourists, however, its most significant association is that with the sacred Hindu symbol after which its famous stretch of sand, Om Beach, is named—an appellation derived from its dual crescents that form the shape of the Om symbol. The destination alternates in identity, donning its dual roles of temple town and beach paradise with ease. Its stone temples reverberate with the clanging of bells and chanting of scriptures by *dhoti*-clad holy men. Outside, on the crowded main street, temple priests try their best to persuade passersby to perform temple rituals (for good health, children, marital bliss, and so on) for a fee. For the beach-happy, there's a variety of shores to choose from, ranging from the popular Om Beach to the quiet Kudlee Beach and the hard-to-get-to Half Moon and Paradise Beaches. Brought to notice, predictably, by the hippies, the beaches have retained their original seclusion and serenity. What is missing, perhaps, is the laidback, happy-go-lucky attitude of the people of its neighboring state—that quintessential Goan vibe.

HISTORY

Gokarna has more mythology than history associated with it and there are several stories that narrate its origins. According to one, it is the place where Rudra, an incarnation of Shiva, was born from the forehead of the god Brahma, as the latter performed penance. At first, Rudra was assigned the task of Creation but Brahma soon changed his mind and took it upon himself to create the universe. Angered, Rudra sought ways to come out of the underworld where he was performing penance and finally emerged from the ear of Mother Earth, giving it the name Gokarna (Cow's Ear).

Mythology also says that the *pranalingam,* mother of all *lingams* that may be found in the Shri Mahabaleshwar Temple in Gokarna, was stolen by Ravana in the epic *Ramayana.* When he stopped to meditate at this spot on his way to Lanka, he was intercepted by Lord Ganesh, representative of the gods. Ganesh is said to have placed the *pranalingam* on the ground, which then rooted itself to the spot even as Ravana meditated.

A third story, according to the ancient scriptures called the *Puranas,* states that when Lord Parashurama formed the state of Kerala by throwing his axe into the sea and causing the waters to recede, his action led to the emergence of an entire body of land, stretching from Gokarna to Kanyakumari.

While little is known of the history of this town, records state that the founder of the Vijayanagar empire at Hampi visited Gokarna (which is also believed to have been part of the same empire at one time) to worship the *pranalingam,* as did the Maratha warrior king Shivaji. In later times, the town became a refuge for Hindu Brahmins escaping persecution from the Portuguese in Goa.

SIGHTS

Gokarna's beaches call for hard work. Be prepared for long treks and steep climbs to get to those tempting white sands and turquoise waters. Apart from beach-trekking, a popular tourist activity is to simply soak in the fervent religiosity that charges the bazaar area as pilgrims, priests, vendors, and cows jostle for space amid narrow, winding alleys outside its temples.

◖ Om Beach

It is a spectacular drive through winding roads on green hillocks suspended over a sheer, sweeping oceanscape to Gokarna's famous Om Beach. The beach derives its name from its dual crescent shape, the form of the symbol "Om" in the Indian Devanagari script, believed in Hinduism to have spiritual vibrations. Palm trees, wooded slopes, and the sound of the ocean greet surprised visitors. A small strip of beach peppered with rocks and the odd swimmer, it is a world away from the frenzied water sport–dominated shores of Goa. A late hippie hangout, Om Beach is enjoyed more for its refreshingly different landscape and makes for an enjoyable trek from the nearby Kudlee Beach. However, like all things fantastic, this golden stretch cannot escape the onslaught of commercialization and its pristine sands are now dotted with a few resorts and beach shacks, including the pioneering and ever-popular Namaste Café.

Kudlee Beach

A vision of white sand and blue ocean, framed by verdant hills, Kudlee Beach is approached by a picturesque little shaded path, just off the road that proceeds to Om Beach. A kilometer of untouched beach inhabited by hermit crabs and a few shacks and thatched stalls, this vast open shore is welcome after the long walk here from town. The currents can get quite strong, however, and it is best not to venture too far out at sea, even during the day. With just one rundown resort, the beach is isolated and can get quite dark at night, making it especially unsafe for a night swim.

Half-Moon Beach

A deserted beach accessed only by boat (Rs 50–75) or by a long and difficult but scenic trek through the rocky hillside from Om Beach, Half Moon Beach is worth the sweat. While there is no trailhead, a narrow dirt path is what most trekkers follow. Keep to the left if the path seems to fork out. After the climb, the descent to the beach is along the cliff. It's best to go in a group, get a local to guide you for a small fee, or go by boat. The beach is inaccessible in the monsoon when the steep hillside turns dangerously slippery and the waters are

© ANIL NAIR

Om Beach derives its name from the om symbol in the Indian Devanagari script.

too choppy for boats to traverse. Once there, however, picnickers will find a few stalls but mostly peace and quiet.

Paradise Beach

The last in a line of four magical beaches, Paradise Beach lives up to its name—but only after testing your willpower and strength. If you thought Half Moon Beach was halfway to the moon, then Paradise lies even farther away. Gokarna's most remote beach, a 20-minute hike from Half Moon on a slippery and rocky path along the beach, it sees only a few ardent climbing enthusiasts. Its isolated sun-drenched shore once attracted nudists, but is now a haven for those seeking solitude and willing to go to great lengths for it.

The beach is beautiful, no doubt, but the route is arduous and it takes about an hour to get to the seashore. For those not quite physically inclined, it is also reached by boat, except during the monsoon. You could hire the same boat to both Half Moon and Paradise Beaches (around Rs 200).

Gokarna Beach

The most easily accessible and also the most avoidable, Gokarna Beach is closest to the town center. Reached by a little alley from near the Shri Mahabaleshwar Temple (Car St.), the beach is littered with rubbish and crowded with pilgrims and holy men.

Shri Mahabaleshwar Temple

A temple town, Gokarna is believed to be a holy place because of the presence of one of the most important *shivlings*, called the *pranalingam*. Believed to have been stolen and brought here by Ravana—the villain of the epic *Ramayana*—on his way to Lanka, this holiest of holy shrines was prevented from being taken away, by the Hindu god Ganesh at the behest of the other gods. Disguised as a hermit, Ganesh is said to have offered to take care of the *pranalingam* for Ravana while he meditated. Mythology says that the *pranalingam* was made so heavy by the gods that it dropped to the ground from Ganesh's hands and took root on this auspicious spot.

The Shri Mahabaleshwar Temple is believed to be the holiest of shrines for devotees of Shiva.

© JANHAVI ACHAREKAR

Today, the said *lingam* is believed to be the one found within the Shri Mahabaleshwar Temple (Car St., 6 A.M.–noon and 5–8:30 P.M. daily, open to all faiths but foreigners not allowed into the sanctum sanctorum, visitors must dress modestly). The beautiful stone temple is also worth a visit for its medieval architecture. It comes alive especially during the *mahashivratri* festival in February when pilgrims arrive in the thousands.

Shri Mahaganpati Temple

Located just down the road from the Shri Mahabaleshwar temple, the Shri Mahaganpati Temple (Car St., 6 A.M.–noon and 5–8:30 P.M. daily, open to all faiths but foreigners not allowed into the sanctum sanctorum, visitors must dress modestly) is dedicated to the elephant God Ganesh for his heroic rescue of the *pranalingam*. The quieter and less commercial of the two temples, it has a magnificent chariot in the courtyard. This carved cart carries Hindu deities during the festival of *mahashivratri* and is taken out into the streets, amid much fanfare.

ENTERTAINMENT AND EVENTS

The temple town was once an unlikely combination of religious festivals and raves. While the parties were banned in 2004, following an increase in drugs and crime, Gokarna continues to celebrate a number of religious festivals through the year. The *mahashivratri* festival held in February, as per the lunar calendar, is the biggest event here and draws crowds from all over. The deity is installed in the big chariot and taken around the street in a colorful procession, to offer a glimpse or *darshana* of the idol to the masses, who accompany it with drumbeats and festivity.

SHOPPING

Gokarna is a small temple town with a few shops selling sweets, eats, and religious souvenirs on the main road. On the beaches, a few stalls propped up with the help of cloth and

Religious souvenirs and personas crowd Car Street in Gokarna.

© JANHAVI ACHAREKAR

bamboo, sell trinkets, beachwear, and "Om" t-shirts.

ACCOMMODATIONS

The temple town lacks the variety of Goa as far as accommodations are concerned. However, its range varies from a few run-down budget lodges and home-stays to a fantastic boutique hotel near the beach. Om and Kudlee also see a few beach shack accommodations (sometimes as cheap as Rs 75 per night) that change every year.

Under Rs 1,000

The name is deceptive because at first glance **Hotel Gokarna International** (Main St., tel. 08386/256-622, hotelgokarn@yahoo.com, Rs 200–700) is a small, unattractive budget hotel popular with pilgrims. If you can ignore the garish lobby and rundown passageways, its rooms are basic but functional. Some rooms are air-conditioned and have balconies, although the view is nothing to write home about. Higher-category rooms also have bathtubs and most rooms come with TVs. The hotel also has a budget resort by the same name at Kudlee Beach.

The popular beachfront restaurant **Namaste Café** (Om Beach, tel. 08386/257-141, Rs 400–600) offers cottages and bamboo huts. The shack accommodation is basic but quiet and serene with the rare advantage of the ocean by the doorstep. The café is popular for its meals and ambience, and also offers Internet and telephone facilities.

Rs 1,000-3,000

Away from the beach on a serene hillock where rustling leaves and crickets are the only sounds you're likely to hear, **(** **Om Beach Resort** (Om Beach Rd., Bungle Gudde, tel. 08386/257-718, www.ombeachresort.com, Rs 2,500–4,000) is a cluster of cottages overlooking hills and valley, with a distant view of the ocean. En route to Om Beach, but a short distance from it, the resort makes for a serene getaway, offering seclusion and holistic living in the form of greenery, Ayurveda, yoga, and meditation. Cottages are spacious with a living area and verandah, as well as a bedroom and an oversized bathroom. Rooms are air-conditioned and service is both friendly and efficient. For local tips and history, speak with the knowledgeable manager, Mudappa, who has been a resident here for a few years. Professionally managed, as part of the larger Kairali chain of hotels in Kerala, the resort also offers special Ayurveda-and-accommodation packages for guests where rates include treatment, room, and vegetarian meals. Trained therapists and masseurs carry out treatments (Rs 900 and up, also open to non-guests) after guests have had a consultation with the in-house Ayurveda doctor; yoga lessons (Rs 500/hr, open to non-guests) are led by trained instructors. Massage rooms are simple and basic but overlook the valley. A buffet and an à la carte menu offer local specialties and a choice of liquor at the restaurant and bar (8–10 A.M., 12:30–3 P.M., and 8–10:30 P.M. daily, Rs 175–225 for a buffet meal), which also provides a beautiful valley view. Try the local fish preparations as you gaze into the misty mountainside. This back-to-nature retreat offers the perfect, rustic getaway after a busy Goan holiday.

Rs 10,000 and Up

Gokarna's most luxurious resort, **(** **Swaswara** (Donibhail, Om Beach, tel. 08386/257-132, www.swasawara.com, Rs 97,000 for five nights, Rs 117,000 for seven nights) is a veritable piece of paradise near Om Beach. Swaswara, meaning "sound of the inner self" makes for a truly introspective, spiritual experience. A luxury eco-resort that resembles a little village with its natural laterite, earth, and straw look, it is spread over 12 hectares of vast, open land. A sanctuary of peace and silence, with gardens, pool, and private path to the beach, it offers holistic living with a package that includes accommodations, meals, yoga, and Ayurvedic treatment. Open showers, a meditation mezzanine, and natural materials make for a wonderful traditional and yet contemporary back-to-nature living experience. The rustic ambience is accentuated with the resort's own vegetable patch, natural waste management, and rainwater harvesting systems. The best feature, however, is its blue meditation dome—a circular cerulean tiled structure reminiscent of a Turkish mosque where yoga and meditation lessons take place. In addition, the resort also has a vast meditation hall overlooking the cliff and ocean. The staff are well trained and very knowledgeable as far as yoga and Ayurveda are concerned. Ayurvedic treatments are carried out by qualified and trained therapists in consultation with an in-house doctor. An open-air restaurant serves organic vegetarian meals and seafood, along with a fine selection of wine.

FOOD

Gokarna has a number of dining options on the beach, ranging from small food stalls to seasonal beach shacks. Apart from the restaurants attached to resorts and small, cheap *thaali* places on the main street, the beachside **(** **Namaste Café and German Bakery** (Om Beach, tel. 08386/257-141, 8:30 A.M.–11 P.M.

daily, mains Rs 30–100) is open through the year. A Gokarna institution, it overlooks the "Om" formation in reverse, with a view of the rising hillocks behind. The café is a popular evening hangout when the sounds of the night fight with the noise of Bollywood music blaring on the boom box. A simple shack with a small bakery and friendly waiters, it serves local, Chinese, Israeli, and European fare. Try the local seafood preparations and wash your meal down with a beer. The place serves everything from pancakes, sizzlers, Israeli salad, and local fish curry to steaks and pasta, in addition to a variety of cocktails.

INFORMATION AND SERVICES
Pharmacies
Medical supplies and toiletries are available on the main street at **Vasudev Medicals** (cell tel. 91/94485-47101, 9 A.M.–1 P.M. and 4–9 P.M. daily), which also organizes taxi services.

Police
In case of emergency, Gokarna has a police outpost (tel. 08386/257-956) at the Shri Mahabaleshwar Temple.

Money
Car Street has a number of small money changers, such as **Pai STD Shop** (near KSRTC bus station, tel. 08386/256-509, 10 A.M.–9 P.M. daily), which also does money grams and Western Union money transfers; **Guru Raghavendra** (tel. 08386/256-898, 10 A.M.–9 P.M. daily); and **Shri Laxmi Finance** (tel. 08386/257-902, 10 A.M.–1 P.M. Mon.–Sat.), which also does Western Union money transfers. Meanwhile, there are **State Bank of India** and **Syndicate Bank** ATMs on the main street.

Postal Services
The **Gokarna Post Office** (Car Street and Main Street crossing, tel. 08386/256-130, 9 A.M.–5 P.M. Mon.–Sat.) meets most postal needs and also receives money transfers from Western Union.

Internet and Telephone
Internet and telephone services are available at **Pai STD Shop** (near KSRTC bus station, tel. 08386/256-509, 10 A.M.–9 P.M. daily), **Shama Internet Corner** (near Mahaganpati Temple, cell tel. 91/99644-28695, 7:30 A.M.–11 P.M. daily), and **Kiran's Internet Floor** (Car Street, tel. 08386/256-251, 9 A.M.–10:30 P.M. daily), among others on the main street. Internet access costs about Rs 40 per hour at all of these places.

GETTING THERE AND AROUND
The nearest airport is Dabolim Airport in Goa; a taxi costs Rs 2,000–2,500 and takes approximately five hours. A number of taxi services are also available from Palolem, while buses from both Madgaon and Palolem come to the Gokarna bus stand. Only a few trains stop at Gokarna Road Train Station. However a number of express trains stop at Ankola and Kumta stations, 25 kilometers away.

JOG FALLS
A destination in itself, about 50 kilometers southeast of Gokarna, Jog Falls (Gerusoppa, Karnataka, 08186/244-732, www.karnatakatourism.org) is a body of four massive waterfalls given the names Raja, Rani, Rocket, and Roarer. At 253 meters, these falls are the highest in India and are created by the gushing Sharavati River. The Linganamakki Dam that lies across the river is responsible for much of the electricity provided to the state of Karnataka, and its gates are usually opened once a month on a Sunday, when the falls are at their most spectacular.

To witness the falls in all their glory, they are best visited in the monsoon season (June–Sept.) or the period just after (Oct.–Dec.). The Raja fall is the highest, and surrounds itself with great clouds of mist as it thunders into the deep gorge below.

While a day trip to the falls from Gokarna is not impossible, it would allow for only a short time at the falls with most of the day lost on bumpy roads getting there and away. For an overnight stay, KSTDC has a modest hotel (KSTDC Mayura Gerusoppa, Jog Falls, tel. 08186-244732, www.karnatakatourism.org, Rs 300 and up) and some forest department guesthouses.

To get to the falls by road, get onto the NH17 and drive toward Honavar via Kumta (approximately 15 km from Gokarna). After Honavar (20 km from Kumta), turn right and get onto the NH206. The falls are located about five kilometers after Gersoppa.

By bus, it is an hour-long ride to Kumta from Gokarna. Change here for a bus to the falls. The whole journey will take approximately six hours.

By rail, the nearest station is out of the way—100 kilometers away—at Shimoga, from where one can take a bus to the town of Sagar (30 km from Jog Falls) and change here for a bus to the falls.

Hampi

The best time to see Hampi is when it is in the throes of twilight. Except for the bustling Hampi Bazaar, the monuments and temples are closed to the public at that time but the blush colors of sunset only serve to accentuate the beauty of the stones, lending a romantic ashes-of-roses aura to the ancient city as the sky above flares a deep pink.

In the day, Hampi's unique landscape never ceases to amaze the first-time visitor. Millions of giant rounded boulders of various shapes and sizes sidle up to the ruins and hide within their crevices a historical treasure or two. And slicing through this spectacular granite landscape is the River Tungabhadra, coursing along the ruins as it did hundreds of years ago.

Hampi's dramatic landscape has a fitting story related to its origins. Legend has it that princes Hakka and Bukka came upon an unbelievable sight during a hunting expedition

© JANHAVI ACHAREKAR

The River Tungabhadra, strewn with boulders and ruins, snakes through historic Hampi.

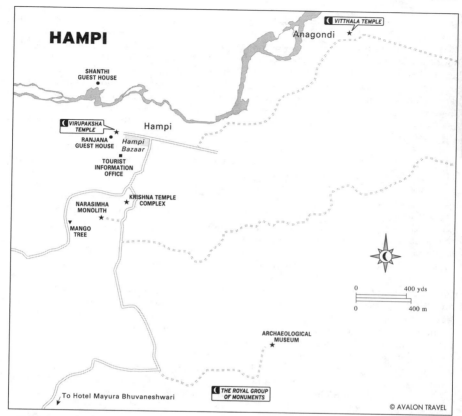

here. A hare that was being pursued by their hunting dogs turned around and gave chase to the hounds, leading the princes to believe that it was a divine sign. When told by sage Vidyaranya that this remarkable incident was indicative of the auspicious nature of the site—where the weak would become mighty—they established their empire here, calling it Vijayanagar: the indomitable City of Victory. For hundreds of years, the glorious Vijayanagar empire reigned supreme and was one of the most resplendent in history. Associated with both myth and history, Hampi continues to enthrall visitors as its temples and monuments regale them with tales from the past. Its fantastic granite boulders are the result of volcanic activity but according to the Hindu epic *Ramayana,* they were hurled down the hillside by the monkey army of simian kings Vali and Sugriva in the days when the town was part of their kingdom, Kishkindha.

Hampi's architecture is among the finest in the world and the site was declared a UNESCO World Heritage Site in 1986. A little path from behind the famous Virupaksha Temple Complex leads to the river where circular "coracle" boats float along the river like saucers in a storm, ferrying people to the more peaceful Sanapur area. The river's boulderscape includes open *mandapas* (halls) and statues of Nandi, Lord Shiva's bull, that emerge from the waters. Hampi's peaceful village scenes—of villagers, pilgrims, holy men, and blue-frocked children in pigtails tied with bright pink ribbons—are juxtaposed with history buffs and neo-hippie tourists from Goa and elsewhere who mill about the ruins, the Bazaar area, or at hangouts such as the riverside restaurant Mango Tree. New to Hampi are rave parties, where marijuana and revelry amid the ruins give this magical destination a whole new meaning to the word "stoned."

HISTORY

Hampi has a rich and glorious history and was established by the princes Hakka and Bukka of the Sangama dynasty in 1336. Its golden era lasted until 1565 when it was invaded and plundered by the Deccan Sultan, after which the city lay deserted and was soon forgotten. It is said that the region was part of the Kampili kingdom that stretched across modern-day Andhra Pradesh, and which was destroyed by the armies of the Delhi sultans. Hakka and Bukka, officers to the Kampili kings, were taken captive and forcibly converted to Islam. However, when they were set free, they returned to Hinduism and established the Sangama dynasty with Hampi or Vijayanagar as it was then called, as their capital. The Vijayanagar kingdom soon rose in might and became the most powerful in the Deccan and the south, protected by its natural rocky fortress. The already existing Virupaksha shrine was now refurbished and became Vijayanagar's chief shrine with Virupaksha as the the patron deity of the Sangama kings. With Hakka or Harihara I (1336–1356) as its first monarch, followed by his brother Bukka (1356–1377), the Vijayanagar army recaptured territories lost to the Muslim invaders, expanding their territory to nearly all of South India. Their successors further expanded the empire, which rose to glory under kings Devaraya I and II in the first half of the 15th century, and stretched as far as the Bay of Bengal. Vijayanagar also became a flourishing center for the arts and developed its own unique style of art, architecture, and sculpture. Islamic influences too

were welcomed and the result was a wonderful cultural amalgamation.

However, later monarchs soon proved to be ineffectual and the empire was taken over by the Saluvas (1485–1505), chiefs in the Vijayanagar kingdom, followed by the reign of the Tuluvas (1505–1565). The empire reached its zenith under Tuluva kings Krishnadevaraya (1509–1525) and his half-brother Achyutaraya (1529–1542). However, the Deccan sultans were provoked by later successor Ramaraya and formed an alliance of Muslim armies, attacking and defeating the Vijayanagar army in the battle of Talikota in 1565. The glorious capital was plundered, destroyed, and reduced to rubble, eventually transformed into a deserted ghost town.

The city lay forgotten until the late 18th century, when it was re-discovered by the British. It became a tourist destination in the 1970s as its monuments began to be steadily restored by the Archaeological Survey of India. In 1986, it was declared a World Heritage Site by UNESCO and is believed the only one of its kind in the world.

SIGHTS

Hampi's sights are spread across a 26-square-kilometer area; given the vast and detailed nature of its ruins, it is best to hire the services of an official tourist guide. Guides can be hired from the **Tourist Information Office** (Virupaksha Temple Rd., tel. 08394/241-339, 10 A.M.–5 P.M. Sat.–Thurs.). The site is generally divided into two broad groups of monuments: the Virupaksha Temple Complex with its surrounding shrines to the south of the river, and the group of monuments known as the Royal Enclosure. The Archaeological Museum at Kamalapuram and the suburban centers of Anegondi lie farther away.

Hampi is also within easy proximity of other attractions, such as the Daroji Bear Sanctuary.

The spectacular historical temples of Badami, Aihole and Pattadakkal are about 100 kilometers away and are destinations in themselves.

Hampi Bazaar

At the entrance to the ruined city and to the east of the towering Virupaksha Temple—where travel agents, streetside, cafés and bike rentals thrive amidst two-story colonnaded structures in stone—is the long market street known as Hampi Bazaar. Once a place that displayed the wealth of the Vijayanagar capital at the height of its glory, with merchants and traders selling gemstones and silks in a vibrant and bustling market atmosphere, its ancient buildings are now either vacant or the domain of hawkers. The street is also the venue for the annual chariot procession during the Virupaksha festival.

Not far from Hampi Bazaar, **Matanga Hill** is a steep climb up an ancient granite staircase. The summit is strewn with ruins and has a bird's-eye view of the ancient city.

C Virupaksha Temple

To the western end of the Hampi Bazaar—or as you clamber over the boulders and past the smaller, nameless ruins near the Ganesh Temple from Hemakuta Hill—you will see the soaring tower of Hampi's central monument. The Virupaksha Temple (8 A.M.–6 P.M. daily, Rs 2, photography Rs 50)—part of a larger temple complex (foreigners Rs 250, Indians Rs 10)—is easily recognized by its carved eastern *gopuram*, or nine-storied tower. Dedicated to Virupaksha—an incarnation of the Hindu god Shiva—and his two consorts Pampa (or Parvati) and Bhuvaneshwari, the temple is the religious epicenter of the ancient town. A temple elephant, tourists, and devotees make up the motley crowd at this spot, the busiest in the ancient city. While the tower of the Virupaksha Temple itself is barely 200 years old, restored with brick and plaster, it leads into a smaller *gopuram* dating to Vijayanagar times, added by Krishnadevaraya at the time of his coronation in 1510. The coronation *mandapa*, the hall within the temple complex itself, is an architectural marvel, with intricate carvings. Also known as the *rangamandapa* or the *kalyanamandapa*, this splendid

The carved *gopuram* of the Virupaksha Temple.

© JANHAVI ACHAREKAR

GETAWAYS AROUND GOA

hall, along with the 100-columned *phalapujamandapa,* are located in the courtyard of the complex. The *rangamandapa* is the most ornate, known for its animal sculptures and ceiling covered with paintings depicting scenes from the epic *Ramayana* and other Hindu religious myths. Built with the intent to create a play of light between the sculpted figures, in the style of shadow puppetry, this is the most magnificent part of the temple complex. In the main sanctuary, devotees continue to pay obeisance to the brass-faced god, while nearby are the shrines dedicated to Pampa and Bhuvaneshwari.

The northern end of the complex opens out into a little pathway (that ultimately leads to the river) lined with ancient pre-Vijayanagar shrines on one side and the **Manmatha Tank**—once a bathing place for pilgrims—on the other. A sandstone shrine dedicated to the goddess Durga is believed to date back to the 9th century A.D. Down by the river, local women wash clothes even as an open *mandapa*, ancient sculptures, and a *nandi*—Shiva's bull—stand mute witness to the flowing waters and riverine scenes.

Hemakuta Hill

Just above Hampi Bazaar is a rocky hillock scattered with the oldest temples and pavilions in Hampi. Hemakuta Hill is one of the most picturesque parts of town, with its rock-carved three-peaked shrines and sweeping views of the surrounding countryside. Built between the 9th and 14th centuries, its pre-Vijayanagar shrines are distinguished by pyramidal roofs, or *shikharas*. Poised dramatically on the hillside, overlooking the rising tower of the Virupaksha Temple, the ruins are marred by electric poles and wires that crisscross the rocky slope. Some shrines show scars from the past, from the time when they were temporary residences for local farmers and workers, before the ancient city was cordoned off as a heritage site.

The colossal monolithic Ganesh sculptures in the deserted **Ganesh Temples** tower above the surrounding lawn and flowers, adding character to the granite landscape.

◖ Vitthala Temple

A small pathway from the Hampi Bazaar leads to the splendid Vitthala Temple complex. Centered around a carved stone chariot, the 16th-century complex is known for its stunning *mahamandapa*, a large open hall with 56 "musical" pillars, each of which mimics the sound of a different musical instrument when struck. The pillars have been damaged over the years by demonstrations of their acoustics and are now out of bounds for tourists, who may only admire the carvings and imagine the sounds produced. The intricate base, or plinth, also has relief carvings of European and Arab horse traders, reflecting global interactions of the time. The *mahamandapa* is at its most magnificent when illuminated during the Hampi Festival in November. The *kalyanamandapa* (marriage hall) nearby is marked by sculptures of amorous couples. Meanwhile, the chariot is a shrine

This carved stone chariot stands at the center of the stunning Vitthala Temple complex.

© JANHAVI ACHAREKAR

dedicated to Vishnu's steed, the vulture Garuda, and its stone wheels could once revolve.

Different parts of the complex were built by various historical figures during the reign of Krishnadevaraya, including the eastern and northern *gopurams* commissioned by his two queens. Just before the gateway is the arched **King's Balance,** where Vijayanagar kings were weighed in gold and the wealth distributed among priests and the needy. A number of other colonnaded halls, ancient inscriptions, and exquisite sculptures make this complex one of the most significant in Hampi.

On the way to the complex, it is worth taking a short detour to the **Tiruvengalanatha Temple,** also known as **Achyutaraya's Temple** for its stone carvings.

Anegondi

Across the River Tungabhadra is the fortressed city of Anegondi, which predates even the Vijayanagar empire. Reached by coracle boat, the town has a crumbling palace complex, step wells, royal memorials, and other structures, but is known particularly for an early Jain temple, the small **Ranganatha Temple,** and a temple complex known as **Chintamani.** Over a kilometer from here is the sacred pool **Pampasarovar,** named after the goddess of Hampi. You can also trek up to the Hanuman Temple for a beautiful view of Hampi. The boats are run by local villagers and there are no fixed timings for excursions to Anegondi.

Krishna Temple Complex and Narasimha Monolith

On the road leading to Kamalapuram is the Krishna Temple complex with its grand entrance built to celebrate the triumph of Krishnadevaraya over the Gajapati kings of Orissa in 1515. It once accommodated the granite idol of the infant Krishna, which was plundered from the Udayagiri Fort and now lies in the Chennai State Museum. A stone inscription records his war exploits.

The complex is dilapidated but the main temple and its surrounding smaller shrines have some carvings and colonnades that are

This *shivling* near the Narasimha Monolith was carved out of a single rock.

© JANHAVI ACHAREKAR

the only remnants of an ancient marketplace, which then lead out onto a path that leads to Hampi's famous monolithic Narasimha, an incarnation of Vishnu. The lion-faced giant sculpture is 6.7 meters high and has been restored, although the four arms of the statue are broken and a smaller image of Vishnu's consort Laxmi is missing. An inscription states that the statue was commissioned by Krishnadevaraya in 1528 and was carved out of a single rock by a Brahmin. Nearby, is the three-meter-high monolithic *shivling*—believed to have been commissioned by an impoverished lady—its crown bright with sunlight streaming from an opening above while its base remains immersed in water.

◖ The Royal Group of Monuments

The most spectacular part of the ancient capital lies south of Hampi Bazaar and north of Kamalapuram. A cluster of royal buildings survives to tell the tale of Hampi in

© JANHAVI ACHAREKAR

The Elephant Stables display the Islamic influence at the Royal Group of Monuments.

the form of splendid palaces, temples, pavilions, baths, and stables. Some of the buildings display a distinct Islamic influence and their soaring arches and domes, interspersed with the Vijayanagar craftsmanship, suggest the influence of the Muslim Bahmani kingdom, as well as an artistic exchange between the two empires. It is debated whether the **Queen's Bath** was really a women's bathing area or a place where male royals sported with women even as perfumed water spouted out of its lotus-shaped fountains. A simple building devoid of carvings and decidedly Islamic in architecture, its arches, domes, and balconies are spectacular but in need of better maintenance.

Nearby is what seems like a fantastic man-made plateau—the **Mahanavami Dibba.** On a vast tract of flat land, this raised granite platform was the venue for royal celebrations of the Mahanavami festival. Constructed after Krishnadevaraya's victory in Orissa, the grand platform once had an elaborate hall and pavilion from where the king watched the colorful festival processions go by. Its only remaining part—the base—has a number of intricate carvings depicting hunts, sport,

foreign visitors, and battles. Just behind the Mahanavami Dibba is a geometrical stepped tank, excavated in the 1980s.

One of the most ornate structures in Hampi, the **Hazara Rama Temple** or "temple of a thousand Ramas," was the king's private shrine. Built by Devaraya I in the early 15th century, it is covered with friezes depicting scenes from the epic *Ramayana*. An inscription near the main entrance also claims that Devaraya was protected by the goddess Pampa. The reliefs on the temple walls narrate the entire story of the *Ramayana* in 108 scenes. The two-story Amman shrine here, built at a slightly later date than the main temple, also has some Narasimha carvings.

The **Zenana Enclosure** is surrounded by broken walls and watchtowers. Although the name suggests a women's enclosure or a harem, its ventilation holes and proximity to the elephant stables suggest that it may have been an armory or courtiers' quarters. Nearby, the two-story **Lotus Mahal** is one of the finest structures in Hampi—built to resemble a lotus in bloom. Its ornate windows, open pavilions, and balconies are a fusion of Hindu and Islamic styles of architecture, with their temple-style pyramidal towers and geometrical, sultanate arches. Believed to be the queen's summer palace, historians are now considering the possibility that this was once the council chamber. Meanwhile, the adjacent **Elephant Stables,** a long and impressive series of arches and domes, are located along a parade ground and next to the **Guards' Quarters.**

The Archaeological Museum and Around

To the south of the Royal Enclosure, the **Archaeological Museum** (Kamalapuram, tel. 08394/241-561, 10 A.M.–5 P.M. Sat.–Thurs., Rs 5) displays reliefs and sculptures, coins, inscriptions, and palm-leaf manuscripts, as well as a model of the ancient city that visitors can study to get their bearings. Nearby, are the **Pattabhirama Temple,** the 14th-century **Ganagitti Jain Temple,** and **Bhima's Gate**—named after one of the heroes of the epic *Mahabharata* and one of the main entrances to the city in ancient times.

Daroji Bear Sanctuary

Only 10 kilometers from Hampi, the Daroji Bear Sanctuary (Vidyaranya, Kamalapuram, tel. 08394/242-869, 6 A.M.–6 P.M. daily, adults Rs 20, vehicles Rs 100, photography permitted) is reached by a picturesque road lined with fields of sunflowers. The sanctuary shelters sloth bears, as well as leopards, hyenas, jackals, wild boar, and other forms of wildlife. From a watchtower, you can see bears charging up the hill from among the boulders at feeding time. (The sanctuary office can tell you when forest guards are scheduled to feed the bears.) The watchtower overlooks the river and offers a sweeping view of the beautiful landscape, with its trees and boulders.

ENTERTAINMENT AND EVENTS

Like Gokarna in previous years, Hampi explores the extremes of religious festivity and rave parties. Alcohol is forbidden in the temple town, but the smaller cafés will discreetly serve you some beer on request. For the most part, however, tourists go to KSTDC's Mayura Bhuvaneshwari at Kamalapuram or to the hotels of nearby Hospet for a drink. Others seek respite by smoking pot with holy men (marijuana and the Hindu religion have a long association that goes back several thousand years) at desolate temples amid the ruins or at discreet raves held nearby.

Hampi's most fascinating events comprise its religious and cultural festivals. The annual **Vijaya Utsav,** or **Hampi Festival,** held annually in November, is the town's biggest draw. Hosted by the Karnataka government, the festival showcases the culture of the region in the form of classical Indian dance, music, drama, and art amid the ruins—which are specially lit for the occasion. A light-and-sound show amid the monuments evokes the history of the ancient city, while traditional handicrafts are sold in the Hampi Bazaar area. Drumbeats, color, art, and gaiety mark the occasion, making it a must-experience event.

Meanwhile, the Virupaksha Temple celebrates a number of religious festivals including the **Chariot Festival,** held as per the lunar calendar in February or March, when the image of the deity and its consort are carried out in a procession along the main chariot street in Hampi Bazaar.

ACCOMMODATIONS

For a town so small, Hampi has a surprising choice of accommodations, ranging from an upmarket resort to small homestays advertised as budget guesthouses. While many prefer the comforts of the fancier Hospet hotels, Hampi and Kamalapuram are infinitely more charming, affording views of the ruins and the surrounding landscape. Don't be taken in by the touts who are likely to approach you at the entrance of Hampi Bazaar. Even as each tries to outsell their own lodge (for which they receive a commission) against the other, try to book yourself into one of the more basic but prettier places across the river. Living on the other side of the river means that the approach is only by coracle boat and you're pretty much stuck there after dark, but most tourists will vouch for the fact that it offers a richer experience of the historical destination.

Meanwhile the KSTDC resort at Kamalapuram is another pleasant option and there are, of course, the numerous smaller guesthouses with tiny terraces and balconies that overlook the action of Hampi Bazaar.

Electricity may be a problem in Hampi, as the lights go off frequently and leave the town in the dark. Those who prefer creature comforts would be better off in Hospet, although the trade-off is having to live among less enchanting surroundings. For those who are content with air coolers in place of air-conditioning, and do not mind the frequent power-cuts or mosquitoes, living amid the ruins of Hampi is an experience like no other.

Under Rs 1,000

The most popular overnight options in Hampi are the budget guesthouses and lodges near the entrance to Hampi Bazaar. Of these, the most famous is **Ranjana Guest House** (behind the government school, Hampi, tel. 08394/241-696, Rs 600–1,200), popularized by historians John Fritz and George Michell in their book on Hampi, as well as a number of guidebooks. However, some recent tourists have reported an unpleasant stay, and that they have faced hostility upon refusing to avail of the taxi/guide service pushed by the guesthouse. The living arrangements here are simple; a small private residence has a few cramped rooms on the lower floor, with a narrow staircase leading up to a special deluxe room with a balcony on the upper story. Home-cooked meals are served to guests—amid pink walls, bronze figurines, and plastic flowers—by the family that runs the place.

Nearby, **Archana Guest House** (Janata plot, Hampi, tel. 08394/241-547, addihampi@yahoo.com, Rs 300–1,000) is a similar two-story structure with cramped, basic rooms. It's located amid more cheerful surroundings: banana plantations and a small canal. All rooms have an attached bath with hot shower, while those on the lower floor have a TV and air-con-

ditioning. The guesthouse has garden seating and a terrace café with a view of the ruins.

Across the river, **Shanthi Guest House** (River Rd., tel. 08394/241-568, Rs 650–800) has small cottages in a picturesque locale. A pretty place with clean rooms and verandahs, it is strewn with hammocks and offers a lovely sunset view. Home-cooked vegetarian food is served and the lodge makes for a great meeting place for travelers.

Rs 1,000–3,000

The only place close enough to the ruins and yet distant enough to be able to serve alcohol, KSTDC's **Hotel Mayura Bhuvaneshwari** (Kamalapuram, tel. 08394/241-474, www.karnatakaholidays.net, Rs 450–5,000) is popular not only for its bar but also for its serene environs and pleasant rooms. Set amid lawns and gardens, this vast, peaceful resort in Kamalapuram—near the Archaeological Museum—is a welcome relief from the cramped lodges of the crowded Hampi Bazaar area. The staff are friendly and efficient, while rooms are generally neat and well kept (although the linen may need some looking into). Rooms cover a wide range, from the un-air-conditioned economy rooms to the spacious (but not quite luxurious) presidential suite—which has housed the president of India, Pratibha Patil, and displays a photograph as proof. The resort also has a good restaurant known for its local *thaali* (the traditional all-you-can-eat platter). On the flip side, the place is slightly out of the way and you will require your own transport to get around.

Across the river and about 15 kilometers from Hampi, **Kishkinda Heritage Resort** (near Broken Stone Bridge Cross, Sanapur, tel. 08533/287-034, www.kishkindaheritage.com, Rs 1,200–2,500) is a tourist complex with an amusement park, children's park, and rustic cottages with thatched roofs. Remote, but luxurious in comparison to other accommodations in the Hampi area, it offers everything from swimming pools and boating to Ayurveda, yoga, and meditation. Cottages (some with air-conditioning) are painted in bright terra-cotta and earthen hues, located amidst well-manicured lawns, and equipped with TVs and phones. There are four deluxe air suites too, and the sprawling property has a restaurant and bar. The resort also offers all-inclusive plans and packages that include meals and lodging.

Rs 3,000-10,000

Across the river and seven kilometers from Hampi, **(Hampi Boulders** (Narayanpet, Bandi Harlapur, tel. 08539/265-939, hampis-bouldersresort@gmail.com, Rs 6,000–10,000 including breakfast, dinner, and tax) is difficult for vehicles to access, thanks largely to a path laden with stones, but is easily one of the best lodging options in the Hampi area. Located on the riverbank, its quaint cottages are spacious and set amid the spectacular boulders of the region. Pleasantly furnished and with verandahs that overlook the stark and unusual surrounding landscape, this wilderness resort offers nature treks, river rafting, rock climbing, bird-watching, fishing, camping, and wildlife-viewing, making it a great place for nature enthusiasts. The resort has a restaurant and bar with a dramatic river-and-boulder view, ideal for bird-watchers. The staff are efficient and knowledgeable, but it's best to call in advance in the low season as they may be missing in action.

FOOD

Hampi has a number of small cafés and restaurants along the main bazaar street where you can sit and watch life go by over a good Indian meal. Local South Indian cuisine is often complemented with Western fare such as pancakes and pastas. Some of the budget lodges also have small terrace cafés with views of the ruins. Since this is a temple town, restaurants serve only vegetarian meals.

Hampi's favorite hangout, **(Mango Tree** (River Side Dr., Hampi, cell tel. 91/94487-65213, 7:30 A.M.–9:30 P.M. daily, mains Rs 70 and up) lies amid the ruins. No visit to the temple town is complete without a visit to this quaint restaurant. Open since 1987, this

family-run establishment, reached by a path lined with banana plantations, is one of the oldest in Hampi. Bench-style, multilevel seating overlooks the spectacular boulders and the river. Mango Tree serves everything from South Indian *dosa* (a paper-thin rice pancake accompanied by spicy curry and chutney), to Israeli cuisine and pancakes. The fruit *lassi* (yogurt drink) is especially popular here.

Great for those who are missing a spot of alcohol and meat, the restaurant at KSTDC's **Mayura Bhuvaneshwari** (Kamalapuram, tel. 08394/241-474, www.karnatakaholidays.net, 6:30 A.M.–10 P.M. daily) is a lovely open café surrounded by lawns and birds. Remarkably easy on the pocket, it offers a variety of Indian, Chinese, and other dishes, along with beer. Both vegetarian (Rs 40) and non-vegetarian (Rs 75, with fish and/or meat) South Indian *thaalis* (all-you-can-eat platters) are prepared in the local style.

Another popular place, but across the river, **Goan Corner** (no tel., mains Rs 70 and up) is aptly named. With its shack-like appearance, hippie atmosphere, and palm groves surrounded by fields and hills, it offers a piece of Goa in Hampi. A thatched roof, hammocks, board games, and books, in addition to local home-style cooking, are offered by the garrulous lady who runs the place. The café also has a few rooms, and this is a great place to meet a varied mix of travelers and interesting characters.

INFORMATION AND SERVICES
Tourist Information

The **Tourist Information Office** (Virupaksha Temple road, tel. 08394/241-339, 10 A.M.–5 P.M. Sat.–Thurs.) provides maps, brochures, specific information on Hampi, as well as 30 trained, official guides (Rs 500 half day, Rs 800 all day, for 1–5 persons). Ask for guides Tipanna Gowda (cell tel. 91/94488-41746) and Kumar (cell tel. 91/94499-04406), who are especially knowledgeable. Tipanna has trained under historians John Fritz and George Michell and is passionate about his job.

All foreigners have to register at the local police station, located at the end of Hampi Bazaar.

Pharmacies
While it has no phone, Hampi's lone pharmacy, **Shri Virupaksheshwara Medical and General Stores** (9:30 A.M.–7:30 P.M. daily) is located just outside the entrance to Hampi and stocks everything from medicine to toiletries.

Money
The Hampi Bazaar area is lined with money changers, such as **Pushpa Tours and Travels** (tel. 08394/241-958, 7:30 A.M.–9 P.M. daily) and **Rahul Tours and Travels** (tel. 08394/241-947, 7 A.M.–8:30 P.M. daily). Travelers' checks may be cashed at **Canara Bank** (Hampi Bazaar, 11 A.M.–2 P.M. Tues., Thurs., Fri. and 11 A.M.–12:30 P.M. Sat.), which also has an ATM.

Internet and Telephone
The Hampi Bazaar area has plenty of travel agents whose offices double up as internet cafés and provide telephone facilities. Among these are **Rahul Tours and Travels** (tel. 08394/241-947, 7 A.M.–8:30 P.M. daily) and **RKS Internet and Travel Centre** (cell tel. 91/94494-71909, 6 A.M.–10 P.M. daily).

GETTING THERE AND AROUND
While Hampi is usually reached by rail or by road, there is an airport 86 kilometer away in Bellary that receives flights from Bangalore and Goa. However, Hampi is generally reached via Hospet (11 km away), which is well connected to both Goa and Bangalore, as well as a number of other Indian destinations. From Goa, the Amravathi Express runs on Wednesdays and Saturdays from Vasco to Vijayawada and stops at Hospet on the way.

By road from Goa, the drive to Hospet and Hampi is via Hubli (NH 63) and past Koppal, known for its historical fort. By bus, the KSRTC has a number of interstate buses that ply between Hospet and other destinations in and around Karnataka. Buses run between Hospet and Hampi 6:30 A.M.–7:30 P.M. Hampi's bus station is located in the Hampi Bazaar area and the drive to the historical town is a pretty one, lined with ancient villages and strewn with ruins.

Auto-rickshaws, cars, and bikes can also be rented to go to Hampi from Hospet, and to travel in and around Hampi once there. Most bike rentals are located in the Hampi Bazaar area.

HOSPET
Hospet is a noisy, crowded town 11 kilometers from Hampi made up of low-rise concrete buildings and little else. The few avenues that it once had for shopping (a handful of state handloom and handicraft stores) are now closed. The only reason for tourists to be here, if at all, is that it has slightly better accommodations options than those in Hampi. A few star-rated hotels offer a spot of luxury in these otherwise charmless environs, and some traditional eateries offer good local fare.

If you do happen to be here and have some time to spare, the **Tungabhadra Dam** is situated about five kilometers from here. Also known locally as TB Dam, at 49 meters in height and two kilometers in length, it is Karnataka's largest dam and derives its name from the Tungabhadra—the river across which it is built. While you could once walk the length of the dam, entry is now restricted to its two ends. The gates of the dam are opened on Independence Day (Aug. 15) each year, and the sight is well worth the visit. The tourism office in Hospet organizes regular coach tours (College Rd., tel. 08394/221-008, depart 9:30 A.M. and return 6 P.M. daily, Rs 175) to the dam.

Accommodations and Food
UNDER RS 1,000
Not quite in Hospet, **Hotel Mayura Vijayanagar** (Tungabhadra Dam, tel. 08394/259-270, www.karnatakaholidays. net, Rs 400–550) lies four kilometers west of town, along the Tungabhadra Dam. A cluster

of rustic cottages with a view of the dam, it may be out of the way from Hampi but is conveniently located for those who also wish to visit the historic destinations of Badami and Aihole. The cottages have double rooms with two beds, and deluxe rooms with three beds. There's a restaurant on the premises that serves both vegetarian and non-vegetarian fare.

RS 1,000-3,000

One of the oldest hotels in Hospet, **Hotel Priyadarshini** (V/45, Station Rd., tel. 08394/227-313, priyainhampi@yahoo.com, Rs 1,400–1,850) offers basic rooms in a dingy, tube-lit ambience. The staff are friendly and cheerful, however, and restaurants are great for those who wish to sample the local cuisine in an equally authentic ambience. The vegetarian restaurant **Naivedyam** (7 A.M.–10:30 P.M. daily) is popular with locals and crowded at lunchtime. Try their South Indian *thaali* (Rs 35), which offers generous portions of various vegetable dishes, lentils, rice, and traditional sweets, among other fare, and is served swiftly and efficiently. The hotel also has a garden restaurant and bar called **Manasa** (noon–10:30 P.M. daily, mains Rs 70 and up) that offers a variety of local and North Indian fare, along with beer and other alcohol.

The first star-rated hotel in Hospet, **(Hotel Malligi** (10/90, JN Rd., tel. 08394/228-101, www.malligihotels.com, Rs 1,000–4,500) is a vast, modern-looking hotel with 175 well-appointed rooms. All rooms are contemporary in decor, and have a television, mini-bar, and air-conditioning. Suites have a kitchenette, as well as Internet facilities, while the honeymoon suite offers romance in the form of a round bed and flowers. The hotel has an Ayurveda center, in-house travel agent, currency exchange, and a bookshop that houses an excellent collection of books on Hampi. Guests have access to the pool and gym. Dining options include everything from Chinese to Indian and European fare at terrace restaurant and bar **Waves** (noon–11 P.M. daily, mains Rs 100 and up), vegetarian cuisine and snacks at **Malligi Café** (6:30 A.M.–10:30 P.M.

daily, mains Rs 100 and up), and multi-cuisine fare at **Temptations** (6:30 A.M.–3 P.M. and 7–11 P.M. daily, mains Rs 100 and up).

RS 3,000-10,000

The newest and most luxurious addition to Hospet's hospitality scene, **(Krishna Palace** (Station Rd., tel. 08394/294-300, www.krishnapalacehospet.com, RS 3,800–7,000, breakfast included) provides the best service and amenities in town. Eager to please, the enthusiastic staff ensures a comfortable stay. Rooms are air-conditioned, equipped with the latest gadgets, Wi-Fi enabled, and come in various categories spread across two floors—the Executive Floor and the more lavish Palace Grande Floor. The hotel has a multi-cuisine restaurant, **Fiesta** (7:30 A.M.–11 P.M. daily, mains Rs 80 and up) that specializes in Chinese fare, while a tea lounge and bar make for pleasant evening hangouts. There's also a pool and fitness center as well as a fancy beauty salon.

Information and Services
TOURIST INFORMATION

The **KSTDC** office (College Rd., tel. 08394/221-008, 7:30 A.M.–8 P.M. daily) provides maps, brochures, and information on Hampi and other destinations in Karnataka. It also organizes guided tours to Hampi and the Tungabhadra Dam (departs 9:30 A.M. and returns 6 P.M. daily, Rs 175 per person).

PHARMACIES

Hospet has plenty of small pharmacies where you can buy medication and toiletries, such as **Poornima Medical and General Stores** (tel. 08394/227-124, noon–5 P.M. and 7 P.M.–midnight, Mon.–Sat.).

MONEY

All the big hotels have their own money changers. Try **Pushpa Tours and Travels** (Hotel Priyadarshini, tel. 08394/225-838, 10 A.M.–9 P.M. daily) or **Hamsa Tours and Travels** (Hotel Malligi, tel. 08394/228-101, chalo_hamsa@yahoo.co.in, 7:30 A.M.–10 P.M. daily).

INTERNET

Hospet has a number of Internet cafés—such as **Sify** (Station Rd., cell tel. 91/99003-37982, 10 A.M.–9:30 P.M. daily) and **Cybernet** (Shivananda Lodge, College Rd., behind bus stand, tel. 08394/222-799, 10 A.M.–10 P.M. daily)—that charge around Rs 30 per hour.

Getting There and Around

The airport closest to Hospet lies at Bellary (75 km away) and receives flights from Bangalore and Goa. Hospet is well connected to Goa, Bangalore, and a number of other Indian destinations by both rail and road. From Goa, the Amravathi Express runs on Wednesdays and Saturdays from Vasco to Vijayawada and stops at Hospet on the way.

By road from Goa, the drive to Hospet and Hampi is via Hubli (NH 63) and past Koppal, known for its historic fort. By bus, the KSRTC has a number of interstate buses that ply between Hospet and other destinations in and around Karnataka.

Buses run between Hospet and Hampi (11 km away) 6:30 A.M.–7:30 P.M. Hampi's bus station is located in the Hampi Bazaar area and the drive to the historical town is a pretty one, lined with ancient villages and strewn with ruins. Auto-rickshaws, cars, and bikes may also be hired to go to Hampi from Hospet. Check with your hotel reception for details.

BACKGROUND

The Land

Located on the western coast of India, Mumbai and Goa share a number of geographical similarities but are distinct in history, culture, and identity. Mumbai became a part of the mainland history only around the 17th century A.D. with colonial expansion into the region. However, the erstwhile seven islands of the city were home to Buddhist monks as early as the 1st century B.C. The second-most populous city in the world, Mumbai generates most of the country's taxes, is home to one of the largest film industries in the world, has one of the busiest stock markets, houses India's elite, and has been a target of terror attacks in recent years.

A small peninsula that juts out of the mainland spanning 437 square kilometers, Mumbai is governed by an elected municipality. It's the capital of the state of Maharashtra, and is located on the west coast along the Arabian Sea. The city is one of the world's most crowded—with a density of about 27,000 per square kilometer. The unique geographical position of the city creates a well-sheltered natural harbor that sees half of the country's maritime trade, a large fishing industry, and one of the best naval fleets in the world. The islands of Elephanta and Uran (located in the bay between the city and the mainland) make beautiful excursions and also house commercial and industrial

© ASHIMA NARAIN

sectors dependent on shipping. There are other islands in the Arabian Sea, numerous beaches and seafronts all along the city's coast, while some areas are protected as natural habitats or for strategic reasons. Recent infrastructural developments have damaged the city's ecology with the steady carving out of hills and flattening of trees, but the city still retains its greenery in patches like the Malabar Hill area, some parts of the suburbs, and in the huge Sanjay Gandhi National Park—located within city limits—which helps maintain a semblance of ecological balance.

The state of Goa, on the other hand, is marked by a 131-kilometer coastline, with partially hilly terrain and two major rivers. About 600 kilometers south of Mumbai, it is situated on the slopes of the Western Ghats (the Sahyadri ranges) and its landscape is dominated by reddish soil and laterite stone, also found along the Konkan coast of Maharashtra. Some of the oldest rocks, many millions of years old, may be found in Goa. Spread across 3,702 square kilometers, the state is rich in mineral resources and known for its agricultural and small-scale industries. In stark contrast with Mumbai, it only has a population density of 363 people per square kilometer. One of India's smallest states, it gained liberation from Portuguese rule and was integrated into India as recently as 1961, and was granted statehood in 1987.

An aerial view of Goa reveals its multiple landscapes.

© ASHIMA NARAIN

GEOGRAPHY

Mumbai has an undulating topography with volcanic hills, natural clay mounds, landfilled *maidans* (sprawling open grounds), and a long coast comprising smooth beaches, rocky shores, heavy marshes and mangroves, and artificial shorelines. Natural creeks, rivers, and drainage canals crisscross the city, swelling during the rains and causing floods due to neglect and haphazard planning. The waters of Mumbai's Mithi River have been depleting steadily and have been pushed back for developmental and reclamation projects, much to the alarm of environmentalists. There are three lakes—Tulsi, Vihar, and Powai—within city limits, in protected areas in and around the national park, which supply most of the city's water.

Goa shares its northern border with the Sindhudurg district of Maharashtra state, and has the Arabian Sea to its west. To its south lies the Karwar district of Karnataka state; while on the east is the Belgaum district of Karnataka. Goa is crisscrossed by rivers, namely, the Zuari, the Mandovi, and their tributaries. A rocky headland divides the harbor of Goa into Aguada at the mouth of the Mandovi in the north, and Mormugao at the mouth of the Zuari in the south.

CLIMATE

Both Mumbai and Goa have a warm and humid climate pretty much throughout the year. Mumbai weather has fluctuated in recent years owing to large-scale construction and topographic changes. The summer months (Apr.–June) at both destinations are hot and sticky owing to their proximity to the sea. Temperatures soar to around 38°C and humidity is almost always above 50 percent. The monsoons last from late June to September and are famous for relentless downpour that can last for days (causing major floods in Mumbai in recent years). The months from November to February tend to be comparatively dry, and the mercury dips to about 10°C on some December and January nights. It tends to be sunny in the day, however, with temperatures of 20–32°C.

Flora

Much of Mumbai's tree cover has been destroyed by commercial and residential construction and by infrastructural development. It is possible, however, to find good floral life in many parts of the city. Goa, on the other hand, is rich in natural resources, and enjoys a forest cover of 1,424 square kilometers with over 1,500 species of plants.

TREES

A significant part of the Mumbai shoreline is covered with mangroves. As most of it is marshy land, these vast protected patches of mangroves keep the city from erosion. Swathes of mangroves can be seen in the suburb of Vikhroli, along the coastal and the creek areas, and these swampy areas make for great biodiversity pools. Trees lining city roads are mostly evergreen—the long-leafed mast tree (Ashoka; *Polyalthia longifolia*) is found in two variations, a tall and slim one and the other, with a broad spread; look for the "gold mohur" *(Delonix regia)* blooming in summer with its flaming red flowers, and the copper pod *(Peltophorum ferruginum)* with its reddish-brown pods. Other species include neem *(Azadirachta indica)*, mango, the broad-leafed banyan and sacred fig (Peepal; *Ficus Religiosa*) tree, the black plum (Jamun; *Syzygium cumini*) tree and the rain tree. The number of laburnum trees has reduced in recent years and there are a few tamarind trees with their sweet-sour fruit.

The coastal areas are conducive for the growth of the areca nut, coconut palms, and the Phoenix palm, which has a delicious watery fruit called the toddy nut, known locally as *taad gola*—the extract of which is used to produce the fermented brew called toddy.

Look for the aptly named cannonball tree in the Horniman Circle gardens. Meanwhile, the Sanjay Gandhi National Park has a much more varied collection, including teak, red silk cotton, acacia, and ziziphus.

Goa's most abundant vegetation includes the coconut and palm trees, seen throughout the coast as well as in the interior. Banana and pineapple plantations as well as fruiting trees and plants such as the mango, cashew, and jackfruit are found across the state. It is also rich in deciduous trees such as teak and sal, while bamboo and cash crops such as sugarcane, areca nut, millet, and rice are plentiful.

© ASHIMA NARAIN

A variety of species of flora coexist with Goa's marine life.

FLOWERS

The common flowering plants found around Mumbai are the red cluster of the ixora, white and red hibiscus, yellow tecoma bushes, the yellow flowers of the copper pod, the red bloom of the gold mohur, and vinca and lantana bushes.

Goa has all these and more. It is also known for blossoms such as the yellow laburnum, bougainvillea, the tiny yellow-red "Pride of India," and the purple arjun; Goan lakes are adorned with lotuses and hyacinths.

VEGETATION ZONES

Mumbai's National Park houses an eclectic growth of vines, trees, ferns, and herbs among huge deciduous and evergreen trees. The streets are tree-lined in most areas, and the south end of the city and the northern suburbs have a fair green cover. The coastal areas have retained most of their palms, and there are protected mangroves all around the coast of the city. Only recently has increasing awareness among citizens made it difficult for developers to chop off trees without penalties. Old Parsi colonies like Malcolm Baug in the suburb of Jogeshwari have retained most of their centuries-old trees. A great place to spot historic trees in the city is the Jijamata Udyan—the city zoo, which doubles up as a botanical garden.

About 62 percent of Goa's forested land comes under Protected Areas in the form of wildlife sanctuaries and parks, and environmental activists have been working relentlessly to stave off developmental activity at the cost of Goa's natural environs.

Fauna

Once known for a great variety of animals, Mumbai's fauna is sadly restricted to the National Park now. Leopards and tigers once roamed the areas where high-rises now soar. Even the city's vast numbers of sparrows was drastically reduced a few years ago—an occurrence that some say coincided with the rising number of cell phones. There are still some surprises in the city, however, as far as animals and birds are concerned.

Goa continues to be rich in fauna, with 275 species of birds, 50 species of animals, and about 60 types of reptiles.

MARINE LIFE

Mumbai and Goa are both located along the Arabian Sea and share a similar marine life. In Mumbai, there was a time when colorful fish and marine creatures like dolphins, octopi, and mollusks were found off the coast of Chowpatty and turtles were known to nest in the sand. Today, however, the city's marine life has receded to as much as 12 kilometers from the shore due to effluents and pollution. The fishing industry survives by fishing farther out, in the deep sea, and in the cleaner waters at the northern end of the city.

The major species of fish found in these waters are the unique Bombay duck, pomfret, seer-fish, mackerel, dog-fish, ribbon-fish, Indian salmon, and the jewfish. Crabs, clams, prawns, squid, and lobsters are also found here, much to the delight of local fishermen. In both Mumbai and Goa, various mollusks and rock oysters are found on the rocky shores, while jellyfish, octopi, and sea snakes live deeper in the sea. Turtles and tortoises, including the unusual mud turtle known for its snout, may be found in and around wells and ponds in Mumbai, while the rare olive ridley turtle nests on the shores of Morjim in Goa.

BIRDS

Both Mumbai and Goa are rich in birdlife, a fact that is obvious from the popularity of the annual Mumbai Bird Race, and from the vast Salim Ali Bird Sanctuary on Chorao Island in Goa. Birds commonly found around the city of Mumbai are the house crow, the jungle crow, the Baya weaverbird or tailor bird, field mynah, house sparrow, bulbul, crow pheasant, coppersmith, snow white egret, and the white breasted kingfisher. Blue rock pigeons are most common, and if you're lucky, you may be able to spot bright yellow ioras and orioles. Pariah kites and Brahmini kites are common birds of prey, as are a few varieties of owls, but the population of scavenging vultures has steadily declined over the years. You will also find the occasional eagle and hawk, and the Malabar Hill area in the heart of the city, surprisingly, has the odd peacock. The National Park has a vast bird population that includes drongos, sun-birds, barbets, shrikes, and other beautiful species like the fairy bluebird and the paradise flycatcher. Not far from the city is the Karnala Bird Sanctuary, a popular spot with bird-watchers.

In recent years, migratory flamingos have arrived in the Sewri Bay in Central Mumbai, and the nearby island of Uran. In a surprising symbiosis of the urbane and the natural, the birds come to feed upon the bacteria that thrive on industrial waste.

Goa's bird life includes much of the same avian population, in addition to a profusion of green bee-eaters, kingfishers, and the Malabar trogon, Malabar pied hornbill, the singing Malabar whistling thrush, and the flame-throated bulbul. Several waders, including sandpipers, may be seen by the beaches.

MAMMALS

Mumbai's mammalian wildlife is largely restricted to its National Park, although signs that say "Go Slow, Leopards Crossing" may be seen on the outskirts of the city. A number of leopards and other wild animals may also be found at the residential neighborhood of Yeoor Hills in the distant central suburb of Thane. Otherwise, you are more likely to find bats, squirrels, and pests like bandicoots and rats. The rat population is so high that the municipality offers a reward per head for rats killed or captured, and professional rat catchers hunt them out at night. At the National Park, you will find leopards, macaques, langurs, civet cats, spotted deer, barking deer, the black-naped hare, mongoose, and other creatures.

Goa's forests and sanctuaries are the habitat

ASHIMA NARAIN

A variety of animals live in Mumbai and Goa.

NESTING GROUND: OLIVE RIDLEY TURTLES

The smallest species of marine turtle in the world – averaging 70 centimeters long and 45 kilograms in weight – the olive ridley turtle gets its name from its olive green color and from H. N. Ridley FRS, who first discovered the species in Brazil in 1887. These rare turtles are migratory by nature and traverse great distances to nest en masse between November and March.

In India, their largest nesting site is in Orissa, though the beaches of Morjim and Galgibaga in Goa also see large numbers every year. Locals claim that there has been a change in the pattern and that numbers have dwindled since the tsunami, which caused large-scale destruction along several coastlines in Asia.

During the nesting season, the turtles arrive on shore after dark and adult females lay 100-150 eggs in the silence of the night. While locals generally afford them the privacy and quiet needed to breed, olive ridleys have been victims of fishing-net accidents and poaching in recent times. The Goan government has taken the initiative to protect them in the form of eco-tourism. The Forest Department now patrols the beaches with local community members, and visitors may join the patrols, provided that silence is maintained at all times. If interested, you can ask the Turtle Protection Center on the beaches for permission to accompany them on a night watch.

of the sloth bear, leopard, flying squirrel, langur, mongoose, barking deer, pangolin, and even the rare black panther.

REPTILES

Both Mumbai and Goa house snakes and crocodiles, although Goa has a considerably larger population of both. Snakes were commonly found within city limits until around a decade ago, but urban development has ensured that they are now few and far between. Snakes found in the National Park, and sometimes in the city, include the Russell's viper, keelback, cobra, rat snake, vine snake, and tiny worm snake; amphibians like bull frogs, toads, and the venomous caecilian are also found around the city. Crocodiles live in the lake near premier engineering institute IIT in the Powai area of Mumbai.

Owing to its vast green cover and tropical climate, Goa is full of snakes, and locals are rarely surprised to find one in their backyard. The king cobra and bamboo pit viper are among the deadlier varieties of venomous snakes found here and are responsible for a large number of deaths in India every year. The Salim Ali Bird Sanctuary at Chorao Island also has crocodiles, pythons, and mudskippers. In mangroves around the Cumbarjua Canal, you will find marsh crocodiles—it's believed that the Sultan of Bijapur kept them to protect the port of Mandovi.

Environmental Issues

In recent years, Mumbai has flooded in the monsoons—caused largely by the destruction of mangroves, increased sewage, drains choked by plastic bags, and increased construction activity. While mangroves are constantly under threat from developers, the city has no space to destroy its garbage. One of the two landfills created for the purpose was closed after it had reached its limit. A lot of the sewage from the city (which includes chemicals from the tanneries located in Dharavi) is let out into the sea. Developers are also thinking up destructive ways for creating space on which to construct buildings—by filling in marshes and mangroves, and by carving out mountains in the northern suburbs. The erosion has destroyed significant green cover and washed out parts of the National Park. Encroachments on the National Park have seen a backlash, with leopards and snakes entering the apartment areas bordering the Park. Trees are being chopped to widen roads, and private gardens surrounding bungalows are being razed to create land for apartment buildings.

A variety of legislation and active citizens groups are trying to preserve the National Park and the trees of the city. Significant legislation includes banning polythene bags of lower grades, and demarcation of a Coastal Regulatory Zone. The latter has been one of the most successful policies, as the river, creek, and sea shorelines are graded in terms of biodiversity. The policy regulates construction, transport, waste disposal, fishing, and dredging.

History

EARLY ORIGINS

Archaeological findings in the region point to early stone-age settlements. Speculation is that people migrated here from the southern part of the peninsula. Rock carvings and stone tools found in Goa date back to the Neolithic and Mesolithic eras, and there are indications of trade with Babylon from the 8th to the 6th centuries B.C.

ISLAND OF THE KOLI FISHERFOLK

The next record is in the 2nd century B.C., when we find that the coastal regions of the mainland and some parts of the city were part of the Maurya Empire of the Emperor Ashoka, proof of which lies in his edicts found north of the city. The settlements from the Stone Age seem to have developed into the fishing tribes—the Kolis. These and the monks—whose monastery at Kanheri (a pilgrimage halt for traders) dates to the same era—were the first inhabitants before the Bhandaris (palm tappers) from the coast and Agris (salt pan workers) migrated to the city. The patron goddess Mumbadevi seems to have been brought from Gujarat a few centuries later. Goa too was under the Maurya empire and together with present-day Ratnagiri and Sindhudurg in Maharashtra, was called Revatidvipa.

ANCIENT HINDU DYNASTIES

The Satavahana dynasty from the southeast of the peninsula controlled Mumbai and its surrounding regions after the fall of the Maurya Empire until around 220 A.D. Following this, the region passed through many small and large empires but was ruled mainly between the Mauryas and the Chalukyas. Goa too was a part of the same western Konkan belt (Revatidvipa) that was passed on as new dynasties controlled the region. Significant in Goa were the Chalukyas, the Rashtrakutas, the Silharas, and the Kadambas. Important nstances include the construction of the first ettlements in Old Goa in the mid-11th century by the Kadambas and then a brief stint by the Yadavas before the invasions by the Bahmani Kings in the 14th century. There was regular maritime and land trade between the Middle East, Africa, and the western coast. Maritime trade history shows growth in trade between the west coast of the subcontinent with the Arabs and the eastern coast of Africa from the 7th–13th centuries A.D. Islands considered unprofitable were passed on from one empire to the next but were mostly under the control of the Silhara dynasty. The oldest surviving structures in the city, like the Walkeshwar Temple and the Banganga Tank, date back to this time, around the late 13th century A.D. The second wave of Zoroastrians from Iran arrived north of the city at this time (the first had arrived in the 7th century). Small empires in the area of Mahim and surrounding areas are also recorded in the next few decades.

MUSLIM INVASION AND PORTUGUESE RULE

By the mid-14th century, the Sultan of Gujarat had taken over the island of Salcette (North Mumbai) and soon acquired the entire archipelago. The mosque at Mahim is believed to date back to this acquisition. In 1508, the first Portuguese ship, commanded by Francis Almeida, sailed into the natural harbor and was followed up with merchants and troops. The Bom Bahia (Good Bay) was ceded by the sultan in 1534 to the Portuguese, who then used the bay as a trading port, converting some of the fisherman to Christianity in the process. The Mount Mary church dates back to this first colonization. The British and the Dutch had acquired ports farther down south along the coast, but the Portuguese cornered most of the trade because of the strategic location of this trade route and port. There were a dozen small settlements along the coast, and physician and botanist Garcia da Orta built a manor house (now demolished, only the gate remains in a protected naval area) on the southernmost island in 1549. For the Portuguese, the center of the city was in the north—most of their original settlements, like the Bassein Fort, lie out of present city limits.

The Bahmanis (a faction of the Mughals) invaded Goa in 1350 and made it a part of their Deccan Kingdom. The Vijayanagar Empire briefly interrupted their hold, but they managed to found a new city for trade on the northern banks of the River Mandovi. The Bahmanis split in 1490 and Goa came under the rule of Bijapur in the southeastern part of the peninsula. On Vasco da Gama's discovery of the west coast of India, the Portuguese realized the need to set up trading posts along the coast. After one unsuccessful attempt, Alfonso de Albuquerque captured the city of Ela in Goa (now known as Old Goa) on November 25, 1510. It became their capital, and Goa was soon called the Lisbon of the East and Goa Dourada (Golden Goa). From 1540 onward, the Jesuits began to proselytize and managed to convert a large part of the populace to Catholicism. St. Francis Xavier, the patron saint of Goa, arrived in 1542.

MUMBAI
British Rule and the Independence Movement

In 1661, the Portuguese handed over the seven mosquito-infested islands now called Mumbai to Charles II of England as a part of the dowry brought by Catherine of Braganza. The crown had little use for the islands and leased them to the East India Company in 1668 for an annual rent of 10 pounds. Owing to threats from the Siddis, the pirates of Malabar, the Marathas, the Dutch, and the French, the East India Company immediately started to build fortifications in the south.

By this time, there was a sizeable British settlement of around 300 people living predominantly in the Fort area. Gerald Aungier, the governor of Bombay (1672–1675) was responsible for restructuring the city by improving the Fort, creating a distinct town plan, founding a mint, establishing a hospital, commissioning a church, and drawing out law and order regulations, among other things. He invited indigenous trading classes and castes to settle within the Fort in order to develop maritime trade. Thus, the foundations of the heterogeneous nature of the city were laid as traders from Gujarat and the Maratha areas, Iranian Parsis, Jewish traders from Armenia, and Africans arrived for the booming trade in ivory, coir, salt, coconut, spices, cloth, and other goods. Aungier's strategy succeeded, and Bombay became a major port well known for tax exemptions and other benefits.

By the late 1600s, the eclectic population of the city rose to almost 75,000. As the port expanded, it drew people to start peripheral commerce like shipbuilding—an industry that moved here from Surat. Artisans like goldsmiths, ironsmiths, and weavers flocked to the islands to sell their wares, and Bombay also became a slave market. These crowds settled immediately north of the Fort area in what became known as the Black Town. Even today, the streets north of CST Station are ghettos of communities that trace their origins to these times.

In 1686, the East India Company moved its base to Bombay, which became the center of maritime trade in the subcontinent. The Church opened in 1718 and a moat was dug around the Fort, a project that was completed in 1745, protecting a 15.5-square-kilometer area.

The seven islands were converted into a singular landmass by reclamation in a project designed by Governor William Hornby. The project lasted from 1784 to 1845. This plan was not approved by the East India Company, but Hornby began work anyway—and was later recalled and discharged of his duty for this very reason. This period also saw the growth of the cityscape as more buildings were constructed. The first railway line in the country was inaugurated between Thana (present-day Thane) and Bombay in 1853, leading to a network that survives even today. Industry too found a footing, with the first cotton mill being established in 1854.

Following the Revolt of 1857, the British crown accused the East India Company of mismanagement and revoked its lease. The American Civil War and the opening up of the Suez Canal led to the growth of Bombay as the new cotton capital, as well as the trading center for the opium that was being shipped to China. The stock exchange dates back to this time. Most of Bombay's landmark buildings also date back to this era of expansion, in 1862, when the Fort walls were pulled down, the moats filled in, and the city expanded into the suburban areas. The railway network had its major terminus here, shipping was pulling in large revenues, and the cotton trade and industry were rising steadily. By this time, the threat of the Marathas and the Dutch was overcome and the Empire consolidated its position here.

With the arrival of Gandhi in 1915, the port of Bombay went into a nationalist frenzy. The large working classes were mobilized by the Congress Party and the Communists, who disturbed the working of the Empire with their sabotages and strikes. The Congress held several sessions in the city and some of the major freedom struggles, like the Quit India Movement, began here. August Kranti Maidan and Mani Bhavan, among other sites, were witness to this period.

Post-Colonial Politics

India won Independence in 1947, which was followed by a period of reconstruction and growth. Bombay developed as a commercial capital owing to its stock market, large mercantile population, trade and shipping, and perfect mix of traders, capitalists, middlemen, labor, and consumers. The Bombay state was divided into the two states of Maharashtra and Gujarat following large-scale protests and clashes on May 1, 1960. Since then, Bombay has been the capital of the state of Maharashtra, but demands continue to be made for it to become a Union Territory (i.e., administered by the central government). The city witnessed great changes in this period as economy and polity saw massive upheavals. Cotton mills were shut down, and the period was also marked by import restrictions and large-scale immigration into the city. Smuggling rings developed, mills declined, unemployment rose, slums blossomed, crime levels soared, militant groups of the hitherto oppressed were formed, and in the midst of all this, the city kept growing as migrants flowed in from around the country. The hard right-wing political party, the Shiv Sena, garnered the support of the unemployed Maharashtrian youth and in subsequent years attacked South Indian migrants to the city, and then North Indians, for appropriating the jobs of native Maharashtrians. The 1970s and '80s were filled with regional, economic, religious, and caste-based clashes. The chaos subsided as the country crept toward economic liberalization in the 1990s.

From Bombay to Mumbai

Bombay moved from the hands of the centrist Congress party to the Shiv Sena in the 1990s, which changed its name to Mumbai, the claimed original nomenclature based on the Goddess Mumba Devi. While the state of Maharashtra has more or less been regained by the Congress, the Mumbai Municipality has been the domain of the Sena for the last two decades. Malls have cropped up on mill lands, satellite townships have sprung up, and infrastructure development is in full flow. Since 1990, economic liberalization has changed the face of Mumbai, giving it the commercial glitzy sheen that it wears today. This hasn't prevented nativism, terrorism, and religious and caste riots from breaking out from time to time, and the damage has been felt by all parts of the city.

Since the 1990s, at least four major terrorist attacks have targeted Mumbai, there is increased flooding during the monsoons, the streets are getting more polluted and crowded—but the city continues to grow steadily.

GOA
Portuguese Rule

By the end of the 16th century and the turn of the 17th century, Old Goa had become one of the richest cities in the world. Trade flourished, and churches, educational institutions, and hospitals emerged in an effort to make it a grander destination than even Lisbon.

© ASHIMA NARAIN

Goa was the domain of the Portuguese until its liberation in 1961.

However, Goa Dourada was marred by the plague, which was brought here by a ship from Europe in 1635. This was followed by a cholera epidemic and the surviving populace moved to Panjim.

The Portuguese stayed on even as their power in the region was reduced thanks to military engagements with the Dutch and the British. Goa became a major trade center for the spice trade and merchandise from the East. In the 1700s, the Marathas, in a bid for expansion, attacked the Portuguese but failed to acquire Goa. The tide changed and the Portuguese managed to acquire new territories, including the outward regions of present-day Goa, by 1791. By this time, the Jesuits were banned and a large number of Hindus managed to retain their religious identities as a result. Portuguese rule continued, although Goans were given increased rights. In 1757, King Joseph I granted Portuguese citizenship and representation to all subjects in Goa and other Portuguese-controlled areas. Panaji was made the official

COMMUNALISM IN A COSMOPOLITAN CITY

The demolition of the Babri Mosque in Ayodhya by right-wing Hindu groups in December 1992 sparked a chain of riots across the country that spread to a city whose very foundations were laid upon its cosmopolitan nature. Bombay, as it was known then, had prided itself for its "unity in diversity," as multiple religious groups and ethnic communities lived amicably as neighbors. The riots, touted as a backlash to the Babri issue, shook this forward-looking city and took it back to the dark ages as friends turned foes and frenzied mobs took to the streets with swords, choppers, knives, and anything else that they could lay their hands on. While the Muslim community was accused of instigating the riots, it is believed that the communal tension was largely a creation of the right-wing Hindu fundamentalist party that was in power at the time – the Shiv Sena.

Many areas shared by Hindus and Muslims – Bombay Central, Jogeshwari, Sewri, Masjid Bunder, and Mahim – saw unabated large-scale violence for a week in December 1992 and another week in January 1993. About a thousand people were killed, and as many went missing, until the army was finally called in and peace restored. The damage in life, trade, and property was felt in the squalid, tense atmosphere of the city in the following months. As much of the violence was planned and instigated by right-wing groups, often in complicity with the police, the Bombay underworld (mostly Muslims) led by Dawood Ibrahim is believed to have holed up outside the country and planned revenge for the Muslims killed in the riots. In a large-scale operation, massive RDX explosions shook Bombay on March 12, 1993, killing 250 people and injuring three times as many. The targets included five-star hotels, a cinema, markets, the stock exchange building, and the Air India high-rise, among others. Repercussions included a crackdown on crime, *mohalla samiti* (neighborhood community watch), strengthening of the Shiv Sena, increased ghettoization of the two religious groups, and a weariness for religious rivalry in the city – which, thankfully, hasn't seen a communal riot since.

An inquiry was conducted after the riots by the Srikrishna Commission, led by Justice Srikrishna. On July 10, 2008, the first of the perpetrators were sentenced to a year's imprisonment. Not surprisingly, they were members of the Shiv Sena. Dawood Ibrahim remains at large, supposedly in Karachi, under the protection of Pakistan. All attempts at negotiation with Pakistan and efforts made by the Indian government to have him extradited have been unsuccessful.

seat of government in 1843 and administration was better established.

Goa Liberation Movement

Throughout the years, there were attempts to overthrow the Portuguese, most notably during the Pinto Revolt of 1787 and the Rane revolts in the 1800s. By the 1900s, Goans educated in Bombay and other places had emigrated to India or set up relations with the Indian National Congress. The Congress in turn sent in leaders to add Goa to the nationalist frenzy for independence in the mainland. The Satyagraha movement of Gandhi was partly successful in Goa before the Portuguese managed to repress it. Nehru tried to initiate negotiations with Lisbon soon after India's Independence, but Lisbon refused to give him audience.

By 1953, diplomatic relations between the two were closed. A number of liberation parties arose in Goa and India, notably the Azad Gomantak Dal, Goa Liberation Council, and the Goan People's Party. Some believed in Gandhi's notion of non-violence; others attacked Portuguese troops and blew up their armories. The Portuguese were thus forced to reinforce their borders. In an almost bloodless coup called Operation Vijay, 30,000 Indian troops captured and integrated Goa on December 19, 1961.

Tourism and the Hippie Era

With the dawning of the hippie era, many found solace by practicing Eastern philosophy while living in India, especially along the sunny beaches of Goa. The 1960s and '70s saw thousands flock to Goa's beaches for a bit of sand and salvation. Tie-dye clothes, dreadlocks, marijuana, and nudity were the norm in these relatively unfettered environs. The hippies introduced Goa to the world, but their movement died out slowly as drugs and crime began to take their toll. Indian moral policing also increased, leading to decreased drug usage in public. Nude beaches were also banned as locals began to reclaim their land.

You may still find the odd hippie old-timer on a Goan beach or in some of the pioneering shacks. One of the notable legacies of the hippie era is the Anjuna flea market. For a colorful account of these times, read Cleo Odzer's account of this era in her book, *Goa Freaks.*

Statehood and Contemporary Politics

Goa was centrally administered as a Union Territory until May 30, 1987, when it became a state. Initial moves to assimilate the region into neighboring states and to drop Konkani as the official regional language were resisted by Goans. Goa soon went on to become India's 25th state, while Konkani came to be recognized as one of the country's official languages.

As one of the last states to join the Union of India, Goa has a distinct identity (which in fact played a major role in its modern statehood). The social, political, and economic nature and problems of the state are different from those elsewhere in the country. It earns sizeable revenue from tourism, and the local population has a stable income from traditional occupations like agriculture and fishing, resulting in a higher per capita income and better standard of living. In recent years, mining, overcrowding of the coastal area, and pollution have been worries, especially in the popular tourist areas.

Because of a small legislature, Goa has had many unstable governments—a total of 14 governments in 15 years! This is largely the result of power shared by the two national parties—the Congress and the BJP—along with local parties that are known to switch sides. Goa continues to be a popular tourist destination despite the rise of crime and terrorist threats in recent years.

Government

ORGANIZATION

The Indian government is a three-tiered system, with a central two-house parliamentary government led by a prime minister, a state government led by a chief minister, and a self-governing body at the local level—a municipality for the urban area and a council for the rural areas. All three levels have distinct administrative functions, each taking care of items in lists defined by the constitution.

Mumbai is mostly administered by the Brihanmumbai Municipal Corporation, though a few administrative details are taken care of by the state government. Being the capital of the state of Maharashtra, Mumbai also has a significant presence of state ministers and administrators. While Maharashtra has a 290-seat lower house, Goa—one of the smallest states in the country—has a unicameral legislature with only a 40-seat house, with some urban areas governed by municipalities.

POLITICAL PARTIES

Indian politics has been dominated largely by two political parties—the moderate Congress party and the right-wing Bhartiya Janata Party (BJP). Of late, neither party has managed to win complete majority in the parliament, resulting in coalition governments with smaller local parties.

In Maharashtra, the Congress allies with Nationalist Congress Party (NCP); the BJP, however, works hand in hand with another right-wing party—the Shiv Sena, which believes in a "Sons of the Soil" ideology that fuels native Maharashtrians to stake their claim on the city. The Mumbai Municipality has been led single-handed by the Shiv Sena for the last two decades, while the state government has changed hands between Congress-NCP and BJP-Shiv Sena.

The Goa legislature has fluctuated between Congress and BJP, and—owing to its small number—has been plagued by members defecting from one party to another for rewards.

JUDICIAL AND PENAL SYSTEM

The Indian judicial system is multi-tiered, with many local tribunals dealing with smaller issues, and a criminal court system that has been plagued by corruption and delayed judgments.

There are three major tiers: the local magisterial courts, the high court (on which Mumbai has a seat and whose jurisdiction extends to Goa), and a Supreme Court of India. The higher judiciary and the prison system are centrally administered, while the lower tribunals are formed within the state.

BUREAUCRACY

India prides itself on the "iron structure" of the bureaucracy that is considered one of the prized legacies left behind by the British. Civil servants are selected on the basis of a rigorous examination system and are specially trained in administration of all possible areas of the country. The Indian Administrative Service wields a lot of legal and administrative power and often clashes with the intentions of political leaders. The Indian Police Service is another rung of the bureaucracy, known for efficient handling of law and order, as well as for its corruption.

Economy

AGRICULTURE

Mumbai and Goa have traditionally been agrarian areas, and the original inhabitants of both area engaged in food production. Even today, Goa produces a substantial crop of cashews, arecas, rice, and coconut. There are subsidiary industries around these crops, which provide most of the local employment. Mumbai does not have any farmlands any more, and it is difficult to believe that areas that now boast the swankiest malls were once paddy fields. Both Mumbai and Goa have always had a significant share in the western coast's fishing industry. While Mumbai supplies the local markets, Goa has several subsidiary industries like tinning and fertilizer production.

INDUSTRY

Mumbai is the hub of commerce and industry in India, with practically every business and entrepreneurial activity you can think of. A majority of commerce in Mumbai is based

© JANHAVI ACHAREKAR

Both Mumbai and Goa have a significant fishing industry.

on the construction boom, with real estate prices in recent years breaking all records. Mumbai is also the financial capital of the country, and most of the national and international banks have their headquarters in the city. Similarly, in recent years, commercial enterprises have been centrally located in specially designated commercial areas of the city, like the Bandra-Kurla complex, and in the satellite township of Navi Mumbai. Recently, several Business Process Outsourcing units (BPOs) have set up office in the northern suburbs of Mumbai.

Goa has significantly protected its land from development, but the scene is slowly changing. Recently, the new urban crowd has snapped up property in the coastal areas, replacing a few old townships and zones by swanky apartments and malls. However, the Urban Task Plan, brought into force by citizen activists, is now paving the way for responsible development.

Bauxite and iron ore mining have also played a significant part in Goa's economy, but issues with environmental degradation and population displacement have plagued the industry in recent years as entire mountains and villages have been carved out of the landscape.

TOURISM

While Mumbai has its share of tourists, most of Goa's revenue production comes from tourism. The annual visitors here rival the population of the state, accounting for up to 12 percent of the country's tourists. However, recent terrorism and natural disasters like flooding in Mumbai, and terrorist threats in Goa, have made a dent in tourism in both destinations.

People and Culture

DEMOGRAPHY

Mumbai is one of the most crowded cities in the world, with a population of more than 13 million people and a density of around 46,000 people per square kilometer. It is difficult to determine who the "original" Mumbaikars (native inhabitants) really were, and the city today is an amalgam of communities, castes, and languages from all over the country.

Goa has a sparse population of around 1.3 million people, dense only around the coastal and the urban areas. The annual number of tourists to Goa is almost equal to its population! The state is largely populated by fisherfolk, landowners, and traders.

RELIGION AND COMMUNITIES

Hindus constitute a majority of Mumbai's population, while Islam, Christianity, Buddhism, and Zoroastrianism are the other prominent religions. There are also small numbers of Jews and Sikhs in the city. Over the years, Mumbai has turned into a heterogeneous mix of people

© ASHIMA NARAIN

Mumbai and Goa are known for their diverse faiths.

MELTING POT: COMMUNITIES OF MUMBAI

Recently, there has been an upsurge in interest concerning Mumbai's "original inhabitants" Nativist parties claim ownership of the city, insisting that it belongs to the "Marathi Manoos" or the native Maharashtrian.

However, the history of the city shows that the foundation of Mumbai lies in its role as a crucible of communities and cultures. The original inhabitants of the islands were the Koli fishing community and the Agri community of salt-pan workers, and Buddhist monks arrived as early as the 2nd century B.C. Fleeing persecution, the Parsis, or the Zoroastrian community from Iran, arrived in the north of Mumbai by the 8th century A.D.; the first of the community settled in the city two centuries later, as their proficiency in ship-building, banking, and commerce attracted them to this growing shipping, industrial, and commercial center. Parsi weavers and artisans too were in demand, and were specially called from Surat, in modern-day Gujarat, by the governor of Bombay. The first city newspaper was started by a Parsi, and the community is as well known for its philanthropy and entrepreneurial skills now as it was then. Jews from Baghdad arrived in the 18th century, for banking and trade. Their numbers have dwindled over the years, especially after Independence, but there are small pockets of settlers in Mumbai and along the Maharashtra coast. David Sassoon, who lends his name to various city icons, was an illustrious Baghdadi Jew, having made his fortune in opium and his name through philanthropy. The Siddis trace their origins to Africa and still live in small numbers in and around the city. The Bene-Israeli Jews, greater in numbers, are an older community, believed to be the descendants of those who first arrived on the west coast when escaping persecution in Galilee. Many continue to live in the city, lending their skills to trade, arts, and society.

Today, the Parsis make up only 2 percent of the population (down from 16 percent at one time), and the Baghdadi Jews have all but disappeared. The Kolis and the Agris have been pushed to the fringes of the city, while right-wing parties stake their claim on a city built by multiple hands, multiple communities.

---

owing to traders who migrated to the city from all over the country; significant communities include the Gujaratis, Shettys, and Keralites, and, more recently, migrants from Uttar Pradesh and Bihar who dominate the service sector.

Goa is dominated by Hindus and Catholics, with small pockets of Muslims. The Church of St. Francis of Assisi was founded here more than 400 years ago and Christianity spread rapidly during Portuguese rule, as a result of mass conversion and missionary zeal. There are also a large number of Bene-Israeli Jews along the coast.

THE GOAN WEDDING

While Goa has a large Hindu population, it is the Goan Catholic wedding that is synonymous with nuptials in the state. A Western-style wedding with uniquely Goan traditions thrown in for good measure, the wedding is a fun, vibrant event. Traditionally, marriages were arranged by parents of the bride and the groom, and once the alliance had been sealed by the two families with a word of honor, the date for the wedding was mutually decided upon. Fortunately, couples have the freedom of choice today.

A number of rituals or customs are precursors to the big day, including a lavish meal to feed the poor and a fun ritual bath in coconut milk on the eve of the wedding, which involves much singing and the customary bottle of *feni*. Traditional songs called the *zoti, vers, ovis,* and *mandos* are sung with great gusto through the wedding preparations. On the day of the wedding, the bride's family delivers her trousseau and traditional Goan sweets to the groom's family, and the two families proceed to church for the ceremony.

HINDU GOA: THE SARASWAT BRAHMIN COMMUNITY

Goa has a large Hindu population, much of which is dominated by the community known as the Gowd Saraswat Brahmins. This Konkani- or Marathi-speaking community traces its origins back to the Vedic Ages (1500–500 B.C.). They're believed to descend from Aryan settlers from Central Asia who settled originally on the banks of the Saraswati River, from which the community derives its name.

The highest in the caste system, the Brahmin community in general was traditionally vegetarian. However, the Saraswats are fish-eating Brahmins – owing to a 12-year famine, according to folklore. The River Saraswati dried by 1000 B.C. as the glacier emptied out and the community migrated in different directions. One faction came westward to Dwarka in present-day Gujarat and set off by ship to Goa. They settled in Goa and were engaged in fishing, farming, and trade. Adopting the names of the regions they lived in as their own, they were soon responsible for the spread of religion, trade, education, and governance. Most of Goa's Hindu and vegetarian cuisine was created and influenced by the Saraswat community.

Over the centuries, the community migrated to the north and the south – myths and temples along the coast tell us how the community came to be here. The arrival of the Portuguese led to a mass exodus of the community and many fled persecution by escaping to South India and modern-day Maharashtra. The community has produced a number of illustrious individuals in the fields of writing, direction, journalism, sports, and politics. It continues to thrive in Goa and the neighboring states, contributing to culture, learning, and trade.

After the nuptials, there is the cutting of the wedding cake, drinking, and dancing to rock and roll while the couple is lifted up in their chairs for a kiss. *Feni* plays a pivotal role in the proceedings and is poured onto the ground as an offering of gratitude, celebration, and prayer, along with traditional songs. Goans are known for their joie de vivre and their weddings are filled with laughter and revelry.

The Goan spirit is infectious and the seascape perfect for a wedding. Wedding tourism has taken off in a big way here, bringing roaring business to hotels and wedding planners. Goa's churches and natural beauty make for a stunning backdrop as couples arrive here from all over the world for their dream wedding.

If you're planning to get married here, make sure that you get your paperwork done as per the law. Lester Melo (The Wedding Boutique, opposite Hotel Delmon, Panaji, cell tel. 91/98221-00170, www.lestermelo.com) is the busiest of all wedding planners in Goa.

LANGUAGE

In Mumbai, you might hear more than five languages in a day: Hindi spoken by auto-rickshaw and taxi drivers, Marathi by bus conductors, English in offices and stores, Gujarati in the trading areas, and Bambaiya—a local tongue that amalgamates the best and the worst of Hindi and Marathi—all over the city.

Konkani is Goa's state language and the most widely spoken here, while Marathi is a primary language in the northern part and a secondary tongue in the rest of the state. Hindi, introduced only after the 1970s, is spoken in parts of the state, but is not native to Goa. English is also spoken fluently in most parts, especially the tourist areas. Portuguese was once the language of the landed elite and upper-crust Goan society. Even today, you will find a smattering of Portuguese spoken in the Latin Quarter and within the old casas that dot the state.

ARCHITECTURE

Both Mumbai and Goa have unique architectural features resulting from varied historical influences. Each has identifiable zones that are exemplary of a particular period or influence of architectural style.

The colonial zones of Mumbai have many neo-classical and neo-gothic buildings—the largest collection of neo-gothic structures after London, in fact. The Indo-Saracenic style, personified by the erstwhile Prince of Wales Museum, incorporates local motifs and stones with neo-gothic architecture. Looming balconies and balustrades, gargoyles replaced by local animals, and elaborate red and black stone domes are some of the features of this style. Mumbai also has the largest collection of art deco buildings after Miami—the stretch on Marine Drive and opposite the Oval Maidan are famous, as are the landmark Regal, Metro, and New Empire cinema halls. In the *gaothan* of Khotachiwadi in the old area of Girgaum, you will find quaint Maharashtrian and Indo-Portuguese-style bungalows, and there are similar hamlets dotting the suburbs.

sculpture at the New India Assurance building in Mumbai

© ASHIMA NARAIN

In Goa, you will find the most spectacular architecture comprising roadside chapels, Hindu courtyard-style homes, grand Indo-Portuguese casas, old gothic churches, and the solitary neo-gothic church of Saligao. Balconies and oyster-shell windows distinguish Goan homes from others, along with bright Mediterranean or earthy colors, clay tile roofs, and sprawling courtyards. The houses are built for the monsoons, and you can see the identifiable Indian modifications made to Portuguese architecture for this purpose. In urban centers like Panaji, there has been an increase in apartment blocks and malls, but its splendid Latin Quarter remains a protected heritage zone and a source of pride.

LITERATURE

Mumbai has developed as a great literary center over the years. Marathi, Gujarati, and English literature have each had their patrons and movements, and have spawned eclectic literary circles. The 1970s saw the Bloomsbury-like group of Kala Ghoda poets, which derived its name from the city's art district. Literary events continue to be held here at the Kala Ghoda Arts Festival, and also in a number of other neighborhood and cultural festivals across the city. The metropolis wends its way into several novels, short stories, and poems—from the days of notable Mumbai poet Nissim Ezekiel to more recent writers like Altaf Tyrewalla. Many writers from across the world and the country have made the city their home and muse, including recent Booker Prize–winner Arvind Adiga. Writer Gregory David Roberts has also been indelibly linked with the city after the phenomenal success of his novel *Shantaram*.

Goa too is known to have an active literary

URBAN ART: MUMBAI ART AND LITERATURE

An unlikely muse, Mumbai wends its way into much of Indian and international art and writing. The city has also been the birthplace of significant artistic movements, including India's modern art movement begun by the Bombay Progressive Artists' Group. Founded by K. H. Ara, S. K. Bakre, H. A. Gade, M. F. Husain, S. H. Raza and F. N. Souza, the group paved the way for a modern Indian form of artistic expression soon after India's Independence, breaking away from the British school of landscape and realistic painting and the Bengal school of art. Their avant-garde works revolutionized the Indian art scene and laid the foundation for India's, and Mumbai's, thriving art scene.

The movement was born at Artists' Centre in the Kala Ghoda art district of Mumbai, where the group's memebers first exhibited their works; the gallery continues to host art shows today and Mumbai is now the center of much artistic activity. Contemporary artists such as Atul and Anju Dodiya, Sudhir Patwardhan, Brinda Miller, Navjot, Gieve Patel, Bose Krishnamachari, Sunil Padwal, Sunil Gawde, and Jitish Kallat are known internationally. Their works, particularly those of Atul Dodiya, Patwardhan, and Patel, are reflective of the city.

Mumbai also finds itself in the throes of a growing literary scene. Legends such as Nissim Ezekiel, Dom Moraes, Arun Kolatkar, Eunice de Souza, and other poets and writers debated and discussed literary theories and each other's works in the 1970s in the same art district that spawned the art movement. Mumbai has found its way into modern literature, ranging from Mumbai-born Salman Rushdie's writings to the works of Mumbai-based writers such as Kiran Nagarkar. Mumbai is also the subject of poetry by poets such as Ezekiel, Kolatkar, Dilip Chitre, and Amit Chaudhuri and it became the focus of international attention when literary phenomenon Gregory David Roberts wrote his autobiographical novel *Shantaram*, the story of an Australian escaped convict who found himself in the thick of the Mumbai underworld. Mumbai's famous gangs are also the subject of author Vikram Chandra's *Sacred Games*, while Nagarkar's *Ravan and Eddie* is set in a Mumbai *chawl* (a low-income tenement). The city has several new and promising writers, such as Altaf Tyrewala, whose novel *No God in Sight* is a series of portraits of Mumbai's Muslim community, and Murzban Shroff, whose *Breathless in Bombay* is a collection of short stories that reflect contemporary Mumbai. The city is also seen in a number of works of non-fiction, prominently in Suketu Mehta's *Maximum City*, which vaulted the city to international fame.

---

scene. An ideal reclusive writer's retreat, it is home to an illustrious list of authors and poets that includes Amitav Ghosh. It has also had its share of Marathi, Konkani, and English literature. Goan resident Maria Aurora Couto is one of Goa's premier authors, while writers such as Damodar Mauzo and Manohar Shetty are known for short stories that evoke the Goan way of life. The Goa Writers' Group comprises the state's resident writers and meets regularly to discuss works and ideas.

VISUAL ART

Mumbai was the birthplace of Indian Modern Art. It was in the district of Kala Ghoda that the group of revolutionary artists called the Bombay Progressives first broke away from the landscape tradition of the British school and the Bengal school, in the year of India's Independence. Today, the area continues to be a vibrant art district that exhibits art everywhere from the pavement to the various galleries that line its roads. Public art exists in the form of the mural of the Kala Ghoda (Black Horse), painted by a different contemporary artist every year, and a famous piece of street-art in the Fort area by noted painter M. F. Husain (one of the Bombay Progressives). In recent years, the art scene has been marked by wine-and-cheese parties, covered extensively by tabloids—in addition to high-profile auctions that have upped art prices to the scale of the real estate boom.

Goa has a vibrant art scene that embraces visiting and resident artists from Goa and around the world. While Mario Miranda is Goa's best-known figure in the visual arts, the state boasts a number of young and established artists whose works may be viewed at the Kala Academy in Panaji. Goa is also known for its Portuguese legacy of *azulejo* tiles, an art revived by a young artist from Panaji.

A POLISHED ART

Among Goa's many Portuguese legacies and influences is the art of the *azulejo* tile. These lovely blue-and-white tiles adorn many a brightly colored balcony, make up murals in five-star hotels, announce names of streets, and double up as name-plates and coasters across Goa. *Azulejos* are glazed, hand-painted ceramic tiles; the name comes from the Arabic word *Al Zulej*, meaning "smooth polished stone," suggesting their origins in Persia. Moorish migrants brought the tiles to the Iberian Peninsula, and 14th-century Spaniards popularized this ceramic art form, which then caught the fancy of the Portuguese. Initially, the tiles had geometric or floral patterns, in keeping with their Islamic origins. However, by the late-16th century, the Portuguese (with the help of Flemish ceramists in Lisbon) had appropriated the art form and added their own touch by introducing human and animal figures or motifs. The original colors of blue, green, yellow, and white too were reduced to stark blue and white – in the style of Chinese porcelain, which had been discovered by Europeans in the age of the great explorations and conquests.

By the 17th century, the Portuguese had taken *azulejos* to other parts of the world, including their prized colony of Goa. The passageway in the building of the Menezes-Braganza Institute in Panaji is testimony to this, with its beautiful 18-square-meter mural depicting Vasco da Gama's journey and the Portuguese conquest of the East. Painted by Jorge Colaco, it also carries verses from *Os Lusiades*, an epic written by Luis Vaz de Camoens – Portugal's national poet. The names of the beautiful, narrow streets of the Latin Quarter in Fontainhas appear on blue-and-white *azulejos*. Although Portuguese tile factories made it easy to reproduce patterns by the 19th and 20th centuries, the traditional hand-painted art survives today in both Lisbon and Goa. Surprisingly, the tiles and murals found in Goa throughout Portuguese rule were imported from Portugal.

The young Goan artist Orlando de Noronha was the first to produce the *azulejo* tile locally, on his return from Lisbon (where he was on a scholarship from the Fundaçao Oriente) in 1998. His Indo-Portuguese designs, produced under the name of Azulejos de Goa, are now seen across Goa, as are those of artists and apprentices who once trained under him.

© JANHAVI ACHAREKAR

The glazed, hand-painted ceramic tile called the *azulejo* is Portuguese Goa's artistic legacy.

PERFORMING ARTS

Mumbai hosts a number classical and contemporary music, dance, and theater performances. You can catch jazz, rock, Indian and Western classical music throughout the year at places like Blue Frog that bring in talent from across the world, and at bars like Not Just Jazz by the Bay. The city hosts a number of music festivals and events through the year, making it a delight for music lovers. Theater too is vibrant, with smaller experimental productions taking place at the Prithvi Theatre and the National Center of Performing Arts. Classical dance performances are held regularly by Indian and visiting artists.

Goa is known for its lively tradition of the performing arts and the Portuguese influence has led to a wonderful tradition of fado dance performances, although seen few and far between. Traditional dances such as the *dekhni* may be seen during festivals, and classical and other performances are held regularly at the Kala Academy in Panaji. However, Goa's most illustrious performing art is the *tiatr*, a traditional farcical art form that is unique to Goa.

Theater

If all the world's a stage, then the Goan *tiatr* is its musical finale. This hybrid local art is steeped in history and tradition—where the word *tiatr* itself is derived from the Portuguese *teatro* (theater). A combination of Italian opera and the burlesque Konkani folk theater, dialogues and songs are delivered in Konkani to maintain its mass appeal. Plays comprise six or seven acts, with each act relieved by lively songs that communicate a social or comic message, often accompanied by a local band. These Brechtian-style musical intermissions are often the most colorful parts of the *tiatr*, where singers (ranging from children to senior citizens) dressed in shiny, bright dresses and tuxedos add to its local flavor. Plots revolve around family sagas, religion, social issues, and political concerns, relying on both melodrama and comedy to elicit laughter and tears from its motley audience. *Tiatr* performances may be caught at a number of places throughout the state, ranging from neighborhood temples during festivals to the Kala Academy in Panaji. The latter hosts an annual *tiatr* competition, where groups from across Goa perform in a marathon *tiatr* festival.

The first *tiatr* performance was staged in Bombay by a young man from Goa called Lucasinho Ribeiro on April 17, 1892. A backstage artist employed by one of the many Italian troupes that hosted operas for the British in Bombay, he evolved his own form from his observation of the Italian opera and knowledge of local folk theater. He was aided by fellow-Goan Joao Agostinho Fernandes, whose wife Regina Fernandes went on to become the first female actor in an era when women were forbidden to step on stage and men played the female parts in their place. *Tiatr* is said to have contributed greatly to Goan society and culture, its most important contribution being the preservation of the Konkani language in colonial times.

FOLK ART AND CRAFTS

Mumbai lacks the folk art and crafts of North India but is fast turning into a center for indigenous arts and crafts thanks to traveling artisan exhibitions from around the country. Handicrafts and textiles may also be found at state emporia in the World Trade Center and the Colaba region, and in specialty stores such as Anokhi.

Goa is known for its coir and shell-craft, found in the government-run store Aparant. Traditional Indian handicrafts from across the country may be found at the flea markets and the roadside stalls of its beaches.

ESSENTIALS

Getting There

Mumbai has long been a famous port well connected with the rest of the world. While travel to the city by sea is rare these days, except on cruise liners and local coastal yachts, it is well connected by air. Today Mumbai has a cramped but well-developed airport, and plans for a larger one on the outskirts of the city are underway. Mumbai is connected to other Indian destinations by an efficient train network, interstate bus services, and budget domestic flights that connect all the major cities (and most minor ones).

Goa, on the other hand, does not have an international airport. The Dabolim Airport near Vasco receives a handful of charter flights, but visitors generally enter via Mumbai or other destinations. There is talk of a new international airport at Mopa in North Goa.

AIR

There are direct international flights to Mumbai's **Chhatrapati Shivaji Airport** (BOM, tel. 022/2681-3000, www.csia.in) from most major cities in the world. The airport is located at Sahar in Andheri, a prominent suburb of the city, and is within reach of all parts of the city. For most visitors, this is the place for a stopover flight to Goa. The domestic terminal at **Santacruz** (tel. 022/2626-4000) is close by and well connected to the

© ASHIMA NARAIN

international terminal by a coach service that runs every 15 minutes.

A number of international airlines fly to Mumbai from the United States. These include United Airlines (toll-free tel. 800/864-8331, www.united.com), British Airways (toll-free tel. 800/247-9297, www.britishairways.com), Air India (toll-free tel. 800/223-7776, www.airindia.com), Jet Airways (toll-free tel. 866/835-9538, www.jetairways.com), Northwest Airlines (toll-free tel. 800/225-2525, www.nwa.com), Emirates (www.emirates.com), Virgin Atlantic (toll-free tel. toll-free 800/862-8621, www.virgin-atlantic.com), Etihad (www.etihadairways.com), Lufthansa (toll-free tel. 800/645-3880, www.lufthansa.com), Continental Airlines (toll-free tel. 800/523-3273, www.continental.com), Swiss (toll-free tel. 877/359-7947, www.swiss.com), and KLM (toll-free tel. 800/447-4747, www.klm.com).

There are many airlines operating flights between Mumbai and **Dabolim Airport** (GOI, Dabolim, tel. 0832/2254-1445) in Goa. No-frills airlines Spice Jet (toll-free tel. 800/180-3333, cell tel. 91/987180-3333, www.spicejet.com), IndiGo (tel. 91/99103-83838 or toll-free tel. 800/180-3838, www.goindigo.in), and Go Air (toll-free tel. 800/222-111, cell tel. 91/92232-22111. www.goair.in) offer tickets for one-third to half the cost of a normal airline ticket. The journey lasts barely an hour and it is usually possible to get tickets at the last minute. The same airlines also fly to other Indian destinations, including Bangalore, Delhi, and Jaipur. For a comprehensive destination/comparison chart while booking, try www.cleartrip.com and www.makemytrip.com. There are daily flights from most major Indian airports twice a day, but these may need advance booking during peak season.

BUS

There are no bus services that you can take from the borders, except from Pakistan, but seats are limited and recent tensions between the two countries point to the disruption of this service, too.

Goa and Mumbai are well connected to each other, and to other destinations in Maharashtra and states such as Karnataka and Andhra Pradesh, by both private and state buses. Of these, the most popular and recommended is **Paulo Travels** (Monalisa, Hill Rd., Bandra, Mumbai, tel. 022/2645-2624 and G1, Cardozo Building, near Kadamba bus stand, Panaji, tel. 0832/243-8531, www.paulotravels.com, Rs 350–750). Their Volvo sleeper and seater luxury coaches make the 12-hour road journey more comfortable than trips with other bus service providers. State-run buses have counters at the Panaji bus terminus. Luxury and air-conditioned buses are available to Mumbai, Bangalore, Hampi, and other destinations. Most private interstate buses arrive and depart from a separate bus stand next to the Mandovi Bridge.

CAR

It is possible to drive in from Nepal with the right permits (visa and international driver's license), but it involves a fair amount of paperwork and dealings with police officials along the way. There are several four-wheel-drive vehicles and cruisers that can take you across the border and drop you off at major transport junctions to catch a connecting bus.

There are a number of car rental and tourist taxi services from Mumbai and nearby destinations to Goa. Car rental services such as **Avis** (domestic and international airports, Mumbai, tel. 022/6556-4697, 24 hr), **Car Care** (Dongersi Road, Malabar Hill, Mumbai, tel. 022/2367-7724, 24 hr), and **Hertz** (Mahakali Caves Rd., Andheri East, Mumbai, tel. 022/6570-1692, 24 hr) are generally safe for the long 12–14 hour journey along the beautiful Konkan coast. Rates vary depending on the type and size of vehicle, but generally range Rs 10–18 per kilometer. This mode of transport is expensive and works only if the cost is shared among passengers and then eventually returned to Mumbai.

CRUISE SHIP

A few cruise ships come into the city. Most of these run coastal tours along the west

special women-only local trains during rush hour in Mumbai

coast and have a fixed route and dates, so you can plan your itinerary accordingly. **Star Cruises** (tel. 022/2219-7000, www .starcruises.co.in) runs cruises from Mumbai to Goa, and from Mumbai to Lakshadweep. Prices are subject to booking time and class. **Royal Caribbean International** (www.royalcaribbean.com), **Oceania Cruises** (www .oceaniacruises.com), **Seabourn Cruise Line** (www.seabourn.com), and **Azamara Cruises** (www.azamaracruises.com) stop over in Mumbai and Goa.

NEIGHBORING COUNTRIES

You can enter by road to India through Nepal, Bhutan, Bangladesh, and Pakistan, but strenuous ties between India and Pakistan keep changing the rules. Inquire in advance about the situation before you attempt to come via the Pakistan border. Make sure you apply for the right permits (visa and international driver's license) to enter through land routes. You can drive in from Nepal, Bhutan, and Bangladesh with these permits.

There are several SUVs that can take you across the border and drop you off at major transport junctions, from where you can catch a connecting bus. There is no organized service for crossing the border, however, and no fixed timings. There are adequate flights out of Nepal and a scary but picturesque one from Bhutan. The Nepal–Bhutan border is part of the Golden Crescent—a triangle of volatile drug and arms trade.

Getting Around

AIR

There are plenty of domestic flights connecting Mumbai to other Indian and international destinations. An increase in the number of budget airlines has made domestic travel cheap in recent years. It's possible to arrange last-minute booking, although the Mumbai–Delhi and Mumbai–Goa routes can get expensive if booked late. There are airports in many small towns and cities in the country, so getting around is rarely a problem.

Transport is easily available from the airport and includes car rental, taxi, auto-rickshaw, and bus services. If you're booking your flight to Goa from Mumbai or any other destination in India, you will get the best deals online (try www.cleartrip.com or www.makemytrip.com). A pre-paid taxi service is available at Goa's Dabolim Airport, but there is no bus service.

TRAIN

The quickest way to get around the country is by rail, and a foreign tourist quota means that you can easily get reservations on the otherwise busy express trains, albeit at a higher cost. If you plan in advance, you can book reservations at normal rates.

The trains have compartments classified into three categories—three-tier sleeper, three-tier AC, and two-tier AC; some trains also have first-class AC coupes. There is also a ladies-only compartment and an overcrowded general compartment that does not require prior reservation.

Train rides are fast and picturesque, but it can take as much as three days if you are traveling from one end of the country to the other—be sure to plan your itinerary accordingly. The **Indian Railways** website (www.indianrail.gov.in) is up to date with train schedules and reservation information. Never buy tickets from touts at the station, and onboard, make sure you keep your luggage chained.

BUS

The Maharashtra and Goa interstate buses have stations in Dadar, Mumbai Central, and Borivli but are a rickety affair that are best avoided. However, the service does run swanky buses to satellite towns like Pune, and there are numerous private bus companies that run air-conditioned TV coaches to most parts of the country, including Goa. These may be found outside bus stations in Mumbai Central, Dadar, and Bandra. **Paulo Travels** (Mumbai, tel. 022/2645-2624; Panaji, tel. 0832/243-8531; www.paulotravels.com) is the most trusted bus service that runs between Mumbai and Goa. Their Volvo coaches also have a comfortable sleeper option. The scenic trip to Goa takes approximately 14–16 hours and costs around Rs 850 for an air-conditioned bus.

For travel within Mumbai, the city's cheap and efficient **BEST bus service** connects all parts of the city at a minimum fare of Rs 4. "Limited" buses, which stop only at selected stops, and air-conditioned buses charge a higher fee. You can also get pre-paid GO cards at railway stations and bus depots.

Goa is well connected by its **Kadamba bus service** (Kadamba Bus Terminal, Panaji, tel. 0832/222-637), which carries passengers across the state.

CAR

You can hire a car (with or without a driver) from the airport or elsewhere in Mumbai. Opting for a driver is strongly recommended, especially in Mumbai, where traffic can get manic at any point in the day or night. If you intend to drive, however, you will need an international driver's license—and don't forget that cars drive on the left-hand side. Some rental agencies provide cars with left-hand drives too, but these are rare.

In Goa, you can easily hire cars and SUVs to get around. Most rental services have fixed daily hours and prices, and charge by the kilometer after that. Rates vary about Rs 800–1,400 for eight hours, and then Rs 10–14 per kilometer beyond working hours. Drivers are paid around Rs 150–300. Make sure you make a note of the kilometers on the odometer at the start of the journey so you calculate the right amount—bargaining with drivers and car rental owners can prove to be a hellish experience. Make sure your car sounds fine and that there is a spare tire and tools in the car.

TAXI

Mumbai's public taxi service is best used for short distances, helping save on time and money spent on parking. Insist on checking the tariff card at the end of your ride, however, or you may end up spending more on your ride than you would have on parking. Basic fare is Rs 13.

Motorcycle taxis are available throughout Goa. Known as "pilots," their origins go back to the hippie era, when motorcycles were a favored form of transport. Licensed motorcycles have a yellow-painted front mudguard and can be found at motorcycle taxi stands in main city areas. They charge Rs 10–15 per kilometer.

MOTORCYCLE AND BICYCLE

Motorcycle rentals do brisk business throughout Goa. Even families and mama-and-papa outfits rent out motorbikes and scooters. Rentals cost Rs 250–500 per day, depending on the type and model of the two-wheeler hired, and the season. In Panaji, **Paulo Travels** (G1, Cardozo Building, near Kadamba bus stand, Panaji, tel. 0832/243-8531, www.paulotravels .com) rents out two-wheelers. An international license is required and some places may ask for your passport details and a small security deposit. Do not leave your passport with them at any cost.

Bicycles are also easily hired in Goa, and make for a pleasant ride along Goan beaches and fields (but impossible in Mumbai). Look out for signs that say Bicycle Rental in the city center and sometimes in the backyards of residential houses. Bicycle rental costs Rs 30–50 per day.

Both motorcycle and bicycle rentals cost less during low season.

AUTO-RICKSHAWS

If traveling in North Mumbai, you can use these quaint three-wheelers to roam around.

© ASHIMA NARAIN

Motorcycles and scooters are a popular mode of transport in both Mumbai and Goa.

Minimum fare is Rs 9, but you should compare the tariff card at the end of the journey to know you are not being taken for a ride. Hint at a tip and the same rickshaw can sometimes be used for the entire day if you plan to cover many stops in one area. Goa also has auto-rickshaws, although they may only be used for short distances.

FERRIES

There are many ferries crossing Goa's rivers and connecting its little islets and islands. Most of these ferries are free for foot passengers (or charge a nominal amount) and charge Rs 5 for bikes and Rs 10 for four-wheelers.

ROAD RULES

Driving on Indian roads can be quite an experience, as lane driving is virtually non-existent, speed limits are archaic and rarely followed, motorcycles and auto-rickshaws can block the fast lane on the highway, and the clichéd cow does make an appearance sometimes.

Roads in Mumbai and the urban centers of Goa are crowded and narrow. Potholes are common during the monsoons and visibility can drop quite low if it is a heavy shower. There is no escaping dangerous overtaking on the highways or even on winding mountain terrain, so keep your eyes on the rearview mirror.

Make sure that your rental car has adequate tools, despite the many repair shops found dotting Mumbai and Goa. Also ensure that your rental car has the necessary papers, insurance, and is registered as a rental vehicle. While riding a motorcycle, wearing a helmet is required by the law.

Traffic police are known to be corrupt, especially on the Mumbai–Goa stretch, and can bother you for the slightest offence. Be wary. Also make sure to get a receipt for any fine that you have to pay.

Indians rely more on hand signals than turning indicators, so look up the actions on www.indiandrivingschools.com—a website that lists traffic rules, signals, signs, offences, and penalties.

INTERNATIONAL DRIVING PERMIT (IDP)

For driving in India you will need an IDP. You can apply for a one-year permit at your local American Automobile Association (AAA) or The National Auto Club office. You need to present your valid U.S. driver's license, two passport-size photographs, and less than $20.

HITCHHIKING

Hitchhiking is strongly advised against anywhere in Mumbai or Goa. Even taking a ride in a respectable-looking car is not worth the risk as there have been cases of attacks and mugging. While taking a ride on the back of the truck is common practice for locals, tourists are warned of its dangers. Women, especially, are warned against these practices.

TOURS

You will find plenty of local travel agents in both Mumbai and Goa. Larger tour operators such as Thomas Cook can be found everywhere, and small operators can be quite resourceful, too, often doubling up as money changers and Internet cafés. These agents book local tours and trips to surrounding areas, and most Goan operators will offer you tempting deals for Gokarna and Hampi.

For guided tours, stick to the certified guides and travel agents. Mumbai has a few upmarket tour operators, which are often better than government-authorized guides. **Bombay Heritage Walks** (Navyug Niketan, ground floor, 185 Walkeshwar Rd., tel. 022/2369-0992, www.bombayheritagewalks.com) and **Mumbai Magic** (cell tel. 91/98677-07414, www.mumbaimagic.com) are two such operators. Goa's **GTDC** (Trionora Apartments, Dr. Alvares Costa Rd., tel. 0832/222-6515, www.goa-tourism.com) also organizes a number of tours.

Visas and Officialdom

VISAS

Travel to India requires a valid passport, and—unless you're a citizen of Nepal, Bhutan, or the Maldives—an Indian visa. Apply at the Indian embassy in your country in advance, as there is no system of visas on arrival in India. The visa procedure is fairly quick and easy, usually only involving a bit of paperwork.

If you are visiting for more than 180 days (tourist visas extend up to six months and give you multiple entry), you should register within 14 days of arrival at the foreigner's registration office (3rd Fl., Special Branch Bldg., Badruddin Tayabji Lane, behind St. Xavier's College, Mumbai, tel. 022/2262-1169). You cannot get visa extensions in Mumbai or Goa, so make sure you have the required residence permit. Temporary Landing Permits, however, are granted to foreigners without visas in case of an emergency. If a visa extension is imperative, you will need to go to an Indian Consulate for information. Many travelers prefer to extend their visa by going to a neighboring country.

CUSTOMS

Drug-screening is quite rigorous at Mumbai and Goa, especially if arriving from Africa. Even domestic flights are regularly checked with sniffer dogs, so be wary of what you carry. You can carry a limited amount of liquor and tobacco in and out of the country, so check the current limits before packing. Visit www.cbec.gov.in/travellers.htm for the latest information.

CONSULATES

The consulates and high commissions in Mumbai are useful to citizens in times of emergency. Most are located in the downtown area. The heavily guarded, fortressed American consulate is located at Lincoln House (78 Bhulabhai Desai Rd., Breach Candy, tel. 022-2363-3611, http://mumbai.usconsulate.gov).

A few European countries have consulates in Goa; it's best to check with your home country about passport issues and travel advisories before you leave for your holiday.

Accommodations

MAKING RESERVATIONS

Most Indian hotels have websites where you can make online reservations—a relatively safe and easy option. Very often, especially during low season, a phone request with definite arrival dates will help block your room even without making a payment. However, this does not always guarantee accommodation.

HOSTELS

Mumbai and Goa have a few hostels, but they are fairly basic and may not offer the facilities or meet the standards of hostels in other parts of the world. However, they are good budget options and are usually clean and well looked after.

HOMESTAYS

The Indian government has proposed the idea of homestays, where willing residents will open up their homes to tourists. The idea has yet to take off but there's a website (www.allindiaguide.com/homestay/mumbai.html) where you can keep yourself updated on developments.

Unofficially, some families welcome tourists into their homes, especially in Goa. Check with the neighborhood shops for information or for informal signs and posters with details. In case of the latter, you should verify the authenticity of the host just to be safe.

BEACH SHACKS

The most popular form of accommodation on Goan beaches, beach shacks can be both a blessing and a pain. While they offer uninhibited access to the ocean, they are often basic and makeshift. Toilets may sometimes be shared and rooms visited by mosquitoes. Flimsy bamboo walls could also mean late-night sounds of the shack party or discotheque filtering into your room at night. Traditionally, shack inhabitants were hippies and budget travelers, but upmarket (and more comfortable) shacks and cabanas such as Ciaran's in Palolem are elevating the standard of the typical Goan beach shack.

HOTELS

Don't let the word fool you. Hotels in Mumbai and Goa can mean anything from a two-room lodge to a 200-room luxury five-star. The destinations offer a wide range of hotel accommodation, varying from modest budget hotels to fancy star-rated accommodations. Three- and four-star hotels can be an excellent bargain, especially during low season when they offer special package rates.

Food

As melting pots of Indian and global cultures, respectively, Mumbai and Goa offer a variety of cuisines at different levels of spice—and hygiene. When you enter a restaurant, look for a small placard that grades the eatery—Grade I, II and sometimes III, are usually clean and safe. Make sure you order bottled water or carry your own. While street food is a must-have for most travelers, it is best avoided by those with a weak stomach or an immune system as yet unexposed to Indian food conditions. Water-borne diseases are as plentiful here as the treats, so it may be safer to enjoy the same flavors at Grade I and II establishments instead. Be careful, particularly during the monsoons when street food and seafood preparations are best avoided. It would be unfortunate to abstain from seafood in Goa, where it is almost always fresh, but it helps to stick to the more reputed eateries.

GOAN CUISINE

Goan cuisine is seafood-dominated and represented by the popular "fish-curry-rice," which is not as simple as it sounds. Curries come in various flavors and colors, depending on the masala or spicy sauces used in the preparation.

Ambot tik is a sour-spicy curry made with spices and tamarind, while the deceptively small fiery Portuguese chili lends its flavor to the exceptionally spicy vindaloo masala, enjoyed only by the brave of stomach. Masalas are not unique to seafood items, and various types of meat and vegetables are also cooked in similar fashion to bring you delicious chicken *cafreal,* vegetable *xacuti* (pronounced sha-coo-tee), and prawn *balchao.* Stuffed fish *reicheado* (pronounced ray-chaa-doe) is another popular seafood preparation. Meanwhile, prok vindaloo is a Goan must-try, as are other pork items such as pork *sorpotel,* best had with fluffed-up *sannas* (rice-flour cakes infused with coconut and the local palm brew called *toddy). Chouricos* (spicy Goan sausages) can be tried with the traditional bread called *pao* or *poi.* After a taste of these tongue-scorching delicacies, most visitors move on to dessert double-quick. Taste buds are easily assuaged by the delicious *bebinca* (a 16-layer baked dessert made of egg, flour, sugar, coconut milk, and nutmeg) and *dodol* (a traditional Christmas sweet prepared with rice flour, jaggery, cashew nuts, and coconut milk).

While most Goan food today is a result of the Portuguese influence (which, in turn, is a

crucible of Arab and African influences) and relished mostly by Goa's Christian population, there's a gastronomical world to be discovered in the state's Hindu kitchens. Fish continues to be a staple, with delicacies such as fish *uddamethi* (fish cooked with fenugreek). There's also a refreshing variety of medium-spicy vegetarian options comprising lentils and delicious preparations made with cashew nuts and vegetables such as pumpkin and French beans. This pre-Portuguese cuisine includes dishes like *tondak* (beans or vegetables cooked in a coconut-based masala) and the alliterative mixed vegetable preparation called *khatkhate,* found in the home of the Hindu Saraswat Brahmin community.

Most Goan restaurants double up as bars. Goan food is generally washed down with the local brew, called *feni.* Cashew *feni* is distilled from the cashew apple, while palm *feni* is derived from sap drawn from the shoot of the coconut tree. For teetotalers, there's the tangy sweet-sour *kokum* juice drawn from the purple-red local fruit.

© MANJIRI ACHREKAR-SMOTHER

Fish curry and rice is the staple diet of Goa.

Conduct and Customs

GENERAL ETIQUETTE

Folded hands, a slight bow of the head, and saying "namaste" is the most formal greeting, but it can be used anywhere. However, in places like Mumbai and Goa, a handshake should do just fine. Kissing on the cheeks as a greeting is accepted in certain strata of society and depends on the degree of closeness between the persons concerned. The commercial areas of Goa are fairly Western in their outlook and lifestyle—and therefore in etiquette. In Mumbai, it may not always be okay for a man to kiss a woman on the cheeks in greeting—this is often restricted to the younger and wealthier sections of society.

Should someone step on your feet, don't do a double take if s/he makes a sweeping gesture seemingly from your foot to their heart. It is a symbolic seeking of forgiveness, as this is considered the highest form of offence. However, this does not necessarily mean that you do the same should you be the offender. A simple "sorry" should suffice.

As far as money is concerned, it has a quasi-divine position and some customs need to be followed. Money is usually extended with the right hand. Do not proffer money pinched between your forefinger and middle finger or toss any money, especially loose change. If someone declines a tip, gently insist but don't push for it if he does not give in.

Avoid stepping on or kicking a newspaper, magazine, or book. Education, too, is considered divine.

COMMUNICATION STYLES

Communicate casually with people providing services—cab drivers, sales people, small shops.

Hail a taxi or auto-rickshaw with a raised hand and ask if he will come to the desired destination. Despite a law that forces them to accept commuters to any destination, some drivers may decline because they do not know the directions, they want a fare to a longer distance or simply because they are heading home in another direction. Whether you want to impose the fare is your call, but complaining to a hovering policeman does wonders.

Bargaining is common practice and often the norm on the streets of Mumbai and Goa. It's a fine art acquired over time, so tourists usually perfect it by the time they leave the country. Vendors at street stalls will quote a high price, often double the usual, in anticipation of the bargain game. It would be silly not to bargain, as prices are hiked when stall owners spot a foreigner. Quote your price—usually half that quoted by the stall owner—and pretend to walk away if he shakes his head. He's bound to call you back and settle for a price only slightly higher than the one quoted by you (it helps to have a local with you). Bargaining is advised especially when buying jewelry and clothes off the street. Don't try it in the larger stores, though, where prices are fixed.

BODY LANGUAGE

Indians are generally very expressive physically and this includes staring. Be prepared to be stared at, especially if you're a woman. It doesn't quite work the same in reverse, however. If you're a man staring at an Indian woman, you're likely to have a male companion or relative pick a fight with you. If a local refuses to make eye contact with you in conversation, it could be out of respect or shyness.

Indians typically have little understanding of the need for physical space, as most live in cramped conditions. If you're a man, don't be offended if someone taps you on the shoulder from behind instead of calling out to you or pushes closer than you would like in public transport. If you're a woman, however, politely ask the person concerned (if male) to back off.

If traveling as a couple, avoid a public display of affection, as it could raise eyebrows, cause stares and giggles, or offend older people. However, in a country where open affection between the opposite sexes is frowned upon, it is perfectly acceptable for male friends (not necessarily gay) to hold hands as a display of friendship.

TABLE MANNERS

Most Indians eat Indian food with their hands and use a knife and fork for other dishes. They frown upon touching food with the left hand, but that is usually a personal choice. They do not usually like to share a spoon or plate, and sharing a bottle or glass of water is a fine art where the mouth is not meant to touch the rim. On the other hand, others may impose themselves upon you, asking to take a bite from your plate or insisting that you try their meal. Ask before taking a bite or politely decline if you are uncomfortable sharing food. Indians are not known for rigid table manners; if eating in a local eatery, don't be surprised if you hear an appreciative belch or two.

CLOTHING AND DRESS

An Indian holiday usually demands that you respect several customs and traditions. While Mumbai and Goa are more progressive in dress and attitude than other destinations in India, it is best to observe a semblance of modesty and deference for tradition. Remove your footwear before entering a place of worship, usually also in the case of private residences. Mosques and some temples may require you to cover your head, and it is important to be appropriately clothed here—Western-style clothing is fine, but shorts, short skirts, and skimpy tops are not.

The beaches of Mumbai and Goa are a study in contrast. In Mumbai, almost nobody wears swimwear, but in Goa, you will even find topless sunbathing in some parts. While nudity is banned in both places, Goan locals will rarely bat an eye on seeing bikini-clad sunbathers. Mumbai's beach-goers, on the other hand, treat their sandy shores as evening entertainment and appear dressed in their finery.

Not only would a bikini be ridiculously out of place here, it would be an uncomfortable crowd puller.

BEGGING

It is not mandatory to put money in the donation box in temples, so be wary of so-called holy men asking for money. Which also brings us to the problem of begging. Mumbai has an "organized" system of begging where gang lords often pay salaries to beggars who hand over their day's income (earned from begging) to them in return. Children and eunuchs are commonly found by the traffic lights—while it is a personal choice to give them food or money, know that taking pity on one kid will have 50 clamoring at your window. This dark side of the city often shocks the Western tourist with its sights and it is important that you brace yourself for it before you arrive.

PHOTO ETIQUETTE

Locals usually love being photographed, but it's best to ask before you take a picture.

Tips for Travelers

EMPLOYMENT AND VOLUNTEERING

There are many non-profit organizations (NGOs) that allow for short-term volunteer work in both Mumbai and Goa. Keep an eye out on the Mumbai University website (www.mu.ac.in) and notice boards for volunteer work. You can also look at the Indira Gandhi Institute of Developmental Research and Tata Institute of Social Sciences for short-term internships. In Goa, some NGOs run special summer programs for foreign tourists in areas ranging from environmental conservation to working with orphanages and HIV/AIDS counseling centers. Visit www.karmayog.com and www.sulekha.com for a list of NGOs in Mumbai and Goa and contact details.

ACCESS FOR TRAVELERS WITH DISABILITIES

India is not quite sensitized to the needs of travelers with disabilities and most places lack the required ramps or guides. While star-rated hotels are equipped to host travelers with special needs, smaller hotels and most public places are not. Wheelchairs and assistance are available on request at the airports and railway stations, and there are special reserved seats on buses and trains. Some public buildings, like the Chhatrapati Shivaji Maharaj Vastu Sangrahalay (Prince of Wales Museum) in Mumbai, have ramps but there is a general apathy and lack of infrastructure. A traveling companion is advised to travelers with disabilities.

TRAVELING WITH CHILDREN

While noise levels, crowds, and pollution in Mumbai may be a cause for concern for those traveling with children, Goa is the perfect place for a family holiday. Food and health are often areas of worry, but you should be safe carrying your own bottled water and prescribed antimalarial and cholera shots or tablets. Baby food and hygiene supplies are readily available in Mumbai, and both Mumbai and Goa have reputed doctors and hospitals in case of emergency. You should avoid traveling by the public bus or train system with kids, however, as the crowds can be frightening. Riding in air-conditioned transport rather than open auto-rickshaws or taxis is advisable to safeguard against the heat and pollution (although children are almost always fascinated by the quaint auto-rickshaws). The clean air and beaches of Goa compensate for Mumbai's polluted air, and, together with wildlife and dolphins, make for a wonderful addition to any child's holiday.

WOMEN TRAVELING ALONE

Women are generally safe in both Mumbai and Goa but incidents of molestation have been on the rise. If traveling alone by train, especially on a night journey, book a two-tier seat. Should your fellow passengers prove to be a nuisance, don't hesitate to complain to the authorities, and in extreme cases, pull the chain that will bring the train to a halt. Indian families make for good fellow passengers if you're a woman and friendly female members will generally take you under their wing, helping stave off any advances you may otherwise have been subjected to. Special seats are reserved for women on buses, while the local trains in Mumbai have special women-only compartments—as well as entire women-only trains. While bus conductors and train attendants are helpful, solo women travelers are warned against depending too much on over-friendly young men in public places. Leering, catcalls, and whispered Bollywood songs are part of what is called "eve-teasing"—if it gets too aggressive, feel free to call the police, as eve-teasing is against the law. In Goa, a police threat works wonders, as the tourist industry is closely monitored. Both Mumbai and Goa have tourist police booths in popular tourist areas.

SENIOR TRAVELERS

Senior travelers needn't worry—most Indians make for helpful traveling companions. There are special reserved seats on public transport, while wheelchairs, porters, and medical assistance are easily available at airports and railway stations. Both Mumbai and Goa are known for their medical facilities in case of emergency, but sneior travelers must take care against the heat and pollution, taking rides in air-conditioned transport rather than open auto-rickshaws or taxis.

GAY AND LESBIAN TRAVELERS

Indian sensibility frowns on homosexuality. While you may see many young men holding hands in an open display of affection, this often has little to do with their sexual orientation and is merely an accepted expression of friendship.

Public displays of affection, even among heterosexual couples, are not very well received, and open displays of same-sex affection will only bring censure. However, the Indian cities are gradually learning to accept same-sex couples and Mumbai recently hosted its first gay pride parade. There are active gay and lesbian communities in both Mumbai and Goa. Some pubs and discos in Mumbai host gay nights, but you must be wary of being solicited at such places.

WHAT TO TAKE

Once you have your passport and visa, there's little else you need to carry. There's no dearth of supplies in Mumbai and Goa, and there's very little that you may have forgotten back home that you're not likely to find here.

There are a few things you should keep in mind, however. Camping equipment, backpacks, and sporting equipment are best carried from home. For a longer stay, you can always have additional **luggage** stored safely at your hotel or luggage-holding facilities. Lock your bags, and carry expensive items in a small shoulder bag or money belt. **Pouches and money belts** are absolute essentials, as Mumbai was once notorious for its pickpockets.

Don't bother with camera peripherals or toiletries, as these are generally available all over. The dust and grime of Mumbai can be quite bothersome, so bring a bottle of hand sanitizer.

Owing to the heat and humidity, loose, cotton **clothing** is the preferred attire. While Mumbai and tourist areas of Goa do not frown significantly on any manner of clothing, make sure you're well covered when visiting religious sites. Some places may require you to cover your head with a scarf. Due to environmental changes in recent years, tropical Mumbai and Goa can get chilly in December and January. It's a good idea to carry a jacket should you be caught in this freak mercury dip.

When you're traveling during the monsoon season, remember to bring a **rain jacket,** as the rain drives quite hard. You can buy cheap umbrellas off the streets in Mumbai.

Health and Safety

Most sanitary and health products (such as disinfectants and first-aid kits) can be purchased locally, and both Mumbai and Goa are known for their excellent medical facilities.

MOSQUITOES AND INSECTS

The menace of mosquitoes is likely to be encountered wherever you travel in India. While most Mumbai and Goa hotels will provide mosquito repellents in your room that work on electricity, it is recommended that you carry adequate mosquito and insect repellent lotion or buy the local varieties from any medical or general store. You may need to apply it quite liberally, especially in the evenings.

Malaria

There is plenty of stagnant water and marshy land in both Mumbai and Goa that breeds malaria-carrying mosquitoes. India has several strains of malaria, including the more dangerous falciparum malaria. UK and US government advisories state the need for anti-malarial drugs to be taken as a precautionary measure before, during, and after travel to India. Recommended drugs include chloroquine, to be taken once a week, along with proguanil. If you want to simply take one precautionary medicine try anti-malarial drug Malarone, which is to be taken daily. Check for variants, brands, dosages, and side effects with your local doctor before you set out on your journey.

HEAT

The heat in both Mumbai and Goa can get quite oppressive and the sun beats down relentlessly even in the so-called winter months. Ensure you carry adequate sunscreen and drink plenty of fluids, especially if you're here in summer when the humidity causes you to sweat off all your essential salts. Wear loose cotton clothing at all times.

DIARRHEA

"Delhi belly" extends to Mumbai and Goa, as diarrhea is a common occurrence—especially after trying out street food or drinking untreated water. Medication is easily available locally, but if symptoms persist for more than a couple of days, you'll need to go to a pathologist to get tested for water-borne diseases like cholera and dengue. Ensure that you have plenty of fluids and essential rehydrating salts like Electral, which are available at all pharmacies. Carry chlorine tablets for emergencies while traveling. Stay safe by eating only at reputed eateries, and avoiding raw greens as well as fresh fruit juices. In the monsoon, abstain from seafood and meat.

DOGS, WILD ANIMALS, AND SNAKES

India is known for its stray dogs and it is not unusual for locals to be bitten by a stray. It is best to take an anti-rabies shot from your local doctor before you depart on your journey; if you haven't been vaccinated in advance, head to the nearest hospital or doctor for an anti-rabies shot should you get bitten by a dog (stray or otherwise) or a monkey. In case of snakebite or attack by a wild animal, rush immediately to the nearest hospital for anti-venom or appropriate treatment. In case of snakebite, do not elevate the limb, tie a tourniquet, use ice packs, or take sedatives before you receive professional medical attention.

VACCINATIONS

Make sure you carry prescribed anti-malarial and cholera tablets and get your tetanus and typhus shots before arriving here. A visit to India requires you to take vaccinations against Hepatitis A and B, encephalitis, typhoid, tuberculosis, yellow fever, rabies, and diphtheria. A typhoid shot safeguards you from the disease for two years, while anti-typhoid pills protect you for longer. Some of these vaccines need to be taken a few months in advance and can have side effects. Contact your local doctor and check the World Health Organization (WHO) website (www.who.int) for more information.

MEDICAL SERVICES

Both Mumbai and Goa are well equipped for medical care and are known for some of the best hospitals in the country. Mumbai is a popular destination for medical tourism and there are 24-hour emergency rooms in the major city hospitals, including Bombay Hospital (Marine Lines, tel. 022/2206-7676), Breach Candy Hospital (Bhulabhai Desai Rd., tel. 022/2363-3651), Jaslok Hospital (Peddar Rd., tel. 022/2493-3333), Hinduja Hospital (Mahim, tel. 022/2445-2222), and Lilavati Hospital (Bandra Reclamation, tel. 022/2645-5920).

For ambulance services, dial 1298 from a landline or 2202-4545. For privately operated ambulances, call 91/98331-69329 or 022/2413-1298. In Goan capital Panaji, there is KLES Hospital Liaison Office (St. Inez, tel. 0832/222-5601), Goa Medical College (Bambolim, tel. 0832/245-8725 or emergency helpline 102), Indian Red Cross (18th June Rd., tel. 0832/222-4601), Laxmibai Talaulikar Memorial Hospital (Dada Vaidya Rd., tel. 0832/242-5625), and Panjim Ambulance and Welfare Trust (c/o Hotel Manoshanti, behind EDC House, tel. 0832/222-7997).

All hospitals have 24-hour pharmacies, and there are a number of day (and night) pharmacies in both cities. Doctor's clinics are scattered across both cities; inquiries at your hotel reception or a call to the 24-hour city helplines (Mumbai "Just Dial" tel. 022/2888-8888 and Goa tel. 0832/241-2121) will point you in the right direction.

INSURANCE

It's best to arrange for travel and medical insurance before you set out, as there are no health policies to cover tourists in India. Contact your local insurance agent for an appropriate policy.

CRIME

Mumbai was once the crime capital of the country, but has now passed on this dubious distinction to Delhi. While the city's pickpockets were once legendary, Mumbai is now relatively safe for travelers. However, it pays to keep valuables close to your person, and larger denominations are best kept out of sight. Chain-snatching incidents are common, so be careful of dangling jewelry and leave valuables in the hotel safe. If taking a taxi late at night, note down the license number that is painted on the windshield. The city is considered the safest in India for women, but incidents of rape and molestation are not uncommon—women are advised not to stay out late on their own or to trust strangers in bars. Goa has been the hub of drug-related crimes, so watch out for food and drink offered by strangers.

POLICE HELPLINE AND EMERGENCIES

Mumbai has a number of helplines for emergencies, ranging from the police helpline (100), fire brigade (101), ambulance service (102), women's helpline (103), child helpline (1098), senior citizen's helpline (1090), and cardiac helpline (126126). Goa has a 24-hour police helpline (100), fire brigade (101), and ambulance service (102 and 108).

Information and Services

MONEY

The common currency is the rupee, made of 100 paise (the Indian equivalent of a cent). The exchange rate has fluctuated between Rs 44–50 per US$1 in recent years.

Traveler's Checks, Credit Cards, and ATMs

Traveler's checks are ideal for safe transactions in the city. Credit cards are accepted in most places and there are plenty of ATMs in both Mumbai and Goa. MasterCard and Visa are most widely accepted, followed by American Express. Some shops have a minimum amount for credit card transactions or charge a 10 percent commission.

Cash

Before doling out Indian money, learn to distinguish between the Rs 1,000, Rs 500, and Rs 100 denominations of notes, which look similar. There is no dearth of licensed money changers in Mumbai and Goa, but beware of touts, agents, and fake currency in popular tourist areas. Avoid carrying too much money on your person but make sure you have plenty of loose change when traveling by public transport. U.S. dollars may come in handy at times, as high-end establishments often accept American currency.

Tax

There is a 12 percent Value Added Tax (VAT) on most services in Mumbai and Goa; check in advance if quoted prices are VAT inclusive. Restaurants may add a 10–15 percent service tax, which will be noted separately in your bill.

Tipping

Tipping is customary at all restaurants in Mumbai and Goa, unless it's a takeaway place. Small change will suffice at a cheap local eatery but a 15 percent tip is generally expected at a larger restaurant. While tipping taxis is not expected, it may help to keep your car rental driver happy. Tour guides are given abysmal rates by the government, so feel free to tip as per your satisfaction. Tipping porters is entirely your choice, as is tipping the home delivery guy—small, loose change will do for both. Gas station attendants are not tipped, nor are grocery store attendants.

COMMUNICATIONS AND MEDIA
Internet

Internet cafés are scattered all over Mumbai and Goa so you needn't worry if your hotel doesn't have Internet. In Goa, most travel agents double up as money changers and Internet cafés so you can meet all your needs at one place. Rates for surfing vary from Rs 20–75 per hour. If you're carrying your laptop and are here for a longish period of time, you could even go to a mobile service provider for an Internet data card—a USB device that you can attach to your computer so you can have Internet on the move. Reliance (www.rcom.co.in), Tata Indicom (www.tataindicom.com), and Vodafone (www.vodafone.in) offer this service for an activation fee; monthly rental and usage charges depend on the plan you choose.

Telephone

If you're carrying your cell phone, it's best to get a temporary pre-paid cell phone number offered by local service providers Airtel (www.airtel.in) and Vodafone (www.vodafone.in), from any of their local agents or stores. However, if your phone was purchased in the United States, you may have to unlock it at a local electronics store for a small fee in order to be able to make local calls. For local calls made by mobile phones, dial the area code—022 for Mumbai and 0832 for Goa—before you dial your local number. However, dialing the area code when calling from a landline is not necessary. There are also a number of phone booths marked "STD-ISD-PCO" from where you can make local, national, and international calls, as well as fax documents.

Calls to Europe cost around Rs 7 per minute; to the United States, it's about Rs 5 per minute. Calls to India from outside the country require you to dial the country code (+91 or 0091) before you dial the area code and number.

Newspapers

There are many English newspapers and tabloids available on the streets of Mumbai and Goa and you can even find foreign editions in Mumbai's Colaba area. Popular local newspapers include the *Times of India, Hindustan Times, Indian Express, DNA,* and tabloids *Mid-Day* and *Mumbai Mirror.*

Radio and Television

India woke up to cable television less than two decades ago but the enormous number of channels found on TV now more than makes up for the lost years. You can watch everything from CNN to BBC and HBO as well as the local MTV channel. Perhaps the one thing you won't get to watch is the Super Bowl. Cable TV is found in most hotels, while pubs and restaurants often screen live sports and music videos.

Radio, sadly, is far behind, with FM radio playing mostly popular Bollywood numbers. All India Radio Rainbow 107.1 plays some good retro music in the mornings and you can catch some fine classical music on AM.

Postal Services

Post offices are found all over Mumbai and in most villages and towns in Goa. The largest post office in Mumbai is the General Post Office (near CST Station, tel. 022/2262-1671). In Goa, the General Post Office in Panaji (MG Road, tel. 0832/222-3704) is the main post office, and there's also the Madgaon Post Office (near Municipal Gardens, tel. 0832/271-5791).

Postcards and letters can be sent inland for Rs 5 and by airmail for as little as Rs 15. Courier services like DHL and Blue Dart are efficient for inland and international services. For mail within Mumbai and Goa, there are many efficient local courier services, such as Vichare Couriers and Professional Couriers.

MAPS AND TOURIST INFORMATION
Maps

The best maps are by Eicher and TTK, and are available at roadside stalls and bookshops. Tourist offices and tourist counters at airports also provide maps for a small fee or free of cost. You can refer to the Indian government website (india.gov.in/maps) and www.mapsofindia .com for detailed political, physical, road, and rail maps of the country.

Tourist Offices

Tourist offices in Mumbai and Goa will be able to help you with most travel information, including maps, hotels, and routes. Tourist booths at airports are generally helpful and friendly. Be prepared for long waits, bored employees, and extended lunch hour in the smaller offices, and don't go expecting the world.

In Mumbai, the Government of India tourist office (opposite Churchgate Station, tel. 022/2207-4333, www.incredibleindia.com) and the Maharashtra Tourism Development Corporation (MTDC, Express Towers, Nariman Point, tel. 022/2202-4482, www .maharashtratourism.gov.in) should be able to help you with tourist information.

In Goa, contact the Government of India tourist office (Communidade Building, Church Square, Panaji, tel. 0832/222-3412, indiatourismgoa@sancharnet.in) or the Goa Tourism Development Corporation (GTDC, Trionora Apartments, Dr. Alvares Costa Rd., Panaji, tel. 0832/222-6515, www.goa-tourism.com).

Film, Photography, and Video

Most photography needs are easily met in Mumbai and in tourist spots in Goa. You can buy film, specialized batteries, memory cards, instant prints, and have CDs burnt as well. Digital camera hardware is cheap in Mumbai, and the Fort and CST areas have adequate stores for photography supplies. Even shopping arcade Heera Panna (Haji Ali, diagonally opposite the Haji Ali Mosque) has plenty of stores that will meet your needs.

WEIGHTS AND MEASURES

India uses the metric system, so distances are in kilometers, weights in kilograms, and volume in liters.

The entire country is on one time zone (GMT +5:30) and there is no daylight saving time.

India uses 240 volts AC usage with round pins on plug points. Inexpensive converters can be bought easily at local electrical stores.

RESOURCES

Glossary

In the general glossary, Hindi terms and phrases are indicated with (H); Marathi terms and phrases are indicated with (M). Many words are the same in both languages and are widely understood in regions where Konkani is spoken.

auto-rickshaw: a three-wheeled taxi cab

baag: (M) garden

bageecha: (H) garden

baksheesh: a soft bribe

BEST: acronym of Brihanmumbai Electrical Supply and Transport, the service that runs the intra-city bus service

bhaajiwalla: vegetable vendor

bhai: (H) elder brother

bhaiyya: (H) brother; term of address for local service providers like taxi drivers and vegetable vendors

bhangi: (H) garbage-collector, also a derogatory word

bhau: (M) elder brother

bhookh: hunger

bungla: bungalow

chaat: tangy, streetside snacks

chappal: Indian footwear, usually flip-flops

chatai: straw mat

chhutta: (H) loose change

chhutti: (H) holiday

coffeewalla: coffee vendor

dabbawalla: tiffin carrier

dada: local bully

dawaa: (H) medicine

dawakhana: doctor's clinic

desi: (colloq.) local, but in urban areas refers to locally brewed potent alcohol (Do not try drinking it.)

dhaba: highway eatery

dhoop: (H) hot afternoon sunlight

firangi: foreigner

gaadi: vehicle

gaon: village

gaothan: village

garam: warm, hot

ghaati: (M) person from the hilly region of Maharashtra; often derogatory

gully: by-lane

hafta: an extorted sum

hajaam: (H) barber

hamaal: coolie

hawaa: air/breeze

hawaldar: constable

kaamgaar: worker

karigar: craftsman

karyalay: office

khaana: (H) food

khanavals: traditional Maharashtrian 'lunch homes'

khet: farm

kirana dukaan: grocery store

kiraya: (H) fare, rent

kurta: long, loose cotton shirt worn as part of traditional attire

maalish: massage

mandir: temple

mantri: minister

masjid: mosque

matka: earthenware pot

mochi: cobbler (found in tiny cupboards by the roadside)

mohalla: (H) local area

neta: politician

nhaavi: (M) barber

oon: (M) hot afternoon sunlight

paani: water
paisa: money, currency
rung: color
saadi: see sari
saala: slang meaning roughly S.O.B., also used affectionately
saheb: sir, officer, boss
sari: traditional garment worn by women
shauchalay: toilet
shetkari: farmer
shivling: sacred phallic symbol of Hindu god Shiva
sit-out: porch or balcony
sona: gold
sui-dhaga: needle and thread
sutti: (M) holiday
tanga: cart
thali: traditional all-you-can-eat-platter
thanda: cold
tiatr: traditional Goan theater
zari fine sparkling embroidery

FOOD AND DRINK

aam: mango
balchao: A spicy gravy sauce made with red chili and vinegar
barfi: condensed milk-based sweet
bhelpuri: popular street food, puffed rice with chopped raw veggies and chutneys
bhutta: corn on the cob roasted on a coal spit and spiced with lemon and powdered peppers
cafreal: a spiced green masala or sauce
chaat: tangy, streetside snacks
chai: tea
chana-seng dana: roasted peanuts and chickpeas sold on the street for small change
chapati: unleavened flat bread roasted on a pan
chettinad: spicy cuisine from the Chettinad region of Tamil Nadu in south India
chhaas: buttermilk
chourico: spicy sausage
dal: thick lentil curry normally made slightly spicy and eaten mostly with rice
dhokla: raised chickpea-flour cakes
dosa: crepe-like rice pancake roasted on an iron griddle and served with coconut chutney and *sambar*

falooda: traditional milkshake with rose syrup and rice noodles
feni: local Goan brew made with cashew apple or coconut
gola: syrupy, flavored ice lollipops
idli: plump steamed rice cake served with coconut chutney and spicy-sour dal or lentil curry called *sambar*
jalebi: sweet fried dough ringlets, orange in color and dipped in sugar syrup
kachori: large, spicy, deep fried canapés served with chutney and yoghurt
khaana: food
kheema pao: spicy mince served with local bread
kela: banana
kulfi: creamy, traditional Indian ice cream
makkhan: butter
meetha paan: a sweet betel leaf and areca nut preparation made with a variety of ingredients including spices like cloves, sweetened coconut powder, rose-petal water, and dried fruits; had after a meal at any of the stalls outside restaurants. There are variations that include tobacco or exclude the hard areca nut
mosambi: sweet lime
namak: salt
nariyal paani: fresh green coconut water
nimbu pani: lemonade
paani: water
paneer: Indian cottage cheese
pani puri: popular street food, puffed canapés filled with spicy water, potato, and pulses
papad: a flour-based crispy, spicy flatbread, served fried or roasted
pav bhaji: a spicy preparation of mixed vegetables mashed up and served with buttered buns
pedha: condensed milk-based sweet
peru: guava, usually served with salt and red chili powder on the street
ragda: potato dumplings served with spicy chickpea curry
reichad masala: a spicy red sauce used both as curry and as stuffing
rollado: a type of beef roll
sambar: a lentil curry often served with *dosas* and *idlis*

samosa: spicy potato mix stuffed inside a deep-fried wheat pastry

sanna: fluffy rice flour cakes infused with coconut and local palm brew called toddy

sev puri: popular street food, specifically flat canapés topped with raw vegetables and chutney

shakkar sugar

sorpotel: a spicy Goan pork dish

tandoori roti: yeasty, starchy flatbread roasted in a charcoal oven

thali: traditional all-you-can-eat-platter

tikka, tandoori: spicy Indian barbecue

unda: egg

vada pav: popular street food, spicy potato patty in a bun

xacuti: a spicy coconut gravy

xec xec: a spicy coconut gravy usually served with crab

MUSIC AND FESTIVALS

dafli: one-sided flat percussion instrument, held against the shoulder.

dandiya: a circular dance, played or performed with wooden sticks or batons

dholak: two-sided percussion instrument played with a stick or by hand

ektara: popular one-stringed instrument played with a bow

ghungru: tiny silver bells tied on the ankle, mostly used in classical dance

jayanti: festive anniversary of a leader or a god

lejhim: vigorous Maharashtrian dance involving clinking and chiming of tiny cymbals on a chain attached to a stick

shehnai: thin flute with a sharp sound, played at Maharashtrian weddings

RELIGIOUS AND CULTURAL ICONS

Ahura Mazda: the highest object of worship, the Creator for Zoroastrians or Parsis

Bhavani: *see* Parvati

Brahma: Hindu god of creation

Dnyaneshwar: Marathi saint, literary figure from the 13th century

Durga: *see* Parvati

Ganesh: (also known as Ganesha and Ganpati) Hindu god of Beginnings and famously known as Remover of Obstacles; patron of arts and sciences, and god of intellect and wisdom; worshipped before every new enterprise or ritual; immensely popular in Mumbai and also among Hindus in Goa

Haji Ali: popular patron saint of Mumbai for people of all faiths, and has a prominent shrine dedicated to him in Mumbai

Hanuman: popular semi-god personified by a monkey-figure in the epic *Ramayana*: led an epic battle against demon Ravana, and is usually depicted lifting a mountain, one of his many feats

Indra: Hindu god of war and weather

Kabir: 14th-century poet and saint belonging to the Bhakti tradition of philosophy

Kali: *see* Parvati

Krishna: Hindu god who played an instrumental role as the philosopher-charioteer in the Hindu epic the Mahabharata. His advice to Arjuna on the battlefield was transcribed as the Bhagavad Gita, Hinduism's most important theological text

Laxmi: Hindu goddess of wealth and prosperity; popular and widely worshipped in the commercial capital

Mumba Devi patron goddess of Mumbai

Namdeo: Marathi saint and writer from the 13th century

Parvati: Shiva's consort and the Mother Goddess – other goddesses Durga, the fierce and invincible embodiment of the feminine force, as well as Kali, goddess of destruction, and Bhavani, creative source and giver of life, are her incarnations. The latter was the patron deity of Maratha chief Shivaji and is also worshipped by Mumbai traders who dedicate their first earning of the day to her

Ravana: the 10-headed King of Demons, defeated by Rama after he abducted Rama's wife, Sita, in the epic *Ramayana*; other versions claim him to be a great scholar, a just king and follower of Shiva

Sai Baba: 19th-century saint revered by both Hindus and Muslims; worshipped extensively in Mumbai

Saraswati: Hindu goddess of knowledge and the arts

Shiva: the Destroyer or the Transformer; together, the three gods Brahma, Vishnu, and Shiva form the *trimurti,* or the holy trinity of Hinduism

St. Francis Xavier: patron saint of Goa

Tukaram: Marathi saint and poet from the 17th century

Varuna: god of sky, rain, and ocean – worshipped largely by fisherfolk

Vishnu: the blue-skinned god; master of the past, present, and future; preserver of the universe

Zoroaster (or Zarathushtra): prophet and religious poet from Iran – revered largely by the Parsi community in Mumbai

Phrasebook

HINDI, MARATHI, AND KONKANI

In Mumbai, Hindi is spoken by all and Marathi by many, though it is hard to tell who speaks which language. Maharashtrians love being spoken to in Marathi and will reciprocate with warmth and small favors. Cops and BEST bus conductors in Mumbai are most appreciative. The local dialect is Bambaiyya, which amalgamates the crudest choice of words from Hindi and Marathi, and is bereft of grammatical rules of respectful addressing, or gender distinction.

Visitors can get by on English and Hindi in the city, while those venturing into destinations that lie in the vicinity of Mumbai – places in interior Maharashtra – will find Marathi especially useful. Besides, Hindi and Marathi share much of their vocabulary and grammar (not to mention a common script), making it easier for visitors to learn both languages at once.

In Goa, Konkani is universally spoken, but visitors rarely need to exercise their local language skills here. While locals tend to appreciate an effort to speak their language, Goa is a multilingual state where English is widely spoken and easily understood in most parts. The state is geared toward tourism, and its Christian English-speaking population dominates the tourist-populated areas. Marathi is also a major language in Goa, and Hindi is easily understood.

PRONUNCIATION
Consonants
Marathi, Hindi, and Konkani have common consonants, and Marathi has a couple of extra ones. Most are the same as in the English alphabet. Marathi is a sharp language with marked **r, t, k,** sounds. Notable is the sharp **n** in Marathi spoken from the back of the palate and the sharp **l** made by clicking the tongue. Hindi is relatively softer – the **t** is spoken softly, there is both a soft and a sharp **d,** and pronunciation is slightly nasal at the end of some words. In all three languages – Hindi, Marathi, and Konkai – the consonants are pronounced completely, especially **r.**

There are combinations with h that soften the consonant sound, as in **kha, gha, bha, dha,** and **tha.**

There is a **ch** sound that is pronounced as in the word "chair."

There is also a **chh** sound that combines **ch** with an exhalation and an extra *h* sound.

Vowels
There are both short and long **a, e,** and **o** sounds, while several words have *au, ou* sounds. Some words, like *nahi* and *nako,* end abruptly with vowels.

Words ending in **-in, -aun,** and **-oun** are slightly nasal. The single **a** signifies a half *a,* or *uh* sound, as in "gun."

The double **aa** sounds like the *a* in "yarn."

The short *oo* sound, as in "look," is indicated by the letter **u.** The short **o,** as in "go," is indicated by a single o.

Where **oo** appears, it sounds like it does in "moon."

Pronunciation Key

Capital letters in this phrasebook indicate sharp pronunciations, for example T sounds like it does in the English word "tin," and D as in "dog."

Lower-case letters are soft, as in din (day), where the d makes the sound of th and is softened with the tip of the tongue, as in the English word "there." The smaller ch is made from the tip of the teeth and the tongue, a much softer sound than the CH of "chair."

HINDI AND MARATHI WORDS AND PHRASES
Numbers

India has its own units for thousands and millions. One laakh is equal to 100,000 (one hundred thousand), and one karoad is the equivalent of 100 laakhs, or 10 million.

English	Hindi	Marathi
zero	shoonya	shoonya
one	Ek	Ek
two	Do	Don
three	Teen	Teen
four	Chaar	Chaar
five	Paanch	Paach
six	Chheh	Saha
seven	Saat	Saat
eight	Aanth	Aath
nine	Nao	Naoo
10	Dus	Dahaa
20	bees	vees
25	pacchees	panchvees
30	tees	tees
35	paytees	passtees
40	chaalees	chaalees
45	paytaalees	paytaaLees
50	pachaas	pannaas
100	sau	shumbhur
1,000	hazaar	hazaar
10,000	dus hazaar	dus hazaar
100,000	laakh	laakh
10,000,000	karoaD	karoaD
half	aadhha	ardhaa
one-fourth	pao	pao

Time

English	Hindi	Marathi
What time is it?	Kitné bajay hain?	Kiti vaazlé?
It is...o'clock.	...bajein hain.	...vaazlé aahet.
an hour	ek ghantaa	ek taas
a quarter till...	pawné...	paoNé...
a quarter past...	sauwwaa...	sauwwaa...
high tide/ low tide	bhurti/ohoti	bhurti/ ohoti
afternoon	Dopahar	Dupaar
night	Raat	Raatri
morning	Sawera	Sakaal
evening	Shyaam	Sandhya-kaal
sunrise	Suryodai	Suryodai
sunset	Suryaast	Suryaast

Days and Months

The English words for the months are generally used while speaking. There is also a lunar calendar that is no longer used except for religious and cultural reasons.

English	Hindi	Marathi
Monday	soamwaar	soamwaar
Tuesday	mangalwaar	mangalwaar
Wednesday	boodhhwaar	boodhhwaar
Thursday	gooroowaar	gooroowaar
Friday	shookrawaar	shookrawaar
Saturday	shaneewaar	shaneewaar
Sunday	raveewaar	raveewaar
today	aaj	aaz
tomorrow	kal	oodya
yesterday	kal	kaal
day after tomorrow	parsau	parwaa
a week	ek hafftaa	ek aaThavDaa
a month	ek maheenaa	ek maheenaa
a year	ek saal	ek varsha

BASIC AND COURTEOUS EXPRESSIONS

There are no translations for certain greetings like "Good morning," and the literal translations will draw blank stares. Words such as "Sorry, Excuse me, Please, Thank you, Welcome, You're welcome," and greetings such as "Hello, Good morning/evening/night" are communicated in English even by locals.

English	Hindi	Marathi
Hello.	namasté	namaskaar
How are you? (respectful)	Kaisé hain?	kashé ahaat?
How are you? (casual)	Kaisé ho?	Kasaa ahés? (masculine), Kushi ahés? (feminine)
Quite well, thank you.	Acchhé hain, shookriyaa	baraa aahe
Good.	Acchha	chaangla
Not so good.	Thheek naheen	bara naahi
So-so.	Thheek	Thheek
And you?	Aur aap?	aaNi toomhhi?
Thank you.	shukriyaa; dhhanyawaad	aabhari aahe

Goodbye.
Marathi and Hindi have no equivalent. Goodbyes generally translate as "See you later," even if you are leaving the country. *Khhuda hafiz* is a formal term for goodbye that finds its origins in Urdu – now considered a language of the genteel.

| See you later. | Phir milengé; aaté hain | bheTooya; yayto |

(The latter literally translates as "I will be back," but is used to say goodbye.)

Yes.	haan	Ho
No.	naheen	naahi
I do not want.	naheen chaahiyé	nako
I don't know.	naheen maaloomt	naahi maahi
Just a moment.	ek minute	ek mintä
Sorry (extremely apologetic).	Maaf karnaa	Maafi maaghto
Pleased to meet you.	acchaa lagaa mil kar	bara waatla bhheToon

How do you say...in Hindi?	Hindi mein...	ko kyaa bolté hain?
How do you say ...in Marathi?	MaraThheet...	la kai boltaat?
What is your name?	aapka naam kyaa hain?	tumcha naav kaai?
Is English spoken here?	yahaan angrezi bolté hain?	ithé ingrujee boltaat ka?

I do not speak Hindi well.
moojhé hindi Thheek bolné nahin aati

I do not speak Marathi well.
malaa barobarr marathi bolta nahi yait.

I don't understand.	mujhe nuheen samajh raha hai	malaa naahi kaLat
My name is...	meraa naam ...hain	maazha naav ...aahé
Let's go to...	...ko challengé	...la zaooya

TERMS OF ADDRESS

The formal and respectful form of address is used for most conversation. It is pleasing and you won't offend anyone if you use it.

The terms "boyfriend" and "girlfriend" have no translations in Hindi or Marathi; the English words are colloquially used. Mrs. and Ma'am are referred to as "Madam."

English	Hindi	Marathi
I	mein	me
we/us	hum	aapuN
you (formal)	aap	toomhee
you (informal)	tum	tu
he/him	woh	toh
she/her	woh	tee
they	woh	té
Mr., Sir	shri, saaheb	shri, saaheb
Mrs., Ma'am	madam	madam
wife	patni	beewee; baiko
husband	patee	navraa
son	laDkaa	mulgaa
daughter	laDkee	mulgee
brother	bhaaee	bhaaoo
sister	behen	buheeN

father	*pitaaji*	*vaDeel*
mother	*maa*	*aai*
grandfather	*daadaaji* (paternal), *naanaaji* (maternal)	*aazoba*
grandmother	*daadiji* (paternal), *naaniji* (maternal)	*aajji*

TRANSPORTATION

Airport, bus stop, train station, taxi stand, and auto-rickshaw stand are terms that are colloquially used. The bus station is called the bus depot.

English	Hindi	Marathi
Where is...?	*...kahaan aahé?*	*...kooThé hain?*

How far is it to...?
...yahaan sé kitnaa door hain? (H)
eethoon...kiti laamb aahé? (M)

How far is it from...to...
...sé...kitna door hain (H)
...té...kiti laamb aahé (M)

What is the way to...
yahaan sé...kaisé jaaengé? (H)
eethoon...la kasa zaaeeché? (M)

Where is this bus/train going?
Yé bus/train kahaan jaa rahee hain? (H)
hee bus/ train kuThé zaat aahé? (M)

Where can I find...?
mujhé...kahaan milegaa? (H)
mulaa...kuThé bhheTel? (M)

luggage	*saamaan*	*saamaan*
Stop here.	*eedhhur rukiyé*	*eethhé thhaambaa*
near	*paas*	*zawaL*
beside	*bagal mein*	*baazoolaa*
behind	*peechhé*	*maaghé*
corner	*kowné pé*	*kopryaavar*
here	*eedhhar*	*eethhé*
somewhere	*yaheen kaheenku*	*ithhé Thhetuhree*
road	*raastaa*	*rastaa*
lane	*gully*	*gully*
north, south	*oottar, dakshin*	*oottar, dakshin*
east, west	*poorav, paschim*	*poorav, paschim*

FOOD

The check is called the "bill." Fruits are identified by their English names. Carbonated water is called "soda." Tea, coffee, wine, and milk are terms that are used colloquially.

English	Hindi	Marathi
I'm hungry/ thirsty	*mujhé bhhook/ pyaas lagee hai*	*malaa bhhook/ tahaaN laagli aahé*
fork	*kaanta*	*kaata*
spoon	*Chammach*	*chamchaa*
breakfast	*naashtaa*	*naashTa*
lunch/ dinner	*khaanaa*	*jaywaN*
prawns	*jhhingaa*	*kowLambee*

Shopping

English	Hindi	Marathi
money	*paisa*	*paishé*
expensive	*mehengaa*	*mahaag*
cheap	*sustaa*	*swastha*
How much does it cost?	*Iska kitna huaa?*	*hyaaché kiti?*

Give me the correct price. This is too much.
Buraabar bataao. Yeh zyaadaa bataa rahé hain. (H)
Thheek bhaav bola. Hé khhoop saangitla toomhi. (M)

I want more/less.
mujhé aur/ kam Chaahiyé (H)
malaa Jaasta/kamee paahijé (M)

HEALTH

Aspirin is not commonly used, generic variations of paracetamol and acetaminophen are used instead for headaches and fever. Regular English words such as bandage, toothpaste, and medicine are commonly used. A pharmacy is referred to as a chemist or druggist.

English	Hindi	Marathi
Help me please.	*meri madad karo*	*maaJhhi madad karaa*

I am ill.
meri tubeeyat Thheek nahi hain (H)
malaa barra naahi aahé (M)

Take me to... *mujhé...*	*malaa...la*
	leké chulo	*ghheoon zaa*
pain	*darrd*	
(...is aching)		*...dookhhat*
		aahé
fever	*buKhhaar*	*taap*
stomach/	*paiT/sirr*	*poTaat/Dokah*
headache	*mein darrd*	*dookhat aahé*
vomiting	*ulTi*	*ulTi*

ANIMALS

English	Hindi	Marathi
monkey	*Bundar*	*Maakad*
cat	*Billi*	*Maanjar*
cow, bull	*Gai, Bael*	*Gai, Bael*
horse	*Ghoda*	*Ghoda*
pigeon	*Kabootar*	*Kabootar*
crow	*Kawwa*	*Kaawla*
dog	*Kutta*	*Kutra*
fish	*Macchli*	*Maasa*
hen	*Murgi*	*Komdi*
pig	*Suwar*	*Dukkar*
(also derogatory slang)		
parakeet	*Tota*	*Popat*

KONKANI WORDS AND PHRASES

Konkani is similar to Marathi in pronunciation. The letter **x** is pronounced as *sh*, as in the word for the culinary sauce *xacuti*, pronounced *sha-kuti*.

Numbers

English	Konkani
zero	*shoonya*
one	*ek*
two	*don*
three	*teen*
four	*chear*
five	*panch*
six	*sov*
seven	*saat*
eight	*aaTh*
nine	*nov*
ten	*dhaa*

Time

English	Konkani
time	*vell* or *vogot*
hours	*orram*
morning	*socaim* or *socallim*
afternoon	*denpar* or *donpar*
evening	*sanje*
night	*raat*

Days of the Week

English	Konkani
Sunday	*aitar*
Monday	*somar*
Tuesday	*moonglar*
Wednesday	*boodhvar*
Thursday	*bherestar*
Friday	*soonkrar*
Saturday	*soonvar*

Basic and Courteous Expressions

As with Hindi and Marathi, English expressions such as please, thank you, sorry, excuse me, good morning, and good night are used colloquially, although they may have Konkani equivalents.

English	Konkani
How are you?	*toom kosso assai ré?* (masculine), *toom koshi assai ghé?* (feminine)
I am fine.	*haanv boro assa*
please	*oopkaar*
thank you	*dev borem korum* (literally "may God bless you")
You're welcome.	*tukai korum* (literally "bless you, too")
Please do me a favor.	*matso oopkaar kor*
Good morning.	*deo boro diss dium*
Good night.	*deo bori ratt dium*
yes	*vhoi*
no	*naka*
What is your name?	*tujem naav kitem?*
My name is...	*mhajem naav...*

How do you say...	...Konkni bhaxent kaxem
in Konkani?	mhuN'tat?
What is that?	tem kitem?

Terms of Address

An important term to know in Konkani is *patrao*. It's a friendly greeting, often used to address a stranger, and roughly translates to "chief" or "boss."

English	Konkani
I	hanv
he	toh
she	tem
we	amim
they (masculine)	té
they (feminine)	tim
mine	mhajem
you	toom
yours	tujem

ours	amchem
for me	maka
for you	tuka
for him/her	teka
for us	amkam
boy	cheddo
girl	cheddum
children	bhurguim
man	dadlo
woman	bail
husband	gho
wife	ghorcarn (formal) or bail
father	bapui
mother	avoi
brother	bhau
sister	bhoin
grandfather	xapai
grandmother	xamai

Suggested Reading

Mumbai and Goa have been written about and celebrated in fiction and non-fiction, both in India and internationally. Most of these books are available in bookstores at both destinations, and may also be found on websites like amazon.com. The academic books may be a little difficult to find, but your local library and the ones in Mumbai may stock some titles.

Chakravarti, Sudeep. *Once Upon a Time in Aparanta*. Penguin. A satirical novel set in contemporary Goa, with all its modern-day socio-political issues.

Chandra, Vikram. *Love and Longing in Bombay*. Faber and Faber. A collection of short stories set in the city.

Chandra, Vikram. *Sacred Games*. A novel set in Mumbai's infamous underworld.

Couto, Maria Aurora. *Goa, A Daughter's Story*. Penguin. The autobiography of Goa's most celebrated writer, interwoven with the state's history.

David, M. D. *History of Bombay*. University of Mumbai. A scholarly work that studies the early city of Mumbai. The precedent for most city historians.

Dwivedi, Sharda and Rahul Mehrotra. *Bombay, The Cities Within*. Eminence Designs. A coffee-table book with great archival images and write-ups that trace the multiple identities of Mumbai.

Dwivedi, Sharda and Rahul Mehrotra. *Fort Walks*. Eminence Designs. A good travel companion for tourists.

Ganesh, Kamala, Usha Thakkar, and Gita Chadha. (eds.) *Zero Point Bombay: In and Around Horniman Circle*. Roli Books. A collection of essays and photographs that look at the architecture, public space, urban identity, commerce, and food of the Horniman Circle area.

Kolatkar, Arun. *Kala Ghoda Poems*. A collection of poetry inspired by Mumbai's art district.

Kaye, Miriam. *Illustrated Guide to Mumbai and Goa*. The Guidebook Co.

Mehta, Suketu. *Maximum City*. Vintage Books. A much-lauded documentation of the city—from its posh areas to the gritty by-lanes, from the police force to the underworld, from Bollywood to commerce.

Miranda, Mario. *Goa, with Love*. Goa Tours. Caricatures of Goa by a true-blue Goan—and one of India's most famous cartoonists.

Mistry, Rohinton. *A Fine Balance*. Vintage Books. A novel that narrates tales of various denizens of the city through its prime years.

Monga, Sunjoy. *The Mumbai Nature Guide*. India Book House. An excellent book for nature walks, trails, and wildlife- and bird-watching sites in and around the city.

Nagarkar, Kiran. *Ravan and Eddie*. Penguin. A hilarious coming-of-age story of two young boys in the *chawls* (community housing) of Mumbai.

Pandit, Heta and Annabel Mascarenhas. *Houses of Goa*. Architecture Autonomous. Journalist Heta Pandit, architect Annabel Mascarenhas, and photographer Ashok Koshy record the eclectic style of the dying Goan tradition of house-building.

Pinto, Jerry and Naresh Fernandes (eds.) *Bombay Meri Jaan*. Penguin. A collection of essays, poems, stories, cartoons, photographs, a play, and a recipe—all to do with the city of Mumbai. Contributors include a Nobel laureate, Booker Prize winners, the city's unofficial poet laureate, and jazz maestro Duke Ellington.

Pinto, Jerry (ed.) *Reflected in Water*. A collection of writings on Goa that includes essays, poems, stories, and extracts from published works.

Roberts, Gregory David. *Shantaram*. Scribe Publications. The fictionalized autobiography of a convict from Australia who escaped to Mumbai and became a part of its notorious underworld. This novel has taken the world by storm.

Rushdie, Salman. *Midnight's Children*. Random House. Winner of Booker of Bookers, a novel that traces the evolution of Mumbai and the country after Independence, in the genre of magical realism.

Shetty, Manohar (ed.) *Ferry Crossing: Short Stories from Goa*. Penguin. The finest short stories from Goa written in Konkani, Marathi, Portuguese (and English), in translation.

Shroff, Murzban. *Breathless in Bombay*. Short stories set in contemporary Mumbai.

Singh, Rashmi Uday. *The Mumbai Good-Food Guide*. Your best guide to eating and drinking in the city.

Tindall, Gillian. *City of Gold*. Penguin. A well-researched and enchanting account of a 300-year history of the city.

Tyrewala, Altaf. *No God in Sight*. Penguin. Powerful vignettes from the life of the Muslim community in Mumbai.

Zaidi, Hussein S. *Black Friday*. Penguin. A detailed account of the 1993 bomb blasts that shook the city, and changed the character of the city. Inspiration for a controversial film by the same title.

Internet Resources

MUMBAI

Mumbai Navigator
www.cse.iitb.ac.in/navigator/
index.html
Just key in your starting point and destination and the website gives you the shortest and fastest bus and train routes to get around the city.

Mumbai on the Net
www.mumbainet.com
A concise website with routes, roads, events, addresses, and basics to get around the city.

My Time Mumbai
www.mumbaieventstoday.com
Daily listings for what is happening where. One-stop site for concerts, recitals, plays, films, exhibitions, and special events.

IndiaMike.com
www.indiamike.com
Great site for travel tips, help, advice, ideas, and travel companions.

Time Out Mumbai
www.timeoutmumbai.net
The website version of the events and city magazine. Up to date with events.

Mumbai Web Guide
www.mumbaiwebguide.com
Basic tips on travel, getting around the city, and saving money.

GOA

GoaCentral.com
www.goacentral.com
For facts and information on Goa.

Goatourism.org
www.goatourism.org
The official government tourism website.

Find All Goa
www.findall-goa.com
For all kinds of useful information ranging from maps and event calendars to contact details of foreign consulates, airline offices, and train stations.

Goa 2 U
www.goa2u.com
Information on festivals, flights, car rentals, and more.

Index

List of Maps

Acknowledgments

The best part about undertaking a project such as this one is the opportunity it offers to meet wonderful people along the way. This book would have been impossible but for the many who extended their support and made the journey even more enjoyable than it was.

Topping the list are Khaliq Parkar—heritage walk volunteer, then student and now lecturer of Political Science—for his diligent assistance, dedication and mapmaking rescue operations. And friend and photographer Ashima Narain for filling in with her skill and talent when my ability to multitask as writer and photographer was beginning to flag.

My gratitude to all those who spent time patiently answering my questions, extended their hospitality and generally went out of their way to enrich my experience. I am particularly grateful to Jack Sukhija of Panjim Inn; Manuella Barboza at the Goa Marriott; Andrew Mensforth, Farrah Fernandez, Chef Asif and the team at Park Hyatt Goa; Allwyn Drego and his team at the Taj Exotica; Shrikant Wakharkar, Capt Paul Moore and the team at the InterContinental Grand Goa Resort; Ewald Rudigere and Biswajit Syam of Kenilworth Hotels; Marius Monteiro of Cavala; Ram Mohan and PV Mudappa at the Kairali Group; Wendell Rodricks; Hari Ajwani; Ravinder Sathasivam of Casino Goa; Sucheta Potnis; Manish Arora of Calizz; Bawmra and Maryam; Sunil Singh and Tina Dehal; Eddie Jorge; Xavier Furtado and his team at Fisherman's Wharf. In Mumbai, I'd like to thank Henry Tham's, Aurus and Albert Amanna of Hotel InterContinental.

I am also grateful to those who shared with me their knowledge on various aspects of Goa. To food critic and director Cidade de Goa, Akash Timblo, for pointing me in the right direction as far as all places gastronomical were concerned. To Mac Vaz, director Madame Rosa, for his invaluable information on feni and for getting me in touch with the right people. To Chand Uppal for inputs on land and property; Derrick Menezes for sharing his experiences as a watersports instructor; Savia Viegas for insights into Goan society and culture; Augusto Pinto for help with the Konkani phrasebook. To Kurt Gidwani for tips on nightlife and food, Debbie for her valuable inputs and Paul for being a great driver.

My thanks to the extremely efficient, organized and friendly team at Avalon. To Elizabeth Hansen for her keen eye for detail and thoroughness as editor. Jehán Seirafi, Elizabeth Jang, Lucie Ericksen, Brice Ticen, Jamie Andrade and all the others kept the communication going as we worked together in virtual space, across continents and different time zones.

Lastly, I'd like to thank friends and family for making me feel at home or joining me at various points during my research trips. Minal and Ashtad for their hospitality; Deepa and Satyajit for a lovely housewarming, Manali and David for a great wedding celebration; Mum, Dad, Manjiri and Jason for letting me be the tour guide; Spacie and Anil for keeping each other entertained while Ashima and I were at work. And to Mathilde, Della and Ian for great new friendships born of chance meetings in Goa.

www.moon.com

DESTINATIONS | ACTIVITIES | BLOGS | MAPS | BOOKS

MOON.COM is all new, and ready to help plan your next trip! Filled with fresh trip ideas and strategies, author interviews, informative blogs, a detailed map library, and descriptions of all the Moon guidebooks, Moon.com is all you need to get out and explore the world—or even places in your own backyard. As always, when you travel with Moon, expect an experience that is uncommon and truly unique.

MAP SYMBOLS

▥ Expressway	**〖** Highlight	✈ Airfield	⚲ Golf Course				
▥ Primary Road	○ City/Town	✈ Airport	**P** Parking Area				
▥ Secondary Road	◉ State Capital	▲ Mountain	▰ Archaeological Site				
▥ Unpaved Road	✪ National Capital	✛ Unique Natural Feature	▮ Church				
▥ Trail	★ Point of Interest		▮ Gas Station				
▥ Ferry	● Accommodation	⤳ Waterfall	Glacier				
▥ Railroad	▼ Restaurant/Bar	⚑ Park	Mangrove				
▥ Pedestrian Walkway	■ Other Location	**T** Trailhead	Reef				
▥ Stairs	△ Campground	⚶ Skiing Area	Swamp				

CONVERSION TABLES

$°C = (°F - 32) / 1.8$
$°F = (°C \times 1.8) + 32$
1 inch = 2.54 centimeters (cm)
1 foot = 0.304 meters (m)
1 yard = 0.914 meters
1 mile = 1.6093 kilometers (km)
1 km = 0.6214 miles
1 fathom = 1.8288 m
1 chain = 20.1168 m
1 furlong = 201.168 m
1 acre = 0.4047 hectares
1 sq km = 100 hectares
1 sq mile = 2.59 square km
1 ounce = 28.35 grams
1 pound = 0.4536 kilograms
1 short ton = 0.90718 metric ton
1 short ton = 2,000 pounds
1 long ton = 1.016 metric tons
1 long ton = 2,240 pounds
1 metric ton = 1,000 kilograms
1 quart = 0.94635 liters
1 US gallon = 3.7854 liters
1 Imperial gallon = 4.5459 liters
1 nautical mile = 1.852 km

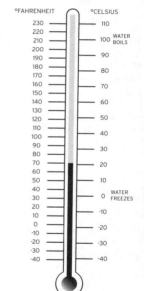

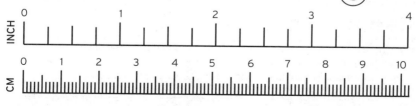

MOON MUMBAI & GOA

Avalon Travel
a member of the Perseus Books Group
1700 Fourth Street
Berkeley, CA 94710, USA
www.moon.com

Editor: Elizabeth Hollis Hansen
Series Manager: Kathryn Ettinger
Copy Editor: Ellie Behrstock
Graphics and Production Coordinator:
   Lucie Ericksen
Cover Designer: Elizabeth Jang
Map Editor: Brice Ticen
Cartographers: Kat Bennett, Mike Morgenfeld
Indexer: Greg Jewett

ISBN-13: 978-1-59880-241-2
ISSN: 2150-9441

Printing History
1st Edition – November 2009
5 4 3 2 1

Text © 2009 by Janhavi Acharekar.
Maps © 2009 by Avalon Travel.
All rights reserved.

Some photos and illustrations are used by permission and are the property of the original copyright owners.

Front cover photo: India, Goa State, Palolem beach © Reflexstock/Hemis/GUIZIOU Franck
Title page photo: Cows soak in the sun on Anjuna Beach, Goa © Manjiri Achrekar-Smothers
Other front matter photos: pages 7, 8-bottom, 10, 13-right, 14, 16-top, 18-bottom, 19, 22, 23-right © Ashima Narain; pages 6, 7-middle, 8-top, 9, 11, 12, 13-left, 16-bottom, 17, 18-top, 23-left: © Janhavi Acharekar; page 20 © Anil Nair; page 24: © Grand Hyatt

Printed in Canada by Friesens

KEEPING CURRENT

If you have a favorite gem you'd like to see included in the next edition, or see anything that needs updating, clarification, or correction, please drop us a line. Send your comments via email to feedback@moon.com, or use the address above.